084

33

Ethics in
SPORT

SECOND EDITION

Ethics in SPORT

EDITOR

WILLIAM J. MORGAN
The Ohio State University

HUMAN KINETICS

Library of Congress Cataloging-in-Publication Data

Ethics in sport / editor, William J. Morgan. -- 2nd ed.
  p. cm.
  Includes bibliographical references and index.
  ISBN-13: 978-0-7360-6428-6 (hard cover)
  ISBN-10: 0-7360-6428-1 (hard cover)
  1. Sports--Moral and ethical aspects--United States. 2. Sports--Social aspects--United
States. I. Morgan, William John, 1948-
  GV706.3.E86 2007
  175--dc22

                                              2006035639

ISBN-10: 0-7360-6428-1
ISBN-13: 978-0-7360-6428-6

Acquisitions Editor: Myles Schrag; **Managing Editor:** Lee Alexander; **Copyeditor:** John Wentworth; **Proofreader:** Sarah Wiseman; **Indexer:** Sharon Duffy; **Permission Manager:** Carly Breeding; **Graphic Designer:** Robert Reuther; **Graphic Artist:** Yvonne Griffith; **Cover Designer:** Keith Blomberg; **Art Manager:** Kelly Hendren; **Illustrator:** Al Wilborn; **Printer:** Sheridan Books

Printed in the United States of America   10 9 8 7 6 5 4 3 2 1

Human Kinetics
Web site: www.HumanKinetics.com

United States: Human Kinetics
P.O. Box 5076
Champaign, IL 61825-5076
800-747-4457
e-mail: humank@hkusa.com

Canada: Human Kinetics
475 Devonshire Road Unit 100
Windsor, ON N8Y 2L5
800-465-7301 (in Canada only)
e-mail: orders@hkcanada.com

Europe: Human Kinetics
107 Bradford Road
Stanningley
Leeds LS28 6AT, United Kingdom
+44 (0) 113 255 5665
e-mail: hk@hkeurope.com

Australia: Human Kinetics
57A Price Avenue
Lower Mitcham, South Australia 5062
08 8372 0999
e-mail: liaw@hkaustralia.com

New Zealand: Human Kinetics
Division of Sports Distributors NZ Ltd.
P.O. Box 300 226 Albany
North Shore City
Auckland
0064 9 448 1207
e-mail: info@humankinetics.co.nz

CONTENTS

PREFACE

I am surely not telling anyone anything they do not already know when I say that the moral standing of contemporary sports at all levels leaves much to be desired. Nor am I saying anything new when I decry the depressingly sorry moral state in which sports presently find themselves; the fact is, they have been feeding at the moral bottom for some time now. Unfortunately, things are likely to get worse before they get better. Take but one example: As refinements in the genetic modification of human beings spill over as they inevitably will into the winning-obsessed and money-crazed world of elite sports they will create moral dilemmas that make those associated with performance-enhancing drugs look like child's play by comparison.

As I see it, the principal moral dangers in current sport are twofold. On the one hand, we must be constantly vigilant that those backers of sport who stand the most to gain from their continued moral degradation are not allowed to sweep these problems under the rug by, among other things, tarring critics of the sport scene as whining discontents with an ideological axe to grind. On the other hand, we must be no less vigilant in ensuring that the critics of sport are not allowed to make too much of their moral failings and simply write off sport as a lost cause. Failures of the first sort confuse moral analysis with hand wringing of a public relations sort, whereas failures of the second sort confuse moral criticism with moral browbeating. The first failure makes a mockery of ethics; the second robs people of the hope they need to think things might get morally better rather than worse—after all, if it is preordained that things can only get worse, why be moral?

It is precisely for reasons such as these that touch on both the theory and practice of ethics that I have tried to gather into the present volume the best of the sport ethics literature to be found. I hope I have provided a sufficiently wide range of material in terms of topics and level of sophistication that are appropriate and relevant both to undergraduate and graduate students. This is no mean feat, to be sure. With this aim in mind, I have chosen to retain a fair number of essays from the previous edition because of their classic and seminal standing in the literature. However, I have also added extensive new material to this body of work that includes, as best as I can tell, thirteen never-before anthologized essays along with three previously unpublished ones.

There will be those who are troubled by my selections or my omissions, or both. Granted, there is plenty to take issue with in this new collection, given the wide range of literature anthologized here. However, I have been helped mightily by two astute reviewers, Nick Dixon and Scott Kretchmar, who offered sage advice and saved me from many errors. They would have saved me from many more, no doubt, if I were wise enough to heed their every suggestion. But there are bound to be disagreements when putting a large collection of essays together, if for no other reason than in compiling such material one can't help but rely on one's own philosophical instincts and commitments and, of course, biases. As the editor of this anthology, I can only hope that I have sufficiently tempered my own ethical tendencies and biases to put together a collection of essays that has wide critical appeal. That, at any rate, was my primary aim.

ETHICS, ETHICAL INQUIRY, AND SPORT: AN INTRODUCTION

William J. Morgan

The field of ethics or morality, which I will treat as interchangeable terms, is an enormously complex one that defies easy characterization. Part of the complexity of the field is owed to the diverse ways in which the field is conceptualized—that is, to the many different ideas in the literature regarding just what counts as an ethical consideration. Any effort to stake out once and for all the precise conceptual boundaries of ethics is not likely to get us far, if only because such an effort adds yet one more conception that is bound to conflict with others that have preceded it. That said, we can shed light easily enough on this area of study and practice so long as we shun attempts to strictly define the area and concentrate instead on the sorts of questions the realm of ethics entertains and the modes of inquiry that are deployed to answer these questions. This will be the strategy I will follow in my ensuing remarks.

Normative (Moral), Objective, and Subjective Questions

Perhaps the best place to begin is to point out that ethics falls within the normative field of study, because the main questions ethics wrestles with and the reasons it trades in are distinctly normative ones. *Normative* questions and reasons are distinguished by the fact that they aim not so much to describe accurately some state of affairs as to prescribe how we should act in certain circumstances. That is, the stock and trade of ethics is to marshal arguments to show why we should abide by certain standards and norms in our actions and interactions with our peers. Thus, the point of normative reasons and arguments is to guide, instruct, recommend, advise, and evaluate how human beings should behave. The point of offering such guidance, of course, is to make claims on how we, in fact, do behave. So when I say to you that you shouldn't eat high-fat food because such food is bad for your health, or that you should avoid prime time television situation comedies (sitcoms) because such shows are mostly mindless, or that selling someone an insurance policy that offers them no substantial protection is wrong, I am not simply stating what I think is the case but also pointedly and strongly urging you not to act in these ways. And my urging that you should act otherwise carries only as much force as is carried by the arguments I use to back up my advice. You have no compelling reason to follow my normative counsel and change your behavior accordingly unless the reasons I furnish you are ones that you can understand and cannot reasonably deny.

That moral questions fall in the normative realm allows us to distinguish such questions from two other sorts of questions commonly asked in and outside of academic circles.[1] The first of these is what might be called *objective* questions, which include such questions as what is the boiling point of water or the atomic weight of copper? In this case, what is meant by the question and what counts as a good answer to the question are as clear as they are uncontroversial. So if I say that the boiling point of water is 212 degrees centigrade and someone takes issue with my answer, I can simply reply, "Okay, then, go look it up for yourself." And if the person does so and alights on the right answer but still insists on treating it as a contested claim, I have good grounds to question his rationality. Because in most cases objective questions have a clear and definitive answer that can be found with relative ease.

A second kind of question, distinct from objective ones, is the *subjective* question (see table 1), of which the following are examples: What is your favorite color? What kind of ice cream do you like best? Did you like that book? In most cases, subjective questions are used to determine people's personal preferences. Unlike objective questions, there is no one correct answer to subjective questions. This is why asking people to justify their answers to subjective questions, or accusing them of being inaccurate in their responses, makes about as much sense as insisting that blue is in fact a better color than green, and that this is true for everyone. (Of course, if I have reason to believe that someone's response to a subjective question is a lie, then I might in fact be justified in voicing my skepticism.) So, if someone forthrightly answers my question by saying she prefers chocolate ice cream to other flavors I have no reasonable grounds to question her answer or to suggest that she might be mistaken. Indeed, any claim of wrongness in such cases will likely only cast doubt on the rationality of the one making the claim.

From our discussion thus far, it should be clear why normative questions cannot be answered either objectively or subjectively, and why it would be a grievous mistake to even attempt to do so, especially in the case of ethical considerations. Unlike objective questions, normative questions do not admit of a single correct answer that can settle a matter once and for all for everyone. The answer to a normative question cannot be located at the back of some textbook. But, unlike answers to subjective questions, normative questions do indeed have answers that are either better or worse than others. This is why it is so important that our answers to these questions can, if necessary, be rationally justified to our peers. What counts as a strong answer to a normative question is one that is well backed by reasons and

TABLE 1 *Three Kinds of Questions*

Normative questions	Objective questions	Subjective questions
What college or university should I attend?	At what temperature does ice freeze?	What is your favorite month of the year?
Was Picasso a great artist?	What is the chemical composition of salt?	Do you like three-piece or two-piece suits?
Would you assist a terminally ill family member to end his or her life if asked to do so?	On what date was Lincoln shot?	What reality show do you like to watch most?

evidence, one that can be supported argumentatively. If I tell you that it is wrong to disrespect another person in the pursuit of your own self-interest, you might go along with me to the extent that I can convince you—through reasons and evidence presented within an argument, or a presentation of my position—that I am right about this. Because arguments and arguments alone do the work of justification when it comes to normative questions, we might well end up accepting reasons for how we should conduct our lives that are not to our personal liking, that in fact go against our own actual desires regarding how we want to lead our lives.

That our normative reasons for living our lives in one way rather than in another often clash with our personal desires in such instances underscores why it is crucial not to lose sight of the important role that normative reasoning plays in our lives. That many people do lose sight of this is partly because of the hard-to-miss, rock-solid reassurance objective claims offer, which prompt many people to confuse normative claims with subjective claims because, well, they are not nearly as reassuring, because they can't deliver the level of truth and certitude that objective inquiry does. When claims such as "the boiling point of water is 212 degrees centigrade" are stacked against claims such as "abortions performed during the third trimester of pregnancy are morally suspect," it is easy to think of the latter as nothing more than an expression of personal preference because its status as a candidate for truth seems so elusive when compared to an objective fact.

As I hinted earlier, though confusing normative with subjective claims is a readily understandable error, it is, nonetheless, an utterly fatal error. This is because if it were true that issues pertaining to how we should live really were just subjective matters in disguise, then our efforts to make normative sense of our lives would fall prey to a vicious relativism. Indeed, the whole idea of trying to make normative sense of our lives would itself no longer make sense, because we would no longer be able to say that one way of acting or living is better than any other way of acting or living. And without any way of justifying or reflectively endorsing the different ways in which we live our lives, there would be no point in even trying to do so.

What makes this particular brand of relativism so unpalatable, then, aside from its general incoherence,[2] is its aim to cut the justificatory legs out from under normative inquiry. Because it is precisely the need to justify what we say when addressing claims regarding how we should live that is, as we have seen, so central to normative queries. It is for this very reason, Simon Blackburn contends, that we find retorts like "that's just your opinion" in moral debates so off-putting—because they are so far off the mark.[3] Moral debates, Blackburn reminds us, are all about offering carefully considered arguments rather than the tossing out of personal opinions. They are about discussions that take their cue from the pro-and-con, back-and-forth exchange of reasons. They are about admitting the possibility that because we could be wrong about certain beliefs we hold and certain desires we harbor to actualize these beliefs, it would benefit us to listen to the carefully considered views of others. By contrast, the statement "that's just your opinion" is not a response to an argument. It is not an invitation to keep a conversation going. It is not a request for a better way to think about some moral quandary. Indeed, such statements generally function as conversation stoppers, as refusals to treat anything that has been said as a good reason to view a moral matter differently from before, and thereby perhaps change a behavior. The retort "that's just your opinion" is, in fact, an insult, a demeaning barb intended to abort a discussion that at least one person recognizes as worthwhile. Such a retort is a vote of no confidence in the value of the serious exchange of ideas. Often, when someone says "that's just your opinion" within a normative discussion, he or she is really saying, "I don't want to think about it" or, worse, "I don't think it's worth thinking about."

What is further unsettling about relativistic putdowns is that they not only gloss over the practical inescapability of normative questions and reason giving—the idea that, as Blackburn so succinctly puts it, "there is no living without standards of living"[4]—but that they would have us believe that we can live without what Koorsgaard rightly claims is perhaps "the most striking aspect about human life," namely, "that we have values" at all. As Koorsgaard explains, "We think of ways that things could be better, more perfect, and so . . . different, than they are; and of ways that we ourselves could be better, more perfect, and so . . . different, than we are."[5] What is so "striking" and truly remarkable about having values in this sense is that they are among the most important driving forces behind life itself, and thus of our effort to make something of that life and of ourselves for the better. Life without values would hardly be worth the effort, and it would certainly not be a pretty sight—Hobbes' description of life in a value-deprived state of nature as "short and brutish" comes to mind. The allegation of relativists that only our "preference rankings" govern our lives insinuates not only that we can do, indeed *must,* do without reasons but without values as well. So much, then, for the normative dimension of our lives.

That this relativistic incrimination of our normative reasoning extends as well to our values should, on reflection, come as no surprise. The normative reasons we rely on to justify our actions receive what sanction they enjoy from the values that serve as their touchstone, because our values furnish us with the standards we need to reflectively appraise our lives. Thus, our normative reasons are only as good, as authoritative, as the values that underpin them. This means, of course, that normative reasons are at bottom value judgments, which is why once moral relativism has wreaked havoc on our reasons, by reducing them to mere preferences, it has also wreaked havoc on the values that stand behind the reasons, which are likewise relegated to the status of mere desires.

Perhaps the best way to see this point is to draw a further contrast between what are commonly called motivating reasons and what we have been calling normative reasons.[6] Motivating reasons explain our intentional action by accounting for the various psychological states and beliefs that accompany them and give rise to the action. Motivating reasons are what prompt us to act in one way rather than another. For example, if asked why I work out on an exercise bike, where the "why" in the question is understood motivationally, I might mention my desire not to succumb prematurely to heart disease and my desire to experience a general sense of well being. By contrast, if asked the same question but this time where the "why" is understood normatively, I would explain my decision in terms of my reasons for riding the exercise bike. That is, I would describe the rational deliberation I went through that led me to take up this particular kind of vigorous experience rather than another. In this case, what I am being asked about is not the desires and beliefs that prompted me to ride an exercise bike, that complex of psychological attitudes that motivated my actions, but the reasons that justify my doing so. In this case, the relevant pairing is not my desires and beliefs, but my values and beliefs. And so I answer by saying that I value a healthy lifestyle over an unhealthy one and I believe that brisk cycling is an optimal way to realize that value—all of which, of course, gives me good (normative) reason to commit myself to this kind of regular, vigorous exercise.

Whereas, then, my motivating reasons explain what I want and end up doing if I follow my desires, my normative reasons explain what I have good reason to do and end up doing if I act rationally. My reasons differ not in their intent to explain my actions but only in the distinct manner in which they go about accounting for what I do.

Some might object at this point, suggesting that what we have here is not a genuine distinction at all, because explaining my behavior by appealing to my desires is hardly different from explaining my behavior by appealing to my values. That is because I typically desire and act on only those things that I value. Thus, valuing and desiring some action or thing often comes to roughly the same thing.

This objection can be met, I believe, by rejecting outright the main premise that drives it—that is, by noting that in fact we often desire things we most assuredly do not value. Frankfurt's example of the drug addict is a case in point.[7] For while there is no doubting the addict wants to do drugs, it is also not hard to imagine that in his more sober moments he thinks he does not really want to feed his addiction, where "what he really wants" is a synonym for what it is rational for him to do. Similarly, as Michael Stocker observes, it is very often the case that because of physical illness, depression, or bouts of weakness of will, people can lack the desire to do what they value. The depressed person, for example, knows full well he should get out of bed and get on with his life, but he can't muster the desire or energy to do so. Perhaps a better because more relevant example is Gary Watson's hypothetical frustrated squash player who, after a resounding defeat, is seized with the desire to smash his opponent in the face with his racket. Again, there is no doubting he does actually desire to inflict such damage, but there is also no doubting that he doesn't value that desire in the least—which is why he finds it so troubling in the first place. For as Watson further insightfully writes, it is not as if the squash player in question gave his desire to retaliate against his opponent an "initial" value that was later overridden after appropriate reflection; rather, there was never a point at which he assigned any value to his desire for revenge. In all these cases, we can explain the behavior of these individuals in accord with their motivating reasons but not their normative ones, and the explanation for this gap between motivating and normative reasons is simply that none of these desires pass muster on the value side of things.[8]

To sum up this first part of our discussion, then, it is apparent that normative reasons are constituted by the justificatory work they do, and by the values that supply the standards that such work cannot get by without. What is true of normative questions and reasons here, of course, goes as well for moral ones, because, as duly noted, the latter are an important variety of the former. But this raises the further question of what distinguishes moral reasons from other kinds of normative reasons. The answer, as we shall see, is by the distinct kind of value moral reasons trade in.

Prudential, Aesthetic, and Moral Values

The values particular to normative judgments come in three basic forms: prudential, aesthetic, and moral (see table 2). The first sort of *prudential* value we have already touched on when we cited the reasons that we should avoid eating high-fat foods. The value at issue here is of the prudential kind because it concerns the value we place on our own well being. This is why it is crucial that we consider not just the short-term, immediate effects of our actions on our well being but also their

TABLE 2 *Three Kinds of Values*

Prudential questions	Aesthetic questions	Moral questions
Should I consider a vocational school if I don't get into college?	Can you detect any patterns in Pollack's abstract paintings?	Is capital punishment justifiable?
What diet works best for keeping one's blood sugar level in a healthy range?	What is the point the author is trying to make in this novel?	What do you mean by equality?
Are high-performance sports healthy?	Do sports have aesthetic properties?	Is it right to intentionally foul your opponent in a game?

long-term effects. For to act without concern for our own future—that is, to act improvidently, recklessly, and incautiously—is to jeopardize that future, and thereby our long-term happiness.

Aesthetic value, by contrast, is rooted not in the kind of enlightened self-interest that informs prudential judgments but rather in the particular way in which we view the world around us, both the natural world and the human-made, artifactual one. When we value something aesthetically, whether it be a sunset or a ballet or a figure skating competition, we consider not what practical purpose it might or might not serve, nor its practical utility, but rather the beauty, grace, and other pleasing features of the object or movements. When we value sport in aesthetic terms, therefore, we focus not so much on the fact *that* a point or goal was scored but on *how* the point or goal was accomplished. From an aesthetic point of view, the aim or purpose of a sport is considered inseparable from the manner in which it is achieved. Of course, just as nearly everything in the world can be considered from an aesthetic perspective but only some objects and activities are more centrally of aesthetic interest than others (works of art, for one), the same is true for sports. Although nearly all sports can be considered from an aesthetic perspective, only some—figure skating, diving, and gymnastics, to name just three—require aesthetic consideration in order to be understood and fully appreciated.[9]

We are now in a better position to see what distinguishes moral judgments from these other two kinds of normative considerations. Moral judgments take their point of departure neither from prudential judgments of well-being nor from aesthetic judgments of beauty but from values that bear directly on our relationships and interactions with others. In particular, moral values concern how we should conduct our lives so that our actions do *right* by others, contributing both to our *own* good as well as that of others. With regard to the "right," moral reasons take their cue from substantive considerations of fairness and justice—in other words, from considerations of equal treatment and moral respect that we owe to others. With regard to the "good," moral reasons take their cue from the qualities of action that make one a (morally) good person—that is, from dispositions such as benevolence that put front and center for our consideration the effects our actions have on others, and from qualities of action that contribute to the good of some end or practice that is itself thought to be vital to living a good life. Of course, reasons for doing the right thing and for doing the good thing are by no means mutually exclusive; on the contrary, they are inextricably bound up with one another. So, moral questions must take into account ways of life that contribute to a good life, to ends or practices that are worthy of our pursuit, and to questions of fairness and justice that importantly bear on the conduct of such practices. As Rawls nicely put it, "Justice draws the limit, the good shows the point."[10] In other words, unless certain ends or practices people take up command not just their attention but their devoted care and even love, there is no point in living in the first place and so no reason to ponder what constitutes a good life. And unless there are justifiable constraints on what it is permissible for us to do in pursuing such ends and practices, there would be no need for us to consider how others are affected by what we do. That is why, in sport, a moral quality such as fairness is indispensable both to our realization of the goods of excellence particular to them and to drawing limits on what is permissible and impermissible for participants to do while engaged in sport.

From what has been said thus far, it should be clear why in theorizing about and doing ethics so much rides on precisely where and how we draw the line between moral and nonmoral considerations. If we draw the line too high, too abstractly, or too strictly, our moral considerations will likely range too far from the concerns and aims that animate our actual lives and give them meaning to be of any relevance; and if we draw the line too low, too concretely, or too loosely our moral considerations are likely to range too close to our actual lives to offer any substantive instruction on how our lives might be better lived.

An example of drawing the line too strictly is famously provided by the eminent English philosopher Bernard Williams, who asks us to consider the example of a man confronted with the choice of saving his wife or a stranger, both of whom are in imminent danger, and who opts to save his wife. Now, someone who holds that moral considerations must, without exception, be impersonal ones might say that "in situations of this kind it is at *least* morally permissible to save one's wife." But Williams rejoins that someone who insists that if we are to give this case a genuine moral hearing we must not only entertain the (personal) thought that this woman is his wife, but the further (impersonal) thought about how anyone else faced with a similar if not identical situation should act is not only guilty of having "one thought too many" but of a serious moral error.[11] For the very fact that it is his wife, Williams insists, is moral reason enough to save her, and to add impersonal considerations in the mix in order to justify such action only shows that he lacks the appropriate love and feelings and thus moral regard for his wife that are characteristic of such intimate personal relations. In other words, the claim that moral considerations must always be impersonal ones sets the bar much too high for what counts as a moral consideration—so high, in fact, that the standard no longer seems a reasonable or relevant one by which to live one's life because it requires that we forsake the very values that give meaning to life.

An example of drawing the line too loosely, by contrast, is apparent in a version of moral contractarian theory (about which we will have much more to say shortly) made famous by the philosopher Thomas Hobbes, who argued that because of our mutual dependence on others, any effort on our individual part to pursue our advantage must involve the cooperation of these others. That is to say, Hobbes' argument is that we have good (nonmoral) reasons to agree to moral principles of conduct with our peers because such agreement is necessary if we are each to get what we want. The problem with this so-called moral theory is that it is not really a moral theory at all but rather a simple strategy for how to use others to advance our own self-interests. As Rawls pithily puts the point, "A man whose moral judgments always coincided with his interests could be suspected of having no morality at all."[12] In this case, then, labeling moral considerations as self-interested ones sets the bar much too low for what counts as a moral consideration because it makes a moral life indistinguishable from a narrowly self-centered one.

A Core Conception of Morality

As I have insinuated throughout, it is a futile task trying to answer with exactitude which reasons and values are moral, and which are not. For starters, the answer to this question depends in part on which moral theory one subscribes to among the several moral theories appearing in the literature. (Sorting out the distinguishing features of each of these theories is a task I will take up in the ensuing and final section of this introduction.) For instance, that literature variously suggests that moral reasons and values are those that can be appropriately generalized and treated as universal principles, or those that produce the greatest balance of good over evil, or those that all relevant and reasonable parties can agree to, or those that a person of good character would be disposed to entertain and act on. But there is also an important feature these different conceptions of morality share in common that, I think, distinguishes them as moral theories in the first place. And that something is an insistence that moral reasons and values are always other-regarding in character rather than strictly self-regarding in character. Let me explain.

What I am getting at here is the very point Rawls expressed in my quotation of him above, namely, that "A man whose moral judgments always coincided with his interests could be suspected of having no morality at all," and the point Williams was trying to make when he wrote, "The idea of something being good imports an idea, however minimal or hazy, of a perspective in which it can be acknowledged by more than one agent,"[13] and when he claimed yet further that "simply to pursue what you want . . . is not the stuff of any morality; if [that] is your motive . . ., then you are not within morality, and you do not have any ethical life."[14] Clearly, moral values are not first-person singular; they are not the subjective kind of values concerned solely, or primarily, with self-interested wants and desires. Rather, moral reasons and values are first-person plural intersubjective; they tell us what we have reason to do or to value as members of a community. The upshot of Rawls' and Williams' remarks is that it is the interpersonal "we" that is the genuine locus of morality, and that this "we" marks off our membership in a community in which there is agreement all around regarding what counts as a moral reason and value.

The claim that moral reasons and values point to a "we" rather than an "I," a reasonably close-knit, and yet far-ranging community rather than a series of largely disconnected individuals, chimes with Blackburn's seemingly provocative claim that human agents are distinctively ethical beings.[15] I say "seemingly" provocative because what Blackburn means by this is not that we humans are disposed to act in ethical, principled ways (which would indeed be not just provocative but downright false since the historical record, alas, suggests rather massively to the contrary) but that we are agents who compare, evaluate, and justify what we say and do. The specifically ethical bit of Blackburn's claim is that what we are constantly sizing up, evaluating, and justifying—not always explicitly, of course—how we should interact with one another. This specifically moral preoccupation with others should not be confused with Hobbes' earlier cited claim that social cooperation is instrumental to getting what we as individuals want, the point of which, after all, is unmistakably egoistic, nor the slightly different because larger claim that cooperation is crucial to the stability of any society, whose emphasis on stability falls short of the solidarity required by a moral community. Rather, Blackburn's point is the decidedly moral one that living with others is itself an inescapably ethical matter because such relationships can only be regarded and treated as valuable ones if they possess "at least enough honesty and integrity so that you are neither a tool in [my] hands nor [I a tool] in yours."[16]

The idea that morality and a certain sense of community go together is to be understood in at least three pivotal senses. The first sense is a social one because our induction into any community, however small or large, is necessarily a moral one. It is through becoming a member of some community or other that we first learn to talk and act in moral ways and to be responsive to the claims of others who reside in these communities. The traditions that inform such communities thus define as well their moral ethos by, among other things, mapping out the moral rules and responsibilities that are supposed to infuse the social roles (parent, teacher, coach) and practices (education, sport, medicine) they sanction. That is why, as MacIntyre was wont to put it, the quest for our own good always begins with these moral particulars, with the moral roles built into these social practices, and although that quest should never, and seldom does, end with them, it at the same time never leaves them completely behind.[17]

Ethical Thinking

What does Blackburn mean when he claims that human agents are distinctly ethical beings?

The second sense in which morality hooks up with the idea of membership in a community concerns the idea that moral reasoning itself necessarily aims at a common point of view that is the trademark of any community rightly understood. That is to say, to claim that some act is wrong or bad requires concurrence from others that it is, in fact, wrong or bad.[18] For this to be the case, it is necessary that those whom I am pitching my arguments to find what I present as reasons for its wrongness or badness persuasive. As Blackburn nicely puts it, "the giving and receiving of reasons" in moral argument presupposes "that what I offer as a reason from my point of view *can* be seen and appreciated as a reason from *your* point of view."[19] That is why moral reasoning cannot help but seek a shared point of view, and why moral argument is parasitic on something called a community. As we have previously remarked, perhaps the chief feature of what makes a social grouping a genuine community is that its members are all of one mind regarding what counts as a good reason for carrying out some action, and thus they agree on what is a right and good way of acting as opposed to a wrong and bad way of acting.[20]

The third, and for my purposes, final sense in which morality needs to be thought of in communal terms is that it requires an acute sense of how our actions affect others. This moral capacity to put ourselves in someone else's shoes, to reverse our perspective to see the world as others do, is a feature that comes rather naturally to members of a genuine community who identify with one another and judge themselves, therefore, by the depth and extent of their fellow feeling rather than by the varying and passing intensity of their preference rankings. What doesn't come quite as naturally, however, is the extension of that identification to others who are not now and never were part of our community. Still, the lessons inevitably learned by all but the most hermetically sealed-off societies in how to enlarge their sense of "we" to accommodate those of their peers unjustly denied full membership in the community (the civil rights and women's movements come immediately to mind) prove invaluable in this regard. For they poignantly show, as Peter Singer once put it in a different context, how our moral horizons need constant expansion if we are to become aware of how we discriminate even against our peers.[21] So learning how to overcome our prejudice toward our compatriots is but a first step in learning how to do the same with regard to strangers, because both of these accommodations depend on our ability to transform a "them" into an "us" by giving greater scope to the things we share in common rather than the differences that separate us. This is why the sense of solidarity and fellow feeling engendered by our identification with a community needs to be an idealized one—that is, one not only open to but encouraging of the reflective process through which we are able to expand the range of our moral acquaintance.

Ethical Thinking

How are we to understand Singer's point that our "moral horizons" need to be expanded constantly if we are to become fully aware of all the ways we discriminate against other human beings?

Before moving on to the next section, I should note that the linkage of morality to a sense of community, to the kind of solidarity that distinguishes more tightly from less tightly wound social groupings, helps to answer a question that has dogged ethicists from time immemorial and that belongs to a subfield of ethics called moral psychology. That question is the obvious one: "Why be moral?"[22] What makes this question so obvious is that thinking and acting in a moral way means that we must often think and act contrary to our own self-interests. What, some might ask, could be more senseless than that? Especially considering that we live in a society where most of us are trying to take advantage of one another. So, why make it easy for others to take advantage of us by not putting our own interests first? By not putting up a fight to ensure we don't get the short end of the stick in trying to realize our own aims and aspirations?

As I said, this is an old question that harkens all the way back to Plato's fable of the "Ring of Gyges," a tale he spins in his important work, the *Republic*. This is a story of a shepherd who, after a "great deluge of rain and an earthquake," spies a gold ring in some newly exposed ground. Much to his delight, he finds that when he puts the ring on and moves it one way he becomes invisible and another way becomes visible again. Equipped with this newfound artifact and knowledge of its inner workings, Gyges immediately arranges to become a messenger to the King "and on coming there he seduced the King's wife and with her aid set upon the king and slew him and possessed his kingdom." The moral of this story is that although we often talk up the importance of doing the right thing, when given the chance to further our own self-interests at little risk or cost to ourselves, as the shepherd in this tale was presented, we are not only apt to take advantage of the situation but to do so without giving it a second thought. So, at least on this accounting, there is no good reason to act ethically, to pursue justice over injustice, when our own self-interests are at stake. This means that anyone who does pursue justice and thereby forsakes his own self-interests is not to be admired but ridiculed, for such a person "would be regarded as most pitiable and a great fool by all who took note of it, though they would praise him before one another's faces, deceiving one another because of the fear of suffering injustice."[23]

A reason Plato's story still resonates with us is that the question "Why be moral?" has assumed even greater urgency for us today. For most contemporary Westerners, putting one's interests first is the most natural and rational thing to do. The reasons for our current state of affairs are fairly complex but, at the danger of oversimplification, I will mention two factors that stand out. The first concerns the growing secularization of Western society (especially in the 17th and 18th centuries), during which the great hold that hierarchical modes of thought held over people were largely broken.[24] The "great chain of being," for instance, assigned human beings their fixed place in the world alongside angels and other heavenly bodies. Other hierarchical social institutions, such as the church, likewise outfitted human beings with social roles and stations they were not to stray from. As these hierarchical modes crumbled over time, people began to take matters into their own hands; they began to think of themselves as autonomous beings capable of forging their own way in the world. This great boost in people's self-confidence that prompted them to choose for themselves what sort of life they wanted to live was further aided and abetted by a second important development: the great upsurge of capitalism, within which whole societies take their marching orders from the market. If there is one thing markets drum into our heads it is that our own individual desires and preferences can easily pass as reasons—and perfectly good and powerful reasons at that—for why we should pursue our self-interests whenever we get the chance. This is why market societies look askance at people who let their other-regarding sentiments and reasons drive their self-regarding ones—because from their perspective such reasons and actions come off not as morally laudable but as plainly irrational. It was because of social developments like these, then,[25] that during our modern period people, as MacIntyre astutely observed, "came to be thought of as in some dangerous measure egoistic by nature; and it is only once we think of mankind as by nature dangerously egoistic that altruism becomes at once socially necessary and yet apparently impossible and, if and when it occurs, inexplicable."[26] In other words, if we humans are hard wired to always think of ourselves first, to reflexively put our interests ahead of everyone else's, then there is really no place for morality in our lives and no reason to downplay or discourage our tendencies toward self-interest. Apparently, then, the brash suggestion presented in Plato's "Ring of Gyges" fable, that acting contrary to one's self-interest is the height of foolishness, not to mention stupidity, is as fitting a description of our society as it was of his.

I say "apparently," of course, not just because if we accede to Plato's and his modern-day counterparts' conception of human agency and practical rationality there would be no point in writing this introduction let alone in gathering the essays that make up this collection, but because their touting of the self-centered, self-resourceful, fully autonomous human agent is misguided and false. The problem here is not only that reasons and desires are *not* the same thing, and therefore that, as we discussed earlier, running them together is a serious error, but more fundamentally that this picture of what Richard Rorty aptly calls the "non-relational self" is at best a social fiction, one that many moral philosophers saw fit to turn into a philosophical fiction, and at worst a pernicious denial of our crucial relationships with and mutual dependence on others. That is to say, once we drop this pretense that we are

Ethical Thinking

Why be moral when doing so requires us to act contrary to our self-interests? Being moral just gets in the way of my getting what I want, so why do it?

"capable of existing independently of any concern for others,"[27] and concede that much, but of course not all, of what we do in life is bound up with our membership in various communities both small and large in stature, it becomes apparent just how indispensable moral reasons and values are in our life. This is especially true in social fare such as sports, in which goals, goods, and values are largely shared. In such social settings, our own individual good (the pursuit of bodily excellence and the living of a life devoted to it) is indistinguishable from the common good that governs these and other similar socially constituted practices (after all, the individual's quest for athletic excellence and the kind of life it demands is one mutually shared by all who take up this quest). This is why it is a mistake to treat these shared goods as if they were individual ones, as if they could be broken up and assigned to this or that person. The cardinal mistake an egoist makes is in his understanding of where his own good lies, a mistake attributable to his failure to see the goods in question as not "his" or "mine" but more fundamentally "ours."

It is this nexus between morality and the life we live in common with others that provides, then, the answer to our puzzling question of why be moral. The answer is not, to reiterate, the nonmoral idea that if we don't cooperate with one another our life promises to be "short and brutish," but the moral idea that we cannot sustain our relationships with our peers unless we can justify our actions to them on grounds they cannot reasonably reject.[28] That is to say, because our moral identity is intertwined with our membership in such communities, we cannot confirm whom we claim to be and what we claim to stand for without squaring our actions with those we share our life with. Williams confirms this for us in rather dramatic fashion when he explains why Ajax, a character in one of Sophocles' plays who commits an act that incurs the wrath and great shame of his peers, concludes he has no alternative but to commit suicide because "he has no way of living that anyone he respects would respect."[29] Indeed, it is no small matter what the fellow members of a community morally think of one another, which is why each of its members is so intent on justifying to the satisfaction of the moral standards held by their peers what and why they do the things they do.

> ## Ethical Thinking
>
> *What does it mean to say that in social practices such as sport the individual's good is in some important sense bound up with the common good?*

Normative Ethics and Normative Ethical Theories

We are now well positioned to sketch out the main moral theories that bear on the ethical considerations of sport featured in the essays to come (see table 3). These moral theories are largely of the normative variety in that they seek to spell out what principles, reasons, and values should guide our actions in particular sporting circumstances. However, the first section of essays deals with another branch of moral inquiry known as "metaethics," in which the primary aim is to explain and justify the status of normative ethical claims themselves. Thus normative questions such as, "Should you treat your opponents in sport with moral respect?" when cast in metaethical terms are transposed into questions of this sort: "What work is being done by the notion of 'should' in this and similar questions?" This asks, among other things, whether "should" in this context is to be understood as

TABLE 3 *Major Ethical Positions*

Utilitarian ethical theories	Deontological ethical theories	Contractarian ethical theories	Virtue ethical theories
Primarily focus on the consequences of our actions	Direct attention mainly to the intrinsic features of our actions rather than their consequences	Argue that moral principles are derived from the agreement of all those who are subject to their dictates	Claim that ethics should devote itself foremost to the development of moral character
Ask what act or rule produces the greatest balance of good over evil	Ask what our moral obligations are in specific circumstances or according to general rules of conduct	Variously claim that moral principles are compromises human agents agree to in order to get what they want, or are derived from the equal moral respect all agents are owed, or are best viewed as conventional solutions to moral problems	Argue that the cultivation of virtues and the pursuit of excellence in all its various forms are essential to good character
Equate the morally good with some notion of pleasure or happiness	Equate the right or good with our basic moral duties	Equate the right and the good with what people can reasonably agree to	Equate the right and the good with what persons of moral character would do in certain contexts

describing certain facts about us as human agents qua athletes or about the nature of sport itself, or whether the term is to be understood as *prescribing* certain ways in which sport is supposed to be valued; or is it to be understood as doing both? (The latter option would require denying any hard and fast distinction between facts and values.) One might also ask whether the moral judgments that back up "shoulds" of this kind are to be understood as ascribing some moral property to our actions in sport, or merely registering our attitudes or desires of approval or disapproval (a view variously called emotivism or expressivism). In metaethical inquiry, then, we are interested in the meaning of moral terms such as "right" and "good" when used in social settings such as those characteristic of sport, and in marking off moral from nonmoral considerations of such social practices. Above all else, however, metaethics is concerned with the justification of moral judgments, of whether the claim "You should respect your competitors in sport" is one that is binding on everyone who engages in sport, or is rather a personal claim of approval binding only on those who likewise approve (or disapprove, as the case may be) of actions like these. In the former sense, moral judgments can be treated as true or false, but in the latter they cannot be treated as either because they lack cognitive standing—that is, they are not the sort of thing than can be shown to be true or false (a view known as noncognitivism).

To reiterate then, metaethical considerations of sport that raise similar claims about whether and how ethical judgments in this arena of life can be justified occupy the attention of the authors of the first section of this anthology. The remaining sections and essays, and thus the bulk of the collection, are devoted to normative ethical considerations of sport that fall into one or more of the following categories of ethical theories.

Consequentialist/Teleological Ethical Theory

The first variety of ethical theory, as its name implies, focuses on the consequences of our actions and thus seeks to locate the rules, principles, and actions that produce the greatest balance of good over bad. If the consideration of such consequences is geared to the good of individuals, then we end up with a position called *ethical egoism*. If such consequences are gauged in terms of the good of all, then the theory we wind up with is called *utilitarianism*. We have good reason, as previously argued, to question whether what is morally right and good can simply be equated with what is in our best self-interests, which if true, as David Gauthier reminds us, would make the appeal to the right and good superfluous because the work these notions are asked to do can be done perfectly fine by nonmoral words such as "benefit" and "advantage."[30] Thus, I shall restrict my attention to utilitarian ethical theory.

As just noted, utilitarian ethical theory holds that moral notions such as right or good are those that either directly or indirectly produce the greatest balance of good over evil. However, utilitarianism comes in two main forms. The first is called act-utilitarianism and asks which of the available actions available to moral agents in a particular set of circumstances are likely to generate the greatest good. The second form is called rule-utilitarianism, and true to its name it asks what rule or rules promise to deliver the most good. In the first case, then, the relevant question is which act or acts have the greatest utility, whereas in the second case the relevant question is which rule or rules have the greatest utility.[31]

Ethical Thinking

Why is "egoism" such a threat to morality?

What utilitarians mean by the good in their calculations of the consequences of acting in certain ways or in following certain rules does vary, but generally they are referring to some notion of pleasure or happiness—both of which are terms that, as their detractors like to point out, are hard to get one's hands around with any great precision. But the utility of our action or rules could also apply to a number of other "good" things, such as power or self-knowledge. In any case, whatever candidate qualifies as the good for utilitarians is one that they seek to maximize to the benefit of the greatest number. That is why Blackburn perceptively characterizes the cast of mind of the utilitarian as that of a "social engineer," as someone who tinkers with social practices, institutions, and goods so as to wring out of them the greatest good possible.[32]

Now, as a well-established and at one time dominant normative ethical theory, utilitarianism has attracted its fair share of critics. Not surprisingly, such critics have questioned whether the notion of utility such theorists work with is itself a moral notion. For example, it may well be the case that the best way to produce the greatest good is to commit a seemingly immoral act, say, by breaking a promise made to someone.[33] Critics have also raised the question of whether the good can be neatly measured and aggregated in the particular ways in which utilitarian types seem to take for granted that it can. Further, critics of this brand of ethical theory have argued that utilitarians impose unreasonable moral demands on human agents, demands that are much too onerous and far reaching for anyone to be held accountable for. This criticism trades on an idea common to ethics generally that *ought* implies *can;* in other words, the moral duties we are held responsible for must be ones that are in our power and capacity to deliver. According to its critics, then, the problem with utilitarianism is that just about anything people do, such as going to a movie, can be criticized on utilitarian grounds, because it could easily be claimed on these same grounds that the money spent to purchase a movie ticket could have been better spent by giving, for example, to Oxfam—a gesture that redounds to the greater good of the greatest number in rather dramatic terms because it takes precious little money to keep someone from starving to death in the poorest regions of the world. One would be hard pressed in the face of demands like this to justify many of the choices we fortunate residents of the rich Western countries routinely make during the course of our daily lives.

Perhaps, however, the most important criticism leveled at utilitarians (mainly by well-respected proponents of the next version of ethical theory we will consider) is that it doesn't take the separateness of persons seriously enough. The charge here is that the utilitarian calculus these theorists employ to effect the greatest balance of good over evil unjustifiably subordinates the interests and aims of the individual to the general welfare, because contributions to the general welfare may well require us to step on the interests and rights of individuals who come out as definite losers in such schemes. Blackburn, however, rightfully reminds us that this criticism isn't entirely fair because utilitarians were responding to what they legitimately saw as a serious moral problem in its own right—namely, that many individuals in modern society display an alarming lack of concern for the plight of others.[34]

Deontological Ethical Theories

Unlike utilitarian theories of the right and good, deontological theories focus mainly on the intrinsic features of our moral actions rather than on their consequences. For theorists of this persuasion, for an action to qualify as a moral action it must be initiated and executed for distinctly moral reasons; that is, the action must be carried out precisely because it is the right and good thing to do. Deontological theory derives from the Greek *deontos,* which means duty. So conceived, a moral action is one performed wholly out of a sense of duty, which further means that moral notions such as the right and the good are to be thought of as binding obligations rather than voluntary preferences. This pivotal distinction between absolute moral commands and relative subjective desires is the same distinction that the eighteenth century German philosopher Immanuel Kant, hands-down the most famous exponent of this ethical position, tried to capture when he distinguished "categorical" imperatives, which single out the moral "must" of irrevocable duty (e.g., I must never break a promise), from "hypothetical" imperatives, which single out the practical "must" of our revocable desires and wants (e.g., I must go to school if I want to be a teacher).[35] Further, not only do deontologists insist that moral imperatives are unconditional ones that make absolute claims on us, they further insist that our actions admit of being only right or wrong, that there are no gray areas when it comes to the evaluation of our moral judgments and the actions that flow from them.[36]

As was the case with utilitarian moral theories, deontological theories also come in two main varieties. The first is called *act-deontological* theory and holds that determining what our moral obligations are is always a matter of figuring out what we should do in the particular circumstances in which we find ourselves. Because these particular circumstances are always changing, we have no choice but to base our moral judgments on the shifting contexts they introduce, which is why we cannot appeal to general principles nor, of course, to abstract calculations of the possible consequences of our actions to guide our actions. It is no wonder then, why act-deontologists look askance at general moral rules or principles, arguing that they are either phantom notions we conjure up to solve moral problems that seem otherwise unsolvable, or are useless platitudes (always honor your promises), or are simply derivative of particular moral judgments we have made in the past.[37] By contrast, *rule-deontological* theory, the second major version of this conception of morality, holds that deciding what our moral obligations are is a matter of determining the standards of right and wrong themselves, of divining what rules should govern our moral duties to ourselves and others. As such, rule-deontological theory regards rules such as "never tell a lie" not as useless general prescriptions but rather as reliable guides to how we should act under particular circumstances. Without appeal to some such rules, adherents of this theory insist, we would be pretty much clueless how to act when we find ourselves, as we often do, in new situations. Just how many of these master rules there are that must be taken into account is a matter of some dispute among rule-deontologists and raises the problem of what we are to do when they conflict with one another. But one solution to this problem, which again is owed to Kant, is to maintain that there is only one absolute moral rule. For Kant, that rule can be found in the first formulation he offers of his "categorical imperative": "Act only according to that maxim by which you can at the same time will that it should become a universal law."[38] Follow this rule of universalization, Kant counsels, and you can rest assured of the soundness of your moral judgments and the rightness of your actions no matter how unfamiliar the social setting in which you make those judgments and perform those actions.

   If the mindset of the utilitarian moral theorist is, as Blackburn earlier related, that of the engineer, the mindset of the deontologist moral theorist is, as Blackburn again instructively relates, that of the judge.[39] That is because both act- and rule-deontologists insist that moral judgments must be made and rendered from an impartial standpoint that is analogous to the impartial standpoint judges employ when deciding cases before them. But unlike judges who are bound by socially and politically settled law, moral legislators of a deontological bent, especially Kantian inspired rule-deontologists, are adamant that we must not only discount our own desires and aims when formulating our moral judgments and determining how we should act, but we must discount as well the social roles and cultural values that define the world we share in common with our peers. That is to say, moral agents must step back not only from the first-person singular frame of reference that informs their individual desires and aims, but also from the first-person plural frame of reference that informs the larger culture in which they live. Instead, then, of asking "how should *I* act" in circumstance X, or "how should *we* act" in circumstance X, the morally relevant (because impartial) question is "how should *anyone* act" in circumstance X.[40] Thus, it is obvious that for rule-deontologists of the Kantian school, moral assessment is not for the faint of heart because it demands nothing less than our complete disengagement from the world as we ordinarily see and know it. We must pry ourselves loose from our more familiar subjective and social perspectives.

   Deontological moral theory receives an ample share of criticism all its own. Much of the criticism takes issue with the rigor that rule-deontologists of a Kantian bent insist must attend our moral judgments. A primary concern is that the necessary impartial standpoint one must take before making moral judgments is too far removed from the "real" world to be relevant to what goes on there. In other words, when we view the world and the actions that take place there from a perspective that is detached from that world, one might plausibly ask what possible counsel or guidance moral principles so adduced can provide our actions? This was the same issue Williams earlier raised with his example of whether he should save his wife or a stranger. In the example, he couldn't save both from the imminent danger they faced, and he concluded it was morally permissible to save his wife rather than the stranger. Remember that Williams' problem with an impartial take in this case was that substituting the impartial point of view of "anyone" when it is "my wife" that needs saving discounts his intimate relationship with his wife. Williams held that such a circumstance should never be discounted in personal cases, including in determining one's moral obligations.[41]

So, the problem in insisting that our moral judgments be strictly impartial is that impartiality closes off moral scrutiny from where it is most needed and required, namely, in the actual situations that crop up in my daily life and in the cultural roles and practices that color and define that life. Because it is in those situations and cultural roles that I live my life and form the important relationships that define who I am and what my ethical obligations are, it is precisely those situations and cultural roles that locate whatever meaning my life might have and makes life worth living in the first place.[42] This is why critics of this ethical position are so insistent that when we remove moral reflection from its rightful place in the fabric of our lives we are not just making a simple intellectual miscalculation, a mere theoretical mistake, but rather a fatal error, one with stark theoretical and practical ramifications, about how we should live our lives.

Contractarian Ethical Theory

This brand of ethical theory is broader in scope than that of utilitarian or deontological ethical theories because its conception of morality cuts across other mainstream ethical theories and thus claims a number of adherents usually identified with those other theories. This is why such eminent and wide-ranging philosophers as Plato, Hobbes, Locke, Rousseau, and Kant have all at one time or another been tagged with the contractarian label. It makes some sense that they are tagged this way because what they share in common, despite the great differences in their views, is the idea that moral norms should be rooted in the agreement of all of those who are subject to the constraints and principles they put in place.[43]

Contractarian moral theory comes in three basic varieties. The Hobbesian version of the theory, which we commented on earlier, claims that we have good nonmoral reasons to be moral. These reasons involve the basic idea that human agents cannot achieve what they want in life without the cooperation of others. Hence, it is our mutual dependence on others that accounts for why we have a compelling reason to cooperate with them, and thus to agree on a set of moral principles that govern our interaction. Simply put, noncooperation would torpedo all of our aims and hopes because it would prevent us from achieving whatever it is we sought to achieve.

According to this notion of morality, principles of morality are best thought of as principles of compromise that we agree to for distinctly self-interested reasons. That is why adherents of Hobbesian contract theory often invoke rules of bargaining or apply strategies gleaned from game theory, especially from Prisoner's Dilemma games,[44] to determine which moral principles should regulate our conduct. These sorts of principles and strategies model well the egoistic transactions that typify this sort of social interaction. And what bargaining and game theory tell us in this regard is precisely what Hobbesian contract theory claims as its main thesis—namely, that we are all better off, meaning we are all more likely to get what we want, if we cooperate with one another rather than seek "immediately available benefits."[45]

The second kind of contractarian ethical theory takes its inspiration from Kant and is most associated with John Rawls' two important books, *A Theory of Justice* and *Political Liberalism*.[46] The Kantian grounding of this theory is evident from the fact that instead of beginning with our individual aims and preferences as Hobbesians do, Rawls and likeminded moral theorists begin with the unmistakable moral idea that all people should be treated with basic moral respect. What is meant by moral respect here is derived directly from Kant's second, and no less famous, formulation of the categorical imperative, "Act so that you treat humanity, whether in your own person or in that of another, always as an end and never as a means only."[47] This rules out in principle Hobbesian and game theoretic notions of morality because these treat others almost exclusively as means rather than as ends—that is, as tools that can and should be wielded to further one's own ends.

Rawls offers two versions of his Kantian-based contractarian theory, one of which trades on the notion of impartiality and the other on a public notion of moral rationality. In his first version, which he develops in his path-breaking book *A Theory of Justice,* Rawls seconds Kant's basic view that moral judgments must be impartial because otherwise they might unfairly work to the advantage of some and the disadvantage of others. However, Rawls does not appeal to a benevolent "God" to secure such a moral vantage point, one whose basic nature and disposition is to view all human agents impartially, nor to Kant's abstract conception of moral reasoning that views the world and what people do there from no particular perspective within it, but to an ingenuous hypothetical device that he calls the "veil of ignorance." The basic idea is that if we want to ensure that our moral decisions are indeed impartial rather than partial, we must deliberate behind a "veil of ignorance" that deprives us of all particular knowledge regarding such things as our social class or status, our natural talents, our particular conception of the good and of the specifics of our life plan, and of our psychological moods and likings.[48] If we are pressed to decide how we should act in the absence of all these particulars regarding our personal and social situation, then our decisions will be genuinely impartial decisions that give fair consideration to the interests of others and that ensure that all concerned will be treated with self-respect. This follows from the idea that when we deliberate behind the veil of ignorance we would not be "in a position to tailor principles to [our] advantage" because none of us, given our reflectively induced state of ignorance, would know enough to be able to do so.[49]

In Rawls' second rendition of contractarian theory he distances himself even further from the Kantian link between impartial moral judgment and maximally detached impersonal reflection. He does so by eschewing the kind of "radical ignorance" achieved by deliberating behind the hypothetical veil of ignorance, and instead opts for a public, political conception of what he calls the "reasonable," which insists that the moral principles that regulate our interactions with one another be grounded in the mutual assent of all relevant parties. The starting point here, then, is not strict impartiality but mutual acceptability, which derives, for Rawls, from our common membership in a moral–political community and the shared intuitions that one picks up and internalizes as a matter of course from such membership. Morality so understood is a public conception that draws "solely upon basic intuitive ideas that are embedded in the political institutions of a constitutional democratic regime."[50] On this notion of moral rationality, as Rorty nicely puts it, we do not claim that "'your own current interests dictate that you agree to our proposal'," the previously remarked Hobbesian contractarian version, "but rather 'your own central beliefs, the ones which are central to your own moral identity, suggest that you should agree to our proposal'."[51] To do anything less for Rorty is tantamount to denying whom one claims to be as an ethical being, in effect, to become one of "them," one of the bad people, and thus to cross the line we ourselves have drawn between moral behavior and immoral behavior.

The third variety of contractarian moral theory takes its cue from Hume, arguing that moral principles are "conventional solutions" to moral problems that crop up in everyday life. Rather than arguing why people have reasons to be moral, as Hobbesians do, or advocating for substantive moral notions like respect for persons, as Kantians do, Humeans endeavor to show that human agents have the particular moral conceptions, evaluative outlooks, and ethical commitments they do as a function of their efforts to cope with the moral issues that life throws their way. This means further, as Sayre-McCord, a prominent exponent of this theory, astutely puts it, that "our [very] capacity to think in moral terms and to talk of reasons depends . . . upon resources that are available only once certain conventions and practices have been established."[52] According to this view, morality itself is a social practice that draws its sustenance from the conventions that human agents conjure up to resolve the moral problems they encounter in the course of their lives; morality can be understood and justified only against this social backdrop. It is not hard to see in this regard why Humeans appeal to considerations of fairness and justice rather than self-interest when it comes to moral matters, because the whole point of moral reasoning, as they see it, is to sort out the moral conflicts that inevitably result when people's particular interests and aims clash.

Criticism of contractarian ethical theories has taken many forms, which is not surprising given the range of views that fall under this category of ethical thought. Critics, for example, question whether parties who deliberate behind a veil of ignorance would choose the particular impartial moral principles of justice that Rawls thinks they would.[53] Other critics have taken Rawls to task for what they see as a too individualistic conception of the self that equates our capacity for choice as the essence of our personhood and that thus wrongly discounts our mutual dependence on others.[54] How fair these criticisms are is a matter of much dispute, but it is not saying too much, I think, to say that the force of some of these criticisms has been muted somewhat by Rawls' political conception of justice that does seem to recognize our important relationships to others and to the moral intuitions that come with membership in a political community. The one strand of this theory that has, however, come in for major criticism is the Hobbesian one. The main charge here, as already noted, is that theories of this kind are not moral theories at all but rather thinly veiled accounts of how cooperation importantly figures into the furtherance of one's own self-interests and, more specifically (and, I would add, more perniciously), how to use others to get what one wants. As the critics see it, the problem is that by starting with the actual desires of individual agents, rather than attempting to neutralize those desires by resort to hypothetical devices or by political appeals, and by insisting only that one compromise one's actual desires rather than critically examine them, the agreements we are able to patch together will merely reflect the "morally suspect differences" that it is the job of moral reasoning to weed out.[55] Indeed, how could it be otherwise, they argue, because those compromises, as we have seen, leave untouched the inequalities that shape the actual circumstances in which these human agents do their bidding and the actual desires they acquire as a consequence. If there is anything that can reasonably be thought of as moral in the working out of these compromises, these critics ask, it is exceedingly difficult to see what it could or might be.

Virtue Theory

The fourth, and last, major ethical position to be discussed in the chapters ahead is virtue theory. Proponents of this theory maintain that ethical considerations should be concerned foremost with the development of moral character rather than the formulation of moral principles or rules or the calculation of the consequences of our action. They argue that to be a person of good character, two factors are especially important. The first is to acquire the virtues on which the formation of good character is dependent, and the second is to adopt what Slote refers to as *aretaic* motives that dispose human agents to seek and achieve excellence in all that they do.[56] This is why virtue theory places a heavy premium on courage, justice, honesty, and integrity in our dealings with one another, and on excellence as the preferred end of human striving.

If virtue theory, as its name implies, accords primacy to the virtues and to evaluative notions such as excellence, then we need to know both how its adherents are using the notion of virtue and what relation they think should obtain among the virtues. The answer to the first question is the relatively straightforward one that virtues are qualities of action or dispositions of character that, as Williams writes, lead us "to choose or reject actions because they are of a certain ethically relevant kind."[57] So acting out of a sense of fairness is crucial to the moral integrity of practices such as politics and sport, just as acting courageously is crucial to the moral conduct of war and similar martial activities. It is important in this respect not to confuse virtuous activity with merely skillful activity; virtues require not only a certain skill in sizing up the situations we find ourselves in but also "characteristic patterns of desire and motivation" that are appropriate to the contexts in which we operate,[58] a developed eye in discerning the relevant moral features of a situation, and a practical sense of judgment on how to achieve ethical ends in specific circumstances. It is also context that gives us the answer to our second question regarding the proper ordering and relation of the virtues. For which virtues should be accorded primacy in our actions and which, if any, role other virtues should play in them depends entirely on the context—that is, on the kind of social practice under scrutiny.

The strong connection virtue theorists make between the just-mentioned notion of practical judgment, or what Aristotle called *phronesis* (practical wisdom), and ethical decision making is a signature feature of their conception of moral reasoning. Because without the counsel of practical judgment, these theorists tell us, our ability to match up the means best suited to the realization of the ethical ends we choose would be severely impaired. And without the counsel provided by the virtues, our ability to select genuinely good ends would be likewise severely impaired. The proper relation between them is summed up nicely in Aristotle's remark that "virtue makes us aim at the right mark, and practical wisdom makes us take the right means."[59] It is no wonder, then, why Aristotle and contemporary exponents of this theory argue as vigorously as they do that when this link between the virtues and practical judgment is severed all is lost from a moral perspective. For when practical judgment no longer is informed by the virtues, moral reasoning turns into a specious form of practical reasoning, one in which, as MacIntyre tells us, our rational deliberations are reduced to "merely a certain cunning for linking means to ends."[60] And when the virtues no longer can depend on practical judgment to deliver the means needed to accomplish the ethical ends they set in our sights, they become little more than quaint—not to mention wholly ineffectual—curiosities. Either way we lose, morally speaking, for although cunning is an important and perhaps even an admirable quality in some practices (bargaining in the market comes quickly to mind), this is definitely not the case in ethical circles where doing the right thing for the right reasons matters most. As for our inability to accomplish the ends we choose to pursue, being ineffectual is hardly a term of praise either in or outside of ethics.

Thus, for a virtuous person, it is not only crucial that the end sought be a morally worthy one, say athletic excellence, but also that it is accomplished in a morally upstanding way, say in accordance with the rules and out of moral respect for our opponents. This is because, for virtue theorists, what distinguishes moral reasoning from other kinds of practical reasoning is that the end sought "cannot be adequately characterized independently of . . . the means."[61] Thus, that some particular end is achieved is of no moral consequence for virtue theorists unless how the end is achieved is not only taken into account but given equal billing. The reason virtuous persons morally deliberate just so, and can be counted on to morally deliberate just so, is because what they choose in the way of ends and how they go about realizing those ends have been duly tutored by the virtues and honed by the repeated exercise of their practical judgment. Unlike Kantians, then, for whom acting morally requires we forsake our desires and inclinations and act exclusively out of a sense of duty, for virtue theorists, acting morally does not require acting contrary to our desires as long as our desires bear the tell-tale imprint of the virtues.

To sum up, virtue theorists claim that what is the right and good thing to do is what a virtuous person would do in a certain context. This explains why they accord special ethical significance to acts committed, for example, in the name of friendship, not done out of a sense of duty or in accord with some ethical principle or other or according to the consequential calculus utilitarians employ, but rather performed out of an intrinsic interest in the welfare of others.[62] It is other-regarding acts such as these, therefore, that for virtue theorists best capture what morality at its core is all about. And we can only expect the virtues to flourish, they further maintain, if we create the right ethical setting for them: one in which virtue is roundly and sincerely celebrated and vice is just as roundly and sincerely condemned.

Despite the fact that this brand of ethical theory has an ancient lineage that can be traced back to Aristotle, it has only relatively lately garnered much attention in philosophical circles. This would explain why the theory has not come in for the same level of critical scrutiny as the other moral theories described here have. That said, it is not as if critics have given virtue theory a free pass. Perhaps the principal criticism leveled by would-be critics concerns whether the claim broadly made by virtue enthusiasts that the virtues alone, apart from any appeal to moral principles and rules, can do all the ethical work that needs to be done with regard to the complicated and often vexing moral problems life throws our way. Critics have been likewise skeptical of virtue theorists for their closely related claim that the moral guidance the virtues furnish truly is uncodifiable—that is, it cannot be neatly encapsulated into clearly demarcated principles and rules of conduct that provide guidance over a wide range of cases. Critics have further wondered aloud how adherents of this view propose to handle situations in which the virtues clash, and in which, therefore, it is not at all clear which virtues should be acted on and which silenced or even rejected. The upshot of this complaint is that it is bordering on naïve, if not duplicitous, to hold that the virtues will always act in concert with one another, that the moral instructions they convey will always point us in the same direction.

Conclusion

This completes my introductory sketch of ethics, of the central questions it asks, of the various modes of inquiry it endorses, and, finally, of the major theories that the field is most identified with. My intent in writing this introduction was to provide readers the background that some of them might need to fully appreciate the ethical questions probed by the authors of the essays in this collection, to gauge the strength and sophistication of the arguments they make, and, more generally, to grasp the ethical perspectives pursued in their critical examinations of sport. Now, it is high time that we turn to the essays themselves and to the important moral issues in sport with which they grapple.

Notes

1. The idea to divide up questions into objective, subjective, and normative ones is one that I borrowed from Professor Martin Benjamin, Michigan State University, in a seminar he conducted on teaching philosophy held at my previous academic institution, the University of Tennessee. I have also taken the liberty of using some of his examples to show how these questions differ from one another.

2. Its incoherence has to do with its self-refuting character. For as the eminent philosopher Hilary Putnam once famously said, if, as relativism says, one view is as good as any other, then why isn't the view that relativism is false as good as any other?

3. Simon Blackburn, *Being Good* (Oxford: Oxford University Press, 2001), 27.

4. Simon Blackburn, *Being Good* (Oxford: Oxford University Press, 2001), 53.

5. Christine M. Koorsgaard, *The Sources of Normativity* (Cambridge, MA: Cambridge University Press, 1996), p. 1. I should note that Koorsgaard's, to my mind correct, contention that one of the more important facts about human beings is that they have values challenges an important distinction between facts and values held by many moral theorists. This point will come up again shortly.

6. I owe this distinction and much of the discussion that follows to Michael Smith's fine book, *The Moral Problem* (Oxford: Blackwell Publishing, 1994), especially chapter 5. I should, however, offer two caveats here. The first is that motivating reasons do not conform to the tripartite division of reasons I have just offered and thus should not be confused for what I earlier called subjective reasons. Motivating reasons, implicitly at least, may well call for justification in a way that subjective reasons of taste never do. For Smith, however, motivating reasons do not qualify, strictly speaking, as normative ones because in asking after them we are only interested in their causal efficacy in prompting us to act in a certain way rather that their justificatory status—which we simply ignore here. The second caveat is that in distinguishing, following Smith, motivating from normative reasons it is neither explicitly claimed nor implied, by Smith or myself, that normative reasons can't be motivating ones—that is, that they cannot cause us to act differently than we would if we simply acted first and only then reflected on what we had done. It would be foolish to claim such, of course, because the very reason that we deliberate about how we should act is precisely because we expect our deliberation to influence the way we in fact do act.

7. This, and the examples that follow, have been lifted from Smith's *The Moral Problem* (Oxford: Blackwell Publishing, 1994), 134-135.

8. Of course, as observed in note 6 above, that motivating and normative reasons may and often do converge in this sense not only goes without saying but is the aim, if not ideal, of moral and other forms of normative inquiry.

9. Those already familiar with the sport philosophy literature will have no trouble in recognizing that my account of the aesthetic and its application to sports derives from David Best's important essay "The Aesthetic in Sport," reprinted in Morgan's and Meier's second edition of *Philosophic Inquiry in Sport* (Champaign, IL: Human Kinetics, 1988), 377-389. It was here that Best offered his important distinction between purposive sports such as football, in which aesthetic considerations figure hardly at all, and aesthetic sports such as figure skating, in which aesthetic judgments themselves determine what counts as athletic success.

10. John Rawls, "The Priority of Right and Ideas of the Good," in *John Rawls: Collected Papers,* ed. S. Freeman (Cambridge, MA: Harvard University Press, 1999), 449.

11. Bernard Williams, *Moral Luck* (Cambridge, MA: Cambridge University Press, 1981), 17-18.

12. *John Rawls: Collected Papers* (Cambridge, MA: Harvard University Press, 1999), 202.

13. Bernard Williams, *Ethics and the Limits of Philosophy* (Cambridge, MA: Harvard University Press, 1985), 58.

14. Bernard Williams, *Shame and Necessity* (Berkeley: University of California Press, 1994), 77.

15. Simon Blackburn, *Being Good,* p. 4.

16. Christine Koorsgaard, *The Sources of Normativity,* p. 11.

17. Alasdair MacIntyre, *After Virtue* (Notre Dame, IN: University of Notre Dame Press, 1984), 221.

18. Such concurrence extends even to the offending party. For as Williams astutely observes, the perpetrator of an act that his peers appraise as morally wrong is not only aware of their negative assessment but concurs fully in their judgment regarding its wrongness. That should come as no surprise because to be a bona fide member of a community means that one has internalized its mores, its constitutive moral beliefs and judgments. See Bernard Williams, *Shame and Necessity,* p. 82.

19. Simon Blackburn, *Being Good,* p. 129.

20. This agreement over what counts as a reason and a good action does not, of course, preclude disagreement about particular issues, such as the abortion question. It also does not suppose that the considered views of a community regarding certain matters are immune to change. Rather, it more basically holds that a community is not a community unless there is general agreement among its members as to what it is rational and good to do.

21. Peter Singer, "Animal Liberation." Reprinted in Morgan et al., *Philosophic Inquiry in Sport* (Champaign, IL: Human Kinetics, 1988), 339.

22. In keeping with our previous discussion, the "why" question asked here is a rational, normative one rather than a psychological, motivational one. This means the answer to this question requires a rational justification for shunting aside whatever desires we might have to act on our self-interests and instead act on the common good.

23. Plato's *Republic.* In *The Collected Dialogues of Plato,* eds. E. Hamilton and H. Cairns (Princeton, NJ: Princeton University Press, 1961), book II, 360 a-e.

24. For more along these lines, see Charles Taylor, *The Ethics of Authenticity* (Cambridge, MA: Harvard University Press, 1992), especially chapter 1.

25. Of course, this championing of individual autonomy is also one of the crowning achievements of modernity, and one that no one in their right mind would or should repudiate entirely. The problem lies with the manner in which this achievement has often been interpreted and understood as suggesting that it requires that we reject not only hierarchical modes of thought and social institutions that have no legitimate standing in contemporary society but also our mutual dependence on others that most definitely does possess legitimacy in this and any other well-ordered society.

26. Alasdair MacIntyre, *After Virtue* (Notre Dame, IN: University of Notre Dame Press, 1984), 228.

27. Richard Rorty, *Philosophy and Social Hope* (New York: Penguin Books, 1999), 77.

28. This latter language is drawn from John Rawls' *Political Liberalism* (New York: Columbia University Press, 1993), 49.

29. Bernard Williams, *Shame and Necessity,* p. 85.

30. As Gauthier further relates in this same vein, the only reason we appeal to moral considerations rather than those of advantage and benefit in such cases is because the latter fail us as appropriate guides about how we should live. David Gauthier, *Morals By Agreement* (Oxford: Clarendon Press, 1986), 1.

31. Frankena, *Ethics*, p. 30.

32. Blackburn, *Being Good*, p. 88.

33. Frankena, *Ethics*, p. 33.

34. Blackburn, *Being Good*, p. 92.

35. Williams, *Shame and Necessity*, pp. 75-76.

36. Blackburn, *Being Good*, p. 88.

37. This point and the rest of my discussion of deontological ethical theory is heavily indebted to Frankena's *Ethics*, p. 15.

38. Immanuel Kant, *Foundations of the Metaphysics of Morals* (NJ: Prentice Hall, 1997), 38.

39. Blackburn, *Being Good*, p. 88.

40. Bernard Williams, *Ethics and the Limits of Philosophy*, p. 65.

41. See p. 15 of the text.

42. Williams says it much better that I do here when he writes, "There can come a point at which it is quite unreasonable for a man to give up, in the name of the impartial good ordering of the world of moral agents, something which is a condition of his having any interest in being around in that world at all." *Moral Luck*, p. 14.

43. My discussion of this variant of moral theory borrows heavily from Geoffrey Sayre-McCord's fine essay, "Contractarianism," in *The Blackwell Guide to Ethical Theory*, ed. H. LaFollette (Oxford: Blackwell Publishers, 2000), 247-267.

44. Prisoner's dilemma games are two-person games that model what occurs in plea-bargaining cases. In other words, two prisoners are questioned separately and offered the same deal. If one of them confesses (defects) and the other doesn't, the defector will get off scot-free and the other will receive a substantial prison sentence. If both confess (defect), then both receive a moderate prison sentence. If both refuse to confess (cooperate with one another), then both receive a light prison sentence. What this game purports to show is that although confession by one prisoner and silence by another is the very best outcome for whomever is the one that confesses, the next best outcome (the second best) results when both prisoners cooperate with one another and remain silent. So the best solution to this game is for both to cooperate and remain silent; otherwise, they will be put in a position that mandates that they choose the third- or fourth-best outcome. For more along these lines, see A. W. Tucker, "Prisoner's Dilemma," in *The Cambridge Dictionary of Philosophy* ed. R. Audi (New York: Cambridge University Press, 1995), 646-647.

45. Sayre-McCord, "Contractarianism," p. 260.

46. John Rawls, *A Theory of Justice* (Cambridge: Harvard University Press, 1971) and John Rawls, *Political Liberalism* (New York: Columbia University Press, 1993).

47. Immanuel Kant's *Foundations of the Metaphysics of Morals*, p. 46.

48. John Rawls, *A Theory of Justice*, p. 137.

49. John Rawls, *A Theory of Justice*, p. 139.

50. John Rawls, "Justice as Fairness: Political Not Metaphysical." In *John Rawls: Collected Papers*, p. 390.

51. Richard Rorty, "Justice as a Larger Loyalty." In *Richard Rorty: Critical Dialogues*, eds. M. Festenstein and S. Thompson (Cambridge: Polity Press, 2001), 232. The alert reader will notice here how contractarian ethical theory veers into a communitarian notion of moral rationality of the sort previously discussed and defended in the opening pages of this introduction.

52. Sayre-McCord, "Contractarianism," p. 263.

53. Ronald Dworkin's discussion of Mackie in this regard, who claims that parties who reason as Rawls suggests here, deprived of knowledge of their own particular situation, would choose a theory of justice based on "average" utility. *Taking Rights Seriously* (Cambridge: Harvard University Press, 1977), 174.

54. Michael Sandel, *Liberalism and the Limits of Justice* (Cambridge, MA: Cambridge University Press, 1982).

55. Sayre-McCord, "Contractarianism," p. 261.

56. Michael Slote, "Virtue Ethics." In *The Blackwell Guide to Ethical Theory*, ed. H. LaFollette (Oxford: Blackwell Publishers, 2000), 325.

57. Williams, *Ethics and the Limits of Philosophy*, pp. 8-9.

58. Williams, *Ethics and the Limits of Philosophy*, p. 9.

59. Aristotle's *Nicomachean Ethics*. In *The Basic Works of Aristotle*, ed. R. McKeon (New York: Random House, 1941), 1144a, 8-10.

60. MacIntyre, *After Virtue*, p. 154.

61. MacIntyre, *After Virtue*, p. 184.

62. Michael Slote, "Virtue Ethics." In *The Blackwell Guide to Ethical Theory*, ed. H. LaFollette (Oxford: Blackwell Publishers, 2000), 333.

I

PART

Metaethical Considerations of Sport

The first essay featured in this section, Bernard Suits' "The Nature of Sport," offers neither a metaethical nor a normative ethical analysis of sport. On the contrary, the aim of Suits' essay is to define sport rather than to mine it for any ethical properties it might or might not possess. This is why his essay begins the collection—because it furnishes a much-needed definitional account of how sport is to be understood in the ethical analyses to come.

To define sport, to set out the necessary and sufficient conditions that qualify some activity as a genuinely sporting one, it first must be established, as Suits sees it, that all sports are games of a particular type. Thus, he begins his essay with an account of what a game is, which, as he sees it, can be defined in reference to four elements. The first element is that games are goal-directed activities, and the goals crucial in this regard are what he calls, first, *pre-lusory* goals, which he characterizes as the specific state of affairs one seeks to achieve in a game—such as putting a ball in a hole or through a round hoop or crossing the finish line first—and, second, *lusory* goals, which he characterizes as winning a game by putting a ball in a hole with the fewest number of strokes or crossing the finish line first by, among other things, going around the oval track rather than across it. Because pre-lusory goals can stand on their own and lusory goals cannot (because they require at least some implicit reference to the rules), and because Suits wants to delineate one by one the features that define a game, he specifies that the first element of a game is that it has a pre-lusory goal.

The second element of a game for Suits is that it has certain means that he calls lusory ones, which mark off permissible from impermissible means to achieve the pre-lusory goal of a game. Of course, restriction to lusory means is a necessary condition of winning a game.

So far so good, as games appear to be much like other sorts of goal-directed activities we engage in that sanction certain ways of achieving them and outlaw other ways they might be achieved.

The third element of a game Suits calls "constitutive" rules because they, along with the pre-lusory goal, spell out the conditions that must be fulfilled in order to be playing a game at all (but not playing it well). This element drives a rather large wedge between games and other goal-oriented activities people take up, because the constitutive rules of games make the attainment of the pre-lusory goal more rather than less difficult to achieve by prohibiting certain useful ways it might be attained. For example, it is useful but forbidden to trip a competitor in a race or to shoot an opponent in a football or baseball game. Thus, unlike most activities people participate in, the rules of a game put "unnecessary obstacles" in our path to make the achievement of its pre-lusory goal more challenging. Of course, games also have rules of skill, such as keep your head down when swinging a golf club, that are meant to aid our surmounting of these unnecessary obstacles, and so, to allow us to accomplish these goals as skillfully as possible. However, because these latter rules, unlike constitutive ones, specify only the conditions of playing a game well, they don't figure further in Suits' account of a game.

The fourth and final element of Suits' account of a game he calls the "lusory attitude," which he defines as "the knowing acceptance of constitutive rules just so the activity made possible by these rules can occur." The purpose of the lusory attitude in Suits' definition of games is to distinguish those rather rare occasions in ordinary life when we rule out more in favor of less efficient means for achieving a goal, say, to get rid of a toothache by shooting ourselves in the head, or to launch a nuclear weapon to intimidate a potential foreign invader, not because we want to engage in some such activity, but because resorting to these very efficient means would lead to a disastrous result—in the first case our own death, and in the second a possible nuclear war. In a game, however, the reason that we rule out using more efficient means to achieve the pre-lusory goal is that is what it takes to play a game—otherwise, we wouldn't be able to play this or any other game.

Although we have yet to discuss sport itself, at least explicitly, we have already come a long way in defining it because, for Suits, as noted, all sports are games. Thus, what qualifies an activity as a sporting one is, to use Suits' shorthand definition of a game, that it is a "voluntary attempt to overcome unnecessary obstacles." However, as a particular kind of game that can be distinguished from other kinds of games, sport possesses the following additional four features. First, it is a game of skill, which marks it off from games of chance, such as dice games. Second, it is a game of physical skill, where the relevant moves involve the skillful and strategic use of one's body, which distinguishes it from other games of skill, such as board games and card games. Third, a sport is a game that has a wide following, which means that it must be more than a local attraction or fad. Fourth, and last, a sport is a game that has achieved institutional stability, which means that a number of social institutions and roles have grown up around it and help to regulate it and establish it as a stable and important social practice.

As I said, the purpose of beginning with Suits' definition of sport is to lay down a few conceptual markers that help set boundaries for the ethical treatments of sport that follow. However, it would be foolish to claim that Suits' rendering of sport is a wholly value-free definition with no implications whatsoever for what sort of ethical treatment it should receive. Doing so would imply something that is not only controversial but that goes against the grain of several of the ethical approaches pursued by the authors in this anthology—namely, that we can speak of facts without speaking of values, that there is indeed an important fact–value dichotomy that one transgresses only at one's peril. In the particular case of Suit's definition of sport, that would mean that any effort to wring evaluative conclusions from his effort to spell out the relevant facts that make sport what it fundamentally is, which in a matter-of-fact manner determine its main point and purpose, would be guilty of running together what supposedly should always be kept apart: facts and values. What makes this illicit coupling of facts and values even more egregious is that this is a very bad way indeed to introduce a set of readings devoted to the ethics of sport because it violates a basic distinction in ethical thinking itself.

But what sort of mistake is supposedly made if we mix facts and values in this way, if we see Suits as not only setting out conceptual markers of sport but moral ones as well? The answer is a logical one, called the "naturalistic fallacy," which argues that one cannot draw an evaluative conclusion from strictly factual premises. The classic and now standard account of this fallacy comes from David Hume:

> In every system of morality which I have hitherto met with, . . . the author proceeds for some time in the ordinary way of reasoning, and . . . makes observations concerning human affairs . . . [by reference to] the usual copulations of is and is not, . . . [when suddenly] I meet with no proposition that is not connected with an ought or ought not . . . . [Because] this ought or ought not expresses some new relation or affirmation it is necessary . . . that a reason or explanation should be given for what seems altogether inconceivable, how this new relation can be a deduction from others which are entirely different from it.[1]

Apparently then, any argument that moves from what the basic nature and point of sport is to a judgment about how sport should be treated is to be roundly rejected on logical grounds, because one cannot deduce a moral "should" from premises that contain nary a single "should."

The point behind the naturalistic fallacy has some force, although not a decisive one. The reason for this involves, to borrow a term from Aristotle, the *ergon* of artifacts and social practices, which refers to the basic function artifacts are expected to perform or the characteristic activity and aim social practices are supposed to serve. For example, the conception of a knife cannot be adequately accounted for independently of the conception of a good knife, because its *ergon* is to cut various things well. Similarly, the conception of sport cannot be adequately accounted for independently of what counts as good sport, because its *ergon* is to produce excellence of a specific bodily kind.[2] Thus, just as the description of artifacts such as knives include within them the standards by which they are to be reflectively appraised, so the description of social practices such as sport include within them the standards of excellence by which they are likewise to be reflectively appraised. If Aristotle errs here, it is for the different reason that he thought that the *ergon* of things such as knives and social practices such as sport are somehow inscribed in human nature itself—that we are, as it were, hard wired to use things and engage in activities in certain ways. It seems much more plausible to suppose that the *ergon* of things and practices is inscribed in how people contingently and historically size up the world in which they live—that is, in the particular cultural meanings they assign to these artifacts and practices in accord with their situated view of the world. Nevertheless, Aristotle's basic point stands: One is not guilty of committing a logical or any other sort of error if one attempts to read off the characteristic purpose of a knife or the characteristic point of sport how either should be evaluated in moral or aesthetic terms.

This important point is not lost sight of in the next two essays of this section. The first of these, Thomas Hurka's "Games and the Good," argues for a distinctively modern account of the value of games that takes its point of departure from Suits's own analysis of games. More specifically, Hurka gives a perfectionist rendering of Suits's conception of games that puts the accent on "good" games, and that argues two grounds of value can be teased from this rendering both of which speak to the intrinsic goodness of game-playing. The first ground of the intrinsic value of games concerns the difficult and complex challenges their (constitutive) rules and (prelusory) goals pose for those intent on achieving them and thereby displaying the excellence they call for. The second ground of the intrinsic goodness of games has to do with the lusory attitude that on Suits's account players are "required" to adopt towards the rules just to make the game possible, but that on Hurka's amended account players willingly adopt just for the sake of the difficulty those rules and goals introduced to the game. Whereas, then, the founding rules of games and their prelusory goals equip them with a good-making feature (as activities that contain complex challenges), the lusory attitude adopted by game-players suggests they pursue these ends precisely because of this good-making feature, precisely because their attainment cannot be had easily, that is, without demonstrating genuine excellence. And while Hurka denies Suits's provocative claim that games are not only intrinsically good, but the chief, supreme intrinsic good, he does allow that they are "paradigmatic" expressions of a distincly modern view of what counts as a good life, one that puts a premium on process rather than product, on the journey itself rather than the end-state sought.

Robert Simon's "Internalism and Internal Values in Sport," the second essay featured in this section, is similarly, as noted, mindful of Aristotle's point about the folly of tyring to separate fact from value. Simon's main thesis is that the moral evaluation of sport should be rooted in the best interpretation that can be given of its main point and purpose—that is, by "appeal to the best interpretation of the game or an inference to the best explanation of its key elements." But before Simon spells out his own moral account, which he dubs "broad internalism," he discusses two other prominent accounts of sport, formalism and conventionalism, which he thinks fail to deliver the normative goods.

Formalism is the view that what counts as a sport, as a move in sport, and as winning a sport, is derived from the formal rules that define the sport. It is from these basic rules that we can divine the aim of sport and draw certain moral conclusions regarding it. These moral judgments are implicated in what formalists, such as Bernard Suits, call the logical incompatibility thesis, which states that one cannot win in sport if one breaks one or more of its governing rules. That means that cheaters in sport cannot only be found wanting on logical grounds—that is, for failing to play the game at all because the moves they made and the end they secured as a consequence were not sanctioned by the rules—but on moral grounds as well, for violating its constitutive rules and thus violating the basic point of how sport should be conducted. The ethical problem Simon flags here, or at least one of the more glaring of such problems, is that many of the ethical dilemmas that arise in sport are not covered by the rules at all. What he has in mind, particularly, is the example of "clubless Josie," which he borrows from an essay in the ensuing section, who arrives at a championship golf match without her clubs because the airline lost them. It turns out that in this hypothetical case her main competitor has a duplicate set of clubs almost identical to Josie's. The question thus arises: Should her competitor lend Josie her clubs so they can proceed with their decisive match? Simon's point in raising this case is the simple but forceful one that nowhere within the rules of golf, or those of any other sport, will anyone find anything that might help determine what should happen next. This goes to show that formalism lacks the normative resources needed to cope with moral problems that often surface in sport.

Much the same fate befalls the second account of sport Simon discusses, what he calls *conventionalism*. Unlike formalism, conventionalist views of sport seek moral inspiration and guidance not from internal elements of sport itself, specifically its main rules, but from larger society, which they then import to handle normative issues that develop in sport. So, for example, because following rules in society has grown rather lax (as a result of certain conventions, or implicit rules of conduct, that have sprung up that condone such laxness), it is not surprising that the same has happened in sport, as perhaps best exemplified by the relatively recent upsurge of what is called strategic fouling. This would explain why in basketball in the closing moments of a game the losing team will often resort to fouling players of the opposing team deliberately in order to stop the clock and thereby gain a competitive advantage. According to conventionalism, because the practice of intentional fouling is a well-established and agreed-upon game tactic, and because each team knows the other team will use this ploy at certain points in the game, such rule violations should not be treated as a breach of fair play or as an instance of cheating. In other words, as conventionalists see the matter, nothing has happened in this example that is morally untoward. But, Simon rejoins, we have two problems here. The first is the same one we saw with formalism in which there might well be no convention applicable to the matter in question. For example, the clubless Josie case is one not only where there is no rule that can be tapped but perhaps no convention as well. If so, we would once again find ourselves morally clueless as to what to do. But suppose a relevant convention exists that could be appealed to here, and suppose that convention suggests we have no moral responsibility to lend Josie our extra set of clubs. This raises a second problem over whether this convention does, in fact, settle the moral issue under consideration, or rather whether it merely begs the question because the convention itself might be the problem rather than the solution here. In other words, there might be a relevant principle of fair play the convention violates that puts its own normative status in jeopardy. After all, conventions are developed by people merely agreeing on how they want to handle certain situations (e.g., whether to drive on the right or the left side of the road) in which questions of justification are seldom if ever raised, and if they are raised are often regarded as irrelevant. This fact alone, to Simon's way of thinking, should give us pause as to whether we should invest moral authority in this or any other convention.

It is against the background of these two morally challenged theories that Simon spins out his own broad internalist account. Like formalism, but unlike conventionalism, Simon thinks there is indeed an internal morality of sport that we can put to good use. However, unlike formalism, that internal morality concerns not so much the constitutive rules of sport but rather the principles that make intelligible the sorts of excellence that are at play in sport. This goes back to Simon's "best interpretation" thesis that we previously mentioned, in which the idea is that moral regard for sport should be rooted in principles that are in some important sense presupposed by sport and, therefore, required to make sense of its major features. This would mean in the case of the clubless Josie example that it would indeed be morally wrong for Josie's opponent not to lend her the clubs because the point of sport is to meet challenges posed by worthy opponents. But, Simon cautions, the moral offense committed does not rise to the level of, say, cheating that warrants punishment in the form of a penalty, which means Josie's opponent is not morally obligated or required to lend her the clubs. Nor does saying that the morally right thing to do in this situation is to lend the opponent the clubs entail further moral responsibilities such as, to use Simon's example, giving one's opponent a golf lesson just before the match.

The third essay of this section, John Russell's "Broad Internalism and the Moral Foundations of Sport," picks up on Simon's internalist account of sport, most features of which Russell finds persuasive, although he argues against Simon that such an account does not require we hold that sport possesses its own autonomous and distinctive morality. Russell's account shares with Simon's account of broad internalism the idea that sport should be morally regulated by principles that provide the best and most coherent interpretation of its basic point and purpose, and that these principles are not social conventions but genuine moral ideals. But Russell parts company with Simon in his thinking that the moral ideals that are specific to sport, and so, provide normative guidance from the inside as to how they should be conducted, are in addition unique to sport. The idea that sport does have its own distinctive morality that differs from the moral system of other spheres of life and from that of everyday life itself lies behind what Russell calls Simon's commitment to the "separation thesis." And while Russell concedes this is certainly a plausible interpretation of broad internalism, it is not the best interpretation of that moral view—a line of argument that, of course, is in keeping with the central interpretive theme of broad internalism itself. On the contrary, Russell argues the best interpretation of broad internalism is one that views the moral principles it appeals to as *continuous* with the moral principles that inform just about everything else it is that people do. This alternative thesis, which he calls appropriately enough the "continuity thesis," argues that the fairness, equality, and respect for persons that is central to the achievement of the standards of excellence of sport is no less central to the achievement of the standards of excellence of other activities people see fit to devote themselves to. This suggests, to use Russell's own words, "that sport represents one distinct way of instantiating and expressing familiar moral ideas," which is all the uniqueness sport or any other practice needs to establish its normative credentials and to show why the moral ideals it covets have something to offer more broadly to the moral education of human agents.

The next and final two essays of this section also take aim at one another. The first of these, Randolph Feezell's "Sport and the View From Nowhere," argues that the best way to come to terms with the morality of sports is to be mindful of Nagel's distinction between the subjective (our immediate, prereflective, take on things), and objective (our mediated, reflective take on those same things) points of view. It is best to approach sport in this twofold manner, Feezell insists, because this approach captures the paradoxical nature of sport itself and offers important clues as to how we should morally cope with this fact about sport. The paradoxical character of sport is easy enough to see once we juxtapose our subjective and objective interpretations of it. From a firsthand, subjective point of view, sport comes off as a highly serious and important undertaking that gives depth and meaning to our lives, at least for those of us for whom such endeavors matter. But these same sporting lives when viewed from a more detached, reflective standpoint—that is, when objectively compared to other projects human agents engage in and dedicate themselves to—come off looking like rather trivial and unimportant fare, and certainly not morally momentous ones. Indeed, from this objective vantage point, sports come across as downright absurd affairs because the seriousness expended on them is far out of proportion to their lowly standing.

Morally speaking, what are we to do, given these tensions in our views of sport and the paradox with which they present us? Feezell's answer is to resist the temptation to dissolve the paradox by favoring the subjective over the objective perspective, or vice versa, because favoring the subjective view of things condemns us to a thoughtless life, one that renounces the important role critical reflection plays in a good life, and favoring the objective view of things would banish most of those activities that give meaning to our lives, one that renounces the very motives that give us a reason to live and enjoy our lives to the fullest. The better, moral way to go is to cope with the paradoxical character of our lives generally and our sporting lives particularly by, first, taking an ironic stance toward those lives, which means for Feezell the same thing it meant for Feinberg—"an attitude of detached awareness of incongruity." In the particular case of sport, this means that we should treat sport "as if" it were a serious affair all the while cognizant that it is anything but. Given the evident absurdity of sport, Feezell thinks a playful regard for sport is in order, one in which we engage in it "without gravity or solemnity" but rather with an "attitude expressed in a wry smile rather than a grimace of discomfort." The second way to cope with the absurdity of sport is by modifying rather than abandoning the objective perspective, which for Feezell means we view sport from a standpoint outside of the immediacy of our subjective involvement in sport, but not so far outside of that perspective that we can no longer see and appreciate the moral qualities to be had by participating in sport. For when viewed from this less detached vantage point, sport does apparently teach moral lessons regarding sportsmanship and fairness that contribute to the development of good moral character.

The final essay of this section, William Morgan's "Why the 'View From Nowhere' Gets Us Nowhere in Our Moral Considerations of Sport," as noted, attempts to take Feezell's moral analysis of sport to task, especially his strong reliance on Nagel's distinction between the subjective and objective points of view. Morgan argues that Nagel's distinction is not well suited to assess the moral properties of practices such as sport because one cannot make moral sense of these kinds of practices, either by clambering inside our subjective selves and endorsing whatever preference rankings they contain or, contrarily, by clambering outside of ourselves in search of some perspectiveless, objective standpoint. Rather, what is needed is an ethical approach that embraces an intersubjective perspective on sport, one that shuns dizzying abstract reflection and stay-on-the-surface subjective scanning. Such an intersubjective perspective, Morgan argues, is best able to capture the shared goods that define sport, as well as the cooperative activity and common understanding that sport and other similarly socially constituted practices require. What recommends this critical intersubjective approach to sport further, Morgan concludes, is that in disabusing us of the notion that moral reflection is per necessity abstract, impersonal reflection, we will be able to indulge both our passion for sport and our reflective commitment not to let that passion stand as the last word in our moral evaluation of it, without raising either the specter of irrationalism or absurdity. After all, if, as Feezell claims, moral reflection strips sport of all meaning and thus reduces it to an absurd enterprise, then, despite his protestations to the contrary, it is hard to see what sense it makes to commit ourselves to sport "as if" it were of some consequence, and it is hard to read his following closing claim as anything other than a false choice: "It is better to approach sport as absurd than to deny our reflective judgments or to give up the joys of sport . . . . Better to be absorbed and absurdly preoccupied than to miss out on all the fun."

Notes

1. David Hume, "A Treatise of Human Nature" in *Hume's Moral and Political Philosophy*, ed. H. Aiken (Darien, CN: Hafner Publishing Co., 1970), 43.

2. I am indebted here to MacIntyre's account of this point found in his book, *After Virtue* (Notre Dame, IN: University of Notre Dame, 1984), 58.

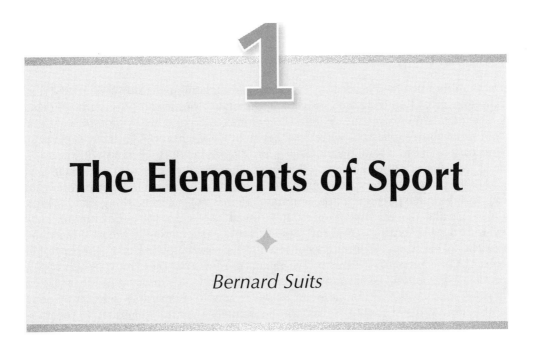

The Elements of Sport

Bernard Suits

I would like to advance the thesis that the elements of sport are essentially—although perhaps not totally—the same as the elements of game. I shall first propose an account of the elements of game-playing, then comment on the relation of game to sport, and finally suggest that the resulting view of sport has an important bearing on the question as to whether sport is or is not serious.

The Elements of Game

Since games are goal-directed activities which involve choice, ends and means are two of the elements of games. But in addition to being means–end oriented activities, games are also rule-governed activities, so that rules are a third element. And since, as we shall see, the rules of games make up a rather special kind of rule, it will be necessary to take account of one more element, namely, the attitudes of game-players *qua* game-players. I add *"qua* game-players" because I do not mean what might happen to be the attitude of this or that game player under these or those conditions (e.g., the hope of winning a cash prize or the satisfaction of exhibiting physical prowess to an admiring audience), but the attitude without which it is not possible to play a game. Let us call this attitude, of which more presently, the *lusory* (from the Latin *ludus,* game) attitude.

My task will be to persuade you that what I have called the lusory attitude is the element which unifies the other elements into a single formula which successfully states the necessary and sufficient conditions for any activity to be an instance of game-playing. I propose, then, that the elements of game are (1) the goal, (2) means for achieving the goal, (3) rules, and (4) lusory attitude. I shall briefly discuss each of these in order.

Reprinted, by permission, from Robert Osterhoudt, editor, 1973, *The Philosphy of sport: A collection of essays* (Springfield, IL: Charles C. Thomas, Publisher Ltd.), 48-64.

The Goal

We should notice first of all that there are three distinguishable goals involved in game-playing. Thus, if we were to ask a long distance runner his purpose in entering a race, he might say any one or all of three things, each of which would be accurate, appropriate, and consistent with the other two. He might reply (1) that his purpose is to participate in a long distance race, or (2) that his purpose is to win the race, or (3) that his purpose is to cross the finish line ahead of the other contestants. It should be noted that these responses are not merely three different formulations of one and the same purpose. Thus, winning a race is not the same thing as crossing a finish line ahead of the other contestants, since it is possible to do the latter unfairly by, for example, cutting across the infield. Nor is participating in the race the same as either of these, since the contestant, while fully participating, may simply fail to cross the finish line first, either by fair means or foul. That there must be this triplet of goals in games will be accounted for by the way in which lusory attitude is related to rules and means. For the moment, however, it will be desirable to select just one of the three kinds of goal for consideration, namely, the kind illustrated in the present example by crossing the finish line ahead of the other contestants. This goal is literally the *simplest* of the three goals, since each of the other goals presupposes it, whereas it does not presuppose either of the other two. This goal, therefore, has the best claim to be regarded as an elementary component of game-playing. The others, since they are compounded components, can be defined only after the disclosure of additional elements.

The kind of goal at issue, then, is the kind illustrated by crossing a finish line first (but not necessarily fairly), having *x* number of tricks piled up before you on a bridge table (but not necessarily as a consequence of playing bridge), or getting a golf ball into a cup (but not necessarily by using a golf club). This kind of goal may be described generally as *a specific achievable state of affairs*. This description is, I believe, no more and no less than is required. By omitting to say *how* the state of affairs in question is to be brought about, it avoids confusion between this goal and the goal of winning. And because any achievable state of affairs whatever could, with sufficient ingenuity, be made the goal of a game, the description does not include too much. I suggest that this kind of goal be called the *pre-lusory* goal of a game, because it can be described before, or independently of, any game of which it may be, or come to be, a part. In contrast, the goal of winning can be described only in terms of the game in which it figures, and winning may accordingly be called the *lusory* goal of a game. (It is tempting to call what I have called the pre-lusory goal the goal *in* a game and the lusory goal the goal *of* a game, but the practice of philosophers like J.L. Austin has, I believe, sufficiently illustrated the hazards of trying to make prepositions carry a load of meaning which can much better be borne by adjectives and nouns.) Finally, the goal of participating in the game is not, strictly speaking, a part of the game at all. It is simply one of the goals that people have, such as wealth, glory, or security. As such it may be called a lusory goal, but a lusory goal of life rather than of games.

Means

Just as we saw that reference to the goal of game-playing was susceptible of three different (but proper and consistent) interpretations, so we shall find that the means in games can refer to more than one kind of thing; two, in fact, depending upon whether we wish to refer to means for winning the game or for achieving the pre-lusory goal. Thus, an extremely effective way to achieve the pre-lusory goal in a boxing match—viz., the state of affairs consisting in your opponent being *down* for the count of ten—is to shoot him through the head, but this is obviously not a means to winning the match. In games, of course, we are interested only in means which are permitted for winning, and we are now in a position to define that class of means, which we may call *lusory* means. Lusory means are means which are permitted (are legal or legitimate) in the attempt to achieve pre-lusory goals. Thus a soccer player may use foot or head, but not hand, in his efforts to achieve that state of affairs wherein the ball is in the goal. And a player who does not confine himself to lusory means may not be said to win, even if he achieves the pre-lusory goal. But achievement of the lusory goal, winning, requires that the player confine himself to lusory means, so that confinement to lusory means is a necessary (but of course not a sufficient) condition for winning.

It should be noticed that we have been able to distinguish lusory from, if you will, illusory means only by assuming without analysis one of the elements necessary in making the distinction. We have defined lusory means as means which are *permitted* without examining the nature of that permission. This omission will be repaired directly by taking up the question of rules. But we may provisionally acknowledge the following definition: *lusory means,* means permitted in seeking pre-lusory goals.

Rules

As with goals and means, two kinds of rules figure in games, one kind associated with pre-lusory goals, the other with lusory goals. The rules of a game are, in effect, proscriptions of certain means useful in achieving pre-lusory goals. Thus, it is useful but proscribed to trip a competitor in a foot race. This kind of rule may be called constitutive of the game, since such rules together with specification of the pre-lusory goal set out all the conditions which must be met in playing the game (though not, of course, in playing the game skillfully). Let us call such rules *constitutive* rules. The other kind of rule operates, so to speak, *within* the area circumscribed by constitutive rules, and this kind of rule may be called a rule of skill. Examples are the familiar injunctions to keep your eye on the ball, to refrain from trumping your partner's ace, and the like. To break a rule of skill is usually to fail, at least to that extent, to play the game well, but to break a constitutive rule is to fail to play the game at all. (There is a third kind of rule in games which appears to be unlike either of these. This is the kind of rule for which there is a fixed penalty, such that violating the rule is neither to fail to play the game nor [necessarily] to fail to play the game well, since it is sometimes tactically correct to incur such a penalty [e.g., in hockey] for the sake of the advantage gained. But these rules and the lusory consequences of their violation are established by the constitutive rules, and are simply extensions of them.)

Having made the distinction between constitutive rules and rules of skill, I propose to ignore the latter, since my purpose is to define not well-played games, but games. It is, then, what I have called constitutive rules which determine the kind and range of means which will be permitted in seeking to achieve the pre-lusory goal.

What is the nature of the restrictions which constitutive rules impose on the means for reaching a pre-lusory goal? The effect of constitutive rules is to place obstacles in the path leading to a pre-lusory goal. I invite the reader to think of any game at random. Now identify the pre-lusory goal, being careful to remember that the pre-lusory goal is simply any specific achievable state of affairs. I think you will agree that the simplest, easiest, and most direct approach to achieving such a goal is always ruled out in favour of a more complex, more difficult, and more indirect approach. Thus it is not uncommon for players of a new and difficult game to agree among themselves to *ease up* on the rules, that is, to allow themselves a greater degree of latitude than the official rules permit means removing some of the obstacles or, in terms of means, permitting certain means which the rules do not really permit. But if no means whatever are ruled out, then the game ceases to exist. Thus, we may think of the gamewright, when he invents games, as attempting to draw a line between permitted and prohibited means to a given end. If he draws this line too loosely there is danger of the game becoming too easy, and if he draws it with utter laxity the game simply falls apart. On the other hand, he must not draw the line too tight or, instead of falling apart, the game will be squeezed out of existence. For example, imagine a game where the pre-lusory goal is to cross a finish line, with an attendant rule that the player must not leave the track in his attempt to do so. Then imagine that there is a second rule which requires that the finish line be located some distance from the track.

We may define constitutive rules as rules which prohibit use of the most efficient means for reaching a pre-lusory goal.

Lusory Attitude

The attitude of the game-player must be an element in game-playing because there has to be an explanation of that curious state of affairs wherein one adopts rules which require him to employ worse rather than better means for reaching an end. Normally the acceptance of prohibitory rules is justified on the grounds that the means ruled out, although they are more efficient than the permitted means, have further undesirable consequences from the viewpoint of the agent involved. Thus, although the use of nuclear weapons is more efficient than is the use of conventional weapons in winning battles, the view still happily persists among nations that the additional consequences of nuclear assault are sufficient to rule it out. This kind of thing, of course, happens all the time, from the realm of international strategy to the common events of everyday life; thus one decisive way to remove a toothache is to cut your head off, but most people find good reason to rule out such highly efficient means. But in games, although more efficient means are—and must be—ruled out, the reason for doing so is quite different from the reasons for avoiding nuclear weaponry and self-decapitation. Foot racers do not refrain from cutting across the infield because the infield holds dangers for them, as would be the case if, for example, infields were frequently sown with land mines. Cutting across the infield is shunned solely because there is a rule against it. But in ordinary life this is usually—and rightly—regarded as the worst possible kind of justification one could give for avoiding a course of action. The justification for a prohibited course of action that there is simply a rule against it may be called the *bureaucratic* justification; that is, no justification at all.

But aside from bureaucratic practice, in anything but a game the gratuitous introduction of unnecessary obstacles to the achievement of an end is regarded as a decidedly irrational thing to do, whereas in games it appears to be an absolutely essential thing to do. This fact about games has led some observers to conclude that there is something inherently absurd about games, or that games must involve a fundamental paradox. (1) This kind of view seems to me to be mistaken. (2) The mistake consists in applying the same standard to games that is applied to means–end activities which are not games. If playing a game is regarded as not essentially different from going to the office or writing a cheque, then there is certainly something absurd, or paradoxical, or simply stupid about game-playing.

But games are, I believe, essentially different from the ordinary activities of life, as perhaps the following exchange between Smith and Jones will illustrate. Smith knows nothing of games, but he does know that he wants to travel from A to C, and he also knows that making the trip by way of B is the most efficient means for getting to his destination. He is then told authoritatively that he may not go by way of B. "Why not," he asks, "are there dragons at B?" "No," is the reply. "B is perfectly safe in every respect. It is just that there is a rule against going to B if you are on your way to C." "Very well," grumbles Smith, "if you insist. But if I have to go from A to C very often I shall certainly try very hard to get that rule revoked." True to his word, Smith approaches Jones, who is also setting out for C from A. He asks Jones to sign a petition requesting the revocation of the rule which forbids travellers from A to C to go through B. Jones replies that he is very much opposed to revoking the rule, which very much puzzles Smith.

> **Smith**—But if you want to get to C, why on earth do you support a rule which prevents your taking the fastest and most convenient route?
>
> **Jones**—Ah, but you see I have no particular interest in being at C. *That* is not my goal, except in a subordinate way. My overriding goal is more complex. It is "to get from A to C without going through B." And I can't very well achieve that goal if I go through B, can I?
>
> **Smith**—But why do you want to do that?
>
> **Jones**—I want to do it before Robinson does, you see?
>
> **Smith**—No, I don't. That explains nothing. Why should Robinson, whoever he may be, want to do it? I presume you will tell me that he, like you, has only a subordinate interest in being at C at all.
>
> **Jones**—That is so.
>
> **Smith**—Well, if neither of you wants, really, to be at C, then what possible difference can it make which of you gets there first? And why, for God's sake, should you avoid B?
>
> **Jones**—Let me ask you a question. Why do you want to get to C?
>
> **Smith**—Because there is a good concert there, and I want to hear it.
>
> **Jones**—Why?
>
> **Smith**—Because I like concerts, of course. Isn't that a good reason?
>
> **Jones**—It's one of the best there is. And I like, among other things, trying to get from A to C without going through B before Robinson does.
>
> **Smith**—Well, *I* don't. So why should they tell me I can't go through B?
>
> **Jones**—Oh, I see. They must have thought you were in the race.
>
> **Smith**—The what?

I believe that we are now in a position to define *lusory attitude:* the knowing acceptance of constitutive rules just so the activity made possible by such acceptance can occur.

Summary

The elements may now be assembled into the following definition. To play a game is to attempt to achieve a specific state of affairs *(pre-lusory goal)*, using only means permitted by rules *(lusory means)*, where the rules prohibit use of more efficient in favor of less efficient means *(constitutive rules)*, and where such rules are accepted just because they make possible such activity *(lusory attitude)*. I also offer the following only approximately accurate, but more pithy, version of the above definition: Playing a game is the voluntary attempt to overcome unnecessary obstacles.

Games and Sport

As I indicated at the outset, I believe that sports are essentially games. What I mean by this is that the difference between sports and other games is much smaller than the difference between humans and other vertebrates. That is to say, sport is not a species within the genus *game*. The distinguishing characteristics of sport are more peripheral, more arbitrary, and more contingent than are the differences required to define a species.

I would like to submit for consideration four requirements which, if they are met by any given game, are sufficient to denominate that game a sport. They are: (1) that the game be a game of skill, (2) that the skill be physical, (3) that the game have a wide following, and (4) that the following achieve a certain level of stability. If I can persuade you that these features or something very much like them are at least the *kind* of differentiating marks we are seeking, I will be satisfied. I have no theory to support the list, except the theory that the features are more or less arbitrary, since they are simply facts about sport. Finally, I have little to say about them aside from presenting them, except as regards the question of skill, which I am interested in taking up on its own account.

Skill in Games

One may agree with my account of what it is to play a game and still find unanswered the rather pressing question why anyone would want to do such a thing (aside from professionals who do so for money and prestige). Smith was no doubt puzzled about this question even after Jones' explanation. Let me propose the following general answer. People play games so that they can realize in themselves capacities not realizable (or not readily so) in the pursuit of their ordinary activities. For example, some people enjoy running competitively, but the opportunities for this are severely limited in ordinary life. One can run for a bus, but even this small range of operations is further limited by the fact that one does not always have the good fortune to arrive tardily at a bus stop. One can, of course, intentionally allow less than enough time for getting punctually to the point of departure, in the hope that a race with the timetable will then be necessary. But such a move is precisely to create a game where there was no game before, by virtue of the constitutive rule requiring you to leave your home or office late. Some kinds of games—such as racing games—have this rather obvious affinity with actions performed aside from games. But most games do not have such a clear counterpart in ordinary life. Ball games which are at all elaborate have affinities with ordinary life only piecemeal; in life, too, one throws and runs and strikes objects, but there is nothing in life which much resembles baseball or football or golf *in toto*. Board games provide similar examples of the hiatus between games taken as wholes and the kinds of structured activities which characterize the rest of life. Thus, with the invention of games far removed from the pursuits of ordinary life, quite new capacities emerge, and hitherto unknown skills are developed. A good golf swing is simply useless in any other human pursuit. And despite the literary mythology which frequently represents superior military and political strategists as being (it is almost presumed to go without saying) master chess players as well, there is as much similarity between those two skills as there is between the skills of golf and wood chopping. Purely topological problems are just vastly different from political and military problems. So people play games not only because ordinary life does not provide enough opportunities for doing such and such, but also (and more interestingly) because ordinary life does not provide any opportunities at all for doing such and such.

Games are *new* things to do, and they are new things to do because they require the overcoming of (by ordinary standards) *unnecessary* obstacles, and in ordinary life an unnecessary obstacle is simply a contradiction in terms.

Although I believe, as I have said, that people play games in order to realize capacities not otherwise realizable (or not readily realizable), and although in most games these capacities are, or intimately involve, specific skills, there are certain activities called games which almost conform to my definition but which do not involve skill. I mean games of chance; that is, games of *pure* chance. Draw poker is not such a game, nor, perhaps, is standard roulette (perhaps a debatable point), but show-down is, and so is Russian roulette. These games do not involve the capacity to exercise a specific skill because no skill is required to play them. Instead of skills, what is put into operation by such games is, I suggest, hope and fear. Bored people are deficient in these feelings, it seems safe to say, since if they were not they would not be bored. But hope and fear can be artificially induced by games of pure chance. (They also appear in games of skill, to be sure, but people to whom games of chance especially appeal are too bored to learn new skills.) What games of chance provide for their players may be described in almost the same words that Jan Narveson has used to describe paranoia: a false sense of insecurity. However, for games of chance the word *false* should be replaced by the word *invented,* for there is nothing false about the capacities which games bring forth, just something new.

All sports appear to be games of skill rather than games of chance. I suggest that the reason for this is that a major requirement in sports, for participants and specta-tors alike, is that what the participants do must be admirable in some respect. The exercise of virtually any skill—even the skills involved in goldfish swallowing or flagpole sitting—will elicit some degree of admiration. But the spectacle of a person sweating in hope and fear as the chamber slowly turns in the revolver evokes not admiration but morbid fascination or clinical interest.

Physical Skill

It is not difficult to draw a line between games which require physical skill and games which do not. It is not necessary first to decide very grave metaphysical issues, such as the relation between mind and body. It is a plain fact that how chess pieces are moved has nothing whatever to do with manual dexterity or any other bodily skill. One can play chess, bridge, and any number of other games solely by issuing verbal commands, as is the case when chess is played by mail. "Physical games" designates a quite definite class of objects, and the term "sport" is confined to this class (though it is not necessarily coterminous with it). The issue is thus wholly terminological; that is, the question "Why do sports have to involve physical skills?" is not a well formulated question. The question should be, "What kind of skill do we find in the class of activities we call sport?" And the answer is "Physical skill." Thus, chess and bridge appear to have all the features requisite for something to qualify as a sport, except that they are not games of physical skill. They do involve skill, and of a high order; they have a wide following and their popularity is of sufficiently long standing so that each of them may be characterized as an institution rather than a mere craze. Each can boast international tournaments, a body of experts, teachers, coaches—all the attendant roles and institutions characteristic of the most well-established sports. It is just that physical skill is not involved.

A Wide Following

I have perfected the following game originally created by Kierkegaard. A high rank- ing official of my university has the constitutional peculiarity that when angry his anger is manifested solely by the appearance of a bead of perspiration at the centre of his forehead which then rolls slowly down his nose, clings for an instant to its tip, and finally falls. If the official's ire continues or recurs, the same steps are repeated. Whenever I have a conference with him I adopt as a pre-lusory goal that state of affairs wherein three separate beads of perspiration shall have progressed through their appointed stages inside of fifteen minutes. And I adopt the constitutive rule that I will refrain from employing as a means to this goal either threats of violence against the person of the official or aspersions on his personal and professional reputation. Although this is, I flatter myself, a pretty good game, I readily admit that it is not a sport. It is too private and too personal to qualify for that status. Imagine my being asked by a colleague in the Faculty of Physical Education what sports I participate in, and my responding that I am very keen on Sweat-Bead.

Still, though Sweat-Bead is not now a sport, it could conceivably become one. If there were a great many people who shared the constitutional peculiarity of my official, and if there were a great many people equipped with the kind of sadism to which this game appeals, and if the rules were clearly laid out and published, and if there were to grow up a body of experts whose concern it was to improve the game and its players, then Sweat-Bead would become a sport. But short of these much to be hoped for developments I must accept the reality that it is simply a highly idiosyncratic game.

Stability

That a game is one of physical skill and that it is very popular is not quite enough to qualify it as a sport. Hula-Hoop, in its hey-day, met these requirements but it would be proper to call Hula-Hoop a craze rather than a sport. The popular follow- ing which attends sports must have a stability which is more than mere persistence through time. Even if Hula-Hoop had lasted for fifty years it would still be a craze, only a very tiresome craze.

What is required in addition to longevity is the birth and flowering of a number of attendant roles and institutions which serve a number of functions ancillary to a sufficiently popular game of physical skill. The most important of these functions appear to be the following: teaching and training, coaching, research and development (Can the sport be improved by making such and such changes?), criticism (sports pundits), and archivism (the compilation and preservation of individual performances and their statistical treatment). Not all sports, of course, require all of these ancillary functions in order to be accepted as sports, but at least some of them will be associated to some degree with every game worthy to be called a sport.

Sport and Seriousness

The conventional wisdom about fun and games which, with brief and infrequent countertendencies, has prevailed from classical antiquity to the very recent past is well expressed by the following observation of Aristotle: ". . . to exert oneself and work for the sake of playing seems silly and utterly childish. But to play in order that one may exert oneself seems right." Play, games, and sport are seen, on this view, as subordinate to other ends, so that they may be taken seriously only if the ends to which they are subordinate are taken seriously. Thus, sports are regarded as serious insofar as they promote, for example, health, which is accepted as a serious matter; but sport unjustified by some such serious purpose is just frivolity. In a "work" ethic, work is the serious pursuit which gives play (and indeed health) what derivative seriousness it possesses. But in a leisure ethic, of the kind which much of the world appears now to be assuming, these old priorities are rapidly changing. For a person in whom the Protestant ethic is quite firmly established it is difficult, if not impossible, to ask the question, "To what further interests is work itself subordinate?" and in times and societies where human and material resources are exceedingly scarce it is perhaps as well for the survival of the human race that such questions are not asked. For under conditions where unremitting labor is necessary for the bare preservation of life, the answer to the question "What are we working for?" is "Just to live." And since the life whose preservation requires continuous toil is just that toil itself, the toiler might well wonder whether the game is worth the candle.

But in a leisure ethic we have not only the leisure to ask why we are working, but the fact of leisure itself provides us with an answer which is not too bleak to bear. The industrial unionist of today who makes a contract demand for shorter working hours is not prompted to do this by Aristotelian considerations. He does not want more time for fishing, bowling, the ballpark, or television so that, renewed and refreshed, he can increase his output on the assembly line on Monday. (In any case, that output will also be fixed by the new contract and cannot be increased.) The attitude of the contemporary worker about work may be expressed as the exact inversion of Aristotle's dictum: "To play so that one may work seems silly and utterly childish; but to work in order that one may play seems right."

I do not think it is too great an overstatement to say that whereas for the Puritan it was work which gave play (as, e.g., exercise) what derivative seriousness it was accorded, it is now play—or at least leisure activities—which gives work a derivative seriousness. Another way to put this is to acknowledge that work is good because it provides us with leisure as well as the means to enjoy leisure. Work is good chiefly because it is *good for* something much better. The things for which it is finally good are good in themselves. They are intrinsic goods. This is not, as a general view, at all novel. It, too, goes back to Aristotle. The only difference in Aristotle's view (and in the view of many others who are in this respect like him) is that for him just a very few things count as intrinsically good, things like virtue and metaphysics. Partisans of this kind have typically managed to get a kind of monopoly on the notion of intrinsic good and have tried, with some success, to persuade the rest of us that only such and such pursuits were worthy of the name. Sometimes it has been holiness, sometimes art, sometimes science, sometimes love. But it seems perfectly clear that any number of things can be intrinsic goods to someone, depending upon his interests, abilities, and other resources, from philately to philosophy (including work itself, if you happen to be Paul Goodman). This view has quite wide, even if tacit, acceptance, I believe, outside of churches and universities.

The new ethic, then, is not only one of greatly increased leisure, it is also one of pluralism with respect to the goods we are permitted to seek in the new time available. It has been some time since our sabbaths were confined to theological self-improvement with the aid of the family bible, of course, but recent changes in our views of leisure activity are just as striking as was our emergence from puritanism. Thus, the view no longer prevails (as it did in the quite recent past) that although leisure was a good thing it was wasted if one did not devote most of it to the pursuit of Culture with a capital C. Today people with the most impeccable cultural credentials may without impropriety savour jazz (even rock) and motor racing.

Although we recognize a class of things which are serious just because they are intrinsically worthwhile, there seems some reason to believe that sports (and games in general) cannot be among these things. It is as though there were something built into the very structure of games which rendered them non-serious. This view is conveyed by the expression, "Of course, such and such is just a game," as though there were something inherently trifling about games. And by the same token, if we find that someone takes a sport or some other game with extraordinary seriousness, we are inclined to say that the pursuit in question has ceased to be a game for him.

This view, though incorrect, may be made quite plausible, I believe, by the following example. Consider The Case of the Dedicated Driver. Mario Stewart (the dedicated driver in question) is a favoured entrant in the motor car race of the century at Malaise. And in the Malaise race there is a rule which forbids a vehicle to leave the track on pain of disqualification. At a dramatic point in the race a child crawls out upon the track directly in the path of Mario's car. The only way to avoid running over the child is to leave the track and suffer disqualification. Mario runs over the child and completes the race.

One is inclined to say that for Mario motor racing is not a sport at all (and certainly not a game!), but a kind of madness. Games (and sports) require a limitation on the means their players may employ, but Mario is obviously the kind of driver who would do anything to win the race. By his insane refusal to stay within proper limits he is no longer playing a game at all. He has destroyed the game.

I submit, however, that we now know what it takes to destroy a game, and that the behaviour of Mario is not what it takes. If Mario had cut across the infield in his efforts to get ahead of the other drivers, or if he had earlier violated a rule governing engine capacity in the construction of his vehicle, then his behaviour would cease to be game-playing, for he would have broken a constitutive rule. It is thus true to say that there is a limitation imposed in games which is not imposed in other activities, and it is also true that the limitation has to do with the means one can legitimately employ. Hence the plausibility of concluding that Mario was not playing a game, since there appeared to be absolutely no means he would not adopt. But it will be recalled that we earlier discovered that more than one kind of goal is associated with games, and more than one kind of means. The plausibility of the claim that racing for Mario had ceased to be a game rests on a confusion between two of these goals. It is perfectly correct to say that not any means whatever may be used to achieve a *pre-lusory* goal, but this limitation in no way entails a quite different kind of limitation, namely, a limitation on the means for *playing* the game (i.e., attempting to achieve what I earlier called the lusory goal of life).

The point of the story, of course, is not that Mario did a terrible thing, but that it is possible to make a game or a sport the over-riding concern of one's life without falling into some kind of paradox. That extreme dedication to a pursuit should somehow destroy the pursuit would be the real paradox. But that a person will do anything to continue playing a game does not destroy the game, even though it may destroy the person. So saying to Mario that motor racing is just a game is very much like saying to the Pope that Catholicism is just religion, to Beethoven that the quartets are just music, or to Muhammad Ali that boxing is just a sport.

I therefore conclude that sports are precisely like the other interests which occur prominently as leisure activities. They are a type of intrinsic good which, along with many others, make up the class of goals to which we ascribe that primary seriousness which provides such things as factories, armies, and governments with the derivative seriousness to which they are entitled.

Acknowledgments

The section of the paper titled *The Elements of Game* is a restatement of the substance of the thesis advanced in "What Is a Game?"[3] However, the language used here is different from the language of that version, and the definition of game-playing that I propose has been somewhat altered. The strategies of the two versions also differ. In "What Is a Game?" I attempted to produce an adequate definition by successively modifying a series of proposed definitions. Here, assuming the adequacy of that definition, I explain and illustrate the elements of game-playing which the definition designates. I should also note that some of the examples used in the present paper were originally used in "What Is a Game?"

Bibliography

1. Kolnai, A.: "Games and Aims," *Proceedings of the Aristotelian Society* (1966).
2. Suits, Bernard: "Games and Paradox," *Philosophy of Science* (1969).
3. Suits, Bernard: "What Is a Game?" *Philosophy of Science* (1967).

Games and the Good

◆

Thomas Hurka

Our societies attach considerable value to excellence in sports. In Canada hockey players are named to the highest level of the Order of Canada; in Britain footballers and cricketers are made MBE and even knighted. And this attitude extends more widely. Sports are a subclass of the wider category of games, and we similarly admire those who excel in non-athletic games such as chess, bridge, and even Scrabble.

I take this admiration to rest on the judgement that excellence in games is good in itself, apart from any pleasure it may give the player or other people, but just for the properties that make it excellent. The admiration, in other words, rests on the perfectionist judgement that skill in games is worth pursuing for its own sake and can add value to one's life. This skill is not the only thing we value in this way; we give similar honours to achievements in the arts, science and business. But one thing we admire, and to a significant degree, is excellence in athletic and non-athletic games.

Unless we dismiss this view, one task for philosophy is to explain why such excellence is good. But few philosophers have attempted this, for a well-known reason. A unified explanation of why excellence in games is good requires a unified account of what games are, and many doubt that this is possible. After all, Wittgenstein famously gave the concept of a game as his primary example of one for which necessary and sufficient conditions cannot be given but whose instances are linked only by looser 'family resemblances'.[1] If Wittgenstein was right about this, there can be no single explanation of why skill in games is good, just a series of distinct explanations of the value of skill in hockey, skill in chess, and so on.

ABSTRACT Using Bernard Suits's brilliant analysis (*contra* Wittgenstein) of playing a game, this paper examines the intrinsic value of game-playing. It argues that two elements in Suits's analysis make success in games difficult, which is one ground of value, while a third involves choosing a good activity for the property that makes it good, which is a further ground. The paper concludes by arguing that game-playing is the paradigm modern (Marx, Nietzsche) as against classical (Aristotle) value: since its goal is intrinsically trivial, its value is entirely one of process rather than product, journey rather than destination.

From T. Hurka and J. Tasioulas, 2006, "Games and the good," *Proceedings of the Aristotelian Society,* Suppl. Vol. 80: 237-264. Reprinted by courtesy of the Aristotelian Society: © 2006.

But Wittgenstein was not right, as is shown in a little-known book that is none-theless a classic of twentieth-century philosophy, Bernard Suits's *The Grasshopper: Games, Life and Utopia*. Suits gives a perfectly persuasive analysis of playing a game as, to quote his summary statement, 'the voluntary attempt to overcome unnecessary obstacles'.[2] And in this paper I will use his analysis to explain the value of playing games. More specifically, I will argue that the different elements of Suits's analysis give game-playing two distinct but related grounds of value, so it instantiates two related intrinsic goods. I will also argue that game-playing is an important intrinsic good, which gives the clearest possible expression of what can be called a modern as against a classical, or more specifically, Aristotelian, view of value.

But first Suits's analysis. It says that a game has three main elements, which he calls the prelusory goal, the constitutive rules, and the lusory attitude. To begin with the first, in playing a game one always aims at a goal that can be described independently of the game. In golf, this is that a ball enter a hole in the ground; in mountain climbing, that one stand on top of a mountain; in Olympic sprinting, that one cross a line on the track before one's competitors. Suits calls this goal 'prelusory' because it can be understood and achieved apart from the game, and he argues that every game has such a goal. Of course, in playing a game one also aims at a goal internal to it, such as winning the race, climbing the mountain, or breaking par on the golf course. But on Suits's view this 'lusory' goal is derivative, since achieving it involves achieving the prior prelusory goal in a specified way.

This way is identified by the second element, the game's constitutive rules. According to Suits, the function of these rules is to forbid the most efficient means to the prelusory goal. Thus, in golf one may not carry the ball down the fairway and drop it in the hole by hand; one must advance it using clubs, play it where it lies, and so on. In mountain climbing one may not ride a gondola to the top of the mountain or charter a helicopter; in 200-metre sprinting, one may not cut across the infield. Once these rules are in place, success in the game typically requires achieving the prelusory goal as efficiently as they allow, such as getting the ball into the hole in the fewest possible strokes or choosing the best way up the mountain. But this is efficiency within the rules, whose larger function is to forbid the easiest means to the game's initial goal.

These first two elements involve pursuing a goal by less than the most efficient means, but they are not sufficient for playing a game. This is because someone can be forced to use these means by circumstances he regrets and wishes were differ-ent. If this is the case—if, for example, a farmer harvests his field by hand because he cannot afford the mechanical harvester he would much rather use—he is not playing a game. Hence the need for the third element in Suits's analysis, the lusory attitude, which involves a person's willingly accepting the constitutive rules, or accepting them because they make the game possible. Thus, a golfer accepts that he may not carry the ball by hand or improve his lie because he wants to play golf, and obeying those rules is necessary for him to do so; the mountaineer accepts that he may not take a helicopter to the summit because he wants to climb. The restric-tions the rules impose are adhered to not reluctantly but willingly, because they are essential to the game. Adding this third element gives Suits's full definition: 'To play a game is to attempt to achieve a specific state of affairs [prelusory goal], using only means permitted by the rules . . . where the rules prohibit the use of more efficient in favour of less efficient means [constitutive rules], and where the rules are accepted just because they make possible such activity [lusory attitude].' Or, in the summary statement quoted above, 'playing a game is the voluntary attempt to overcome unnecessary obstacles.'[3]

This analysis will doubtless meet with objections, in the form of attempted counter-examples. But Suits considers a whole series of these in his book, showing repeatedly that his analysis handles them correctly, and not by some ad hoc addition but once its elements are properly understood. Nor would it matter terribly if there were a few counterexamples. Some minor lack of fit between his analysis and the English use of 'game' would not be important if the analysis picks out a phenomenon that is unified, close to what is meant by 'game', and philosophically interesting. But the analysis is interesting if, as I will now argue, it allows a persuasive explanation of the value of excellence in games.

Suits himself addresses this issue of value. In fact, a central aim of his book is to give a defence of the grasshopper in Aesop's fable, who played all summer, against the ant, who worked. But in doing so he argues for the strong thesis that playing games is not just an intrinsic good but the supreme such good, since in the ideal conditions of utopia, where all instrumental goods are provided, it would be everyone's primary pursuit. The grasshopper's game-playing, therefore, while it had the unfortunate effect of leaving him without food for the winter, involved him in the intrinsically finest activity. Now, I do not accept Suits's strong thesis that game—playing is the supreme good—I think many other states and activities have comparable value—and I do not find his arguments for it persuasive. But I will connect the weaker thesis that playing games is one intrinsic good to the details of his analysis more explicitly than he ever does.

Consider the first two elements of the analysis, the prelusory goal and constitutive rules. By forbidding the most efficient means to that goal, the constitutive rules usually make for an activity that is reasonably difficult. They do not always do so. Rock, paper, scissors is a game whose prelusory goal is to throw rock to one's opponent's scissors, scissors to his paper, or paper to his rock, and the rules forbid the easiest means to this goal by forbidding one to make one's throw after he has made his. But though the rules make achieving this goal more difficult than it might be, they do not make it by absolute standards difficult; rock, paper, scissors is not a challenging activity. But then rock, paper, scissors is not a very good game, and certainly not one the playing of which has much intrinsic value. It is characteristic of good games to be not only more difficult than they might be but also in absolute terms reasonably difficult. They cannot be so difficult that no one can succeed at them, but also cannot lack all challenge; they must strike a balance between too much and too little difficulty. In what follows I will defend the value only of playing good games, because they realize what seems an internal goal of the design of games. If the constitutive rules of a game make achieving its prelusory goal more difficult than it might be, this is surely because they aim at making it simply difficult.

If the prelusory goal and rules of a good game make succeeding at it reasonably difficult, they will also give it one ground of value if difficult activities are as such intrinsically good. And I believe that difficult activities are as such good. Though not often explicitly affirmed by philosophers, this view can be defended in at least two ways.

Many contemporary philosophers include among their intrinsic goods achievement, by which they mean not just moral but also non-moral achievement, for example, in business or the arts.[4] But what exactly is achievement? It clearly involves realizing a goal, but not every such realization counts as an achievement; for example, tying one's shoelace does not unless one has some disability. And among achievements some are more valuable than others; thus, starting a new business and making it successful is a greater achievement than making a single sale. If we ask what explains these differences—between achievements and non-achievements, and between greater and lesser achievements—the answer is surely in large part their difficulty: how complex or physically challenging they are, or how much skill and ingenuity they require. It is when a goal is hard to bring about that doing so is an achievement. So reflection on our intuitive understanding of the value of achievement suggests a first reason for holding that difficult activities are as such good.

A second reason, which is complementary but more abstract, is suggested by Robert Nozick's fantasy of an 'experience machine'.[5] This machine, which can electrically stimulate the brain to give one the pleasure of any activity one wants, is intended as a counterexample to the hedonistic view that only pleasure is good, but it also makes a positive point. If life on the machine is less than ideal, this is largely because people on it are disconnected from reality. They have only false beliefs about their environment and never actually realize any goals: they may think they are discovering a cure for cancer or climbing Everest, but in fact they are not. This suggests that an important good is what we can call 'rational connection to reality', where this has two aspects, one theoretical and one practical.[6]

The theoretical aspect is knowledge, or having beliefs about the world that are both true and justified. The beliefs' truth means there is a match between one's mind and reality; their being justified means the match is not a matter of luck but something one's evidence made likely. But a full account of this good must explain which kinds of knowledge are most worth having. Classical philosophers like Aristotle thought the best knowledge is of the intrinsically best objects, such as the divine substances, but the more plausible view is that the best knowledge has the most of certain formal properties that are independent of its subject matter. More specifically, the best knowledge is explanatorily integrated, with general principles that explain middle-level principles that in turn explain particular facts. This integration results in an explanatory hierarchy like that represented in figure 1, where items of knowledge higher up in the hierarchy explain those below them. And this hierarchy embodies more intrinsic value than if one knew only isolated unexplanatory facts, like the number of grains of sand on seven beaches (figure 2). We can give an artificial but illustrative model for measuring this value if we imagine that each item of knowledge initially has one unit of value in itself, but gains an extra unit for every other item of knowledge subordinate to it in a hierarchy. Then the seven isolated items in figure 2 have just one unit of value

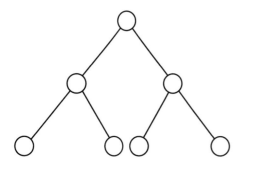

FIGURE 1

FIGURE 2

From T. Hurka and J. Tasioulas, 2006, "Games and the good," *Proceedings of the Aristotelian Society,* Suppl. Vol. 80: 237-264. Reprinted by courtesy of the Aristotelian Society: © 2006.

each, for a total of seven units. But in figure 1 the middle items have three units, since they each explain two further facts, and the top item has seven units, for a total of seventeen units in the hierarchy as a whole. The explanatory relations between them give an integrated set of beliefs more value than ones that are unconnected.

This model can be enriched. We may think it especially valuable to give unifying explanations of diverse facts, or to make surprising connections between what seemed unrelated phenomena. If so, we can count not just the number of individual items a given item of knowledge has subordinate to it, but the number of items of different kinds, so there is more value in explaining more types of fact. We may also value precision of knowledge, such as knowing that the constant of gravitational acceleration is not just somewhere between 5 and 15 m/s^2 but exactly 9.8 m/s^2. And we can capture this view both by giving more value to precise knowledge in itself and by giving it more additional value for explaining further precise truths.

Finally, we may think that knowing truths concerning many objects is better than knowing highly particular ones, even apart from the former's explanatory role; thus, knowing a scientific law is better than knowing the number of grains of sand on some beach even if one has not used the former to explain anything else.

The practical parallel to knowledge, and the other value missing on the experience machine, is achievement, or realizing a goal in the world given a justified belief that one would do so. Here again there is a match between one's mind and reality, though now reality has been made to fit one's mind, and a justified belief that makes the match not just lucky. Again we must specify which achievements are best. A classical view might say they are of the goals that are independently best, but we can maintain the parallel with knowledge, and give a better account of achievement as achievement, if we say they are of the goals with the most of certain formal properties that again centre on hierarchical integration. This time, however, the integrating relation is not explanatory but means–end. Thus, in figure 1 we achieve the goal at the top of the hierarchy by achieving the two middle-level goals as means to it, and each of those by achieving the two below them. And if each non-luckily achieved goal has one unit of value in itself plus an additional unit for every other goal achieved as a means to it, the achievements in this hierarchy again have seventeen units of value as against the seven in seven unrelated achievements. Just as more complex explanatory relations make for more value in knowledge, so more complex means–end relations make for more value in achievement.

Again this model can be enriched. We may think achievements are especially valuable if they require subsidiary achievements of varied kinds, and can capture this view by counting the number of goals of different types a given one has subordinate to it. More strongly, we may deny significant value to achievements that involve only subordinate goals of the same repetitive type. We may also value precision in achievement—hitting a particular target rather than just some vague area—and can give achievements additional value for that. And we can think that, apart from means–end relations, achieving goals whose content extends more widely, through time or in the number of objects they involve, is likewise more valuable.

This model deepens the value of achievement by showing it to be parallel to knowledge and, with it, one aspect of a more abstract good of rational connection to reality. It also makes many difficult activities good for the very properties that make them difficult. First, the more complex the means–end hierarchy an activity involves, the more places there are where one can fail at something crucial and the harder success in the activity becomes. Second, the more complex the hierarchy, the more deliberative skill it requires, since one has to monitor one's progress through a more elaborate sequence of tasks. There is a further increment of difficulty if the hierarchy involves a greater variety of subordinate goals, since then it requires a greater variety of skills, and likewise if the activity demands more precision. And it is more difficult to achieve goals with more extended contents, both because holding them in one's mind is more difficult and because achieving them requires changing more of the world.[7]

Moreover, these are precisely the aspects of difficulty found in good games. These games usually require one to go through a complex sequence of tasks rather than do one simple thing such as throw rock, paper or scissors. The tasks in question often demand varied skills: thus, golf requires one not only to drive the ball a long distance but to drive it accurately, play from bunkers, putt, and make strategic decisions. Good golfers are also precise, hitting their approach shots to a particular part of the green rather than just somewhere near it. And many games, such as chess, hockey and basketball, require players to grasp an extended content, including all the pieces on the board or all the players on the ice or court, in a single act of consciousness. That again is difficult, and requires years of practice to master.

Not all the difficulty in games involves this complex ratiocination. Weightlifters have to go through a precisely ordered sequence of moves in order to lift their weights, but also need brute strength: if one of two lifters has less perfect technique but is stronger and therefore lifts more, he wins the competition. Boxing, too, depends in part on raw power. These purely physical forms of difficulty do not instantiate the value of rational connection, and their role in making game-playing good is unclear. Why do we value the physical aspects of weightlifting and boxing but not those found in, say, pie-eating contests? Does this reflect just the historical accident that weightlifting and boxing began long enough ago that we can value them now for their traditions? Or do we value physical difficulty only when it accompanies more rational forms of challenge but not on its own? I will not pursue this issue, taking the rational connection model to capture what makes purely cerebral games such as chess difficult, and also much of what makes sports such as golf and hockey difficult.

I have argued that the prelusory goal and constitutive rules make playing a good game difficult, and have given two reasons to believe that difficulty is as such good. But I have not yet used the third element in Suits's analysis, the lusory attitude. Let us examine it more closely.

In his 1907 book *The Theory of Good and Evil* Hastings Rashdall remarked that '[s]port has been well defined as the overcoming of difficulties simply for the sake of overcoming them'.[8] This definition is close to Suits's, but differs on one point. It in effect takes the lusory attitude to be one of accepting the rules because they make the game difficult, whereas Suits takes it to be one of accepting the rules because they make the game possible. For Rashdall, the golfer accepts the rule against improving one's lie because it makes golf harder; for Suits, it is because it makes golf golf. Which view is correct?

Suits's view is preferable if we are analysing the generic concept of playing a game. Consider what we can call a pure professional golfer, who plays golf only as a means to making money and with no interest in the game for itself. He does not cheat as a means to making money; he knows that to make money he must play golf, which means obeying all its rules. But his only reason for accepting the rules is to make money. If we used Rashdall's view to define the generic concept, we would have to say the pure professional is not playing golf, which is absurd. But on Suits's view he is playing golf: though he accepts the rules only as a means to money, he does accept them in order to play golf and so has the lusory attitude.

But though Suits defines the generic concept of game-playing, this is not what he defends as the supreme intrinsic good. His argument, recall, is that in utopia, where all instrumental goods are provided, game-playing would be everyone's primary activity. But this description of utopia implies that it would contain no professional players; since no one would need to play a game as a means to anything, all players would be amateurs who chose the game for itself. But then they would have Rashdall's lusory attitude of accepting the rules because they make the game difficult, and Suits explicitly agrees. He describes how one utopian character decides to build houses by carpentry rather than order them up telepathically because carpentry requires more skill. And he starts his discussion of utopia by saying he will defend the value of game-playing as a specific form of play, where he has earlier denied that playing a game necessarily involves playing: to play is to engage in an activity for its own sake, and a pure professional does not do that.[9] So the activity Suits defends as supremely good is game-playing that is also play, or what I will call 'playing in a game'. And that activity involves accepting the rules not just because they make the game possible, but also because they make it difficult.

I will follow Suits here and narrow my thesis further: not only will I explain the value only of playing good games, I will explain the value only of playing *in* these games, or of playing them with an at least partly amateur attitude. But this is not in practice much of a restriction, since most people do play games at least partly for their own sakes. Consider Pete Rose, an extremely hard-nosed baseball player who was disliked for how much he would do to win. Taking the field near the end of the famous sixth game of the 1975 World Series, and excited by the superb plays that game had involved, he told the opposing team's third base coach, 'Win or lose, Popeye, we're in the fuckin' greatest game ever played'; after the game, which his team lost, he made a similar comment about it to his manager. Intensely as he wanted to win, Pete Rose also loved baseball for itself.[10]

So the game-playing whose value I will explain involves accepting the rules of the game because they make it difficult. But then the elements that define this type of game-playing are internally related: the prelusory goal and constitutive rules together give it a feature, namely difficulty, and the lusory attitude chooses it because of this feature. More specifically, if difficulty is as such good, the prelusory goal and rules give it a good-making feature and the lusory attitude chooses it because of that good-making feature. This connects the lusory attitude to an attractive view that has been held by many philosophers, namely that if something is intrinsically good, the positive attitude of loving it for the property that makes it good, that is, desiring, pursuing and taking pleasure in it for that property, is also, and separately, intrinsically good. Thus, if another person's happiness is good, desiring, pursuing and being pleased by her happiness as happiness is a further good, namely that of benevolence; likewise, if knowledge is good, desiring, pursuing and being pleased by knowledge is good. Aristotle expressed this view when he said that if an activity is good, pleasure in it is good, whereas if an activity is bad, pleasure in it is bad,[11] and it was accepted around the turn of the twentieth century by many philosophers, including Rashdall, Franz Brentano, G. E. Moore, and W. D. Ross. And it applies directly to playing in games, which combines the good of difficulty with the further good of loving difficulty for itself. The prelusory goal and constitutive rules together give playing in games one ground of value, namely difficulty; the lusory attitude in its amateur form adds a related but distinct ground of value, namely loving something good for the property that makes it so. The second ground depends on the first; loving difficulty would not be good unless difficulty were good. But it adds a further, complementary intrinsic good. When you play a game for its own sake you do something good and do it from a motive that fixes on its good-making property.

This two-part explanation deepens Suits's claim that playing in games is an intrinsic good, by connecting it to more general principles of value with application beyond the case of games. At the same time, however, it makes playing in games a derivative rather than a fundamental intrinsic good. It would not appear on a list of basic goods, since it combines two other, more fundamental, goods in a particular way.

But a good that is not fundamental can nonetheless be paradigmatic because it gives the clearest possible expression of a certain type of value. If difficult activities are as such good, they must aim at a goal: it is achieving that which is challenging. But their value does not derive from properties of that goal considered in itself, depending instead on features of the process of achieving it. Yet this can be obscured if the goal is independently good, since then the activity, if successful, will be instrumentally good, and this can seem the most important thing about it. If the farmer who works by hand successfully harvests a crop, his work contributes to the vital good of feeding his family, and this can distract us from the value it has in itself. But there is no such danger if the goal is intrinsically valueless, as it most clearly is in games. Since a game's prelusory goal—getting a ball into a hole in the ground or standing atop a mountain—is intrinsically trivial, the value of playing the game can depend only on facts about the process of achieving that goal. And this point is further emphasized by the lusory attitude, which chooses that process just as a process, since it willingly accepts rules that make achieving the goal harder. Game-playing must have some external goal one aims at, but the specific features of this goal are irrelevant to the activity's value, which is entirely one of process rather than product, journey rather than destination. This is why playing in games gives the clearest expression of a modern as against an Aristotelian view of value: because modern values are precisely ones of process or journey rather than of the end-state they lead to.

The contrary Aristotelian view, which denigrates these values, was expressed most clearly in Aristotle's division of all activities into the two categories of *kinēsis* and *energeia,* and his subsequent judgements about them.[12] An Aristotelian *kinēsis*—often translated as 'movement'—is an activity aimed at a goal external to it, as driving to Toronto is aimed at being in Toronto. It is therefore brought to an end by the achievement of that goal, which means that a *kinēsis* can be identified by a grammatical test: if the fact that one has *X*-ed implies that one is no longer *X*-ing, as the fact that one has driven to Toronto implies that one is no longer driving there, then *X*-ing is a *kinēseis.* But the main point is that a *kinēsis* aims at an end-state separate from it. By contrast, an *energeia*—translated variously as 'actuality', 'activity', or 'action'—is not directed at an external goal but has its end internal to it. Contemplation is an energeia, because it does not aim to produce anything beyond itself, as is the state of feeling pleased. And *energeiai* do not pass the above grammatical test, and therefore, unlike *kinēseis,* can be carried on indefinitely: that one has contemplated does not imply that one is not contemplating now or will not continue to do so. Contemplation, like driving to Toronto, is an activity, but it does not aim to produce anything apart from itself.

Now, Aristotle held that *energeiai* are more valuable than *kinēseis*, so the best human activities must be ones that can be carried on continuously, such as contemplation. This is because he assumed that the value of a *kinēsis* must derive from that of its goal, so its value is subordinate, and even just instrumental, to that of the goal. As he said at the start of the *Nicomachean Ethics*, 'Where there are ends apart from the actions, it is the nature of the products to be better than the activities.'[13] But it is characteristic of what I am calling modern values to deny this assumption, and to hold that there are activities that necessarily aim at an external goal but whose value is internal to them in the sense that it depends entirely on features of the process of achieving that goal. Suits cites expressions of this modern view by Kierkegaard, Kant, Schiller, and Georg Simmel,[14] but for an especially clear one consider Marx's view that a central human good is transforming nature through productive labour. This activity necessarily has an external goal—one cannot produce without producing some thing—and in conditions of scarcity this goal will be something vital for humans' survival or comfort. But Marx held that when scarcity is overcome and humans enter the 'realm of freedom' they will still have work as their 'prime want', so they will engage in the process of production for its own sake without any interest in its goal as such. Or consider Nietzsche's account of human greatness. In an early work he said the one thing 'needful' is to 'give style to one's character', so its elements are unified by 'a single taste', and that it matters less whether this taste is good or bad than whether it is a single taste.[15] Later he said the will to power involves not the 'multitude and disgregation' of one's impulses but their coordination under a single predominant impulse.[16] In both discussions he deemed activities good if they involve organizing one's aims around a single goal whatever that goal is. So for both Marx and Nietzsche a central human good was activity that on the one side is necessarily directed to a goal but on the other derives its value entirely from aspects of the process of achieving it. This is why the type of value they affirm is paradigmatically illustrated by playing in games; when one's goal is trivial, the only value can be that of process. Marx and Nietzsche would never put it this way, but what each valued is in effect playing in games, in Marx's case the game of material production when there is no longer any instrumental need for it, in Nietzsche's the game of exercising power just for the sake of doing so.

Playing in games also clearly straddles Aristotle's division between *kinēseis* and *energeiai*. It has the logical structure of a *kinēsis*, since it aims at a goal external to itself, and passes the relevant grammatical test: if one has parred a golf hole or climbed a mountain, one is no longer doing so. But it also has value in itself, as an *energeia* does, based on properties internal to it as an activity. We can show this more precisely using our formal model of the value of achievement, on which the value of any goal depends in part on the number of other goals achieved as means to it. In figure 1 the lower-level goals are pursued as means to higher-level ones, and contribute to those goals' value only if they are both successfully achieved and contribute causally to them. And the higher-level goals must themselves also be successfully achieved. Since the hierarchy is precisely one of *achievements*, a highest-level goal that is not achieved does not qualify for inclusion in the hierarchy, and so does not gain any value from having other goals achieved as attempted means to it. This means that if two people go through the same complex process as a means to a given goal, and the first achieves the goal while the second through bad luck does not, the first's activity has more intrinsic value: his hierarchy contains his highest-level goal, which has his greatest value, but the second's does not. (If Pete Rose's opponents played as well as he did but Rose's team won the World Series, his play was intrinsically better.) So the activities valued by our formal model are directed at an external goal, as *kinēseis* are, and have their full value only if that goal is achieved. But their value does not depend on properties of the goal considered by itself; if the same goal were achieved without complex means, it might have just one unit of value. Instead, their value depends on means–end relations between their components, and so depends on internal features of the activity as does that of an *energeia*.

If playing in games is the paradigm expression of modern values, it helps us see similar value in other activities not normally associated with games. One, emphasized by Nietzsche, is a life organized around a single goal; it embodies through a longer stretch of time the same hierarchical structure present in individual difficult activities. The relevant activities also include ones in business and the arts. Business activity sometimes aims at an independent good such as relieving others' suffering or increasing their comfort. But often its goal is just to win market share and profits for one company, which is morally trivial; there is no intrinsic value in people's drinking Coke rather than Pepsi or using Microsoft rather than Apple. Aristotle should therefore deny this activity value, and he did, arguing that if money has no intrinsic value, the activity of money-making must likewise have no value.[17] But if winning market share is difficult, requiring a complex series of finely balanced decisions, a modern view can grant it significant worth. And its pursuit can also involve something like the lusory attitude, since business people who aim partly for profits can also value the exercise of business skill just as skill, or for its own sake. Artistic creation too, to cite a different activity, has an independently good product if it aims, say, at communicating truths that cannot be communicated by non-artistic means. But a distinctively modern view (which is not to say the only view held nowadays) says that art aims only at beauty, where that consists in organic unity, or having the different elements of a painting, novel or piece of music form a coherent, dynamic whole. This view makes the value of artistic production rest on its intentionally creating all the complex relations that define its product's beauty, that is, on its itself being complex. And its value will be greater if it has more of the supplementary qualities mentioned above: if it unifies more varied elements, if it requires more precise brushstrokes, notes or words, and if it involves grasping more extended contents in a single act of consciousness, as Henry Moore could see his sculptures from all sides at once.[18] And of course artistic creation can involve a lusory attitude, if the artist enjoys and values the skill his work involves for its own sake.

But playing in games is also in one respect a lesser good, and I want to close by explaining why. Imagine two activities that are equally complex and difficult, one of which produces an intrinsically good result while the other does not. Perhaps one is political activity that liberates an entire nation from oppression while the other involves winning a high-level chess tournament. The first activity will, of course, be instrumentally better, because it produces a separate intrinsic good. But it will also arguably be on that basis intrinsically better. Consider Derek Parfit's example of a person who spends his life working for the preservation of Venice. Parfit claims, plausibly, that if after this person's death Venice is preserved, and in a way that depends crucially on his efforts, that will make his life and activities intrinsically better than if Venice had been destroyed.[19] This conclusion already follows from our formal model of achievement, since any realization of a topmost goal adds value to a hierarchy. But I think there is an extra ground for its truth if, as Parfit clearly intends, the preservation of Venice is independently good. Whatever additional value there is in achieving a goal just as a goal, there is further value in achieving one that is good. When an activity aimed at a valuable end successfully achieves that end and therefore is instrumentally good, its being instrumentally good is an extra source of intrinsic goodness.[20]

Now, because game-playing has a trivial end result, it cannot have the additional intrinsic value that derives from instrumental value. This implies that excellence in games, though admirable, is less so than success in equally challenging activities that produce a great good or prevent a great evil. This seems intuitively right: the honour due athletic achievements for themselves is less than that due the achievements of great political reformers or medical researchers. Whatever admiration we should feel for Tiger Woods or Gary Kasparov is less than we should feel for Nelson Mandela. It also implies that, whatever their other merits, Suits's utopia and Marx's realm of freedom would lack an important intrinsic good. Their inhabitants could play the game of, say, farming or medicine by going through the same complex procedures as farmers and doctors today. But if food could be produced and diseases cured by pushing a button, as they can in Suits's vision, their activity would not have the additional intrinsic value that comes from actually feeding or curing people and that is found in present-day farming and medicine.[21] The very perfection of Suits's and Marx's utopias prevents them from containing the distinctive good of producing intrinsic goods that would not otherwise exist.

The point that an ideal world may exclude certain intrinsic goods should not be unfamiliar: G. E. Moore noted that the best possible world could not contain compassion for real pain, which he plausibly held was a greater good than compassion for merely imaginary pain.[22] And Suits's and Marx's utopias can still contain, alongside such goods as pleasure and knowledge, the distinctively modern good of achieving a difficult goal regardless of its value. Moreover, their doing so can help make them better on balance than any world in which successful instrumental activity is possible. Many philosophers have assumed, with Aristotle, that the value of a process aimed at producing some end-state must derive entirely from the end-state's value, so if the latter is negligible so is the former. But there is no reason to believe this. Even if some of the process's intrinsic value depends on its instrumental value, in the way just described, there can also be intrinsic value in its properties just as a process and apart from any value in its product. To return again to figure 1, this value will depend not on any qualities of the topmost goal considered in itself, but only on the means–ends relations between the various goals whose sequential achievement constitutes the process. I have argued that this distinctively modern value is illustrated most clearly by playing in games, especially when that is analysed as in Bernard Suits's wonderful book *The Grasshopper.*[23]

Notes

1. Ludwig Wittgenstein, *Philosophical Investigations*, 3rd edn, trans. G.E.M. Anscombe, Oxford: Blackwell, 1972, Sect. 66.

2. Bernard Suits, *The Grasshopper: Games, Life, and Utopia*, Toronto: University of Toronto Press, 1978; repr. Peterborough, ON: Broadview Press, 2005, p. 41/55 (page references are first to the University of Toronto Press edition, then to the Broadview Press edition).

3. Ibid., p. 41/54-55.

4. See, for example, James Griffin, *Well-Being: Its Meaning, Measurement and Moral Importance*, Oxford: Clarendon Press, 1986, p. 67.

5. Robert Nozick, *Anarchy, State, and Utopia*, New York: Basic Books, 1974, pp. 42-45.

6. I give a fuller account of this value in my *Perfectionism*, New York: Oxford University Press, 1993, Chs 8-10.

7. Some may deny that difficulty is as such good, on the ground that an activity aimed at evil, such as genocide, is not in any way made good by its difficulty. The issue here is complex (see my *Virtue, Vice, and Value*, New York: Oxford University Press, 2001, pp. 144-52), but those moved by this objection can retreat to the weaker claim that only activities with good or neutral aims gain value by being difficult. This weaker claim is sufficient to ground the value of games.

8. *The Theory of Good and Evil,* 2 vols, London: Oxford University Press, 1907, vol. 2, p. 105.

9. Suits, *The Grasshopper,* pp. 166/149, 144/130.

10. Tom Adelman, *The Long Ball: The Summer of '75—Spaceman, Catfish, Charlie Hustle, and the Greatest World Series Ever Played,* New York: Back Bay Books, 2003, p. 313.

11. Aristotle, *Nicomachean Ethics,* trans. W.D. Ross and J.O. Urmson, Oxford: Oxford University Press, 1980, 1175b24-30. I discuss this view at length in *Virtue, Vice, and Value.*

12. *Nicomachean Ethics,* 1094a1-7, 1174a13-b8, 1176b1-8, 1177b2-4.

13. Ibid., 109414-5.

14. Suits, *The Grasshopper,* pp. 93-94/92.

15. Friedrich Nietzsche, *The Gay Science,* trans. Walter Kaufmann, New York: Vintage, 1974, Sect. 290.

16. Nietzsche, *The Will to Power,* trans. Walter Kaufmann and R.J. Hollingale, New York: Vintage, 1968, Sect. 46.

17. *Nicomachean Ethics,* 1096a5-10. An obvious suggestion is that an activity like money-making can be a *kinēsis* when described in one way and an *energeia* when described in another. But, plausible though it is, this does not seem to have been Aristotle's view. He seems to have treated the distinction as a metaphysical one, between types of activities as they are in themselves. Nor could he have accepted the suggestion and continued to give his arguments about the inferiority of money-making and the superiority of contemplation, however described, based on their properties as *kinēsis* or *energeia.*

18. Howard Gardner, *Frames of Mind: The Theory of Multiple Intelligences,* New York: Basic Books, 1983, p. 188.

19. Derek Parfit, *Reasons and Persons,* Oxford: Clarendon Press, 1984, p. 151.

20. On this see Shelly Kagan, 'Rethinking Intrinsic Value', *Journal of Ethics,* 2, 1998, pp. 277-97; and my 'Two Kinds of Organic Unity', *Journal of Ethics,* 2, 1998, pp. 299-320.

21. This claim is defended, with specific reference to Suits, in Shelly Kagan, 'The Grasshopper, Aristotle, Bob Adams, and Me', (unpublished ms).

22. G.E. Moore, *Principia Ethica,* Cambridge: Cambridge University Press, 1903, pp. 219-21.

23. I am grateful for helpful conversations to my former student Gwendolyn Bradford, whose essay, 'Kudos for Ludus' first linked the value of game and the details of Suit's definition of a game.

References

Adelman, Tom 2003: *The Long Ball: The Summer of '75—Spaceman, Catfish, Charlie Hustle, and the Greatest World Series Ever Played.* New York: Back Bay Books.

Aristotle 1980: *Nicomachean Ethics.* Trans. W.D. Ross and J.O. Urmson. Oxford: Oxford University Press.

Gardner, Howard 1983: *Frames of Mind: The Theory of Multiple Intelligences.* New York: Basic Books.

Griffin, James 1986: *Well-Being: Its Meaning, Measurement and Moral Importance.* Oxford: Clarendon Press.

Hurka, Thomas 1993: *Perfectionism.* New York: Oxford University Press.

_____1998: 'Two Kinds of Organic Unity'. *Journal of Ethics,* 2, 1998, pp. 299-320.

_____2001: *Virtue, Vice, and Value.* New York: Oxford University Press.

Kagan, Shelly 1998: 'Rethinking Intrinsic Value'. *Journal of Ethics,* 2, 1998, pp. 277-97.

_____unpublished: 'The Grasshopper, Aristotle, Bob Adams, and Me'.

Moore, G.E. 1903: *Principia Ethica.* Cambridge: Cambridge University Press.

Nietzsche, Friedrich 1968: *The Will to Power.* Trans. Walter Kaufmann and R.J. Hollingdale. New York: Vintage.

_____1974: *The Gay Science.* Trans. Walter Kaufmann. New York: Vintage.

Nozick, Robert 1974: *Anarchy, State, and Utopia.* New York: Basic Books.

Parfit, Derek 1984: *Reasons and Persons.* Oxford: Clarendon Press.

Rashdall, Hastings 1907: *The Theory of Good and Evil,* 2 vols. London: Oxford University Press.

Suits, Bernard 1978/2005: *The Grasshopper: Games, Life and Utopia.* Toronto: University of Toronto Press. Repr. Peterborough, ON: Broadview Press, 2005.

Wittgenstein, Ludwig 1972: *Philosophical Investigations,* 3rd edn. Trans. G.E.M. Anscombe. Oxford: Blackwell.

Internalism and Internal Values in Sport

♦

Robert L. Simon

At least since our days in elementary school or its equivalent, most of us who have been involved in sports and athletics, whether as participants, fans, observers, or critics, have been told that sports have a close connection with values. Indeed, sport has been regarded as an important source of values by a great variety of individuals for long periods of human history. In the *Republic*, Plato declares that "there are two arts which I would say some god gave to mankind, music and gymnastics . . . not for the soul and body incidentally, but for their harmonious adjustment," while centuries later, Camus reportedly maintained that the context in which he really learned ethics was that of sport.[1] Sport has long been identified as an important source of values in the popular culture as well, and its alleged role in character building and even in promoting patriotism has frequently been stressed. On the other hand, many critics of competitive sports have not denied that sports promotes values, but affirm that it is the wrong values that get promoted.

But just how is sport connected to values? One position, which I will call *externalism*, denies that sport is a special source of values, although sophisticated externalists may claim that sport helps reinforce values already in the culture and socializes participants to accept them. On this view, the values sport promotes or expresses simply mirror, reflect, or reinforce the values found in the wider society. Thus, to take a perhaps too crude example, in a predominantly capitalist society, sports will emphasize such capitalist values as intense competition and rivalry and may, in addition, socialize athletes and their fans to make such values their own.

Internalists, on the other hand, hold that sport has a significant degree of autonomy from the wider society and supports, stands for, or expresses a set of values of its own which may run counter to the values dominant in the culture. William Morgan,

Adapted, by permission, from Robert L. Simon, 1999, "Internalism and internal values in sport," *Journal of Philosophy of Sport* 27: 1-16.

for example, in his *Leftist Theories of Sport* (9), defends the idea that there is a "gratuitous logic" of sport, which does not merely reflect or reinforce the values dominant elsewhere. Similarly, in last year's Presidential Address to the PSSS, Drew Hyland argued that sport, rather than functioning as a mirror of external social values, can actually subvert them.[2]

In what follows, I will try to explore the view that sport has a kind of internal ethic, what might be called an internal morality of sport, that is tightly (some would say conceptually) connected with the idea of athletic competition. In particular, I will try to suggest how one approach to explicating this internal ethic of sport, one that has been suggested by many writers but perhaps not clearly distinguished from positions it resembles, such as formalism, sheds light on the role of values that are internal to sport. I will call this view broad internalism, and will contrast it with narrower formalistic versions of internalism, noting that some versions of broad internalism resemble closely and in some cases explicitly draw upon the interpretative approach to philosophy of law defended by Ronald Dworkin (3 and 4). Although there is surely very little new or original in what I have to say, as much of my paper will try to place the work of others within a framework for analysis, I hope the framework I examine proves illuminating for understanding the basis of internal values of sport.

I. Formalism

"Formalism" is the name given to a position, or more accurately, a family of positions that characterize games and game derivative notions primarily in terms of their formal structure, particularly their constitutive rules (8: p. 1; 2: p. 7). Thus, in a narrow sense, formalism has been characterized as the view that such game derivative notions as "a move or play within a game" and "winning a game" are definable by reference to the constitutive rules of the game. In a broader sense, formalism may be thought of as the view that games (and sports to the extent that sports are games of physical skill) can be defined primarily by reference to the idea of constitutive rules and goals or obstacles designated by the rules themselves, which are unintelligible apart from them. A move within a game is what is permitted or required by the constitutive rules, while what counts as winning a game also is defined by such rules. For example, using a tank during a football game to run over the opposing team's defensive players is not a move within the sport, since such moves may be made only in accord with the constitutive rules. There are different versions of formalism, so "formalism" might best be regarded as an umbrella term covering a family of positions which, although closely related, sometimes differ on points of varying degrees of significance.

Much of the literature has focused on whether formalists have provided an adequate definition or characterization of games and sports, or of such derivative notions as "winning a game," but formalism also has normative implications. Perhaps the most best known of the normative implications of formalism is the incompatibility thesis, which denies that cheaters can win competitive games or sports. According to this thesis, since cheaters violate the rules, they fail to make moves within the sport and hence fail to play it. Since one can win the game only by playing it, and since cheaters do not play, cheaters can't win. In addition, formalists tend to characterize sportspersonship as playing fair, where playing fair is understood as respecting the letter and perhaps the spirit of the rules.

The emphasis of formalists on the constitutive rules of the game has been salutary, particularly in contributing to our understanding of the nature of games. However, whatever its merits or demerits as a characterization of game and game-derivative concepts, formalism lacks the normative resources to address many of the moral problems that arise in connection with sport.

Issues of sportpersonship, for example, often go beyond conformity to the formal rules of a sport or game. Thus, to modify an example discussed most recently by Robert Butcher and Angela Schneider (1: p. 6), consider the case of clubless Josie, a top amateur golfer who arrives at a national amateur golf championship without her clubs.[3] Clubless Josie has lost her clubs, not because she is clueless, but due to an error made by her airline. Josie's chief rival, Annika, has a spare set of clubs virtually identical to those Josie has lost. Should Annika lend poor clubless but not clueless Josie the spare set of clubs so Josie can compete in the tournament? It is unclear that formalism has anything to say about this question, since the issue does not concern the application of the rules.

Some formalists might reply that their view, sympathetically interpreted, supports lending the clubs to Josie. If we correctly understand the spirit or point of the rules, which is to promote competition, we should perform the act that enhances competition. However, in appealing to the spirit of the rules or their underlying point, formalists go beyond a narrow version of formalism and raise the question of how we are to understand such notions as the spirit of the rules or their underlying point. In answering these questions, I suggest they move beyond formalism to a different version of internalism that needs to be assessed on its own merits.

In addition to lacking the resources to address ethical problems in sport that do not clearly fall under the rubric of the rules, formalism suggests a less than plausible account of the ethics of rule violations in certain situations arising in athletic competition. I refer, of course, to the analysis of strategic fouls given by some writers who appear sympathetic to a formalist approach. A strategic foul is a rule violation designed to secure an advantage within the sporting contest to the team or individual who fouls. A widely discussed example is the strategic foul at the end of a basketball game, where the losing team fouls in order to stop the clock and in the hope that the opposing team will miss its foul shots thereby increasing the chances of a come back. According to critics of this practice, such fouls are intentional violations of the rules and therefore are not legitimate moves within the game. In particular, they violate the understanding or implicit contract that must hold between opponents to play the game by the rules. On this analysis, strategic fouling is a form of cheating.

However, almost all practitioners of the game deny that strategic fouling is a form of cheating and view it instead as an established part of the game. Of course, the practitioners might just be wrong, but as we will see, an analysis of strategic fouls different than that provided by the formalist critics is available, one that goes beyond formalism without simply accepting the opinion of the practitioners that established custom is the basis of the ethic of the sport. If this alternate analysis is plausible, formalism may not be adequate even on what seems to be its strongest ground, where violation of central rules of the game is concerned.

Formalism also has problems with the ethics of rule change and rule formation, a problem that was brought to our attention at the last annual meeting of the PSSS by Alun Hardman. How are proposed changes in the rules, or sets of rules for new sports and games, to be assessed? Of course formalists might point out that the rules of many sports include what Hart calls rules of change. A rule of change for golf might state that a proposal becomes a rule of golf if and only if it is accepted through established procedures by the governing golf organizations of an area, such as the United States Golf Association in America and the Royal and Ancient in Britain. However, while such rules of change might establish when a rule change becomes official, they do not establish whether the change is desirable or undesirable, or good or bad for the game. Consider, for example, the proposed rule that anyone who commits a strategic foul in the last 4 minutes of a basketball game is thrown out of the game and the injured team is awarded 30 straight foul shots. Because it is so penal, such a rule might eliminate strategic fouling if adopted. But is it a good rule? It is not clear that formalism as a theory has much to contribute to this issue. Of course, theorists regarded as formalists may have something to say on the ethic of rule change, but my contention is that when they do, they no longer speak as pure formalists but extend the formalist approach in a way that will be useful to make more explicit.

II. Conventionalism

Many theorists who are dissatisfied with formalism argue that in emphasizing the formal constitutive rules of given sports, the formalists have ignored the implicit conventions accepted by the participants which apply to the actual practice of participating in the sports in question. These conventions are sometimes referred to as the "ethos of the game" (2: p. 7-18). For example, with respect to the practice of strategic fouling in basketball, conventionalists are prone to argue that there is a convention in basketball permitting such fouls as a legitimate strategic move within the game. Since the players all accept the convention, and since each team knows the other team will strategically foul at appropriate points in a contest, no team has a special advantage over others. Therefore, strategic fouling is not cheating, but is legitimized by actual practice and widely accepted social conventions that apply within that practice.

But can social conventions be a source of value in sports? Conventionalists certainly have made a contribution to our understanding of actual sporting practice by exploring the role of the ethos and cultural context of games. But does the ethos have normative force? Do the conventions express what ought to take place as well as describe what does take place in sporting practice?

Consider, for example, the case of clubless Josie. For one thing, if such a case were highly unusual, there might be no applicable convention. In that case, conventionalism, like formalism, would not tell us what should be done. Suppose, however, that there was an applicable convention according to which players were under no obligation to lend equipment to fellow competitors. Would that settle the issue or would it simply raise the deeper issue of whether that convention itself was ethical or reflected appropriate standards of fair play? Thus, one major problem with conventionalism is the ethical status of the conventions themselves.

This is true even in the case where conventionalism has a great deal of plausibility—namely, its analysis of strategic fouls in sports such as basketball. But even here, it is far from clear that the mere existence of conventions settles the issue raised by critics of strategic fouling. The critics of strategic fouling acknowledge that they are opposing present practice, and the underlying understandings upon which practice is based, but they argue that appeal to central values implicit in the logic of sports requires reform of present practice. Unless we are to immunize conventions from criticism and in effect always choose to preserve the existing understandings of sport, challenges to existing conventions cannot be dismissed simply on the grounds that they counter our present conventional understandings of sporting practice.

In this respect, conventionalism resembles the view in ethical theory, sometimes called normative ethical relativism, which states that individuals ought to follow the moral norms dominant in their own cultures. Just as normative cultural relativism suggests that reformers within a culture must be wrong a priori, since they propose to change the moral norms dominant in their own culture, so conventionalism in sport, when taken as a normative theory, imply that existing conventions are in effect immune from criticism, since it is precisely those conventions which are determinative to begin with.

It also is unclear how conventionalism can respond to our second set of issues involving the evaluation of proposed changes in the rules or conventions of a sport. When is a change for the better? How are we to evaluate a proposed change to the conventions of basketball, for example, to the effect that players on a losing team should not foul simply to gain a strategic advantage. Just as appeal to the existing rules alone cannot settle the issue of whether a proposed rule change is or is not an improvement, so appeal to existing conventions cannot be the sole basis for evaluation of proposals for reform and change. In either case, arguments for and against the proposed changes, either in the rules or the conventions, would have to come from elsewhere. But from where?

Postmodernists who emphasize that ethical discourse ultimately must be ethnocentric in that it ultimately can appeal only to intellectual resources already available within the existing social framework may maintain that the conventionalists are on the right track but have not gone far enough. That is, the conventionalists are quite right to emphasize the social and historical setting of sport within a particular cultural context but have remained too much on the surface focusing on specific surface conventions tied to sporting practice rather than looking deeper into the cultural resources available for ethical argument. However, such an ethnocentric approach need not lead to an externalist theory of the source of values in sport. Rather, as in the case of Morgan's *Leftist Theory of Sports*, it can lead instead to the view that an ethnocentric but critical and rationally grounded investigation of the conceptual resources found in actual sporting practices leads us to recognize an internal "gratuitous logic" or internal morality of sport.

So far, then, I have tried to suggest that both pure formalism, understood as a narrow version of internalism, and conventionalism, a well known form of externalism, lack the intellectual resources to deal with such issues as sportspersonship, strategic rule violations, and the desirability of proposed changes in the rules and conventions of sport. More broadly, it is hard to see how emphasis either on existing formal rules of sport or social conventions can provide a basis for the resolution of some fundamental moral issues that arise in sport, or for the kind of moral and educational development that many expect sport to provide. Perhaps a third position, which I will call broad internalism, can do better.

III. Broad Internalism

In a series of writings in jurisprudence, Ronald Dworkin has criticized legal positivists, particularly H.L.A. Hart, for holding too narrow a view of the nature of law (3 and 4). According to Dworkin, the positivists have identified law with a model of formal rules. One of Hart's major contributions to this area is to show the diverse kinds of rules that make up law, ranging from criminal sanctions to rules of change and adjudication, to the Rule of Recognition which identifies the rules of the legal system and distinguishes them from non-legal rules. Dworkin has argued that in addition to rules, there are legal principles, which have normative force within the legal system. What makes these principles legal ones, rather than simply moral principles imported by judges from beyond the law and applied according to the particular political and ethical commitments of individual judges, is that they are in some sense presupposed by the legal system or are required to make sense of its key elements.

For some time, a significant number of writers have been developing what appears to be an analogous position in the philosophy of sport. While many have close ties to or are clearly sympathetic to many aspects of formalism, or may in some cases even view themselves as formalists, they at least go beyond narrow versions of formalism in developing resources for the ethical assessment of behavior in sports that can be distinguished from rules without being mere conventions. Rather, the kinds of considerations they point to seem to be presuppositions of sporting practice in at least the sense that they must be accepted if our sporting practice is to make sense, or perhaps make the *best* sense. Before developing this account of the view I will call broad internalism, let me give some examples of what I believe are instances of it.

In a recent article, aptly called "Fair Play as Respect for the Game," Robert Butcher and Angela Schneider (1: p. 9) maintain that "if one honors or esteems one's sport . . . one will have a coherent conceptual framework for arbitrating between competing claims regarding the fairness . . . of actions." Where does this conceptual framework come from? Butcher and Schneider suggest that sports themselves have interests. Respect for the game can be articulated in terms of athletes making the internal interests of the game their own. Thus, they claim that "the idea of the interests of the game provide a means for judging one's own action in relation to the sport . . . . Taking the interests of the game seriously means that we ask ourselves whether or not some action we are contemplating would be good for the game concerned, if everyone did that" (1: p. 11). Butcher and Schneider illustrate their position by applying it to the case of poor clubless Josie (who in earlier versions of the example is a racquetless squash player rather than a clubless but not clueless golfer).

> The notion of respect for the game provides ample reason for lending Josie the racquet. At the personal level . . . you would forgo a valuable experience and personal test if you decline to play Josie. At a more general level, the sport of squash is enhanced by people playing and competing at their best whenever possible. Squash at the institutional level would not be served by neglecting to play a . . . scheduled match. You should want to lend Josie your racquet. (1: p.18)

What makes this an example of broad internalism is that appeal is being made to norms or principles internal to the idea of sport. These norms or principles are not mere social conventions and indeed may run counter to and provide a basis for criticizing existing social conventions, which might support requiring Josie to forfeit the match. Neither are they formal rules of the game. Although broad internalists might well want to avoid the metaphysical complications attached to the notion of games having their own interests independent of those of human agents, perhaps all that internalists need to assert is the metaphysically more minimalist claim that the point of playing competitive squash would be best achieved if the match was played.

A second and very instructive example of broad internalism is provided in a recent paper by J.S. Russell entitled "Are Rules All an Umpire Has to Work With?" (13) In this paper, Russell, who explicitly appeals to Dworkin's views in jurisprudence, argues against the view that rules are all an umpire has to work with. He discusses a variety of ingeniously selected cases from the history of American baseball, cases which call on umpires and officials to extend, change, or interpret the rules, which by themselves may be indecisive or indeterminate when applied to hard cases. Russell, applying Dworkin, suggests that "we might try to understand and interpret the rules of a game, say, baseball . . . to generate a coherent and principled account of the point and purposes that underlie the game, attempting to show the game in its best light" (13: p. 14). Russell cites as an example of a principle that might underlie such competitive sports as baseball the injunction that "rules should be interpreted in such a manner that the excellences embodied in achieving the lusory goal of the game are not undermined but are maintained and fostered" (13: p. 15).

Broad internalism, then, is the view that in addition to the constitutive rules of sports, there are other resources connected closely—perhaps conceptually—to sport that are neither social conventions nor moral principles imported from outside. These resources can be used to adjudicate moral issues in sports and athletics. In William J. Morgan's terms, sport has an independent "gratuitous logic" of its own that makes it more than a mirror simply reflecting the values of society. This underlying logic may be interpreted in a variety of ways.

IV. Three Approaches to Broad Internalism

Broad internalism claims that in addition to the rules of various sports, there are underlying principles that may be embedded in overall theories or accounts of sport as a practice. But what is the relationship between the rules and the underlying principles or theories? What form do these theories take? Do the principles apply to sport as a general practice or to particular sports, or both? If the latter, what is the relationship between the more general principles underlying sport and those underlying specific sports, say, soccer or basketball or golf?

These are difficult questions to which I wish I had acceptable and well worked out answers. Unfortunately, all I can do is offer suggestions for development of broad internalism that I hope are capable of advancing the discussion but which assuredly are far from definitive.

First, however, a critic might ask why we need to appeal to broad principles or theories of sport in the first place. For practical purposes, intuitive reactions to individual cases might work quite well. To cite one of Russell's cases, an umpire in baseball might intuitively understand that the rule prohibiting base runners from interfering with fielders should be interpreted to also prohibit a runner who has crossed home plate (and so in a narrow sense is no longer on the bases) from tackling the catcher to prevent him from tagging the next runner out.

But while intuitive judgments of wise practitioners may stand us in good stead in individual cases, problems arise when we want to see if the set of individual judgments about particular cases coheres. Thus, if a critic challenges us to show that our judgment about case A can fit coherently with our judgment about case B, we need to provide a justification. Moreover, in other individual cases, expert and wise practitioners may disagree about the correct resolution, and need principles and theories to help adjudicate the dispute. Individual judgments about specific cases may nevertheless be invaluable, as in the method of reflective equilibrium, in helping us formulate hypotheses about the correct principles which apply to sports. However, it is difficult to see how we can avoid the appeal to an underlying account of sports if we are to provide any kind of deep justification for our decisions in a variety of specific instances.

It is possible to find at least three approaches in the literature to the kind of underlying account of sport postulated by broad internalism. The first is contractual. The sports contest is seen as governed, not only by the rules, but by a social contract that has among its terms an agreement to play by the rules. Presumably, the strongest version of such a theory postulates that the contract is a hypothetical one reflecting the agreement athletes would make under fair conditions of choice. For example, Kathleen Pearson argues that strategic fouling "destroys the vital frame of agreement which makes sport possible" (11: p. 118), while Warren Fraleigh maintains that "it cannot be stated unequivocally that all participants agree to performing the good foul by agreeing to play basketball" and hence the permissibility of such fouling cannot be assumed to be part of the underlying social contract (5: p. 42). Others, myself included (14: p. 80-84), have argued that rational and impartial athletes would not agree on a social contract for competitive sports that allows the use of potentially harmful performance enhancing drugs.

A second approach appeals not to an underlying social contract but, as we have seen in the case with Butcher and Schneider, to the interests of the game. As they articulate the idea that "sports are practices and practices are the sorts of things that can have interests" (1: p. 9). On their account, "the athlete takes on the interests of his or her sport. . . . Because the interests of the game are now our own interests, we have a motivation for striving for the good of the game" (1: p. 11). This transformation of interests has important consequences. "The athlete who respects the game wishes to play as well as possible against a worthy opponent playing as well as possible. . . . It is not, therefore, in your interest to have your opponent play below his or her best, except where your methods of bringing that about are part of the game itself" (1: p. 15). It is not surprising, then that Butcher and Schneider conclude that Annika should lend poor clubless Josie her spare set of golf clubs.

A third more directly Dworkonian or *interpretive* version of broad internalism derives the principles and theories underlying sport neither from a hypothetical social contract nor a conception of respect from the game but rather from an appeal to the best interpretation of the game or an inference to the best explanation of its key elements. Certain principles and theories must be *presupposed* if we are to make sense of key elements of sport, such as the rules, the skills that are tested, and possibly the history, traditions, and central elements of the ethos of particular sports. This is the approach Russell takes in the article referred to earlier. While I am not sure just what kind of presupposition is involved here, I tend to view it as at least partially pragmatic. The form of the argument is that a particular activity, competitive sport, would lack a point, be not fully intelligible, or make no sense (or at least less sense than otherwise) were not certain underlying principles taken as normative or as applying to the activity in question.

Which approach is philosophically best? While I suspect the three approaches differ primarily in heuristic value and tend to yield similar results in similar cases, I also suggest that the third approach is perhaps the most fundamental. It is more fundamental in the sense that proponents of the other approaches need to implicitly rely upon it in ways that interpretivists need not rely on the other views. Thus, it is difficult to see how we are to decide just what the interests of a sport actually are without an appeal to a kind of theory of the nature of the sport, which either purports to be the best interpretation of its central features or the best explanation of them. However, interpretivists need not deal with the special metaphysical issues raised by the claim that sports are the sort of entities that can have interests (although their own view may have metaphysical commitments of a different sort). So theories appealing to interests of a sport implicitly appeal to an interpretation or explanation of it, but the appeal need not go the other way.

Similarly, contractualists will need to build some account of the nature and point of competitive athletics into their specification of the initial situation under which hypothetical contracts are formed, but interpretivists need not appeal to contracts other than as heuristic devices. For example, the analysis of strategic fouling as a violation of the contract among athletes presupposes that the penalties for such acts are *punishments* designed to penalize rule violations rather than prices designed to set the *cost* for exercising an allowable strategic option. Thus, the contractual analysis presupposes a prior theory of the point and nature of the game to even get off the ground. I suspect, then, that while all three versions of broad internalism are valuable and provide important frameworks for illuminating the assumptions underlying moral arguments, approaches which rely on hypothetical contracts or the best interests of a sport are best understood as heuristic devices for illustrating important features of still deeper underlying moral theories.

V. Broad Internalism and an Internal Morality of Sport

We began our discussion by asking in what way sport was connected to values. Can broad internalism help us answer the question? After all, even if the main thesis of broad internalism is accepted, what reason is there to believe that the principles or theory underlying sport is *moral* in content? Dworkin suggests that in choosing among theoretical interpretations of such legal systems as those of Britain and the United States, we should select the *morally* best reading. To what extent does such a claim also apply to sport?

If we view sports as paradigmatically games of physical skill, the formalist characterization of the nature of games suggests that moral content is built in. On that analysis, perhaps most famously developed by Suits, sports, qua games, have rules that create obstacles simply for the purpose of challenging the competitors. Hence, sports contests can be regarded as tests of the competitor's abilities to meet the challenge created by the rules. More broadly, sports are arenas in which we test ourselves against others, where we attempt to learn and grow through our performances, and where we attempt to develop and exhibit excellence at overcoming the sport specific obstacles created by the rules.

This overall theory of the nature and function of sport, however roughly and sketchily characterized here, is not part of the constitutive rules but may be thought of as the best explanation of why the rules have such characteristics as the creation of artificial obstacles to achieving pre-lusory goals that often are easily achievable outside the context of the sport. Russell's example of a principle, "Rules should be interpreted in such a manner that the excellences embodied in achieving the lusory goal of the game are not undermined but are maintained and fostered," basically requires us to interpret the rules of different sports in a way that maximizes their function as a challenge and incentive to the pursuit of the excellences required for competitive success.

But what has this to do with an internal morality of sport? A preliminary attempt might emphasize that the pursuit of excellence is itself a value and the qualities such as dedication that are required to achieve it, along with the self-examination and honesty about one's strengths and weaknesses that success in competitive sport calls for, are virtues. But is this enough to establish moral content? After all, success at becoming a leading burglar may involve some of the same factors but lacks moral standing.

However, that a concern for excellence can be used for the wrong ends no more shows that it is not a value than the fact that there can be justice among thieves shows that justice lacks moral standing. Probably any single quality, when placed in the wrong context, can foster immoral ends. What gives moral force to the virtues and excellences required in sport is their connection within the practice to respect for certain qualities of human beings.

Because sports are activities involving obstacles that are challenging for us to overcome, their logic commits the competitive athlete to competing against worthy opponents. While all of us as individuals will sometimes hope for an easy contest, say to allow us to qualify for a championship, the best explanation of the rules of well designed sports is that they create a test. An athlete who never wanted to face a worthy opponent, and instead wished only to win in a blow-out, might well value such normally external goals of sport as fame and fortune but would at best have only minimal commitment to sport.

This suggests that if we regard competition in sport at its best as constituting a test of excellence through creation of challenges, principles requiring an ethic of respect for the opponent and a commitment to fair play are a consequence. This ethic, first of all, requires competitors not to interfere with their competitor's ability or capacity to compete under the rules. For example, competitors may not intentionally injure fellow competitors or deceive them, say by lying to them about the time or location of a contest in the hopes of winning by default, or attempt to win a contest by bribing officials.

More positively, competitors also are at least encouraged to create conditions under which opponents may perform at their best.[4] Since sport is best understood as a practice within which competitors seek to pursue excellence through meeting challenges, participants would undermine the practice by continually seeking less than worthy opponents. Moreover, since the internal point of participation is to expose oneself to competitive opponents so that one can truly test one's skills, one should act within reason to promote conditions under which opponents can play their best. Noted golfer David Duval expresses how a good competitor should view opponents when he discusses the possibility of contending against Tiger Woods in a major championship,

> One of the great things about golf is that you don't have to have any ill-will in this game. If I come head-to-head against him at say, the U. S. Open, I want him to be playing as good as he can play because I want to beat him when he's playing his best. It would be a heck of a lot better, if you know he gave you all he's got, and you beat him.[5]

Thus, impartial athletes might agree to encourage and support the creation of conditions that would allow athletes to function as worthy opponents. Athletes want to compete at their best, and so value such conditions for themselves, and so, if impartial, would have to apply to all athletes the principles they want applied to themselves. Moreover, it would be hard to understand how an athlete could be genuinely committed to athletic competition without wanting to play against worthy opponents. Athletes who intentionally played only against vastly inferior opponents would rightly be suspected of being concerned only with external goods of sport and not with the value of athletic competition itself.

In addition, broad internalists can argue that part of the explanation of why sports have the features they do, as well as a justification of why they should have such features, is a conception of the good life for human beings. According to this conception the good life, or (more plausibly) at least a significant part of it, consists of meeting challenges for their own sake and developing our capacities in order to do so. On this conception, some activities are worth doing not because of the external rewards we can acquire as a result, but because of the nature of the activities themselves. In this regard, Drew Hyland has suggested that sports at their best can be part of a Socratic process of self-examination, in which we learn about our strengths and weaknesses, and those of others, and try to develop together through the common challenge of achieving competitive excellence (7).

Of course, there are athletes who compete for external rewards, such as fame, trophies, or incredibly large salaries. However, while many professional players may not be motivated to play largely by the ideal of meeting challenges for their own sake, their large salaries are still parasitic on that ideal. For if the players did not in fact try to meet the challenges set by the rules within the framework of the sport, but instead tried to win through such external means as deliberately injuring opponents or bribing referees, they would undermine the structure of their own practice and perhaps, if the behavior was sufficiently widespread, destroy it. Thus, regardless of the personal motivations of the players, they must meet the challenge set by the sport on its own terms and will be rewarded to the extent that they actually do so.

VI. Applications

Let us briefly review how a broad internalist might address the three cases with which we started—namely, the case of clubless Josie, the issue of strategic fouls, and the assessment of proposed rule changes in sport.

As Butcher and Schneider have argued, Annika should lend the clubs to Josie. Sporting contests are designed to be tests, and competitors should not avoid a worthy opponent. However, I would suggest that while Annika should be encouraged to lend the clubs to Josie, and may be subject to moral criticism on the basis of poor sportspersonship for not doing so, she is not morally required to make the clubs available to Josie and should not be formally punished or penalized for failing to do so. Failing to lend her opponent the clubs is in a different moral category than, say, trying to deliberately disable an opponent or bribe an official. External interference with competitors, say by deliberately trying to injure them or by bribing officials, makes the good sports contest impossible and clearly undermines the very point of competitive sports. However, the idea that competitors take positive steps to promote good play on the part of opponents, while worthy of support, is open ended and not so clearly essential to the good sports contest. Thus, it is controversial what level of support should be provided in what contexts—suppose Josie needed a lesson from Annika just 5 minutes before teeing off—and so it is unclear that when culpable noncompliance takes place, let alone what degree of noncompliance is worthy of punishment.[6]

To turn to our second case, is fouling for strategic purposes a form of cheating? As I have suggested elsewhere (14: p. 48-49), this would depend on whether the best theory of the sport in question views the penalty as a *punishment* for misbehavior or as a *price* for exercising a strategic option. To develop this point further, the decision as to whether the penalty is a price or a punishment depends on an overall conception of the point and purpose of the game, and the nature of the test it provides. For example, I would argue that since foul shooting is an important skill in basketball, and the award of two foul shots is appropriate compensation to the offended team, fouling at the end of the game is not cheating but permissible strategy. It creates a test of nerve, which the offended team may pass by making its foul shots. Opponents of this view need to make a case in view of their overall conception of the game that the penalty in question, the award of foul shots, is best understood as a punishment designed to sanction a prohibited act rather than the price of a permitted option.

What about rule change? Basketball might be a better game, for example, if the penalty for fouling late in the game was changed to make it clearly a punishment, for example through setting the cost of fouling so high that it is no longer a sound strategic option. Defending such a view would involve ultimate appeal to a theory, not just of sport but of the specific sport of basketball and the skills it is best construed as testing. For example, if one sees it as a game of flow and constant motion, one will want to limit stops in play at the end of the game and hence may advocate more extreme penalties than exist at present for strategic fouls, in effect making clear that they should be viewed as a punishment and not a price.

Unlike the case of clubless Josie, the issues of strategic fouling and the assessment of proposed rule changes, while they raise questions of values, are not primarily moral issues. Rather, both involve an appeal to an overall theory of how the sport of basketball should be conceived. There is a moral element inherent in constructing such a theory, since we are trying to understand it as a fair and challenging test through which human agents can develop important physical and mental skills and characteristics. And, of course, whether or not the strategic fouler cheats is a moral issue. But constructing the best theory of a sport like basketball also involves issues that are not primarily moral ones, such as the role that skill in shooting fouls under pressure should play in the game. This suggests that the best overall conception of a game or sport need not necessarily be the morally best one, although all sports as such will presuppose the requirement of non-interference, as well as the encouragement of support for worthy competitors, and express the ideal of the good life as encompassing personal growth through the meeting of challenges.[7]

It might be objected that the kind of moral principles discussed so far are not necessarily distinctive to sport. For example, the prohibition against external interference with the performance of others clearly has broader application throughout the body politic. (Indeed, questioners at the presentation of this address at the IAPS annual meeting in Bedford argued forcefully that my analysis says nothing special about sports and ethics, and that similar principles can be derived from other practices. To take one of their examples, if tubaless Teddy shows up for the concert without his tuba, surely other tuba players who have a spare tuba should lend it to him.)

However, broad internalists need not claim that *all* the principles to which they appeal are distinctive or restricted to the context of sport. Indeed, if the internalist analysis came up with principles that contradicted well supported and well known moral rules, we would be right to at least question the ethics of sport, not the traditional ethical theories. What the internalist should want to claim, then, is not that internalist analysis yields an entirely new ethic (although it is plausible to think that some of the principles uncovered may well be unique to sport) but that it provides grounds internal to sport for important ethical principles.

Moreover, what makes sport such a powerful moral medium is not only its public character which is accessible to peoples throughout the world. In addition, sporting activity at its best, along with performances in some other areas such as the arts, is chosen by practitioners and spectators for its own sake, and its values often are internalized by the members of the sporting community themselves. A major implication of broad internalism, then, is that the sporting community, when operating according to its own principles, illustrates and expresses fundamental ethical norms that people adopt for themselves and apply in common within practices to which they owe allegiance. Thus, it can not only be a model of an important version of the moral life for us all but also a means of promoting allegiance to fundamental values as well.

VII. A Concluding Note on Ethnocentrism

Philosophers sympathetic to postmodernism, as well as the neo-pragmatism of philosophers such as Richard Rorty, may maintain that no such result can be had. At best, we can have a localized historically situated understanding justifiable to a particular group in a particular context. Justification, after all, must be ethnocentric starting and finishing with the resources available to specific historical communities. Appeal to transcendent principles, on the other hand, must always be specious, perhaps even involving appeal to the dreaded "God's eye view," the ultimate philosophical insult in some philosophical quarters. So rather than an internal logic of sport itself, what we may arrive at is at most a localized understanding of what is involved in sport as practiced within specific communities.

In my view, we should not accept too extreme a version of ethnocentrism in part for the reasons articulated so well by William J. Morgan. As Morgan suggests (8: p. 189), ethnocentrism in some of its forms seems committed to saying, "it always boils down to saying something such as 'we are in a privileged position simply by being *us* . . . that truth can only be characterized as the outcome of doing more of what we are doing now.'"[8] Indeed, it is difficult to see how what Morgan calls vulgar or noncritical forms of ethnocentrism can avoid extreme moral relativism according to which it is possible, as Sartre suggested, that Nazism might become the "truth of man" if accepted to a sufficient degree. Morgan suggests that we reject vulgar ethnocentrism and embrace a more reflective variety which attempts to avoid contradiction, seeks coherence, and appeals to the deeper critical principles of the society.

However, I would add to Morgan's argument that to regard these critical principles as justified is not to view them as merely beliefs deeply embedded in our cultural web of belief. That is, if it is unacceptable to rely on shared agreements merely because we agree to them, isn't it just as unacceptable at the deep level as at the surface level? Rather, deep principles of justification have normative force precisely because they have survived rational criticism from diverse quarters, including cross-cultural inquiry, and make an intellectual claim to us on their merits.[9]

Reflective ethnocentrists will want to emphasize, however, that even the kind of justification about which I am speaking is contextual and historically situated. What else can justification be but deriving conclusions from factors that already have made the deepest claims to our assent? I cannot give a full answer to that retort here except to suggest that in some cases, the best explanation of why some principles, premises, or other justifiers to which we appeal are regarded as deep is because they have at least provisionally passed intellectual tests that confer normative force upon them. We agree to them because of the intellectual considerations in their favor rather than find them intellectually favored because we agree. The alternative is simply to privilege the belief of existing communities just because they are believed, a view which has the dismaying consequences that Morgan himself has pointed out.

Thus, assuming that a critically reflective theory or set of principles of sport survives extended rational evaluation and criticism, then there is a case that such an account of sport is not merely a reflection of deep cultural understandings but may be a novel extension of them, or even a repudiation of prevailing norms, depending upon the nature of the surrounding cultural context.

Because broad internalism supplies us with a set of principles that arguably have normative force and that can be used to criticize contemporary sporting practice, it seems to suggest to many an excessively purist, some would say Platonic, conception of sport. Indeed, Morgan views what he calls the gratuitous logic of sport as a ground for criticizing what he regards as the corruption of sport in capitalist societies. Are broad internalists committed to the view that actual sporting practice is largely corrupt?

First of all, if the charge of wholesale corruption is warranted, it applies well beyond the scope of capitalist societies. Second, it is important to keep in mind the diversity of sporting practices ranging from major international competition and different professional sports all the way down to the level of local communities and clubs. As Drew Hyland reminded us in last year's Presidential Address, the former are not necessarily representative of the latter.

That having been said, there is no question that commercial interests have changed major sports at the highest levels, sometimes for the worst. Pressure to win can constrain sportspersonship, overemphasize winning, and lead to changes in sport that make them more entertaining or more marketable but less viable as pure contests between worthy opponents. The frequent media sponsored time-outs in televised American basketball games, which allow more commercials but undermine the flow of the game, are a case in point. On the other hand, not all changes are necessarily bad. The introduction of the shot clock and the three-point shot in basketball in the U.S. not only made the game more entertaining to mass audiences but arguably made the game better in its own terms as well. A number of sports at the highest level, professional and top amateur golf perhaps being the best example, retain not only the minimal ethic of no external interference with opponents but also implement and illustrate the idea of respect and support for opponents to a significant extent. Moreover, at least some prominent athletes, Michael Jordan being a primary example, illustrate and express respect for their sport at the highest levels, showing that love of the game is compatible with professionalism at its best. The degree, then, to which a broad internalist will find contemporary sport corrupt is itself a complex issue depending at least as much upon specific evaluations of sporting practice in context as upon the abstract principles the broad internalist finds presupposed by sporting practice.

What I have tried to suggest, however, is that much of the current literature in philosophy of sport supports the value of a broadly internalist approach to understanding not only the nature of sport but its underlying values and presuppositions. I have tried to identify and briefly speak to some of the issues raised by such an approach. If my suggestion has force, sport is an independent source of important values and contains within itself the basis for a critical evaluation of sporting practice.

To the extent sport is true to its underlying ideals, it provides a defensible internal basis for an ethic of athletic competition.

Notes

1. The quotation from Plato is from *The Republic,* Book III, Section 412. Albert Camus, "The Wager of Our Generation," in *Resistance, Rebellion, and Death* (Justin O'Brien, trans.). New York: Vintage Books, 1960, p. 242.

2. Hyland's address was presented to the PSSS Annual Meeting in Boston in August 1998.

3. Robert Butcher and Angela Schneider (1: p. 6) employ this example, but see A.S. Lumpkin, S. Soll, and J. Beller, *Sports Ethics: Applications for Fair Play* (St. Louis, MO: Mosby, 1994) for an even earlier use of it.

4. Using the framework defended by Bernard Gert, one might say that the prohibition of external interference is a moral rule and the encouragement and support of competitors as facilitators is a moral ideal. (For Gert's most recent views on moral rules and ideals, see 6: chapters 7–10.)

5. *The New York Times,* Feb. 3, 1999, p. D4.

6. Again the distinction here draws on Gert's distinction between moral rules and ideals. This distinction might also be made contractually. A sketch of such an argument would be that all athletes who consider the matter impartially would want external interference with all competitors to be prohibited. However, while I believe they would want to encourage competitors to take steps to insure that opponents performed well, I know of no argument that would establish universal agreement on the level of support that would be required, how often support must be given, and under what if any circumstances participants who fail to provide such support should be penalized or punished.

7. Perhaps particular sports, such as basketball, can be defined as the conjunction of their rules and whatever principles must be presupposed by the rules and the central features of the sport in question. What the relationship of definitions of particular sports to definitions of the more inclusive or general account of "sport" would be a further problem for those broad internalists with definitional agendas. I have hoped to avoid these questions in the present paper, however, by focusing only on the normative rather than the definitional implications of a broad internalist approach.

8. The quotation is from Richard Rorty, *Consequences of Pragmatism* (Minneapolis: University of Minnesota Press, 1982, p. 173), who Morgan quotes for purposes of criticism. See also, the critique of Morgan's distinction between vulgar and reflective ethnocentrism in Terence J. Roberts, "Sporting Practice Protection and Vulgar Ethnocentricity" (12). Morgan replies in his "Ethnocentrism and the Social Criticism of Sports: A Response to Roberts," *Journal of the Philosophy of Sport,* XXV: 82-102, 1998.

9. As Thomas Nagel suggests (10: p. 73), "This is the general form of all failures of reduction. The perspective from inside the region of discourse or thought to be reduced shows us something that is not captured by the reducing discourse." In the present case, the claim that justification ultimately can be reduced to shared agreement or consensus among members of the relevant community, if it is to rationally persuade dissenters of its own worth and be a basis for justified agreement, must appeal to standards of reasoning whose worth cannot be merely that we agree to them.

Bibliography

1. Butcher, R., and Schneider, A. "Fair Play as Respect for the Game." *Journal of the Philosophy of Sport.* XXV:1-22, 1998.

2. D'Agostino, F. "The Ethos of Games." *Journal of the Philosophy of Sport.* VIII: 7, 1981.

3. Dworkin, R. *Taking Rights Seriously.* Cambridge: Harvard University Press, 1977.

4. Dworkin, R. *Law's Empire.* Cambridge, MA: Harvard University Press, 1986.

5. Fraleigh, W. "Why the Good Foul Is Not Good." *Journal of Physical Education, Recreation, and Dance.* January:41-42, 1982.

6. Gert, B. *Morality: Its Nature and Justification.* New York: Oxford University Press, 1998.

7. Hyland, D. *The Question of Play.* Latham, MD: University Press of America, 1984.

8. Morgan, W.J. "The Logical Incompatibility Thesis and Rules: A Reconsideration of Formalism as an Account of Games." *Journal of the Philosophy of Sport.* XIV:1-20, 1987.

9. Morgan, W.J. *Leftist Theories of Sport: A Critique and Reconstruction.* Urbana, IL: University of Illinois Press, 1994.

10. Nagel, T. *The Last Word.* New York: Oxford University Press, 1997.

11. Pearson, K. "Deception, Sportsmanship, and Ethics." *Quest.* XIX:115-118, 1973.

12. Roberts, T.J. "Sporting Practice Protection and Vulgar Ethnocentricity: Why Won't Morgan Go All the Way?" *Journal of the Philosophy of Sport.* XXV:71-81, 1998.

13. Russell, J.S. "Are Rules All an Umpire Has to Work With?" *Journal of the Philosophy of Sport.* XXVI:27-49, 1999.

14. Simon, R.L. *Fair Play.* Boulder, CO: Westview, 1991.

Broad Internalism and the Moral Foundations of Sport

J.S. Russell

It is easy to be puzzled by sport's relation to morality. Does sport reflect or represent important everyday moral ideals, or does sport encourage values that are separate from and potentially at odds with familiar moral ideals? Can sport act as a foundation for moral education about virtue and moral principle, or are there significant limitations to using sport to educate about morality? These are important questions for philosophy and practice, and answers to them are not straightforward. The puzzles they present are undoubtedly prompted in part by the exceptional nature of sport: by its separation from what we call "real life," by the distinctiveness (or—let's be honest—the oddity) of some sporting activities, by the apparent triviality of those activities, and of course by the sometimes extraordinary moral misadventures of participants on and off the field, to name a few obvious reasons. The puzzles are also pressed by the diversity of conduct found within sport, much of which seems morally questionable at best. Thus, many participants, fans, and critics must at least occasionally ask themselves how an activity such as American football, which on the surface appears to promote some of the worst human vices—violence punctuated by committee meetings, as one observer put it[1]—could represent or reflect any important moral ideals. American football is hardly unique in this respect.

We cannot avoid confronting these issues, and not just because of the ubiquity of sport in modern culture but also because moral evaluation in sport is ever present and richly diverse. Thus, we readily and confidently condemn poor sportsmanship, unfairness, failures to make sacrifices for the team, and the moral poverty evident in some particular contests, and we praise their opposites—though we often disagree over what counts as what. In light of the variety of moral opinions expressed about both the nature and conduct of sport, many would agree that a clearer understanding of sport's relation to morality would be valuable.

One way of responding to the ambiguities over the connection between sport and morality is to acknowledge the evident role of morality and moral reasoning in sport and to consider whether some moral values are distinctive to sport. If so, what are these values, and to what extent do they occur in sport? Does the uniqueness of sport reflect and entail a distinct and separate morality? That is, should sport and the concerns of sport be viewed through their own moral lens rather than the one we use for everyday living?

My aim in this paper is to look closely at these and similar questions regarding morality and sport. Mainly, I want to challenge the view that there is much that is distinctive or autonomous about morality or moral reasoning in sport. I shall call the view I want to challenge "the separation thesis," which I shall understand as the claim that sport morality has some significant moral values of its own that are neither reflections of nor expressions of moral values found outside sport. In other words, the separation thesis claims that sport supports, stands for, or expresses a set of moral values that are uniquely its own. I shall contrast this position with what I shall call "the continuity thesis," which claims that moral values that are most fundamental to sport—namely, those that are constitutive elements of sport—are expressions or reflections of more basic moral values found outside of sport. Once we reject the separation thesis in favor of the continuity thesis, we will have a clearer picture of the moral foundations of sport and of sport's relation to morality, and we will then be in a better position to answer questions such as those posed earlier.

Before moving ahead, we should first point out what an ambitiously strong claim the separation thesis makes. We should also understand that the continuity thesis does not have to assert that there is nothing at all distinctive about sport morality. Thus, not just any examples of specialized moral duties or values will prove the separation thesis and refute the continuity thesis. Human institutions are replete with examples of specialized duties and values that regulate behavior in particular contexts but that do not therefore indicate any interesting separation or autonomy from familiar moral ideas or values. On the contrary, this is frequently how familiar general moral ideas are connected to particular practices. Thus, lawyers have moral obligations not to disclose certain personal information about their clients without consent. If we accept the common claim that a lawyer's obligations of privilege are the highest ones, the specific duties or values that are implied may be unique to that profession. But this does not yet show that law has a separate or distinct morality of its own. Indeed, it is evident that the duties and the general principles of client privilege rest on more general moral principles of respect for privacy, trust, justice, and liberty. Thus, it is also evident that the particular professional duties regarding protection of client information support, stand for, or express more general moral values found elsewhere.

Now if this type of example illustrates the sort of distinctiveness or autonomy of moral value that the separation thesis claims, this is hardly an interesting idea, for we are all familiar with how general moral values inform and regulate unique practices and duties in specific contexts, and this is all the example describes. For the claims of the separation thesis to be interesting, there must be some more fundamental separation between at least some of the moral values in sport and moral values found outside of sport. Thus, the separation thesis must claim that something genuinely autonomous exists in some of the moral values found in sport;

these values can neither be reflections nor extensions of more general moral values found outside of sport. In other words, the separation position must hold that sport supports, stands for, or expresses moral values that are uniquely sport's own. I will have more to say about this later.

The separation thesis has a fairly long history among commentators on sport, although it has never been worked out systematically. For example, the thesis is strongly suggested in Johan Huizinga's classic analysis of play as "a stepping out of 'real' life into a sphere all its own," a sphere that is "outside the range of good and bad" (9: p. 8, 1.I).[2] In a recent paper, Claudia Pawlenka reviewed how these sorts of ideas have been taken up by a number of contemporary German philosophers who have claimed that sport has its own "particular" morality that stands independent of general morality to a significant degree (12).[3] There is no clearly articulated movement that represents a counterpart in Anglo-American philosophy. However, an influential discussion that touches on these issues is Robert L. Simon's analysis of "internalist" accounts of sport (18). According to Simon, "'internalists' hold that sport has a significant degree of autonomy from the wider society and supports, stands for, or expresses a set of values of its own" (18: p. 2). He cites as a statement of the basic internalist idea William J. Morgan's view that sport has an "independent 'gratuitous logic' of its own" and does not simply reflect or reinforce values found elsewhere. (18: pp. 2, 7). Simon's own version of internalism, which he calls "broad internalism," takes the more specific view that sport contains certain normative moral principles that "are neither social conventions nor moral principles imported from outside." Thus, the internalist analysis holds that there is a special "internal ethic" or "internal morality" of sport. (18: p. 7). This is contrasted with externalist views of sport that hold that sport is regulated by moral values that are not found within sport per se but that are applied to sport from outside, perhaps drawn from society generally or from moral values found outside sport itself.

Simon's own internalist position, broad internalism, is developed through generalizing from my arguments that certain normative principles are constitutive features of sporting games in addition to the rules that make them up and that a Dworkinian interpretivist approach to adjudication based on an ideal of integrity best explains how to understand and apply these principles (15, 18: pp. 6-10). I am sympathetic to Simon's use of this work, but I want to test the possible connections between a broad internalist analysis of sport and the separation and continuity theses. More specifically, I shall argue that broad internalism is best understood as endorsing the continuity thesis and, thus, as rejecting the separation thesis. I will follow this with a more detailed discussion of the ways in which sport is continuous with certain familiar and basic moral ideals found outside sport, in effect outlining the moral foundations of sport. I will conclude with a discussion of further implications of the relation between sport and everyday morality and moral education generally.

Internalism and the Separation and Continuity Theses

The internalist analysis of morality and sport just described seems at least consistent with the separation thesis and might even be read to entail it. Which is it, then? In a later discussion, Simon states that a broad internalist analysis of sport incorporates a commitment to fundamental moral values such as fairness, liberty, and equality (19). But this certainly seems to soften the point of the internalist analysis given earlier, and how any of this is reconciled with the previous statements of internalism or broad internalism is not worked out. However, as a response to the objection that broad internalism does not identify moral principles that are necessarily distinctive to sport, Simon asserts what is surely right—namely, that not all moral principles to which broad internalists appeal must be unique to sport (18: p. 13). This does not yet answer the objection, but it does tell us that broad internalism need not deny a role for familiar moral ideals in sport. Simon goes on to claim that the key issue should be for internalists to show that there are "grounds internal to sport for important ethical principles," or in effect that the nature of sport incorporates certain specific moral principles within itself. This apparently answers the objection—moral principles internal to sport need not be distinctive to sport at all—but that seems to soften the internalist analysis further. Broad internalism, in particular, becomes the view that important moral principles are found simply in the nature of sport itself. This might include only reflections or extensions of values that are present elsewhere, but they would not be external to sport and imposed from outside to regulate it.

This understanding implies that an internalist analysis is consistent with the continuity thesis. That seems contrary to the apparent intention of the internalist analysis, which claimed that sport "supports, stands for, or expresses a set of values of its own" and thus has a significant degree of autonomy, including having its own "independent 'gratuitous logic'" that does not merely reflect or reinforce values found elsewhere. In the same discussion, however, Simon clearly wants to preserve the prospect that sport might have some truly distinctive or autonomous moral values. Thus, he acknowledges that internalists, including broad internalists, might come up with moral principles that contradict established and well-supported moral rules and theories (18: p. 13). This is an acknowledgment that the internalist analysis is consistent with the separation thesis and that that thesis might apply to sport in a particularly strong form. But of course these remarks do not identify or resolve any potential conflicts.

The best reading of these remarks, then, is that, despite some ambiguities and appearances to the contrary, Simon's presentation of internalism in general, and broad internalism in particular, should be understood to be consistent with both the separation and continuity theses. Moreover, the internalist analysis pointedly raises the issue of whether the best defense of internalism in sport should incorporate the separation thesis. This is an issue raised in Simon's own discussion. Moreover, the issue is raised by internalism generally, for if there are moral values found internally within the nature of sport in some sense, it is natural to ask if they are unique to sport. Simon's discussion, thus, provides a fruitful starting point for considering a number of issues of fundamental importance in philosophy of sport. Indeed, because Simon's analysis is so sensible and thoughtful in recognizing connections between sport and what we traditionally think of as morality, it is a rich starting place for sorting out issues related to the separation and continuity theses.

It follows, then, that the account of internalism should be revised to acknowledge clearly that it is consistent with both the separation and continuity theses. I shall argue now that broad internalism is best interpreted as rejecting the separation thesis and embracing the continuity thesis. In effect, I shall argue that Simon's own commitments are best served by revising broad internalism to explicitly accept the continuity thesis.

Broad Internalism and Morality

Simon defends broad internalism, in part, by arguing that two competing theories of sport, formalism and conventionalism, are inadequate. Game formalism, roughly the view that the nonnative content of games is exhausted by the rules that constitute them, is inadequate because it lacks normative resources to address and resolve ethical problems that are regularly posed by games but that are not clearly addressed by a game's constitutive rules. Thus, formalism cannot clearly enough understand efforts to regulate games that make reference to the spirit of games, nor can formalism make an adequate distinction between rule violations involving strategic fouling and cheating, nor can formalism account for various problems in interpreting and changing the rules themselves, all of which seem to require reference to normative moral resources that go beyond the constitutive rules of games (18: pp. 2-4). Simon then goes on to consider whether these shortcomings could be addressed by recognizing social conventions associated with games as a source of value external to sport. But Simon rejects conventionalism mainly on the grounds that it fails to explain how conventional values can themselves be subject to meaningful criticism and how we can understand when resolutions of various ethical problems represent improvements or changes for the better (18: pp. 4-5). The argument here trades on construing conventionalism as a variety of moral relativism and focuses on familiar difficulties relativists face making sense of moral progress in moral reasoning and deliberation. According to Simon, broad internalism addresses the problems posed by formalism and conventionalism by claiming that there are extra-rule normative moral principles internal to sport that are, thus, "neither social conventions nor moral principles imported from outside" (18: p. 7). Those moral principles fill the normative gap that formalism leaves, and they provide a nonconventional basis for moral progress grounded in moral commitments contained within sport itself.

Simon's argument is convincing that formalism and conventionalism cannot adequately account for the normative moral content and deliberations we find in sport.[4] And he makes a strong case that certain normative moral principles are found within sport itself, and so this establishes the merits of broad internalism. That leaves the issue of whether Simon's analysis of the normative content of broad internalism supports the separation or the continuity thesis.

Simon considers a number of approaches in the literature of sport philosophy that could be construed as versions of broad internalism, including social contract approaches proposed by Pearson and Fraleigh (7, 13) and Butcher and Schneider's analysis of fair play as respect for the game (3). He then argues, rightly in my view, that a Dworkinian interpretive approach is presupposed by the others and so is fundamental (18: pp. 7-9). Thus, he calls his position "interpretive broad internalism." This approach is built on two related normative principles that were presented in my paper on adjudication. The first is a moral principle asserting a general interpretive approach to games—namely, that we should understand and interpret the rules of a particular game "to generate a coherent and principled account of the point and purposes that underlie the game, attempting to show the game in its best light" (15: p. 35). The second principle more specifically directs the application of the first. It asserts that "rules should be interpreted in such a manner that the excellences embodied in achieving the lusory goal of the game are not undermined but are maintained and fostered" (15: p. 35).

I argued in my earlier paper that the first principle is simply an application to sport of a general moral ideal of integrity, drawn from Dworkin's theory of law. Simon does not directly mention it as an extension of the ideal of integrity, but it is implied in his acceptance of a Dworkinian interpretive approach to sport. Indeed, for Dworkin, the moral virtue of integrity is fundamental to his interpretive theory of law; in fact, he regards the virtue of integrity as the fundamental moral virtue of law (6: ch. 7-8). Thus, according to Dworkin, in an adjudicative context the moral virtue of integrity requires that judges try to give a coherent, principled account of the system of law, attempting to show the law in its best light by providing the best moral interpretation of previous judicial decisions. In my paper on adjudication, I argued, and Simon later seemed to agree, that this ideal applied to sport and games generally (15: pp. 34-39). (In fact, I went further than this, suggesting that Dworkin's ideal of integrity applied less problematically to sport than to law.) But although sport has its own version of a moral principle of integrity, there is nothing interestingly autonomous or unique about this ideal. The nature of sport is such that it supports, stands for, and expresses a general moral ideal that is arguably part of any human legal or quasilegal institution, including sport. What this discussion shows, then, is that the moral ideal of integrity that interpretive broad internalism argues is part of sport is powerful evidence against the separation thesis and for the continuity thesis. Indeed, it is direct support for the continuity thesis.

There are other potential problems here for the separation thesis. In particular, interpretivism presupposes, as Dworkin argues, a fundamental commitment to moral equality via its commitment to the moral ideal of integrity (6: p. 213). If that is right, then interpretivism as a theory of sport seems to recognize that the moral foundations of sport are informed by basic considerations of moral equality—namely, that participants are entitled to equal concern and respect. This presses the question of whether there could be any truly autonomous or unique moral ideals of sport, as the separation thesis holds. There is room for this, however. There may be distinctive moral principles or ideals in sport that are not expressions or reflections of specific moral ideals found elsewhere but that are also regulated and informed by a basic notion of moral equality. This is a very plausible way of regarding the separation thesis. It connects morality in sport to morality in general but would still allow for a morality or set of moral principles that is unique to sport. That would still raise the issues of tensions between sport and moral values found elsewhere and of how useful sport might be in educating about morality generally. An obvious candidate for such a principle would be the second principle described above—namely, that rules should be interpreted in such a manner that the excellences embodied in achieving the lusory goal of the game are not undermined but are maintained and fostered. Indeed, Simon uses this principle to generate an argument for certain sport-specific moral values. What I want to consider now is to what extent, if at all, this lends any support to the separation thesis.

Simon argues that this principle presupposes certain commitments to develop and challenge one's skills in ways that demand that competitors pursue and foster contexts for genuine competition. Thus, sport makes moral demands that participants pursue genuinely worthy adversaries and even that they take reasonable measures to promote conditions that would allow competitors to function as worthy adversaries (18: pp. 10–11). Let's call these "duties to foster a context of competition." A real-world example that illustrates these ideas would be boxing champions who fail to seek out, or who avoid, worthy opponents. This seems to be a competitive moral failure. And if a worthy opponent is not available because technical impediments prevent him or her from being an opponent (say, there are contractual impediments to fighting across federations), then this approach suggests there are moral obligations to take reasonable measures to eliminate those impediments.

Do such duties to foster a context of competition, then, reflect values that are unique to sport? I doubt it. These sorts of values are present not merely in sport but in many, perhaps all, situations in which institutions for the promotion of human excellence exists. Thus, as a philosopher, I have obligations to test my ideas in contexts in which they are likely to be subject to the most informed and cogent criticism. Little is accomplished if I test my ideas only against undergraduate philosophy students and then present the ideas as important contributions to philosophy (tempting as that can be at times). A commitment to philosophical excellence demands that I test my ideas against informed and thoughtful audiences and critics, and the more informed and thoughtful, the better (difficult as that can be sometimes). In effect, I have professional obligations to seek out worthy critics, including worthy adversaries. We can characterize these exchanges aptly as a mutual striving for excellence, just as competition in sport is often characterized. Thus, I should be committed to fostering contexts in which ideas can be fairly and robustly exchanged and tested; and thus I should also be committed to removing impediments to such contexts, in part because this is a means to testing and furthering my own contributions to philosophy. Of course, such mutual striving for excellence also demands certain requirements of fairness, impartiality, respect, and tolerance toward those whose work is in competition with one's own. Thus, certain processes are built into publication of philosophical work, such as peer review and double-blind reviewing, to name just two examples. Philosophy is not unusual in any of these respects. The same or similar obligations can be found in all areas of serious intellectual and artistic endeavor. All of these points have parallels in the case of sports, as Simon and others have observed (19). But in all these matters, then, it appears that the special moral commitments to competition that are internal to sport are continuous with and reflect and reinforce moral commitments that flow more generally from the pursuit of excellence, and thus are not distinctive to sport per se. There does not, then, seem to be anything here yet that identifies a distinctive or unique internal morality of sport. The moral values associated with competition support, stand for, or express familiar values that can apparently be found in all institutions that exist to promote human excellence.

There is at least one further prospect for the separation thesis that flows from this discussion. Perhaps the *aim to win* represents a distinctive moral ideal in games and in sport. This is an obvious candidate for a distinctive internal moral value of sport, given the importance that is often given to winning in competitive sports. Indeed, the pursuit of winning seems to be a fundamental attitude that one takes toward participating in sport (20), and so perhaps it should be considered a separate and distinctive moral value. Thus, one has a distinct competitive duty in sport to strive to win. However, the aim to win is not found only in sport but also in games generally as well as in other competitive contexts. Thus, I might aim to win an essay competition or a grant or an award. Moreover, the pursuit of winning seems part of framing a competitive context in which excellences can be displayed and measured; thus, its value seems grounded in its general role in contributing to the promotion of human excellence, similar to the other virtues of competition just discussed. As is often remarked, winning or its pursuit seems designed to provide a public and objective proof of superior excellence through competition (9: pp. 11, 5, 13). It remains to be shown, then, that striving to win in sport identifies some particular moral value distinctive to sport.

It is difficult to imagine a different characterization of the purpose of winning that makes sense. Even winning for the purposes of achieving values external to sport, such as fame or money, presupposes that the competitor's worthiness in realizing such external values is because superior excellence has been demonstrated in victory. The value of winning seems to lie, then, in its contribution to constructing certain competitive contexts that will foster the exercise and display of distinctive sporting excellences, particularly contexts that attempt to measure and record superior displays of such excellence.[5] Indeed, all must acknowledge that this is what winning is designed for. The only issue that remains is whether pursuit of winning is valuable because it demonstrates superiority of sporting excellences valued for their own sake or valued instrumentally in promoting external values, such as fame or money. In either case, it is difficult to see how the pursuit of winning stands on its own as a distinctive value within sport. Indeed, its value is apparently as an instrument that is wholly subsidiary to promoting principles and values that are realized within or that are external to sport. The pursuit of winning seems to be just one more value that, although certainly internal to sport, is not distinctive to sport and has its value principally in its role in contributing to a particular sort of context of competition that displays and promotes human excellence.

In our discussion so far we have not yet seen a compelling argument for the separation thesis. Indeed, the main evidence that has been advanced—in particular, the recognition of an ideal of integrity and ideals related to fostering a context of competition in sport—clearly supports the continuity thesis. Perhaps this is not quite a refutation of the separation thesis, but it does seem to establish a burden of proof on those who wish to defend the separation thesis. Our position also supports the idea that broad internalism should reject the separation thesis in favor of the continuity thesis. In the next section, I will further support these positions by showing that certain basic moral ideas found in sport are continuous with moral ideas found outside it.

The Continuity Thesis Defended

In a paper following my work on rules and adjudication, I argued that there were two key moral principles that are constitutive aspects of sport in addition to their rules. I dubbed these the "external" and the "internal" principles of games (16). The external principle of games reflects the idea that games are institutions grounded in a principle of consent, and thus they embody a basically Kantian idea of respect for persons, at least in the sense that games are voluntary activities for game participants. Thus, one of the things that the external principle does is to regulate how individuals become participants, how they enter and leave games, when they have status as a genuine game player and when they do not, and so on. The internal principle, by contrast, is perhaps the most general normative principle that governs the behavior of participants once they have entered a game as a player, umpire, or coach. The internal principle is essentially a generalization of the earlier principle of adjudication—namely, that rules shall be interpreted and applied so that the context in which the excellences the game makes possible are not undermined but are maintained and fostered. This principle is typically what informs attempts to recognize and promote the spirit and integrity of games. As we have seen, this principle is closely connected to a moral ideal of integrity. More specifically, it seems drawn from a general commitment to promote human flourishing, for games and sporting games in particular are institutions that foster human flourishing by providing opportunities for humans to develop, realize, and enjoy a variety of distinctive human physical, intellectual, and emotional excellences. Both of these principles, then, reflect familiar general moral ideas related to the promotion of respect for persons and of human flourishing. If I am right that they are fundamental to the nature of sport, that presents a powerful case for the continuity thesis and for the claim that broad internalism reflects the continuity thesis.

Games are institutions that seem quite clearly to embody Kantian principles of respect for individuals. This is represented clearly in Suits' summary definition of games as "the voluntary attempt to overcome unnecessary obstacles" (20: p. 41). Indeed, it is difficult to think of a human institution that has a more profound commitment to a Kantian consent principle than sport and games generally. This principle is, in particular, key in determining whether someone is actually a player or participant in a sport in a proper, full sense of the term. One is not properly a player or a genuine sport participant unless one consents to be a player or participant. One can of course be coerced to participate in sporting activities, but then one is not fully engaged in *sport* but rather in forced labor or punishment (or self-defense or war, if one is, say, forced to participate in a sport involving martial combat).

The moral implications of the consent principle run very deep; in particular, this principle sets the moral boundary of permissible conduct in sport. Thus, when hockey players like Marty McSorley or Todd Bertuzzi commit acts of violence against an opponent, a key moral and legal question is whether the victims can be said to have consented to accept such acts as part of what is involved in participating in hockey. If they can, then it seems clear that the action can be regarded as part of the game (although adequate reasons might exist for prohibiting such behavior in games). However, in both the McSorley and Bertuzzi incidents many would argue that there was no consent, and further that no rational person would ever consent to the sorts of actions that were committed. If so, the claim that their actions were part of the sport of hockey is rejected by the external principle. In fact, in the McSorley case, Judge William Kitchen observed that all parties agreed that an assault to the head with a stick was not part of the game, even taking into account the "unwritten" rules of professional hockey. Judge Kitchen held, further, that even a major stick slash to the shoulder of a vulnerable player was "too dangerous for the players to consent to" and thus fell outside the boundaries of the sport (15: para. 61, 74-75).[6] These remarks reflect clear applications of the external principle. In a real sense, McSorley's assault fell outside the boundaries of the game because according to the court the participants either did not, or could not, consent to such actions as part of the game. What Judge Kitchen found, then, in effect through an application of the external principle, was that McSorely's slash fell outside the activity of the sport and thus was simply an everyday criminal assault.

Such applications of the external principle represent one of the clearest ways in which we can argue morally that certain instances of violence in sport can be subject to criminal law. It is sometimes argued that even egregious acts of assault between sporting participants should be handled "in house" as part of the game (hockey is a good example). But the application of the external principle helps us determine who counts as a genuine sporting participant and, by extension, what counts as in-house activity and what does not. If the argument had been compelling in the McSorley case that the offending behavior had been consented to as part of the game, then the case for excluding the criminal law and addressing the misdeeds in house would have been very strong indeed. Of course, in this particular case the nature of the behavior made that just about impossible.

In a more pedestrian vein, the external principle also neatly explains why cheating is specifically regarded as falling outside sport—because cheating is unacceptable activity that occurs in the context of a particular sport. Thus, according to the external principle, cheaters are not really playing the game, which is how cheating is usually characterized. By contrast, certain types of rule infractions can be fully anticipated and expected (indeed they can be unavoidable) elements of participating in a sport. They are thus a recognized, and therefore a permissible, part of the game. Such behavior falls within the bounds of sport. Although infractions like those committed in, for example, strategic fouling involve obtaining prohibited advantages, they do not count as full-blown cheating, according to the external principle, because they are a permissible feature of any informed choice to participate in a game,

I cannot carry out a complete analysis of the external principle here, but I want to mention that also packed into the external principle are further ideals involving respect for the dignity of persons. These are often reflected in principles and practices of sportsmanship. For example, the practice in soccer of kicking the ball into touch to permit an injured opponent to receive medical attention is, at least in part, an expression of a moral principle. To be meaningful, consent always presupposes capacity (or competence) of some sort, and in sport we may presume consent involves capacity to participate in the sport's activities. Consent to play a game with no capacity or competence at all to play is not interesting or meaningful consent, just as consent in medicine or law without capacity or competence is not genuine consent. Furthermore, there is a presumption that absence of capacity vitiates consent, and thus, the incapacitated player can be presumed to be no longer a game player according to the external principle. Kicking the ball into touch recognizes this and displays respect for the injured player as a person by recognizing important moral limits on his or her role as a game player via an application of the external principle.

Sportsmanship is, of course, a moral ideal too complex to be represented by only the external principle. Again, though I cannot provide a full analysis of sportsmanship here, we can extend our current discussion to show that the principled moral position I am defending is capable of acknowledging the depth of this moral ideal and its connection to fundamental general moral ideas.

In an influential discussion, Peter Arnold argued that sportsmanship is a virtue in part for its role in building community among players, which in turn helps to establish a context in which the goals of a sport can be fostered (1). There can be little doubt that a principle of respect for persons as embodied in the eternal principle is an essential component of building such community. But, also, if we take fostering the goals of a sport to be connected fundamentally to the promotion of its distinctive excellences, as surely we must, sportsmanship appears to be also informed in part by the internal principle. Moreover, it is certainly arguable that the internal principle is also at work in the soccer example just presented. That is, the internal principle would hardly foster a context in which the excellences of a game could be displayed if players knew that injuries derived from the acts of pursuing those excellences were unlikely to be treated in a timely fashion (or would be ignored altogether). Knowing that one will be left for dead if one gets injured in the course of play is surely no incentive to take chances displaying, let alone extending, the more demanding physical skills required by a sport.

It is also implied, as Arnold notes, that sportsmanship is altruistic to an important degree because there is often a prudential cost to being a good sport. (Kicking the ball into touch might give up an advantage that cannot be compensated by having the ball returned on the in-bound throw.) Perhaps such altruism itself reflects a deeper everyday moral principle that is part of sport. But more than this is implied. Altruism is implied respectively by the moral demands of respect for persons and respect for the point and purposes of games that are promoted by both the external and internal principles. What is also implied by these principles besides altruism are commitments to fairness and impartial treatment and, indeed, to moral equality. Thus, we have seen that it is unfair to treat participants in ways that fail to respect their dignity as persons. As well, the demands of fostering a context in which the distinctive excellences of a sport can be fostered and maintained will require impartial treatment of participants, for example, through impartial adjudication, among other things. All of this presupposes that a rich and familiar notion of moral equality underlies participation in sport. We have seen this already in the application of a Dworkinian ideal of integrity to sport. But moral equality is also a commitment evident in the external and internal principles in their role of institutionalizing respect for consent and the promotion of human flourishing within sport. Thus, we might say that McSorley's behavior failed, whereas the soccer player succeeded, in demonstrating equal concern and respect for his opponents.

There is nothing, then, in this brief discussion of sportsmanship and its connection to the external and internal principles that seems to aid the separation thesis, and there is much here with which the thesis must contend. We can add to this case by looking more closely at the moral origins of the internal principle. This principle seems clearly drawn from a general moral ideal of promoting human flourishing. That is, the internal principle requires the fostering of special contexts for the development, creative exercise, and enjoyment of distinctive human capacities and character traits. Virtually all moral theories recognize either direct or indirect duties to promote such human flourishing. For example, Kantian deontology, utilitarianism, and Aristotelian perfectionist theories all recognize the moral importance of developing human talents and capacities. Sporting games institutionalize the production and development of excellences that contribute to such human flourishing by promoting certain physical, emotional, and intellectual excellences. The internal principle in games clearly reflects and extends these moral commitments. As we saw, the internal principle is also supported by related general duties that are connected to fostering a context of competition in which such flourishing can occur. All this systematically ties the internal principle to general and theoretical moral concerns to foster human flourishing.

If I am right about all this, a strong case is made that moral values and principles found in sport (specifically as expressed in the external and internal principles, the principle of integrity, and in related commitments to fairness, impartiality, and moral equality) show that sport is profoundly informed by ideals that are continuous with and represent, reflect, extend, and reinforce more basic moral values found outside sport in everyday life. There may, of course, be other everyday moral or other values represented in sport that I have not identified. However, I suspect that these could be shown to be drawn from these general moral commitments. It follows that the separation thesis is at least in need of more clarification and defense and, indeed, looks to be undermined by these remarks. Given the depth and generality of the application of these principles to sport, I doubt that anyone can prove the existence of an interesting distinctive or separate morality of sport. The moral values we have seen at work here seem to undergird and inform all aspects of sport. The evidence I have presented shows that sport is a human institution that reflects, and is broadly continuous with, some of our most basic moral ideals. In effect, then, I have argued that an accurate way of describing the relation between moral value and sport is not to suggest that sport has its own distinct morality but to say that sport represents one distinct way of supporting and expressing familiar moral ideas.

Conclusions About the Moral Foundations of Sport

There is nothing original about arguing that sport is generally continuous with morality as we normally think of it. However, the position I have developed gives systematic defense to this idea and allows us to make several other important points. In particular, we have seen that it is not that moral ideals that inform sport are distinct ideals that are separate and perhaps in uneasy conflict with general moral ideals found outside sport, but rather that a proper understanding of sport shows that sport itself is fundamentally continuous with familiar and basic moral ideals. This philosophical point is potentially of significant practical import. It can explain clearly and compellingly why, for example, sport is potentially such a morally instructive institution. To say that sport embodies in itself commitments to human dignity and flourishing and to moral equality and to integrity can explain why sport, properly understood, might figure prominently as part of a foundation for moral education. We might even see how sport can be tried as a vehicle to promote respect and peace among people who find it difficult to live together. Indeed, duties to foster contexts of competition will at times require a willingness to break down cultural, social, or racial barriers, but in ways that also exemplify basic standards of respect for persons. Thus, we can argue that the elimination of the color barrier in baseball was required not only by commitments to racial equality but also in part by moral commitments within sport to athletic excellence and merit that make race irrelevant. In doing so, sport also demands respect for the dignity of participants and fair treatment of them. Properly understood, then, sport can represent a profound moral example for the broader society, and it is no surprise that movements such as De Coubertin's Olympism have the ambitious goal of making a contribution to social justice generally. This is not just because sport can hold up a mirror for important values reflected by good sportsmen and sportswomen who just happen to accept certain lofty ideals. Even more fundamentally, these values, including requirements to respect persons and to foster a context for promoting human flourishing, are required by the very foundations of sport that are themselves extensions of more basic moral values. Being a good sport, then, is something required by sport; it is not something that is optional or supererogatory in sport. Thus, being a good sport should be taught as part of what is required by sport because sport reflects and extends certain fundamental moral requirements that all must acknowledge. Being a good sport, then, reflects and extends important ideals of being a good person.

Some might think that the analysis given here overlooks the ways in which sport can also be at odds with everyday moral commitments and virtues. For example, because a remarkable diversity of activity is permitted in sport by the principle of consent, it is natural to be concerned that some sporting excellences will encourage traits that have antisocial implications. Thus, training violent or aggressive behavior in some sports, for example, can have its dangers. More generally, it is often remarked that sporting competition is typically highly self-centered and egoistic and thus permits a release from everyday requirements to be concerned about others, so that even if competition is constrained in the ways described in this chapter, competitive attitudes might arise that interfere with effective moral reasoning in contexts that require more careful consideration of others' interests. These are reasonable concerns, and some of them are supported by literature in the social sciences (2, 17).

However, the analysis given here can recognize these limitations of sport and help to address the tensions that can exist between sport and morality in other contexts. We can achieve this by placing sport in its proper context and by qualifying some of the criticisms of sport. For example, the self-centered nature of sporting competition is not evidently any sort of moral failure considered on its own, because it is the purpose of competition to provide competitors with mutual opportunities to test and demonstrate their sporting skills to the full extent of their abilities. Indeed, in a genuinely competitive context in which competitors are each striving to demonstrate athletic excellence, it is a display of mutual respect to pursue one's own (or one's team's) advantage to the best of one's ability, because doing so best allows opponents to test and demonstrate their own skills and abilities. Of course, it is natural to be concerned that such focused pursuit of self-interest through competition can spill over and undermine relations with others in other contexts in which more direct concern for others is morally appropriate. But this is a familiar problem that pervades moral reasoning and is not unique to sport. That virtues or moral rules appropriate in one sphere of life might not be relevant to the same degree (or not at all) in other spheres of life is a fact that should be recognized both in and out of sport. Thus, the degree of care or concern shown family members and other intimates is often out of place in other contexts, such as in a teacher–student relationship or in business relations. That certain competitive attitudes or virtues acquired through participation in sport might be inappropriate in other contexts does not show that there is any moral shortcoming within sport, any more than a teacher treating his or her son or daughter within the formality and distance of a teacher–student relationship reflects some moral shortcoming within the institution or practice of being a teacher.

It is a remarkable fact, now so often overlooked that it holds considerable irony, that sport properly understood has great potential to teach us about just these things. What sport emphasizes so clearly by its nature and proper example is that *human goals must be accomplished by overcoming obstacles with the use of permissible means that themselves satisfy requirements of respect for persons and, also, respect for the integrity of the institution or practice in which those means are exercised.* This is of course a fundamental moral lesson, perhaps *the* fundamental moral lesson, and it may be the deep moral lesson of sport. This lesson is not only reflected in the internal constitution of sport, as we have seen, but also in the very diversity of sport that exemplifies the idea that different goals with distinctly identified obstacles require acceptance of different permissible means that are themselves constrained by certain general moral requirements. The simplicity and transparency of sport in comparison with the complexity and opacity of ordinary life can make sport particularly well suited to demonstrating this. Sport, at least in this abstract and general sense, can be a moral mirror for how we are to live elsewhere. What needs reminding, then, when attitudes developed in the context of pursuing sports interfere with appropriate moral relations and moral reasoning outside sport, is that sport by its nature and proper example directs us to be attentive to the limitations and appropriateness of the means we employ to achieve our aims so that these reflect due respect for the persons, institutions, and practices involved. This is a lesson we can apply to all aspects of our lives. When sport seems to have lost its potential to reflect or teach about these things, we should be concerned that its basic example has been lost on its practitioners and that sport has been misused or corrupted by some of its participants or by broader elements of society, or by an entire culture. Sport as a foundation for moral education should start from these points and use them to illustrate their applicability to other contexts.

It is appropriate to conclude these remarks by tying this discussion to our point of departure, namely, Simon's defense of interpretive broad internalism. I am sure that Simon would agree with much of what has been described in this chapter. He has, for example, argued cogently for the value of sport in promoting moral education, including that sport "illustrates a framework of universal moral values" that can be taught across cultures, in particular because of its simplicity, accessibility, and near universality (19: p. 26). My main point of criticism, and it is a very friendly one, is that these contributions fit most aptly and are better supported within a framework that recognizes an even deeper relation between morality and sport than broad internalism initially acknowledged, a relation that we have seen is implied in much of Simon's defense of broad internalism. Thus, demonstrating that basic moral commitments we find in morality are foundational within sport clarifies and makes even more compelling the point that sport, properly understood, can and should be used to promote moral ideals, including ideals of equality and fairness. It does so by arguing that these ideals are not only contained in the very notion of sport but that there is no further special moral content to sport that uniquely separates and distinguishes its morality from morality generally. Thus, when we participate in sport we are not in any fundamental sense leaving one moral sphere and entering another, as broad internalism initially suggested could be true. Amending broad internalism to recognize the continuity thesis helps to encourage healthier moral attitudes within and outside of sport.

In an earlier discussion of broad internalism, Nicholas Dixon made two important points that help to draw our discussion to a close (4). First, broad internalism presupposes a commitment to moral realism. This is implied in the Dworkinian interpretive approach, which is avowedly moral realist, and it is also required by Simon's critique of conventionalism. Second, Dixon remarked that a better account of the autonomy of sport from sources of value in social convention was to be found in the more general autonomy of morality and its capacity to serve as a basis for critical reform of the status quo within and outside sport. I accept both of these points. The main point I have to add is that the current discussion shows more precisely how such critical reforms are to be carried out. We are to conceive of the distinctive practices, duties, and values of sport as grounded in, and thus expressing, extending, and reflecting, important moral values found in morality generally. Thus, to address important moral issues and problems in sport is simply to engage in familiar moral debate about how to make our human institutions better reflect and serve general moral ends. Such debate is required not only by morality but by the moral nature of sport itself.[7]

Notes

1. Thus observed social commentator George F. Will: "Football combines two of the worst features of American life: it is violence punctuated by committee meetings." (21: p. 68).

2. See also the quotations from sociologists and psychologists of sport in Shields and Bredemeier (17).

3. Pawlenka has a similar objective to mine in showing the connection of sport to morality generally. However, she acknowledges that her approach is different in that it is not concerned with exploring whether there is an internal normative basis for morality in sport, as argued in Simon's and my own work, and how this affects sport's relation to morality (12: 57n3). Her piece usefully complements the current discussion.

4. I would add a list of other objections to conventionalism, including that more sophisticated versions confuse truth with justification (16).

5. Of course, such measures can be imperfect, depending not only on luck and bad officiating but also on imperfections in the nature of games themselves. See Kretchmar (10)

6. In the Bertuzzi incident in the late winter of 2004, a similar attack occurred from behind, but without a stick. In both cases, the opponents suffered serious head injuries. Bertuzzi pleaded guilty to assault, so there were no reasons for judgment in his case. However, the reasoning in Judge Kitchen's decision clearly set an important precedent for this case (both were heard in Vancouver, Canada) and was undoubtedly a factor in Bertuzzi's decision to plead guilty.

7. I am indebted to an audience at a meeting of the North American Philosophy of Sport Society at the University of New Brunswick in June 2005 and also to Alister Browne, Ted Palys, and Bob Simon for comments on various ancestors (some of them distant) of this paper.

Bibliography

1. Arnold, P.J. "Three Approaches Toward an Understanding of Sportsmanship." *Journal of the Philosophy of Sport* 10 (1983): 61-70.

2. Bredemeier, B. and D. Shields. *Character Development and Physical Activity.* Champaign IL: Human Kinetics, 1994.

3. Butcher, R. and A. Schneider. "Fair Play as Respect for the Game." *Journal of the Philosophy of Sport* 25 (1998): 6-22

4. Dixon, N. "Canadian Figure Skaters, French Judges, and Realism in Sport." *Journal of the Philosophy of Sport* 30, no. 2 (2003): 103-116.

5. Dixon, N. "On Winning and Athletic Superiority." *Journal of the Philosophy of Sport* 28 (1999): 10-26.

6. Dworkin, R.M. *Law's Empire.* Cambridge, MA: Harvard University Press, 1986.

7. Fraleigh, W. "Why the Good Foul Is Not Good." *Journal of Physical Education, Recreation, and Dance* (January 1982): 41-42.

8. Guest, S. *Ronald Dworkin.* Stanford: Stanford University Press, 1991.

9. Huizinga, J. *Homo Ludens: A Study of the Play Element in Culture.* Boston: Beacon Press, 1950.

10. Kretchmar, S. "Game Flaws." *Journal of the Philosophy of Sport* 32, no. 1 (2005): 36-48.

11. Morgan, W.J. "Moral Anti-Realism, Internalism, and Sport." *Journal of the Philosophy of Sport* 31, no. 2 (2004): 161-183.

12. Pawlenka, C. "The Idea of Fairness: A General Ethical Concept or One Particular to Sports Ethics?" *Journal of the Philosophy of Sport* 32, no. 1 (2005): 49-64.

13. Pearson, K. "Deception, Sportsmanship, and Ethics." *Quest* 29 (1973): 115-118.

14. *Regina* v. *Marty McSorley,* 2000 BCPC 0116. Available at http://www.provincialcourt.bc.ca/judgments/pc/2000/01/p00_0116.htm. Accessed June 5, 2005.

15. Russell J.S. "Are Rules All an Umpire Has to Work With?" *Journal of the Philosophy of Sport* 26 (1999): 27-49.

16. Russell, J.S. "Moral Realism in Sport." *Journal of the Philosophy of Sport* 31, no. 2 (2004): 142-160.

17. Shields, D.L. and B.L. Bredemeier. "Moral Reasoning in the Context of Sport." Available at http://tigger.uic.edu/~lnucci/MoralEd/articles/shieldssport.html. Accessed June 4, 2005.

18. Simon, R.L. "Internalism and Internal Values in Sport." *Journal of the Philosophy of Sport* 27 (2000): 1-16.

19. Simon, Robert. "Sports, Relativism, and Moral Education." In *Sport Ethics,* ed. Jan Boxill, Oxford University Press, 2002.

20. Suits, Bernard. *The Grasshopper: Games, Life and Utopia.* Toronto: University of Toronto Press, 1978.

21. Will, George F. *Bunts, Curt Flood, Camden Yard, Pete Rose and Other Reflections on Baseball,* New York: Scribner, 1998.

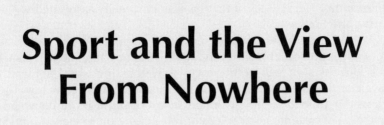

Sport and the View From Nowhere

♦

Randolph Feezell

Part I: Nagel's Problem

In a number of well-known papers, many of which have been collected in *Mortal Questions* (14), and in *The View From Nowhere* (15), Thomas Nagel has analyzed a single problem that reappears in a variety of perennial philosophical disputes. Early on he spoke of this as the problem of "Subjective and Objective,"[1] that is, the problem of the conflict or opposition between two very different viewpoints we can take toward ourselves and our experience of the world. On the one hand, we experience life from a particular perspective. We drag along the contingencies of particularity as we make our way through the world. On the other hand, we can step back from our immediate involvement in life and take a new viewpoint which includes within it the original, more particular perspective. The possibility of transcending one's subjective viewpoint and seeing it from a larger perspective appears to be a permanent possibility for a complex reflective being. As we will see, this possibility occasions a number of puzzling personal and philosophical questions.

Nagel later speaks of objectivity as the "view from nowhere" and he systematically explores this problem in the book by the same name. The problem is "how to combine the perspective of a particular person inside the world with an objective view of the same world, the person and his viewpoint included" (15: p. 3). Like Nagel, I find it natural to view the human situation in terms of the opposition

Reprinted, by permission, from R. Feezell, 2001, "Sport and the view from nowhere," *Journal of the Philosophy of Sport* 28: 1-17.

between these two standpoints, and I identify with the need to investigate strategies for reconciling them. But I wish to focus on an area of life that Nagel has ignored at least in his published work. Like many people, involvement in sports has been a significant part of my life since childhood. But as a philosopher I have found this involvement puzzling and not easily understood. I find Nagel's approach quite helpful in understanding the sources of the forms of perplexity associated with thinking about sports participation.

In this paper I would like to show the implications of Nagel's approach when applied to sport. I borrow from him the basic structure, and some remarks about its analysis. But the spin will be my own, as well as the way I apply it to sport. Once I have clarified the structure in the next section, I will show how the opposition between our immediate involvement in sport and a more detached view of this involvement occasions the problem of reconciling these viewpoints. Strategies arise for avoiding the conflict—none of which succeed. Finally, I will show that there are certain attitudes toward sport that are more appropriate expressions of the paradoxes that arise because we can, and should, view sports activities in two very different ways. Moreover, these attitudes have important moral implications for participation in sports.

Part II: Subjectivity and Objectivity

Let us return to the basic idea and begin our discussion with two common examples from ordinary life. Suppose a teacher is supervising two small children playing together when one child becomes aggressive and mean. The teacher intervenes, stops the hurtful behavior, and offers the expected moral lesson: "Would you like it if someone did that to you? How would that make you feel?" The child is asked to step back from her personal stance and take a new perspective in which this more personal perspective is included. The child is asked to consider that all persons have feelings, or all persons have reasons not to be hurt, so she must consider herself as simply one person among all persons, with no special or distinctive status.

For our second example, consider a parent whose child is a substitute on a high school basketball team. The child badly wants to play, is miserable on the bench, and feels unfairly treated. When the parent feels terrible because the child isn't playing, the perspective is one step away from a subjective viewpoint that is wholly self-preoccupied and ignores other persons altogether. But we often say that the parent needs to judge relative abilities more accurately, where the judgment is less tainted by subjective concerns.

From these two ordinary examples it is easy to extract the structure that gives rise to numerous perplexities. From the more subjective viewpoint our perspective is conditioned by the specific aspects of being a particular human being. Here the specific and contingent aspects of individuality shape our experience: our particular desires, needs, perceptions, sensations, goals, values, etc. But we have the capacity to step back from the subjective perspective and gain a new perspective which includes the original one in it. As Nagel says, to gain "a more objective understanding of some aspect of life or the world, we step back from our initial view of it and form a new conception which has that view and its relation to the world as its object. . . . we place ourselves in the world that is to be understood" (15: p. 4).

The opposition may at first have the appearance of an "either-or" where objectivity means a "factual, scientific" perspective, subjectivity means a "value-laden" perspective, and science always wins the epistemic game. However, this is mistakenly oversimplified. In various places Nagel points out that the distinction between the internal and external views is a "matter of degree" (15: p. 5), a "polarity" (14: p. 206) in which the distinction is "relative" (14: p. 206). "A view or form of thought is more objective than another if it relies less on the specifics of the individual's makeup and position in the world, or on the character of the particular type of creature he is" (15: p. 5). In our original example, we might see the moral point of view as more objective than the original personal aggressive perspective, because it is the standpoint from which a particular person can consider the interests of *all* sentient beings (including herself) when she acts.

The sport example suggests another important issue involved in clarifying the basic structure. When the parent steps back from the situation and attempts to perceive accurately the relative basketball abilities of the child, this new and more objective perspective seems to offer a more accurate view of things. Here objectivity is a way to understand the way things are, and an objective understanding of the situation generates beliefs and attitudes that render the more subjective perspective as a source of mere "appearances." This broader perspective includes these personal judgments and feelings, and explains them. There is no problem, in one sense, of what to do with the more subjective viewpoint, since it has been corrected—although the residual psychological aspects may still be difficult to deal with. This analysis may lead us to "think of reality as a set of concentric spheres, progressively revealed as we detach gradually from the contingencies of the self" (15: p. 5).

Thus a second important element in the analysis of the internal–external dynamic is this: while the distinction is relative, when we abstract from the personal we seem to be headed in the direction of truth. This is because increasing objectivity seems to be the attempt to approach the way the world is in itself and not just for some individual. Because the development of objectivity seems truth-guided, the objective viewpoint may appear to dominate any relatively subjective viewpoint, and it may exert certain "pressures toward a more external viewpoint" (15: p. 208).

Yet if the situation were so simple, there would be no problem associated with the distinction between subjectivity and objectivity. That is, there would be no problem of combining the two perspectives, since the point of developing an increasingly objective view of life would be to give up "appearances" in favor of a truer, more objective understanding of "reality." But there is a problem, or, rather, there are a number of problems, because it isn't clear that it's always more "truthful" to negate the subjective in whatever way seems appropriate for a more objective way of understanding. Consider our first example of moral education. It may be true that a social scientific account of morality, as simply a set of rules conventionally agreed upon, is "objective" in some sense, but it doesn't appear to be a true account of morality, for a variety of reasons.[2] There are other possible objective or scientific explanations of our moral life (e.g., biological explanations), but, *prima facie*, they seem to leave behind, in their explanations, our immediate sense of some things being "really" right or wrong, good or bad. It is always possible that the subjective sense of moral value conflicts with an objective account of morality as a set of conventionally accepted rules; for example, when the 19th century Abolitionist in America embraced the notion that it is really wrong to own another human being, regardless of the social approval involved in slavery. Here a conflict arises. "The opposition between subjective and objective can arise at any place on the spectrum where one point of view claims dominance over another, more subjective one, and that claim is resisted" (14: p. 206).

There is nothing distinctive about the way this problem arises in ethics, as a theoretical reflection on our moral life. As Nagel insists, the "internal-external tension pervades human life, but it is particularly prominent in the generation of philosophical problems" (15: p. 6). To give just two examples: from the inside of life, I seem to be an agent who performs free actions, and for whom autonomy means the ability to do otherwise. However, when I step back from my actions and see them as events or processes with causal explanations, and I see myself not as some mysterious immaterial nugget but as the locus of various causally produced biological and psychological processes, agency seems to vanish.[3]

Likewise, from the internal viewpoint, I seem to have privileged access to my own subjective mental states. I am directly aware of tastes, sounds, feelings, etc., and I assume that there's "something it's like" to be a particular human being.[4] When I step back, however, and see myself as a part of nature, it's not clear how dualism could be true, in part because it has so little explanatory power when contrasted with various forms of materialism, and because the interaction between immaterial mental processes and brain processes would be so mysterious.[5] In both of these examples, the objective perspective confronts something that resists its reductive or eliminative impulses. As Nagel remarks: "the trouble occurs when the objective view encounters something, revealed subjectively, that it cannot accommodate. Its claims to comprehensiveness will be threatened. The indigestible lump may either be a fact or a value" (14: p. 210).

For our purposes, the way the objective threatens our *values* is most important, and the threat is not simply a scientific one. Let's consider this and then turn our attention toward sport. When people decide what to do in life—or what kind of person to be—their goals may be relatively personal. I may save my hard-earned money for a vacation in Cancun. But I may also consider the fact that my desires for rest and relaxation on the beach are relatively unimportant when I contrast my situation with the plight of people who are starving, homeless, or oppressed. I could give my money to a service organization or spend my time directly helping others. From the standpoint of overall good, I could develop other-directed motives that recognize the triviality of my concerns in relation to some larger moral perspective. In ethics there are enormous problems that arise on the continuum from subjective to objective, because moral judgment seems to force one from a more self-centered, personal, even egoistic viewpoint to a more impersonal viewpoint that is other-directed.[6] Yet how do we legitimately integrate our personal concerns into an acceptable moral outlook?[7]

If the development of objectivity in ethics is driven by the desire to "get outside of ourselves," there are no obvious final resting stops in the movement from the personal, to the relatively impersonal, to the extremely impersonal or even centerless view. For the consequentialist (utilitarian), the pursuit of overall good trumps personal goals, as well as appeals to individual rights, special obligations, and perfectionist ends.[8] (Obviously, it's not clear that consequentialism is therefore the most acceptable ethical theory because it is most objective.) But consequentialism may be transcended in a more objective philosophical reflection. Any justification of value may be skeptically undermined.

> Objectivity itself leads to the recognition that its own capacities are probably limited, since in us it is a human faculty and we are conspicuously finite beings. The radical form of this is philosophical skepticism, in which the objective standpoint undermines itself by the same procedures it uses to call into question the prereflective standpoint

of ordinary life in perception, desire, and action. Skepticism is radical doubt about the possibility of reaching any kind of knowledge, freedom, or ethical truth, given our containment in the world and the impossibility of creating ourselves from scratch. (15: p. 7)

We are left with a very perplexing situation. Sometimes the objective standpoint offers a truer way of understanding the world. When we transcend our prejudices and presuppositions, we are able to see the way our particular nature distorts our perspective. The success of science constitutes a powerful testament to the belief that objectivity should be our ideal for understanding reality. But the movement toward objectivity has problems in both directions. In the direction of subjectivity, it leaves behind some (much?) of what it means to be a particular, highly specific human being, whether it be autonomy, mind, or meaning. It seems to lead to reductionism. At the other extreme, in the direction of the most "centerless" form of objectivity, the attempt to recognize our epistemic limitations may inevitably lead to a skepticism or nihilism that undermines both objective knowledge and any values to which we are personally attached. How do we decide where the legitimate claims reside in the continuum from subjective to objective, from the internal to the "view from nowhere"? How do we determine a method for sorting out the truth-claims of personal metaphysical and axiological appearances, impersonal moral demands, scientific models of explanation and reduction, and various arguments offered by both local and global skeptics?[9] Now we are in a better position to understand the perplexities associated with our (subjective) attachments to sport.

Part III: Sport and Conflicting Perspectives

As I have suggested, the problems associated with sports participation are related to the problem of the meaning of life—at least insofar as the problem of the meaning of life arises—because we have the capacity to step back from our immediate involvement in life and take a detached viewpoint from which our life seems not to matter much at all. We struggle to get through school, get a good job, raise a family, worry about the bills—to what end? As Nagel has said, "From far enough outside my birth seems accidental, my life pointless, and my death insignificant, but from inside my never having been born seems nearly unimaginable, my life monstrously important, and my death catastrophic" (15: p. 209). From the outside, from the view from nowhere, my life seems to be an accidental and insignificant moment in the entire scheme of things; my attachments as well seem as accidental as my life, objectively insignificant from the standpoint of a skeptical reflection that denies the ultimate justification of value.[10]

Now, if it is difficult to follow Nagel to the furthest reaches of objectivity from which the problem of the meaning of life arises, it is certainly not difficult to see the way in which the path toward objectivity threatens some of our cherished attachments in life. I am most interested in the sports participant for whom sport matters, in a relatively significant way. For such a person, sport is an important part of life. Think especially of players and coaches at all levels of play, and at all ages. From the inside of this involvement, nothing seems to matter more than what happens in their respective sport. Participants spend countless hours at practice, worry about improvement and execution, and often think the fate of the world—*their* world—depends on who wins the game. There is often a pervasive spirit of *seriousness* when participants engage in sports.[11] Players are praised for the intensity of their competitive serious-ness. From the internal viewpoint, life seems often to present itself at its subjectively best—or worst—in sports. Internally, experience is enhanced when structured by the rhythms of games, contests, and seasons. Sports participation seems to give life some dramatic or narrative shape as the pursuit of athletic success unfolds.[12] However, subjective attachment to sport is only part of the picture, precisely because we are complex, reflective beings who can step back from our particular involvement and scrutinize them.

How does a more objective view of an individual's involvement in sport arise? Consider the obvious and commonplace examples. The young player strikes out with the bases loaded and the team loses the Big Game. Someone attempts to console the distraught young person: "It's only a game." Death or illness in the family causes a player to miss a practice or game. Someone is severely injured in a game. The other stunned players look on and later say: "Something like this puts sports into perspec-tive." In the movement from subjective to objective, one doesn't have to travel far to see sport as less important than other things in life. You step back and compare sport to other parts of your life, you see your involvement in relation to other things that seem to matter, and sport loses. It still seems "important," sometimes overwhelm-ingly so, but you're not sure why.

At this point, the central problem concerning subjectivity and objectivity arises. Recall that the "opposition between subjective and objective can arise at any place on the spectrum where one point of view claims dominance over another, more subjective one, and that claim is resisted" (14: p. 206). From the internal view-point, sports participation is serious, sometimes all-consuming, and "monstrously" important. But even for people who are not disposed to being very reflective, an objective viewpoint insinuates itself into experience and suggests that sport is rela-tively unimportant. How are these two viewpoints to be reconciled? How can they co-exist? After all, it may be within the same person that the two standpoints clash. The objective viewpoint claims that sport is not important. Subjective involvement resists that judgment and wants to return to its prereflective attachment unaffected by the objective perspective.[13]

The problem increases when the gap between subjective and objective increases. If we want to reflect on our involvement and attempt to understand why sport seems less important than other things in life, then we must attempt to understand the nature of sport itself.[14] Here we reflect not simply about the relative importance of attachments; we want to understand something about sport itself, in order to reflect back on the appropriateness of these very attachments. Obviously, much has been written about the nature of sport, but for our purposes, we need only to highlight the essentials. First, it is plausible to assert that sport involves the playing of games. This thesis is associated with Bernard Suits, who argued in an early essay: "I would like to advance the thesis that the elements of sport are essentially—although not totally—the same as elements of game" (22: p. 8). He later qualifies this thesis by distinguishing between games and performances (like diving and figure skating) because of the apparent differences in the way rules function in refereed games as opposed to the way ideals function in judged performances (22: p. 19). However, I agree with Klaus Meier that Suits' earlier view is the more accurate, because perfor-mances are in fact rule-governed in the required way, so the minimal qualifications of game-playing are satisfied (13: p. 28).

What are these qualifications? Here is Suits' original account of game-playing:

> To play a game is the attempt to achieve a specific state of affairs (pre-lusory goal), using only means permitted by rules (lusory means), where the rules prohibit use of more efficient in favor of less efficient means (constitutive rules), and where such rules are accepted just because they make possible such activity (lusory attitude). I also offer the following only approximately accurate, but more pithy, version of the above definition: Playing a game is the voluntary attempt to overcome unnecessary obstacles. (22: p. 11)

Of course, it is plausible to insist that sports involve other important elements, such as physical skill, institutionalization, or competition.[15] But Suits' original account of sport as essentially involving game-playing is already quite suggestive. Consider these activities: Putting a little ball in a small hole in the ground some distance away. Carrying a leather ball to a point many yards away. Hitting a thrown ball with the intention of allowing one to run around in a circle, arriving at precisely the point from which one starts! In Suits' language, the pre-lusory goal can always be brought about in much more efficient ways than the means permitted by the rules. If I wanted to put the little white ball in the hole in an efficient manner, I could simply walk or run to the hole and place it in the cup with my hand. From the standpoint of ordinary life, games are by their very nature rather silly. Suits recognizes this, but denies the inherent absurdity of games. As he says, "in anything but a game the gratuitous introduction of unnecessary obstacles to the achievement of an end is regarded as a decidedly irrational thing to do, whereas in games it appears to be the absolutely essential thing to do" (22: p. 10). However, Suits rejects the implication that games are thereby irrational or absurd, because:

> The mistake consists in applying the same standard to games that is applied to means–end activities which are not games. If playing a game is regarded as not essentially different from going to the office or writing a cheque, then there is certainly something absurd, or paradoxical, or simply stupid about game-playing. (22: p. 10)

Suits is only half right in saying this. From the internal standpoint of the player, games are decidedly different from means–end activities of ordinary life. It is a mistake, from the subjective perspective, to apply the standard of rationality as efficiency to the realm of game-playing. But we can also step back from our game-playing and see it from a perspective which does, in fact, judge game-playing as trivial, irrational, and absurd. The same person who invests game-playing with seriousness, intensity, and concern can also see it for what it is—from a perspective outside the immediacy of participation. There is no "mistake" here; or rather, it is a mistake only from a certain point of view. Both viewpoints make legitimate claims, with each resisting the dominance of the other, and this conflict may take place within the unity of the consciousness of a single player.

Isn't it curious that we engage in such unnecessary and seemingly trivial activities? What could be the end or goal of activities that are inherently irrational by ordinary standards? Once again, Suits' account is suggestive, although I will take it in a direction with which he would disagree. For Suits, if the goal of the activity is to bring about a state of affairs in an inefficient manner, the player must have an attitude that recognizes this but affirms that the activity itself is still worth doing. The "lusory attitude" of the player is "the knowing acceptance of constitutive rules just so the activity made possible by such acceptance can occur" (22: p. 11). In my judgment, this attitude toward an instrumentally trivial or absurd activity must affirm the intrinsically satisfying or valuable nature of the activity—at least in the genesis of the game, or the player's introduction to it. So we are led to the neighborhood of play with this understanding.

The relation of sport and play is a complex and contentious issue, and I don't wish to get sidetracked by this important debate. Suffice it to say that from the internal standpoint many participants identify strongly with Huizinga's original description of play, stressing the freedom and joy of playing, "outside" of real life concerns, with utmost seriousness about and absorption in such an intrinsically valuable but "superfluous" activity (8).[16] Even college and professional athletes will often lament that the "fun" has been taken out of the game and express a certain nostalgia for their original experience of playing sports. For some, the internal standpoint is filled with the radiance of play, whose inherent worth resists objective dismissal.

It is possible to widen the gap between subjective and objective even further. As I have suggested, the arguments about the meaning and value of sport participation are similar to the way in which Nagel approaches the problem of the meaning of life. The difference is simply how far we "step back" from the immediacy of particular involvement in life and where we find ourselves when we land as a result of the distancing made possible by this reflective metaphor. If an "objective" philosophical reflection finds sport to be trivial and irrational, then, *a fortiori*, at the furthest reaches of skepticism, whatever values we experience in sport are undermined. In his well-known essay, "The Absurd," Nagel argues that a situation is absurd "when it includes a conspicuous discrepancy between pretension or aspiration and reality" (14: p. 13). For example, at 50 years of age a person quits his well-paying job and leaves his family in order to pursue the dream of playing in the NBA. This would be absurd, as would be the single-minded attempt to communicate with plants (Nagel's example), or devoting one's life to collecting as many clipped toenails as possible, at the expense of many things we normally think are constitutive of the good human life—fulfilling work, friendship, etc. For Nagel, life as such is absurd because it inevitably involves a "collision between the seriousness with which we take our lives and the perpetual possibility of regarding everything about which we are serious as arbitrary, or open to doubt" (14: p. 13). From this standpoint, sport is absurd because life is absurd, not simply because our seriousness in sport collides with the recognition that there are many more important things in life than improving one's backhand or winning games.

In any case, the pressures exerted by the reflective movement toward the "view from nowhere" are real, and they occasion the fundamental problem, which we will call the "problem of coherent attitudes." Nagel is interested in this problem in general, for any of our attachments in life. We are most interested in how this problem is experienced in one specific area of life: sport. The problem arises because of the claims made from the standpoint of reflective detachment.

> The same person who is subjectively committed to a personal life in all its rich detail finds himself in another aspect simultaneously detached; this detachment undermines his commitment without destroying it—leaving him divided. And the objective self, noticing that it is personally identical with the object of this detachment, comes to feel trapped in this particular life—detached but unable to disengage, and dragged along by a subjective seriousness it can't even attempt to get rid of. (15: p. 210)

The problem of coherent attitudes is the problem of how to respond to such worries, which Nagel calls the "discomfort of objective detachment." These worries alienate some persons from themselves. Objective transcendence brings with it some inevitable degree of disengagement or dissociation from the original subjective engagement, and the problem is how the objective self rejoins the subjective self. For the reflective sports participant the problem is significant. "Some of us feel a constant undertow of absurdity in the projects and ambitions that give our lives their forward drive. These jarring displacements of the external view are inseparable from the full development of consciousness" (15: p. 211). From the internal standpoint, seriousness is uncontested. The pursuit of excellence, the exuberance of play, and the satisfaction of victory give meaning to the life of the sports participant. Yet once the self expands to include the external point of view with its concommitant judgments, the objective self returns, reconstituting the activity. If a person now finds, from an external point of view, that a significant part of his life is objectively insignificant, how is he to deal with this? Sport is meaningful and significant. Sport is trivial and absurd. Is there a way out of this impasse? Can this inner conflict be eliminated? Are there attitudes that can reduce, but not eliminate, this opposition?

Part IV: Unsuccessful Responses

The logic of possible strategies in response to the opposition between subjective and objective in sport is quite clear.[17] One might attempt to deny the subjective importance of sport by wholly affirming the objective viewpoint, one might attempt to deny the objective viewpoint altogether, or one might argue that no "solution" is called for because the whole issue is misguided or unreal. This would be the attempt to dissolve the problem. I don't believe any of these strategies work, but there are more or less appropriate ways to alter our attitudes and behavior such that the extremity of the conflict between objective detachment and subjective engagement is reduced. First, let's briefly consider these unsuccessful ways of dealing with the problem.

The first solution would be to embrace the objective perspective by denying the claims of the internal viewpoint. At its most extreme, this would probably mean a relatively radical negation of sports altogether, depending on one's personal situation: no playing, coaching, watching, or reading about it. Complete unconcern about the sportsworld would be the result, or extreme cynicism if one were forced to sustain some uncomfortable relationship with the sportsworld.[18] I have certainly known people who seem to embody this viewpoint toward sport, who simply can't see the point of all the mindless, pervasive involvement. In another context, Nagel offers an apt image of detachment: "Watching the human drama is a bit like watching a Little League baseball game: the excitement of the participants is perfectly understandable but one can't really enter into it" (15: pp. 217-218). On the one hand, many people at Little League baseball games certainly need more detachment, since they do seem to be absurdly serious about a trivial event. There ought to be an unmistakable "undertow of absurdity" in the life of an intensely serious Little League coach, or perhaps *any* intensely serious coach for that matter. On the other hand, to use Nagel's image, the problem of subjective and objective in sport is that one is simultaneously observer and participant.

It is like sitting in the stands watching the game and judging it to be trivial while at the same time playing or coaching with utmost seriousness, playing or coaching *as if* it really mattered. From the internal perspective, it does really matter to practice and play hard, to try to become better, to compete intensely, and to attempt to win. Subjectively, there's too much good involved in sport to allow objective skepticism to negate it. If there's really joy, fun, camaraderie, and achievement in the experience of sport, the extinction of subjective value for individual participants is misguided. These values need not be endorsed by objective reflection in order to survive.

For the sports enthusiast the other strategy is the more important one to consider. Some subjective concerns survive, in some form, the attempt by the objective to extinguish them. "Playing in a Little League baseball game, making pancakes, or applying a coat of nail polish are perfectly good things to do. Their value is not necessarily canceled by the fact that they lack external justification" (15: p. 220). This merely means that the subjective self need not succumb to the most extreme pressures of objectivity. But these pressures are real. The objective self is as much a part of a person, in principle, as the more subjective one. The denial of objective insignificance might take various forms. It would be natural to inflate the objective pretensions of certain subjective concerns, in order to satisfy the demands of objectivity and reduce the conflict. In a moment I'll pursue this strategy, but it seems doomed when we consider the value of what so many are concerned with in sports: winning.

Another way to avoid the conflict would be to forget the claims of objectivity and simply ignore the deliverances of such an assessment of sport. But this is dishonest. Forgetfulness doesn't negate the legitimacy of the objective assessment of sport. Finally, there are those who seem not to be bothered by the objective insignificance of sport, perhaps because they are ignorant of this standpoint or have not developed the capacity to step outside the immediacy of subjective attachment. But this isn't a solution or strategy which denies the objective; for such people, objective reflection is available as a development in human consciousness—it has merely not developed in relation to an understanding or sport.

Therefore, the denial of either aspect of the polarity in favor of the other is misguided. The final strategy is to deny the status of the objective viewpoint, not its judgments, by claiming that the objective self is unreal. To experience objective discomfort is "to forget who you are. There is something deranged in looking at one's existence from so far outside that one can ask why it matters" (15: p. 220). The objection may seem appropriate for the more global problem of the meaning of life than for an objective reflection that remains within it and works its skepticism piecemeal on various aspects of life. But I agree with Nagel that the "view from nowhere," at its most skeptical extreme, is still a part of us, as is any moment on the continuum from objective to subjective. The problem cannot be dissolved by asserting the unreality of objective detachment. As Nagel says, "The objective self is a vital part of us, and to ignore its quasi-independent operation is to be cut off from oneself as much as if one were to abandon one's subjective individuality. There is no escape from alienation or conflict of one kind or another" (15: p. 221).

So the attempts to solve the problem by avoiding the conflict between the internal and external standpoints are unsuccessful. We must live with the conflict. What this means is that our participation in sports is, or should be, plagued by what I would like to call a kind of "double consciousness" that affirms both perspectives. They must be allowed to co-exist. How are we to understand and live with this conflict?

Part V: Playing Ironically

The problem of reconciling subjective and objective attitudes is to find ways of regarding sporting activities that produce as much harmony as possible between the perspectives.

The appropriate attitude for the reflective sports participant is irony.[19] This is a somewhat unusual way of speaking of irony. What I have in mind refers neither to ironic uses of language nor to the irony of unexpected events. Rather, irony refers to "an attitude of detached awareness of incongruity."[20] Irony is a way to regard sports participation, including the pursuit of athletic excellence and the desire for victory, *as if* it really matters, while at the same time recognizing that it is relatively trivial in the larger scheme of things. Like Nagel's image of watching a Little League game, we become simultaneously a player who is passionately involved and a detached spectator who views the spectacle from a distance. I take irony to be a unifying attitude that is positive, not negative; it is an awareness of the paradoxical nature of sport as competitive play, serious nonseriousness, or nonserious seriousness. Irony is an attitude that embraces the basic incongruity of our devotion to triviality, our celebration of absurdity every time we compete intensely and play games seriously. The ironic competitor, or the athletic ironist, is a person whose engagement is modified by objective detachment and whose detachment is mediated by immediate engagement.

Joel Feinberg nicely describes irony as a "cosmic attitude" appropriate to the human situation in general. His description also fits the athletic ironist's attitude toward sport. Irony

> is a state of mind halfway between seriousness and playfulness. It may even seem to the person involved that he is both very serious and playful at the same time. The tension between these opposed elements pulling in their opposite ways creates at least temporarily a kind of mental equilibrium. . . . One appreciates the perceived incongruity much as one does in humor, where the sudden unexpected perception of incongruity produces laughter. Here the appreciation is more deliberate and intellectual. (6)[21]

I also welcome Nagel's suggestion that humility is an attitude that promotes harmony and integration between the internal and the external. Humility is a consequence of the objective perspective on sport (and life). In general, humility works against our tendency to inflate the significance of our personal projects and successes. In particular, humility in the sportsworld works against the athlete's natural reaction to our culture's glorification of athletic success. Humility for the sports participant realistically deflates the seeming global pretensions of our merely local athletic concerns. Humility is a way to come to grips with our capacity to step back from our participation in sports while at the same time sustaining our commitment. As Nagel says about this attitude:

> Humility falls between nihilistic detachment and blind self-importance. It doesn't require reflection on the cosmic arbitrariness of the sense of taste every time you eat a hamburger. But we can try to avoid the familiar excesses of envy, vanity, conceit, competitiveness, and pride—including pride in our culture, in our nation, and in the achievements of humanity as a species. (15: p. 222)

Of course, Nagel is talking about humility as a fundamental general attitude in life, but what he says seems particularly pertinent when we think of the excesses of pride, vanity, and competitiveness in sports. Moreover, this also suggests that we are talking about attitudes that have practical consequences in our life. The ironic competitor, who embraces an attitude of humility toward his or her athletic talents and successes, will *act* differently from the pretentious and arrogant participant who lacks this perspective.

If humility is an appropriate effect of the objective perspective, I believe our subjective involvement is itself double-edged, as has been suggested in the discussion of irony. From the internal standpoint, commitment to a particular sport requires a competitive attitude in order to become better and excel. Moreover, attempting to become good in a sport is a source of significant personal satisfaction. Performing well is an important good, internal to the practice of a particular sport.[22] Competition is essential to sport, since it provides the possibility for achieving the internal goods made possible by participating in such a practice. On the other hand, since sport involves participation in activities whose external significance is originally minimal, and whose value is for the most part intrinsic to the activity, sport inevitably is associated with play. For most who will never be paid to play or supported in order to promote national pride, if it ain't fun, it ain't worth it. From this standpoint, it's a mistake to say: "If the point is not to win, what is the point?" The response is: "The point is to play—else why was the game created?" The athletic ironist is a playful competitor, whose playfulness reinforces his humility and moderates his competitiveness. This suggests that in the midst of spirited competition, the playful competitor attempts to sustain a certain lightheartedness. If sport is objectively insignificant and participation is absurd, it's more appropriate to participate without gravity or solemnity, to reinforce the possibilities of play with an attitude expressed in a wry smile rather than a grimace of discomfort.

There is one final strategy of integration that is extremely important. Recall that our first example of the movement from subjective to objective was one in which the moral viewpoint was described as a perspective from which one considers how actions affect others as well as oneself. In a broad sense, the development of moral sensibilities and moral character is the attempt to mold a self whose actions and dispositions can be endorsed by a more objective viewpoint. As Nagel says, "Morality is a form of objective reengagement. It permits the objective assertion of subjective values to the extent that this is compatible with the corresponding claims of others" (15: p. 222). If, from some relatively objective viewpoint, we insist that sport is in itself relatively trivial and insignificant, there is certainly also a standpoint outside of the immediacy of internal attachment that affirms the importance of the moral qualities made possible by sports participation. To state the obvious: in sport we must confront the possibility of isolation and failure. Sport is an arena in which courage and responsibility may be developed.

Since sport is rule-governed and embodies standards of achievement for those who attempt to become good, players may exhibit an understanding of justice as they respond to their own competitive situation in relation to others. Since they must compete with others who challenge them to become better, they may develop respect for opponents, without whom the achievement of excellence would be impossible.[23] Because sport requires officials to enforce rules, sport offers the opportunity to respect the guardians of order within the game. Since sports develop historically, participants may develop a respect for tradition and past excellence that expresses a certain broadness of appreciation and opens the self to the rich possibilities of historical consciousness.[24] In short, sport is an arena within which it is possible to develop and display the excellence of good moral character, and the development of good character can be endorsed by an objective viewpoint.[25]

Objectivity here is seen as a kind of filter. What is filtered out of sports participation is the objective significance of the supposed end of games, winning, and the external value of athletic excellence itself. What is objectively retained as significant is the moral atmosphere of sports participation: possibilities for developing sportsmanship, excellence of character, and the important attitudes that are essential to good character in sport. Sportsmanship involves attitudes of respect for opponents, teammates and team, coaches, officials, and the game itself.[26] As Nagel says about various forms of morality, they involve to some degree "a position far enough outside yourself and other people to reduce the importance of the difference between yourself and other people, yet not so far outside that all human values vanish in a nihilistic blackout" (15: p. 222).

This position should not be misunderstood. It's not as if the only justification of sports participation is the old character-building argument. From the internal viewpoint, sport is significant because of the personal satisfactions and values involved, whatever they are. From a more objective standpoint, sport is insignificant and the collision between our seriousness and its objective insignificance makes our participation absurd. From the most extreme objective vantage, the view from nowhere delivers a judgment of global insignificance on our life. Yet one way to bring a degree of harmony to the opposition between subjective and objective is to see the way in which "morality as objective reengagement" reduces the opposition. This means that developing attitudes associated with sportsmanship is an appropriate way to respond to the paradoxical nature of sport.

Part VI: Can the Good Competitor Be Detached?

There is one final important question. In this paper I have recommended a certain attitude, or a set of attitudes that should be embraced by the sports participant who wants to respond truthfully to the nature of sport. The sports participant—the athlete, player, coach—should embody irony, humility, playful competitiveness, and the respectful attitudes of sportsmanship. But all of these attitudes are the result of a detachment from the kind of unreflective immediacy characteristic of intense involvement in sports. Wouldn't these attitudes tend to dull the competitive edge? Doesn't sport require complete involvement, passion, and a commitment to excellence and winning that are incompatible with the detached, ironic stance that I have described? Aren't irony, humility, playfulness, and respectful attitudes incompatible with the very nature of sport as competitive, as a contest whose ultimate goal is winning and defeat of the opponent?

Let's call the position from which this criticism comes the "Kierkegaardian competitor." Recall that Kierkegaard recommends faith as an infinitely committed relation of subjectivity to an objectively uncertain object.[27] For Kierkegaard, the very nature of faith excludes the possibility of an objective reflection that could endorse it through the pursuit of arguments or rational support. Likewise, the Kierkegaardian competitor recommends complete involvement and dedication to the internal goals of sport, such that any reflective detachment would be contrary to the proper relation of the "true competitor" to his sport. For the Kierkegaardian competitor, the double-consciousness of the ironic competitor is untrue to sport, just as the tentative religious believer's stance distorts a proper relationship of faith within the subjectivity of the "authentic believer."[28] At its higher levels, sports participation often requires a total passion and dedication incompatible with the doubt of reflective detachment. The "winner" is infinitely committed, says the Kierkegaardian competitor. The ironist "doesn't want it enough"; hence both ultimate success and the most intense forms of sports experience will elude the partially disengaged ironist.

However, I do not think the ironic competitor is required to engage in sport listlessly or halfheartedly, nor are the benefits of sports participation denied to the reflective participant. An objective perspective is the consequence of the development of self-consciousness about one's life. The problem of finding coherent attitudes toward sport arises because we have the ability to step back from our life and reflect on it. I do not see how the external viewpoint can be denied, since this capability is an essential aspect of what it means to be a person.[29] The ability to step back poses the problem of re-engagement or co-existence, and the attitudes I've recommended are appropriate responses that confront the problem instead of ignoring or denying it. It's not as if the ironic competitor must continually mutter to herself, "Sport is absurd, sport is absurd," as she shoots every jumper or fields every ground ball. The athletic ironist can practice hard and compete intensely; she need not be denied the heightened experiences of sport. Yet her attitudes will make a difference in how she comports herself—how she competes within the constraints of rules, how she relates to others in the sportsworld, how she reacts to victory and defeat, how she handles her life in sports in relation to the rest of her life, what she expects and what she hopes for, etc. The ironist's attitudes work as dispositions to behave, sources of emotions as covert judgments about aspects of sports experience, and reminders about the very nature of sport.

Absurdity in life arises because of the incongruity between our desires and aspirations, that is, our seriousness, and the reality of the situations within which we find ourselves. Nagel's analysis of the absurd extracts the fundamental structure from various situations in life—the pursuit of an NBA career by a middle-aged man—and generalizes it to apply to life as such. He seems to miss one of the interesting implications of his analysis. Situations are sometimes absurd, life as a whole may be absurd, and persons are or can be absurd to the extent that a part of their life is absurd.[30] For example, given certain assumptions about the depth of their commitment and the time and energy expended in the public display of their beliefs, either the priest or the atheist is an absurd person. Moreover, the more extreme the commitment, the more absurd is the person for whom the object of commitment is trivial, futile, worthless, or even nonexistent. Where we have the reflective resources to determine, in some way, the objective insignificance of our attachments, the more extreme the form of seriousness, the more absurd the person becomes.

With this in mind, it is hard not to come to the conclusion that the sportsworld is populated by many absurd persons. In one sense, everyone who is serious about sport is absurd. Yet, based on the analysis I've offered in this paper, it is possible to reduce, without entirely eliminating, the absurdity of sports participation. The crazed Little League coach or fan, the ruthless, cheating high school or college competitor or coach—even the professional athlete who is suicidal after defeat—all are absurd. Yet if we see sports from an external viewpoint and return to our competitive play with a suitable amount of detachment, the integration of the viewpoints lessens our absurdity and salvages what really matters in sport.

Nagel may be right about life in general.[31] If that is true, the case I've made for how to view sport follows rather obviously. For those who find Nagel's larger position difficult to swallow, it's much easier to see the way in which the "view from nowhere" insinuates itself into segments of our life. For Nagel, the backward step undermines our egocentric self-absorption throughout life. He concludes his discussion of the meaning of life with these remarks:

> Our constitutional self-absorption together with our capacity to recognize its excessiveness make us irreducibly absurd even if we achieve a measure of subjective–objective integration by bringing the two standpoints closer together. The gap is too wide to be closed entirely, for anyone who is fully human. (15: p. 223)

For the reflective and honest sports participant, it is better to approach sport as absurd than to deny our reflective judgments or to give up the joys of sport. "It is better to be simultaneously engaged and detached and therefore absurd, for this is the opposite of self-denial and the result of full awareness." Our situation is comic, not tragic, and deserves an ironic smile as we reflect on the foibles of human existence. Better to be absorbed and absurdly preoccupied than to miss out on all the fun.

Notes

1. See the essay having this title in (14).
2. The standard argument against such conventionalism (also called *normative relativism, prescriptive relativism,* or *conventional ethical relativism*) can be found in most introductory ethics textbooks. For example, see (17) or (18).
3. See Chapter VII, "Freedom" in (15) and "Moral Luck" in (14).
4. See Nagel's widely discussed arguments in "What Is It Like to Be a Bat?" in (14).
5. Richard Taylor offers a clear discussion of the "interaction problem" in (23). Also, see Paul Churchland's arguments against dualism in (1), Chapter 2.
6. For a clear defense of this notion of the "moral point of view," see the introductory chapter in (21).
7. See, for example, Bernard Williams' criticism of utilitarianism in (26), Wolf (27), or Nagel's "Living Right and Living Well" in (15).
8. See Nagel's discussion of "The Fragmentation of Value" in (14).
9. For example, see (24) for a contemporary defense of global skepticism. A more local skepticism might deny that we can have, for example, moral knowledge or metaphysical knowledge, while arguing that scientific claims remain secure.
10. See Nagel's essay, "The Absurd" in (14).
11. See Huizinga's classic discussion (8: pp. 18-21).
12. I have discussed this more thoroughly in (4).
13. The judgments about sports we might make from a relatively "objective" perspective—the distinction is a matter of degree—are not unitary. I do not believe that sports are reduced to absurdity based on all objective views of it. Later I will argue that the development of moral character in sport represents a form of "objective reengagement" after reflective detachment has seemed to undermine the objective significance of sports participation. Some kind of objective viewpoint can obviously recognize valuable aspects of sports participation, including psychological, physical, and social benefits as well as the intrinsic value of noninstrumental activities. Nevertheless, at some point objectivity generates a perspective from which judgments about the relative triviality of sports participation are occasioned, especially when certain aspects are emphasized to the exclusion of others. Likewise, "subjectivity" in sports is a complex phenomenon. It includes intersubjective elements insofar as sports are social practices that involve shared goods, as well as more subjective elements like the joys of playful exuberance, personal well-being, and a sense of achievement. I wish to thank the thoughtful and useful comments of a reviewer and the editor for helping me clarify these points.
14. For a tidy summary, see Chapter 2, "Sportsmanship and the Nature of Sport," in (2).
15. See (22).
16. Also see (20).
17. I am following Nagel's structure here. See (15: pp. 218-221).
18. See Michael Novak's insightful discussion of the "new sportswriters" in (16), chapter 14, "Jocks, Hacks, Flacks, and Pricks."
19. See Nagel's discussion of irony in "The Absurd" (14). Also, see (6).
20. Feinberg refers to this definition in his article.
21. The reference is to the appearance of the article in an introductory anthology, *Philosophy and the Human Condition,* edited by Beauchamp and Feinberg, Prentice Hall, 1984, pp. 601-602.
22. The distinction between the internal and external goods of a practice is made by MacIntyre (10: chapter 14).

23. See (2: Chapter 3).

24. See George Will's discussion in the "Conclusion" of (25).

25. I have discussed this more extensively in (5).

26. See (2).

27. See Kierkegaard's discussion (9: pp. 177-188).

28. See Robert McKim's analysis and defense of the appropriateness of "tentative" religious belief because of the "widespread and deep disagreement" about religious matters among those with "intellectual integrity and some relevant expertise" (12). McKim's defense of tentative religious belief is analogous to my defense of the appropriateness of an ironic attitude in sports: Both require a detached awareness of the conditions that undermine a more robust and immediate attachment to the relevant concerns.

29. Heidegger uses quite different language to make the point that persons are ontologically unique because they can reflect upon their life and choose what to be and do. Da-sein, or human being, is "being about which this being is concerned" (7: p. 39). "And because Da-sein is always its possibility, it *can* 'choose' itself in its being, it can win itself, it can lose itself, or it can never and only 'apparently' win itself" (7: p. 40).

30. Feinberg makes this interesting point in (6).

31. I have argued in (3) that Nagel is not right about his global claims of life's absurdity.

Bibliography

1. Churchland, P. *Matter and Consciousness* (Rev. ed.). Cambridge, MA: MIT Press, 1988.

2. Clifford, C., and Feezell, R. *Coaching for Character: Reclaiming the Principles of Sportsmanship.* Champaign, IL: Human Kinetics, 1997.

3. Feezell, R. "Of Mice and Men: Nagel and the Absurd." *The Modern Schoolman* LXI(4): 259-265, 1984.

4. Feezell, R. "Sport, the Aesthetic, and Narrative." *Philosophy Today* 39: 93-104, 1995.

5. Feezell, R. "Sport, Character, and Virtue." *Philosophy Today* 33: 204-220, 1989.

6. Feinberg, J. "Absurd Self-Fulfillment." In: *Freedom and Fulfillment: Philosophical Essays.* Princeton, NJ: Princeton University Press, 1992, pp. 297-330.

7. Heidegger, M. *Being and Time* (Joan Stambaugh, Trans.). Albany: State University of New York Press, 1996.

8. Huizinga, J. *Homo Ludens.* London: Routledge and Kegan Paul, 1950.

9. Kierkegaard, S. *Concluding Unscientific Postscript* (Walter Lowrie, Trans.). Princeton, NJ: Princeton University Press, 1971.

10. MacIntyre, A. *After Virtue.* Notre Dame, IN: University of Notre Dame Press, 1981.

11. Mackie, J.L. *Ethics: Inventing Right and Wrong.* Hammondsworth: Penguin, 1977.

12. McKim, R. "Religious Belief and Religious Diversity." *Irish Philosophical Journal* 6:275-302, 1989.

13. Meier, K. "Triad Trickery: Playing With Sport and Games." In: *Philosophic Inquiry in Sport* (2nd ed.), W.J. Morgan and K.V. Meier (Eds.). Champaign, IL: Human Kinetics, 1995, pp. 23-35.

14. Nagel, T. *Mortal Questions.* Cambridge, UK: Cambridge University Press, 1979.

15. Nagel, T. *The View From Nowhere.* New York: Oxford University Press, 1986.

16. Novak, M. *The Joy of Sports.* New York: Basic Books, 1976.

17. Pojman, L. *Ethics: Discovering Right and Wrong* (3rd ed.). Belmont, CA: Wadsworth, 1998.

18. Rachels, J. *The Elements of Moral Philosophy* (3rd ed.). Boston: McGraw-Hill College, 1999.

19. Sayre-McCord, G. (Ed) *Essays on Moral Realism.* Ithaca, NY: Cornell University Press, 1988.

20. Schmitz, K.L. "Sport and Play: Suspension of the Ordinary." In: *Sport and the Body: A Philosophical Symposium,* E. Gerber and W.J. Morgan (Eds.). Philadelphia: Lea and Febiger, 1979, pp. 22-29.

21. Singer, P. *Practical Ethics* (2nd ed.). Cambridge, UK: Cambridge University Press, 1993.

22. Suits, B. "The Elements of Sport." In: *Philosophic Inquiry in Sport* (2nd ed.), W.J. Morgan and K.V. Meier (Eds.). Champaign, IL: Human Kinetics, 1995, pp. 8-15.

23. Taylor, R. *Metaphysics* (4th ed.). Englewood Cliffs, NJ: Prentice Hall, 1992.

24. Unger, P. *Ignorance: A Case for Skepticism.* Oxford, UK: Clarendon Press, 1975.

25. Will, G. *Men at Work: The Craft of Baseball.* New York: Macmillan, 1990.

26. Williams, B., and Smart, J.J.C. *Utilitarianism: For and Against.* Cambridge, UK: Cambridge University Press, 1973.

27. Wolf, S. "Moral Saints." *Journal of Philosophy* 79:419-439, 1982.

Why the "View From Nowhere" Gets Us Nowhere in Our Moral Considerations of Sport

◆

William J. Morgan

In a recent essay, Feezell (2) provocatively argued that coming to terms with the morality of sports is best approached mindful of Nagel's famous distinction between the subjective (our immediate, pre-reflective take on things) and objective (our mediated, reflective take on these same things) points of view. It is this tension, he insisted, between our personal, particular, qualified understandings of the moral qualities of sports and our impersonal, universal, and unqualified understandings of such qualities that sports ethics should train its focus and concentrate its efforts.

But I remain unconvinced. My quarrel with Feezell's account and his heavy reliance on Nagel, however, does not extend to Nagel's essentially Kantian characterization of morality itself, which holds that the difference between a morally informed relationship with others and a morally uninformed one is the difference between treating others as ends-in-themselves and treating them as mere means—in other words, that moral reasons are the sort of reasons that lead us to treat others and the projects they take up in value laden non-instrumental ways.[1] Rather, my quarrel with Feezell is that

I want to thank two anonymous reviewers for their helpful comments on an earlier draft of this manuscript.

Reprinted, by permission, from W.J. Morgan, 2003, "Why the 'View from nowhere' gets us nowhere in our moral considerations of sport," *Journal of the Philosophy of Sport* 30(1): 51-67.

his effort to steer us in this morally non-instrumental direction by strictly adhering to Nagel's subjective–objective distinction backfires, that, contra Nagel himself, the distinction is not well suited to this moral aim. For social practices like sports cannot be made ethical sense of, either by clambering inside our subjective selves and endorsing whatever preference rankings they harbor or, contrarily, by clambering outside of ourselves in search of some perspectiveless, objective vantage point. Rather, what is needed here in the way of moral reflection is a third, intersubjective perspective, one that eschews both dizzying abstract reflection and stay-on-the-surface subjective scanning. Said another way, sports demand an interpersonal moral take, one that combines critical reflection with an appreciation of the cultural and historical situatedness of sports. And it is because Feezell's allegiance to Nagel's subjective–objective divide gets in the way of such a moral approach to sports, indeed undercuts such an approach, that I am forced to reject his account. In short, I think Feezell's Nagelian commitments get the better of him here.[2]

Sports Subjectively and Objectively Considered

What sort of account of sports is Feezell able to spin out using Nagel's subjective–objective distinction as his guide? The answer is a paradoxical one, since sports look entirely different depending on whether one takes a subjective or objective view of them, and since, on his account, there is no way one can avoid sizing them up in both of these ways.

On the subjective side, they come off not only as highly serious undertakings, at least to those for whom sports already "matter"—Feezell's focus here—but as "monstrously" important undertakings. I am reminded as I write this, during the 2002 World Cup, of the South Korean fan who set himself ablaze in order to spur his fellow countrymen on to victory. Obviously, for this poor soul and many others, most of whom, fortunately, manage to express how much sports mean to them without immolating themselves, sports could hardly be more important. No doubt, from this vantage point just about every thing pales in significance when stacked up against sports.

The reason why this is so is not especially difficult to divine when we see more clearly what goes into a subjective appraisal of sports. For to view sports subjectively is to evaluate them exclusively from the standpoint of our own personal beliefs, desires, needs, perceptions, sensations, goals, and values (2: p. 2), what Williams pithily called our "subjective motivational sets."[3] As such, we are to take sports pretty much as we find them, whether as engaged participant or as rapt fan and admirer. Morally speaking, this means that whatever we immediately and intuitively think is right and good for us to do while engaged in sports is, in fact, right and good to do. So our individual reasons for getting involved in sports and for acting within and on them turn out to be the very same reasons we deploy for evaluating them. Not surprisingly then, when the world is considered from these individual motivational sets, in which the apercus of subjective assessment guide us untouched by the ardor of reflection, sports look like big deals indeed, for many the biggest of deals.

When viewed objectively, however, Feezell insists that a radical reevaluation of sports is in order. For here the standards of appraisal derive not from subjective batches of beliefs, intentions, and values, but from a detached standpoint in which reflection, as opposed to our first-order desires, governs what is good and right for us to do in sports. Reflection thus initiates a chain of reasoning that enjoins we step back from our personal, immediate, pre-reflective preoccupation with sports, and assume an impersonal, mediated, objective outlook. And when one separates oneself from one's firsthand attachment to sports in this carefully contrived reflective way, their luster not only fails to shine through, but their very significance and moral import is stripped away as well. For when sports are objectively compared to all the other activities humans pursue, they look downright trivial and irrational, and/or when they are caught in the gaze of a reflection, which has severed all first-personal ties to the world, they are revealed as altogether absurd human undertakings.

We should resist the perhaps natural temptation, Feezell cautioned, to view this distinction as a hard and fast, either/or one, for at least two reasons. First, it is not a rigid distinction but a continuum in which the further removed we are from the particular beliefs and values of individuals and their particular positions in the world, the more objective our reflective grasp of sports becomes. So while we can easily identify clear points along the continuum that demarcate an intimately personal from a maximally impersonal viewpoint, there are, in fact, a number of more fine-grained points that can be marked along it as well that distinguish a more objective from a more subjective view of sports and the world. It is this more or less objective or subjective outlook that militates against any reading of this distinction as a fixed, inflexible one.

It should also not be construed as a strict distinction in the second sense that the move from the personal to the impersonal side of the continuum is not always a move in the direction of truth or moral rightness and goodness. That is because some things are better understood and evaluated from a less objective perspective, and sports, Feezell contends, are one of those things because their subjective side plays its own independent and indispensable role in assigning them their importance and meaning.

That said, it must also be made clear that for both Nagel and Feezell, with one possible exception in the latter's case that I will take up in the next section of my paper, moral reflection is, ipso facto, impersonal reflection. For moral reflection mandates that we put in question our personal and self-interested attachment to sports, our egocentric estimate of their significance, and normatively evaluate the warrant of that estimate from the impersonal, objective side of the reflective continuum.

Nagel could not, I think, be clearer on this point, when he argued that the first step on the path to ethics is to admit generality into our practical judgments, and the second step is to come up with universal, agent-neutral principles that are neither "merely" personal nor "merely" social (8: p. 119, p. 10). Nagel makes a useful analogy here to perceptual cases, for just as the epistemological validation of perceptual beliefs requires that we adopt an external standpoint that forces us to think about the world and not ourselves (our perceptions of the world), so too does the validation of moral values require that we adopt an external standpoint that forces us to think about the world (what good moral reasons we can divine to live a moral life that does justice to that world) and not ourselves (our own subjective estimate of what is a good moral reason to act). Feezell is no less clear in the case of the moral treatment of sports, for the relevant vantage points that do most of the moral work in his essay, the "relatively" impersonal (where sports are compared to other human activities) and the "extremely" impersonal (where sports are viewed from a maximally detached point of view), fall, as the names themselves give away, on the impersonal, universal side of the subjective-objective divide.

I said earlier that Feezell's use of Nagel's distinction commits us to a paradoxical conception of sport. How so? Because it suggests that we are inextricably pulled in both a subjective and objective direction in our sporting lives and, of course, outside them. The internal pull is easy enough to understand, since our very attraction to sports, our sense that they fill our lives with a sense of purpose and significance they would otherwise lack, is supplied by our subjective attachment to them. It is our subjective side, as Feezell felicitously puts it, that "gives our lives their forward drive" (2), that stokes the fire within us to pursue sports with the seriousness we have grown accustomed to seeing in the contemporary era. The objective pull, however, is also not difficult to fathom. For it is our objective side that impels us to stand back from our various projects and reflect on their true significance. To refuse this external, objective dimension of our selves is to condemn ourselves to the status of what Koorsgard (6) calls a "wanton," someone who acts on every impulse that crosses her consciousness. So to defer to every one of our subjective whims at the expense of our objective judgments is to fail to be a fully conscious agent and, therefore, to be a morally conscious and responsible agent.

What the unavoidability of this clash between the personal and impersonal suggests in the case of sports, Feezell argued, is that sports are seen both as highly serious and valued activities and as trivial and absurd ones. Since there is, on his and Nagel's account, no apparent way of getting around this distinction in or outside of our sporting lives, no way to forsake one for the other that does not condemn us either to a thoughtless life or a meaningless one, we have little choice but to live out our lives in the paradoxical crosshairs of this distinction.

Yet, Feezell thinks there are better and worse ways of coping with the fundamental paradox of sports. To be exact, he thinks there are two better ways of doing so.

The first strategy involves taking an ironic stance towards sports, whereby irony is meant what Feinberg meant, "an attitude of detached awareness of incongruity" (2: p. 10). The incongruity in question is the great seriousness that we invest in sports, which are, when considered in the larger scheme of things, relatively trivial affairs. A properly ironic take on sports, then, is one that treats them *as if* they were serious matters, knowing full well they are not. What this evidences is how our subjective view of sports mediates our detached outlook on them, and how our detached view of them mediates our subjective outlook. And what this suggests about how we should engage in sports is nicely summarized by Feezell, "If sport is objectively . . . absurd, it's more appropriate to participate without gravity or solemnity, to reinforce the possibilities of play with an attitude expressed in a wry smile rather than a grimace of discomfort" (2: p. 12). What we end up with here, then, is a full-throated affirmation of sports' paradoxical character, as things that are highly competitive yet playful, as deadly serious practices yet non-serious ones.

The second strategy is a distinctly moral one in which he cashes in on his earlier point that not all objective takes on sports yield a unitary judgment of irrationality and absurdity.[4] Aside from objective assessments of the non-significance of sports, he wrote, "there is certainly also a standpoint outside of the immediacy of internal attachment that affirms the importance of moral qualities made possible by sports participation" (2: p. 12). While he is silent where, exactly, this "objective" view of sports falls on the subjective–objective continuum (specifically, whether it is to be located on the personal or impersonal side), and how this less extreme notion of objectivity comports with Nagel's own clear strictures on moral reflection, points I will take up in due course, the implication is clear: Sports are, after all, important sources of moral values. The specific moral values he cited in this regard all pertained in one way or another to moral character, and included, among other things, lessons sports can teach us about how to deal with failure, virtues like courage that sports frequently call upon, and a sense of justice and respect for others that sports often encourage. On this second moral strategy, then, the best way to cope with the contradictory subjective and objective tensions of sports is to encourage sportsmanship, attitudes that foster the development of moral character and that downplay the importance of winning.

Why a Subjective Moral Account of Sports Falls Short of the Mark

I am already on record as stating that neither side of Nagel's subjective–objective divide serves sports ethics well. What I now want to say more precisely and perhaps more strongly is that it is Feezell's own bifurcated moral approach to sports that proves to be paradoxical, rationally inexplicable, not sports themselves. In other words, I want to argue that there is nothing paradoxical about incorporating a reflective moral perspective into our sporting lives so long as two points are kept in mind: first, that the significance of our sporting lives is not attributable to a bald, primitive subjectivism, to whatever happen to be the particular subjective beliefs and values we hold at any given time and, second, that moral reflection is not reducible to impersonal reflection, to a view of the world from nowhere within it. Put otherwise, I want to argue that sports are at bottom social, intersubjective practices, and that if morally construed in these interpersonal terms, any supposed paradoxy of sports dissolves, as does the efficacy of Feezell's ironic and moral strategies to cope with it.

Let's begin with the subjective side of the distinction. We have already seen that for Feezell sports matter when they do because they resonate with and excite our subjective motivational sets (hereafter referred to as S), those subjective beliefs and values which we bring with us to sports as individual participants and observers. When sports chime with our S, and so predispose us to pursue them with utmost seriousness, this tells us two further important things: first, that S ensures that sports will, by and large, matter to all of us in roughly the same non-instrumentally serious way and, second, that S provides an internal, insider view of sports and their basic workings.

Now, one thing that can and should be said on behalf of Feezell's account of our subjective attachment to sports is that it mines a rich source of the autobiographical reasons that have prompted many of us to get involved in sports in the first place, and explains why a lot of us continue to find them deeply engaging enterprises throughout our lifetime. And it goes without saying, I suppose, that many of these reasons are not transparent even to our closest teammates and friends, as was the case of my own early involvement in sports in which I was constantly working out my conflicted relationship to my father who was also my coach. It would be foolish to slight this autobiographical side of sports, and its explanatory value, in accounting for why sports appear to be so important and moving to vast numbers of us.

But as an account of the rationality of sports themselves and their moral salience, it leaves much to be desired. That is because while our personal, autobiographically sensitive reasons for taking up sports may explain our desire to play and watch them, it does not account for the rationality of sports themselves nor their moral good. For considerations regarding the rationality of sports necessitate we consider, not our personal interests in them per se, but rather the way of life and standards of excellence they exemplify and the demands they make on those who partake of them. Similarly, the moral goodness of sports is not a matter of gauging our own personal good about what we expect to gain by participating in sports, but of gauging the good of the forms of life embodied in sports. The first instance explicates why among the (personal) reasons we may have for engaging in sports, we must have a reason for playing the sport itself, for taking seriously the demands it throws up to us and the skills, virtues, and commitments it imposes. And the second instance explicates why it is always in point to ask of some individual action taken in sport whether it was good, where that good is, and is understood to be, synonymous with the good of the game. A mistake in the first case, then, amounts to a mistake to realize what sports rationally demand of us as participants and devotees, and a mistake in the second case amounts to a failure to see where one's good qua participant in sports lies.

Since what is at issue here is what makes my involvement in sports rational and moral, rather than what personal reasons I may have for getting involved in sports, it should be clear by now why trying to answer the former question by referencing our motivational sets sends us in the wrong direction. For what counts as a reason for action and valuing that action in the game itself, as interpreted, to use MacIntyre's (7) language, by its relevant practice community and traditions, might well be at odds with the personal reasons individuals may have for actually playing them.

However, Feezell might retort that since his focus is on those for whom sports already matter, not those for whom they might at some point matter or, certainly, those for whom they might never matter, we can safely presume that their individual motivational sets will include the requisite game reasons and values discussed above. Indeed, he might contend that is precisely what it means to say sports matter to these practitioners. So with this group at any rate, there should not be any serious mismatch between their personal reasons and values for playing sports and the perfectionist way of life sports require.

Admittedly, this point is not without force. That is because some people do live and die for sports precisely because they find the contrived challenges they pose intrinsically worthy of their pursuit—in which case it can be said that their good is co-extensive with the goods internal to sports. It was for much the same reason that philosophers like Dewey have warned us not to distinguish too sharply between morality and self-interest. Dewey's point was that since the boundaries of the self are elastic ones, we cannot dismiss the possibility that they include rather than exclude a concern for others, which means that it is just as plausible to say of some people that doing good or seeing to it that there is more justice in the world is the guiding aim of their lives, as it is to say that getting rich is the guiding aim of other people's lives. Since the boundaries of the self are no less elastic in sports than outside them, the same, as already noted, is true of sports. So it is not far fetched to say that for some people, pursuing their individual good in sports is conducive to the perfectionist way of life instantiated in sports, indeed, that one cannot distinguish the former from the latter.

But it would be sociologically naïve to say something like this and treat it as some sort of privileged given. For it is no secret that at least for those of us who live in market societies, interest in sports and in things like morality is more often than not instrumentally driven. The reason why is that markets operate exclusively according to the canons of instrumental reason, in which the point is to use others and whatever else happens to be available to get what you want. Since markets make it possible to do just this, to pursue our self-interests in complete indifference to the reasons and values of others (but not, of course, their first-order desires) and the things and activities they get involved in, they are perfectly suited for such instrumental posturing. When we couple this point with the further one that nowadays the encroachment of the market into sports, politics, and practically everything else that human beings do, is a fait accompli, Feezell's take on our subjective regard for sports begins to look less sure.

What this all means is that for far too many contemporary practitioners, sports matter because of the instrumental payoff they provide, the usual suspects include money and fame, not the intrinsic requirements of skill and excellence they pose. As such, we can expect to find many features of the motivational sets of contemporary athletes and their minions that not only do not mesh with those of game-reasoning and game-valuing, but directly conflict with them. That is to say, many of these people take sports seriously not in the sense of absorbing them "intensely and utterly," but in the instrumental sense of seeking external goods they covet through their involvement in sports. For this, alas, ever growing group, sports are not independent aims but sheer instruments, the implications of which are as clear as they are contrary to Feezell's account of our subjective attachment to sports: We can expect the personal interests that fuel their involvement in sports to be at odds with the goods internal to sports, goods that give sports their sense of purpose and moral cachet.

Of course, it hardly needs to be said further that this prevailing subjective regard for sports as instruments is not merely an unmediated subjective expression of meaning, an element of our S. Rather, it bears as well the stamp of the dominant way in which most players and observers are inducted and socialized into sports today. In this sense, it reveals what has become of sports once the money game has spilled over into the game itself. This is, as Feezell contended, an internal view of sports so long as we equate internality with S, that is, with whatever beliefs and values practitioners happen to hold regarding their involvement in sports. But we have already argued that agent-internalism is not a fit substitute for practice-internalism, since the more perspicacious insider's view of sports is one that takes its point of departure from the rationality, values, and forms of life embodied in sports themselves. Strictly speaking, then, Feezell's subjective, insider's view of sports is actually an outsider's view, and as such accessible even to those who know next to nothing about sports but a lot about the money exchanged in their name.[5]

Still, Feezell might continue to insist that his notion that sport "matters" applies only to those for whom sports are aims not instruments. But I am not sure at this point the objection goes anywhere. For whether he either wrongly assumed that S, *simpliciter,* furnishes a perspicacious account of social practices like sports, or whether he assumed his account of S spoke only to what one's motivational state looks like when sports matter in a quite specific sense (where that means it is the goods particular to sports and not the goods particular to those who play them that are in point), the fact remains that he left something important out of his account of our subjective attachment to sports. And that something is a feature Williams does include in his account of S, which shows, or so I want to argue, that the only personal attachment to sports that does them justice as social practices is, in fact, an intersubjectively mediated one.

Williams argued that among the features that can be counted as S are "non-egoistic projects of various kinds, and these equally can provide internal reasons for action" (14: p. 105). Sports qualify as projects of this non-egoistic, interpersonal kind because they are foremost social practices whose goods are not only, as MacIntyre nicely put it, "achieved by means of cooperative activity and shared understanding of their significance, but in key part constituted by cooperative activity and shared understanding of their significance" (5: p. 240). So what shape these common goods take in sports, and what standards of excellence and forms of life they install, can only be learned through interaction with other members of the practice community, and through a consideration of the traditions that inform them. That is why sports are put in jeopardy by those who seek only to further their self-interests through them, who mistakenly think that the common goods of sports are merely the sum of the individual goods of those who engage in them.

As we have seen, these common, practice goods and individual, agent-specific goods need not always collide. In the present moral climate of sports, however, which, as we have also seen, is awash in money and other external goods, they are more likely to conflict than not. And for those participants for whom they do not conflict, and for whom, therefore, sports provide their own internal reasons for action, it is seldom the case that they come by their intrinsic interests in sports naturally.

However, whether they do or not is, ultimately, beside the point. For even if they do, they still must make an intersubjective move to ensure their self-interests are conducive to the good of the game, the very same intersubjective move that other practitioners quite consciously and deliberately make, which consists of subordinating their own personal reasons for playing the game to those that the game itself inspires and requires. It should be clear by now why this slide to the intersubjective is necessary, since the common goods of practices like sports are characterizable, to use MacIntyre's (5: pp. 225-226) words again, "antecedently to and independently of" the individual goods of those who engage in them. When we take this intersubjective step and, therefore, make our good the good of the game, we will come to see that "the identification of my good, of how it is best for me to direct my life, is inseparable from the identification of the common good of the [practice] community, of how it is best for that community to direct its life" (5: p. 240).

The point not to be lost sight of here, then, is that what underlies, mediates, and colors our subjective attachment to sports, where that attachment secures our access to the goods internal to sports as opposed to our access to our own private, idiosyncratic interests, is itself a carefully cultivated and crafted intersubjectivity. And it is precisely this intersubjective dimension of sports, which is as crucial to their social constitution as it is vital to their flourishing, that Feezell—take your pick—either glosses over or leaves unremarked. In either case, it proves fatal, I believe, to his effort to root sports in the furthest, most subjective point of Nagel's subjective–objective scheme, in our bare subjectivity.

Why an Objective Moral Approach to Sport Fails Us As Well

I want to argue next that intersubjectivity turns up unbidden as well in Feezell's retooled objective moral rendering of sports but, owing to his allegiance to Nagel's account of moral reflection, is in the end rejected in favor of a decidedly impersonal objective view of sports. But I am already getting ahead of myself since, as previously noted, the latter impersonal version of objectivity does the brunt of the moral work in Feezell's essay. It is here, therefore, that we need to begin our interrogation of his objective assessment of sport's moral importance.

To recap, there is not much to be said about sports, morally or otherwise, from this impersonal objective slant, since no matter what impersonal perspective we take on sports they yield, according to Feezell, the same unitary judgment: Sports are utterly senseless, manifestly absurd practices. More particularly, whether we view sports from a "relatively" impersonal perspective, in which they get compared to all other human undertakings, or from an "extremely," maximally detached impersonal perspective, in which they, and everything else, are viewed abstractly from afar, sports turn out to be morally vacuous affairs.

It is in this sense that Feezell's adaptation of Nagel's views on moral reflection begins to look considerably more inflexible and rigid than it first seemed. For while it can scarcely be denied that the latter's subjective–objective way of dividing up the world is a continuum, one in which objective judgments can be rendered less as well as more abstractly, it also can scarcely be denied that the continuum itself turns on a fixed moral axis. And that axis is an impersonal one, since Feezell, again taking his cue from Nagel, makes it clear that it is on this side of the continuum that moral reflection is located. This is why the distinction between a "relatively" impersonal moral view of sports and an "extremely" impersonal moral view of sports is a difference that does not seem to make a difference. This is so not only because they both generate the conclusion that sports are anything but serious moral undertakings, but because they both start their moral inquiries from the same exalted view from nowhere. Any claim that the "relatively" impersonal, comparative vantage point is any less exalted than the maximally impersonal detached one, is dashed by Nagel himself, when he declares in no uncertain terms that "the task of ethical theory is to develop and compare conceptions of how to live which can be understood and considered from no particular perspective" (9: p. 151). So the summary deflationist judgment that sports are bereft of moral importance is foreordained, rather than argumentatively secured, by the impersonal point of departure they both make the starting points of their moral inquiries.

It thus appears that the transition from a personal to an impersonal point of view is no ordinary transition in at least two senses: First, it marks off the distinction between a moral and non-moral view of the world and, second, it unequivocally and unqualifiedly consigns sports and other like particular fare to moral irrelevance. It is hard to see how it could be otherwise since, for both Nagel and Feezell, the personal–impersonal boundary is, apparently, an impermeable one in which all traces of the particular must be expunged if moral reflection is to claim its rightful empyrean standing as a truly universal reflection. True to form, Nagel minces no words in this regard, arguing that universality is a necessary feature of moral judgments—not, as it was for Kant, because the free will is a form of causality that must, therefore, operate in a universal, law-like manner—but because of "the externality of the reflective view" itself (10: p. 202). In other words, moral reflection just is general, universal reflection, and one whose philosophical and moral importance lies in the irrevocable distinction it draws "between appearance and reality, between how things seem from our personal point of view and how they really are" (10: p. 202).

This is why it is so difficult to see what Feezell's distinction between the "relatively" and "extremely" impersonal point of view comes to, since there does not seem to be anything relative about impersonal reflection; it either is impersonal, and so devoid of all first-personal reflective marks be it of the singular "I" or the plural "we" variety, or it is not. And if it is not, then reflection cannot escape its first-personal character, which shatters any moral pretensions it might have. The long and short of it, then, is that Nagel provides no moral middle ground here, one in which the fact that my reflection is of the first-person kind does not in itself count as a nullification of its moral force and import. And since Feezell is operating in Nagel's shadow here, he offers no moral middle ground either. Which is all to the bad for sports, apparently, since when viewed from afar, from no particular place within the world, there is nothing that can be said on behalf of sports morally or in any other important sense that suggests they are substantive, worthwhile pursuits.

But this may not be a fair criticism of Nagel himself, as he would likely be the first to point out. Since he does offer at least one argument, which, if successful, shows that his characterization of moral reflection as impersonal reflection is not as dismissive or as clueless regarding particular human pursuits like sports as I have alleged. And his argument does seem to support a distinction that looks very much like the one Feezell tried to make between the "relatively" and "extremely" objective viewpoint. So if his argument goes through, it offers a way to rehabilitate Feezell's distinction and the argument that accompanies it as well. Let me explain.

In the *View From Nowhere,* Nagel conceded that the impersonal form of philosophic and moral reflection he champions might, at first blush, seem utterly vapid. As he wrote, "It is true that with nothing to go on but a conception of the world from nowhere, one would have no way of telling whether anything had value" (9: p. 147). This rendition, I take it, reasonably passes for the "extreme" form of objectivity that Feezell singled out in his essay. Nagel, however, in a sentence that immediately follows the preceding one, distinguished this maximally detached view of the world from a less detached one: "But an objective view has more to go on, for its data include the appearance of value to individuals with particular perspectives, including oneself" (9: p. 147). This less detached and abstract conception of the impersonal view seems to chime nicely with the other half of Feezell's distinction, his characterization of "relative" objectivity. If so, then Nagel's way of drawing the distinction between these two forms of objectivity seems to breathe new life into Feezell's own distinction and suggests that we think of the less detached form of objectivity as at least close enough to the world that it is able to recognize the moral value of particular human pursuits like sports.[6]

But this alleged particularist-friendly version of relative impersonal reflection is not as accommodating of sports and other practices as it seems. The reason why is that the objective *recognition* of the moral value of sports is one thing, but the objective *justification* of that moral value is quite another. Nagel makes this very point when he distinguishes "what can be valued from an objective standpoint and what can be seen from an objective standpoint to have value from a less objective standpoint" (9: p. 166). And it is the primary job of moral reflection on Nagel's account to tell us which value judgments we make regarding sports are objectively justified ones. So the initial data this view from nowhere has to go on are just that—the initial "reasons that appear from one's own point of view" (9: p. 149) to suggest that practices like sports are suffused with moral value. Of course, these initial, first-person reasons must pass reflective muster before the court of universal reason before they warrant moral sanction. And it is here that we get a strong whiff of just how dismissive and particularist-unfriendly this form of universal reflection is. For if Feezell is to be believed, each and every one of our first-person reasons for believing sports are a source of moral value fail to survive this "relatively" impersonal reflective test, which means that sports are adjudged, without exception, to be irrational, trivial, morally insignificant practices.

If there is a lesson to be learned here, it is not to run together what can be seen from an objective standpoint to have value with what can be justified from an objective standpoint to have value. Since acknowledging the reasons why people think sports have value from a first-person point of view does not curry justificatory favor from an objective point of view, in other words, since what counts as a moral reason for action in the former instance does not count as a moral reason for action in the latter instance, Nagel's version of the distinction between these two impersonal objective views has no more to recommend it than Feezell's stillborn version. Notwithstanding, then, Nagel's worries in the *View From Nowhere* and in his other books and essays about how far moral reflection can range outside the forms of life that impel us forward without becoming irrelevant to the course of those lives, he resolutely comes down on the side of moral universalism. As he wrote, "How far outside ourselves we can go without losing contact with . . . the forms of life in which values . . . are rooted . . . is not certain. But I believe that ethics . . . requires more than the purification and intensification of internal human perspectives. It requires detachment from particular perspectives and transcendence of one's time and place" (9: pp. 186-187).

It thus seems safe to conclude that Feezell's and Nagel's effort to distinguish a relative from an extreme form of impersonal reflection is untenable, and so, that their brand of moral universalism is untenable as well. That is why it comes off more so as a recipe for moral obfuscation rather than for clear-headed moral objectivity, one reflectively attuned to the moral nuances of our actual lives.

However, Feezell might reasonably complain that the view from nowhere is not the only moral line he pursues in his essay, that so far I have ignored his later advocacy of an "objectively reengaged" brand of moral reflection. On this view of moral reflection, it will be recalled, sports were found to be an important source of moral virtues.

I think there is much force to this objection; in fact, I even want to argue for a version of it in the last section of my paper—though my account differs from Feezell's on several key points. But whatever force this argument for a reengaged form of moral reflection possesses is lost within the Nagelian philosophic framework Feezell compels it to do its moral bidding. For had he troubled to consider where this latter form of objective morality is located within this framework, specifically, whether it reflected a personal or impersonal outlook,[7] and the possible implications of such a consideration, he might well have seen the folly of taking reflection so far in the impersonal, abstract direction that one had to retrace one's steps, in his words, to "reengage" the forms of life in which our values are rooted, in order to hook reflection back up with our lives. In other words, he might have seen the wisdom of abandoning his unswerving commitment to Nagel's moral universalism and of anchoring moral reflection instead in a more situated and historically informed point of view. More about this shortly.

For now, however, I want to direct my attention to the fact that his reengaged notion of moral objectivity was fashioned only to cope with, rather than solve, the reflective and moral lurch Nagel's subjective–objective distinction leaves us in—the fact that the former endorses the moral value of sports and the latter endorses their moral insignificance. This seems odd if only because this reworked notion of moral reflection was intended, on the one hand, to confirm reflectively what those of us who love sports already intuitively know—that sports, at least in some contexts and places, are rife with moral value and, on the other hand, to engage our reflective capacity without succumbing either to a mind-numbing egocentrism or an impossible moral altruism—a universal standpoint that gives no moral weight to our own particular moral perspectives. To put it straightforwardly, this "reengaged" moral outlook seems to resolve Nagel's subjective–objective conundrum rather than merely making it possible to endure it better, by turning reflection back on the forms of life in which our moral estimates of their value are based.

Why, then, is Feezell indisposed to saying anything stronger regarding such a suitably chastened moral objectivity? The only reason I can divine is that he is simply unwilling to give up on Nagel's universal moral outlook. As he has repeatedly remarked, the impersonal reflective point of view is an indelible part of who we are as reflective agents, and even if we can at times safely ignore "the most extreme pressures of objectivity" (2: p. 10), we cannot ignore its less extreme pressures without becoming wantons, beings incapable of moral reflection. When all is said and done, then, Feezell's reengaged objective moral standpoint is parasitic on the view from nowhere, not vice versa, and so takes its marching orders exclusively from it. This is why for Feezell it can only serve as a palliative rather than as a substitute for moral universalism, which is just another way of saying that in the present case, coping-talk must trump resolution-talk so long as Nagel's view from nowhere serves as the point of departure.

But the crucial question that must be asked here is: Do the rest of us have any reason to follow Feezell's lead and summarily buy into Nagel's conception of moral reflection and the view of the world it makes accessible to us? I think the answer to this question must be no; for if our previous arguments have any force, then Nagel's view from nowhere does not. And if we can free moral reflection from the abstract, universal trajectory Nagel insists it must follow, we will be able to indulge both our passions for sports and our reflective disposition not to let those passions stand as the last word in our moral evaluation of them, without raising either the specter of irrationalism or absurdity.

For much the same reason I find Feezell's moral antidote to the subjective–objective dilemma weak tea, I find his ironic antidote that asks us, it will be remembered, to treat sports as if they are serious moral undertakings when we know full well they are not, weak tea as well. To the charge that an ironic take on sports cannot but diminish our passion for and commitment to sports, Feezell rightly responds that the ironic competitor need not incessantly mutter to herself during the game, "sport is absurd," "sport is absurd." But I must demure when he says that "for the reflective and honest sports participant, it is better to approach sport as absurd than to deny our reflective judgments or to give up the joys of sport. . . . Better to be absorbed and absurdly preoccupied than to miss out on all the fun" (2: p. 15).

I must demure since the view that sports are absurd, it scarcely needs to be said, is hardly fertile ground for sowing a sporting life, or any other sort of life. For just as surely as an absurd view of the world saps life of its meaning, it also saps it of its dynamism. After all, what's the point if everything is in vain, if meaning and uplift are nowhere to be found in sports or in any other sphere of life. The haunting thought that absurdity induces in us, then, that nothing really matters, is certainly strong enough to wear down even the most hardened practitioners and devotees of sports, to say nothing of their aspiring counterparts.

So it is clearly better, when we can pull it off, neither to be absurd nor to forsake our reflective judgments and pleasures in sports. This would, of course, be mere pie-in-the-sky wishful thinking were it not for the fact that the absurdity of sports as here conceived is a philosophic fiction rather than a bona fide existential dilemma, an example of the kind of reflective overkill that runs through much of contemporary moral philosophy, especially of the Kantian sort, and gives philosophy a bad name in non-philosophical circles. For the plain point, to reiterate, is that it is possible both to enjoy sports and flex our reflective muscles, to, as the saying goes, have our cake and eat it too, so long as we understand by reflection not some universal capacity that resides deep within us and decrees that we all should think of the world in a certain, binding way,[8] but rather as something in evidence whenever people try to justify their claims to each other, as opposed to bargaining in the market, or working out a *modus vivendi,* or simply threatening each other.[9] If we conceive of practical reason and the reflective life in this socially based communicative way, in which we view the world from some intersubjective vantage point within it, then we should be able to bring our intuitions and reflections concerning sports into reflective equilibrium. I am not saying by any means that this an easy task, but to my way of thinking, it is neither an impossible one nor an insalubrious one.

Concluding Remarks

I have argued that Feezell's use of Nagel's subjective–objective distinction is ill suited to sport ethics because it gives us a distorted picture of the moral character of sports, one which holds that conflicting personal and impersonal claims for their moral significance cannot be brought into reflective equilibrium and, more strongly, that all claims touting the moral potency of sports cannot be reflectively vindicated. But I do not want to let matters stand here, on this note of disagreement, because I believe Feezell's alternative, reengaged moral account of sport does show real promise for sports ethics. In order to cash in on that promise, however, we must first jettison Nagel's moral universalism and, second, following my own earlier advice, ask how this particularist-friendly moral reflection might best be characterized. As far as I can tell, there are three possible candidates here: the subjective (first-person singular "I"), the intersubjective (first-person plural "we"), and the objective (impersonal, universal, view from nowhere).

The first and third candidates that, of course, make up Nagel's hallowed distinction, can be quickly dispatched for reasons already adduced. To begin with Nagel's view from nowhere, the reason why this impersonal standpoint cannot serve as a placeholder for this reengaged notion of moral objectivity is simply that it reflectively quashes any claims that sports are a source of moral values, whereas Feezell's refashioned version reflectively buttresses such claims. It stands to reason, therefore, that Feezell's reworked account, notwithstanding his claims to the contrary, must involve some form of first-person reflection.

But it is equally clear that this first-person reflection cannot be of the singular "I" variety, the other half of Nagel's distinction, for at least two reasons. First, as Feezell has repeatedly remarked, no trace of reflection can be found within this intimately personal standpoint. So to appeal to our bare subjectivity for moral direction is to conflate moral judgment with the immediate satisfaction of our desires, to conflate being a moral agent with being a wanton. And what is clearly preposterous about this conflation is that if there is one thing a wanton is not, it is a moral agent.[10]

The second reason why this appeal to the first-person singular cannot play host to Feezell's retooled notion of moral reflection is that this sort of reflection, as Nagel reminded us, is distinguished by the fact that it gives us non-instrumental reasons to interact with others and participate in the projects they undertake. By contrast, the "I" of the subjective standpoint only furnishes instrumental reasons for engaging in practices with others. That is because from this personal vantage point what "I want" or desire counts itself as a reason for action, which means that my involvement with others has either to do with the fact that they stand in the way of what "I want," or that I need their cooperation to get what "I want." In either case, my reason for hooking myself up with them, and insinuating myself in the various projects they pursue, is to further my own self-interests. And since everyone else, on this account, reasons and acts from this same personal perspective, all human interactions are colored in this instrumental way. That this instrumental regard for others is not conducive to their moral welfare should be obvious by now, since it crowds out any moral concern for their well-being as well as the well-being of the practices in which they are mutually involved.

This leaves the second candidate, the intersubjective sphere, as the only plausible locus of Feezell's reengaged brand of moral reflection. And rightly so, for the move from the first-person "I" to the first-person "we," I want to argue, requires an expansive understanding of our practical identity, one that includes others, and in the particular case of practices like sports, others that are collectively committed to a perfectionist way of life. Further, it includes a reflective regard for that practical identity, one that seeks the best account of it that can be mustered. In the case of sports, the best account is one that provides the most perspicacious answer to the following key question: What forms of life and standards of excellence best exemplify the practice of sports? If I am right about this, then the transition from the "I" to the "we," enacted in sports and other social practices as a condition of our involvement in them, supplies the two features we earlier identified as central to moral reflection: a point of view that opens up a space for the consideration of others, and a reflective regard for those others and the shared goods that define the projects to which they are mutually bound that goes beyond individual calculations of utility.

A moral life, therefore, the kind of life sports at their best still provide to those who seek it out, is only possible if one is capable of seeing oneself as a member of some community, a community in which its members are ready and willing to come to one another's aid because each member matters to the others in distinctly non-instrumental ways.[11] So considered, moral justification requires answerability to others rather than to the world or some divinized part of ourselves. In sports, of course, that means answerability to other members of the practice community, such that, by persuasion rather than coercion or finesse, these particular others come to see that certain actions and reasons for actions are in the best interests of the game itself. Moral deliberation thus turns out to be precisely the sort of thing that Scanlon (12) and others have said it is, a matter of justifying our moral beliefs and reasons for action, at least at first, to one's peers in terms they cannot reasonably reject. And it is because social practices like sports situate individuals in larger, practice communities to which their actions and, when called for, reasons for action are held accountable, that historicist philosophers like MacIntyre have singled them out as ideal types of the moral life, as the places where a virtuous life is most likely to flourish.[12]

My linkage of a moral life, and more specifically, moral justification, to the intersubjective sphere in general and practice communities of the sort that sprout up around sports in particular, does not mean we must despair of all moral judgments that claim to be universal in scope. For I have only claimed that moral justification is, in the first, but certainly not last, instance a matter of convincing one's peers. In this first instance, answerability to others means that moral justification has to do with what people like us are persuaded is the right and good way to lead our lives.

But agreement at the local level, among people like "us," does not preclude agreement on a larger scale, among people that, at least before the agreement is actually secured, fall into the category of "them." In other words, we are capable of larger moral identities, of extending the reference "us" to larger and larger groups of people. Something very much like this is what Rawls had in mind by his notion of an overlapping consensus whereby, through persuasion rather than force, we are able to fashion larger, more inclusive moral communities. And what I am trying to get at here is what he tried to get at by distinguishing between two kinds of universality, what he called universal in "authority" and universal in "reach." Universal in authority involves just the kind of answerability to the world or to some core rationality that we discussed previously and rejected, in which "the universality of the doctrine is the direct consequence of its [rational] source of authority" (11: p. 45). This kind of rational authority begins moral inquiry with universal rational principles already in hand that "apply to all reasonable beings everywhere," even though they played no deliberative part in their formulation. By contrast, universal in "reach" involves the kind of answerability to others that we also discussed above and accepted as a way of doing moral philosophy, in which, in the course of trying to persuade others and through a series of modifications that stem from these argumentative encounters, principles are arrived at that apply to all those who have reflectively considered and endorsed them. Universality so understood, comes at the end rather than the beginning of moral inquiry, and only after all parties to the inquiry have had their say. The analogue in sporting circles would be international athletic festivals like the Olympic Games and the World Cup, in which some overlapping consensus about how sports should best be treated and regulated is required just to be able to stage such global events.

To sum up then, I think Feezell's reengaged notion of moral reflection opens up a fertile path for moral inquiry into sports, but only if it is fashioned in something like the communicative terms I have sketched above. If such a communicative rendering would prove acceptable to Feezell, then it would at least stake out some common ground between our respective moral approaches to sports. In other words, instead of just carping at one another, we would actually have something substantial to agree about. The problem here, however, is the same one that has dogged his embrace of Nagel's views on moral reflection from the outset, which is that as long as Nagel's moral universalism is the point of departure of moral inquiry, any communicative approach to sports ethics is doomed to failure.

Notes

1. As Nagel writes, moral reasons supply us with "a noninstrumental reason to consider the interests of others" (8: p. 120).

2. One reason for thinking so is that he has written perceptively and with keen insight into sports in a number of other essays. See, for example, (3).

3. With one important exception, which I shall take up in my criticisms, Williams's characterization of a subjective motivational set matches Feezell's Nagelian characterization of the subjective standpoint. As Williams writes, these sets include, besides desires, "dispositions of evaluation, patterns of emotional reaction, personal loyalties" (14: p. 105).

4. He also mentions here that intersubjective elements like shared goods play an important role in sports. Unfortunately, he relegates this point and the one just cited to footnote text, largely ignoring them in the main arguments.

5. The very standard, it seems, in which most candidates for athletic organizations and institutions are judged today.

6. The reason why I claimed earlier that if Nagel's argument is successful here it rehabilitates Feezell's argument, rather than rescues it just as it is, is that while it redeems his distinction between the "relatively" and "extremely" impersonal, it puts into question his use of the first part of this distinction to discredit sports. That is because if a "relatively" objective view of the world is able to detect the value of particular human practices, then the question arises as to why it would not also be able to detect and vouch for the value of sport practices. I can find no argument in Feezell that such an objective view of the world itself forces such a conclusion on us. For if we were to see how the different practices humans engage in all hang together, then, as Suits himself argued in his brilliant book *The Grasshopper* (13), we would see that it is precisely non-instrumental activities like sports that give instrumental activities like work their purchase. In other words, the purpose of work is to get to the point where we do not have to work anymore so that we can engage in non-instrumental activities like sports to our heart's content. I suspect that what really lies behind Feezell's insistence that the value of sports cannot survive reflective scrutiny even of the relative sort is no universal judgment but a particular judgment that gives pride of place to instrumental activities—in other words, that violates Suits's admonition not to compare sports to other means–ends activities if we hope to grasp their point and value.

7. For reasons that already have been adduced, and will be adduced subsequently, I argue that such a reflective stance must be rooted in the personal, intersubjective side.

8. This means that for Nagel, as for Kant, the path to a moral point of view outside oneself must pass through one's self. As he puts it, "Thus I find within myself the universal standards that enable me to get outside of myself" (9: p. 117).

9. The communicative account of practical reason I offer here is, of course, inspired by Rawls's and Habermas's work.

10. Of course, we can import reflection into our personal standpoint, as the ethical egoist does, by arguing that everyone would be better off, morally and otherwise, by acting according to his or her own self-interests. Two problems stand in the way of such a move, however. First, it incorporates a third-person perspective into the discussion. Second, it fails the second test of moral reflection, which is that moral reasons are the sorts of reasons that enjoin us to treat people and the projects they take up in non-instrumental ways. With regard, then, to this attempt to anchor morality in the first-person singular, I am completely sympathetic to Nagel's complaint that "the temptation to offer an egoistic answer to egoism has been a weakness of ethical theory since the dawn of the subject" (10: p. 206).

11. Sportscaster, and former coach of the Oakland Raiders, John Madden offered a poignant reminder of this very point. When he went to the hospital to visit New England Patriots' Daryl Stingley, paralyzed after a devastating tackle by one of Madden's players, he was horrified to find no players or coaches from either team there. He promptly called the airport and had the Patriots charter plane stopped from taking off until they sent someone over to stay with Stingley. As he explained his actions, "To me football is a brotherhood . . . we're all in this together" (1: p. 30).

12. More analytic philosophers are similarly disposed. For example, Stuart Hampshire argued that "the true communities in modern life are to be found in professions and shared pursuits, in the communities of people who work together. Most lawyers, most actors . . . most athletes . . . and most diplomats feel a certain solidarity in the face of outsiders, and, in spite of their differences, they share . . . a common ethic . . . and a kind of moral complicity" (4: p. 45).

Bibliography

1. deJonge, P. "Man's Best Friend." *The New York Times Magazine*. July 21, 26-31, 2002.
2. Feezell, R. "The View From Nowhere." *Journal of the Philosophy of Sport*. XXVIII:1-17, 2001.
3. Feezell, R. "Sport, the Aesthetic, and Narrative." *Philosophy Today*. 39:93-104, 1995.
4. Hampshire, S. *Justice Is Conflict*. Princeton, NJ: Princeton University Press, 2000.
5. Knight, K. *The MacIntyre Reader*. Notre Dame, IN: University of Notre Dame Press, 1998.
6. Koorsgaard, C. *The Sources of Normativity*. Cambridge, UK: Cambridge University Press, 1997.
7. MacIntyre, A. *After Virtue*. Notre Dame, IN: University of Notre Dame Press, 1984.
8. Nagel, T. *The Last Word*. New York: Oxford University Press, 1997.
9. Nagel, T. *The View From Nowhere*. New York: Oxford University Press, 1986.

10. Nagel. T. "Universality and the Reflective Life." In: *The Sources of Normativity*, Koorsgaard, C. (Ed.). Cambridge, UK: Cambridge University Press, 1997, pp. 200-209.

11. Rawls, J. "The Law of Peoples." In: *On Human Rights: The Oxford Amnesty Lectures*, Shute, S., and Hurley, S. (Eds.). New York: Basic, 1993, pp. 41-82.

12. Scanlon, T.M. *What We Owe to Each Other*. Cambridge, MA: Harvard University Press, 1998.

13. Suits, B. *The Grasshopper: Games, Life, and Utopia*. Toronto: University of Toronto Press, 1978.

14. Williams, B. *Moral Luck*. Cambridge, UK: Cambridge University Press, 1981.

II
PART

Competition and Fair Play

Considerations of Winning, Cheating, and Gamesmanship

Paul Gaffney's "The Meaning of Sport: Competition as a Form of Language" begins this section with a probing analysis of the meaning of competitive sport. Unlike sociological analyses of the meaning of sport, which tell us *that* sport matters, philosophical analyses, Gaffney argues, purport to tell us *why* sport matters. In this regard, he distinguishes three different senses in which sport can be said to be a meaningful practice. The first sense stakes the meaning of sport to its importance as a highly valued enterprise, to the fact that people care deeply about sport and regard it as central to a good life. The second sense in which sport is meaningful is that it can serve as a surrogate either for our most noble aspirations, for example, as having appropriated from religion the primary role of expressing our spiritual needs, or our basest tendencies, for example, as having appropriated from war the expression of our aggressive dispositions. The third sense in which sport is considered meaningful is the one that Gaffney favors and that borrows from H. Paul Grice's theory of meaning. The idea here is that sport can be considered as a kind of language game in which participants engage one another in a dynamic and interactive manner that calls both for recognition and response. Gaffney argues that competitive sport requires participants to signal to one another both their intent to engage the other in a contest and to telegraph that intention clearly to the other. Because this kind of communicative interplay mimics that of language itself, it is not surprising why Gaffney thinks this semantic account best captures what the competitive striving specific to sport is all about.

This part's second essay, Rob Butcher's and Angela Schneider's "Fair Play as Respect for the Game," turns our attention from competition to the important moral ideal of fair play. The authors begin by identifying five different conceptions of fair play in sport, all of which they find unsatisfactory, and then offer up their own account, which, they hold, can overcome the shortcomings of the previous conceptions. The first rendering of fair play they consider views fair play as a "bag" of assorted virtues, such as compassion, integrity, and sportspersonship, which they reject mainly because the order of primacy and general relation among these virtues is never clearly spelled out. The second conception likens fair play to play itself, understood, as Keating famously conceived it, as an intrinsic regard for sport that requires participants to be treated with generosity. The problem here, the authors maintain, is that this approach does not give sufficient weight to the importance of winning in sport and thus to the standards of excellence that underpin athletic success. The third account links fair play to the idea of a fair contest in which participants agree to abide by and observe the rules of the game. The shortcoming of this account is that it offers a rather impoverished view of fair play, one that merely equates it with the absence of cheating. The fourth conception of fair play claims that it involves showing respect for the governing rules of sport. This proves inadequate for Butcher and Schneider because many of the moral situations that crop up in sport—such as their example of Josie who, through no fault of her own, shows up for a championship squash match without her racket—are not covered by the rules, and so, no normative guidance to speak of is provided. The fifth, and last, conception of fair play they explore defines fair play as a contract in which participants agree to play the game according to the rules, and by agreeing to do so bind one another to those rules. However, because such agreements are typically tacit ones, it is not exactly clear what it is these participants have agreed to do or not do. With these failed efforts to account for the moral thrust and content of fair play as their backdrop, Butcher and Schneider proceed to offer their own conception of fair play, which they hold is best rendered as respect for the game itself. What they mean by "respect" is not mere compliance with the rules but a fairly robust sense of honoring, esteeming, and valuing both the rules of sport and the form of life it embodies.

James W. Keating and Randolph Feezell's ensuing essays, entitled respectively "Sportsmanship as a Moral Category" and "Sportsmanship," as their titles reveal, take on the important notion of sportsmanship. Armed with his well-known distinction between sport (a diversion whose main aim is a pleasurable experience) and athletics (a competitive contest whose main aim is victory), Keating starts things off by claiming sportsmanship is not the all-embracing moral notion that many have taken it to be. Rather, he argues that its moral role is restricted and thus tailored to cultivate the festive atmosphere required to ensure the mutual pleasure of all in sport, but that in the separate case of athletics sportsmanship functions only as a legal constraint on what participants are permitted to do in their quest for victory. Feezell rejects Keating's partitioning of sportsmanship into a moral code for sport and a merely legal code for athletics, arguing that the attitudes of participants in competitive sport properly reflect a balance of pleasure and joy and of dedication to victory. So construed, Feezell thinks sportsmanship is crucially linked to the preservation of a playful spirit in sport, which he interprets according to Aristotle's famous conception of the mean: To be a good sport is to be both serious and nonserious in the right proportion—that is, to avoid the excesses of both caprice and overseriousness.

Nicholas Dixon's chapter, "On Winning and Athletic Superiority," tries to answer the question of what constitutes athletic superiority by examining various cases of what he aptly calls "failed athletic contests" in which the "better" team did not come out on top as a result of unjust outcomes. In the course of his analysis, he effectively shows why athletic superiority cannot be treated as a synonym for winning, and why qualities of action (e.g., guile, poise, and playing well under pressure) are not always good measures of athletic excellence. Dixon suggests that one reason athletic competitions fall short is errors made by officials, a result either of incompetence or simple bias. When such errors are responsible for swinging a contest one way rather than another, the team favored by these errors cannot be regarded as the better team. Another, more obvious, sense of a failed athletic contest is when an outcome is determined by cheating, which Dixon characterizes as deceitful rule breaking. Such rule violations mean that one or more participants have failed to observe the rules or have not properly recognized the equality of opportunity necessary to ensure a fair contest. A third example of a failed athletic competition is when victory is a consequence of one competitor or opponent besting another by cunning play or gamesmanship. Gamesmanship, unlike cheating, does not involve explicit or deceitful rule breaking but rather such behavior as trash talking, psychological trickery, or strategic fouling in which the penalty levied is less than the advantage gained. Here again, the winning team cannot be said to be the better team. A final example Dixon cites as leading to a failed contest is simple bad luck, in which an errant blast of wind or a freakish play results in an undeserved score. Once again, victory goes here not to the most excellent but to the most fortunate. The cumulative weight of these examples, as Dixon skillfully concludes, should be sufficient to demolish both the commonly held claim that athletic superiority can be equated with winning and that a playoff system that rewards teams not with the best overall record but with the best postseason record of playing well under pressure is the best way to measure athletic excellence.

Scott Kretchmar's and Tim Elcombe's essay, "In Defense of Competition and Winning: Revisiting Athletic Tests and Contests," aims to answer critics like Dixon who think winning is overrated as a measure of genuine athletic excellence. They do so by revisiting Kretchmar's important distinction between tests and contests. This chapter's authors do not intend to challenge the main features of this distinction but want to develop and enrich the distinction further so that it is not confused with another dichotomy they do not support—namely, the characterization of competitive sport as mainly a zero-sum game that divides players into winners or losers. On this expanded account, tests and contests are further analyzed in terms of whether the challenges they present are open ones (such as in golf in which the problem is never solved but only more closely approximated) or closed ones (such as with certain puzzles in which the problem can indeed be solved and once it has been solved loses its allure), and in terms of whether the skills tested or contested are normed so that we have a better understanding of the level of skill achieved. Adding to the richness of this extended account is the authors' use of MacIntyre's notion of a social practice to characterize tests and contests in which the narrative of excellence they make possible and the traditions that surround these game problems highlight their historical resonance with those who play and watch them.

Edwin Delattre's classic piece, "Some Reflections on Success and Failure in Competitive Athletics," further attacks the simplistic idea that athletic success and failure can be reduced without remainder to winning and losing. He persuasively argues that this is a crude and impoverished conception of athletic success and failure because, among other things, it fails to note the contribution "worthy" opponents make to a well-played game and overlooks the importance that all competitors both morally respect their opponents as individuals in their own right and respect the game itself as a pursuit of excellence that places a heavy onus on precisely how that excellence is accomplished.

Delattre's essay serves as a nice foil for Oliver Leaman's controversial contribution, "Cheating and Fair Play." Leaman's piece is controversial partly because it argues that cheating, except in the most obvious of circumstances (say, when the offensive line of a football team pistol whips their defensive adversaries) is never easy to get one's conceptual hands around because it is a much more complex notion than most people imagine. Leaman further contends that there is nothing morally wrong with "nondisruptive" forms of cheating and that, indeed, clever cheating adds to the range of skills contested in sports and thus makes them more exciting to play and watch. This is Leaman's most controversial view of all, perhaps because it challenges our most basic moral intuitions regarding how competitive sports should be conducted.

The final two essays of this section, Warren Fraleigh's "Intentional Rule Violations—One More Time" and Robert L. Simon's "The Ethics of Strategic Fouling: A Reply to Fraleigh," debate the moral standing of the ever-increasing resort to "strategic fouling" in contemporary sports.

Fraleigh helpfully notes that the disagreement about the moral permissibility of strategic fouling is owed to a larger controversy over whether the rules alone, as formalists maintain, or the rules plus the *ethos* (social agreements), as conventionalists maintain, determine what sport is about and how it should be morally treated. What further contributes to this moral disagreement is that no rule or set of rules can determine how a rule or rules will be interpreted. So the crux of the problem is what counts as an "appropriate" interpretation of the point and purpose of sport. For Fraleigh, the answer to this important question is whether the interpretation of sport ventured supports and maintains the relevant skills contested in it and so the excellence sought or detracts from and perhaps even countermands those skills and that excellence. To answer that question, Fraleigh argues we need to appeal to Torres' important distinction between "constitutive" skills, those skills basic to sport and to the central challenge they pose (in basketball, shooting, dribbling, passing), and "restorative" skills, those skills that come into play when a penalty-bearing rule is broken (in basketball again, primarily foul shooting). Armed with this distinction, Fraleigh concludes that the strategic foul is indeed morally problematic because it gives too prominent a role to what are only "restorative" skills and thereby discounts the greater role "constitutive" skills should play in athletic contests. Because this is, according to Fraleigh, the better interpretation of sport, it trumps Simon's claim that strategic fouls can be morally justified because the penalty-bearing rules they violate are not prohibited actions as such but rather a cost paid for exercising a certain strategy.

Simon's response to Fraleigh begins on a note of agreement, as Simon credits Fraleigh for taking the moral dispute about strategic fouling beyond the larger dispute between formalists and conventionalists, and for showing that the dispute centers more on what Simon earlier called a broad internalist account of sport in which the way we answer moral problems like this one is by appealing to that interpretation that best captures the main point and purpose of sport. Simon, however, is not convinced that Fraleigh's treatment of the strategic foul is in fact the best interpretation of its place in sport. He tries to show this by arguing that Torres' insightful rendering of "restorative skills" rests on two assumptions:

1. that the function of restorative skills is to get games back on track when certain rule violations occur (which essentially defines what these skills are), and
2. that since restorative skills are mere back-ups as it were for constitutive ones they are less interesting and complex (which justifies their subordinate status to constitutive skills).

Simon contends, however, that a wide range of restorative skills are as interesting as and even more complex than their constitutive counterparts, and he offers as examples penalty-killing in hockey, the psychological intensity surrounding foul shooting in pressure-packed situations when a basketball game is on the line, and the mundane exhibition of basic skills such as dribbling out the clock in basketball. Simon further argues that in a match between teams of relatively equal constitutive skills those teams that are superior in their restorative skills do seem genuinely to be the better team, which shows that in some contests at least restorative skills are as crucial and relevant to athletic success as constitutive skills. Simon concludes that strategic fouls that involve the complex performance of restorative skills are not morally objectionable, allowing them a legitimate ethical place in competitive sport.

Further reading on the topics covered in this section would include at the top of the list Simon's newly revised, second edition of *Fair Play: The Ethics of Sport*.[1] A newly published essay that discusses the main important German philosophical literature dealing with the issue of fair play is Pawlenka's "The Idea of Fairness: A General Ethical Concept or One Particular to Sport Ethics?" and a recent survey of the literature on fair play is Sheridan's "Fair Play: A Review of the Literature."[2] The literature on sportsmanship is voluminous, but more recent as well as classic treatments of this subject include Sessions' "Sportsmanship as Honor," Kreider's "Prayers for Assistance as Unsporting Behavior," Dixon's "On Sportsmanship and 'Running Up' the Score," Arnold's "Three Approaches Toward an Understanding of Sportsmanship," and Pearson's "Deception, Sportsmanship, and Ethics."[3] The topic of gamesmanship is critically analyzed in Howe's "Gamesmanship." And the ethical treatment of the strategic foul is taken up in Simon's previously mentioned book, *Fair Play: The Ethics of Sport* and in Fraleigh's first essay on this topic, "Why the Good Foul Is not Good."[4]

Notes

1. Robert Simon, *Fair Play: The Ethics of Sport*, 2nd ed. (Boulder, CO: Westview Press, 2004).

2. Claudia Pawlenka, "The Idea of Fairness: A General Ethical Concept or One Particular to Sport?" *Journal of the Philosophy of Sport* XXXII, no. 1 (2005): 49-64; Heather Sheridan, "Fair Play: A Review of the Literature," *European Physical Education Review* 9, no. 2 (2003): 163-184.

3. William Lad Sessions, "Sportsmanship as Honor," *Journal of the Philosophy of Sport* XXXI, no. 1 (2004): 47-59; Anthony J. Kreider, "Prayers for Assistance as Unsporting Behavior," *Journal of the Philosophy of Sport* XXX, no. 1 (2003): 17-25; Nicholas Dixon, "On Sportsmanship and Running Up the Score," *Journal of the Philosophy of Sport* XIX (1992): 1-13; Peter Arnold, "Three Approaches Toward an Understanding of Sportsmanship," *Journal of the Philosophy of Sport* X (1983): 61-70; Kathleen Pearson, "Deception, Sportsmanship, and Ethics," *Quest* XIX (1973): 115-118; Leslie Howe, "Gamesmanship," *Journal of the Philosophy of Sport* XXXI, no. 2 (2004): 212-225.

4. Warren Fraleigh, "Why the Good Foul Is Not Good," *Journal of Physical Education, Recreation and Dance* (1982): 41-42.

7

The Meaning of Sport: Competition As a Form of Language

Paul Gaffney

Three Ways in Which Sport Is Meaningful

Practically no one would deny that sport possesses some kind of meaning, insofar as it plays an important role in the lives of many individuals, and virtually all societies. We could measure this importance empirically—for instance, in terms of the investments of time, or money, or sheer emotion—and the findings would surely be impressive. Indeed, even an unsympathetic observer would have to be impressed, if not alarmed, by the story the numbers would tell about our cultural and personal estimation of sport. And there may well be reason for some alarm, especially when we contrast the emphasis placed on sport with that placed on other cultural and personal values.

My investigation into the meaning of sport is related to but different from the approach just described. The difference is this: An empirical, sociological study tells us *that* sport matters, but it does not tell us *why* sport matters; it argues merely from the outside. A philosophical study, on the other hand, attempts to explain the data from the inside. In my view, the inside perspective enjoys a conceptual priority vis à vis the outside perspective, in a manner reminiscent of the distinction famously introduced by Socrates in Plato's *Euthyphro*: Sport is not meaningful because so many people engage in it; rather, so many people engage in sport because it is meaningful (5: 10a, p. 14).

To begin, I distinguish three senses of the concept of "meaning" that people typically ascribe to sport. All three senses are, in my opinion, valid and relevant, but I think we can identify a certain ordering among them that helps reveal the true nature of sport.

First, we often talk about sport as meaningful in the sense that it is important, or that it possesses value. For some, sport is significantly defining of the self and the good life in much the same way that art or music, for example, might be for others. People care intensely about the games or the competitions they engage in, they care about their performance, and they care about winning and losing. In fact, it is not unusual to hear people speak seriously about loving a particular sport, showing respect for it, or protecting its integrity. Furthermore, this attitude characterizes not only participants but also spectators, officials, and, especially, fans.

Second, we sometimes talk of sport as a kind of surrogate for other, perhaps more basic, human needs or expressions. In this sense, sport is meaningful because it provides a substitute for the deeper longings of the human condition, or perhaps because it prepares one for the so-called "real" challenges of life. For example, in a recent book, Michael Mandelbaum refers to sport as "a variety of religious experience" (4: pp. 1-39) because he recognizes the striking psychological and behavioral resemblances between the respective devotees of religion and sport. Understood properly, neither sport nor religion is concerned primarily with the basic requirements of physical survival; rather, each addresses needs of the spirit. Mandelbaum thus surmises that in modern sport we find satisfactions previously furnished by religion, such as diversions from working routines, focuses of coherence and community spirit, and heroic models. Of course, there are many who see in sport a surrogate not for humankind's highest aspirations but for its basest tendencies. According to that perspective, sport is a relatively harmless domestication of our essentially antisocial or aggressive nature, a point underscored by the shared vocabularies of warfare and sport. Some emphasize the cathartic power of competitive sports, whereas others express the fear that sport actually aggravates problems. In either case, however, those who understand sport as surrogate agree that its meaning derives from this deeper reality.

Third, I will explore the idea that sport can be thought of as meaningful in much the same manner that propositions are. This is, I take it, an obvious implication of Wittgenstein's famous invocation of "language games"(*Sprachspiele*) as an explanatory device:

> We can also think of the whole process of using words . . . as one of those games by which children learn their native language. I will call these games "language-games" and will sometimes speak of a primitive language as a language-game. (7: section 7, p. 4)

The analogy is doubling revealing: Just as it is helpful to think of language acquisition and understanding as similar to participation in a game, with its regulated moves and predictable responses, it is worthwhile to consider how the playing of a game represents a kind of communication, or intersubjective achievement. In other words, my discussion can be understood as an attempt to turn the tables back on Wittgenstein's "meaning as use" theory of semantics. In fact, if my thesis is correct, there is something of a circularity in Wittgenstein's discussion: He explains the concept of "meaning" by reference to "use," which is a helpful and persuasive insight precisely because we already intuit that coordinated practice, especially as exemplified in games, is inherently meaningful.

Of the three senses of sport's meaningfulness—sport as *valuable*, sport as *surrogate*, and sport as *semantic*—I want to suggest that the third sense is the most fundamental and in fact explains the other two.

The Meaning of "Meaning":
The Semantic Theory of H. Paul Grice

Our initial task is to identify precisely what we mean by the word "meaning." My strategy will be to outline the classic semantic theory of H. Paul Grice and then use this theory as a kind of a structure to explain competitive engagements, which is where I suggest the real meaning of sport resides. Grice first distinguishes between what he calls "natural meaning" and "nonnatural meaning" (which is roughly equivalent to the distinction between natural and conventional signs) (1: p. 215). For example, consider expressions such as "These spots mean measles" or "Smoke means fire" on the one hand and compare them to expressions such as "Three rings of the bell means the bus is full" or "When Smith says he cannot survive without trouble and strife he means that his wife is indispensable" on the other. Strictly speaking, according to Grice, the semantic notion of meaning is always of the latter, nonnatural, kind. The first two expressions are not really instances of meaning at all; they are better understood to indicate causal relationships or relationships of entailment. For instance, it makes no sense to say, "Those spots mean measles, but in fact he doesn't have measles" although it does make sense to say, "The three rings mean the bus is full, but in fact it isn't full." One of the characteristics of semantic meaning, in other words, is that it can be used dishonestly.

Both natural and nonnatural meaning cause some belief to be induced into the recipient mind, but the psychological mechanisms in the two cases differ. "Natural meaning" occurs between one mind and some external association, such as that between smoke and fire. "Nonnatural meaning," on the other hand, involves two minds: the mind of speaker A interacting with the mind of audience B. In the remainder of his discussion, Grice attempts to present the structure and nature of this interaction; specifically, he is concerned to show that the interaction is not a one-directional, active to passive, transaction.

We are given the following example: A leaves C's handkerchief at the scene of a murder in order to induce a belief X into the mind of a detective B. In Grice's view, the handkerchief, or A's leaving it at the scene, means nothing, even if it does induce the belief as intended. In this situation, A attempts to engineer something that will strike B as a natural association, and this might put the belief in B's mind, but he himself has not had a meaningful interaction with detective B. What is missing? It might appear that the problem is that A's intention to induce belief X into B is covert; a meaningful exchange would seem to require not only that A intended to induce belief X into B, but also that A intended B to recognize the intention to induce belief X. But Grice argues that nonnatural meaning requires more than these two intentions. To illustrate, let us consider two other examples:

1. A shows B a photograph of C displaying undue familiarity with Mrs. B.
2. A draws a picture of C displaying undue familiarity with Mrs. B., and gives it to B.

Both examples have moved beyond the problem of covert intentions; in both, A's intention to induce belief X is coupled with A's intention that B recognizes A's intention to induce belief X. And we can suppose that both examples would successfully induce a belief into B's mind. But, as Grice tells us, there is an important difference between "deliberately and openly letting someone know" on the one hand, and "telling" on the other; in his view, only the latter example represents a meaningful exchange (1: p. 218).

The difference is this: In the drawn picture example we could say that A meant something because there his intention that he be recognized as intending to induce belief X plays an essential role in the exchange. The picture exchange takes place through, and in virtue of, the fact that B recognizes that A is trying to communicate something with him; A is not just doodling or producing a work of art. There is truly a meeting or an engagement of the minds. B recognizes and, in a sense, accepts what A initiates, even when the information accepted is unwelcome. By contrast, in the photograph example it is the photograph that is actually doing the work; A's intentions there are actually irrelevant to the induction of belief. (Exactly the same induction would occur even if A had accidentally left the photograph lying around and B had found it.)

Grice's summary reads as follows: For meaning to exist "A must intend to induce by X a belief in an audience, and he must intend his utterance to be recognized as so intended. But these intentions are not independent; the recognition is intended by A to play its part in inducing the belief, and if it does not do so something will have gone wrong with the fulfillment of A's intentions" (1: p. 219). The important insight here is the transforming power of the second intention: Not only does A want to induce a belief into B's mind; A also intends that B recognizes A's intention to do so, because the induction takes place only *through* that recognition. The recognition changes the character of the exchange from causal to collaborative. Meaningful communication, in other words, is not something that A does *to* B but rather something that A does *with* B.

We can now connect the two main points. A meaningful exchange is something nonnatural, or conventional. But a hearer can only recognize the convention *as* convention when and if he is able to discern the double intention behind it. For example, let's say B hears a foreigner pronounce something that sounds like a vulgar insult in English. Does that pronouncement mean anything? Should the pronouncement be identified with the insult? Here one would be asking whether or not the foreigner could be understood to have used the convention, and that determination turns on whether or not B would be able to divine that the foreigner intended to communicate this insult to him, and intended him to recognize this as his intention. Thus we observe the intimate connection between intentions, convention, and meaning.

Although the foregoing analysis of semantic meaning might appear to be quite complex, this dynamic, if Grice is correct, actually structures the simplest conversational exchanges. My thesis is that the same structure obtains in competitive sport, which explains why we so naturally use the word "meaning" to describe its appeal. In the remainder of my paper I want to use my analysis to support and connect two theses relevant to the competitive engagement in sport.

1. Competition is best understood as a positive and irreducible kind of relationship.

2. Sport typically devises nonnatural conflicts in place of natural conflicts (to recall Grice's terminology), which thematizes and enhances the meaningfulness of the engagement.

The Intentional Structure of Competition

I begin by distinguishing a competitive relationship against two foils: competitors confront one another *within the event* neither as friends nor as enemies. Both friendship and enmity are relatively simple phenomena. In the former one seeks the good of the friend as one's own; in the latter, the intention is to suppress or to destroy. Competitors are not friends, however, because they devote their energies to frustrate and deny the desires of the other—the more merciless, the better. When tennis players look across the tennis net during a match, for instance, they want to see self-doubt, confusion, and despair in their opponent. They do everything they can, within the rules of the engagement, to elicit these feelings. They might consistently hit the ball to their opponent's weaker side; they might vary the placements of their shots in an effort to tire the opponent; and they might even feign confidence or energy in an attempt to discourage or intimidate.

But competitors are not enemies for the simple reason that they need each other. Moreover, they need each other to thrive, at least to some extent, in order to sustain the competition. If a player looks across the net and sees that his or her opponent has succumbed to those negative feelings, he or she is, on another level, disappointed. The activity that both players sought out is thereby terminated. The worth of the victor's achievement as competitor is precisely a function of, and limited by, the excellence of the opponent. Competitors, although they are not friends, give their opponents something otherwise unavailable: the opportunity to prove to themselves and to others that they are winners and deserving of esteem. And they do this precisely because, with all of their energies, they are trying to prevent just that.

Thus, competitors enter into a relationship—a kind of intimacy, really—that should not be understood as an approximation of some other type of engagement, such as friendship or warfare. Nor does competition represent some kind of uneasy balance between the contrary impulses of those engagements; rather, competition is a special type of collective activity that requires more than simultaneity and mutual appreciation. Competition is a reciprocal, intentional, and dynamic interaction.

Here we can identify some parallels with Grice's semantic account. The activity of competitor A is driven by two desires or intentions. First, A desires victory; he or she wants to defeat opponent B, and thereby gain all the spoils of victory. Second, A desires that B recognize this desire to defeat B, because it is not possible, in my view, to compete against someone anonymously. True competition requires recognition and response. Furthermore, as in the semantic structure, the two desires or intentions of the competitor are intimately connected. Grice had insisted that audience B's recognition of speaker A's intent to induce belief—a recognition A also intends—must "play its part" in inducing the belief. Similarly, opponent B's recognition of A's intention to defeat him or her—a recognition A also intends—is precisely how the game gets set in motion. Competitor A wants opponent B to recognize the activity for what it is; that is, A wants B to recognize that the challenge has been declared and is awaiting a response. Only through this intersubjective connection does the possibility of victory exist.

B's recognition of A's two competitive intentions manifests itself in two ways. First, B engages in a reciprocal effort against A; this is what "recognition" means here.

Structurally, we can put it this way: A intends to defeat B, and also intends that B recognize that he or she intends to defeat B, but this is only half of the dynamic; B intends to defeat A, and also intends that A recognize that he or she intends to defeat A. The structure of intentionality underlying the competitive encounter, therefore, is something like the Gricean account squared. For that reason, my discussion in the preceding paragraph in terms of a "competitor" and "opponent" is overly simple and misleading. For whereas the semantic account breaks down into distinguishable roles of speaker and audience, the competitive account does not. The second manifestation of opponent B's recognition of A's desire to win is that B responds according to the rules or conventions that define the activity. Again, this point finds its parallel in language usage: The speaker discovers whether or not the hearer has understood what was said by the appropriateness of the hearer's response. One cannot look into another's mind; one can only infer the other's thoughts from his or her next move in the language game.

Two Understandings of Human Conflict: Hobbes and Hegel

To understand fully how the competitive relationship in sport becomes meaningful, we must first situate that relationship within a general theory of human conflict. In this section I outline two of the most important and comprehensive theories of human struggle. Perhaps the best-known account is that offered by Thomas Hobbes, which famously presents the natural state of humankind as a universal war of all against all, a zero-sum struggle over scarce goods, including glory. In *Leviathan*, Hobbes asserts:

> So that in the first place, I put for a generall inclination of all mankind, a perpetuall and restlesse desire of power after power, that ceaseth only in Death. (2: chapter XI, p. 49)

The quintessential Hobbesian value is physical survival, and all conflicts can be understood as intimations of this ultimate struggle.

> And therefore if any two men desire the same thing, which neverthelesse they cannot both enjoy, they become enemies; and in the way to their End, (which is principally their owne conservation, and sometimes their delectation only,) endeavor to destroy and subdue one an other. (2: chapter 13, p. 63)

The conflict Hobbes describes takes place between fully formed individuals, and it should be understood in material terms. That is to say, there is no meaning, development, or inherent value to the Hobbesian struggle; nor is there any possibility of an internal resolution. The war ends only because of the development of the Leviathan, the overawing power that scares the combatants into obedience of their contractual agreement to maintain peace.

An alternative account is offered by Georg W.F. Hegel, who, like Hobbes, understands the original condition of humankind to be one of struggle but differs in that he sees the struggle to be essentially about something beyond the material realm, namely, recognition (*Anerkennen*). In Hegel's view, a necessary stage in the development of self-consciousness is that the self transforms what was formerly only a subjective self-certainty into an objective truth, and this can occur only through the recognition provided by another self-consciousness that is, necessarily, engaged in the same pursuit.

> Self-consciousness exists in and for itself when, and by the fact that, it so exists for another; that is, it exists only in being acknowledged. (2: section 178, p. 111)

Two self-consciousnesses confront one another, each seeking recognition while refusing to grant it to the other. This creates a "life and death struggle" that ends only when one self-consciousness relinquishes its claim because it cannot or will not risk its life.

> The individual who has not risked his life may well be recognized as a *person,* but he has not attained to the truth of this recognition as an independent self-consciousness. (2: section 187, p. 114)

Thus arises the relation of "master and slave," which Hegel depicts as a temporary and mutually dissatisfying stage because the slave is forced to recognize the master through his or her work, and the master fails to find an adequate other to provide recognition of himself or herself. This stage will be overcome as the slave finds dignity in the work he or she is forced to do and will soon rise up against the master, seeking his or her own recognition.

> Through this rediscovery of himself by himself, the bondsman [slave] realizes that it is precisely in his work wherein he seemed to have only an alienated existence that he acquires a mind of his own. (2: section 196, pp. 118-119)

With a new-found strength and sense of self, the former slave is able to trade places, as it were, with the former master, but the new ordering simply replicates the dissatisfactions and instability that characterized the original domination. This pattern of alternating dominations repeats itself in a dialectical escalation in much the same way that the best games or contests exhibit a back-and-forth tension.

Hegel understands conflict and struggle to be reciprocally constitutive of the self, and thus inherently meaningful. In Hegel's view, the self desires more than anything else, more than life itself, to be esteemed by others, not so much as a matter of vanity but rather of ontology: I am precisely that which a resistant other is compelled to recognize. Accordingly, an antagonist must be regarded as a collaborator of some sort. It is important to note that the encounter between the antagonists is always *over* some "work" (*Arbeit*) but it is not *about* the work. Work simply provides the occasion or the material that supports the struggle and could be variously understood as physical labor, the body, or, I would suggest, an athletic contest.

These two interpretations of human struggle imply very different understandings regarding the value and meaning of sport. The Hobbesian view must understand competitive sport as a domestication of the basic problematic of the human condition. According to this approach, any competitive engagement is valuable as a means to an end, whatever the scarce good might be, and thus the opponent presents himself or herself as a mere obstacle. The whole point of an athletic contest conceptualized in Hobbesian terms would be the goods attained after the encounter. In the Hegelian version, on the other hand, the struggle is something of an end in itself because it is *through* this encounter, indeed, *in* this encounter that the self realizes its full being. The opponent is not only necessary but is indeed the very thing that presents the possibility for the self's full realization, thereby determining the value of an achievement. Here, the whole point of the encounter is the encounter itself, in its pure, coordinated, and reciprocal character.

Competition, Convention, and Meaning

We are now in a position to combine the Hegelian account of human conflict with the Gricean semantic structure, which together explain the true meaningfulness of sport. Because we recognize the constructive character of human antagonism, insofar as it allows for the progressive emergence of self-consciousness, it makes sense to set up occasions for such encounters in order to enhance and frame the positive benefits. In addition to the natural conflicts of human society, therefore, we fashion nonnatural conflicts, the whole point of which would be to allow for the pure encounters as I have described. Athletic competitions are the prime examples of such nonnatural conflicts, and they possess their purity precisely because the "work" over which the antagonists struggle has been purposely stripped of its natural value and invested with conventional value. There is, for example, no natural value in hitting a tennis ball over a net consistently, or in kicking an inflated ball into a goal, or even in running a hundred meters a fraction of a second faster than others. In sport—in principle at least—nothing is at stake except for recognition.

To use John Searle's terminology, athletic events typically devise constitutive rules that essentially create an activity (6: pp. 224-226). Regulative rules, on the other hand, govern preexisting activities, such as struggles over scarce goods, that would be necessary within the Hobbesian understanding of human conflict. The contrast between regulative and constitutive rules recalls the distinction Grice was making between natural and nonnatural meaning—namely, that sports, like semantics, arise in and through the development of accepted conventions. They are both meaningful as intersubjective engagements mediated by conventions; they are not engagements between a mind and some natural value.

In my view, the tendency to formalize our basic conflicts with one another (i.e., establish the rules and conventions according to which we understand the engagement) confers meaning on what would be otherwise merely brute struggles. I would conceptualize all conflicts on a spectrum of nature and meaning, which are inversely related.

- *Natural conflicts.* At one end of the spectrum we have war, which is a zero sum confrontation over the most basic natural values, such as life and land. In warfare, one seeks to annihilate the other, the confrontation has no inherent importance, so there is nothing constitutive or meaningful in the engagement.

- *Mixed conflicts.* In the middle, we have mixed modes of human "competition" that increasingly make up our institutional arrangements, such as adversarial law, market capitalism, and political elections. There are natural values at stake in the institutional competitions, such as justice, political authority, and market shares, but these engagements have been made more meaningful insofar as they have been formalized and ritualized. The participants have come to accept common procedures for the resolution of the inevitable conflicts that these values create; the manner in which we resolve these conflicts has become as important as the resolution itself. In other words, what were once causes for war have become something like sports. Of course, litigation is not a game, but lawyers adopt something of the attitude and stance of competitive athletes toward one another.

- *Meaningful conflicts.* At the other end of the spectrum, we have those nonnatural engagements that have their meaning precisely in virtue of their conventional character. Sport is best understood as an instantiation of this type. Athletic competition is not about external values, and it cannot be understood merely as a means to an end because a victory easily won is hollow and unsatisfying, for both the winner and the loser (in much the same way that the lopsided recognition in the first stage of the master–slave dialect frustrates both antagonists). The athletic engagement is complete in itself, positive and irreducible, and is always, strictly speaking, an amateur enterprise.

Sport resembles language not only because they both can be presented according to this structure of meaning—which is something of a static view—but also because of the dynamic activity that takes place in virtue of this engagement. In other words, in both arenas there is an interplay between what is determinate and what is indeterminate: The rules and conventions provide the structure and the methods of the contest or the language game, but within these boundaries is a realm of genuine freedom, creative expression, and unscripted play. In both competitive sports and language games there is generally a pattern of call and response; we often, for example, speak of great competitors who are able to "answer" the charges of their opponents with responses of their own. Furthermore, as we previously noted, because the ultimate reality underlying all this activity is a simultaneous and reciprocal engagement of minds, there is always the need to discern intentions, and this allows for the possibility of strategy and deceit (in the sports arena) as well as for metaphor and fiction (in language games). And that is where both derive a great deal of their interest.

Two Objections

I conclude by addressing two obvious objections. First, does meaning in sport require competition? The premise of my argument has been that sport gains its meaning through the competitive engagement, which implies that noncompetitive sports and athletic endeavors are meaningless. But this stance seems overly restrictive, prejudicial, and even arrogant. Why does one have to intend to defeat another to gain meaning? In response, I would remind the reader that I have deliberately used the term "meaning" in a specific sense, and not as a summation of all possible virtues. No one could deny the many positive features of noncompetitive sports: They build health, they are often beautiful, they provide pleasure and entertainment, their physical demands carry both risks and rewards, and they have some educational significance, even if people debate over exactly what the significance is. All of these aspects are important, and many are unquestionably positive. But meaning is special and, in my view, represents the chief virtue of sport. Although noncompetitive sport possesses and promotes many values, something very important is added when the exercise of one's skills and capacities are put to the test against a resistant other. In fact, all of the other positives are reshaped and revitalized when done in a competitive context. Now they become aspects of an interpersonal engagement; they are realized through the constitutive activity of the other.

Second, does competition require otherness? Doesn't one compete against oneself when, for example, a runner seeks to better his or her previous times on a daily route? Isn't the competitive challenge always a matter of forcing oneself to go beyond one's *own* presumed limits? While there is some plausibility to this objection, I think the idea that one can compete against oneself faces something like the private language objection made by Wittgenstein. That is, no matter how hard I push myself, no matter how scrupulous I am in recording my scores and times, I cannot be sure if I challenge myself as much as an opponent would. I cannot be sure if I can perform under pressure, because this is a condition I cannot simulate by myself. I cannot even be sure if I am following the same rules that define the sport because, as Wittgenstein suggests, rules are interpersonal, behavioral phenomena and not concepts in the mind (7: section 154, p. 52). At the most fundamental level, this objection raises a question about the ontology of personhood. The thesis I have been exploring takes the position that there is no real self, in any adequate understanding of the word, prior to relationship or engagement. Competitive sport thus represents an exemplary instance of the basic human need for meaningful encounters with others.

Bibliography

1. Grice, H.P. "Meaning." *Studies in the Way of Words*. Cambridge, MA: Harvard University Press (1989): 213-223. Originally published in *The Philosophical Review* 66 (July 1957).

2. Hegel, G.W.F. *Phenomenology of Spirit*. Trans. A.V. Miller. Oxford University Press, 1977.

3. Hobbes, T. *Leviathan*. Buffalo, NY: Prometheus Books, 1988.

4. Mandelbaum, M. *The Meaning of Sports*. New York: Public Affairs, 2004.

5. Plato, *Five Dialogues: Euthyphro, Apology, Crito, Meno, Phaedo*. Trans. G.M.A.Grube. Indianapolis: Hackett Publishing, 1981.

6. Searle, J. "What Is a Speech Act?" *Philosophy in America*, ed. Max Black. Ithaca, NY: Cornell University Press (1965): 221-235.

7. Wittgenstein, L. *Philosophical Investigations*. 3rd ed. Trans. G.E.M. Anscombe. Oxford: Blackwell, 2001.

Fair Play As Respect for the Game

◆

Robert Butcher and Angela Schneider

Despite the prevalence and intuitive force of the term *fair play*, its precise content is much debated. Most historical introductions to the idea trace its roots to 19th century British Public Schools and the "Muscular Christianity" movement that, in turn, claim roots in classical Greek sport. In the mid-19th century, the term did not need much in the way of detailed explanation. Because sport was the preserve of an homogeneous elite (i.e., moneyed, educated, aristocratic, leisured males), their shared values spilled over into their sporting practices. Any decently brought up young man simply knew that certain things were "not cricket." But things rapidly began to change. McIntosh, in *Fair Play: Ethics in Sport and Education* (15), quotes contemporary 1891 discussions around the introduction of the penalty kick in soccer:

> It is a standing insult to sportsmen to have to play under a rule which assumes that players intend to trip, hack, and push their opponents and to behave like cads of the most unscrupulous kind. I say that the lines marking the penalty area are a disgrace to the playing field of a public school. (15: p. 80)

The reasoning behind the statement is interesting. A player might trip, hack, and push his opponent by accident or by design. If it occurred by accident, no penalty was required. No gentleman sportsman would ever intentionally consider such behavior. Sport was played by gentlemen, so either way, the penalty kick and penalty area were clearly unnecessary and insulting.

The democratization of sport, itself a good thing, admitted players from a far wider variety of backgrounds. Indeed, even women were permitted to participate

The authors would like to thank the Canadian Centre for Ethics in Sport for funding the research for this article.

Reprinted, by permission, from R. Butcher and A. Schneider, 1998, "Fair play as respect for the game," *Journal of the Philosophy of Sport, 25:* 1-22.

in sport! The old certainties were no longer shared, and assumptions made in the offices and boardrooms of sport governing associations were sometimes not reflected in the practices of athletes. This broadening of the base of participation in sport was both positive and healthy, but it carried a price: What was once taken for granted had now to be explained, debated, and justified.

Fair play has always been an applied concept. Many treatments of fair play were, and still are, motivated more by the desire to use sport to teach some set of positive values, than by the goal of understanding the nature of the concept itself. It is generally agreed that sport teaches values, but the content of those values—indeed whether the values are good or ill—depends upon the way in which sport is played, taught, and practiced. *Fair play* is often the phrase used to capture the view that sport *should* be used to teach positive social values, with the chosen values forming the content of the concept. On this view, fair play forms a subset of general moral or social values applied to, and taught through, sport and physical activity.

We begin this paper with a survey and analysis of the contemporary debate on fair play. We will map out and examine five different philosophical treatments of fair play and show how they are each intellectually unsatisfying. The approaches we will examine may be summarized as follows: (a) fair play as a "bag of virtues"; (b) fair play as play; (c) sport as contest and fair play as fair contest; (d) fair play as respect for rules; and (e) fair play as contract or agreement.

We will then present our own positive approach. We will argue that seeing fair play as "respect for the game" provides both philosophical grounding and intellectual coherence while fitting neatly with general intuitions. We will argue that the notion of fair play has its grounding in the logic of sport itself. This approach has a number of advantages:

1. Sport forms the conceptual grounding for fair play;
2. Fair play is a conceptually coherent concept;
3. The motivation for acting fairly will thus be found in the activity (sport) itself; and
4. There is a logical framework for discussions of the fairness of particular practices.

Naturally, there are some drawbacks to this approach. Fair play does not turn out to be the sum total of morality, nor does it answer all questions about the applicability of general moral concepts to sporting situations. What it does provide, however, is a method for determining right conduct in sport which refers directly to sport itself and not to a set of external, culturally determined, and variable values. In the final section, we will summarize our conclusion on fair play as respect for the game.

The contemporary debates around fair play have focused on a number of related issues: (a) content of the concept—what fair play is; (b) grounding of the concept—how to justify the claim that some action is and is not fair; (c) definitions of cheating and sportspersonship; and (d) the moral status of rule-breaking and cheating. A discussion of the different methods of grounding the concept of fair play will be our route to an examination of the varied approaches to the other issues. By and large, the philosophical grounding adopted for fair play dictates what can then be said about the other issues.

Bag of Virtues

The bag-of-virtues approach takes a list of not necessarily related virtues, praise-worthy attributes, or behaviors and associates them with, or applies them to, sport. It is easy to see how this method is derived from research in the social sciences. Here the need is to operationally define measurable behaviors so that data can be collected and analyzed. For the purposes of social scientific research, *fair play* has been defined positively as handshaking with opponents, congratulating teammates, or negatively, as penalty minutes, incidence of violence, or verbal intimidation.

An additional impetus to this approach comes from the desire to use sport to teach social values. On this model, sport is the vehicle by which a set of approved values can be efficiently delivered.

The most developed contemporary work, from this perspective, has been conducted by Bredemeier and Shields, whose 15 years of work is brought together in *Character Development and Physical Activity* (1). They propose four elements of character—compassion, fairness, sportspersonship, and integrity—that can be taught through properly structured sports programs (1: pp. 193-194). These elements of character are derived from their developmental model of moral reasoning, then applied to sporting situations.

A similar practical motivation lies behind Lumpkin, Stoll, and Beller's four fundamental moral values or principles that, when taken together, are proposed as the basis of a reasoning strategy for fair play behavior (13). They propose justice, honesty, responsibility, and beneficence as their four fundamentals. These are selected on the grounds that they can all be found in historical guides such as "the Bible, the Pali Cannon [sic], the Book of Koran, and most societal ethics" (13: p. 21). Fair play thus becomes the application of these general moral principles to sporting situations. Different theoretical (or cultural) models of morality thus generate different conceptions of fair play.

The drawbacks of this approach are apparent. While *justice* (or fairness) is common to both lists and *responsibility* and *honesty* could be collapsed into *integrity*, the lists while compatible, are not identical.[1] Different views of ethics as such translate into different characteristics as the foundations of fair play, and just as we have no good method of arbitrating between the competing claims of different moral systems, we have no corresponding way of adjudicating between rival claims concerning fair play. Similarly, it is always open to the relativist to claim that a culturally grounded conception of fair play is not relevant to the enterprise upon which he or she is embarked. In the world of international and inter-cultural relations, these difficulties also arise and, depending on the task at hand, are either dealt with, glossed over, or avoided altogether. In sport, the situation is interestingly different. The very nature of a sporting contest requires that the participants be engaged in the *same* activity. If fair play can be grounded in sport itself, we have the ideal method for claiming the allegiance of all sportspeople.[2]

The bag-of-virtues approach is discussed, and consequently dismissed, by both Keating (8) and Feezell (5) (although neither of them recognize it as such an approach). It is dismissed, as argued above, because it offers no defensible method of deciding which characteristics or actions should fall within the relevant definitions and no method of arbitrating between competing claims. The approach that is the standard for philosophical writers has been, not surprisingly, a conceptual analytic approach that looks first to the nature of sport and seeks to generate from that nature the moral ideals of fair play and sportspersonship.

Before we turn to these other, sport-based analyses of fair play, it is worth pointing out the difficulties highlighted by Bredemeier and Shields (1), and Lumpkin et al. (13). Because sport is conducted by human beings, it falls within the realm of morality. That is, the general rules of moral life apply to sport. Sport and any action which occurs within sport is, thus, amenable to moral discussion and analysis. However, what would count as a violation of the moral order is determined both by the nature of sport itself and the agreement of the competitors to modify or suspend the scope of general moral rules.

The most obvious examples of the modification of normal moral rules comes in the area of violence. In everyday life, pushing, shoving and diving into people is generally prohibited. However, on the rugby field those actions are constitutive of the game. One could not play rugby without engaging in those activities. By agreeing to play rugby, one accepts that one will be subjected to and must inflict actions that would be both illegal and immoral in other contexts. So in rugby, a morally culpable act of violence might be a punch or a kick but not a crushing tackle. (And, of course, this is true even if the tackle causes more physical harm than the punch.) What is true of violence is also true in other areas. Various forms of deception are game-related skills in most sports. As such, those acts (referred to as "strategic deception" by Pearson [18]) are not morally wrong. Lying about a line call in tennis, however, would be.

The observation that participation in sport modifies general moral rules raises two issues. The first issue concerns just what it is that one agrees to when one decides to participate in a sport. One certainly agrees to accept actions that are permissible within the rules of the game. One also agrees to accept accidents that are a foreseeable consequence of the game. What is less clear is whether one also agrees to accept actions which, while against the rules, are common practice in a given game. (We will look at this issue of agreement in more detail below.)

Second, we might, on moral grounds, wish to limit the possible content of the sorts of "agreements to compete" into which people can enter. Bare-knuckle boxing is currently banned in many countries (despite the argument that it is, in fact, safer than boxing with protective equipment because there is less brain damage, because the boxers cannot sustain as many blows to the head). That is, on moral grounds, we do not allow willing competitors to suspend the usual social rules against this form of violence to the extent bare-knuckle boxing would require. (Whether we should ban bare-knuckle boxing is, of course, subject to debate. The point to be made here is that the general requirements of morality can be brought to bear to limit actions in the realm of sport.)[3]

The relationship between general morality and fair play in sport is, thus, complex and nuanced. Although general moral rules still apply, they are limited and modified by the nature of the game that defines the ways in which one can do wrong and may even create new possibilities to act immorally. The nuanced nature of this relationship also provides further reasons for rejecting the view that fair play in sport can be understood simply as a subset of general moral values.

Fair Play As Play

In broad terms, much of the philosophical analysis of sport and its relationship to fair play has focused on the ideas that sport is play and sport is a contest. On the sport-is-play approach, the central feature of sport is its nature of being set apart. Sport is not a part of everyday life; it is freely chosen and entered into for its own sake. The appropriate attitude is, therefore, one of playfulness.[4] Keating (8) takes this to mean that the purpose of sport is the creation of enjoyment of the activity and that to do this, the appropriate attitudes are generosity and magnanimity. Keating claims that *sport* can be radically distinguished from *athletics*, the purpose of which is victory in a contest.

This distinction has been soundly criticized and rejected by Feezell (5) and others as unworkable, unhelpful, and false to the facts. On Feezell's Aristotelian account, sportspersonship is a mean, the balanced recognition and acceptance of the essential non-seriousness of sport combined with the utmost dedication and commitment in its pursuit.

While Feezell's objections to Keating's distinction are sound, it would be a mistake to reject out of hand Keating's emphasis on the freely-chosen nature of sport participation along with his distinction between sport and athletics. We will argue below that Keating has, in effect, missed a step in his argument. He moves directly from the set-apart, freely-chosen nature of sport to the conclusion that enjoyment is the goal. The step he misses is an understanding and explanation of just why it is that sport is both freely-chosen and enjoyable. That is, he argues as if the pleasure or enjoyment of sport was somehow separable from the practice of sport itself. On Keating's account, it is not clear why a person who sought enjoyment through the practice of some sport wouldn't just switch to stamp collecting—or indeed take a good drug—if they held out the prospect of greater enjoyment. We will argue that it is the activity of sport itself that brings its own rewards and pleasures. It is through commitment to a sport and the standards and skills it requires, that we gain enjoyment in its practice. We do not seek pleasure, then plug in means to that end. Rather, we commit to activities, then derive pleasure from them.[5]

Sport As Contest: Fair Play As Fair Contest

An alternative approach is to look at sport as a test or contest and try to derive fair play or sportspersonship from that. Within this general approach, the greatest debate has centered on the precise definition of the nature of the test or contest in which competitors are engaged. Most approaches start with the analysis that sports competitions are examples of games. Because they are games, they are created and defined by their rules, as are the permissible means of scoring goals or runs, and hence, winning. Athletes agree to test their skill against each other at a sport. The sport defines the nature and limitations of skill. If an athlete breaks the agreement to compete, he or she ceases to compete, and so, can no longer be in a position to win. That is, if one cheats one cannot win.[6] This is an essentially negative conception of fair play and sportspersonship, one which starts from a definition of cheating, then proposes that fair play and sportspersonship are the absence of cheating. This has two problems, the first definitional and the second evidential. The definitional problem concerns the nature of cheating. If we accept that cheating is the breaking of an agreement, we need to identify precisely the content of the agreement. Some authors (7, 18) argue that the agreement is defined by the rules of the sport. If one breaks a rule (especially if one intentionally breaks a rule), then one has broken the agreement to compete to test skill, so one has cheated, and hence, cannot win.

This position is viewed as too restrictive by both Leaman (11) and Lehman (12) who argue that the nature of the agreement must make some reference to the way the game is, as a matter of fact, played. If the game is generally taken to include the possibility of a "professional foul," then a player will not have cheated, or ceased to compete, if he or she commits a professional foul (11, 12).

The moral status of cheating flows from its definition. If cheating is all rule-breaking or even all intentional rule-breaking, then not all cheating is morally wrong.[7] However, if cheating is breaking one's agreement, then all cheating is morally wrong, but not all rule-breaking is cheating.

The evidential problem is that we tend not to view fair play or sportspersonship as the mere absence of cheating. While we may reject the overblown excesses of the early part of this century, fair play certainly has positive rather than merely negative connotations. To say that someone exhibits fair play seems to say more than: He or she clearly follows the rules or keeps to his or her agreements.

Just as Keating's analysis, while inadequate, stressed the important points that sports are participated in for their own sakes and bring enjoyment, the analysis of sport as contest, while also inadequate as an account of fair play, stresses the essential point that agreement must lie at the heart of contest.

In what follows, we will look in a little more detail at two common conceptions of fair play that develop the idea of sport as an agreement based on rules. We will argue that neither approach captures our positive sense of what constitutes fair play or sportspersonship. We will then move to our own positive conception of fair play as "respect for the game."

Fair Play As Respect for Rules

The International Council for Sport and Physical Education (ICSPE) defines *fair play*, first and foremost, as respect for the rules of the game. Fair play "requires, as a minimum, that [the competitor] shows strict, unfailing observance of the written rule" (1: p. 23). This is glossed by the suggestion that respect is due the spirit, rather than the letter of the rules, but the intent is the same. This understanding of fair play is important in that it draws attention to the rule-governed and -defined nature of sport. Games exist and are defined by their rules. This position is also important, because it acts as the foundation of the logical incompatibility thesis, the thesis which demonstrates that one cannot win if one cheats (21).

Fair play as respect for rules is, however, an inadequate formulation for capturing some of our intuitions about the idea. For example, we sometimes want fair play to apply to situations within sport but outside of the rules of the sport. For instance, Lumpkin et al. (13) pose the case of Josie, the squash player. Josie is your opponent in an important match and has arrived (not to her fault) without a racquet. She will forfeit the game. You use the same kind of racquet and grip as she, and you have a back-up racquet. She is the only competitor at this event who could seriously challenge you and without her, you would almost certainly win the championship. The game against her will be tough, and you are far from certain you can win. What should you do?

The fair play answer seems clear. Indeed one of the earliest fair play awards (to bobsledder Carlo Monti in 1952) was presented in a similar case. Monti loaned another team his brake when theirs was inoperable. The other team went on to beat Monti. You should lend Josie your racquet. But why?

Respect for rules does not help. You break no rule in declining to lend Josie your racquet. Lumpkin et al. (13) use the case as an illustration of the principle of beneficence. This is a standard moral notion, the idea that one ought, generally, to do nice things for people. As a general moral principle it certainly applies here. Anyone who could, should lend Josie a racquet. But you are in a special position—you are her opponent—and as such, have better reasons than generalized beneficence for lending her your racquet. (Although, at first glance, it appears that it is in your self-interest not to lend her your racquet.) As we will argue below, a formulation of fair play as respect for the game will show just why it is you would want to give Josie your racquet.

As an aside, the general applicability of beneficence to sport is unclear. While fair play dictates that you must let your opponents play and that you will only use legal means to stop them, there is no compulsion to be nice to them, for instance, by allowing them to make their best shots or play to their strengths.

Fair play as respect for rules cannot account for actions we take to be required by fair play but which are not directly covered by any rule.

The rule-based conception can also err in the opposite direction. As Lehman (12) has argued, before one can make judgments of cheating or unfairness, one must consider more than just the rule book and should look at the context in which the game is played.[8] If the contestants agree that, for instance, undetected spitballs are an accepted part of modern professional baseball, then "Spitball Perry" did not cheat.[9] Similarly so for the so-called "professional foul" when a player performs an illegal act and willingly accepts a penalty, because it would seem to create a competitive advantage to do so. While we can argue with Lehman about the best approach to take to the rules of a game—should one play to their spirit, to their letter, or to what one can get away with undetected or insufficiently punished—he makes an important point, similar to D'Agostino's (3): Games are played in a context, a context that uses more than just the rule book to define cheating. Fair play as "respect for rules"—which is primarily derived from what D'Agostino has referred to as a "formalist account of games"—does not take into account the variety of sport as played and practiced.

Fair Play As Contract or Agreement

It could be argued that fair play can be seen and explained on the model of a contract or agreement. While this is an interesting and important component of fair play, it is insufficient to characterize the concept fully. Fair play as contract starts from the position, mentioned above, that games are created by their rules. A sporting competition is, thus, a test of skill within the parameters prescribed by the rules. When athletes enter a contest, they agree, and form a tacit contract, to test their skills in the ways permitted by the game concerned. On this account, unfairness or cheating is wrong, because it breaks the agreement. Fair play as contract is open on the content of the agreement. On some versions of this view, the content of the contract is created solely by the rules. In other versions, it is the rules as practiced and understood by the athletes.

This approach is important, because it shows the athlete's own role in accepting the rules of his or her own sport. By making an agreement to compete, the athlete binds him- or herself with self-imposed conditions. This approach does not permit the athlete to view the rules (and the officials who enforce them) as somehow "out there" imposing rules against the athlete's will and interest. The contest is defined by the rules, and in entering the contest, the athlete agrees to measure skill, defined by the rules, against competitors doing the same.

Because this account leaves open the exact content of the agreement, it is flexible enough to account for the variability in the way in which the same sport is played in different places and at different competitive levels. Here the agreement to compete would be framed by the rules but with the added clause "as defined or interpreted" at the relevant level (3). On this account if, for instance, the game is played to the referee—that is, one is expected to break certain rules if the referee is not looking—then the two opponents could agree to a match played in this way, and it would be fair.

This method of viewing things accounts for a number of problems. Athletes often dismiss calls for fair play with the derisive response that "the game is not played that way." Their claim is that their agreement defines what is fair, not simply the rules. Some competitive discrepancies can also be accounted for by the tacit nature of the agreement. If one team is playing the game one way, for instance to the referee, and the other practices a different ethos, for instance, playing to the spirit of the rules, then they may well not have agreed to compete in the same way. This inevitably leads to bitterness and charges of unfairness. This problem could be solved by making as public as possible the nature of the tacit agreement to compete. Note, however, that the central idea is still one of agreement. This rules out the possibility of one team, or player, playing fairly, but operating by a different set of rules from their opponents.

The alternative view would rule out consideration of the ethos of the game by insisting that the content of the agreement be taken as the rules of the game and nothing more. This renders the fair-play-as-agreement position very similar to fair play as respect for rules, with the added benefit of emphasizing the athlete's role in accepting and living up to his or her part of the agreement.

Fair play as agreement is an important further step, but it does not go far enough. The idea of governing sport by contract reduces fair play to an essentially negative concept. Fairness is the absence of unfairness, and unfairness is defined by the breaking of one's word or contract. So fair play is merely doing no less than you said you would do. Without wishing to get overly romantic about the concept, fair play is generally taken (and sportspersonship is always taken) to be something positive, something that cannot be fully explained by mere adherence to one's word, although that is certainly required. When we talk of fair play, the standard we tend to adopt is one that refers to the spirit of the game, rather than the letter of its rules.

For example, some sports still carry rules against "unsportsmanlike conduct" or "bringing the game into disrepute." These rules go undefined, and of course, they can readily be abused to punish people unfairly. However, despite their lack of clarity, we will argue that these sorts of rules can not only be rendered coherent and justified, but that they carry an important concept, a concept we should do our best not to lose.

The Josie-the-squash-player example from the last section is again useful here. Your contractual agreement with Josie is to play fairly, to keep to the rules of the game. You break no rule, and hence, break no promise, by declining to lend her your racquet. Yet we want to say that fair play dictates that you lend her your racquet. So, fair play cannot be reduced entirely to keeping an agreement. It may be a necessary condition but not a sufficient condition.

In the next part of this paper, we will examine fair play as respect for the game and argue that this idea builds on the nature of the sporting agreement and provides the positive structure of our concept of fair play—a structure that will give a logical account for the intuitions in Josie's case.

Fair Play As Respect for the Game

We wish to defend the position that fair play in sport can be understood as respect for the game. As we unpack this idea, we will see the behavioral implications that flow from this central attitude. We will argue that the standard intuitive ideas of fair play are linked, and conceptually grounded, in the idea of "fair play as respect for the game."

There are two commonly used and rather similar senses of respect. In the first, weaker sense, one can respect merely by observing or following. In this sense, we respect the rules of the road by adhering to the speed limit, stopping at stop signs, and so on. The second sense of respect is stronger and carries connotations of honoring, holding in regard, esteeming, or valuing.

It is this second sense of respect that is operative in moral discussions of respect for autonomy, or equal respect for persons. Here, the idea is that one should, from a moral point of view, value the interests, rights, preferences, and so on, of others as one values one's own.

In the context of sport, it is easy to run the two senses together. Because sports are games made up by their rules, there is the requirement that we respect the rules of the game. This could mean that we treat the rules of the game in the same way we treat the rules of the road. We observe or follow them, perhaps for the sake of expediency or as a courtesy. However, it is not obvious how one could honor or esteem traffic regulations. But it is precisely in this latter sense that we wish to defend the idea that fair play can be understood in terms of respect for a game. We will argue that if one honors or esteems one's sport, not only will one wish to exhibit fair play, but one will also have a coherent conceptual framework for arbitrating between competing claims regarding the fairness, or otherwise, of actions.

We will argue below that sports are practices and that practices are the sorts of things that can have interests. Respect for the game will thus entail respect for the interests of the game (or sport) as a practice.

Sports Are Games

As we accepted earlier, sports are games. This means they are artificially constructed from their rules. Participation in a game takes one outside of everyday life. A game creates its own world with its own standards of excellence and its own ways of failing. What counts as skill and what counts as winning and losing are defined through its rules within the game.

Respect for the game, therefore, entails respect for the rules of the game. The rules of a sport make the activity itself possible. Because participation in a game is chosen, because the activities of sports are inherently worthwhile,[10] the rules that make those activities possible are due honor and respect.[11] But respect is a critical and reflective notion. One can criticize while still respecting. In fact, if one respects, one has a duty to criticize. But the criticism must be open and public and should be constructive rather than destructive.

Sports Are Contests

As noted above, although fair play cannot be straightforwardly derived from sport-as-contest, the test and contest nature of sport are important components of our approach. As Kretchmar points out, a contest is always against another and consists in the competitors trying to do the same thing better than each other (9). That the competitors are engaged in the same activity is crucial. If two people are engaged in different activities, there is no one activity they can be competing in. This begs questions about the identification, and identity, of actions or activities. In the sports context, we support the view that contests are defined by a combination of rules and ethos. The rules, constitutive and regulative, form the basis of an agreement that can then be modified by practice and further agreement—the ethos of the game. The fluid nature of the ethos of a particular game played at a particular level reinforces the necessity of agreement between the competitors. Because there are choices to be made about the way the game is to be conducted, we need to agree on what will count as fair in the contest and what will not. Otherwise we run the risk of engaging in different enterprises and thus failing to contest at all. If players wish to contest, they must agree on the precise nature of the contest.

Sports Are Practices

MacIntyre in *After Virtue* defines a *practice* as:

> any coherent and complex form of socially established co-operative human activity through which goods internal to that form of activity are realized in the course of trying to achieve those standards of excellence which are appropriate to, and partially definitive of, that form of activity, with the result that human powers to achieve excellence, and the human conceptions of the ends and goods involved, are systematically extended. (14: p. 187)

He then goes on to cite chess and football as examples of practices in the sense he intends. What practices do is create opportunities to pursue goods and to extend, expand, and realize our conceptions of what is worthwhile in life. MacIntyre makes the (by now) commonplace distinction between internal and external goods. Internal goods are those benefits or goods only available through the practice concerned. External goods, such as money or fame, can be pursued through a variety of means.

Being engaged in a practice means standing in a particular relationship to the practice itself and to other practitioners:

> A practice involves standards of excellence and obedience to rules as well as the achievement of goods. To enter into a practice is to accept the authority of those standards and the inadequacy of my own performance as judged by them. It is to subject my own attitudes, choices, preferences and tastes to the standards which currently partially define the practice. (14: p. 190)

This should not be taken to mean that a practice requires slavish and unquestioning obedience. MacIntyre stresses that practices have histories and traditions and form living, vibrant, and changing entities. Practices change—they must—but the change comes from within and operates inside the context formed by tradition.

It is the latter part of that last quotation—the idea that, as a practitioner of a practice, one's preferences, tastes, attitudes, and choices are partially shaped by the practice—that is most significant for our present purposes. We will argue that "respecting one's game" requires that one takes on or assumes the interests of that game.[12]

Respect for the Game As an Assumption and Transformation of Interests

If you are engaged in a practice, if you respect a practice, you acquire and assume a new set of interests—those of the practice itself. It may seem a little odd to speak of the interests of a practice, but we think the idea can be made clear enough. Let us take the practice of philosophy as an example. It is in the interests of philosophy for there to be innovative scholarship, lively and vigorous debate on contested issues, the study and analysis of historical work, a vibrant community of scholars (highly paid tenured faculty?), broad teaching of the concepts and techniques of philosophy, and so on. Philosophy should make a difference in people's lives. It is not in the interests of philosophy for its research to become sterile, its teaching stale, or its issues irrelevant. And, of course, philosophy being what it is, there should continue a lively debate about just what should constitute the interests of philosophy.

As philosophers we take on those interests as our own. If we care about philosophy, we care about our own roles and performance within the practice. We take on the interest in creating innovative scholarship, engaging in debate, teaching, and so on. We wish to add our own little brick to the philosophical edifice. Excellence in philosophy is in our interests, just as it is in the interests of philosophy itself.

This acquisition of interests has important consequences. To continue the philosophical example, as philosophers, we are committed to the quest for truth—wherever that might lead. That means that we are committed to following the argument, even if the argument runs against our most cherished positions. It is in the interests of a philosopher, as a philosopher, to see his or her own positions demolished in the name of truth.

The same principle holds good for other practices. To return to sport, the athlete takes on the interests of his or her sport. Those interests become the interests of the athlete. If you respect the game, you honor and take seriously the standards of excellence created and defined by that game. For example, an athlete who respected the game of soccer would take seriously its requirements and standards. Such an athlete would care about soccer skills and tactics. He or she would accept the fitness requirements of the game of soccer and would strive to meet them. Because such an athlete accepts the standards of soccer excellence, he or she would work to acquire and exhibit soccer skills. This general point is true whatever one's level of ability or commitment to training. Even if we can commit only small periods of time to our game, or even if we recognize that we will never have the skill to be truly great, the person who respects a game will still accept the standards imposed by the sport. (Naturally, one can also respect a game one does not play, for instance, as a spectator or official—but in all cases the same point applies: One accepts the standards of the game concerned and acts accordingly.)

The idea of the interests of the game provides a means of judging one's own actions in relation to the sport. We approach any activity with mixed motivations and interests. Taking the interests of the game seriously means that we ask ourselves whether or not some action we are contemplating would be good for the game concerned, if everyone did it.[13]

The transformation of interests that occurs when we take on the interests of a game has a second important consequence. Because the interests of the game are now our own interests, we have a motivation for striving for the good of the game. As we will see, this means we have a motivation both to play fairly and strive for excellence.

Respect for the Game and Intrinsic Motivation

The connections between fair play, respect for the game, intrinsic motivation, and the internal goods of a practice—really require a paper of their own. The association of respect for the game and intrinsic motivation offers rich practical and conceptual implications that warrant detailed analysis. However, for our present purposes, it is sufficient to introduce the ideas and draw the conceptual connections. It is a commonplace observation that people participate in sport for an enormous range of reasons. A very few participate because they are paid. Many participate for fitness and companionship or to achieve the respect and admiration of others. But for the great mass of people, the reasons for participating in sport lie within sport itself: People play games because they are fun. For many, perhaps most, participants in sport, its activities are intrinsically rewarding. They bring a feeling of pleasure and provide experiences that are enjoyable and worthwhile.

In the literature of the psychology of sport, the phenomenon of performing an action or activity for its own sake has been studied as an issue of *intrinsic motivation*. What follows is a brief synthesis and review of that literature, which is necessary to defend the premises of our argument on fair play as respect for the game.

The standard contrast in discussions of motivation is between intrinsic and extrinsic motivation. Extrinsic motivation is available for a variety of activities. For instance, one can acquire money or fame in a variety of ways. One might become a lawyer or a pop star, so, insofar as one wants fame or money, one is motivated to be a lawyer or a pop star. If one is motivated by the desire for fame or money, the question one faces is merely of the most efficient means of achieving those ends. For those who are physically gifted, professional sports may well provide the means to both money and fame. But extrinsic motivation is more pervasive than that. The admiration that comes from one's peers for outstanding athletic performance or for the beauty of one's body are extrinsic motivations for pursuing sporting achievement. This is similarly true for "most valuable player" awards, trophies, and the like. Engaging in sport to prove one's own self-worth is also a form of extrinsic motivation (23).

In contrast, an action or activity is intrinsically motivated if it is engaged in for its own sake. This idea has been operationally defined in the psychological literature in two quite different ways: (a) actions or activities engaged in, in the absence of external rewards, or (b) activity in which participants express an interest or enjoyment (4). The difference between the two definitions is important. In the first, one cannot be intrinsically motivated if one receives any extrinsic reward for the activity in question. This begs the question of the relationship between intrinsic and extrinsic rewards. At this stage, we would like to leave open the interchange and relationship between intrinsic and extrinsic motivation.[14]

So far we have merely contrasted intrinsic and extrinsic motivation and suggested that intrinsic motivation is connected to performing an activity for its own sake. But what is it about an activity that makes performing it for its own sake worthwhile? There seem to be four key components for an activity to be experienced as sufficiently worthwhile to be intrinsically motivating.

1. The activity must be interesting. There must be room for the individual participant to express creativity, to experiment (perhaps within limits) with new ways of performing the task.

2. It must be challenging. That is, the task the person is presented with must extend, but not over- or under-extend the person's competence to perform the required action. If the task is too simple, it will be boring, and if it is too difficult it will be stressful. This notion of challenge embraces the possibility of mastery. If the activity is appropriately challenging, the person will feel that he or she has the prospect of meeting and mastering that challenge.

3. The activity must provide feedback. The person needs to be able to assess how well or badly he or she is performing the task at hand.

4. The activity must be freely chosen. Participation should be uncoerced or voluntary (4, 23, 24).

The perfect example of the effects of deep intrinsic motivation can be found in the experience first described by Czikszentmihalyi (2, 6) over 20 years ago as "flow." When one is in flow, all of one's energies and attention is focused on the task at hand. Time seems to stop moving as one is absorbed in the activity. Czikszentmihalyi has researched this phenomenon in a number of sport and nonsport settings. For the flow experience, one should be engaged in a task that is interesting and challenging but within one's capabilities.

As it stands, this is dry and uncompelling. Flow, in fact, is the pinnacle of sporting experience. Flow is the joy of sport distilled. It is the experience felt when one's self and one's environment are one, when the plays are flowing as they should, when one's teammates are moving with almost mystical grace and ease, when one's whole being is focused on the moment, the movement, when the ball or the puck moves as if on wires, when everything in the game is right. The flow experience is highly variable and highly prized. It can also be had at any level of sport. Because an activity that permits the flow experience must be challenging, the level of the game required to create the flow experience will improve as the player becomes more and more skilled.

Flow is the experience one has as one is achieving the internal goods of a sport. As can probably be detected from the above, discussions of flow are notoriously difficult. While the features of flow—focus, attention, absorption, and so on—are common to all flow experiences, the feelings will be different for the flow experience of the basketball player, the chess player, and the surgeon.

Interaction Between Intrinsic and Extrinsic Motivation

The obvious assumption, when one considers motivation, is that motivations would be additive. If you have one reason for doing something, then two reasons would motivate you even more. The relationship is not this straightforward. Several studies show that the presence of extrinsic motivations, such as money, food, and good player awards, all tend to decrease intrinsic motivation (4, 23).[15] It would be premature, however, to assume that extrinsic rewards automatically decrease intrinsic motivation. In another study on scholarship athletes, it was found that those in high profile sports, like basketball and football, showed decreased intrinsic motivation in the presence of extrinsic rewards, whereas those in low profile sports, such as wrestling, and women with scholarships did not (4).

The theoretical explanation for these differences, and the complexity of the interaction between intrinsic and extrinsic motivation, lies in the way the extrinsic rewards are perceived. If the extrinsic rewards are seen as controlling or coercive, they will tend to diminish intrinsic motivation. Typically, extrinsic rewards are used to pressure or coerce people into doing things they do not otherwise wish to do. By association, therefore, extrinsic rewards can be seen as coercive and controlling. But this result is not logically necessary. It is suggested that women athletes, and those in low profile sports, do not tend to view scholarships as controlling but rather see them as informational feedback and a recognition of competence and skill.

An essential component of intrinsically motivated activity appears to be that it is freely chosen. Conversely, if people perceive their actions to be controlled, they are less likely to be intrinsically motivated to perform the actions concerned (even when the same, inherently interesting tasks are examined [23]).

Although there is relatively little research on the direct effects of intrinsic motivation on sport performance and perseverance, the general position on intrinsic motivation is that people who are intrinsically motivated to perform an action, or engage in an activity, get more enjoyment from the activity and persevere longer than those who have been extrinsically motivated (23). People who are intrinsically motivated also tend to be more creative in their approach to the tasks at hand, whereas those who are extrinsically motivated tend to do the minimum required in order to receive the reward.

The connection between intrinsic motivation and internal goods of a practice should be obvious. In effect, internal goods and intrinsic motivation are the philosopher's and the psychologist's view of the same phenomenon. The substance of intrinsic motivation is the internal goods of a practice.

The psychological literature of intrinsic motivation and how it is enhanced and nurtured and how it is affected by different treatments of opponents, competition, and so on, offers a rich source for practical approaches to teaching fair play. For our purposes right now, intrinsic motivation emphasizes the achievement of internal goods that, in turn, reinforce a commitment to the process of playing a game. A commitment to the process of playing the game is a commitment to, and respect for, the game itself, with all that that implies. Because respect for the game requires respect for its rules and traditions, intrinsic motivation is its natural practical ally and support.

Practical Implications

We can think about the implications of viewing fair play as respect for the game at two levels. At the personal level of the individual athlete, fair play as respect for the game will provide guidelines as he or she considers what ought to be done. At this personal level, respect for the game will influence actions on the field of play, attitudes toward one's opponents, and even one's own level of commitment to the game. Fair play as respect for the game also has implications for actions and decisions at the level of policy. Most sports have, in MacIntyre's sense, institutions. These institutions are comprised of sports governing bodies, rule committees, administrative superstructures, and so on. At this level, too, fair play and respect mandate particular decisions—decisions that refer to the best interests of the game concerned.

For any game or sporting contest, it is possible to describe an ideal against which other contests might be measured.[16] While the particular description will naturally vary from sport to sport, we can identify some necessary conditions. Each item on the list can be justified and explicated in terms of promoting the interests of the game.

1. The contestants should be evenly matched. The ideal contest requires that the contestants be at comparable levels of skill and fitness;

2. The contestants should play at or near their best;

3. The outcome of the contest should be in doubt until the end. (This should be guaranteed by having evenly matched contestants playing at their best.)

4. The outcome of the contest should be determined by sporting skill or ability, not extraneous factors such as egregious luck or errors in officiating. Conditions of play, such as weather, may create additional obstacles but must not be so severe as to undermine the exhibition of skill;

5. The match must be fairly contested, that is, played within the rules of the game;

6. For an ideal match, the contestants must have a high degree of skill. Good contests can, however, take place between evenly matched opponents at any level of skill.[17]

The structure of sports and games is such that skills cannot be tested or demonstrated in isolation. The interests of both athletes and the game itself lie in excellent competitions. Athletes who respect and honor their sport have an interest in participating in good sporting contests. One shows and measures one's sporting skills in competition against others seeking to do the same. For the athlete, a competition is a chance to show and test his or her skills, to play the best game that he or she is capable of. In this case, the interests of the athlete are in producing the best possible game. But the best possible game, from a sporting point of view, is not a lop-sided contest where one player or team demonstrates its skill while the other helplessly looks on. In the best possible competition, excellent, evenly matched competitors push each other to the limits of their ability.

The competitive interest of an athlete who honors his or her sport is to play the best possible game against evenly matched opponents playing their best possible game. This interest dictates an important attitude toward one's opponent. The best possible game requires not only that you play to your best, but also that your opponent does. It is not, therefore, in your interest to have your opponent play below his or her best, except where your methods of bringing that about are part of the game itself. For instance, it is part of basketball to pressure a player as he or she attempts to shoot—defensive skill is all about creating such pressure, and shooting skill is about dealing with it—but it is not permissible to cough while your opponent serves in tennis.

Respect for the game, thus, creates important behavioral consequences in competition. The athlete who respects the game wishes to play as well as possible against a worthy opponent playing as well as possible. The only legitimate reason for wanting your opponent not to show his or her skill to its best advantage is where the limitation is imposed by your sporting skill. This means that you allow your opponent every opportunity—as defined by the game—to play his or her best.

If you ask athletes what their goal is in playing sport, they may say "winning." This appears to describe the athlete's interest in sport as winning and makes no reference to the manner in which the victory is achieved. Without question, any athlete who respects his or her sport will try his or her best to win whenever he or she plays. However, respect for the game requires that the athlete view winning only as a good if it comes as a result of a particular process: the well-played, well-matched game.

The athlete who honors the game has taken on the interests of the game as his or her own. It is not in the interests of sport to have undeserving competitors win. If it is not in the interests of sport, it is not in the interests of athletes who respect sport.

Winning is important only if it comes to the player or team that has played best on a given day. (And even then, it may be tainted if the teams or competitors are unevenly matched or if one team plays well below its capabilities.) If winning comes as a result of a well-played, evenly-matched game, both the victor and the vanquished can view the win as providing important performance feedback, an essential part of intrinsic motivation.

Because respect for the game entails an understanding of the relationship between a game and its rules, the athlete who respects the game realizes the truth of the logical incompatibility thesis. If one cheats one ceases to play, and if one does not play one cannot win. Because such an athlete values the process of playing, he or she has no motivation to cheat and would not value a victory awarded as a result of any unfairness.

A victory won through cheating is worthless. While a certain amount of luck is part of any sporting contest, there are some situations where the luck all seems to run one way. In such a case the winners would feel that the outcome was not a true representation of the display of skill in the contest. The further a contest is from the model of the ideal described above, the less satisfaction is available for the victor.

The attitude of respect for the game can be seen to lead readily to an attitude toward one's opponents. If one values and seeks the well-played game, one cannot view one's opponents as an obstacle to be overcome in one's drive for victory. Rather, one's opponents are an essential part of one's quest for the well-played game. Not only can an athlete not get what he or she wants without opponents, what is desired cannot be achieved without those opponents playing as well as they are able. Opponents must therefore be seen as co-questors for excellent sport (in Fraleigh's term, *facilitators*). One's competitors share the same goals and hold the same game in the same respect. They must therefore be seen as colleagues and compatriots, not enemies.

Violence outside of the rules is a form of cheating and so would be avoided by any athlete who honors or respects his or her game. Violence within the rules is more difficult. Many games make a virtue of physical strength and power. In these contact sports, an important part of the game may be to inhibit your opponent's actions and movements by means of your physical strength. The critical issue has to concern injury and potential injury. It cannot enhance the game to take an opponent out of the game by injuring him or her (which is, as a matter of fact, precisely the goal of boxing). Intending to injure would thus be unfair and should be avoided. Causing pain is a different matter. It is perfectly legitimate, for instance, to try to disrupt a quarterback's play by tackling him hard but fairly. If his fear of a legitimate but painful tackle causes him to rush his game, your team has fairly gained a tactical edge. Football (and rugby and hockey and wrestling and boxing and many other sports) test physical courage and strength as part of their tests of skill. Fairness as respect for the game does not rule out as unfair games that permit the infliction of pain.

While it could be argued that such sports are barbarous and should be banned or seriously modified, that moral claim operates from outside of the sport rather than from within. As such it is not really an issue of "fair play" at all. The claim would thus need to be made on moral or social policy grounds rather than fair play. This indicates the limitations of the view that fair play is respect for the game. The concept of fair play should not be expected to provide an answer to any and every moral problem that arises in or around the practice of sport. What our approach can do is provide a framework for settling fair play issues that is grounded in the nature of sport itself.

Intimidation needs sport-by-sport analysis. It may be argued that verbal intimidation may have a place in physical sports such as those listed above. Where the intimidation takes the form of boasting about one's physical prowess and the vigorous things you intend to do, and where it takes place within or around the game, it may be unpleasant but not morally reprehensible. Where it takes place outside of the game, or in the context of noncontact sports, it seems far less appropriate. Lumpkin et al. (13) recount the case of a football coach who used to send dead flowers and obituary notices to his team's opponents and another case of tennis players coughing during the opponent's serve or deliberately failing to let their opponents warm up properly. Both examples seem somewhat pathetic, as well as inappropriate. The respect for the game model of fairness can be used to support this feeling. Do these practices enhance the playing of the game? Do they make for better sport? Do they test game-related skills? Quite obviously not, so on the grounds of fair play, they should be avoided.

It is possible to take two quite different views of rule infractions and their penalties. One view says that a rule against, for instance, handling the ball in soccer, means that handling the ball is prohibited, then dictates a penalty (a direct free-kick) if the rule is broken. On this view, a player should not handle the ball. Another view says that handling the ball is generally imprudent (in sporting terms) because the cost—a direct free-kick—normally outweighs any possible benefits. But this is a defeasible condition. In some circumstances, for instance to stop a certain goal near the end of a vital game, the cost, the free-kick, may be worth paying. Such offences, as we discussed earlier, are usually referred to as "professional fouls," and the view that gives rise to them is one that values the outcome over the process of playing.

In effect these two views describe different games. In one game (soccer 1) the players do not consider handling the ball. In the other (soccer 2) handling is always an option to be assessed in light of its consequences. The two games would measure and test different skills, one of which (soccer 2) would be the tactical skill of assessing consequences of rule infractions. (For if this attitude is taken to the rule against handling the ball, it could, presumably, be taken for any rule.) Is the latter game, soccer 2, better, more skillful, more interesting to play and watch than soccer 1? Respect for the game will not dictate an answer, only a process for reasoning. Rules and our attitude toward them are constructed and can be changed. What is required is a debate and a decision that refers to the interests of the game of soccer.

While we cannot lay out this debate in its entirety, we can point to the sorts of arguments that might be raised. Soccer is a game where, relatively speaking, the play is continuous. Allowing players to constantly consider the relative cost of breaking the rule is likely to result in more rule infractions and hence more stoppages. This would change the nature of the game for the worse. Soccer skills include dribbling the ball with the feet and beating opponents. If handling the ball is a constant option (especially outside of the penalty area), traditional soccer skills will become of less value. This will make for less skillful soccer and would be a bad thing. Of course, proponents of soccer 2 may wish to argue that the new attitude will permit the development of new skills—strategic penalty evaluation, for instance, and they will further have to argue that these developments make soccer better. As the debate gets deeper, we will come closer to the heart of what makes soccer the game that it is. We cannot specify the outcome of this debate in advance, but the ground rules for discussion are the nature and interests of soccer itself. The outcome of the debate will be a decision.

Once that decision is made, we have the content of the agreement we enter into when we play. If the soccer community decides soccer 1 is better and promulgates that view, introduces harsher penalties for relevant infractions, and so on, it will not then be open to a player or team to play soccer 2, for that would constitute a breach of the agreement.

Respect for the Game and Racquetless Josie

In our analysis of the inadequacy of the rule- and agreement-based conceptions of fair play, we made use of the example of poor racquetless Josie. By now, it should be obvious that the notion of respect for the game provides ample reasons for lending Josie the racquet. At the personal level, if you respect the game, you enjoy the process of playing, competing, and testing your skills. You are intrinsically motivated to compete at your sport. You would forego a valuable experience and personal test if you decline to play Josie. At a more general level, the sport of squash is enhanced by people playing and competing at their best whenever possible. Squash at the institutional level would not be served by neglecting to play a possible and scheduled match. You should want to lend Josie your racquet.

Unfortunately, we do not have the time in this paper to explore in any depth the connections between our view of fair play and sportspersonship. (While we feel the connections are interesting, we do not feel that our account of fair play stands or falls on its relation to the concept of sportsperson.) In the context of sporting activity itself, we feel that fair play as respect for the game captures the attitude of the sportsperson. Such a person will be committed to the highest possible standards of play—for both himself or herself and his or her opponents. The attitude of the sportsperson is one that subsumes personal interest under the interests of fair and excellent play. This attitude is clearly grounded in our notion of fair play as respect for the game.

But there is more to the concept of the sportsperson than mere fair play and conduct within games. A person may be called a good sport for importing the general claims of morality into a sporting situation and for exporting a game playing attitude outside of sport.

In the latter case, we might call someone a sportsperson if he or she demonstrated the characteristic sporting attitude in situations outside of sport. In this type of case, the person may subsume personal interests under a broader commitment to the task at hand. For instance, to return to the academic example we used above, it would be sporting for someone to pass on information about a job or position to a potential rival. The concern that any qualified person be considered and the hope that the best person get the job is an obvious extension of the principles of fair play as respect for a practice applied outside of sport.

But there is an additional use of the concept sportsperson that does not obviously fit with our model. In cases of this type, the term is applied to someone who imports the general requirements of morality into a sporting situation. For example, in the 1988 Olympics in Seoul a Canadian yachtsman abandoned his race (when apparently, he had an excellent chance of winning a medal) to save another yachtsman in distress. If it was indeed the case that the other man would have died without the intervention, then the action is hardly one of moral heroism. We would all agree that it is right to save a life over completing a race. However, the more likely scenario is that many of us would judge that someone else could have completed the rescue, while we go on. Our hero's actions are good sporting behavior precisely because he was not willing, even in a situation as dramatic as an Olympic final, to allow the increased risk of waiting for someone else to make the rescue. What such a person appears to have is a fine sense of the relative importance of sport. Sport can be all-absorbing, and great sport is always pursued with the utmost dedication and commitment. But in the end, it is not worth a life. It is not clear to us how this sense of sportsperson fits within our model. We do not, however, take this use of sportsperson as a counterexample to our position that fair play can best be understood as respect for the game.

Conclusion

We set out to argue that standard views and treatments of fair play were incoherent and indefensible. Rather than presenting a unified conception of fair play, they either present a shopping cart of miscellaneous values or fail to capture our intuitions.

Respect for the game is a rich and powerful conception of fair play. It captures our intuitive understanding of the concept while providing a fully-worked out philosophical foundation for those intuitions. Respect for the game, rather than presenting ready made solutions to the issues of fair play, provides a process—a process that is grounded in sport—for working out what we should do.

Because of the connection between respect for the game and intrinsic motivation, the concept has its own, sport-based motivations for fairness. Teaching fair play as respect for the game increases intrinsic motivation, and teaching intrinsic motivation enhances fair play. The result is a philosophically credible and practically effective approach to fair play. Fair play as respect for the game is applicable at all levels of sport and readily lends itself to adaptation and implementation in education programs.

One could object that fair play as respect for the game preaches only to the converted. That is, it is applicable only to those who antecedently participate in sport for its own sake. It is true that fair play as respect for the game will resonate most clearly with those who already see sport in this way. We believe, however, that the approach is important even for those who do not currently have this view of sport. Our argument is both moral and psychological. On the moral side we are happy to argue that sport should be participated in for its own sake. Sport is only coherent if it is taken seriously on its own terms. The claims of fair play, however construed, will always be unheeded by those who insist on viewing sport instrumentally. (If one is not interested in sport itself, only the rewards that come from being hailed as the winner, there is no possible reason not to cheat if one thinks one can get away with it.)

From a psychological perspective and as a matter of fact, not only do people typically come to sport for intrinsic reasons, people who continue to play for intrinsic reasons have more fun. Those of us who care about sport and who care about fairness have an obligation to promote a view of sport that sees it practiced for its own sake.

Fair play as respect for the game is philosophy in action. It is an attempt to ground the treatment of actual sporting concerns and issues on philosophically sound foundations. As such it lays itself open to criticism from the members of two practices: sport and philosophy. As practitioners of both disciplines and, as we hope, good sports, we invite your criticism and collaboration as we attempt to make the world a slightly better place—through sport and through philosophy.

Notes

1. Although we do not support this method of understanding fair play, one could certainly do worse than apply the four cardinal virtues: wisdom, courage, justice, and self-control (temperance) to sporting situations.

2. We have made a similar point elsewhere. In *The Ethical Rationale for Drug-Free Sport* (19), we distinguish between arguments for banning doping that work from the "outside-in" and those that work from the "inside-out." The former rely on general moral principles and apply them to the specific issue of doping, while the latter work from principles found in sport itself. There, as here, we prefer the latter.

3. It could also be argued that games not only modify the scope of moral rules by limiting their applicability, but they also create new ways in which one can do moral wrong. On this view, intentionally handling the football during a game of soccer (assuming one is not the goalkeeper) and concealing that one did so, would constitute a moral wrong, one only possible given the rules of the game of soccer. We think that what would constitute the immorality of handling the soccer ball lies in the nature of the agreement of the players to compete. As such, the immorality would come from the general prohibition against breaking one's agreements rather than from soccer, which merely provides the context and content of the agreement.

4. Suits refers to this attitude as *autotelicity* (20).

5. This argument has a long history in ethical discussions of the self-defeating nature of simplistic views of hedonism. See *Reason at Work* (6).

6. Suits refers to this as the "logical incompatibility thesis" (21).

7. We can illustrate this with an example from golf. If, when playing alone, I throw my ball out of the rough, I break a rule of golf but do no moral wrong. (Although, we could say that I stop playing golf and start playing my own, modified version of golf.) If, however, I then tell others what my score was, or if I were playing against other people, without indicating my modification of the rules of golf, I would have committed the moral wrong, in the former case, of misrepresentation or, in the latter, of breaking my agreement to compete.

8. D'Agostino refers to this as the *ethos* of the game (3).

9. For a full account of this kind of discussion see Morgan (15).

10. It could be objected that sports are, in fact, paradigm examples of activities that are inherently worthless. In the grand scheme of things, it is irrelevant whether one can adequately perform a lay-up or put topspin on a backhand. This debate turns on what one takes to be worthwhile. We accept the position that activities that bring pleasure or meaning to lives (provided they are not ruled out on the basis that they cause harm to others) are candidates for being classified as worthwhile. Sports are often such activities.

11. This point applies particularly to the constitutive (and regulative) rules of a sport.

12. It could be objected that only individuals capable of having experiences or sensations are capable of interests at all. In what sense, then, could a practice have interests? At best, on this account, the interests of a practice would be the aggregate of the interests of its practitioners. Obviously we reject this view. The interests of a practice in one sense do derive from the interests of persons. Practices are human enterprises. There would be no such practice if human needs, desires, or preferences were not somehow behind the practice. But a practice takes on a life of its own and has the power to transform the lives and interests of those who participate. When this happens, the practitioner takes on the interests and values of the practice, to the extent sometimes of neglecting or abandoning other aspects of regular human life. A devotee can even sacrifice himself or herself to the practice he or she loves. In this context it is natural and helpful to talk of the interests of a practice.

13. The requirement of universality is included for two reasons. First, if we are considering the good of the game we must assume that innovations be accessible to all practitioners. Second, the contested nature of sport requires that each competitor be permitted to use the same means to achieve the goal of the game.

14. We argue elsewhere (20) that the mere presence of payment does not necessarily obliterate intrinsic motivation.

15. Similar results are also found for college athletes with scholarships. Athletes who were on athletic scholarships listed more extrinsic reasons for playing and expressed less enjoyment of their sports than did college athletes without scholarships.

16. See, for example, Fraleigh's description of a good badminton match (7: pp. 30-33).

17. This list owes much to discussions by both Fraleigh and Kretchmar.

Bibliography

1. Bredemeier, B., and D. Shields. *Character Development and Physical Activity*. Champaign, IL: Human Kinetics, 1994.

2. Czikszentimihalyi, M. *Beyond Boredom and Anxiety*. San Francisco: Jossey-Bass, 1975.

3. D'Agostino, F. "The Ethos of Games." In: *Philosophic Inquiry in Sport*, W. Morgan and K. Meier (Eds.). Champaign, IL: Human Kinetics, 1988, pp. 63-72.

4. Deci, E., and R. Ryan. *Intrinsic Motivation and Self-Determination in Human Behavior*. New York: Plenum, 1985.

5. Feezell, R. "Sportsmanship." In: *Philosophic Inquiry in Sport*, W. Morgan and K. Meier (Eds.). Champaign, IL: Human Kinetics, 1988, pp. 251-262.

6. Feinberg, J. "Psychological Egoism." In: *Reason at Work*, S.M. Cahn, P. Kitcher, and G. Sher (Eds.). San Diego, CA: Harcourt Brace Jovanovich, 1984, pp. 25-35.

7. Fraleigh, W. *Right Actions in Sport: Ethics for Contestants*. Champaign, IL: Human Kinetics, 1984.

8. Keating, J. "Sportsmanship as a Moral Category." In: *Philosophic Inquiry in Sport*, W. Morgan and K. Meier (Eds.). Champaign, IL: Human Kinetics, 1988, pp. 241-250.

9. Kretchmar, S. "From Test to Contest: An Analysis of Two Kinds of Counterpoint in Sport." In: *Philosophic Inquiry in Sport*, W. Morgan and K. Meier (Eds.). Champaign, IL: Human Kinetics, 1988, pp. 223-230.

10. Kretchmar, S. *Practical Philosophy of Sport*. Champaign, IL: Human Kinetics, 1994.

11. Leaman, O. "Cheating and Fair Play in Sport." In: *Philosophic Inquiry in Sport*, W. Morgan and K. Meier (Eds.). Champaign, IL: Human Kinetics, 1988, pp. 277-282.

12. Lehman, C. "Can Cheaters Play the Game?" In: *Philosophic Inquiry in Sport*, W. Morgan and K. Meier (Eds.). Champaign, IL: Human Kinetics, 1988, pp. 283-288.

13. Lumpkin, A., S. Stoll, and J. Beller. *Sport Ethics: Applications for Fair Play*. St. Louis, MO: Mosby, 1994.

14. MacIntyre, A. *After Virtue* (2nd ed.). Nortre Dame, IN: University of Notre Dame Press, 1984.

15. McIntosh, P. *Fair Play: Ethics in Sport and Education*. London: Heinemann, 1979.

16. Morgan, W. "The Logical Incompatibility Thesis and Rules: A Reconsideration of Formalism as an Account of Games." *Journal of the Philosophy of Sport*. 24:1-20, 1997.

17. Morgan, W., and K. Meier. *Philosophic Inquiry in Sport*. Champaign, IL: Human Kinetics, 1988.

18. Pearson, K. "Deception, Sportsmanship, and Ethics." In: *Philosophic Inquiry in Sport*, W. Morgan and K. Meier (Eds.). Champaign, IL: Human Kinetics, 1988, pp. 263-266.

19. Schneider, A., and R. Butcher. *The Ethical Rationale for Drug-Free Sport*. Ottawa, Canada: Canadian Centre for Drug-Free Sport, 1993.

20. Schneider, A., and R. Butcher. "For the Love of the Game: A Philosophical Defense of Amateurism." *Quest*. 45:460-469, 1993.

21. Suits, B. "Words on Play." *Journal of the Philosophy of Sport*. 4:117-131, 1977.

22. Suits, B. *The Grasshopper: Games, Life and Utopia*. Toronto: University of Toronto Press, 1978.

23. Vallerand, R., E. Deci, and R. Ryan. "Intrinsic Motivation in Sport." In: *Exercise and Sport Sciences Reviews* (Vol. 15), K. Pandolf (Ed.). New York: Macmillan, 1987, pp. 398-425.

24. Weiss, M., B. Bredemeier, and R. Shewchuk. "An Intrinsic/Extrinsic Motivation Scale for Youth Sport Settings: A Confirmatory Factor Analysis." *Journal of Sport Psychology*. 7:75-81, 1985.

Sportsmanship As a Moral Category

◆

James W. Keating

Sportsmanship, long and inexplicably ignored by philosophers and theologians, has always pretended to a certain moral relevancy, although its precise place among the moral virtues has been uncertain. In spite of this confusion, distinguished advocates have made some remarkable claims for sportsmanship as a moral category. Albert Camus, Nobel Prize winner for literature in 1957, said that it was from sports that he learned all that he knew about ethics.[1] Former President Hoover is quoted as saying: "Next to religion, the single greatest factor for good in the United States in recent years has been sport."[2] Dr. Robert C. Clothier, past president of Rutgers University, paraphrased the words of Andrew Fletcher and commented: "I care not who makes the laws or even writes the songs if the code of sportsmanship is sound, for it is that which controls conduct and governs the relationships between men."[3] Henry Steele Commager, professor of history at Columbia University, has argued that it was on the playing fields that Americans learned the lessons of courage and honor which distinguished them in time of war. Commager sums up: "In one way or another, this code of sportsmanship has deeply influenced our national destiny."[4] For Lyman Bryson, of Columbia University, sportsmanship was of extraordinary value:

> The doctrine of love is much too hard a doctrine to live by. But this is not to say that we have not made progress. It could be established, I think, that the next best thing to the rule of love is the rule of sportsmanship. . . . Some perspicacious historian will some day write a study of the age-old correlation between freedom and sportsmanship. We may then see the importance of sportsmanship as a form of enlightenment. This virtue, without which democracy is impossible and freedom uncertain, has not yet been taken seriously enough in education.[5]

Reprinted, by permission, from J.W. Keating, 1964, "Sportsmanship as a moral category," *Ethics: An International Journal of Social, Political, and Legal Philosophy* 75(1): 25-35, and published by The University of Chicago Press.

Pope Pius XII, speaking of fair play which is widely regarded as an essential ingredient of sportsmanship, if not synonymous with it, has said:

> From the birthplace of sport came also the proverbial phrase "fair play"; that knightly and courteous emulation which raises the spirit above meanness and deceit and dark subterfuges of vanity and vindictiveness and preserves it from the excesses of a closed and intransigent nationalism. Sport is the school of loyalty, of courage, of fortitude, of resolution and universal brotherhood.[6]

Charles W. Kennedy was a professor of English at Princeton University and chairman of its Board of Athletic Control. His small volume, *Sport and Sportsmanship*, remains to this day probably the most serious study of sportsmanship conducted in America. Kennedy's commitment to sportsmanship was not merely theoretical and scholarly. As chairman of Princeton's Board of Athletic Control, he severed athletic relations with Harvard when unsportsmanlike conduct marred the relationship.[7] For Kennedy it was not sufficient that sportsmanship characterize man's activities on the athletic field; it must permeate all of life.

> When you pass out from the playing fields to the tasks of life, you will have the same responsibility resting upon you, in greater degree, of fighting in the same spirit for the cause you represent. You will meet bitter and sometimes unfair opposition. . . . You will meet defeat (but) you must not forget that the great victory of which you can never be robbed will be the ability to say, when the race is over and the struggle ended, that the flag you fought under was the shining flag of sportsmanship, never furled or hauled down and that, in victory or defeat, you never lost that contempt for a breach of sportsmanship which will prevent your stooping to it anywhere, anyhow, anytime.[8]

Similar eulogies by other distinguished men with no professional or financial interest in sport or athletics could be multiplied without difficulty, but perhaps the point has already been made. The claims for sportsmanship as a moral category deserve some investigation. It is surprising that the experts in moral theory, the philosopher and the theologian, have seen fit to ignore so substantial an area of human conduct as that occupied by sport and athletics.

Three interrelated problems will be considered in this study: (1) the source of the confusion which invariably accompanies a discussion of sportsmanship and the normal consequences resulting from this confusion; (2) the essence of genuine sportsmanship, or the conduct and attitude proper to sport, with special consideration being given to the dominant or pivotal virtues involved; (3) sportsmanship as applied to athletics—a derivative or analogous use of the term. Once again special attention will be directed to the basic or core virtues which characterize the conduct and attitude of the well-behaved athlete.

The Source of Confusion and Its Consequences

What is sportsmanship? William R. Reed, commissioner for the Big Ten Intercollegiate Conference, is most encouraging: "It [sportsmanship] is a word of exact and uncorrupted meaning in the English language, carrying with it an understandable and basic ethical norm. Henry C. Link in his book 'Rediscovery of Morals' says, 'Sportsmanship is probably the clearest and most popular expression of morals.'"[9] Would that this were the case. Reed, however, does not define sportsmanship or enumerate the provisions of its code, and the briefest investigation reveals that he is badly mistaken as to the clarity of the concept. The efforts of no less a champion of sportsmanship than Amos Alonzo Stagg presage the obscurities which lie ahead. In addition to a brilliant athletic career at Yale and forty years as head football coach at the University of Chicago, Stagg did a year of graduate work in Yale's Divinity School and would thus seem to have the ideal background of scholarly training in moral theory and vast practical experience to discuss the problem. Yet his treatment leaves much to be desired. He defined sportsmanship as "a delightful fragrance that people will carry with them in their relations with their fellow men."[10] In addition, he drew up separate codes of sportsmanship, or Ten Commandments of sport, for the coach and for the football player and held that both decalogues were applicable to the business world as well. The second, and by far the most unusual, commandment contained proscriptions seldom found in codes of sportsmanship. "Make your conduct a worthy example. Don't drink intoxicants; don't gamble; don't smoke; don't use smutty language; don't tell dirty stories; don't associate with loose or silly women."[11] Stagg's position is undoubtedly an extreme one, but it calls attention to a tendency all too common among the champions of sportsmanship—the temptation to broaden the concept of sportsmanship until it becomes an all-embracing moral category, a unique road to moral salvation. As always, there is an opposite extreme. Sportsmanship, when not viewed as the pinnacle of moral perfection, can also be viewed as a moral minimum—one step this side of criminal behavior. "A four point program to improve sportsmanship at athletic events has been adopted by the Missouri State High School Activities Association."[12] The first and third provisions of bylaw No. 9 detail penalties for assaults or threats upon officials by players or fans. Such legislative action may be necessary and even admirable, but it is a serious error to confuse the curtailment of criminal activities of this sort with a positive promotion of sportsmanship.

What, then, is sportsmanship? Another approach is by way of the dictionary, everyday experience, and common-sense deductions. Sportsmanship is conduct becoming a sportsman. And who is a sportsman? One who is interested in or takes part in sport. And what is sport? Sport, Webster tells us, is "that which diverts and makes mirth"; it is an "amusement, recreation, pastime." Our problem, then, is to determine the conduct and attitude proper to this type of activity, and this can be done only after a more careful consideration of the nature of sport. Pleasant diversion? Recreation? Amusement? Pastime? Is this how one would describe the World Series, the Masters, the Davis Cup, the Rose Bowl, the Olympic Games, or a high-school basketball tournament? Do the "sport" pages of our newspapers detail the pleasant diversions and amusements of the citizenry, or are they preoccupied with national and international contests which capture the imaginations, the emotions, and the pocketbooks of millions of fans (i.e., fanatics)? It is precisely at this point that we come face to face with the basic problem which has distorted or vitiated most discussions of sportsmanship. Because the term "sport" has been loosely applied to radically different types of human behavior, because it is naïvely regarded as an apt description of (1) activity which seeks only pleasant diversion and, on the other hand, (2) of the agonistic struggle to demonstrate personal or group excellence, the determination of the conduct proper to a participant in "sport" becomes a sticky business indeed. Before proceeding with an analysis of sportsmanship as such, it is necessary to consider briefly an all-important distinction between sport and athletics.

Our dictionary definition of sport leans upon its root or etymological meaning. "Sport," we are told, is an abbreviation of the Middle English *desport* or *disport*, themselves derivatives of the Old French *desporter*, which literally meant to carry away from work. Following this lead, Webster and other lexicographers indicate that "diversion," "recreation," and "pastime" are essential to sport. It is "that which diverts and makes mirth; a pastime." While the dictionaries reflect some of the confusion and fuzziness with which contemporary thought shrouds the concept of athletics, they invariably stress an element which, while only accidentally associated with sport, is essential to athletics. This element is the prize, the *raison d être* of athletics. Etymologically, the various English forms of the word "athlete" are derived from the Greek verb *athlein*, "to contend for a prize," or the noun *athlos*, "contest" or *athlon*, a prize awarded for the successful completion of the contest. An oblique insight into the nature of athletics is obtained when we realize that the word "agony" comes from the Greek *agonia*—a contest or a struggle for victory in the games. Thus we see that, historically and etymologically, sport and athletics have characterized radically different types of human activity, different not insofar as the game itself or the mechanics or rules are concerned, but different with regard to the attitude, preparation, and purpose of the participants. Man has probably always desired some release or diversion from the sad and serious side of life. This, of course, is a luxury, and it is only when a hostile environment is brought under close rein and economic factors provide a modicum of leisure that such desires can be gratified. In essence, sport is a kind of diversion which has for its direct and immediate end fun, pleasure, and delight and which is dominated by a spirit of moderation and generosity. Athletics, on the other hand, is essentially a competitive activity, which has for its end victory in the contest and which is characterized by a spirit of dedication, sacrifice, and intensity.

When this essential distinction between sport and athletics is ignored, as it invariably is, the temptation to make sportsmanship an all-embracing moral category becomes irresistible for most of its champions. In 1926 a national Sportsmanship Brotherhood was organized for the purpose of spreading the gospel of sportsmanship throughout all aspects of life, from childhood games to international events.[13] Its code consisted of eight rules:

1. Keep the rule.
2. Keep faith with your comrades.
3. Keep yourself fit.
4. Keep your temper.
5. Keep your play free from brutality.
6. Keep pride under in victory.
7. Keep stout heart in defeat.
8. Keep a sound soul and a clean mind in a healthy body.

The slogan adopted by the Brotherhood to accompany its code was "Not that you won or lost—but how you played the game." In giving vigorous editorial support to the Sportsmanship Brotherhood, the *New York Times* said:

> Take the sweet and the bitter as the sweet and bitter come and always "play the game."
> That is the legend of the true sportsmanship, whether on the ball field, the tennis court,
> the golf course, or at the desk or machine or throttle. "Play the game." That means

truthfulness, courage, spartan endurance, self-control, self-respect, scorn of luxury, consideration one for another's opinions and rights, courtesy, and above all fairness. These are the fruits of the spirit of sportsmanship and in them . . . lies the best hope of social well-being.[14]

Dictionaries that have suggested the distinction between sport and athletics without explicitly emphasizing it have remained relatively free from this type of romantic incrustation and moral exaggeration in their treatment of sportsmanship. Beginning with nominal definitions of sportsmanship as the conduct becoming a sportsman and of the sportsman as one who participates in sport, they proceed, much more meaningfully, to characterize the sportsman by the kind of conduct expected of him. A sportsman is "a person who can take loss or defeat without complaint or victory without gloating and who treats his opponents with fairness, generosity and courtesy." In spite of the limitations of such a description, it at least avoids the inveterate temptation to make sportsmanship a moral catch-all.

The Essence of Genuine Sportsmanship

Sportsmanship is not merely an aggregate of moral qualities comprising a code of specialized behavior; it is also an attitude, a posture, a manner of interpreting what would otherwise be only a legal code. Yet the moral qualities believed to comprise the code have almost monopolized consideration and have proliferated to the point of depriving sportsmanship of any distinctiveness. Truthfulness, courage, spartan endurance, self-control, self-respect, scorn of luxury, consideration one for another's opinions and rights, courtesy, fairness, magnanimity, a high sense of honor, co-operation, generosity. The list seems interminable. While the conduct and attitude which are properly designated as sportsmanlike may reflect many of the above-mentioned qualities, they are not all equally basic or fundamental. A man may be law-abiding, a team player, well conditioned, courageous, humane, and the possessor of *sangfroid* without qualifying as a sportsman. On the other hand, he may certainly be categorized as a sportsman without possessing spartan endurance or a scorn of luxury. Our concern is not with those virtues which *might* be found in the sportsman. Nor is it with those virtues which *often* accompany the sportsman. Our concern is rather with those moral habits or qualities which are essential, which characterize the participant as a sportsman. Examination reveals that there are some that are pivotal and absolutely essential; others peripheral. On what grounds is such a conclusion reached? Through the employment of the principle that the nature of the activity determines the conduct and attitudes proper to it. Thus, to the extent that the conduct and attitudes of the participants contribute to the attainment of the goal of sport, to that extent they can be properly characterized as sportsmanlike. The primary purpose of sport is not to win the match, to catch the fish or kill the animal, but to derive pleasure from the attempt to do so and to afford pleasure to one's fellow participants in the process. Now it is clear that the combined presence of such laudable moral qualities as courage, self-control, co-operation, and a spirit of honor do not, in themselves, produce a supporting atmosphere. They may be found in both parties to a duel or in a civil war. But generosity and magnanimity are essential ingredients in the conduct and attitude properly described as sportsmanlike. They establish and maintain the unique social bond; they guarantee that the purpose of sport—the immediate pleasure of the participants—will not be sacrificed to other more selfish ends. All the prescriptions which make up the code of sportsmanship are derived from this single, basic, practical maxim: Always conduct yourself in such a manner that you will increase rather than detract from the pleasure to be found in the activity, both your own and that of your fellow participants. If there is disagreement as to what constitutes sportsmanlike behavior, then this disagreement stems from the application of the maxim rather than from the maxim itself. It is to be expected that there will be differences of opinion as to how the pleasurable nature of the activity can best be maximized.

The code governing pure sport is substantially different from a legalistic code in which lawyers and law courts are seen as a natural and healthy complement of the system. In fact, it is in direct comparison with such a system that the essence of sportsmanship can best be understood. In itself, sportsmanship is a spirit, an attitude, a manner or mode of interpreting an otherwise purely legal code. Its purpose is to protect and cultivate the festive mood proper to an activity whose primary purpose is pleasant diversion, amusement, joy. The sportsman adopts a cavalier attitude toward his personal rights under the code; he prefers to be magnanimous and self-sacrificing if, by such conduct, he contributes to the enjoyment of the game. The sportsman is not in search of legal justice; he prefers to be generous whenever generosity will contribute to the fun of the occasion. Never in search of ways to evade the rules, the sportsman acts only from unquestionable moral right.

Our insistence that sport seeks diversion, recreation, amusement does not imply that the sportsman is by nature a listless competitor. It is common practice for him, once the game is under way, to make a determined effort to win. Spirited competitor that he often is, however, his goal is joy in the activity itself and anything—any word, action, or attitude—which makes the game itself less enjoyable should be eliminated. He "fights" gallantly to win because experience has taught him that a determined effort to overcome the obstacles which his particular sport has constructed adds immeasurably to the enjoyment of the game. He would be cheating himself and robbing the other participants of intense pleasure if his efforts were only halfhearted. Yet there is an important sense in which sporting activity is not competitive but rather co-operative. Competition denotes the struggle of two parties for the same valued object or objective and implies that, to the extent that one of the parties is successful in the struggle, he gains exclusive or predominant possession of that object at the expense of his competitor. But the goal of sporting activity, being the mutual enjoyment of the participants, cannot even be understood in terms of exclusive possession by one of the parties. Its simulated competitive atmosphere camouflages what is at bottom a highly co-operative venture. Sport, then, is a co-operative endeavor to maximize pleasure or joy, the immediate pleasure or joy to be found in the activity itself. To so characterize sport is not to indulge in romantic exaggeration. It is indisputable that the spirit of selfishness is at a very low ebb in genuine sport. Gabriel Marcel's observation concerning the relationship of generosity to joy may even have a limited applicability here. "If generosity enjoys its own self it degenerates into complacent self-satisfaction. This enjoyment of self is not joy, for joy is not a satisfaction but an exaltation. It is only in so far as it is introverted that joy becomes enjoyment."[15] In comparison with sport, athletics emphasize self-satisfaction and enjoyment; sport is better understood in terms of generosity, exaltation, and joy.

Although there is no acknowledgment of the fact, the concern which has been shown for sportsmanship by most of its advocates has been almost exclusively directed to its derivative meaning—a code of conduct for athletes. To the extent that the Sportsmanship Brotherhood was concerned with athletics (and their code of conduct would indicate that was their main concern), their choice of a slogan seems singularly inappropriate. "Not that you won or lost—but how you played the game." Such a slogan can be accommodated in the world of sport, but even there the word "enjoyed" should be substituted for the word "played." Application of this slogan to athletics, on the other hand, would render such activity unintelligible, if not irrational.

"Sportsmanship" in Athletics

Careful analysis has revealed that sport, while speaking the language of competition and constantly appearing in its livery, is fundamentally a co-operative venture. The code of the sportsman, sportsmanship, is directed fundamentally to facilitating the co-operative effort and removing all possible barriers to its development. Mutual generosity is a most fertile soil for co-operative activity. When we move from sport to athletics, however, a drastic change takes place. Co-operation is no longer the goal. The objective of the athlete demands exclusive possession. Two cannot share in the same victory unless they are teammates, and, as a result, the problems of competition are immediately in evidence. "Sportsmanship," insofar as it connotes the behavior proper to the athlete, seeks to place certain basic limitations on the rigors of competition, just as continual efforts are being made to soften the impact of the competitive struggle in economics, politics, international relations, etc. But we must not lose sight of an important distinction. Competition in these real-life areas is condoned or encouraged to the extent that it is thought to contribute to the common good. It is not regarded as an end in itself but as the only or most practicable means to socially desirable ends. Friedrich A. Hayek, renowned economist and champion of competition in economics, supports this position:

> The liberal argument is in favor of making the best possible use of the forces of competition as a means of co-ordinating human efforts, not an argument for leaving things just as they are. It is based on the conviction that, where effective competition can be created, it is a better way of guiding individual efforts than any other. It does not deny, but even emphasizes, that, in order that competition should work beneficially, a carefully thought-out legal framework is required and that neither the existing nor the past legal rules are free from grave defects. Nor does it deny that, where it is impossible to create the conditions necessary to make competition effective, we must resort to other methods of guiding economic activity.[16]

A code which seeks to mitigate the full force of the competitive conflict can also be desirable in athletics. While an athlete is in essence a prizefighter, he seeks to demonstrate his excellence in a contest governed by rules which acknowledge human worth and dignity. He mistakes his purpose and insults his opponent if he views the contest as an occasion to display generosity and magnanimity. To the extent that sportsmanship in athletics is virtuous, its essence consists in the practice of fairness under most difficult conditions. Since the sportsman's primary objective is the joy of the moment, it is obvious from that very fact that he places no great emphasis on the importance of winning. It is easy for him to be modest in victory or gracious in defeat and to play fair at all times, these virtues being demonstrated under optimum conditions for their easy exercise. The strange paradox of sportsmanship as applied to athletics is that it asks the athlete, locked in a deadly serious and emotionally charged situation, to act outwardly as if he were engaged in some pleasant diversion.

After an athlete has trained and sacrificed for weeks, after he has dreamed of victory and its fruits and literally exhausted himself physically and emotionally in its pursuit—after all this—to ask him to act with fairness in the contest, with modesty in victory, and an admirable composure in defeat is to demand a great deal, and, yet, this is the substance of the demand that "sportsmanship" makes upon the athlete.

For the athlete, being a good loser is demonstrating self-control in the face of adversity. A festive attitude is not called for; it is, in fact, often viewed as in bad taste. The purists or rigorists are of the opinion that a brief period of seclusion and mourning may be more appropriate. They know that, for the real competitor, defeat in an important contest seems heartbreaking and nerve-shattering. The athlete who can control himself in such circumstances demonstrates remarkable equanimity. To ask that he enter into the festive mood of the victory celebration is to request a Pagliacci-like performance. There is no need for phony or effusive displays of congratulations. A simple handshake demonstrates that no personal ill-will is involved. No alibis or complaints are offered. No childish excuses about the judgment of officials or the natural conditions. No temper tantrums. To be a good loser under his code, the athlete need not be exactly gracious in defeat, but he must at least "be a man" about it. This burden, metaphorically characterized as sportsmanship, bears heavily upon all athletes—amateur or professional. But there are added complications for the professional. Victories, superior performances, and high ratings are essential to financial success in professional athletics. Too frequent defeat will result in forced unemployment. It is easy, therefore, for a professional athlete to view his competitors with a jaundiced eye; to see them as men who seek to deprive him of his livelihood. Under these circumstances, to work daily and often intimately with one's competitors and to compete in circumstances which are highly charged with excitement and emotion, while still showing fairness and consideration, is evidence of an admirable degree of self-mastery.

Attempts have been made to identify sportsmanship with certain games which, it is contended, were the private preserve of the gentleman and, as a result, reflect his high code of honor.

> Bullying, cheating, "crabbing" were all too common in every form of sport. The present movement away from muckerism probably should be attributed in large measure to the growing popularity of golf and tennis. Baseball, boxing, and many of our common sports trace their origin to the common people who possessed no code of honor. On the other hand, golf and tennis, historically gentlemen's games, have come down to us so interwoven with a high code of honor that we have been forced to accept the code along with the game. . . . The effect of the golf code upon the attitude of the millions who play the game is reflected in all our sports.[17]

It is true that in England the terms "gentleman," "sportsman," and "amateur" were regarded as intimately interrelated. The contention that the common people, and consequently the games that were peculiarly theirs, had no comparable code of honor may be correct, but it awaits the careful documentation of some future social historian. One thing is certain, however, and that is that there is nothing in the nature of any game, considered in itself, that necessarily implies adherence to a moral code. Some games like golf and tennis in which the participants do their own officiating provide greater opportunity for the practice of honesty, but if a high code of honor surrounds the "gentleman's games," it is due principally to the general attitude of the gentleman toward life rather than to anything intrinsic to the game itself. The

English gentleman was firmly committed to sport in the proper sense of that term and eschewed the specialization, the rigors of precontest preparation, the secret strategy sessions, and professional coaching which have come to be regarded as indispensable for the athlete. "The fact that a man is born into the society of gentlemen imposes upon him the duties and, to some extent, the ideas of his class. He is expected to have a broad education, catholic tastes, and a multiplicity of pursuits. He must not do anything for pecuniary gain; and it will be easily seen that he must not specialize. It is essentially the mark of the bourgeois' mind to specialize."[18] Moreover, "too much preparation is contrary to all English ethics, and secrecy in training is especially abhorrent. Remember that sport is a prerogative of gentlemen. And one of the earmarks of a gentleman is that he resort to no trickery and that he plays every game with his cards on the table—the game of life as well as the game of football."[19]

It is the contestant's objective and not the game itself which becomes the chief determinant of the conduct and attitudes of the players. If we take tennis as an example and contrast the code of conduct employed by the sportsman with that of the athlete in the matter of officiating, the difference is obvious. The sportsman invariably gives his opponent the benefit of the doubt. Whenever he is not sure, he plays his opponent's shot as good even though he may suspect that it was out. The athlete, however, takes a different approach. Every bit as opposed to cheating as the sportsman, the athlete demands no compelling proof of error. If a shot seems to be out, even though he is not certain, the athlete calls it that way. He is satisfied that his opponent will do the same. He asks no quarter and gives none. As a result of this attitude and by comparison with the sportsman, the athlete will tend toward a legal interpretation of the rules.

The athletic contest is designed to serve a specific purpose—the objective and accurate determination of superior performance and, ultimately, of excellence. If this objective is to be accomplished, then the rules governing the contest must impose the same burdens upon each side. Both contestants must be equal before the law if the test is to have any validity, if the victory is to have any meaning. To the extent that one party to the contest gains a special advantage, unavailable to his opponent, through an unusual interpretation, application, or circumvention of the rules, then that advantage is unfair. The well-known phrase "sense of fair play" suggests much more than an adherence to the letter of the law. It implies that the spirit too must be observed. In the athletic contest there is a mutual recognition that the rules of the game are drawn up for the explicit purpose of aiding in the determination of an honorable victory. Any attempt to disregard or circumvent these rules must be viewed as a deliberate attempt to deprive the contest of its meaning. Fairness, then, is rooted in a type of equality before the law, which is absolutely necessary if victory in the contest is to have validity and meaning. Once, however, the necessary steps have been taken to make the contest a true test of respective abilities, the athlete's sole objective is to demonstrate marked superiority. Any suggestion that fair play obliges him to maintain equality in the contest ignores the very nature of athletics. "If our analysis of fair play has been correct, coaches who strive to produce superior teams violate a fundamental principle of sportsmanship by teaching their pupils, through example, that superiority is more greatly to be desired than is equality in sport. . . . But who today would expect a coach to give up clear superiority—a game won—by putting in enough substitutes to provide fair playing conditions for an opposing team?"[20] Thus understood, sportsmanship would ask the leopard to change its spots.

It rules out, as illegitimate, the very objective of the athlete. Nothing shows more clearly the need for recognition of the distinction between sport and athletics.

Conclusion

In conclusion, we would like to summarize our answers to the three problems set down at the outset.

1. The source of the confusion which vitiates most discussion of sportsmanship is the unwarranted assumption that sport and athletics are so similar in nature that a single code of conduct and similar participant attitudes are applicable to both. Failing to take cognizance of the basic differences between sport and athletics, a futile attempt is made to outline a single code of behavior equally applicable to radically diverse activities. Not only is such an attempt, in the nature of things, doomed to failure but a consequence of this abortive effort is the proliferation of various moral virtues under the flag of sportsmanship, which, thus, loses all its distinctiveness. It is variously viewed as a straight road to moral perfection or an antidote to moral corruption.

2. The goal of genuine sport must be the principal determinant of the conduct and attitudes proper to sporting activity. Since its goal is pleasant diversion—the immediate joy to be derived in the activity itself—the pivotal or essential virtue in sportsmanship is generosity. All the other moral qualities that may also be in evidence are colored by this spirit of generosity. As a result of this spirit, a determined effort is made to avoid all unpleasantness and conflict and to cultivate, in their stead, an unselfish and co-operative effort to maximize the joy of the moment.

3. The essence of sportsmanship as applied to athletics can be determined by the application of the same principle. Honorable victory is the goal of the athlete and, as a result, the code of the athlete demands that nothing be done before, during, or after the contest to cheapen or otherwise detract from such a victory. Fairness or fair play, the pivotal virtue in athletics, emphasizes the need for an impartial and equal application of the rules if the victory is to signify, as it should, athletic excellence. Modesty in victory and a quiet composure in defeat testify to an admirable and extraordinary self-control and, in general, dignify and enhance the goal of the athlete.

Notes

1. *Resistance, Rebellion and Death* (New York: Alfred A. Knopf, Inc., 1961), p. 242.
2. In Frank Leahy, *Defensive Football* (New York: Prentice-Hall, Inc., 1951), p. 198.
3. "Sportsmanship in Its Relation to American Intercollegiate Athletics," *School and Society,* XLV (April 10, 1937), 506.
4. Henry Steele Commager, in *Scholastic,* XLIV (May 8-13, 1944), 7.
5. Lyman Bryson, *Science and Freedom* (New York: Columbia University Press, 1947), p. 130.
6. Pope Pius XII, *The Human Body* (Boston: Daughters of St. Paul, 1960).
7. "Athletic Relations between Harvard and Princeton," *School and Society,* XXIV (November 20, 1926), 631.
8. Charles W. Kennedy, *Sport and Sportsmanship* (Princeton, N.J.: Princeton University Press, 1931), pp. 58-59.

9. William R. Reed, "Big Time Athletics' Commitment to Education," *Journal of Health, Physical Education, and Recreation,* XXXIV (September, 1963), 30.

10. Quoted in J.B. Griswold, "You Don't Have To Be Born with It," *American Magazine,* CXII (November, 1931), 60.

11. *Ibid.,* p. 133.

12. "Sportsmanship," *School Activities,* XXXII (October, 1960), 38.

13. "A Sportsmanship Brotherhood," *Literary Digest,* LXXXVIII (March 27, 1926), 60-61.

14. *Ibid.,* pp. 60-61.

15. Gabriel Marcel, *The Mystery of Being, Vol. II: Faith and Reality* (Chicago: Henry Regnery Co., 1960), pp. 133-34.

16. Friedrich A. Hayek, *The Road to Serfdom* (Chicago: University of Chicago Press, 1944), p. 36.

17. J.F. Williams and W.W. Nixon, *The Athlete in the Making* (Philadelphia: W.B. Saunders, 1932), p. 153.

18. H.J. Whigham, "American Sport from an English Point of View," *Outlook,* XCIII (November, 1909), 740.

19. *Ibid.*

20. Frederick R. Rogers, *The Amateur Spirit in Scholastic Games and Sports* (Albany, N.Y.: C.F. Williams & Son, 1929), p. 78.

Sportsmanship

◆

Randolph M. Feezell

I

There is a movement in contemporary moral philosophy, attempting to return our attention to thinking about the centrality of virtue in the moral life. Until recently the language of virtue had seemingly fallen into disfavor in our 20th-century philosophizing about moral matters. We heard much talk about the naturalistic fallacy, verificationism, the expression of attitudes, prescriptivity, universalizability, the principle of utility, and the like, but little talk about *being* a certain kind of person, having certain dispositions or characteristics that we have always thought to be central to living life in a civilized moral community. In the move toward thinking about lived moral experience, philosophers began talking about issues of pressing social concern, such as abortion, euthanasia, and war. The mistaken impression occasioned in our students and in the community may have been that the return to relevancy, to "real" moral concerns, involved the necessary connection between applied ethics and social ethics. Again, one wonders what happened to the texture of individual moral experience, moral discourse, and moral education, in which we stress the importance of friendliness, compassion, fairness, truthfulness, and reliability. Perhaps an important part of applied ethics involves trying to understand individual virtues. For example, what do we mean or what are we recommending when we speak of aspects of the virtuous life such as compassion or boldness?

In this context I believe it is relevant to think about the virtue of sportsmanship. Sports have a prevalent place in American cultural life, as well as in numerous foreign countries. Spectator sports set attendance records, yet crowd behavior is often atrocious. More adults participate today in sports with differing degrees of seriousness. There are vast numbers of young people playing sports, coming of age morally, as they devote a large amount of time to their athletic endeavors. Impressive claims are made about the role of sports in the development of character and how important

Reprinted, by permission, from R. Feezell, 1986, "Sportsmanship," *Journal of the Philosophy of Sport,* 13: 1-13.

sports are as a preparation for later competitive life. It would be interesting, and indeed important, if one could enlighten us as to what it means to be a good sport. Parents often stress to their children the importance of being a good sport, but it is not apparent what that means.

It should be helpful to start with a few examples before turning to the main arguments of this paper. The paradigm case of a bad sport is the cheater. Consider a high school basketball game. At the end of a close game, a flurry of activity takes place beneath the basket. A foul is called and the coach sees that the referees are confused about who was fouled. He instructs his best foul shooter to go to the free throw line to take the shots although he knows, as does his team and most of the crowd, that another player, a poor foul shooter, was actually fouled. The wrong player makes the free throws and his team wins.[1] In this case the coach has cheated. He has instructed or encouraged his players to cheat, and we would say he is a bad sport or, in this instance at least, whether acting out of character or not, he has acted like a bad sport.[2] He has displayed poor sportsmanship.

Why is the cheater a bad sport? What is wrong with cheating? The answer is not difficult to find. Two teams agreed to play the game of basketball, defined by certain rules that constitute what it means to play basketball. By cheating, the coach intentionally broke a rule, thereby violating the original implied agreement. In this sense cheating is a kind of promise-breaking or violation of a contractual relationship. Notice that the moral reason that explains the wrongness of cheating is not unique to playing basketball; an ordinary moral rule has been broken. In the language of virtue, the coach has been found lacking in trustfulness and integrity. He has attempted to gain an unfair advantage by breaking a rule. Perhaps being a good sport is simply an extension of being a good person—in one sense this is an obvious truism—and the meaning of the virtue of sportsmanship is not unique to the activity in question.

Consider some other examples. The intent to injure would usually be a serious moral violation, but acting in such a way that one *might* injure an opponent is often morally ambiguous. Think of a hockey player fighting or a pitcher in baseball throwing one "under the chin." Should one yell at an opponent in hopes of rattling him? Certainly how one responds to defeat or victory is often thought to be an important part of sportsmanship. Should one ever refuse the traditional handshake after the contest? What about running up the score on an opponent or refusing to give credit due to an opponent who has defeated you? In such cases our judgments are more ambiguous and our explanations less obvious. Certainly no rule is violated when one team runs up the score on another, or when a tennis player continually whines, complains, throws his racket, interrupts play, and questions calls. But we want to say this type of behavior is bad form, somehow inappropriate because it violates the nature of what sport is about.

Is there some essential meaning of the virtue of sportsmanship? How can we unify our concept of sportsmanship? Are some aspects of it more central than others? In this paper I will attempt to respond to these questions. First I will critically discuss James Keating's views. Keating (14) first published his analysis of sportsmanship in 1964, and it has become a standard part of the literature in philosophy of sport.[3] As late as 1978, in the introduction to *Competition and Playful Activities* (13), which contains a revised version of his original paper on sportsmanship, he maintained that his view had not been extensively criticized. In speaking of his views of amateurism, winning, and sportsmanship, he said, "To the best of my knowledge there has been no concerted attack upon any of them in the literature" (13: p. iii). I intend to do just that in this paper. Keating has offered an excellent framework within which to initiate an understanding of sportsmanship, but I do not believe he is correct in radically separating sports and athletics. I will conclude the paper with some more positive, less critical suggestions about sportsmanship.

II

Keating's paper is a valuable resource for a number of reasons, not the least of which is his overview of the many and varied claims made about the nature of sportsmanship. Some have made extraordinary assertions about the importance of this notion, as if it is *the* most important virtue in American cultural life. The interpretations of the essence of sportsmanship have included numerous other virtues: self-control, fair play, truthfulness, courage, endurance, and so forth (13: p. 39-42). Keating attempts to unify our understanding by providing a tidy scheme that shows which virtues are essential and which are of only accidental importance. His argument is simple and compelling. Sportsmanship is the conduct that is becoming to a sportsman, or one who engages in sport, so we simply have to understand what sport is. Here we have the crux of the argument, because the term refers to "radically different types of human activity" (13: p. 43). Keating could not be more emphatic in stressing the extreme separation of sport as playful activity and sport as competitive athletic contests. On three different occasions he speaks of them as "radically different types of human activity," and at one point says (13: p. 47) that "a drastic change takes place" when we move from playful activity to athletics.

What, more precisely, is the distinction? Taking hints from dictionary definitions and etymology, Keating argues that sport refers both to the pleasant diversion of play and to spirited competitive athletic contests. To understand the true meaning of sportsmanship, we must carefully distinguish conduct and attitude appropriate to play and conduct and attitude appropriate to athletics.

> In essence, play has for its direct and immediate end joy, pleasure, and delight and which is dominated by a spirit of moderation and generosity. Athletics, on the other hand, is essentially a competitive activity, which has for its end victory in the contest and which is characterized by a spirit of dedication, sacrifice, and intensity. (13: pp. 43-44)

Thus the virtues of the player are radically different from the virtues of the athlete. Insofar as the activity determines the conduct appropriate to it, the player should conduct himself or herself with an attitude of "generosity and magnanimity," keeping in mind his or her obligation to maximize the pleasure of the event and reinforce the ludic character of the activity. Play is essentially cooperative. On the other hand, the athlete is engaged in a competitive struggle whose end is exclusive possession of victory. In the words of G.J. Warnock (23: Ch. 2), this is a situation in which things have the "inherent tendency to go badly"[4] unless moral restraints are put on the rigors of competition. "Fairness or fair play, the pivotal virtue in athletics, emphasizes the need for an impartial and equal application of the rules, if the victory is to signify, as it should, athletic excellence" (13: p. 52). In athletics, generosity and magnanimity are misplaced, as they supposedly are in other areas of life that are essentially competitive. Your opponent expects only that you fairly pursue your self-interest, not that you are to be interested in his or her goal, for you cannot be. Victory is the *telos* of the activity and an exclusive possession. Once the contest ends, the athlete, like the victor or vanquished in war, should face victory or defeat with modesty or a strength of composure.

Since Keating's view of sportsmanship depends so heavily on the sharp distinction between sport as playful activity and sport as athletic competition, we should look more closely at that distinction. How does Keating arrive at it? He begins by citing Webster's definition of sport as "diversion," "amusement," and "recreation." However, since so many sporting events (he mentions, among others, the World Series, the Davis Cup, and even a high school basketball tournament) would be inaccurately described in these terms, there must be another important sense given to this notion. Etymologically, the English forms of the word "athlete" suggest the centrality of contest and the struggle for excellence and victory, so sport, he concludes, must refer to "radically different types of human activity." Although there might already be something misleading about placing such emphasis on etymology and dictionary definitions, the distinction ultimately is a phenomenological one. We should look at lived experience for the basis of the distinction, for play and athletics are radically different "not insofar as the game itself or the mechanics or rules are concerned, but different with regard to the attitude, preparation, and purpose of the participants" (13: p. 43). Now curiosities arise, of a logical, psychological, and moral nature.

Consider one of Keating's own examples, a high school basketball tournament. Suppose Team A is coached by Smith, who views sport as little short of war. The opponent is the enemy, who must be hated and scorned in order to produce maximum intensity and effort. Practices and games are pervaded by a spirit of overarching seriousness. He yells at his players and at referees. He never lets up because he views sport as real life or, if not quite like real life, of great importance as preparation for the harshness of the "real" world. There is a certain ruthlessness in his pursuit of victory and anything goes, short of outright cheating, although even here he is inclined to think that it's all right if you don't get caught. For example, he wouldn't hesitate to run up the score if it might enhance his team's rating and its future tournament seeding. He expects no less from his opponent.

On the other hand, Team B is coached by Jones, whose whole approach to basketball is fundamentally different. He is also a spirited competitor who instills in his player–athletes the value of excellent performance and victory. However, he never forgets that basketball is a game, an arbitrary construction of rule-governed activities invented in order to make possible an intrinsically satisfying activity.[5] For Jones there is always something magical about the world of basketball, with its special order, its special spatial and temporal rhythms. It is set apart from the concerns of ordinary reality. To play and coach basketball is to engage in joyful activities, and the pleasure is increased by improving skills, being" challenged to perform well, inventing strategies, and achieving one's goals. He sees the opponent not as an enemy but as a friendly competitor whose challenge is necessary to enhance the pleasurable possibilities of his own play. He realizes it is difficult to sustain the spirit of play within spirited competition, but that is his goal. His seriousness about the pursuit of victory is always mediated by an awareness that basketball is just a game, valuable for the moment, whose value consists primarily in the intrinsic enjoyment of the activity. Fun is an essential element in his understanding of sport.

Are these two coaches engaged in fundamentally different human activities? The example suggests that Keating's distinction is plausible. In one sense, the coaches' attitudes are so dissimilar that we want to say they are engaged in different activities. But the most important question here is moral, not psychological. I see no reason to take Smith's attitudes as normative. Although the picture of Smith may appear to be overdrawn, it is undoubtedly a correct description of the understanding and attitudes some people have regarding sport. However, it doesn't follow that their attitudes are correct. Keating's argument is logically curious. Recall that play and athletics have been characterized as being radically different with regard to attitudes, but later he states (13: p. 44) that "the nature of the activity determines the conduct and attitudes proper to it." Without further clarification, this appears to be circular and uninformative concerning how our original attitudes toward sport should be formed. I would say that Smith has an impoverished view of sport, an impoverished experience of sport, and it is just such views and attitudes that tend to generate unsportsmanlike behavior in sport.

There are two main problems with Keating's analysis, vitiating his account of sportsmanship. First, because he takes his understanding of play simply from Webster's definition of sport as "diversion," "amusement," and "recreation," he fails to describe adequately the nature of play so as to understand how sport could be seen as an extension of play. Second, and probably because of his limited clarification of play, he incorrectly ascribes a false exclusivity to the psychology of the player and the athlete. The latter point will be discussed first.

The player and the athlete are to be radically distinguished supposedly on the grounds that they differ with regard to attitude, preparation, and purpose. The previous example made such a distinction plausible, but failed to show why one set of attitudes should be normative. In numerous other cases, however, the distinction is difficult if not impossible to make, precisely because the attitudes of the participants are mixed. Consider an ex-college basketball player engaged in a pickup game. Is this person a player or an athlete? What virtues should characterize his conduct? On Keating's model it would be difficult to say. Suppose the basketball player intends to play well, puts out maximum effort, competes hard, and pursues victory. Why? Because he still loves the game and still enjoys the competitive play, the very feel of the activity.

Each game is a unity, the development of a totality with its own finality. Something is at issue, and this is an arena in which the issue at hand will be decisively resolved. He finds the dramatic tensions satisfying, as well as the frolicking nature of running, jumping, and responding to the physical presence of other players. He enjoys the sheer exuberance of the experience. He is serious about his play because such seriousness enhances the activity and heightens the experience. He is serious because the internal logic of the activity demands the pursuit of victory, yet he realizes that in a profound sense his seriousness is misplaced. It doesn't really matter who wins the game, although it does matter that the festivity occurs. Such an attitude toward the pursuit of victory acts as an inner negation of his original seriousness and produces moderation. One might go on here with an extended phenomenological account, but the point is already clear. His attitudes and purposes are extraordinarily complex. He is simultaneously player and athlete. His purpose is to win the contest *and* to experience the playful and aesthetic delights of the experience. His attitudes are at once both playful and competitive, and these color his relationship with his fellow participants. He sees his opponent as both competitor and friend, competing and cooperating at the same time. These are the attitudes that guide his conduct.

Such a fusion of attitudes and purposes may be unsatisfying to some, but I think such a picture of the player–athlete is a truer one than the one offered by Keating. His radical distinction between play and athletics is an excellent example of what Richard Taylor calls polarized thinking. In the context of showing how such thinking leads to metaphysical puzzlement or confusion he says the following:

There is a common way of thinking that we can call *polarization,* and that appears to be the source of much metaphysics. It consists of dividing things into two exclusive categories, and then supposing that if something under consideration does not belong to one of them, then it must belong in the other. "Either/or" is the pattern of such thought, and because it is usually clear, rigorous, and incisive, it is also often regarded by philosophers as exclusively rational. (21: p. 106)

Such sharpness and precision are sometimes bought at the expense of truth, for reality is far too loose a mixture of things to admit of such absolute distinctions, and sometimes, both in our practical affairs and in our philosophy, we are led into serious errors, which are fervently embraced just because they seem so clearly to have been proved. (21: p. 107)

Keating offers only one extended example to show what his polarized view of sportsmanship would look like in practice, and his conclusions are odd.

It is the contestant's objective and not the game itself which becomes the chief determinant of the conduct and attitudes of the players. If we take tennis as an example and contrast the code of conduct employed by the player with that of the athlete in the matter of officiating, the difference is obvious. The player invariably gives the opponents the benefit of any possible doubt. Whenever he is not certain, he plays his opponent's shot as good even though he may believe it was out. The athlete, however, takes a different approach. Every bit as opposed to cheating as the sportsman, the athlete demands no compelling proof of error. If a shot seems to be out, the athlete calls it that way. He is satisfied that his opponent will do the same. He asks no quarter and gives none. As a result of this attitude by comparison with the player, the athlete will tend toward a legal interpretation of the rules. (13: p, 50)

I have played tournament tennis and find this example not only unconvincing, it is simply inaccurate in some respects. It bears little comparison to my own experience and that of those with whom I play. First, based on Keating's model, it would be impossible for me to know whether I am a player or an athlete in the context of my tennis playing. I should say I am both, since I compete for victory, but also find great fun in the activity and recognize my opponent as a partner of sorts. Moreover, the conventions of tennis render Keating's example misleading and of little value in helping us to understand sportsmanship. If one is not certain that a ball is out, one plays it. *Only* if one is sure the ball is out is it to be called out. If a call is made but disagreement arises, a let is called and the point is replayed. Giving the benefit of the doubt to the opponent isn't generosity here; it is simply recognizing the relevant conventions. Actually, Keating's description of the so-called athlete sounds suspiciously like an example of bad sportsmanship, since such a person's zeal in the pursuit of victory ignores the unwritten rules of playing without officials and tends to destroy the spirit of play. A more playful spirit would mediate against a zealousness that fuels inappropriate conduct and an ignoring of the rules.

The other main problem with Keating's view of sportsmanship is his account of the nature of play and its relationship to sport. Such a topic demands an extended treatment, and I have attempted to do this elsewhere.[6] Briefly, the most accurate and inclusive phenomenological accounts of experience in sport are those which focus on the nature of play and which show, either explicitly or implicitly, that sport is a formal, competitive variety of human play.[7] I agree with Kenneth Schmitz when he says (18: p. 22) that "sport is primarily an extension of play, and that it rests upon and derives its central values from play." Huizinga's classic account of play stresses that it is an activity freely engaged in when someone metaphorically "steps out" of ordinary life and becomes absorbed in an alternative world of play, with its own order and meaning, constituted by its own rules, experiential rhythms, traditions, tensions, and illusory quality. He also stresses the element of fun as essential. He sums up his account in the following passage:

> Summing up the formal characteristics of play we might call it a free activity standing quite consciously outside "ordinary" life as being "not serious," but at the same time absorbing the player intensely and utterly. It is an activity connected with no material interest, and no profit can be gained by it. It proceeds within its own proper boundaries of time and space according to fixed rules and in an orderly manner. (10: p. 13)

Schmitz (18: p. 23) strengthens the analysis of play by distinguishing four types: frolic, make-believe, sporting skills, and games. The movement from frolic to sport is a continuum from less formal, spontaneous, animal-like behavior to more formal activities guided by rules, in which knowledge, preparation, and understanding are called for. In all forms, Schmitz, like Huizinga, stresses the movement from the ordinary to the world of play by a free decision to play. "Such a constitutive decision cannot be compelled and is essentially free. Through it arises the suspension of the ordinary concerns of the everyday world" (18: pp. 24-25). Such a decision constitutes an act of transcendence beyond the natural world, in which a new totality is opened, and experienced with a sense of exhilaration and celebration. Schmitz compares the transcendence of play with religion and art. Also akin to Huizinga's account, Schmitz stresses, especially for the more formal varieties of play, the new order of the world of play with its new forms of space, time, and behavior. It is a "transnatural, fragile, limited perfection . . . delivering its own values in and for itself, the freedom and joy of play" (18: p. 26). Finally, Schmitz (18: p. 26) argues that it is a "distinctive mode of being. It is a way of taking up the world of being, a manner of being present in the world . . . whose existential presence is a careless joyful freedom."

The problem for the play-theorist of sport is how to connect such a striking description of play with sport. Many think, as Keating seems to, that this account necessarily excludes essential elements of sport, including the striving for excellence and good performance and contesting for victory. But the strength of the play theory of sport is the way in which it can provide both a rich phenomenological account of the experience of play within sports and an explanation of the prominence and appropriate value of good performance and victory. No one would deny that the pursuit of victory is essential in sport; after all, a contest is not mere frolic. But why *do* so many engage in sport? Why do we create our games and begin and continue to play them? The critics of sport give us an important perspective here when they wonder why so many people become obsessed with things like hitting a ball with a wooden stick, or throwing a ball into a hoop, or clubbing a little ball around expansive fairways. They can understand why children, lacking maturity and experience, could enjoy the exuberance of such activities. But grown people? Compared with suffering, friendship, and possible nuclear annihilation because of deep-rooted human conflicts, playing games and treating them with utmost seriousness seems silly. Bernard Suits brings this out well in attempting to define game-playing.

> it is generally acknowledged that games are in some sense essentially non-serious. We must therefore ask in what sense games are, and in what sense they are not, serious. What is believed when it is believed that games are not serious? Not, certainly, that the players of games always take a very light-hearted view of what they are doing. A

> bridge player who played his cards randomly might justly be accused of failing to play the game at all just because of his failure to take it seriously. It is much more likely that the belief that games are not serious means what the proposal under consideration implies: that there is always something in life more important than playing the game, or that a game is the kind of thing that a player could always have reason to stop playing. (20: p. 14)

The important insight here is that the "nonseriousness" at the heart of play is based on the recognition that there are obviously more important vales in life than the value of improving sporting skills and winning games. A correct attitude concerning sport would place these values in an appropriate hierarchy. Suits goes on to deny such nonseriousness as the essence of game-playing on the grounds that one could take a game so seriously as to consider it supremely important, taking over one's whole life and forcing one to avoid other duties. But his point is psychological, not moral. Undoubtedly someone *could* have such an attitude but ought not. Suits sees this clearly:

> Supreme dedication to a game . . . may be repugnant to nearly everyone's moral sense. That may be granted; indeed insisted upon, since our loathing is excited by the very fact that it is a game which has usurped the place of ends we regard as so much more worthy of pursuit. (20: p. 15)

Suits concludes his attempt to define game-playing by arguing (20: p. 17) that when we play a game we accept the arbitrary way in which means are used to achieve certain ends—for example in golf our goal is not just to put the ball in the hole but to do it in an extraordinarily limited way—because we simply want to make the activity possible. Evidently such activity, without external practical ends, is intrinsically satisfying.[8]

This analysis leads us to a point where we can see the attitudinal complexity of the player—athlete. We might distinguish between internal and external seriousness. The activity of playful competition calls for pursuit of victory. As Suits suggested, if someone isn't serious in this sense he might be accused of not playing the game at all. On the other hand, there is an external perspective from which the internal seriousness of competition is mediated by an awareness that the activity is a form of play, infused with its own values and qualified by the values of life outside the play-world. The activity engaged in is both competition and play, serious and nonserious. This is the understanding of the activity that gives rise to a more adequate understanding of sportsmanship. The spirit of play may be absent within sport, but it ought not to be if, as has been argued, sport is intimately and in some sense originally related to the playful activity of game-playing. Once again Schmitz offers helpful comments:

> sport can be carried out without the spirit of play. Nevertheless, in the life of individuals and in the history of the race, sport emerges from play as from an original and founding posture. Sport is free, self-conscious, tested play which moves in a transnatural dimension of human life, built upon a certain basis of leisure. . . . There is certainly a return to seriousness in the discipline of formal sport. There is training, performance and competition. But the objectives of sport and its founding decision lie within play and cause sport to share in certain of its features—the sense of immediacy, exhilaration, rule-directed behavior, and the indeterminacy of a specified outcome. (18: p. 27)

Let us turn now to a positive account of the virtue of sportsmanship.

III

In my view, instead of a rigid and precise distinction between play and athletics, we must be content with a fuzzy picture of the fusion of these activities, a picture in which edges are blurred and complexity of attitudes is retained. Keating's view embraces tidiness at the cost of truth. Still we want to ask, What is the essence of sportsmanship? I tend to think that the question is misleading and the phenomenon is dispersed in our experience in innumerable particular instances. We ought to be hesitant about attributing to this notion an abstract unity that is not found in experience. Wittgenstein's admonition that we ought to be suspicious of such talk and appeal to particular cases is well taken here, as always. However, if we view sport as an extension of human play, we can offer an understanding of the virtue of sportsmanship that will be somewhat more satisfying intellectually, although it will not always generate easily purchased moral recommendations. This shouldn't surprise us.

Keating is right to see that we must understand sportsmanship as conduct flowing from our attitudes, and he is correct in attempting to describe the attitudes appropriate to sport. He is simply incorrect about the attitudes. If sport is understood as an extension of play, then the key to sportsmanship is the spirit of play. Within the arena of competition the play-spirit should be retained. It would be helpful to think of this in Aristotelian terms. Recall Aristotle's description of virtue:

> By virtue I mean virtue of character; for this pursues the mean because it is concerned with feelings and actions, and these admit of excess, deficiency and an intermediate condition. We can be afraid, e.g., or be confident, or have appetites, or get angry, or feel pity, in general have pleasure or pain, both too much and too little, and in both ways not well; but having these feelings at the right times, about the right things, toward the right people, for the right end, and in the right way, is the intermediate and best condition, and this is proper to virtue. Similarly, actions also admit of excess, deficiency and the intermediate condition. (1: 1106b)

In fact, Aristotle's description of the virtuous person reinforces the previous attempt to ascribe a certain psychological complexity to the player–athlete. The courageous or brave person, according to Aristotle (1: 1107), is neither excessively fearful, else he would be a coward, or excessively confident, else he would be foolhardy and rash. He feels appropriately fearful, which moderates his confidence, and he feels appropriately confident, which moderates his fear. His virtuous acts are expressions of such moderation and a result of experience and habit. Likewise, the good sport feels the joy and exuberance of free, playful activity set apart from the world, and feels the intensity of striving to perform well and achieve victory. Sportsmanship is a mean between excessive seriousness, which misunderstands the importance of the play-spirit, and an excessive sense of playfulness, which might be called frivolity and which misunderstands the importance of victory and achievement when play is competitive. The good sport is both serious and nonserious, in a sense which by now should be understandable.

Many, if not most, examples of bad sportsmanship arise from an excessive seriousness that negates the play-spirit because of an exaggerated emphasis on the value of victory. Schmitz has a superb comment on such exaggeration:

> The policy of winning at all costs is the surest way of snuffing out the spirit of play in sport. The fallout of such a policy is the dreary succession of firings in college and professional sport. Such an emphasis on victory detaches the last moment from the whole

game and fixes the outcome apart from its proper context. It reduces the appreciation of the performance, threatens the proper disposition towards the rules and turns the contest into a naked power struggle. The upshot is the brutalization of the sport. And so, the sport which issued from the play-decision, promising freedom and exhilaration, ends dismally in lessening the humanity of players and spectators. (18: pp. 27-28)

Such exaggeration of victory goes hand in hand with the way we view our relationship to our opponents. The play-spirit will moderate, not negate, the intensity with which we pursue victory, and will introduce a spirit of friendship and cooperation in what would otherwise be a "naked power struggle."[9] Thus, the good sport doesn't cheat, attempt to hurt the opponent, or taunt another. A certain lightness of spirit prohibits uncivil displays of temper, constant complaints to officials, and the like. Throughout the activity, self-control and kinship with others are necessary to maximize the possible values of the play-world.

What does all this mean in more particular instances and over a wider range of examples? Once again Aristotle is helpful. First he insists that it would be misguided to expect an extreme degree of exactness, clarity, or precision in our present moral inquiry. We should expect that degree of precision appropriate to the inquiry, and in ethical theory "it will be satisfactory if we can indicate the truth roughly and in outline" (1: 1094b). In addition, when speaking of moral virtue we seek the mean "relative to us." Virtue is not alike to all people in all situations. Terence Irwin comments:

> Aristotle warns against any misleading suggestion that his appeal to a mean is attended to offer a precise, quantitative test for virtuous action that we can readily apply to particular cases—as though, e.g., we could decide that there is a proper, moderate degree of anger to be displayed in all conditions, or in all conditions of a certain precisely described type. The point of the doctrine, and of Aristotle's insistence of the "intermediate relative to us," is that no such precise quantitative test can be found. (1: p. 313)

To see the virtue of sportsmanship as a mean between extremes is not to be given a precise formula for interpreting acts as sportsmanlike or not, but to be given an explanatory and experiential context within which we can learn and teach how we ought to conduct ourselves in sports. From the standpoint of teaching and moral education, an appeal to exemplars of this virtue will always be useful, for they will show us what it means to be playful and cooperative in our sport experience. I cannot see that the moral philosopher is required to do more.[10]

Notes

1. There is, of course, some dispute whether we should say that the cheating coach's team won. Bernard Suits (20: pp. 12–13) argues that in a strict logical sense one cannot win by cheating. The game is defined by it rules, so one cannot win the game by breaking the rules since, in that case, one would not be playing the game at all. Craig K. Lehman (15) argues that the conventions of a sport may allow some breaking of the rules (e.g., Gaylord Perry throwing a spitball or an offensive lineman holding) without thinking that the violator has ceased to play the game because of such nonobedience. I am sympathetic to Lehman's arguments, but the so-called "incompatibility thesis" is not crucial to my arguments in this paper. I simply attempt to start with a paradigm example of unsportsmanlike behavior, and the cheating coach is a good place to start since such behavior violates the rules of basketball and the unwritten conventions of proper conduct in the sport.

2. Here I am using the term "bad sport" simply to describe the cheater as someone who displays poor sportsmanship. Bernard Suits (19: Ch. 4) distinguishes the trifler, the cheater, and the spoilsport. What I mean by "bad sport" is not what Suits means by "spoilsport." In the broad sense in which I am using the notion, the trifler, cheater and spoilsport are all bad sports.

3. Keating's views are extensively discussed in (17). His views are noted by Carolyn Thomas (22) and by Warren Fraleigh (9).

4. Warnock's comments attempt to describe generally "the human predicament" and the way in which morality serves to better the human predicament by countervailing "limited sympathies."

5. See Suits (20).

6. See Feezell (4; 5; 6; 7).

7. See Huizinga (10), Caillois (2), Novak (16), Schmitz (18: pp. 22-29), Fink (8: pp. 73-83), Esposito (3: pp. 102-107), and Hyland (11: pp. 94-101) and (12: pp. 133-140).

8. The conclusion concerning intrinsic satisfaction is mine, not necessarily Suits.' I leave open the question whether his account of "lusory attitude" would agree or disagree with this conclusion. See his discussion (19: pp. 38-40, pp. 144-146). His comments on page 40 seem close to the conclusion I offer, but his later comments on professional game playing may lead elswhere.

9. Drew Hyland (12: pp. 133-139) offers an excellent analysis of how competition always involves the risk of degenerating into an alienating experience, but it need not. Competitive play can be a mode of friendship.

10. I wish to thank members of the editorial board and the editor of the *Journal of the Philosophy of Sport* for their helpful comments.

Bibliography

1. Aristotle, *Nicomachean Ethics*. Translated by Terence Irwin. Indianapolis: Hackett, 1985.

2. Caillois, Roger. *Man, Play, and Games*. Translated by Meyer Barash. The Free Press of Glencoe, 1961.

3. Esposito, Joseph. "Play and Possibility." *Sport and the Body: A Philosophical Symposium. Second Edition*. Edited by Gerber and Morgan. Philadelphia: Lea & Febiger, 1979.

4. Feezell, Randolph M. "Of Mice and Men: Nagel and the Absurd." *The Modern Schoolman*, LXI(4) (May, 1984), 259-265.

5. Feezell, Randolph M. "Play and the Absurd." *Philosophy Today* (Winter, 1984), 319-328.

6. Feezell, Randolph M. "Play, Freedom, and Sport." *Philosophy Today* (Summer, 1981), 166-175.

7. Feezell, Randolph M. "Sport: Pursuit of Bodily Excellence or Play? An Examination of Paul Weiss's Account of Sport." *The Modern Schoolman*, LVIII(4) (May, 1981), 257-270.

8. Fink, Eugene. "The Ontology of Play." *Sport and the Body: A Philosophical Symposium. Second Edition*. Edited by Gerber and Morgan. Philadelphia: Lea & Febiger, 1979.

9. Fraleigh, Warren. *Right Actions in Sport: Ethics for Contestants*. Champaign, IL: Human Kinetics, 1984.

10. Huizinga, Johan. *Homo-Ludens: A Study of the Play-Element in Culture*. Boston: Beacon Press, 1955.

11. Hyland, Drew. "Athletics and Angst: Reflections on the Philosophical Relevance of Play." *Sport and the Body: A Philosophical Symposium. Second Edition*. Edited by Gerber and Morgan. Philadelphia: Lea & Febiger, 1979.

12. Hyland, Drew. "Competition and Friendship." *Sport and the Body: A Philosophical Symposium. Second Edition*. Edited by Gerber and Morgan. Philadelphia: Lea & Febiger, 1979.

13. Keating, James. *Competition and Playful Activities*. Washington: University Press of America, 1978.

14. Keating, James. "Sportsmanship as a Moral Category." *Ethics*, LXXV (October, 1964), 25-35.

15. Lehman, Craig K. "Can Cheaters Play the Game?" *Journal of the Philosophy of Sport* VIII (1981), 41-46.

16. Novak, Michael. *The Joy of Sports*. New York: Basic Books, 1976.

17. Osterhoudt, Robert. *The Philosophy of Sport: A Collection of Original Essays*. Springfield, IL: Charles C Thomas, 1973.

18. Schmitz, Kenneth L. "Sport and Play: Suspension of the Ordinary." *Sport and the Body: A Philosophical Symposium. Second Edition*. Edited by Gerber and Morgan. Philadelphia: Lea & Febiger, 1979.

19. Suits, Bernard. *The Grasshopper: Games, Life and Utopia*. Toronto: University of Toronto Press, 1978.

20. Suits, Bernard. "What is a Game?" *Sport and the Body: A Philosophical Symposium. Second Edition*. Edited by Gerber and Morgan. Philadelphia: Lea & Febiger, 1979.

21. Taylor, Richard. *Metaphysics, Third Edition*. Englewood Cliffs, NJ: Prentice-Hall, 1983.

22. Thomas, Carolyn. *Sport in a Philosophical Context*. Philadelphia: Lea & Febiger, 1983.

23. Warnock, G.J. *The Object of Morality*. London: Methuen, 1971.

11

On Winning and Athletic Superiority

◆

Nicholas Dixon

How do we decide which team or player is better in a competitive sporting contest?[1] The obvious answer is that the winner is the superior team or athlete. A central purpose of competitive sport is precisely to provide a comparison—in Kretchmar's terms (7), a contest—that *determines* which team or player is superior. However, we can easily find undeserved victories in which this purpose is not achieved—in other words, contests in which the player or team that wins is not, according to both our intuitions and plausible accounts of the goal of competitive sport from the philosophy of sport literature, better than the losing player or team.[2] This paper is an examination of several such situations in which competitive sport fails to provide an accurate measure of athletic superiority. For brevity's sake, I will at times refer to such events as "failed athletic contests," meaning contests that have failed in their central comparative purpose, even though they may have succeeded in other goals like entertaining spectators.

My purpose is threefold. First, studying various ways in which athletic contests fail to achieve their central comparative purpose is intrinsically interesting. While the philosophy of sport literature is replete with discussions of the purpose of competitive sport, it does not, to my knowledge, address the question of how well athletic contests fulfill that purpose. An instrumental benefit of this discussion is that a clear delineation of the wide variety of sources of unjust outcomes in sporting contests, showing that winning is not the be-all and end-all of athletic superiority, may help to weaken the motivation to resort to morally objectionable means to

---

An early draft of this paper was presented at the Philosophic Society for the Study of Sport conference in Clarkston, WA on Oct. 3, 1996. This final draft has greatly benefited from suggestions by the editor of the *Journal of the Philosophy of Sport* and three anonymous referees, to all of whom I am most grateful.

Reprinted, by permission, from N. Dixon, 1999, "On winning and athletic superiority," *Journal of the Philosophy of Sport, 26:* 10-26.

secure victory. Second, in the process of examining unjust victories, we will deepen our understanding of the concept of athletic superiority. More specifically, we will be forced to confront the issue of how much weight we should give to such psychological traits as guile and poise in our determinations of athletic superiority. Third, consideration of how much weight we should give to one particular psychological trait—the ability to perform well under pressure—in our judgments about athletic superiority will lead to the conclusion that the "playoff" system by which championships are determined in American team sports is a relatively inefficient method of determining which team is best.

For the first four sections, I will use "the better team" as interchangeable with "the team that deserves to win." Both expressions refer to the team that performs better (however we choose to define superior performance) in a particular athletic contest. In section 5, the two concepts diverge, as I discuss the possibility that the team that performs better and deserves to win may still not be the better team.

Refereeing Errors

Suppose that a soccer referee is either incompetent or openly biased in favor of the home team. He or she disallows as offside three perfectly good goals for the away team, even though replays clearly indicate that all the attacking players were onside. The home team wins by a single goal after the referee awards a "phantom" penalty, even though replays conclusively show that no contact was made with the attacker who slumped to the ground in the penalty area. Furthermore, the away team was constantly on the attack, pinning the far less skillful home team in its own half throughout the entire match. In this case, I suggest, the home team did not deserve to win. The better team did not win.[3] Several different views on the goal of competitive sport support this claim, assuming that the team or player that best meets this goal is the better one and deserves to win. For instance, Robert Simon's view that competitive sport is "the attempt to secure victory within the framework set by the constitutive rules" (11: p. 15) indicates that the away team is superior, since, had the referee applied the rules of the game correctly, it would have won. The injustice of the home team's victory follows from another of Simon's views, namely "the idea of the sports contest as a test of skill, a mutual quest for excellence by the participants" (11: p. 50), since the away team displays more skill and excellence. For the same reason, the away team's superiority also follows from Kathleen M. Pearson's view that the purpose of competitive sport is

> to test the skill of one individual, or group of individuals, against the skill of another individual, or group of individuals, in order to determine who is more skillful in a particular, well-defined activity. (10: p. 183)

But let us pause to consider some objections that would deny that refereeing errors lead to undeserved victories and, hence, to failed athletic contests.

First, we might insist that the referee's word is final and that, as long as no cheating occurs, any results based upon the referee's decisions are just. As a long-serving baseball commentator in Detroit was apt to point out, when people challenged an umpire's calls, tomorrow morning's box scores will always prove that the umpire was right after all. The problem with this argument is that it clumsily conflates power with infallibility. The jury in the first trial of the LAPD officers who assaulted Rodney

King certainly had the power to acquit them. Those of us who disagreed with the verdict believed that, even though the correct *procedures* for a jury trial may have been followed, the *outcome* was unjust. Similarly, even though the procedural rules of soccer do indeed give the referee the final word, this in no way guarantees that the referee's calls will be correct. And referees' errors can lead to unjust results.

Second, and rather more plausibly, some people argue that a great team should be able to overcome bad calls by the referee and win anyway. There may be some truth to this claim, but it does not undermine my thesis, which is that the *better* team can be prevented by refereeing errors from winning, not that great teams can be. The away team in my example may not be good enough to overcome the referee's poor calls, but it is certainly the better team, and deserved to win, according to the rules of the game.

A third objection takes a very different tack. Rather than denying that the winning team (in my example, the home team) is superior, this final objection consists in arguing that the home team does not win at all. For instance, Suits (12: p. 9) argues that "a player who does not confine himself to lusory means may not be said to win, even if he achieves the pre-lusory goal." Thus the home team's alleged victory, which has been achieved by methods that violate the permitted lusory means, even though the referee negligently failed to punish these violations, is not a victory after all. This approach has an interesting parallel in natural law theory's treatment of unjust laws. In justifying his violation of segregation laws, Martin Luther King cited St. Augustine's view that "an unjust law is no law at all" (6: p. 89). Just as an unjust law, according to natural law theory, is superseded by the moral law that it violates, so an apparent victory by illicit means is nullified by the very rules that have been violated.

A problem with this approach is that, in preserving the justice of the outcome of sporting contests by legislating out of existence victories by inferior teams due to refereeing errors, it creates the suspicion of an ad hoc maneuver designed to respond to a troubling objection by stipulation rather than by argument. More important, in considering the analogy with natural law theory, we need to examine a rival theory, that of legal positivism. According to legal positivism, whether a statute is indeed a valid law, we need only consider its "pedigree" (that is, whether it was enacted in accordance with the constitution or whatever other "rule of recognition" is operative) without deciding on its moral justifiability. So a bad law is still a law. The problem with natural law theory, according to legal positivists, is that it conflates the concepts of "law" and "good law," and fails to allow for the very possibility of a bad law. We would do better, they suggest, to focus our attention on moral evaluation and criticism of immoral laws than to dispute their status as law.[4] The implication of legal positivism for our debate over refereeing errors is that, rather than disputing the fact that the home team won the game, we should instead concentrate on describing the injustice of this victory. Ordinary usage has a meaning for the expressions "hollow victory" and "undeserved victory," and we should be suspicious of an approach that would render these concepts meaningless by fiat.

Showing that refereeing errors can lead to undeserved victories by inferior teams has not required us to make any controversial assumptions about our criteria for athletic superiority. The fact that the visiting team was far superior in terms of physical skills and performance seems sufficient, in our example, to identify it as the better team. In the next section, however, we will have to broaden our concept of athletic superiority beyond mere physical prowess.

Cheating

My purpose in this section is not to offer a comprehensive account of cheating, a complex topic that deserves a much more detailed discussion than is possible in the confines of this paper. I offer instead what I hope will be an uncontroversial sufficient condition for cheating—namely, an attempt to break the rules of a game while escaping detection and punishment. Whatever else may count as cheating, we can be sure that anything meeting this description does. My goal is to explore the implications of this minimal definition for my topic of the relationship between victory and athletic superiority.

A victory that depends in large part upon cheating seems neither deserved nor a sign of athletic superiority. This is, presumably, why Ben Johnson was stripped of his gold medal in the 1988 Olympic Games after he tested positive for illegal steroids. Granted, Johnson did outperform his rivals. But he would also outperform them if he spiked their food or drink with a performance-impairing drug. In neither case does Johnson's victory prove him to be a superior athlete, because his violation of the rules gives him an unfair advantage over his opponents, thus subverting the race as a legitimate test of athletic excellence. Cheating can also occur *during* a game: A golfer may move the ball from a bad lie when her opponent is not looking, a pitcher may doctor the baseball, or a player in a tennis match without an umpire may wrongly call a ball out. An especially infamous act of cheating was committed by Diego Maradona, one of the most gifted soccer players of all time, who illegally punched the ball into the net to score a goal for Argentina against England in a 1986 World Cup quarterfinal. The referee did not spot the infraction that replays revealed, and Maradona afterwards boasted that the "hand of God" had scored his goal. In general, the reason why cheats do not deserve to win is that their victories are due not to their athletic superiority, but to their violation of rules which their opponents, in contrast, obey. This claim is based on the assumption that the athlete who deserves to win is the one who performs better *within the game's rules* and *under conditions of equality*.

However, we need to consider an audacious defense of cheating as playing a legitimate role in competitive sport. Oliver Leaman (8) describes cheating as the use of "wits" in addition to skill and strategy and suggests that it adds a new dimension that makes sport more interesting. As long as cheating occurs in the context of *overall* obedience to the rules by the cheater and other competitors, it will not result in anarchy, and the overall character of games will be preserved. Moreover, if we were to recognize cheating as a *legitimate* tactic for athletes to use, then the cheater would no longer have an unfair advantage, since *all* athletes would feel free to cheat. Indeed, the ability to cheat without being detected might even become a prized aspect of athletic skill. So, if Leaman is correct, even the orthodox view that the best athlete, the one who deserves to win, is the one who displays most skill does not necessarily preclude cheating. Perhaps Maradona's ability to deceive the referee into believing that he had used his head and not his hand to score the infamous goal against England is itself evidence of his genius. Machiavellian conflict between ruthless competitors would be the best test of this new, broader concept of athletic prowess.

Regardless of the merits of Leaman's defense of cheating, he has said enough to indicate that we need to broaden our concept of athletic superiority to include more than mere physical prowess. An excellent athlete must not only have superior physical skills but also the acumen to use them wisely, employing shrewd tactics and strategy that are designed to maximize the benefits of his or her skills while simultaneously neutralizing those of opponents. A soccer team that has exquisite ball control skills, but unwisely commits all 11 players to a constant onslaught on the opposing team's goal will often leave itself vulnerable to fast breaks from the opposition. Should the opponents win the game by virtue of a goal scored during just such a fast break, the technically superior losers cannot justly claim to be the superior team, since they have failed to exhibit an integral part of athletic excellence. If, as Leaman argues, the ability to cheat is itself a legitimate component of the "strategy and tactics" dimension of athletic excellence, then perhaps the cheating winners listed at the beginning of this section did after all deserve their victories.

Of course, moral condemnations of cheating in sport are easy to formulate.[5] However, Leaman's point is precisely that athletes are protected by a kind of moral immunity to the criticisms that would rightly be directed at them were they to cheat outside the context of sport.[6] We might compare this immunity to that enjoyed by defense attorneys in the U.S. Even when an attorney is convinced that her client committed a despicable crime, she is professionally obligated to mount a zealous defense, trying to get key evidence excluded on constitutional grounds, challenging truthful prosecution witnesses, and trying to persuade the jury of alternative possibilities that she herself believes did not happen. The end product of the attorney's actions may be the acquittal of a dangerous, factually guilty defendant.

Now the attorney's moral immunity is an essential part of the legal adversary system, which is itself justified by the belief that even the most despicable defendant deserves a loyal ally to protect his or her rights. Whether or not Leaman's argument for the moral immunity of athletes succeeds depends on the existence of a similar rationale for allowing cheating in sport. Is cheating essential to sport in the way that an attorney's loyalty to clients is essential to the legal adversary system? The answer seems to be no. Granted, widespread cheating would add an extra layer of intrigue and excitement to sport, but it hardly seems to further any of sport's central values. On the contrary, it sabotages one of competitive sport's least controversial goals: to determine which team has most athletic skill, including, as we have just seen, mental abilities like shrewd tactics as well as physical prowess, *as permitted by the rules of the game*. Certainly, successful cheating requires some skill and cunning and even, in some cases, considerable physical ability, but this is very different from the kind of legitimate use of tactical and physical prowess that competitive sport aims to test.[7]

My goal in this subsection is not morally to condemn cheating, even though good reasons exist for doing so. It is, instead, to evaluate the relationship between cheating and athletic superiority. However, for the same reason that teams cannot claim moral immunity for their acts of cheating—that is, they subvert the test of athletic skill that is a central goal of competitive sport—the claim that the team that uses cheating to win is *ipso facto* the best team and deserves to win is unconvincing. This judgment is reflected in the heavy penalties that sporting federations have imposed on athletes whom they catch cheating. More than the long-term suspension that was imposed on Ben Johnson for his illegal drug use, the fact that his Olympic gold medal was taken away from him indicates the belief that he did not deserve to win. In terms of the abilities that competitive sport is designed to test, Johnson was *not* the best athlete. So, at least in some cases, cheating can prevent competitive sport from providing an accurate measure of athletic superiority.

Gamesmanship

Gamesmanship is a slippery concept that is hard to define. Unlike cheating, it does not involve violating the rules of the game in the hope of avoiding detection. Examples include using legal but morally dubious designed tactics to unsettle opponents: trash talking, taking an inordinate amount of time between points in a tennis match, and so on. A different kind of gamesmanship is the so-called "professional foul," which is committed in order to prevent an opposing player from scoring an easy goal or lay-up. Unlike outright cheating, such fouls are committed openly, in the expectation that a penalty will be imposed. Perhaps what all gamesmanship has in common is an apparent violation of the *spirit* of a game.[8] My purpose here is not morally to assess gamesmanship. It is, rather, to argue that an athlete or team that successfully uses gamesmanship as a major weapon in securing victory may not deserve to win in the sense of being the best athlete or team. Gamesmanship, then, provides another category of situations in which athletic contests can fail in their aim of accurately determining athletic superiority. We should note that at this stage we may only call gamesmanship an *apparent* violation of the spirit of a game. Should we conclude that successful use of gamesmanship is one sign of a good athlete, then we must withdraw the judgment that it violates the spirit of competitive sport.

I begin by considering the professional or "strategic" foul. Some philosophers of sport outright condemn such fouls,[9] while Robert Simon has given a nuanced, qualified defense of professional fouls in some circumstances (11: pp. 46-49). He points out that in basketball, for instance, the intentional foul is widely regarded as a legitimate strategy. The only issue, on Simon's view, seems to be the prudential one of whether preventing an easy lay-up is worth the penalty incurred for intentional fouls. For the sake of argument, I will grant Simon's point that a professional foul is sometimes a legitimate strategy. My goal in this section is to show that sometimes it is *illegitimate* and subverts the goal of measuring the relative athletic ability of the contestants.

For such an example, let us consider a soccer game that has been dominated by the home team but that remains scoreless going into the final few minutes. The home team finally mounts a decisive attack, and one of its players is about to tap the ball into an empty net when he is brutally rugby-tackled by an opponent, preventing him from scoring. The goalkeeper then saves the resultant penalty. In the final seconds of the game, the away team mounts a similar attack. The home team, in contrast, refrains from resorting to a professional foul to prevent the attacker from scoring, and the away team scores the winning goal with the last kick of the game. In such a case, I suggest, the away team did not deserve to win, because it did not demonstrate superior athletic skill. Its victory is due, instead, to its cynical willingness to exploit the rules of the game that "permit" the professional foul to teams willing to incur the resultant free kick or penalty. The recent (but unevenly enforced) decision by FIFA (the Federation of International Football Associations) to automatically penalize the professional foul by ejection from the game (without substitution) indicates that soccer's highest governing body regards it as a violation of the game's spirit.

How we view a professional foul may depend on the type of foul involved: we naturally view hard fouls more harshly that risk injuring opponents. Especially in basketball, we are more apt to condemn such fouls when they occur late in the game, since they are more likely to determine its outcome than those that occur earlier. The difference in attitude to the professional foul in basketball and soccer is arguably attributable to the vastly different impact that it can have in each sport. Basketball is a high-scoring sport, in which preventing a lay-up and requiring the offensive player to earn points from the free throw line normally has a minimal impact on a game's outcome. Soccer, in contrast, is a low-scoring sport, in which a single professional foul can prevent what would have been the decisive winning or equalizing goal. In such sports, a team that wins as a result of a professional foul is not necessarily the best team, in terms of the criteria we have so far allowed as relevant for athletic excellence: physical skill and tactical acumen, both exercised within the rules of the game.

The use of psychological tricks—for example, trash talking or delaying the game—to try to unsettle opponents is a very different kind of gamesmanship that forces us to confront another dimension of our concept of athletic excellence. We have already widened the concept to include mental as well as physical attributes. We now need to consider whether the mental element of athletic superiority should include such emotional characteristics as coolness under pressure, in addition to the cognitive abilities (for instance, strategy) that we have already added. In favor of such a widening of our understanding of athletic excellence is the view that players who allow themselves to be distracted by such tactics do not deserve to win. Truly great players, one might argue, will use their vastly superior skill to compensate for whatever loss of composure they suffer as a result of opponents' psychological tricks. However, we need to remember that the question here is not whether *great* players always win but, rather, whether the *better* player wins when gamesmanship is a decisive factor. And we can easily imagine examples in which a clearly superior, but not great, player is so rattled by her opponent's gamesmanship that she loses her cool and the game. According to the uncontroversial view that the primary purpose of competitive sport is to determine which team or player has superior athletic skill (understood as including both physical ability and astute strategy as permitted by the game's rules), players who use this kind of gamesmanship to win do not appear to deserve their victory.

In response, apologists for gamesmanship will respond that it *is* a legitimate strategy in competitive sport. If the ability to use gamesmanship (and to remain impervious to opponents' use of it) is part of athletic excellence, then the technically superior player who allows herself to be unsettled by her opponent's psychological tricks is deficient in one of the mental elements of athletic excellence and is not, after all, the better athlete. The issue, which we may safely leave unresolved at this stage, hinges on whether we include "psychological coolness" or temperament as part of the mental element of our definition of athletic excellence. In section 5, I will discuss in more depth the relationship between temperament and athletic excellence. I will conclude there that, while repeated defeats due to extreme nervousness may disqualify a team's claim to be the best, we must also allow for the possibility that a team that loses a big game due to nervousness may nonetheless be the better team. What has already emerged from this section is that at least one kind of gamesmanship—the professional foul in low scoring games like soccer—can result in undeserved victories in which the better team does not win, and the athletic contest has failed.

Bad Luck

The next set of putative failures of athletic contests to accurately measure athletic superiority involves neither mistakes by referees nor misconduct by players. It arises, rather, in games in which one team dominates the other but still manages to lose the game, because of a succession of strokes of bad luck.[10] The distinction between high- and low-scoring games is relevant here. In a high-scoring game like basketball, a few unlucky breaks are unlikely to sway the outcome. In contrast, in a low-scoring game like soccer, a small number of unlucky breaks can be decisive. Nor do we have to resort to thought experiments: most soccer fans have seen games dominated by one team that hits the woodwork several times and still ends up losing to a single goal scored on one of its opponents' few serious attacks. Suppose further that the dominant team has several goal-bound shots deflected by erratic gusts of wind, others stopped by thick mud on the goal line, and others still inadvertently stopped by a poorly-positioned referee. When, moreover, the winning goal is caused by a freakish deflection by a defender, the dominant team may justly claim that it was the better team and deserved to win. Unlucky losers appear, therefore, to provide another category of failed athletic contests. Let us pause to consider some objections.

First, mirroring an argument we have already considered, one might insist that a great team makes its own luck, and teams that fail to do so do not deserve to win. But this argument is vulnerable to a response already given: While a truly great team may indeed be able to salvage victory despite horrendously bad luck, a less talented team may be unable to do so, while still being clearly the better team and deserving to win. Granted, if a team with a long-term poor record claims that its losses were all due to bad luck, we would suspect self-deception and suggest that its players take a little more responsibility for their performances. Luck does tend to even out in the long run. However, in the short run—for instance, an individual game—we may plausibly say that a team was unlucky and did not deserve to lose.

A second objection reminds us that the purpose of any competitive game is to score more points than opponents. When a team dominates the action, keeping the opponent pinned in its own half, yet still manages to lose, it may be the lack of two legitimate considerations in determining athletic superiority, a killer instinct and good strategy, not bad luck, that accounts for its losses. Such charges were made, for instance, against the French soccer team in the 1982 World Cup, when it played beautiful, crowd-pleasing soccer but was eliminated in the quarter-finals. However, even granting for the sake of argument that some dominant teams do not deserve to win, we can still produce cases in which a team loses undeservedly due to bad luck. In the hypothetical case at the beginning of this section, the dominant team did not play pretty but innocuous soccer. It employed shrewd strategy and displayed a killer instinct, translating its dominance into several accurate shots on goal that were stopped only by the woodwork and by aberrational interventions by the wind, the mud, and the referee. Had these interventions not taken place, had any one of these shots gone just a few inches inside, and had the freakish deflection not occurred, the team would have won. Under these admittedly far-fetched circumstances, the better team did not win. However, more mundane examples of unlucky losses do occur in the real soccer world. Even the best players cannot direct their shots to the nearest inch, and the precise placement of any shot is partly a matter of luck. When a team repeatedly hits the goalpost without scoring, it is usually unlucky.

A final objection draws a line in the sand and insists that, no matter how close a team may have been to scoring several goals, it does not deserve to win if it does not score. According to this defense, the team that wins by a freakish goal on an isolated attack, despite several lucky escapes, including having its own goal's woodwork rattled repeatedly throughout the game by opponents' shots, deserves to win. The problem with this impregnable-sounding argument is precisely that it is *too* impregnable. Instead of honestly confronting the role of luck in sport, it tries to legislate it out of the picture by simply *defining* the best team as the one that scores most points. Arguments, not question-begging stipulative definitions, are needed to decide the question. And the arguments that I have presented in this and previous sections indicate that refereeing errors, cheating, unacceptable gamesmanship,[11] and bad luck can all result in undeserved victories by inferior teams.

Before moving on to a different aspect of the relationship between winning and athletic superiority, I pause to consider an argument that stipulative definitions of the kind I have just criticized are not necessarily question-begging. According to this argument, winning is an *operational definition* of the concept *the better team* in the same way that a score on an IQ test is an operational definition of the everyday concept of intelligence, and a legal verdict of guilty is an operational definition of the intuitive concept "that guy did it!" Operational definitions generally provide clear, objectively-ascertainable criteria for concepts whose everyday usage is more ambiguous and complex. (Legal guilt is an exception, in that rules of evidence and burden of proof requirements may make determinations of guilt appear more complex than the intuitive sense of "he did it!" Nonetheless, like all operational definitions, it provides an objective decision procedure—in this case, has the prosecution proven beyond a reasonable doubt that the defendant performed the *actus reus* with the requisite *mens rea?*—for determining a question that might otherwise be subject to arbitrary personal preference.) Since operational definitions do not claim to capture all the connotations of the everyday concepts that they replace, we should not be surprised by divergences between the two. People whom we judge very intelligent may perform poorly on IQ tests, and people who we know committed the act of which they are accused may be *correctly* found legally innocent. These divergences need reflect no fault in the operational definitions but, rather, the mere fact that they are operational definitions.

In support of viewing winning as an operational definition of athletic superiority, one goal of athletic contests is precisely to *determine* which team is better, and they have been designed to provide an accurate measure of excellence. Moreover, we sometimes modify rules in order to make contests a more accurate test of athletic superiority, for instance the offside rule in soccer, which prevents the tactic of booting the ball upfield to strikers who are permanently camped in front of the opposing goal, and encourages teams to play a more skillful passing game. To the extent that winning the contest is an operational definition of athletic superiority that has evolved over the years in the sporting world, it appears to be immune from the critiques that I have made, since my critiques are made from the point of view of the intuitive, everyday concept of athletic excellence. As we have seen, operational definitions do not claim to coincide with the everyday concepts that they are designed to replace.

In response, I do not deny that regarding winning as the criterion for athletic superiority is, *qua* operational definition, irreproachable. However, critiques of operational definitions from the point of view of intuitive concepts still perform two useful functions. First, too great a divergence between an everyday concept and its operational definition casts doubts on the adequacy of that definition. This is precisely what has happened with the concept of IQ, which has been criticized because of major discrepancies between it and intuitive judgments about intelligence. Victories by inferior teams or athletes, on the other hand, are sufficiently rare to indicate that this particular criticism is not applicable to regarding the winner as the better athlete, which remains a workable operational definition. Second, and most important, "external" critiques from the point of view of everyday concepts serve to remind us that such concepts as legal guilt *are* only operational definitions. They remind us that a defendant may really have "done it," even though he was correctly found legally innocent. And, in the case of the intuitive concept of athletic superiority,[12] they remind us that, while regarding the winner as the better athlete is generally a harmless convention, on some occasions it leads to inaccurate judgments of athletic superiority. I intend this paper, in part, as just such a reminder.

Inferior Performances by Superior Athletes

Steffi Graf dominated women's tennis for several years from the late 1980s until the mid-1990s. Suppose that in the middle of her period of dominance, she plays devastating tennis to reach the final at Wimbledon without losing a set. Her opponent is an unseeded player who has battled her way to the final by means of a series of gutsy three-set victories over technically superior players. And suppose, finally, that the unseeded player continues her string of upsets with a famous victory over Graf in a long, desperately close game. Her victory is fair and square. It involves no refereeing errors, no cheating, no gamesmanship, and no notably good luck. She deserves her victory because, on that day, she is the better player. However, in another sense, she is not the better player. Steffi Graf, who would almost certainly beat the player nine times out of ten, is the better player. She just had an off day.

So we appear to have found another sense in which an athletic contest can result in an inaccurate measure of athletic excellence: The winning player can deserve to win and yet still be an inferior athlete. Superior athletes do sometimes have bad days and lose. Few people would deny this claim in the case of my Steffi Graf example, but when it comes to other sports, some sectors of the sporting community are surprisingly reluctant to concede the possibility of this source of failed athletic contests. Concurrent with discussing their obvious relevance for my central topic of the relationship between winning and athletic superiority, I will point out the implications of such inaccurate measures of athletic superiority for the playoff system used in the U.S. to determine the winners of team sports championships.

According to a popular approach in the U.S. sporting community, a football team with the best record during the National Football League's regular season and playoffs, winning all its games easily but losing the Super Bowl, is not after all the best team in the NFL. The surest sign of the best team, the view continues, is the ability to save its best performances for the biggest occasions, and this is precisely what the winning team does, despite its indifferent play during the regular season and the playoffs. Evidence of the prevalence of this view is provided by the astonishing scorn directed at the Buffalo Bills football team in the U.S. for a series of Super Bowl losses in recent years. Even though it had the best record in American football for several years and was agonizingly close to winning one of its Super Bowl games, the mere fact that it lost several of these finals not only prevented it from being considered the best team but also made it a despised laughingstock among many sport journalists.

Michael Jordan's status as an all-time great was secured in the opinion of many American basketball fans the first year he led the Chicago Bulls to a National Basketball Association championship, even though his play, both quantitatively and qualitatively, may have been just as outstanding in previous seasons. Once again, the underlying belief is that the best players, especially great ones, are those who come through to achieve victory when it matters most: post-season playoff games.

More generally, the playoff system in the best-known professional team sports in the U.S.—baseball, basketball, football, and hockey—clearly presupposes that victory in the biggest games is the best measure of athletic superiority. The championship is awarded not to the team with the best regular-season record but rather to the team that excels in a relatively brief playoff tournament involving some of the teams with the best regular-season records. Athletic excellence is understood as the ability to perform well under pressure, when the stakes are highest, rather than as the ability to perform well over the course of an entire season.

As a matter of contingent fact, the two rival criteria for athletic excellence—performance over an extended period (a season) versus performance in a brief, high-pressure playoff tournament—usually point to the same player or team. With rare exceptions, playoff winners tend to have very strong regular-season records, if not the best. Strong teams win most of their games, including high-pressure playoff games. The most interesting cases from the point of view of our discussion of athletic superiority, though, are those where a team with a mediocre regular-season record wins the playoffs, for example a wild-card team winning the Super Bowl. What reasons exist for the belief that this Super Bowl winner is, *ipso facto*, that season's best NFL team? Think back to the example about Steffi Graf, where a single defeat in a major tournament to an unranked player would not have dislodged our belief that she was the best women's tennis player in the world during her years of dominance. By analogy, why don't we also believe that the team with a perfect regular season record, which has dominated its opponents throughout the regular season and playoffs, is still the best team in the NFL, despite its subpar performance in its Super Bowl loss to a wild-card team? Certainly, a difference of degree exists between the two situations. Whereas a single loss in a major tournament is relatively insignificant in the context of Steffi Graf's dozens of victories in many other tournaments, the Super Bowl is clearly the most important game in a very brief NFL season, consisting of a *single* tournament with a maximum of only 20 or so games. However, this difference in degree seems insufficient to support the view that the team that wins the playoffs for the championship is necessarily the best team. My scenario in which the season's dominant football team has an off day and loses the Super Bowl makes a strong enough *prima facie* case that it is still the best team in the NFL to require in response an *argument* for, and not just an assertion of, the accuracy of the playoff system in measuring athletic excellence.

And perhaps such an argument is not too hard to find. The ability to perform well under pressure, so the argument goes, is a sign of *psychological toughness*, which is an essential ingredient of excellence in competitive sport. We have already encountered in section 3 one element of psychological toughness, namely the ability to remain impervious to opponents' gamesmanship. Now little doubt exists that psychological toughness is an important quality for winning athletic contests. The key question is how much weight we assign to it in assessing athletic excellence.

I agree that a claim to athletic excellence would be hollow in the case of an athlete who *always* choked in any competitive game, not just big games in big tournaments. We would suspect that a general lack of athletic ability, and not just a suspect temperament, is responsible for the repeated losses. Furthermore, we could even require a baseline of psychological toughness as a prerequisite for athletic excellence, and concede that, however gifted an athlete may be, repeated losses in major tournaments due to nerves, undue sensitivity to opponents' gamesmanship, or a failure to be "up" for the occasion preclude us from considering her as the best athlete in her field. However, we also need to avoid the danger of setting our standard for psychological toughness so high that only actually *winning* the tournament or playoff series or Superbowl qualifies us as mentally strong enough to be the best athlete or team. In other words, we should leave conceptual space for regarding the team that has shown supreme skill, strategy, *and* psychological toughness throughout the entire regular season and playoffs, before losing the final game in the playoffs in a subpar performance, as nonetheless the best team. If we fail to allow for this possibility, the belief that the best team always comes through on the big occasions has become an article of faith rather than a hypothesis that is open to confirmation or falsification by open-minded examination of our concept of athletic excellence.

To further challenge the centrality of psychological toughness to athletic excellence, consider, by analogy, the importance that we place on the ability to perform well under pressure in other activities. For instance, is excellence in teaching best judged by a job candidate's classroom performance during a one-day campus visit, or by observing her classes for an entire semester? While we admire the candidate who rises to the occasion to deliver a dynamic guest lecture, most search committees recognize that nerves caused by the momentousness of the occasion can obscure the ability of even excellent teachers. A far better, but logistically impractical, way to evaluate a candidate's teaching ability would be to observe her over a longer period of time in a more relaxed setting. Why should we regard performance under pressure as so much more important in judging athletic excellence when in other fields we regard pressure as a factor that can *obscure* excellence? Of course, important disanalogies exist between teaching and sport, which is by its very nature competitive and tense. However, this does not explain why people regard performance under the greatest pressure as *the best* indicator of athletic excellence.

One reason for this may be that we in the U.S. are accustomed to the playoff system, which puts a premium on performing well in a small number of high-pressure games. And the very fact that we do have such a system may cause teams to approach the season in such a way that does indeed make the playoff system a reasonably accurate measure of excellence. In other words, professional teams in the U.S. recognize that reaching and sustaining a peak level of performance during the playoffs is far more important for winning the championship than compiling the best regular-season record. They may, therefore, regard the regular season primarily as a training period of little intrinsic importance, the main purpose of which is to allow them to fine-tune their skills and strategy for the playoffs for which they reserve their maximum effort. Given that we have such a system, the best teams will successfully channel their talents into developing the ability to produce excellent performances under extreme pressure in the brief playoff period.

However, we should not let this blind us to the more fundamental question of whether the playoff system is the best way of measuring talent in the first place. The force of my arguments in this section is that it is not. We seem to have fetishized the ability to perform well under pressure and given it far more importance as a criterion of athletic excellence than it deserves. It is instructive to compare the playoff system with the organization of professional sports in other countries. For example, in professional soccer leagues in Europe and South America the most prestigious trophy goes to the team with the best record at the end of the season. No post-season or playoffs exist. Single-elimination cup tournaments also exist, but they run concurrently with and independently of the so-called league championship. The underlying belief is that the most accurate measure of athletic excellence is performance against all rival teams over an entire season. Why does the introduction of the high pressure that accompanies playoff series provide a better measure? A further advantage of the "over the entire season" method of evaluation is that it minimizes the impact of refereeing errors, cheating, gamesmanship, and luck, much of which will tend to even out over the length of a season, whereas any one of them may be decisive in a playoff tournament.

In the case of international tournaments such as the soccer World Cup or the Olympic Games, simple logistics require a brief, high-pressure "knockout" or single elimination tournament. A season-long series of games or track meets would not be feasible for such international competitions. And doubtless powerful financial considerations underlie the American playoff system, in that it sustains fans' interest and attendance at games far deeper into the season than does the league table approach, which can effectively eliminate most teams from contention well before the season ends. None of my arguments in this section are intended to diminish the value of success in such tournaments or in post-season playoff series in American professional sports. The ability to rise to the occasion and succeed in competition against the best athletes in the nation or the world is indeed a sign of athletic excellence. In the absence of crucial refereeing errors, cheating, unacceptable gamesmanship, and exceptional luck, winners of these tournaments are fully deserving of our admiration. They are indeed the best athletes and teams, in the sense that they performed best on the days of the tournament and deserved their victories. In most cases, they are also the best athletes and teams, judged on their form throughout the current or past season.

My objections have been directed solely at the view that insists that the winning team or athlete in a playoff or a similar tournament is *by definition* the best one, not just on the day but for the entire season or year. My point has been that a subpar performance resulting in a loss, whether due to nerves, insufficient motivation, or some other psychological factor, does not necessarily negate an athlete's or a team's claim to be the best. Psychological toughness is a legitimate component of the mental element in athletic excellence, and a serious deficiency in it greatly weakens an athlete's claim to athletic superiority. But we should beware giving psychological toughness so much importance in our understanding of athletic excellence that it eclipses all other elements.

The most important consequence of my reasoning in this section is that we should reexamine our attitude toward the playoff system in American professional sport. The best way to measure relative ability in domestic professional sport is the system used in European countries for such sports as soccer: a league championship, which is awarded to the team with the best record after an entire season of play. This system minimizes the impact of unjust results in individual games due to such factors as poor refereeing, cheating, gamesmanship, and bad luck. And while end-of-season games will sometimes involve enormous pressure, and while the ability to perform well under this pressure is a legitimate aspect of athletic excellence, the over-a-season method of evaluation is superior to the playoff system in not placing an inordinate weight on this ability in determining which team wins the championship. Unlike international tournaments like the Olympics and the World Cup, logistics do *not* demand that we base championships in American professional sport on brief tournaments. If we persist in using the playoff system, we need to acknowledge that this is a choice, not a necessity. And this choice involves sacrificing a more accurate measure of athletic excellence—the season-long championship—in order to enjoy the financial benefits of the playoff system. By choosing this system, we decrease the probability that the best team wins the championship.

Justice and Results in Sport

Despite the relatively uncontroversial nature of the list of situations I have described in which a sporting contest fails to provide an accurate measure of athletic superiority (sections 1-4), we are reluctant to concede that sometimes sporting contests may have unjust results. We like to think of sport as a supremely democratic arena where ability and dedication are the only determinants of success, at least in those sports that do not require expensive equipment and country club memberships. And there is some truth in this belief: A child from the shanty-towns around Rio may face insurmountable socio-economic obstacles that prevent him from any realistic chance of becoming a lawyer, but exquisite soccer skills may by themselves be sufficient to raise him to fame and fortune with the Brazilian national team. My conclusion that even sport is not a pure meritocracy may, therefore, appear to tarnish its image. However, the fact that a conclusion may disappoint us is not a good reason for rejecting it.

A helpful parallel to my thesis about sporting results exists in ethics. A venerable tradition associated with Kant holds that I am morally responsible only for what is within my control. I am not responsible for any consequences of my actions that I did not intend and had no reason to foresee. Strictly speaking, the only human actions that are subject to moral evaluation are our *intentions*, which, unlike the consequences of our actions, seem to be fully within our control. However, in the last 25 years or so, philosophers have realized that *moral luck* may play a significant role in determining our moral "record."[13] Factors beyond our control, including genetics, upbringing, and even where and when we happen to be born, influence what kind of people we become and even what kind of intentions we form. Nor does recognizing the role of moral luck require that one make controversial metaphysical assumptions about the absence of free will. Even if we grant that people have free will, we must concede that two people with exactly similar moral character may be faced with vastly different challenges and obstacles during their lives, resulting in one's leading an unobjectionable life, while the other becomes a moral monster. But for the historical accident of living in Germany during Hitler's rise, a Nazi war criminal might well have led a morally innocuous life, while his morally innocuous counterpart who spent his entire life as a farmer in South America might have played a gruesome role in the Holocaust had he lived instead in Nazi Germany.[14] Yet if we were to try to strip away the unfair influence of these external factors and confine our moral evaluation to the part of ourselves over which we have complete control, we would be left with no subject for our ethical judgments.[15] If we are to have moral assessment at all, we have to concede the role played by moral luck.

Similarly, my arguments show that displaying superior athletic skill, strategy, and mental toughness to those of our opponents—in other words, doing everything that is within our control while obeying the rules and spirit of the game—does not guarantee victory. Poor refereeing decisions, cheating, gamesmanship, and bad luck can all deny us the victory that we deserve. Perhaps the realization that morality itself is sometimes unfair, in the sense that we are not in complete control over our moral record, will soften the blow of the unfairness that sometimes arises in sporting results.

In contrast, my discussion of inferior performances by superior athletes (section 5) does not indicate any unfairness in the results of sporting contests. After all, the team that plays better on the day against superior opponents *deserves* to win. What my arguments in that section do show is that even a just result is sometimes not an accurate indicator of the relative athletic excellence of the teams. The only sense in which such a result is unjust is reflected in the statement that the losing team did not do justice to itself.

So we have seen many factors that can prevent the better team from winning. Bad refereeing decisions, cheating, gamesmanship, and bad luck can result in a loss for the team that performed better and deserved to win. And a subpar performance can result in a deserved loss by a team that is better than its opponents. The concept of athletic superiority that has emerged from our examination of these situations includes not only physical prowess but also mental attributes. And relevant mental attributes include not only cognitive skills like astute strategy but also affective qualities like poise and toughness. However, we should beware of placing undue stress on these affective qualities in our determinations of athletic superiority. A welcome consequence of our realization that a wide range of situations exists in which the better team or player does not win may be to weaken the obsession with winning that exists among some athletes, especially in the U.S. Putting winning and losing in a saner perspective may reduce the motivation to resort to cheating, distasteful forms of gamesmanship, and trash talking and other forms of taunting. And, while the desire to win is a necessary ingredient of competitive sport, realizing that winning is not the be-all and end-all of athletic excellence may help to foster the cooperation that is part of healthy competition and prevent it from degenerating into alienation.[16]

Notes

1. For the sake of convenience, I will refer throughout most of this paper to the "better" team or player. While the comparative "better" applies most naturally to contests between pairs of players or teams, I also intend my discussion to include competitions involving several players or teams. Understanding "better" in such contexts to mean "better than the rival(s)" will enable me to avoid the cumbersome construction "better or best."

2. For the sake of brevity, I will henceforth usually refer only to the better team, except when explicitly discussing individual sports, in which case I will refer to the better player. The reader should understand, however, that my entire paper pertains to both team and individual sports.

3. An actual example of a victory resulting from a refereeing error was the University of Colorado football team's infamous "5th down" win over the University of Missouri in 1990.

4. For an excellent summary of this central tenet of legal positivism, see Hart (4: sec. 1).

5. See, for example, Edwin J. Delattre's critique (2).

6. "Cheating in sport need not be compared morally to cheating in our everyday affairs since sport is 'just a game' and not simply a reflection of our everyday behavior. It may be morally acceptable to do certain things in sport which are not acceptable in everyday life" (8: p. 196).

7. See Simon (11: pp. 37-51) for a very perceptive analysis of the incompatibility between cheating and sport as a test of athletic skill.

8. Fine questions arise concerning whether a professional foul can be such a violation of D'Agostino's concept of the ethos of a game (1) that it constitutes an outright act of cheating rather than gamesmanship. Such questions, while of great intrinsic interest, are beyond the scope of this section. My concern is with whether such acts, *however* we characterize them, can result in an undeserved victory by an inferior team, and with what implications this has for our concept of athletic superiority.

9. See Warren Fraleigh (3) for a persuasive example of such critiques.

10. By luck I mean factors that are beyond the control of either team and that have, hence, no bearing on the teams' athletic ability, whether understood in purely physical or psychological terms. Uncontroversial examples of bad luck are being on the wrong end of a net cord in tennis or losing a golf game when one's opponent's tee shot on the final hole rebounds freakishly from a tree into the hole.

11. I add the qualifier *"unacceptable gamesmanship"* to allow for my concession to Simon, for the sake of argument, in the previous section—namely, that some gamesmanship may be permissible. By implication, a team that succumbs to opponents who use *legitimate* gamesmanship may have lost the right to call itself the better team.

12. I remind the reader that what I refer to as the "intuitive" concept of athletic superiority is not a blind appeal to intuition. The account developed in this paper is based on uncontroversial views on the purpose of competitive sport by such philosophers of sport as Kretchmar, Simon, and Pearson, and modified in the light of Leaman's radical critique.

13. Two ground-breaking articles are Thomas Nagel (9) and Bernard Williams (13).

14. This is a variation on an example that Nagel gives (9: p. 26).

15. Nagel: "The area of genuine agency, and therefore of legitimate moral judgment, seems to shrink under this scrutiny to an extensionless point" (9: p. 35).

16. For an excellent account of healthy, non-alienated competition in sport, see Drew A. Hyland (5).

Bibliography

1. D'Agostino, F. "The Ethos of Games." *Journal of the Philosophy of Sport.* 8:7-18, 1981.

2. Delattre, E.J. "Some Reflections on Success and Failure in Competitive Athletics." *Journal of the Philosophy of Sport.* 2:133-139, 1975.

3. Fraleigh, W. "Why the Good Foul Is Not Good." *Journal of Physical Education, Recreation and Dance.* 53(1):41-42, 1982.

4. Hart, H.L.A. "Positivism and the Separation of Law and Morals." *Harvard Law Review.* 71:593, 1958.

5. Hyland, D.A. "Opponents, Contestants, and Competitors: The Dialectic of Sport." *Journal of the Philosophy of Sport.* 11:63-70, 1984.

6. King, M.L. "Letter from a Birmingham Jail." In: *I Have a Dream: Writings and Speeches That Changed the World.* San Francisco: Harper Collins, 1992.

7. Kretchmar, R.S. "From Test to Contest: An Analysis of Two Kinds of Counterpoint in Sport." *Journal of the Philosophy of Sport.* 2:23-30, 1975.

8. Leaman, O. "Cheating and Fair Play in Sport." In: *Philosophic Inquiry in Sport* (2nd ed.), W.J. Morgan and K.V. Meier (Eds.). Champaign, IL: Human Kinetics, 1995.

9. Nagel, T. "Moral Luck." In: *Mortal Questions.* Cambridge, UK: Cambridge University Press, 1979.

10. Pearson, K.M. "Deception, Sportsmanship, and Ethics." In: *Philosophic Inquiry in Sport* (2nd ed.), W.J. Morgan and K.V. Meier (Eds.). Champaign, IL: Human Kinetics, 1995.

11. Simon, R.L. *Fair Play: Sports, Values, and Society.* Boulder, CO: Westview Press, 1991.

12. Suits, B. "The Elements of Sport." In: *Philosophic Inquiry in Sport* (2nd ed.), W.J. Morgan and K.V. Meier (Eds.). Champaign, IL: Human Kinetics, 1995.

13. Williams, B. "Moral Luck." In: *Moral Luck: Philosophical Papers 1973-1980.* Cambridge, UK: Cambridge University Press, 1981.

In Defense of Competition and Winning

Revisiting Athletic Tests and Contests[1]

Scott Kretchmar and Tim Elcombe

Over 30 years ago, Kretchmar (14) argued that a key element in understanding the attraction of games lay in the distinction between tests and contests. This analysis had an analytic flavor to it because tests and contests were depicted as distinctive kinds of endeavors—activities that have clean edges to them and that stand in a variety of invariable logical relationships to one another. Kretchmar indicated, for instance, that these two kinds of projects have distinctive purposes. Tests are designed to measure simple achievement, whereas contests are structured to assess superiority and inferiority. Years later, Dixon (9) would agree with these analytic-tending conclusions by noting that competitive sport has a "central comparative purpose"—namely, "the determination of athletic superiority" (p. 10).

Understood in these unequivocal terms, sport provided a target for certain critics of competition, including Dixon (9) himself. Dixon argued that, for a variety of reasons, sporting projects do not always assess superiority accurately. Because of this, winning is often overrated and misunderstood. Other commentators, including Carr (4), Ennis (10), and Fraleigh (11), questioned the significance of victories and argued that the purported zero-sum relationship between winning and losing raises significant moral concerns. All of these writers suggested that the competitive elements of sport, as well as the athlete's quest for victory, be de-emphasized or re-conceptualized—particularly in educational and youth settings. More radical critics, such as Kohn (13), went even further, arguing that competitive activities, including athletic contests, should be avoided altogether.

These conclusions, we believe, are excessive given what appears to be a pervasive human attraction to athletic competition that has transcended time, location, and culture (1, 18). In addition, sharp-edged, categorical conclusions about sporting purposes, as well as winning and losing, seem to miss the mark when compared to the variety of nuanced experiences available in sport. In light of this, we raise the possibility that contesting forms of sport are actually rich, meaningful, and potentially uplifting forms of human behavior.

In this chapter we will revisit Kretchmar's original analysis of athletic tests and contests and point out how its analytic conclusions resulted in incomplete understandings of competitive activities. Following this review, we will reconsider tests and contests from a more anthropological, phenomenological perspective. Finally, to reveal the potential that competitive sport holds for human flourishing, we will employ three arguments related to the work of Alasdair MacIntyre in *After Virtue* (20).

Analytic-Tending Distinctions Between Tests and Contests

Kretchmar's original attempt to understand tests and contests produced clear distinctions between these two versions of sporting activity. He even claimed that tests and contests stood in fixed logical relationships to one another. For his efforts, Kretchmar would have been identified by Boisvert (2) as among the friends of *mathema* in contrast to *bios*.

> They are attracted to fixed forms, computational certainties, and the unambiguous clarities associated with numbers. The safest generalization about all branches of this family is that they . . . . prize discrete, individualized, clearly separated elements. Purity is an important family ideal. Messy entanglements are its greatest scandal (p. 132).

Kretchmar avoided the messiness of more pragmatic-tending analyses by indicating that tests and contests are grounded in two distinct kinds of counterpoint: opposition by cut and degree. Opposition by cut is inherent in facing the ambiguous difficulty posed by tests. The difficulty of tests is ambiguous because tests at once show faces of vulnerability ("I can do this!") and impregnability ("Maybe I cannot do this.").

This "maybe-yes-maybe-no" kind of experience can occur, for example, when trying to reach the top of a high mountain. Alternately, in cases in which the foundational test itself is not sufficiently difficult, the project may involve completing the feat with unnecessary time or equipment restrictions. Regardless, in all these cases, when a genuine test is in place, the possibility exists of meeting some achievement criterion point or not. It is the validity of the problem or test that renders reaching the goal or criterion measure of the project "iffy" or uncertain.

This becomes clear, Kretchmar argued, by noting that tests can disappear in one of two directions—toward gratuity, on the one hand, and toward impossibility, on the other. Importantly, both directions produce foregone conclusions and, because of this, the cut disappears. Neither the simple task nor the impossible challenge provide *both* the "can" and the "cannot." "Can" applies only to simple tasks, whereas "cannot" applies only to impossible tasks. Either way, the cut vanishes. This is why gamewrights must be adroit in developing game challenges that are neither too hard nor too easy (27).

Kretchmar proceeded to note that tests can be put to the service of contests. That is, two or more individuals can share a test and make a commitment to outperform one another in solving its problems. This introduces a second kind of contrariety—namely, opposition by degree. In sharing a common problem, competitors attempt do the same thing, only better than one another. The contest outcomes that we call "victories" and "defeats" are misleadingly dichotomous surrogates for this variable difference by degree. These outcomes can mislead because they stand, in principle, for *all* differences—from those that are so close they are difficult to measure to those that are so disparate we call them "blowouts" or "laughers."

Contests, Kretchmar argued, presuppose valid tests. This is so because opposition by degree is predicated on the ability to show differences. When the test dissolves into the forgone conclusion of gratuity or impossibility, the capacity to show difference disappears. In the inappropriately easy "test," everyone scores 100. In the patently impossible "test," everyone scores 0. Because no opposition by cut exists, the test disappears. Without a valid test, the ability to show difference is lost. Consequently, competing and experiencing opposition by degree are also forfeited.

To put this line of reasoning in analytic terms, competition in the absence of a valid test is unintelligible. Conversely, however, testing in the absence of a valid contest does not introduce a conceptual dilemma. Facing a test, in other words, is a coherent project all by itself. Tests and contests thus stand in a classic one-way relationship of dependency. Contests are parasitic on tests, whereas the reverse is not the case.

Kretchmar used this conclusion to suggest that tests lie at the heart of our human fascination with games, whereas contests are derivative or secondary. We form "testing families" and identify ourselves as golfers, distance runners, and hang gliders, not as nomadic or homeless competitors. But he also noted that contests "are captivating" and they too provide their own "sweet tension." In other words, both kinds of opposition—the kind produced by the testing cut and by the contesting degree, produce "auras of uncertainty" that have the power to seduce and delight. Because contests require both kinds of tension, Kretchmar concluded, competitive projects can be more attractive and, for this reason, may actually enjoy an advantage over more foundational testing activities.

We agree with Kretchmar's suggestion that contests may offer a richer resource for human flourishing than mere tests, but his analytic descriptions did not go far enough in promoting this provocative idea. In fact, they encouraged us to see both tests and contests as simple phenomena. They depicted competitive activities as uniform, comparative, zero-sum endeavors. They suggested that sport involves clinical comparisons of testing skills that produce superior and inferior performances. They implied that the greater the victory by the dominant side, the less there is for the inferior party to salvage from the experience.

As noted previously, this kind of clean-edged, mathematically inclined thinking provided fodder for critics like Dixon, Carr, Fraleigh, Ennis, and Kohn. If sport is simply about comparisons of relative skill, an inability to produce accurate measurements of these skills would strike a blow to the heart of the enterprise (9). Furthermore, if sport is simply about skill, and if skill is grounded in our initial genetic endowment and other factors that lie outside our control, the assignment of merit associated with victory is compromised or lost (4). Additionally, if sport is simply about superiority, and thus winning, and if victory can be secured by only one party, it would be difficult to defend sport as a mutually valuable project (11).

Also, if sport is simply about showing superiority, it smacks of Social Darwinism, making for a rather crass "survival of the fittest" view of life. As such, sport might not be appropriate for educational settings (10). Finally, if the primary purpose of sport is to secure victories, sporting contests may well tear at the social fabric (13). Perhaps it would be best to agree with Kohn (13) and avoid sporting competition altogether.

This conclusion is premature, we believe, because games are understood differently by the so-called "friends of *bios*." Games address the complex and messy human needs for challenge and its attendant uncertainty. Unlike the more logical, reductive analyses performed by "friends of *mathema*," pragmatically-inclined philosophers inquire into the lived experiences of "concrete human beings who have bodies, are parts of families, make up the fabric of a particular culture, and in general are imbedded in a network of caring relations" (2, p. 144). While this approach need not contradict insights derived analytically, it should at least add important information that could produce a persuasive defense of competition and winning.

A Pragmatic-Tending Reconceptualization of Tests and Contests

As embodied, habituated, socialized, constrained, intelligent, and still-evolving biological creatures, we need problems at many levels and for different reasons.[2] From our chemistry and cells, to our biological systems, all the way to the more complex social, political, and intellectual levels, atrophy can result when we fail to exercise our "problem-solving muscles." Holistic laws of use and disuse, homeostasis, growth and decline, and interaction and isolation affect us not as "minds" but as thoroughly ambiguous creatures—as thoughtful animals, as symbolically animated flesh, as intelligent beings who can be destroyed by problems but who also, curiously enough, need problems and seek them out.

We have many ways to meet these needs for the stimulation produced by difficulty. Among them is inventing and confronting those artificial problems we call games. But games come in different shapes and sizes. Some are relatively simple and others more complex; some are plain and temporary, others far richer and more durable; some produce impoverished meanings, and others carry us away on the wings of delight (16). In short, some games (and some ways of engaging them) work better than others.

Why is this so? Tests can be evaluated in terms of the nature and quality of their problems. For example, an open-ended problem, one that invites repeated confrontations of its difficulties, has obvious advantages over closed problems, the kind that lose their attractiveness once they are solved. Golf is an example of the former kind of game. Even with improvement and good scores, the core problem is never exhausted. All races are like this too. No matter how fast one runs, swims, drives a race car, or rides a horse, improvements are conceivable, and new challenges forever present themselves.

An interlocking ring puzzle is an example of the latter kind of game problem, the closed problem. Once we see how the rings need to be juxtaposed to get them apart, we can do it again easily. Once solved, always solved! New challenges do not appear. The game is no longer of service.

Challenges can also be understood in terms of the meaning that is produced. Some game results make little sense and produce insignificant meanings. Other game results have far more potential to "say" things to us, to evoke emotions and provide important information. A test that has not been normed, for instance, is a relatively sterile problem. Simon (26), borrowing from work by Nozick (24), described an isolated villager who made 15 jump shots out of 150 tries. Fifteen successes is an unambiguous numerical result, but what does it mean? In the absence of a norm, it is hard to say. If the villager shot day in and day out, the meaning would improve in the context of his own shooting history, but still it would be difficult for him to draw any conclusions about either his rate of improvement or the significance of his achievement. In the absence of interpersonal comparisons—either norms or direct observations of the foul shooting of others—the testing activity remains relatively uninformative and thus uninteresting.

This helps us to see that information can grow incrementally from tests that lack norms to simple self-normed or self-improvement challenges to interpersonal-normed tests to in-person comparisons of testing performances among two or more people to impersonal and potentially asynchronous contests in which commitments to surpass are in place but the progress of an opponent cannot be seen—all the way to robust, simultaneous in-person competition. The resources for meaning that are available in sport improve, if only gradually, from a first experience with a novel test to norm-referenced, face-to-face competition.

This enhancement of meaning can be seen in Kretchmar's (15) analysis of the evolution of diving as a game. The fictional athlete in this account first tastes the sensuous quality of diving by jumping off a cliff into the waters below to avoid a dangerous bear in hot pursuit. Wanting to relive this heightened experience, the young man eventually changes how the diving occurs—first by tantalizing the bear to increase the tension in the event, then by limiting the degrees of freedom through which he can enter the water after diving off the cliff's edge. This, Kretchmar argued, is how tests grow. The impregnability and vulnerability that produce the testing cut are "lived," modified, and recreated rather than encountered as analytical categories. The addition of a second diver with competitive intentions adds complexity and potentially further meaning to the event, which suggests that contests are not merely parasitic upon tests in a logical sense but also expand their experiential potential in a variety of ways.

This all makes sense because information from competition comes from at least two general sources—from both the richly normed testing score (and what it means) and the potentially dramatic contest result (and what it means). In effect, competition provides a powerful second source of meaning without eliminating all the information that comes from the test itself.

A golfer, for instance, who shoots a 74 in his club tournament and also wins the event has achieved two important and symbolically rich contexts for meaning. The testing information related to the 74 provides one group of meanings specific to the testing family of golfers and what counts as excellence in the testing environment provided by golf courses. But this individual also has information related to the contest and the commitment to take the test in a superior fashion. Was a particular strategy employed to win the day? Were gambles taken? Were nerves calmed at a crucial time when, perhaps, an opponent took the lead by a stroke? The contest and competition and the winning and losing provide enhanced meanings that tell us more about who we are and what we have accomplished. We will have more to say about enhanced meaning later in the chapter.

The quality of tests and contests rests on a host of other factors in addition to durability and meaning. For example, some tests, such as those involving skiing, hiking, and swimming, are sensuously rich. Other tests, such as checkers and crossword puzzles, have less sensuous content. Some games are culture-reinforcing in nature and thus come alive in certain historical and political settings. Others are misplaced. Their structure and symbol systems rub against the socialized grain of the people playing them and thus need to be partly revised and reinterpreted, or simply replaced (12, 22, 23).

Undoubtedly, many other important variables affect our experiences in both tests and contests, but enough has been written to show how a pragmatic-tending analysis opens up new avenues for understanding competition and appreciating its rich possibilities. To better see at least three such avenues, we now turn to Alasdair MacIntyre's conception of practice communities, internal goods, and virtues, as developed in *After Virtue* (20).[3]

Durable Sport Practices: Enhancing Dynamism, Complexity, and Cooperation

MacIntyre pictured healthy human beings as story-telling creatures who develop coherent personal narratives related to one or more roles or positions in life. These narratives, he believed, should always be directed toward some end, or *telos,* related to one's identity as, say, a warrior, musician, parent, philosopher, or athlete. The vehicle that promoted this view of the good life is something he called a "practice."

> By a 'practice' I am going to mean any coherent and complex form of socially established cooperative human activity through which goods internal to that form of activity are realized in the course of trying to achieve those standards of excellence which are appropriate to, and partially definitive of, that form of activity, with the result that human powers to achieve excellence, and human conceptions of the ends and good involved, are systematically extended. (p. 187)

Central to MacIntyre's argument is the demarcation of practices from other lesser but nearby phenomena. Isolated competencies stand as a case in point. The so-called technical skills such as throwing a football, according to MacIntyre, are not practices. Football, however, is a practice. Erecting a wall is not a practice, but architecture is.

The difference between the two rests on a cluster of characteristics. The more something is dynamic, complex, and a product of social collaboration, the more it is likely to be a practice. Practices require community and participant cooperation, the recognition of authority and achievement, respect for standards, and occasional risk taking—all of this in order to provide opportunities for humankind to excel and otherwise flourish (20: p. 193). Furthermore, a practice "has its own history and a history that is more and other than that of the improvement of the relevant technical skills" (p. 194).

This background information on MacIntyre's concept of "practice" brings us to the central question of this section: Could it be that contests provide a better foundation for practices than tests do? Does competitive behavior, for example, require higher levels of complexity, dynamism, and cooperation than does testing activity? We believe that it does.

The shift of an activity from testing to contesting promotes complexity in several important ways.[4] For example, a contest requires a more complex intentionality and forces participants to face a double uncertainty. This is the case because testing formats require only a singular focus on solving the puzzle or problem. For the contestant, however, intentionality runs in two directions at once: toward solving the test as well as one can *and* toward solving it better than one's opponent can do.

This enriched intentionality is paralleled by a magnified experience of "sweet tension" or, more plainly, uncertainty. Test takers face the uncertainties and meanings generated by the problems of the test. They ask themselves, "Can I do this or not?" or "How well can I do this?" In contrast, contestants experience a more complex set of uncertainties and meanings. They ask themselves, "Even if I *can* do this, can I do it better than my opponent? or "Even though both of us might be able to do this, what exactly is the difference between us?"

These dual sets of meanings and uncertainties add considerable dynamism to the competitive project. An individual could be acing the test but losing the contest. Conversely, someone might be having an off-day and performing poorly but still be leading an opponent who is performing even worse. Thus, competition involves the interweaving of at least two stories into one—stories that, at day's end, might leave the contestant with any number of complex, mixed emotions.

For example, concomitant experiences of hope and despair, though relatively uncommon in testing environments, are not unusual in a single contest. Improvement in the face of the test provides one story line—in this case a positive one. The athlete is playing about as well as he or she can play. But a second narrative progresses at the same time. The athlete is losing to a long-standing adversary, say, for the seventh straight time. Some bitterness and disappointment might accompany this unfolding drama.[5]

The move from test to contest also places additional demands on community, specifically on important interpersonal agreements. Tests, by nature, do not require collaboration. All that is needed is a challenging goal, a set of means, and a way of measuring success. If the test does not satisfy, changes in any of these factors could be made unilaterally. Even if more than one person wants to take the same test, little is at stake if someone defects. Because we are not worried about comparing our scores to determine a victor, disparate tests simply produce disparate and potentially incommensurate test scores. Thus, few if any demands on community or cooperation are present.

In contests, communitarian demands extend further. For example, new issues of fairness emerge. If competitors do not take the same test, comparisons of achievement become difficult, and verdicts might be hollow or meaningless. Any individual or team deprived of test-taking means that were available to the other side would have good reason to claim foul. Additionally, should any of the competitors wish to change the means or ends of the test, this would require full agreement and understanding by the opposing sides. Moreover, for more meaningful and robust experiences to occur in contests, the competitors must commit to superior performances—that is, to try their hardest (within the rules) to defeat their opponent(s). Any defections in this regard often "leave a bad taste" and once again minimize the experiential potential made possible by the competitive project.[6] Finally, when scores are close—or alternately when games become lopsided—additional interpersonal pressures related to cooperation come to the fore: pressures that are not commonly found in individual or group testing environments.

In sum, contests, in a sense, are embellished or upgraded tests. In other words, contests include all the assets of tests—and then some. Contests invariably offer more complexity and dynamism than tests do, and they place greater demands on cooperation than are found in base-level testing environments. For these reasons alone, their credentials as sites for durable MacIntyrian practices—and thus as forms of life that make room for human flourishing—would seem to be superior. However, these advantages lead to additional arguments that can be made on behalf of competition.

More Meaningful Sport Practices: Expanding the Availability of Excellences

Practices are sites for what MacIntyre calls internal goods or excellences. Seeking these excellences in a practice provides a *telos* for humanity and unity for our narrative. Internal goods are specific to practices. In other words, the excellences of baseball are different from those of teaching or sculpting, and only those within the respective practice communities can be expected to know and appreciate their own community's excellences when they pursue or see them. Most important, these excellences cannot be gained except by submitting to the standards and disciplines of the practice. In contrast, external goods such as fortune and fame can be achieved through any number of means. Dedication to external goods can thus produce an opportunistic, disconnected pattern of living. MacIntyre accordingly places a clear premium on the quest for internal goods or excellences as a defining feature of the good life and a resource for its coherence.

This analysis of excellences could be used to support a testing version of sport, one that deemphasizes competition or eliminates it altogether. The argument might go something like this: At base level, the display of excellences requires only a problem, dilemma, or puzzle of some sort or other against which one's mettle will be tested. The internal goods of sport are attached to the abilities, skills, and virtues needed to negotiate the valid test. Although comparative testing, including the public sharing of both performances and test scores, would be understandably important in MacIntyre's practice communities, it is not clear what role *exclusionary* comparative testing would play. Such zero-sum testing, in which only one side wins and everyone else loses, might be seen as superfluous at best, or harmfully divisive at worst.

It is conceivable in golf, for example, that scoring consistently below par would provide honored membership in the golfing community and also be grounded in a full complement of excellences ranging from the virtue of honesty to the motor skills that provide a magical touch around the greens. Defeating an opponent on any given afternoon would then seem unnecessary in that the victory would not add anything substantial to the internal goods already achieved.

This might be a hasty conclusion, however, because contests can provide a second resource for the development of excellences. It is one thing to show testing excellence, but it is another to display contesting capabilities. Just as contests provide a richer resource for meaning, as we saw earlier, they also provide a richer foundation for the development and display of excellences. Of course the meaning and excellences are very closely related.

This argument concerning the expansion of excellences depends on our ability to see two things: first, that winning is a process distinct from achieving and, second, that this process of winning has excellences associated with it that are, once again, distinct from the excellences tethered to achieving.

The first distinction, discussed in the literature by Kretchmar (14) and others (e.g., 11), is not particularly contentious. It seems clear that someone could be doing poorly on a test (achieving very little) and still, if his or her opponent is faring even less well, comparing favorably in the contest—that is, winning. Of course, the opposite can also occur. An Olympic sprinter, for example, might achieve testing excellence by setting a world record but still lose the contest because an opponent broke the record by a greater margin.

The second distinction, regarding excellences of winning in contrast to those of achieving, is not well represented in the literature. When MacIntyrian excellences are cited, they typically involve the skills, tendencies, and knowledge related to the practice, the sport—that is, the testing arena of hitting, running, aiming, throwing, catching, and the like.

However, when practices are converted into contests, new opportunities for fine performances appear to present themselves. Contests introduce a host of additional excellences related to the processes of winning, such as, leading, taking the lead, holding a lead, gambling for a lead, delaying strategically for a reversal late in the contest, intentionally forfeiting a lead, mustering resources that would not be needed just to do well on the test but are necessary to surpass an opponent, intentionally and skillfully deceiving an opponent into thinking that a lead has been lost when it has not, identifying the precise moment when a move will have its greatest impact, and sensing when an opponent is flagging and vulnerable. Clearly, these processes involve a second group of excellences, a group that has been missed or ignored by most commentators.

If this argument is not convincing, consider the following: We know that individuals can be good at a sporting practice itself—say, running long distances in unusually short periods of time—but still be mediocre when it comes to comparative standings, such as pacing oneself relative to the field, deciding when to make a move, choosing to draft at the right times or take the lead, intuiting when one is actually winning even though he or she is literally behind, or simply producing the concentration and effort required to provide that whisker of a difference that brings victory. The talented individuals who always seem to "leave their best game on the practice field" provide further evidence to the claim that excellences related to competing and winning transcend those of simply playing well. In short, to take a test successfully involves one set of capabilities or excellences. To take that same test in a competitive environment, where a new comparative objective is present and where the progress of one's opponent is now crucial, appears to demand additional perceptions, motivations, strategies, and skills.

On MacIntyrian grounds, then, contesting excellences might demand the same respect usually accorded testing capabilities. When we compliment an athlete by noting that he or she is an excellent marathon distance runner *and* a remarkable competitor, we are not being redundant. The running and the competing involve different sets of challenges and, correspondingly, separate sets of capabilities.

If this argument is at all persuasive, winning takes on a different life than the one often associated with it. Victory is not simply a crass product or end state associated primarily with extrinsic goods such as fame and fortune. Rather, winning is an ongoing process that requires its own set of capabilities. It is not just a zero-sum outcome or product, a treasure eventually possessed by only one individual or team.

Rather, winning involves a series of relationships in which the excellences related to superiority can be (and usually are) exhibited by both teams on the way to the final verdict. And, also important: Winning is not just an object with a luster that wears off soon after it is gained. Rather, winning represents a distinct set of capabilities and achievements that can be appreciated and valued as part of our life narratives long after the event has taken place.

These expended capabilities and achievements are accompanied, however, by the additional stresses and strains that come with contesting forms of sport—which leads us to a third and final argument in defense of competition. This argument is related to the virtues needed to reap the benefits of sport.

More Responsible Sport Practices: Cultivating and Expanding the Virtues

MacIntyre argued that virtues must be cultivated and exercised if the good life is to be realized (20: p. 191). A life built on problem solving and striving for excellences in the various roles we adopt requires the deployment of such virtues as courage, honesty, and justice. This is the case because we might be tempted to shortcut the considerable challenges that stand in the way of experiencing internal goods—for instance, the training, practice, and dedication required to excel. The deployment of virtues is also needed because institutions like the National Collegiate Athletic Association (NCAA), Little League Baseball, Inc., or the National Basketball Association (NBA), with their inherent focus on such external goods as visibility and profit, might corrupt sport.

Morgan (22) analyzed the corruptive tendencies of institutions in a sport context arguing that they often co-opt the internal goods of sport practices. With an exclusive focus on external goods, institutional operations strive for efficiency and effectiveness—values embodied in MacIntyre's stock character called The Manager (20). The managerial mentality, operating within an amoral, instrumental framework, threatens the integrity of the sporting practice. For instance, cost–benefit thinking can lead to illegal drug use, the admission of illegitimate collegiate athletes, the modification of games to satisfy the dictates of television, and pandering to the masses while ignoring the needs of the more discriminating connoisseurs of the activity.

Both MacIntyre and Morgan acknowledge that institutions are not inherently harmful to practices and that a complex symbiotic relationship exists between them. Nevertheless, a tension is always present, and the temptation to choose what is institutionally expeditious over what is required by the practice is always present. Virtues help us to resist this temptation. MacIntyre summarized the role of virtues as follows:

> The virtues therefore are to be understood as those dispositions which will not only sustain practices and enable us to achieve the goods internal to practices, but which will also sustain us in the relevant kind of quest for the good, by enabling us to overcome the harms, dangers, temptations and distractions which we encounter, and which will furnish us with increasing self-knowledge and increasing knowledge of the good (20: p. 219).

With this understanding of virtues in hand, we can return to the issue of tests and contests. Certainly the opportunity and need to exercise virtues, including MacIntyre's three central dispositions of courage, honesty, and justice, are available in sport tests. A runner, for example, can cheat in the face of her test even if she is running alone for nothing more than a personal record. Institutional pressures for external goods can also influence sport testing environments because money, prestige, and position are often associated with high test scores. Nevertheless, contesting forms of sport place amplified and unique pressures on the virtues.

First, the essential public aspect of contests raises the stakes of sport performances, demanding the cultivation and embodiment of virtues. Contests, unlike tests, must be public. They require, at minimum, a second party—another person, another team, or groups of individuals and teams. Successes and failures are witnessed. Accordingly, temptations to find performance-enhancing shortcuts are often increased.

In addition, contests, far more often than tests, draw spectators, who are there to witness the performances, the highs and lows of athletic competition. The virtual impossibility of hiding testing or contesting incompetence or weakness places additional pressures on such virtues as courage and perseverance. In short, the interpersonal forum of the contest includes all the stresses and strains inherent in the sporting test while adding those public pressures of face-to-face competition and, often, interested observers. These expanded pressures require a corresponding expansion and strengthening of the virtues.

Some might doubt that gratuitous activities such as sport generate real existential fear and require true courage.[7] However, living a virtue such as courage in sport contests, in part because of its public nature, is a realistic requirement. Corlett suggested that the fear faced by athletes is genuine, yet they "choose to participate in the circumstances that produce the fear that debilitates them" (5: p. 52). Consequently, Corlett concluded that sport is a worthwhile social practice and thus worthy of true courage: "[Athletes] actively seek the opportunity to challenge themselves and know beforehand that if the challenge were trivial, there would be no point" (p. 52). Every athlete, at every level, in every contesting circumstance has the opportunity to publicly encounter injury, embarrassment, disappointment, and corruption. Courage "does feel like something, and affords great accomplishments in the face of threats to one's physical, mental, or social well-being of the kind perceived regularly by competitive athletes" (5: p. 52).

The second factor that enhances the demands placed on the virtues in contests is its inherent structure. Competitive sports produce winners and losers. Contests take potentially negligible differences in test scores and use them to determine all-or-nothing outcomes. In a contest, a 91.8 might signal defeat, while a 91.9 produces the victory. Such negligible differences can determine winner from loser, champion from also-ran, and gold medalist from silver medalist. This comparative structure, and the irony and drama it creates, increases the demands placed on the virtues.

The increased demands occur because exceedingly small differences between victory and defeat might tempt athletes to find that small edge to eliminate these potentially infinitesimal gaps. These small disparities can be erased by such acts as violating unenforceable rules, intentionally breaking rules whose penalties do not fit the crimes, taking banned substances surreptitiously, intimidating opponents, manipulating officials, and finding loopholes in rules. Small indiscretions, to say nothing of their more robust cousins, can lead to not-so-small victories. Once again, this realization places increased demands on the virtues, particularly those related to integrity.

A second inherent structure of contests—namely, "playing until the end" to enhance the validity of achievement comparisons—introduces unique demands on virtuous behavior. For instance, the dispositions of cooperation and perseverance are lived differently in tests and contests. Anyone taking a test who faces insurmountable odds and recognizes the overwhelming impregnability of a problem can choose to quit without directly affecting others who might also be facing this problem. A climber at the base of a seemingly impossible rock formation can turn back without influencing fellow climbers working on other parts of the mountain. In a competitive situation, however, a climber's choice to turn back destroys the contest. It eliminates, or at least substantially reduces, the possibility of all parties realizing contesting excellences. Consequently, the demands on a contestant's will to persevere and commitment to cooperate are greatly amplified and lived in unique ways during competitive situations.

Finally, it is important to note that contests, far more than tests, are vulnerable to the corrupting tendencies of institutions. Money, visibility, power, influence, and other external goods are associated far more with the powerful lure of the so-called big game than with scrimmages, practices, or other testing formats. With the rise of external goods comes pressure to secure them. With pressure to secure them, sport participants are tempted to substitute expeditious achievement for the excellences that could be won in the practice.

To be sure, tests, practice sessions, displays, recitals, scrimmages, noncompetitive challenges, and exhibitions garner interest. On occasion, such events draw a crowd and are even televised. But in contemporary society they are not often seen as a culminating event, as offering a climax or anything particularly dramatic or special. And, also important, they do not as readily attract the attention, control, and potentially corrupting influences of institutions.

It is those who compete well who receive college scholarships as amateurs, make multimillion-dollar salaries as professionals, serve as ambassadors for political purposes, and have their face posted on the cover of *Sports Illustrated*. Of course, those who compete well must also be expert on the test. But as noted before, those who leave their best game on the practice field will not have full access to external goods or, correspondingly, be as readily tempted by them. Such temptation requires firm commitments, well-developed virtues, and an array of dispositions that can allow competitors to weather the variety of distractions that come with visibility and institutional coercion.

MacIntyre reminds us that where the virtues can be found, the vices may also thrive. Nowhere is this more the case than in competitive settings. The public nature of competition, the structure of the contest that turns small differences into either-or results and requires persistence to the end of the activity, and the connection of competition to institutions and a plethora of external goods requires that we both expand our array of virtues and embed them ever more fully in our character. To be sure, the exercise of the virtues is required by tests. But this requirement is magnified when we enter contests.

Conclusion

Analytic approaches to understanding sport are useful. In point of fact, we have employed in this essay a number of the insights provided by Kretchmar's early work on the logical distinctions between tests and contests. That said, an analytic approach also reduces what would otherwise be a rich and varied experience in sport to a set of relatively clean characteristics and relationships. This, we noted, provided a target for scholars such as Dixon, Carr, Ennis, Fraleigh, and Kohn, who highlighted various problems with competitive versions of sport. In some cases, the target merited the slings and arrows directed toward it. Competitive enterprises have their weaknesses.

Without a doubt, structural imperfections of various sorts, as well as a robust array of vices, can readily be found within competitive contexts.

We have argued, however, that an anthropological, phenomenological account of sport presents a more balanced picture of the values of competition and the quest for victory. We sided with the friends of *bios* by describing some of the nuances of testing and contesting experiences. Phenomena with clean edges were complemented with messy and overlapping experiences. Fixed logical relationships were expanded to include a variety of encounters that might or might not be found within them. In short, the target of past critiques was shown to be richer than analytic approaches had shown it to be. We have not necessarily invalidated criticisms based on these perspectives, but we hope we have raised doubts about their sufficiency.

We cited MacIntyre as a friend of *bios* who attempted to draw distinctions among such overlapping and interacting phenomena as practices, technical skills, institutions, and virtues. He speculated that a coherent, narrative life grounded in the pursuit of excellences can provide deep human satisfactions. We used those ideas to show how testing activity provides a foundation for practices, permits the pursuit and acquisition of excellences, and requires the utilization of virtues. But we also argued that tests raised to the level of competition include all those values in addition to others. Contests, in contrast to tests, provide a firmer foundation for practices, they extend the excellences available to participants, and they present additional challenges for the virtues. As "enriched tests," we believe that contests and the pursuit of victory provide material for a human story that is clearly worth telling.

Notes

1. Portions of this paper were taken from Kretchmar's "In Defense of Winning" (17) published in Boxill's *Sports Ethics: An Anthology* (3).

2. Evolution and biology, for instance, rest on the basic principles of homeostasis. Too much and too little resistance are both dangers. Overstimulation and understimulation can damage an organism. More to the point here, where we focus on games as an artificial stressor, it is important to note that a lack of stimulation leads to stasis at best and, more likely, to decline and ultimate extinction. For more on the centrality of challenge and homeostasis in understanding evolution and human development see, e.g., Damasio (6, 7) and Pinker (24).

3. MacIntyre's early work in *After Virtue* admittedly has less *bios* in it than some later writings. For instance in *Dependent Rational Animals* (21), MacIntyre admitted to a degree of forgetfulness "of our bodies and how our thinking is the thinking of one species of animal" (p. 5). But even with MacIntyre's rationalist tendencies in *After Virtue*, his arguments transcend the clean distinctions and logic preferred by many analytic philosophers.

4. It is important that readers recognize that our comparison is of testing and contesting forms of the same athletic activity. In other words, we are comparing oranges to oranges (throwing a football to playing the game of football) rather than apples to oranges (climbing Everest as a test compared to playing basketball as a contest).

5. Some great athletes or teams have had their legacies diminished because they competed at the same time as superior opponents. John McEnroe, for example, likely would have won numerous Grand Slam titles if he had been able to beat Bjorn Borg more often. Similarly, today's young tennis stars entering their prime, such as Andy Roddick, Lleyton Hewitt, and Marat Safin, must compete for championships at a time when Roger Federer's record-breaking level of play stands at its apex.

6. Many participants in competitive sport can point to the hollowness of a game experience when the other team or competitor does not commit to pursuing victory. For example, pick up basketball games in which opponents fail to make a defensive transition, or when opponents perceive the game as unimportant and stop competing, leave the competitive project uninteresting. Such a game also fails to make contesting excellences available.

7. MacIntyre (20) defines courage as "the capacity to risk harm or danger to oneself" (p. 192).

Bibliography

1. Blanchard, K. *The Anthropology of Sport: An Introduction.* (A revised edition.) Westport CT: Bergin and Garvey, 1995.

2. Boisvert, Raymond D. "Heteronomous Freedom," In John J. Stuhr (Ed.) *Philosophy and the Reconstruction of Culture: Pragmatic Essays after Dewey.* Albany, NY: State University of New York: 131-149, 1993.

3. Boxill, Jan (Ed.). *Sport Ethics: An Anthology.* Malden, MA: Blackwell, 2002.

4. Carr, David. "Where's the Merit if the Best Man Wins?" *Journal of the Philosophy of Sport* XXVI (1999): 1-9.

5. Corlett, John. "Virtue Lost: Courage in Sport," *Journal of the Philosophy of Sport* XXIII (1996): 45-57.

6. Damasio, Antonio. *The Feeling of What Happens: Body and Emotion in the Making of Consciousness.* New York: Harcourt, 1999.

7. Damasio, Antonio. *Looking for Spinoza: Joy, Sorrow and the Feeling Brain.* New York: Harcourt, 2003.

8. Dixon, Nicholas. "On Sportsmanship and 'Running Up the Score,'" *Journal of the Philosophy of Sport* XIX (1992): 1-14.

9. Dixon, Nicholas. "On Winning and Athletic Superiority," *Journal of the Philosophy of Sport* XXVI (1999): 10-26.

10. Ennis, Catherine. "Students' Experiences in Sport-Based Physical Education: [More Than] Apologies Are Necessary," *Quest* 48 (1996): 453-456.

11. Fraleigh, Warren P. *Right Actions in Sport: Ethics for Contestants.* Champaign, IL: Human Kinetics, 1984.

12. Gruneau, Richard. *Class, Sports, and Social Development.* Champaign, IL: Human Kinetics, 1999.

13. Kohn, Alfie. "Why Competition?" *The Humanist* 40 (1980): 14-15, 49.

14. Kretchmar, R. Scott. "From Test to Contest: An Analysis of Two Kinds of Counterpoint in Sport," *Journal of the Philosophy of Sport* II (1975): 23-30.

15. Kretchmar, R. Scott. "On Beautiful Games," *Journal of the Philosophy of Sport* 16 (1989): 16, 34-43.

16. Kretchmar, R. Scott. "Moving and Being Moved: Implications for Practice," *Quest* 52 (2000): 260-272.

17. Kretchmar, R. Scott. "In Defense of Winning," In: *Sports Ethics: An Anthology,* ed. Jan Boxill (Malden, MA: Blackwell, 2002): 130-135.

18. Kretchmar, R. Scott. "Why Do We Care So Much About Games? (And is this Ethically Defensible?)," *Quest* 57 (2005): 181-191.

19. Kretchmar, R. Scott. "Game Flaws," *Journal of the Philosophy of Sport* XXXII (2005): 36-48.

20. MacIntyre, Alasdair. *After Virtue,* 2nd ed. Notre Dame, IN: University of Notre Dame, 1984.

21. MacIntyre, Alasdair. *Dependent Rational Animals: Why Human Beings Need the Virtues.* Chicago: Open Court, 1999.

22. Morgan, William J. *Leftist Theories of Sport: A Critique and Reconstruction.* Urbana, IL: University of Illinois, 1994.

23. Morgan, William J. Patriotic sports and the moral making of nations. *Journal of the Philosophy of Sport* XXVI (1999): 50-67.

24. Nozick, Robert. *Anarchy, State, and Utopia.* New York: Basic Books, 1974.

25. Pinker, Steven. *The Blank Slate: The Modern Denial of Human Nature.* New York: Penguin Group, 2002.

26. Simon, Robert L. *Fair Play: The Ethics of Sport,* 2nd ed. Boulder, CO: Westview Press, 1991.

27. Suits, Bernard. "What is a Game?" *Philosophy of Science* 34 (1967): 148-156.

Some Reflections on Success and Failure in Competitive Athletics

✦

Edwin J. Delattre

The initial objects of my reflections are the great and transporting moments of participation in competitive athletics. Reflection on these moments draws our attention to the conditions under which they are possible and to the kinds of people who are capable of achieving them. Reflection on these, in turn, enables us to see at once the touchstone relationship of competitors, and the moral and logical incompatibility of competing and cheating. Most of all we are reminded throughout these reflections that success in competitive athletics is not reducible to winning, nor failure to losing.

Richard Harding Davis was sensitive to the great and transporting moments of participation in competitive athletics. In the late fall of 1895, he wrote a gripping account of the recently contested Yale–Princeton football game. He captured both the involvement of the spectators and the struggle of the participants in revealing ways.

With the score at 16-10 in favor of Yale, but amidst a Princeton comeback, the description proceeds:

> It was obviously easy after that to argue that if the Tigers had scored twice in ten minutes they could score at least once more . . . or even snatch a victory out of defeat. And at the thought of this the yells redoubled, and the air shook, and every play, good, bad, or indifferent, was greeted with shouts of encouragement that fell like blows of a whip on one side and that tasted like wine to the other. People forgot for a few precious minutes to think about themselves, they enjoyed the rare sensation of being carried completely away by something outside of themselves, and the love of a fight, or a struggle, or combat, or whatever else you choose to call it, rose in everyone's breast and choked him until he had either to yell and get rid of it or suffocate. (2: p. 9)

Reprinted, by permission, from E. Delattre, 1976, "Some reflections on success and failure in competitive athletics," *Journal of the Philosophy of Sport, 2:* 133-139.

Forgetting "for a few precious moments to think about" oneself, being "carried completely away," can be among the high points of human existence. Yet being so transported in the wrong way, or in the wrong context, becomes fanaticism, irresponsible loss of self-control, even madness. Here we will not concern ourselves with the problematic dimensions of being "carried completely away," since they are not relevant to our reflections.

As the objects of eros are many, we can become passionately involved in diverse pursuits and activities, concerns, persons, even places. Inquiry can be transporting, the quest to discover—was anyone ever more obviously carried completely away than the Leakeys at Olduvai Gorge? The love of another, a symphony, dance; the range of our passionate concerns is virtually endless. In this list, of course, is the game: competitive athletics. Because of its special place on this list, which will emerge in our discussion, competitive athletics merit our attention and reflection.

Let us return then to Davis' description for it becomes even more revealing about the transporting moments in competitive athletics:

> The clamor ceased once absolutely, and the silence was even more impressive than the tumult that had preceded it. It came toward the end of the second half, when the light had begun to fail and the mist was rising from the ground. The Yale men had forced the ball to within two yards of Princeton's goal, and they had still one more chance left them to rush it across the line. While they were lining up for that effort the cheering died away, yells, both measured and inarticulate, stopped, and the place was so still that for the first time during the day you could hear the telegraph instruments chirping like crickets from the side line. (2: p. 9)

What is crucial in this passage is not the silence of the crowd, but the occasion for it. The silence is occasioned by the resolution of the game into this moment, this spellbinding moment when the competition is most intense. Think of the moment not as a spectator, but as a competitor. Think of the overwhelming silence of the moments when the game is most of all a test, the moments of significance in the game, the turning points, which all the practice and diligence and preparation point to and anticipate.

Such moments are what make the game worth the candle. Whether amidst the soft lights and the sparkling balls against the baize of a billiard table, on the rolling terrain of a lush fairway or in the violent and crashing pit where linemen struggle, it is the moments when no let-up is possible, when there is virtually no tolerance for error, which make the game. The best and most satisfying contests maximize these moments and minimize respite from pressure. When competition achieves this intensity it frequently renders the outcome of the contest anti-climactic, and it inevitably reduces victory celebrations to pallor by contrast.

We see here the basic condition of success in competitive athletics. We must be able mutually to discover worthy opponents, opponents who are capable of generating with us the intensity of competition. Exclusive emphasis on winning has particularly tended to obscure the importance of the quality of the opposition and of the thrill of the competition itself. It is of the utmost importance for competitors to discover opponents whose preparation and skill are comparable to their own and who respect the game utterly.

We are recalled to this insight by the applicability to competitive athletics of the phrase "testing one's mettle." The etymological roots of "mettle" are the same as those of metal; indeed these were originally variant spellings of the same word. Just as the quality of a metal ore was determined long ago by the intensity of the color streak produced by rubbing it against a mica-like material called a touchstone, so in competition, one's opponent is his touchstone. In rubbing against a worthy opponent, against his skill, dedication and preparation, the quality of a competitor's mettle is tested.

As all philosophers know, Socrates employed the metaphor of the touchstone in the dialogues. Fellow participants in dialogue are the touchstones by which one tests the epistemic quality of his beliefs. That I have used the same metaphor must not be allowed to obscure the point that inquiry, dialogue, is, without qualification, not competitive. To view inquiry as competition, argument as something won or lost, is to misunderstand both. Dialectical inquiry is the shared and cooperative pursuit of the best approximation of the truth. In successful dialogues, false and confused beliefs are exposed as such, and those who held them benefit by the disclosure of their inadequacy. The testing of one's mettle in competitive athletics is quite another thing. The distinction is vital because when inquiry is treated as competition it is destroyed as inquiry.

Competition, contesting, if you will, thus requires commensurate opponents. The testing of one's mettle in competitive athletics is a form of self-discovery, just as the preparation to compete is a form of self-creation. The claim of competitive athletics to importance rests squarely on their providing for us opportunities for self-discovery which might otherwise have been missed. They are not unique in this by any means—the entire fabric of moral life is woven of such opportunities—but there is no need for them to claim uniqueness. They provide opportunities for self-discovery, for concentration and intensity of involvement, for being carried away by the demands of the contest and thereby in part for being able to meet them, with a frequency seldom matched elsewhere. It is in the face of these demands and with respect to them that an athlete succeeds or fails. This is why it is a far greater success in competitive athletics to have played well under the pressure of a truly worthy opponent and lost than to have defeated a less worthy or unworthy one where no demands were made.

We may appreciate this last point through a final look at Davis' chronicle:

> And then, just as the Yale men were growing fearful that the game would end in a tie, and while the Princeton men were shrieking their lungs out that it might, Captain Thorne made his run, and settled the question forever.

> It is not possible to describe that run. It would be as easy to explain how a snake disappears through the grass, or an eel slips from your fingers, or to say how a flash of linked lightning wriggles across the sky. (2: p. 9)

We cannot separate the significance of the Yale victory and the Princeton defeat from the fact that there was involved a player capable of such a run. For Princeton to have played well against a team with such a back, to have held a back of such quality to a single long run, to have required magnificence of Thorne for him to score, is a great success in itself.

How different this is from the occasion for Jack London's concluding lament in his coverage of the Jack Johnson–Jim Jeffries fight:

> Johnson is a wonder. No one understands him, this man who smiles. Well, the story of the fight is the story of a smile. If ever man won by nothing more fatiguing than a smile, Johnson won today.

> And where now is the champion who will make Johnson extend himself . . . (4: p. 513)

Jeffries was game in that fight, and he took a terrible beating. But the fight was no real competition because the opponents were not commensurate. Worse, Jeffries was ill-prepared, he was not the opponent he might have been. Accordingly, the extent of success possible for Johnson was extremely limited by the time the fight began.

As we noted previously, more is required for successful competition than commensurate opponents. Opponents, to be worthy, must utterly respect the game. Let us return now to explore that claim, for it involves not only important moral considerations but also rather more subtle logical or conceptual ones. An example will help us to expose and deal with both.

It is well known that during his career as a golfer, Bobby Jones several times called penalty strokes on himself. By 1926, he had won the American and British Opens and the American amateur title. In that year he granted an interview on golf style to O. B. Keeler, who asked Jones about those self-imposed penalties:

> "One thing more, Bobby. There is a lot of interest in those penalty strokes you have called on yourself. At St. Louis and Brookline and at Worcester—they say that one cost you the championship—and the one at Scioto, in that awful round of 79 when the ball moved on the green—" Bobby held up a warning hand. "That is absolutely nothing to talk about," he said, "and you are not to write about it. There is only one way to play this game." (3: p. 222)

From the point of view of morality, competitors must consider it unworthy of themselves to break deliberately the rules of the game. When a person violates the rules which govern competition, he treats his opponents as means merely to his end of victory. The symbols of victory have status or meaningfulness only because they stand for triumph in competition; without the opposition, they are worthless. Attainment of these symbols by cheating is therefore the exploitation of those who competed in good faith. Competitors are equally reduced to means merely in cases where the end of the cheater is prize money or gambling profit. Without the competition there can be neither prize nor wager, and the cheater simply uses the bona fide competitors solely for his own gain. Cheating is thus a paradigm case of failure to act with respect for the moral status of persons as ends.

From the point of view of logic, the need for the players' utter respect for the game is equally crucial. Competing, winning and losing in athletics are intelligible only within the framework of rules which define a specific competitive sport. A person may cheat at a game or compete at it, but it is logically impossible for him to do both. To cheat is to cease to compete. It is for this reason that cheaters are the greatest failures of all in competitive athletics, not because of any considerations of winning or failing to do so, but because they fail even to compete.

In the case of golf, as in the Bob Jones example, failure to impose a penalty on oneself where it is required by the rules is to cease to compete at golf. For one can compete with others only in accordance with the rules which govern and define the competition.

Or consider the case of pocket billiards. In all pocket billiard games it is a rule violation to touch any object ball or the cue ball with one's hands or clothing, etc. during play. It is also a violation for the cue to touch any object ball in the execution of a shot; any player who violates these rules has committed a foul. The penalty for a foul in all cases is termination of one's inning or turn. Now suppose that during a game of straight pool in the execution of a shot where the cue ball must be struck at a steep angle because of an object ball immediately behind it, a player knowingly touches that object ball with his finger, undetected by his opponent or a referee. If he continues to shoot, if he does not terminate his inning voluntarily, he has ceased to compete at straight pool. And because he is no longer competing, he cannot win at straight pool. He may appear to do so, he may pocket the prize money or collect on the wager or carry off the trophy, but since he is not competing any longer, he cannot win. The cheater is logically prohibited from competing and therefore from winning. He can lose by disqualification.[1]

We may wish here to recall Bernard Suits' discussion of rules in "The Elements of Sport." Suits distinguishes the constitutive rules of a game, those which proscribe certain means of achieving the end of the game, from rules of skill which apply to how to play the game well or effectively. He points out that to ". . . break a constitutive rule is to fail to play the game at all." (5: p. 52) He mentions also a third kind of rule, namely the kind of rule which if violated requires the imposition of a specific penalty, the sort of rule we have been discussing. He urges rightly that violating such a rule is neither to fail to play the game nor to fail to play it well, since the penalized action may be nonetheless advantageous to the competitor. But he also notes that such rules are extensions of the constitutive rules. This is the emphasis of my argument. In particular, to commit an act which merits a penalty, to do so knowingly and not to incur the penalty is to cease to play the game. To ground a club in golf or to commit a foul in pool is not to cease to play the game. But to ignore the penalty imposed by the rules surely is, and it is in this sense that we understand rules with penalties as extensions of constitutive rules.

Both morally and logically, then, there is indeed only one way to play a game. Grantland Rice makes clear his appreciation of this insight in his autobiography, *The Tumult and the Shouting.* For emphasis, he employs the example of a rookie professional offensive lineman. The athlete responds to Rice's praise for his play during his rookie year by observing that he will be better when he becomes more adept at holding illegally without being caught. Of course, to Rice this confused vision of successful competition is heartbreaking.

We have seen now that success in competitive athletics requires being and discovering worthy opponents, and that worthy opponents must be relative equals with utter respect for the game and their fellow competitors. We have related success to competing well, performing well, under pressure. No one can be a success in competitive athletics if he fails to compete, either by avoiding worthy opposition or by cheating.[2]

Of course, our treatment of competitive athletics is rather narrow; it does not deal with the variety of reasons and purposes people have for engaging in competitive athletics. Our reflections do not really pertain to people who play at competitive games merely for fun or relaxation or exercise, who use, as it were, the format of competitive games for purposes largely indifferent to competing and to winning. We are talking only about people who seek to compete with those whose investment in a game, whose seriousness of purpose and talent, are comparable to their own and who therefore play to win.

Now people vary greatly in talent and available time for preparation, opportunity, training and so on. This means that success in competitive athletics cannot be tied unconditionally to absolute quality of performance. Whether a competitive athlete is a success hinges on numerous relevant factual considerations. We acknowledge this point as part of our sense of fairness through handicapping, establishment of weight divisions in boxing and wrestling, age divisions in junior and senior competition, and division of amateur and professional, to mention only a few.

What then of the athlete as competitor, the athlete who competes with equals, who, in the very act of competing, sets victory among his goals? Is winning everything in such competition, the only thing, the sole criterion of success?

We have been told so often enough, and we have seen the young encouraged to believe that winning and success are inseparable, that those who win are "winners" and those who lose, "losers." This view, however, must be tempered by our previous insights; we must not become preoccupied with individual victories to the exclusion of recognition of the importance of patterns of outstanding performance. As Thackeray saw, "The prize be sometimes to the fool. The race not always to the swift." (6: p. 57)

Sometimes performance in victory is mediocre, in defeat awesome. Many Super Bowls are testimonial to the former. There are countless other examples of mediocrity in victory, from Little League games to professional contests. So too of excellence in defeat. To cite only one:

> Anyone who saw Wohlhuter's heroic performance in Munich won't soon forget it. In the first qualifying heat, he tripped, and his pipestem body scraped along the track. Scrambling to his feet, he chased after the field—but was shut out by a stride.

> "I was startled," he recalls. "To this day, I don't even know why or how I went down. When there're 80,000 people watching you, you want to have a good day. I had a choice—walk off the track or give it a try. I chose to be competitive." (1: p. 48)

To stress victory to the point of overlooking quality of performance is to impoverish our sense of success in competitive athletics.

It matters whether we win or lose. It also matters whether we play the game well or badly, given our own potential and preparation. It matters whom we play against and whether they are worthy of us, whether they can press us to call up our final resources. Satisfaction in victory is warranted only when we have played well against a worthy opponent. Otherwise victory is no achievement, and pride in it is false.

Notes

1. We might ask whether other members of a team are competing if one member is cheating. We would ask immediately whether they knew of it, and deny that they were competing if they knew and did nothing. We would be more perplexed if they did not know. But we would still deny, I think, that the team as a unit was competing. Notice that a team can be disqualified for the violations of one member. The same considerations apply to cheating in the form, say, of recruiting violations.

2. Obviously there is no failure involved in the decision not to participate in athletic or nonathletic competition. Some people are constitutionally unsuited for athletics, some for competition, while others find the demands of games artificial or fabricated and therefore unsatisfying. That there is failure in cheating or in constantly playing unworthy opponents neither suggests nor entails that there is anything wrong with unwillingness to enter at all into competition.

Bibliography

1. Bonventre, Peter. "The Streaker," *Newsweek* (February 17, 1975).

2. Davis, Richard Harding. "Thorne's Famous Run," *The Omnibus of Sport*. Grantland Rice and Harford Powel (eds.). New York: Harper and Brothers, 1932. Reprinted from: "How the Great Game Was Played," *The Journal* (November 24, 1895).

3. Keeler, O.B. "Bobby Jones on Golf Style," *The Omnibus of Sport*. Grantland Rice and Harford Powel (eds.). New York: Harper and Brothers, 1932.

4. London, Jack. "The Story of a Smile," *The Omnibus of Sport*. Grantland Rice and Harford Powel (eds.). New York: Harper and Brothers, 1932.

5. Suits, Bernard. "The Elements of Sport," *The Philosophy of Sport: A Collection of Original Essays*. Robert G. Osterhoudt (ed.). Springfield, Illinois: Charles C Thomas Publisher, 1973.

6. Thackeray, William M. "Sportsmanship," *The Omnibus of Sport*. Grantland Rice and Harford Powel (eds.). New York: Harper and Brothers, 1932.

Cheating and Fair Play in Sport

◆

Oliver Leaman

It is not as easy as it might initially be thought to define cheating in sport, and it is just as difficult to specify precisely what is wrong morally with such behaviour, and why fair play should be prized. In this article I intend to try to throw some light on the notions of both cheating and fair play, and to suggest that stronger arguments than those so far produced in the literature are required to condemn the former and approve the latter.

Let us try to deal first with the definitional problem of what sorts of behaviour constitute cheating, and come to the ethical issue later. Gunther Luschen boldly starts his essay on cheating in sport with this definition:

> Cheating in sport is the act through which the manifestly or latently agreed upon conditions for winning such a contest are changed in favor of one side. As a result, the principle of equality of chance beyond differences of skill and strategy is violated. (1976, p. 67)

A problem with this definition is that it omits any consideration of intention. After all, if a player unwittingly breaks the rules and thereby gains an unfair advantage he will not necessarily have cheated. For example, if a boxer has a forbidden substance applied to bodily damage without his knowledge, then he has not cheated even though the rules have been broken to his advantage. Were he to be penalized or disqualified, it would not be because of his cheating but due to the rules having been broken by those who attend to him in the intervals.

Reprinted from *Sport and the Humanities: A Collection of Original Essays* (pp. 25-30), (1981), edited by William J. Morgan, Bureau of Educational Research and Service, University of Tennessee.

A superior account of cheating is then provided by Peter McIntosh, who claims that:

> Cheating . . . need be no more than breaking the rules with the intention of not being found out . . . Cheating, however, implies an intention to beat the system even although the penalty, if the offender is found out, may still be acceptable. (1979, pp. 100-101)

But McIntosh next claims that:

> This definition, however, is too simple. It is not always the written or even the unwritten rule that is broken; tacit assumptions which one contestant knows that the other contestant acts upon may be rejected in order to gain an advantage . . . A more satisfactory definition is that of Luschen. (1979, pp. 182-3)

McIntosh's adaptation of Luschen's account makes possible the useful distinction between intending to deceive, which he calls cheating, and breaking the rules without having that intention. He concludes that: "Cheating is an offence against the principles of justice as well as against a particular rule or norm of behaviour" (1979, p. 185). This is presumably because the attempted deception is an attempt at unfairly putting the cheater in a superior position vis-à-vis the person cheated. This distinction is made clearer if we compare cheating with lying. We may tell someone an untruth without at the same time lying, because we may not intend to present the audience with a proposition which we know not to be true. This comparison suggests that McIntosh's dichotomy is not sufficient since it does not cover those cases where the rules are deliberately broken without any intention to deceive. A player may commit a professional or tactical foul in front of the referee or umpire because he considers that it is better to break the rules and suffer the penalty rather than not to commit the foul at all. Of course, such a player would *prefer* the offense to be unobserved, but cannot reasonably expect it in those circumstances to be overlooked. It is not obvious whether this sort of case is an example of cheating or not. If the intention to deceive is a necessary condition of cheating, then obviously such a case is not one of cheating, for not only did the player not intend to deceive, but he could not even reasonably have expected such an intention to be realized. Yet the rules of the game have been broken, and it might well be argued that it is the intention to break the rules rather than the intention to deceive which will do as a necessary condition of cheating. We can see why this should be so if we return to the analogy of telling an untruth. There is nothing wrong with telling an untruth as such; the fault lies in intending to tell an untruth. If I intend to tell an untruth then my action may or may not deceive you. The falsehood may be so blatant that it is obviously not intended to deceive, but perhaps merely to confuse or gain time. Such a falsehood may nonetheless be called a lie since it seeks to place its author in a position of undeserved superiority vis-à-vis the audience, and this runs against a principle of justice, other things being equal, namely, that the truth ought to be told. If I tell you that p is the case, and I know that p is false, *and* I intend to deceive you with respect to the truth of p, then this is no doubt a more serious lie than if I just intentionally tell an untruth without attempting to deceive. Other things being equal, we have a right to be told the truth, and if we are lied to then we are not dealt with justly. The injustice is magnified if we are at the same time deceived, or if there is an intention that we be deceived, but the injustice is there whether we are deceived or not, and whether there is any intention to deceive or not.

We may now be a bit clearer about the nature of cheating, but there are nonetheless problems in specifying precisely when a player cheats. Luschen's definition refers to a principle of equality over and above differences in skill and strategy. Using such a definition makes it difficult to give determinate answers to a variety of cases. For example, it might be that player A knows that player B is put off his play by such actions as A's coughing, or doing up his shoe-laces, or altering the pace of the game by doing things which are not directly part of the game, and so on. There are, of course, all sorts of actions which can put players off which are not in themselves illegal. A player may have considerable skill at a game and yet be quite easily beaten by an opponent who understands what sorts of (legal) behaviour the superior player dislikes. If such behaviour is indeed legal, must we say that A is cheating because he is breaking one of the "latently agreed upon conditions for winning such a contest"? It might well be argued that A is cheating since the sorts of skill and strategy which are acceptable in a game involve being better at the motions of the game than one's opponent and successfully exploiting his weaknesses and one's own strengths. Such weaknesses and strengths should be limited to the moves of the game and not to the defects in psychological make-up which are not directly related to the moves of the game. On this view, if B is put off his tennis by A's continual practice of doing up his shoe-laces, and A acts thus because he knows that it puts B off, then A is cheating by acting in this way even though he is not doing anything illegal. (There is naturally a continuum of cases here, where the yelling of hostile imprecations of a sexual nature by A at B would no doubt be adjudged illegal.)

It might be thought that calling A's actions in this sort of case an example of cheating is to go rather too far. After all, perhaps it should be up to a sportsperson to conquer his feelings about slowing a game down by tactics such as A's when such actions are within the rules of the game. B may be a "better" player in terms of skill and strategy than A, yet also more temperamental than A, and A might play on this defect to win more often than B in their contests. This sort of case emphasizes yet again the unsatisfactory nature of the definitions of cheating which Luschen and McIntosh offer. The latter's description involves trying to beat the system and deception, which A's behaviour does not necessarily do. A may take no pains to hide the fact that he is trying to put B off, and he is not trying to beat the system in so far as he is keeping to the explicit rules of the game. So on the McIntosh model A is not cheating at all. On Luschen's account A might be cheating, since he is violating "the principle of chance beyond differences in skill and strategy." However, as we have just suggested, it might be argued that being a good player involves being able to control one's emotional states and overcome annoyances of the time-wasting variety.

What we can conclude is that both accounts fail to tell us how to classify this very common form of behaviour in sport. McIntosh is clear in having to think that A is not cheating, yet this is only because of a simplistic view of the limited possibilities of cheating which is based upon deception and which has already been criticized. Luschen can provide no answer at all. The question of cheating can either be answered in terms of B's obligation as a skillful player to control his temperament (in which case A is not cheating) or in terms of A's behaviour violating a "latently agreed upon" condition for winning a contest (in which case A is cheating). The latter disjunct may seem temptingly acceptable, yet it should be pointed out that there are serious problems with talking about "latent agreements," especially when in practice quite a few players do not act in accordance with such agreements. Non-compliance by some players makes the problem of identifying precisely what the latent agreement is allegedly about insoluble. In fact, we frequently resort to talking about latent agreements when some people do not want to comply with a behavioural norm and we are trying to prove that they ought to by appealing to some non-explicit rule which they are obliged to follow. Yet this sort of argument is always open to attack by saying that no person is obliged to abide by an agreement, explicit or latent, to which he is not a party.

The tentative conclusion, then, is that there are a good number of difficulties in defining cheating in sport. Now it remains for me to argue that there are similarly many difficulties in specifying precisely what is *wrong* with cheating. It is a commonplace of the literature that cheating in sport is rather like lying in our everyday affairs, and falls under the same moral reproach. That is, if I am not morally entitled to hit someone over the head when competing for a business contract, then I am just as ethically constrained from injuring a competitor in a sporting contest. After all, the practice of sport comes under the same moral rules as the carrying out of any other interpersonal activity (see the work of Aspin, Keenan, Osterhoudt and Zeigler on this topic). Indeed, this rather unexciting comparison has been used to suggest that physical education has a large part to play in moral education. Huizinga has expressed the generally accepted view of what is wrong with cheating in sport by arguing that: "To our way of thinking, cheating as a means of winning a game robs the action of its play-character and spoils it altogether, because for us the essence of play is that the rules be kept—that it be fair play." Aspin makes an interesting observation on this passage. He claims that it ". . . underlines the point about the central virtue of athletic competitions . . . that their whole framework rests upon our desire to see excellence achieved according to rules which attempt to ensure equality, fairness, and impartiality for all" (1975, p. 55). Now, as we have just seen, it is not at all clear what "equality, fairness and impartiality for all" means in a sporting context, nor when they are being denied to a player or players in a contest. It is not a simple matter to determine when the rules of the game are being kept—it depends upon whether a narrower or broader interpretation of the notion of the rules of the game is accepted. So Huizinga's justification of fair play in sport does not as it stands explain why players are morally obliged to reject cheating.

Let us consider a more radical argument concerning fair play. Why should keeping the rules, on whatever interpretation of that expression, be "the essence of play"? In a very basic sense it is obvious that if all or some of the players in a game disobey the rules as a matter of course in their entirety, then they are not playing the game in an ethically dubious manner—they are not playing it at all. Yet this general breakdown of the rules, and consequently of the game, is not what is meant by cheating. The cheater's behaviour is on the whole conforming, since otherwise he would not be allowed to break the rules of the game. Someone who does not in any way conform to the rules of the game will presumably be forbidden, at some stage or other, to continue in it. The cheater seeks to gain an advantage over the opposition in a game and through the game, and so he wants to stay in the game and not destroy it. In addition, those occasions in which he intends to deceive would be robbed of their possible success if it is obvious that he is not adhering to the rules of the game.

If it is acceptable to assert that the presence of cheating in a game does not necessarily invalidate the game, then does it really follow that either the players or the audience should be in favour of fair play in a contest? It might be suggested that many competitions, especially those with some sort of authority present to regulate cheating, would be more interesting if cheating takes place within it, or if several players try to stretch the rules. Such deviant behaviour adds a new dimension to the game which can also add to its interest. Now, I do not want to suggest that cheating cannot disturb the game's rhythm and so make it less interesting to both players and spectators. Perhaps this is what happens in the majority of cases where cheating is prevalent in sport. Yet it need not be the case in all sporting contests. In so far as the contest is one of wits as well as one of skill and strategy, it can be exciting to compete with and against someone who uses his wits to try to cheat and it can be exciting for an audience to observe such intelligent behaviour.

It might be argued that if both players and spectators have such a laissez-faire attitude to cheating, then they will suffer, or be likely to suffer, harmful influences upon their moral character. We have already referred to the link which is sometimes taken to hold between physical and moral education, to the idea that someone who is taught to break the rules of hockey (or to enjoy watching those rules broken) when it suits his side is more likely to break social rules when it is in his personal interest to do so. Whether any such link exists is an unproved empirical proposition, and there is surely no a priori way of establishing its truth or otherwise. On the other hand, it is surely true that it is possible to inculcate virtues into players and spectators by giving them the opportunity to interact with other people on the sports-field in a morally acceptable manner and thereby to practice such mutually beneficial roles which they might then apply later in a purely general public context. Yet my argument seems to be that it does not matter how players behave provided that it does not interfere with the interest of the game. Any such claim that sport is amoral in nature would collapse, however, since the actions of players fall under the same very general moral rules as any other sort of behaviour which affects the welfare of others. What I am suggesting is that the fact that people may cheat is part of the structure of sport and is taken into consideration in the rules of the sport, so that cheating in a sport can be built into audience and player perceptions of the game. If it is true that cheating is recognized as an option which both sides may morally take up, then in general the principles of equality and justice are not affected. It may be that player A is a better cheater than player B, yet if cheating is recognized as part of the skill and strategy of the game, then A's advantage is merely an aspect of his being a better player than B. If we dislike the idea of cheating being part of the structure of the game, then perhaps we might consider this passage from Huizinga:

> . . . the game depends upon the temporary acceptance by the players of a set of rules which 'cut off' the activity within the games from events in the 'real' world . . . Play as type of leisure activity . . . entails the temporary creation of a sphere of irreality. . . .

Huizinga's remarks support the idea that cheating in sport need not be compared morally to cheating in our everyday affairs since sport is "just a game" and not simply a reflection of our everyday behaviour. It may be morally acceptable to do certain things in sport which are not acceptable in ordinary life. In his description of violence in hockey, Vaz comments that the

> . . . implicit objective is to put the opposing star player out of action without doing him serious harm. Illegal tactics and 'tricks' of the game are both encouraged and taught; rough play and physically aggressive performance are strongly encouraged and sometimes players are taught the techniques of fighting. Minimal consideration is given to the formal normative rules of the game, and the conceptions of sportsmanship and fair play are forgotten. . . . Gradually the team is molded into a tough fighting unit prepared for violence whose primary objective is to win hockey games. (1972, p. 230)

If this is an accurate description of the general preparation for the playing of professional hockey then both the players and (Vaz suggests) the spectators will expect a skillful player to be good at cheating, where this involves breaking the rules when it is most advantageous to his side. Where such a policy is generally pursued there is no general deception practiced, and players are on equal terms in so far as the conditions for winning the contest are concerned. It is difficult then to see what is morally wrong with such behaviour. After all, it is presumed that the players and spectators are free agents in their participation and attendance. The players know how they are going to behave and the spectators know what they are going to see, namely, cheating carried out when it is considered to be in the best interests of the cheater and his side. If our objection to this practice is to be more than empty romanticism then some stronger arguments in favour of the moral obligatoriness of fair play in sport must be produced.

Perhaps, though, we have unduly stressed what actually happens in some sports at the expense of what ought to happen. That is, if people undertake to play a game, then they may be taken to have understood and agreed to the rules of the game and the principles upon which any fair victory in that game must rest. As Keenan puts it: ". . . if cheating in any form occurs among those parties to the game, they simply fail to adopt the principle of fair play and the morality of justice" (1975, p. 117). As Robert Nozick has expressed this argument: ". . . the principle of fairness . . . holds that when a number of persons engage in a just, mutually advantageous, cooperative venture according to rules and thus restrain their liberty in ways necessary to yield advantages for all, those who have submitted to these restrictions have a right to similar acquiescence on the part of those who have benefited from their submission" (1974, p. 90). Yet what are "the rules of the game" to which players supposedly commit themselves when they enter a game? If we look at the ways in which some sports are played it becomes evident that the rules of the game involve following the formal rules in so far as it is to the advantage of one's own side and breaking them when that is perceived, perhaps wrongly, to be to the side's advantage, where the possibility of suffering a penalty is taken into account. The existence of an authority in games enshrines cheating in the structure of the game; the authority is there to ensure that cheating does not interfere with the principle of fairness in a game. He is there to regulate cheating so that it does not benefit one side more than the other except where one side is more skillful at cheating than the other, and to see that the amount of cheating which takes place is not so great as to change the general form of a particular game. That is, the formal rules of the game must in general be adhered to by all players since otherwise in a clear non-moral sense the game is not being played. But if we are profitably to discuss the notion of the rules of the game, and of cheating and fair play, we must address ourselves to the ways in which players and spectators perceive those rules rather than to an abstract idea of the rules themselves. The next step is to determine what notion of fair play is applicable within the context of the ways in which players actually participate in sporting activities. An injection of realism into philosophical discussions of cheating and fair play in sport is long overdue.

Bibliography

1. Aspin, D. "Ethical Aspects of Sport and Games and Physical Education." *Philosophy of Education Society of Great Britain,* 1975, 49-71.

2. Huizinga, J. *Homo Ludens: A Study of the Play Element in Culture.* Boston: Beacon Press, 1950.

3. Keenan, F. "Justice and Sport." *Journal of the Philosophy of Sport,* 1975, 2, 111-123.

4. Luschen, G. "Cheating in Sport." In D. Landers (Ed.) *Social Problems in Athletics.* Urbana: University of Illinois Press, 1977.

5. McIntosh, P. *Fair Play: Ethics in Sport and Education.* London: Heinemann, 1979.

6. Nozick, R. *Anarchy, State and Utopia.* Oxford: Blackwell, 1974.

7. Osterhoudt, R. "The Kantian Ethic as a Principle of Moral Conduct in Sport and Athletics." In R. Osterhoudt (Ed.) *The Philosophy of Sport.* Springfield, Illinois: Charles C Thomas, 1973.

8. Vaz, E. "The Culture of Young Hockey Players: Some Initial Observations." In A. Taylor (Ed.) *Training: Scientific Basis and Application.* Quebec: Laval University, 1972.

9. Zeigler, E. "The Pragmatic (Experimentalistic) Ethic as It Relates to Sport and Physical Education." In R. Osterhoudt (Ed.) *The Philosophy of Sport* (op. cit.).

Intentional Rules Violations—One More Time

Warren P. Fraleigh

The topic of intentional rules violations has been discussed extensively in the literature over the past 30 years. In what follows I will try to clarify the underlying issues
and differing positions taken on them and then will offer my own conclusions. My
conclusions will be used to distinguish among several levels or categories of intentional rules violations and extend my earlier critique of such violations in what I
think is a fuller and more defensible manner.

Formalism and Ethos

Differences with regard to the acceptability of intentional rules violations show a
tension between the relative importance of the rules and of the ethos of sport. The
formalist account of sport (4, 5, 9, 10, 14), simply stated, says that the rules of sport
are its definition and, therefore, intentional rules violations are either not playing
the game and, logically, eliminating the possibility of winning; playing a different
game than prescribed by the formal rules and, thus, potentially voiding the possibility of contest; or playing a defective instance of the game prescribed by the rules.
From the formalist position, intentional rules violations are not acceptable because
of either violation of a contestant's agreement or some form of cheating.

In reaction to formalism, several authors (3, 6, 7, 15) state that the social context of
sport must be accounted for in our understanding of what sport is. This, in differing

Reprinted, by permission, from W.P. Fraleigh, 2003, "Intentional rules violations—One more time," *Journal of the Philosophy of Sport* 30:166-176.

versions, is called the ethos argument. The unifying factor in this argument is that some sort of agreed interpretation of the formal rules is needed to comprehend what our sports are. According to some ethos arguments, some intentional rules violations are "part of the game" because they are interpreted as socially acceptable. What constitutes the ethos and what acceptable interpretations of the rules are, however, take several forms. D'Agostino (3: p. 42) says the ethos is "those conventions determining how the formal rules . . . are applied in concrete circumstances." Leaman (6: p. 197) and Lehman (7: p. 43) say it is the ways in which the players and the spectators perceive the rules. Tamburrini (15: pp. 30-31) says, "'The sport practitioners' ethos—the particular understanding of the game entertained by the players—is the most relevant indication of how the game should be played." Butcher and Schneider (2: pp. 34-35) recommend an ethos derived from "respect for the game." Loland (8: p. 105) refers to a "just" ethos, and Morgan (9: pp. 61-62) favors an ethos of sport understood as a MacIntyrian social practice.

In the cited ideas of ethos there are two primary concepts of conventions regarding application of the rules to circumstances. One is that the conventions are determined by some sort of agreement (tacit or otherwise) among the participants. The other is that such conventions should be informed by something beyond social acceptability, for example, "respect for the game," justice, or the internal values of sport as a social practice.

Issues

As a result of the differences between formalism and ethos, several issues are relevant to the acceptability of intentional rules violations. These can be stated in the form of questions:

- What is the agreement we make when we agree to engage in sport?
- What constitutes cheating?
- What are the reasons that make cheating wrong?
- Is intentional violation of the rules always cheating?
- Should acts of intentional tactical rules violations be acceptable?

With respect to the agreement made the issue is whether its content is completed by the rules or the rules plus the ethos. There is no doubt that the rules play an indispensable role. The fact that no instance of a particular sport can occur without the kind of actions prescribed by the constitutive rules of that sport is clear. One cannot do basketball without throwing the ball (passing, dribbling, or shooting). One cannot do soccer without kicking the ball (passing, dribbling, or shooting), except for the goalie and for throw-ins. Thus, if one agrees to engage in a particular sport, one *by necessity* agrees to perform the actions prescribed by the constitutive rules. So, an individual who agrees to play basketball and then engages in wholesale kicking is not doing basketball as constituted by the rules. If two teams agree to engage in basketball but also agree that no free throws will be awarded and that the fouled team will take the ball out of bounds, they have agreed to a modified game—different from the game constituted by the formal rules. The point of these two examples is that there has been *explicit* agreement as to what constitutes the rule-defined contest and, thus, on what basis a winner can be determined. In the first example, however, the content of the agreement is determined by the constitutive rules, whereas in the second case, agreement content is composed by an explicitly stated change of the rules. In both cases a known set of rules is agreed upon. In the first case, the agreement is *implicitly necessary,* whereas in the second it is *explicitly stated* in advance. Accordingly, sports in which intentional rules violations occur might or might not be the same game and, thus, a contest, depending on whether or not all participants have *explicitly* agreed to the same sort of intentional rules violations. The *assumption* of rules-violation agreement is not as logically strong as the explicit *necessity* of agreement to perform the actions required by the constitutive rules.

Cheating

What constitutes cheating is related to the potential acceptability of intentional rules violations. Pearson (10: p. 184) equates cheating with what she calls "definitional deception," that is, when someone "has contracted to participate in one sort of activity and then deliberately engages in another sort of activity." Because Pearson takes a strict formalist position that a sport "is no more (in terms of its careful definition) than its rules" (10: p. 183), all intentional rules violations are failures to honor one's contractual obligation. Tamburrini (15: pp. 13-14) says, "Cheating is a violation of the written rules of a game, performed in order to gain an illicit advantage for oneself or for one's team over rival players." Fraleigh (5: p. 72) states, "We understand cheating to be deliberate violation of the rules to gain advantage while avoiding a penalty so that the opponents are not now facing the same test." Simon (12: p. 40) defines cheating as "probably best identified with intentional violation of a public system of rules in order to secure the goals of that system for oneself or for others for whom one is concerned." Loland (8), in a more complete definition, says,

> Simply defined, cheating is an attempt to gain an advantage by violating the shared interpretation of the basic rules (the ethos) of the parties engaged without being caught and held responsible for it. The goal of the cheater is that the advantage gained is not eliminated or compensated for. (p. 96)

Some of the conceptions of cheating are more inclusive than others. As a basis for a stipulative definition of cheating, analysis reveals several elements. These are an intentional violation of a shared interpretation of the rules and the intention to be undetected and to gain advantage for oneself or one's partisans while escaping penalty. Accordingly, the following stipulative definition of cheating will be used for examining the acceptability of intentional rules violations: *Cheating is an intentional act that violates an appropriate interpretation of the rules shared by the participants, done to gain advantage for oneself and/or one's teammates, while trying to avoid detection so as to escape penalty.*

Most commentators find cheating unacceptable when it is "a violation of the written rules of a game, performed in order to gain an illicit advantage for oneself or for one's team over rival players" (15: pp. 13-14). Two, however, offer differing and atypical responses to cheating so defined. Both Leaman (6: p. 196) and Tamburrini (15: p. 21) find, in an ethos in which cheating is regarded as acceptable, that it is not wrong because all have access to the acceptable act of cheating and, therefore, no unfair advantage occurs, because the cheater has not violated a shared interpretation of the rules. This assumes that an ethos derived solely from social agreement among the participants is an appropriate ethos.

Leaman (6: p. 196) further states that cheating can provide for a more interesting contest involving the use of one's wits for creative cheating. How this can provide for a more interesting contest is puzzling inasmuch as highly skilled and successful cheating often goes undetected because it is intended to be hidden from the opponent, the spectators, and the officials.

With the exception of Leaman and Tamburrini, commentators consider cheating wrong. As Butcher and Schneider (2) observe,

> The moral status of cheating flows from its definition. If cheating is all rule-breaking or even all intentional rule-breaking, then not all cheating is morally wrong. However, if cheating is breaking one's agreement, then all cheating is morally wrong, but not all rule-breaking is cheating. (p. 27)

Several reasons are given for the unacceptability of cheating. Pearson (10: p. 184) and Fraleigh (5: p. 73) both state that cheating denies the implicit agreement or contract into which competitors enter and, accordingly, negates the agreed-upon contest. Negation of the agreed-upon contest then involves Suits' logical incompatibility thesis, that is, it is logically impossible to win a game if one is not engaged in it (12: p. 24). Fraleigh (5: p. 73), referring to Delattre (4: p. 136), says that denial of the implicit promise to follow the rules "is a moral concern because it is an 'exploitation of those who competed in good faith.'" Simon (12: pp. 40-41) states that "the cheater acts in a way that no one could rationally or impartially recommend that everyone in the activity act," and "cheaters arbitrarily subordinate the interests and purposes of others to their own, and so violate the fundamental moral norm of respect for persons." Loland (8: p. 97) says, "The very foundation of the fairness ideal, mutual respect between persons and respect for the shared ethos according to which all compete, is violated." So the objections to cheating are of two kinds, logical and moral.

Is intentional violation of the rules always cheating? If we use the stipulative definition of cheating offered previously the answer is no. Instances in which a contestant intentionally violates a rule with the expectation that he will be detected and penalized are not covered by the definition. Therefore, such instances of "tactical use of the rules" do not qualify as cheating. To sharpen the focus on such "tactical use of the rules," I will eliminate the kinds of acts covered by the definition. All instances of cheating as defined are either logically or morally, or both, unacceptable for the reasons cited previously.

Intentional Tactical Rules Violations

From this point, I shall focus on intentional tactical rules violations. These violations are defined as an intentional act that violates the rules in a way in which the rule violator expects to be detected and penalized but expects some benefit to his or her competitive effectiveness.

This type of act is often referred to as the "good" or "professional" foul and is frequently shared by competitors in an ethos composed entirely by social agreement.

Now, the question at issue is, should acts of intentional tactical rules violations be acceptable, that is, should such acts be acceptable in the ethos of a sport? It is very clear that certain intentional tactical rules violations are socially accepted in some sports and are part of the ethos of those sports. For example, in college basketball in the United States, players on the team behind toward the end of a close game will intentionally foul a member of the team ahead and in possession of the ball in order to stop the clock. This is done so as to be detected by officials and with the expectation of a penalty. There are several objections to the acceptance of such intentional tactical rules violations supported by social agreement, including the following:

- It gives the ethos the power to determine what is a legitimate game (9: p. 58).
- It "confuses social description with normative justification" (9: p. 57).
- It results in existing conventions becoming immune to criticism (9: p. 57; 13: pp. 13-14).
- It provides a base for ethical relativism (13: p. 14).

Nonetheless, it is the case that rules cannot determine their own interpretation. If we examine actual rulebooks we see that, indeed, they often include parts called interpretations. It seems then that we must find a source for the content of the phrase *appropriate interpretation of the rules*. What is needed is clarity on the substance of an *appropriate* socially agreed-upon ethos among sports participants.

Internalism and an Appropriate Ethos

As indicated previously, many authors have provided insights as to the appropriate content of an ethos. Together, these sources might be subsumed under what Simon calls broad internalism. He says (13: p. 7), "Broad internalism, then, is the view that in addition to the constitutive rules of sports, there are other resources connected closely, perhaps conceptually, to sport that are neither social conventions nor moral principles imported from outside."

What are some suggested resources? Butcher and Schneider (2: p. 34) cite "respect for the game," meaning "you honor and take seriously the standards of excellence created and defined by that game." Loland (8: p. 10) says, "The goal of sports competitions is to measure, compare and rank two or more competitors according to athletic performance." Similarly, Fraleigh (5: p. 41) states, "The purpose of the sports contest is to provide equitable opportunity for mutual contesting of the relative abilities of the participants to move mass in space and time within the confines prescribed by an agreed-upon set of rules." Simon (13: pp. 9-10) adds, "Sports contests can be regarded as tests of the competitors' abilities to meet the challenge created by the rules." Russell continues (11: p. 35), "Rules should be interpreted in such a manner that the excellences embodied in achieving the lusory goal of the game are not undermined but maintained and fostered." Morgan (9) maintains that if we understand sport as a social practice whose purpose, rationality, and internal goods are indicated by formal rules, this provides an ethos wherein

> the exercise of the specific skills of a game will be taken seriously and accorded significance, that the players will commit themselves to achieve the goods of the game, that an esteem for the sporting excellence and the risks it entails will be maintained. (p. 61)

Together these focused views expound a central point that inherent in the structure of sport qua sport is the contesting and pursuit of excellence in *rule-defined skills,* and that this is a basis for us to ascertain acceptable actions. In short, actions that support and maintain contesting the rule-defined skills that test the relative excellence of the participants are acceptable, and those that reduce or negate the contesting of those same skills are unacceptable.

Intentional Tactical Rules Violations and an Appropriate Ethos

How then do we evaluate intentional tactical rules violations as defined here? First, it should be clear that a legitimate contest can be completed, even though this is unlikely, without inadvertent or intentional rules violations. This makes engaging in intentional tactical rule violations unnecessary, logically, to completing a legitimate contest. At the same time, it is clear that it is logically impossible to complete a contest in a sport without performing what Fraleigh (5: pp. 75-76) called previously the "positively prescribed skills" of the game. One cannot do basketball without throwing the ball, either by passing, dribbling, or shooting. Even so, what is *logically* necessary for a contest does not exhaust what might be acceptable.

To evaluate intentional tactical rules violations we must examine the logic of the central test of a sport. Here, the recent work of Torres (16) is useful and significant. He argues that the formal rules of a sport provide two sets of skills that have fundamentally different significance for the contest. One set of skills is called the constitutive skills, which "define and shape the character of games. They exist to bring games to life and, in terms of such skills, players are to show their superiority" (16: p. 86). In basketball such skills include forms of throwing that must be done—passing, dribbling, and shooting. In soccer, with specified exceptions, players must kick the ball—passing, dribbling, and shooting. In short, these constitutive skills are prescribed by the constitutive rules and specify how the game problem is to be accomplished. "In other words, constitutive skills provide solutions to game problems in their own right and, in principle, are sufficient" (16: p. 85). A second set of skills is called restorative, and these are generated by the regulative rules (16: p. 85). Such rules

> Prescribe precise penalties and methods for re-establishing the lusory project, but in doing so they generate additional skills that are employed during what may be labeled the regulative phase of the game, the period during which an interruption occurs and a need arises to put the game back on track. (16: p. 85)

Such skills are, indeed, part of the game, but their significance is derivative. They come into being when the central lusory project has been interrupted. Although they are part of the game their importance is not necessary in the same way that constitutive skills are. Again, it is logically possible to complete a game using only constitutive skills. In basketball, restorative skills include free throws and the throw-in, whereas soccer has the throw-in, corner kick, and so on. These sports exhibit a clear time between when the constitutive skills and the restorative skills are employed. Those times are demarcated by the official's signal of a whistle or horn. When these sounds are heard, the central lusory project, as defined by the constitutive skills, is interrupted because of a rule violation. Then the central lusory project is restored by means of the restorative skills that penalize or compensate.[1,2]

Are the penalties specified by the regulative rules always punishments? Simon offers an interesting interpretation: "Not all penalties in sports are sanctions for prohibited acts" (12: p. 48). Using the example of the unplayable-lie rule in golf, he states that the one-stroke penalty "is the price of exercise of the option rather than a sanction for doing what is forbidden" (12: p. 48). The only example Simon has provided for the idea of a price rather than a punishment is golf's unplayable-lie rule. Although there might be other examples in the regulative rules of sport in which the price for an option overrules the idea of punishment, the unplayable-lie rule in golf cannot carry the critical weight Simon assigns to it. There are at least three things about this rule that make it different from more typical regulative rules that prescribe penalties. First, for an unplayable lie in golf, the player who makes the choice invokes the penalty on himself—it is not imposed by an official. Second, such a rule is necessary because golfers, unintentionally, hit the ball into places that are either unsafe or impossible from which to play the next shot—high up in trees or imbedded in bushes so thick that swinging a golf club is impossible. Thus, a golfer, in some cases, cannot not choose this option. Third, this option for the golfer does not interfere with the play of an opponent—often at issue in tactical rules violations.

Simon (13: p. 12) extrapolates the unplayable-lie golf rule to "I would argue that since foul shooting is an important skill in basketball, and the award of two foul shots is appropriate compensation, . . . fouling at the end of the game is not cheating but permissible strategy." It appears, however, that Torres's countervailing argument that foul shots in basketball are restorative skills designed to restore the central lusory project and "put the game back on track" (16: p. 85) would trump Simon's example of acceptable intentional tactical rules violation. Torres's view trumps Simon's point in precisely the appropriate way that Simon suggests as legitimate (13: p. 12) because it establishes a theory of the skills of sport that assign secondary, derivative importance to the restorative skill of foul shooting in basketball. Fraleigh (5), speaking about regulative rules in 1984, said,

> These proscriptions and their penalties are in the rules so that such actions do not become skills of contesting. The spirit of such rules is that intentional fouls are not part of the officially agreed-upon skills and tactics of basketball. (p. 78)

There are several ways of testing the validity of the contrary views of Simon and those opposite. They deal with ascertaining what the intent of the rules is with regard to tactical rules violations. First, if such records exist, historical researchers can examine consideration of regulative rules by rules makers. Second, the development of penalties over time can reveal the direction of the intent—either toward a price or toward a punishment. For instance, in American intercollegiate basketball the rule with regard to intentional rules violation has moved definitely toward a punishment. Within my lifetime it has evolved from a point where there was no such rule (because the ethos did not consider such violations appropriate) through several less stringent penalties to the present penalty of two free throws and the ball out of bounds for the offended team. Similarly, in soccer the penalty for tackling from behind, on an offensive player ahead of the defense, has progressed to where it now draws a red card automatically, whereas in English soccer decades ago it was done almost routinely. Both of these examples show that rules makers have concluded that these tactical rules violations are not acceptable and that the penalty is a punishment and not a price. Third, the particular actions of intentional tactical rules violations can be evaluated in terms of their compatibility with a theory of each sport and, as Simon stated, "the skills it is best construed as testing" (13: p. 12). This is what Torres has argued effectively by means of the distinction between the function of constitutive skills in defining the central skills to be contested and the regulative rules establishing restorative skills that return a contest to its primary test.

To say that sports contests have a set of constitutive skills that embody the central test of excellence for participants does not imply some sort of Platonism of ideal forms. The *details* of the central test of a sport can change over time as a result of the creative efforts of participants to improve performance. Although the central-skills test maintains a measure of integrity (basketball is still fundamentally a test of skillful throwing, soccer remains a test of skillful kicking, and golf continues to be a test of skillful striking), history clearly reveals many instances of improved ways of performing the central skills. The jump shot in basketball, "bending" the ball in soccer, and the "flop" shot in golf are all instances of skillful improvements. Also, rules makers over time attempt to maintain a certain consistency in the relative importance of elements of sports. In basketball, rules changes dealing with goal tending and the 3-point shot have been instituted to prevent tall players from extreme dominance of the game. Likewise, as indicated with respect to the penalties for intentional fouls in basketball and tackling from behind in soccer, rules changes have attempted to maintain or restore the integrity of the central test. As Fraleigh (5: pp. 76-77) stated in 1984, rules makers apply an implicit "zone of consistency" test to ascertain what innovations will fit well into the continuing central test. Some will be acceptable; some will not be. Radical changes in the central test are infrequent because they would markedly change the particular challenge of each sport. To allow "handballs" in soccer would violate the nature of the test of soccer. To allow wholesale holding in basketball would transform it into wrestling.

Categories of Intentional Tactical Rules Violations

Not all kinds of intentional tactical rules violations seem to have the same kind of impact on the central, rule-defined test of sports. Following are several categories of such violations based in two principal elements. One is that the act is intentional, proscribed in the rules of the sport, and the second is that in performing the pro-scribed act the violator judges that the result will be some improvement in his or her competitive effectiveness or a decrease in the effectiveness of the opponent.

Acts that intend injury to an opponent in order to reduce his or her effectiveness. Examples are undercutting a leaping opponent in basketball, throwing a bean ball in baseball, and hitting an American football quarterback after release of the ball. This category must be unacceptable for two reasons. The first is application of the principle of nonmaleficence—it is wrong to intentionally injure someone else unnecessarily. Second, it contradicts the contesting of the central skills of the sport by attempting to deny legitimate opportunity for an opponent to perform the constitutive skills.

Acts that intend to negate the earned advantage of an opponent. Examples are holding a basketball player in possession of the ball who has eluded the defender and has an unimpeded route to the basket, tackling from behind an opposing soccer player in possession of the ball who has no defender between her and the goalie, and trip-ping or hooking an opposing ice-hockey player in possession of the puck who has no one between him and the goalie. This category must be unacceptable because it removes an advantage gained in the central test of the constitutive skills by means of a prohibited act.

Acts that interfere with the movements of an opponent who is not in a position of earned advantage. Examples are holding a basketball player in her own backcourt and trip-ping a soccer player not in possession of the ball in his defensive field. This category must be unacceptable because it gratuitously denies an opponent the opportunity to perform the constitutive skills by means of a prohibited act.

Acts that are intended to attain an illicit advantage for the violator without interfering with an opponent. Examples are a "handball" in soccer, improving one's lie in golf, and reaching over the net in volleyball to spike the ball. This category must be unacceptable because it substitutes a prohibited skill for a constitutive skill and, thus, changes the central test of the sport.

Acts that are intended to reduce a negative impact of time or geographic position on the violator's effectiveness. An example is delaying the game in American football so that the penalty will provide a longer field for a punter. This category seems to be innocuous in that it does not compromise the central test or does not interfere with effective use of the constitutive skills by an opponent.

I do not know that these categories encapsulate all possible instances of intentional tactical rules violations. Nonetheless, their organization around the idea of the central, rule-defined test of a sport is helpful in reaching judgments about whether actions that fall within these categories ought to be acceptable or not.

If we accept the conclusions offered in each category and the primary importance in sports of the rule-defined constitutive central test, there is still need to establish the basis for such importance. Several authors offer compatible pieces for a broad internalism and have been previously identified by Simon (13: pp. 7-9). Behind and supportive of such importance for the rules are presuppositions that explain why we engage in such activities. According to Simon (13), "sports are arenas in which we test ourselves against others, where we attempt to develop and exhibit excellence at overcoming the sport specific obstacles created by the rules" (p. 10). Boxill (1) states, "Constitutive rules are designed to develop and exhibit distinct sets of skills and talents. In combination these rules impose a discipline and create a framework for self-expression and self-development" (p. 4). Loland (8) says that "sport possesses a special potential to provide an arena for human flourishing and so find a place as one among many possible practices constitutive of a good life" (p. 149). Finally, Simon (13) continues,

> This overall theory of the nature and function of sport . . . is not part of the constitutive rules but may be thought of as the best explanation of why the rules have such characteristics as the creation of artificial obstacles to achieving pre-lusory goals that are often easily achievable outside the context of sport. (p. 10)

In summary, we engage in sport in order to test ourselves in unnecessary rule-defined tasks, the experiences of which constitute a kind of human flourishing. Although there are many other individual reasons for people to engage in sport, this reason is internal to sport and common to all who engage in it. At the same time, this common reason might or might not be primary in the thinking of any individual sport participant. This analysis and its conclusions provide small latitude for an appropriate interpretation of the rules (an ethos) that finds intentional tactical rules violations acceptable. Indeed, as Loland (8) said, "If the ethos of a sport tolerates a high number of rules violations, its rule system may lose clear meaning and no longer serve as a conceptual framework for the practice at all" (p. 8). Also, he states, "The ideal must still be to minimize the number of accepted rule violations" (8: p. 9).

Notes

1. The fact that the constitutive skills define the central lusory project is affirmed by ongoing, common experiences of good sports contests. While the contest is going smoothly there is little interruption in the continuity. For example, in basketball, one team's series of throwing actions ends in a field-goal attempt. If the attempt is successful, the opposing team takes the ball out of bounds and proceeds with its own throwing actions to attempt a field goal. If an attempt is unsuccessful, one team secures the rebound and a new series of actions toward a field goal begins. All this continues and there is no interruption in performance of the constitutive skills. If, however, a rules violation occurs,

an official blows a whistle and the game stops, time is out, the ball is not in play, and contesting constitutive skills ceases. Then, on an official's signal, time is in and restorative skills such as the throw-in or the free throw become a prelude to reestablishing the constitutive phase of the game. The pause in action brought on by the rules violation is a break in contest continuity. I observed an extreme of such continuity breaks in the 1976 Olympic Games water-polo matches in which very frequent whistles, in reaction to almost continuous underwater rules violations, made me wonder what skills were being contested. Such extremes were often the case in American intercollegiate basketball, and the closing minutes sometimes became a boring parade to the free-throw line until the recent changes in the penalty for intentional rules violations.

2. A perceptive referee raised an interesting question in the review of this manuscript: "Do all sports have restorative skill?" The referee asked specifically about baseball. Although I cannot attempt to answer this question now, it might be that the regulative rules of some sports provide only compensation or a penalty, for example, awarding a hit batsman first base, but do not generate specific restorative skills other than an official's decision. Nonetheless, even in such a sport the rules violation and the procedure to rectify it result in an interruption in continuity.

References

1. Boxill, J. "Introduction: The Moral Significance of Sport." In *Sport Ethics, An Anthology,* J. Boxill (Ed.). Oxford: Blackwell Publishing, 2003, pp. 1-12.

2. Butcher, R., and Schneider, A. "Fair Play as Respect for the Game." In *Ethics in Sport,* W.J. Morgan, K.V. Meier, and A.J. Schneider (Eds.). Champaign, IL: Human Kinetics, 2001, pp. 21-48.

3. D'Agostino, F. "The Ethos of Games." In *Philosophic Inquiry in Sport,* W.J. Morgan and K.V. Meier (Eds.). 2nd ed. Champaign, IL: Human Kinetics, 1995, pp. 42-49.

4. Delattre, E.J. "Some Reflections on Success and Failure in Competitive Athletics." *Journal of the Philosophy of Sport.* II, 1976, 133-139.

5. Fraleigh, W.P. *Right Actions in Sport*: *Ethics for Contestants.* Champaign, IL: Human Kinetics, 1984.

6. Leaman, O. "Cheating and Fair Play in Sport." In *Philosophic Inquiry in Sport,* W.J. Morgan and K.V. Meier (Eds.). 2nd ed. Champaign, IL: Human Kinetics, 1995, pp. 193-197.

7. Lehman, C.K. "Can Cheaters Play the Game?" *Journal of the Philosophy of Sport.* VIII, 1979, 41-46.

8. Loland, S. *Fair Play in Sport*: A *Moral Norm System.* London & New York: Routledge, 2002.

9. Morgan, W.J. "The Logical Incompatibility Thesis and Rules: A Reconsideration of Formalism as an Account of Games." In *Philosophic Inquiry in Sport,* W.J. Morgan and K.V. Meier (Eds.). 2nd ed. Champaign, IL: Human Kinetics, 1995, pp. 50-63.

10. Pearson, K.M. "Deception, Sportsmanship and Ethics." In *Philosophic Inquiry in Sport,* W.J. Morgan and K.V. Meier (Eds.). 2nd ed. Champaign, IL: Human Kinetics, 1995, pp. 183-184.

11. Russell, J.S. "Are Rules All an Umpire Has to Work With?" *Journal of the Philosophy of Sport.* XXVI, 1999, 27-49.

12. Simon, R.L. *Fair Play, Sports Values and Society.* Boulder, CO: Westview Press, 1991.

13. Simon, R.L. "Internalism and Internal Values in Sport." *Journal of the Philosophy of Sport.* XXVII, 1999, 1-16.

14. Suits, B. *The Grasshopper: Games, Life and Utopia.* Toronto: University of Toronto Press, 1978.

15. Tamburrini, C.M. *The 'Hand of God?' Essays in the Philosophy of Sports.* Goteborg, Sweden: Acta Universitatis Gothoburgensis, 2000.

16. Torres, C.R. "What Counts as Part of a Game? A Look at Skills." *Journal of the Philosophy of Sport.* XXVII, 2000, 81-92.

The Ethics
of Strategic Fouling

A Reply to Fraleigh

Robert L. Simon

In a recent article, Warren Fraleigh made a significant advance in the discussion of the ethics of strategic fouls (1: pp. 166–176). Strategic fouls occur when a competitor in an athletic contest deliberately and openly breaks a rule expecting to be penalized and with willingness to accept the penalty, in order to obtain a strategic advantage in the contest.[1] Examples include fouling by the losing team to stop the clock in the last few minutes of a basketball game and interfering with a pass receiver in (American) football who otherwise would break free and possibly score a touchdown.

The discussion over the ethics of strategic fouling is much more than a narrow debate over the use of a tactic in sport. Critics of strategic fouling admit that the practice is prevalent and tend to regard it as an example of how emphasis on winning has undermined the deeper and more fundamental values that make sport a morally attractive enterprise. In particular, critics fear that strategic fouling alters the kind of test that should be fundamental to a sports contest and so in effect gives priority to winning while undermining the kinds of skills that when exercised properly give winning its true significance. Undue emphasis is placed on results, and the external rewards such as fame and fortune that come with winning, and not enough on the integrity of the activity itself.

Philosophers of sport have discussed the ethics of strategic fouling from a variety of perspectives. Those who view the ethics of strategic fouling from perspectives influenced by formalism have stressed that such fouls are violations of the constitutive rules of the game. By this view, the rules are the basis of the (implied or explicit)

Reprinted, by permission, from R.L. Simon, 2005, "The ethics of strategic fouling: A reply to Fraleigh," *Journal of the Philosophy of Sport* 32(1):87-95.

contract between the competitors, or at least the basis of the public understanding that all competitors should be expected to follow. Hence, strategic fouls either violate the fundamental norm of conformity to the constitutive rules of the game or are perhaps not part of the game itself. According to the latter interpretation, strategic foulers are not really playing the game at all and so are unable to truly win, because the game is defined by the constitutive rules that determine what are and are not permissible moves within it.

Other writers who emphasize the social context of sport have argued that social conventions and practices, often referred to as the ethos of the game, legitimate strategic fouls in a way ignored by formalists, who focus too exclusively on formal elements of sport, particularly constitutive rules. Thus, there is alleged to be a common understanding among basketball players that losing teams will foul at the end of games to stop the clock. Because all teams do this and expect others to do so, as well, there is nothing illegitimate about such tactics.

A third group of theorists, including myself, has agreed with the conventionalists that formal rules are not necessarily all ethicists in sport have to take into account; they also have been wary of endorsing the conventionalist view that a practice is legitimate just because current practitioners of a sport accept it (4: pp. 1–16; 3: pp. 50–52). These theorists have argued that in addition to rules, a broad interpretation of the best understanding of the game, including respect for its internal norms and values, can be fundamental to the ethical assessment of practices in sport. In my own case, I have tried to defend a theory of penalties that distinguishes punishments for prohibited behavior from prices for the exercise of strategic options and have argued that in some cases, such as fouling late in a basketball game to stop the clock and force the team in the lead to make foul shots, the penalties for strategic fouls are prices for allowable strategic choices rather than sanctions of moves not allowed in the game.

Fraleigh's recent contribution takes the discussion farther by presenting new arguments, drawing in part on the work of Cesar Torres (5: pp. 81–92), against the acceptability of strategic fouling and by maintaining that the best overall theory of competitive sports supports the view that strategic fouls are unacceptable. Moreover, Fraleigh uses this line of argument to undermine the use of the price–sanction distinction to defend strategic fouling.

As we would expect given his distinguished contributions to the field, Fraleigh's discussion significantly advances the debate. In fact, I myself feel its pull and find that his arguments not only deserve careful consideration but also are quite plausible. But are they correct? Perhaps, but there also are points to be made on behalf of the judicious use of strategic fouls that deserve consideration and might not have been given adequate weight in Fraleigh's article. After briefly summarizing Fraleigh's arguments, I will try to develop these points in order to show why strategic fouling might sometimes be appropriate (and ethically defensible) in a hard-fought sports contest.

Fraleigh's Critique of Strategic Fouling

Fraleigh draws heavily on Cesar Torres's distinction between the constitutive and restorative skills of a sport. Constitutive skills are those required to meet the challenges set by the constitutive rules. In basketball, they would include dribbling, passing, moving without the ball, and shooting field goals. In soccer they would include kicking the ball, dribbling it, and moving into the right position when action is elsewhere on the field. Restorative skills, on the other hand, are those employed when something has gone wrong in the game, as when rules are violated. They set matters right and get the game back on course. Foul shooting is a restorative skill in basketball, and shooting penalty kicks is one in soccer.

The point of this distinction is that constitutive skills are fundamental to the game in a way that restorative ones are not. Restorative skills apply only "when the central lusory project, as defined by the constitutive skills, has been interrupted by a rules violation" (1: p. 171). Restorative skills then can be employed in order to "put the game back on track" either by penalizing or compensating the offending or offended team or player (5: p. 85; 1: p. 171). As Fraleigh maintains, "Torres's view trumps Simon's point in precisely the appropriate way which Simon suggests as legitimate since it establishes a theory of the skills of sport which assign secondary, derivative importance to the restorative skills of foul shooting in basketball" (1: p. 172). Part of what makes Fraleigh's argument significant, then, is that it advances the discussion beyond the formalist–conventionalist debate by maintaining that those who take a broadly interpretivist view of sport, including those who appeal to such notions as "respect for the game" and "the most defensible overall interpretation of the sport," should conclude that strategic fouling is ethically inappropriate in competitive athletics.

Fraleigh's case, then, is that in the best interpretation of sports, contests should be decided on the basis of the skilled exercise of constitutive skills, which after all are the skills that the constitutive rules test. Although restorative skills inevitably play a role in actual contests, competitors are not showing the appropriate respect for the game or, to put it another way, are undermining the central challenge the sport presents by deliberately transforming the game from one in which constitutive skills, the skills that sport is best construed as testing, dominate to one in which restorative skills can be determinate.

Finally, Fraleigh points out that rules makers over time have made it clearer that certain penalties are to be construed as punishments for prohibited behavior rather than as prices for exercising strategic options. For example, "in American intercollegiate basketball the rule with regard to intentional rules violation has moved definitely toward a punishment" (1: p. 172).

This critique of strategic fouling has considerable force, but before it is accepted we need to examine three distinctions more closely. The first is the distinction between constitutive and restorative skills, the second is between different kinds of strategic fouls, and the third is between a critique of indiscriminate strategic fouling and a critique of strategic fouling in specific situations in which it might add not only to the excitement and interest of the contest but also to the test it presents to competitors.

Constitutive and Restorative Skills

What exactly is the distinction between constitutive and restorative skills? In part, it is one of function. Restorative skills are those employed to get the game back on track after a constitutive rule has been violated. In part, the restorative skills might resemble physically the same skill when exercised in the normal course of play. Foul shooting in basketball resembles in many respects the movements of open shooters who have their feet set when launching the ball. As Torres points out, however, there are important contextual differences (5: pp. 86–89). Foul shooting is fixed and repetitive compared with the fluid motions of normal play in basketball. There is no opponent trying to defend against the shot. The shooter does not have to move to get open in the first place. Foul shooting, in other words, is less complex and therefore less interesting than shooting field goals. It is perhaps for this reason that fans at a basketball game marred by frequent fouling often feel that the game is spoiled and call to the referees to "let them [the athletes] play the game," something that would make no sense if foul shooting were regarded as a central skill of basketball.

All these points support the analysis of Torres and the use Fraleigh makes of it. But consider further. There seem to be two accounts of restorative skills presupposed by this discussion, or at least two separable claims about them. The first is that restorative skills are defined by function; their role is to put the game back on track after certain sorts of violations of constitutive rules. The second is that exercise of restorative skills is less interesting or complex than exercise of constitutive ones and so should not be construed as skills the game is designed primarily to test. (Perhaps the first condition should be regarded as the definition of restorative skills and the second a reason or justification for regarding them as less central to the sport than constitutive skills.)

But do all restorative skills fit both of these conditions? Consider, for example, the art of killing penalties in ice hockey. The skills involved are hardly simple and repetitive. Penalty killing and the correlative power plays associated with it often are especially interesting and exciting parts of the game. Although a hockey game constantly disrupted by penalties can be regarded as defective to one degree or another and even spoiled in extreme cases, the skills employed by both sides during power play often are as intrinsically interesting or complex as those employed in the regular course of play.[2] (I assume here that because the numerical disadvantage assigned to the team that has violated the rules turns the situation into a restorative one, the skills exercised during the power play are restorative ones. Perhaps, however, Torres and Farleigh would argue that the skills involved are constitutive ones. If so, they may avoid my point that restorative skills can be complex but only at the price of blurring the distinction between constitutive and restorative skills to a dangerous extent.) Moreover, even though the physical motions of making a foul shot in basketball might be less complex than normal field-goal attempts, making crucial foul shots at the end of a close game may be as psychologically complex and difficult as exercising constitutive skills in the normal course of play.

Moreover, aspects of regular play might in themselves also lack complexity and exhibition of high levels of skill, such as a basketball player dribbling out the clock or a physically dominant player constantly scoring easy layup shots from under the basket against clearly mismatched opponents.

Finally, we need to distinguish between the complexity of an action during a game, such as shooting a foul shot, and the strategic complexities generated by the possibility of strategically fouling and sending an opponent to the foul line. The possibility of what I will later call the judicious strategic foul generates a whole set of complex options and choices that can make the overall game more interesting than otherwise for participants and spectators alike.[3]

Accordingly, we can conclude that the second condition, lack of complexity and interest—although it applies to some, perhaps most, exercises of restorative skills—does not apply to all of them. Moreover, the exercise of some skills during the regular course of play can sometimes lack complexity and be uninteresting, as well. Hence, the second condition does not provide an overarching justification for always regarding the exercise of restorative skills as inferior to the exercise of constitutive ones.

What is the significance of this for Fraleigh's argument? First, it suggests that the use of restorative skills in a sports contest does not *necessarily* make that contest less complex or less interesting than otherwise, although it might often in fact do so. Fraleigh's argument suggests that the perfect contest would not involve restorative skills at all because there would be no rule violations calling for the use of restorative skills. But contrary to that suggestion, sometimes a sports contest in which restorative skills are employed can be a better test of more varied abilities than one in which only constitutive skills are employed. For example, an ice-hockey game with some power plays might provide more of a test of more varied skills than one in which two evenly matched teams continually struggle at center ice with few shots on goal by either side. And, as I will argue below, basketball games that involve the judicious use of strategic fouls might be more complex and interesting and provide a more stringent test for the participants than one in which such a practice is disallowed or absent.

Fraleigh (and perhaps Torres) might accept this point but reply that unintentional rule violations might be an inevitable part of a hard-fought contest between evenly matched teams and might indeed add interest to the game, but intentionally violating the rules to gain a competitive advantage is another matter. Let us turn to that point, keeping in mind, however, that the use of restorative skills might in certain contexts add to rather than undermine the interest, strategic complexity, and excitement of a contest.

Types of Strategic Fouls

Although the distinction between constitutive and restorative skills might be complex, the main point of Torres's distinction is that constitutive skills are those the game is best construed as designed to test (5: p. 89). Accordingly, intentional fouling changes the nature of that test and disrespects the central value of the game by eclipsing the role of constitutive skills and elevating restorative skills beyond their proper station. The true test of which team or athlete is best is found in the exercise of constitutive skills, not restorative ones. Thus, we judge who are the best defensive backs in football by such factors as their speed and quickness, their intelligence in reading plays and anticipating the moves of receivers, and their ability to make interceptions, not by how good they are at committing pass interference!

This argument is a strong one, and I believe it does establish strategic fouling as (at least presumptively) unethical in at least two kinds of cases. The first is when a less skilled team or player resorts to strategic fouls in order to disrupt the style or eliminate the advantage of skills of a superior team—in other words, to prevent the other team from exhibiting superior constitutive skills by disrupting the normal flow of the game so no room is left for skillful play. For example, an ice-hockey team that cannot skate anywhere near as well as its opponents might resort to illegal roughhouse play thinking it has a better chance to win that way, even taking into account the likelihood of penalties being called, than if it had to match its constitutive skills in the normal course of play.

A second related kind of strategic foul, identified by Fraleigh, occurs when a foul is committed in order to deprive an opponent of an advantage already gained through superior use of constitutive skills. This category would include intentionally fouling in basketball, soccer, or hockey in order to prevent a player who has broken away ahead of the defense from scoring a goal or deliberately committing pass interference in American football against a receiver who is about to break into the open for a touchdown.

Each of these kinds of strategic fouls is presumptively unethical for precisely the reason identified by Fraleigh; namely, it violates the principle that sports contests should be primarily tests of constitutive skills by either preventing opponents from establishing superiority in use of such skills in the first place (the ice-hockey example) or preventing players from gaining the advantages earned through the use of such skills. Not all strategic fouls, however, fall within these two categories.

First, and perhaps the less interesting kind of example for the issues involved here, are what might be called mixed or impure strategic fouls. Mixed strategic fouls occur when athletes play more aggressively at key points in the contest, knowingly taking on the increased risk of fouling because the price of fouling might be strategically worth paying. For example, basketball players on a team a few points behind in the last few minutes of a game might try to steal the ball from the offensive team but do so in a much more aggressive fashion than normal because, even if fouls are called, the offensive team might miss its foul shots. Here, the intention is to steal the ball, but the defenders are deliberately less inhibited in their attempts to get the ball because the price of being called for a foul is considered worth paying. Although it obviously will be hard to distinguish mixed from pure strategic fouls in practice, the difference nevertheless might be a real one. Because players who commit mixed fouls intend only (or at least intend mainly) to play aggressive defense, they arguably do not fall under the prohibition against strategic fouling.[4]

A kind of case that more directly challenges Fraleigh's argument is a strategic foul that does not deprive an opponent of an advantage already gained but that prevents play from being executed in the first place, that is, preventive strategic fouls. Thus, a basketball player might foul the recipient of a pass before the ball handler can pass, dribble, or make a move to shoot. Clearly, if a team repeatedly fouls in such a way, a basketball game can have no flow and the game is spoiled. A clearly inferior team that continually fouls in the hope of making the game so lacking in flow that the superior skills of the opponent are negated might be justly criticized. It does not follow, though, that this is the only kind of case in which a strategic foul of this kind might be employed. Let us consider the point further.

Judicious Strategic Fouls

In particular, even if some preventive strategic fouls are open to legitimate moral criticism, it does not follow that the judicious use of strategic fouls of this sort in close games is similarly inappropriate. Consider the following example. Teams A and B are meeting for the third time this basketball season. Team A won the first game by 3 points and Team B the second game by 4. So far in the deciding contest of the season, the teams remain equally matched. Let us suppose that play so far in all three games clearly indicates that in terms of constitutive skills the teams are roughly equal in ability. In the present game, which determines a slot in the postseason playoff, the score is tied until the last few seconds when Team A scores a go-ahead field goal. B misses its chance to tie the game. Team A has a lead of 2 points and possession of the ball with 9 seconds left in the game.

Team B's coach realizes that his team's chances of stealing the ball with just 9 seconds to play are remote. Players on Team A might just hold the ball and not even attempt to advance it up the court. The coach also knows, however, that although both teams are roughly equal in constitutive abilities, Team A's players are not good foul shooters. He orders his team to foul to stop the clock, reasoning that if the opponents miss their foul shots, Team B will have a chance to tie or win the game.

Is this choice of strategy unethical? From the point of view of broad internalism (or interpretivism), we need to ask if basketball is a better game if judicious use of strategic fouling is regarded as appropriate. Although the answer certainly is debatable, it is not unreasonable to think that the game in question is a better one if it remains competitive until the end rather than ending anticlimactically by Team A simply holding the ball or not trying to advance it for the final 9 seconds.

What about the point that contests should, as far as possible, be determined by use of constitutive rather than restorative skills? This principle is presumptively correct, but in the previous example, it already has been established that the opponents are roughly equal in constitutive skills. Neither is better than the other in that regard. Although the suggestion that a tie might be the fairest resolution has merit, a tie is not feasible in this context because only one team can advance to the playoffs. (See 6: pp. 144–158 for an argument defending the importance and legitimacy of ties in sports.) In such a case, if both teams are equal in terms of constitutive skills but one team is much better at exercising restorative skills, why isn't that team the better of the two? In other words, it is appropriate for differences in restorative skills to be tiebreakers. That is what Team B is trying to do by making Team A go to the foul line. After all, Team A could have improved its foul shooting. If foul shooting is its weakness, and the teams are equal in all other respects, why is it unethical for Team B to try to establish its superiority by exploiting the weakness of its opponent?

Of course, this example is an extreme case, but it does suggest a more general thesis. According to this thesis, strategic fouls are not ethically inappropriate when the following conditions are satisfied. First, it is reasonable to believe that the opponents are roughly matched in constitutive skills. Second, the team that strategically fouls has no alternative strategy based on the use of constitutive skills that gives it a reasonable chance to win. Third, the penalty for the foul must reasonably be regarded as the price of action rather than punishment for it; that is, the penalty must provide reasonable compensation for the offended team. Last, the strategic foul must not take away an advantage in play that the opponents have already earned through the exercise of constitutive skills. For example, this would rule out tripping from behind a hockey player who has broken away on an open goal. (We might also add that teams not employ a series of strategic fouls designed to prevent opponents from exhibiting constitutive skills by disrupting the flow of the game.)

One difficulty with this approach is that in my basketball example, it is not clear that the second condition is satisfied. Team B could try to double-team or trap players on Team A in an attempt to steal the ball. Such attempts sometimes are successful and involve the use of constitutive rather than restorative skills. But while this point has force, it is not clear that it applies fully to evenly matched teams with only a few seconds left in the game. A player on Team A might simply hold the ball and let the clock run out. So although this criticism does show that it might be difficult to determine when a strategic foul is judicious, I do not think it shows that strategic fouls in the kind of situation I have described in a basketball game are always injudicious or illegitimate.

Another difficulty, a critic might argue, is that the third condition is not satisfied. Penalties for many strategic fouls have been elevated to resemble punishments rather than prices. As we have seen, Fraleigh maintains that the evolution of the rules of basketball makes it clear that intentional strategic fouls are to be punished rather than purchased for a fair price (1: 172).

Are the rules best interpreted as Fraleigh suggests? Perhaps so, but consider two difficulties for such a view. First, referees do not treat clearly strategic fouls as different from ordinary ones unless they are blatant, that is, risk injury to a player or take away an advantage earned by the use of constitutive skills, such as fouling a basketball player who has a breakaway layup from behind. Perhaps this is merely a conventionalist point, that referees, contrary to the intent of the rule makers, accept the (ethically indefensible) social convention that strategic fouling is part of the game. But two other possibilities exist. For one thing, referees might be unable to distinguish pure from what I called mixed strategic fouls and hence give the defenders the benefit of the doubt. Another interpretation is that the referees understand the rules as prohibiting certain kinds of strategic fouling but not as eliminating strategic fouling from the game.

In fact, one structural feature of the rules of basketball supports this last suggestion. This is the rule that allows a losing team to in effect trade two foul shots for the opportunity to attempt to make a 3-point basket. That is, a losing basketball team can strategically foul, giving the opponent the opportunity to make two foul shots, and then when it gets possession of the ball, attempt a 3-point shot. In a sense, this feature of the rules encourages losing teams to commit strategic fouls in such situations because this strategy gives them a reasonable chance to come from behind, especially against opponents who do not shoot foul shots well.[5] Is this a flaw in the rules, or does it provide the opportunity for strategic choices and excitement in the last few minutes of a contest that actually enhance the game? If, as I have suggested, the judicious use of strategic fouls in basketball games raises the competitive intensity of the game, making it a better test for the players, and if restorative skills can help determine which of two otherwise evenly matched opponents is superior, such fouls can have a defensible place in the game.

Conclusions

By placing the issue of strategic fouling in the framework of interpretive or broad internalist theory and by applying Torres's distinction between constitutive and restorative skills, Fraleigh has raised the discussion to a new level. In my view, his argument is most successful when directed against the use of strategic fouling to prevent a superior opponent from exercising constitutive skills. Serial strategic fouling of this kind turns an athletic contest into a test of restorative rather than constitutive abilities and is wrong for just the reasons provided by Fraleigh and Torres. The use of strategic fouling to deprive an opponent of an advantage already earned through the exercise of constitutive skills also is morally questionable.

Nonetheless, I have suggested that in specific contexts, particularly close games in basketball, the judicious use of preventive strategic fouls can be morally appropriate. For one thing, when the teams are evenly matched in constitutive skills, differences in restorative skills become relevant to determining which team has best met the test of the contest. Second, judicious strategic fouling in close basketball games raises the competitive intensity of the game and creates more of a test for the players than simply letting the leading team run out the clock. Third, some features of the rules create an incentive for teams to strategically foul at the end of close games in order to trade 2 points for a chance of making 3, thereby calling into question whether in such contexts foul shots really are intended to be punishments for forbidden behavior or the price of strategic choices.

How far these points apply to strategic fouling in sports other than basketball is difficult to say and depends heavily on the individual features of each. I hope my discussion of strategic fouling, which does focus most fully on basketball, suggests how the analysis of such behavior in other sports might proceed, but that is a broader topic than can be considered here.

In any case, Fraleigh's discussion undoubtedly sharpens the discussion and advances powerful arguments against the practice of strategic fouling. Whether he has shown that strategic fouling is always unethical, however, remains debatable.

Notes

1. Typically, those who commit strategic fouls acknowledge that others may permissibly do the same and regard the practice as common to participants in the game. Thus, they do not employ a tactic the use of which they would deny to others.

2. Perhaps a similar point can be made about corner kicks in soccer, as well.

3. I owe this point to Warren Fraleigh, whom I would like to thank for helpful critical comments on an earlier draft.

4. Fraleigh also considers "mixed" strategic fouls acceptable (2: pp. 79–80).

5. Even if the offended team makes both foul shots and scores 2 points, the team that fouls can score a 3-point field goal, thereby cutting the opponent's lead by 1 point. By repeating the process, a lead of several points can be eliminated in a relatively short time. Fraleigh might argue that such repeated use of strategic fouls is not judicious and gives restorative skills like foul shooting too much of a role in determining the outcome. I agree here that "judicious" is somewhat open-ended and that it is not easy for someone who holds my position to say just where the cutoff lies. Even so, it does not follow that strategic fouls are *never* judiciously or defensibly employed.

References

1. Fraleigh, Warren. "Intentional Rules Violations—One More Time." *Journal of the Philosophy of Sport.* XXX, 2003, 166-176.

2. Fraleigh, Warren. *Right Actions in Sport.* Champaign, IL: Human Kinetics, 1984.

3. Simon, Robert L. *Fair Play.* 2nd ed. Boulder, CO: Westview Press, 2004.

4. Simon, Robert L. "Internalism and Internal Values in Sport." *Journal of the Philosophy of Sport.* XXVII, 1999, 1-16.

5. Torres, Cesar R. "What Counts as Part of the Game? A Look at Skills." *Journal of the Philosophy of Sport.* XXVII, 2000, 81-92.

6. Torres, Cesar R., and Douglas McLaughlin. "Indigestion: An Apology for Ties." *Journal of the Philosophy of Sport.* XXX, 2003, 144-158.

III
PART

The Limits of Being Human

Doping and Genetic Enhancement in Sport

The essays in this section consider the moral permissibility of using performance-enhancing drugs in sport; currently, these drugs appear to be widespread at nearly all levels. These chapters also deal with the emergent and, for many, frightening specter of the genetic modification and enhancement of athletes; this issue poses its own special moral problems. As we shall see, the moral disrepute and fury that doping in sport often elicits is beginning to cast a similar moral pall over the genetic enhancement of athletic performance. The authors of these essays, however, are interested in probing whether there are any good arguments to support the strong public disapproval of so-termed "artificial" methods of generating athletic excellence. Some believe that good arguments exist, whereas others remain unconvinced.

The first of the essays devoted to performance-enhancing drugs, John Hoberman's "Listening to Steroids," whose title is borrowed from Kramer's best-selling book *Listening to Prozac*, puts this issue in both a historical and critical perspective. For although drugs to enhance athletic performance have been banned for some thirty-five years now, they have been around much longer—dating at least to the early 1920s. The outlawing of these drugs, Hoberman persuasively argues, was owed to the dominance of a conservative attitude that Kramer dubbed "pharmacological Calvinism," which encouraged people to look askance at drugs used for other than the treatment of bona fide medical conditions. Today that conservative attitude is under siege both in and outside of sports, a development that Hoberman traces to the emergence of the "therapeutic ideal," which blurred the distinction between enhancement and the treatment of medical disorders and other similar bodily maladies. This elastic conception of therapy extended easily to the use of performance-enhancing drugs in sport and helped break down resistance to their use. The rise of the therapeutic ideal also led to the gentrification of drug use devoted to enhancement in all spheres of life, which explains the widely prescribed use of low doses of testosterone today to restore the virility and vitality of millions of middle-aged men suffering from no known medical incapacity other than aging. Under such favorable cultural conditions, Hoberman conjectures, efforts to stem the use of performance-enhancing drugs in sport will soon come to an end, to be replaced by a conception of athletes as superhuman beings whose use of drugs will not only be then condoned by the general public but promoted by pharmacological companies to sell these drugs by affixing their corporate logos on the uniforms and equipment of elite athletes.

The following cluster of three essays—Robert L. Simon's "Good Competition and Drug-Enhanced Performance," W. M. Brown's "Paternalism, Drugs, and the Nature of Sports," and Michael Lavin's "Sports and Drugs: Are the Current Bans Justified?"—argue the moral pros and cons of athletes' efforts to boost their performance by using drugs. Simon's essay begins by arguing that many of the arguments successfully enlisted to ban these drugs in the first place—that these drugs harm athletes, that their use is coercive, that they harm others, especially impressionable children who idolize famous athletes—are remarkably weak. The main problem with them is that they overstep their paternalistic bounds and end up trampling on the individual freedom of athletes. However, he does think that a ban on such drug use can be justified if the argument for banning them is aimed at what the point and purpose of sport is. For if we take into account that the point of an athletic contest is to gauge the athletic excellence of its participants, in short, what they are capable of achieving in a highly trained state, then we will be hard pressed to find a legitimate place for performance-enhancing drugs in such a contest. The reason is that when our performance is improved as the result of such drug use, the improvement is essentially because our body just so happens to respond well to the drug, and how our bodies contingently responds to drugs is, argues Simon, most definitely not the purpose of competitive sport.

Brown is not persuaded by Simon's argument, but only with respect to adult athletes who are fully capable of making their own autonomous and responsible judgments about how they want to live their lives in and outside of sports. However, in the case of youth sports in which we are dealing with athletes who are not autonomous decision makers owing to their youth and inexperience, it is morally justified, Brown contends, to ban drugs from competition. But in such cases the justification for doing so is not pitched to any account of the nature of sport but to the just-stated incapacities of the performers themselves. For these incapacities suggest adults have the right to act paternalistically—that is, to interfere with the freedom of these young athletes in order to protect them and the sports they play from the physical, psychological, and social harms associated with use of performance-enhancing drugs. However, when it comes to adult athletes and sports, Brown insists all bets are off because paternalistic interference with the freedom of such autonomous athletes regarding how they want to engage in sports and more generally how they see fit to live their lives is morally impermissible. Simon-like appeals to the nature of sport won't work at this level either, because, argues Brown, there is no such thing as *the* nature of sport but only a variety of competing and equally compelling conceptions of sport, some of which encourage risk taking and experimentation not just with drugs but with novel forms of equipment as well.

Lavin's final essay of this cluster comes down, like Simon's, on the prohibition side of the issue. But unlike Simon, Lavin insists there is no need to overreach and claim that there is just one morally privileged way of doing sports that warrants the banishment of drugs that boost performance. Rather, all we need is a democratic conception of sport to justify such a ban. What he means by a democratic conception is an understanding of sport that enjoys wide public approval and that appeals to certain core ideals of what counts as good sport. It must be a genuine consensus or else the resultant bans will come across to those that are subject to them as capricious limitations on their individual liberty. And it must be a true democratic consensus because limitations on what groups of people can and cannot do are considered morally acceptable if and only if they reflect such a consensus.

Christian Munthe's contribution, "Selected Champions: Making Winners in the Age of Genetic Technology," broaches the issue of the genetic enhancement of athletes and argues that most forms of genetic intervention to boost the performance of elite athletes are not analogous to doping and thus cannot be morally condemned on the same grounds. He goes further and claims that such genetic interventions are not only morally permissible but perhaps even morally laudable. But these claims require some stage setting, which is what Munthe spends much of his essay doing. He begins by noting that all living organisms are a product of their environment (which includes, among other things, the substances they imbibe, the training they undertake, and the climatic conditions in which they live and exercise) and their genetic inheritance. It has long been possible to alter one's environmental conditions to bolster athletic performance; only in the last couple of decades has it become possible to alter one's genetic makeup. The advances in genetic technology suggest that this may soon change, that in the next decade or so we might well be able to manipulate our genetic endowments in ways that lead to improvements in athletic excellence. Munthe skillfully lays out four ways in which such genetic modification relevant to sport might occur. The first is by fine-tuning training and nutrition by keying them to the genetic characteristics of the individual athlete. The second is by somatic genetic modification in which the somatic cells of the body (that is, our normal body cells responsible for the composition of our blood and bodily organs) are manipulated to increase, say, red blood cell production, thereby bolstering performance in high-endurance sports; such interventions would have to be local and so targeted to specific bodily organs and would not be inherited by the modified athletes' offspring. A third way to genetically boost athletic performance involves germ-line genetic modifications that regulate the basic structures of the body and determine our physiological capacities. Because this form of genetic intervention must occur very early on, either the sperm, or the unfertilized egg, or the just-fertilized egg is manipulated to enhance physical performance—obviously this kind of intervention is performed before the actual person that results is born and thus will be passed on to his or her offspring. The fourth and final way to raise athletic excellence by genetic means involves the selection of individuals for elite athletic competition based on their genome. Munthe concludes his ethical analysis by arguing that because of the novelty of most of these forms of genetic modification, with the possible exception of somatic cell modifications that change the biochemistry of the body in ways that are similar to doping, the ethical arguments that have been advanced to ban doping do not work in the case of genetic modification. For example, genetically uninformed decisions about training methods and special diets may well be more unsafe than genetic modifications, and germ-line genetic modifications produce different individuals than those born through normal procreation, thereby further complicating any argument based on harm. For this and other reasons, Munthe argues we will have little choice but to accept genetic modifications in sport. Perhaps in the future, after their novelty wears off, we may even be persuaded to treat them as a welcome contribution to elite sport because of the greater knowledge they provide of how humans function.

Claudio Tamburrini gets the last say on this issue in his essay "After Doping, What? The Morality of the Genetic Engineering of Athletes." His contribution to the ethical debate over genetically modifying athletes to enhance their athletic prowess not only defends such intervention but goes so far as to suggest that it will lead to "the flourishing of human character in sport." Tamburrini lays out his argument in much the same way Munthe does, first outlining the different ways genetic technology might be employed in sport and then rejecting moral arguments imported from the performance-enhancing drug controversy (for instance the argument from harm) on the grounds that they are not applicable to genetic efforts to raise athletic standards of excellence. The new twist Tamburrini provides in his essay has to do with the argument that genetic modification should be banned because it makes the competition unfair. He not only rejects this argument but turns it on its head by showing that genetic interventions can, in fact, make sports fairer enterprises than they presently are by nullifying the huge advantage the winners of the genetic lottery have over the losers when it comes to practices such as sport. For as things presently stand no amount of training or other similar compensatory efforts can overcome the advantage those participants with superior genetic endowments enjoy in sport. And it is in this sense that Tamburrini thinks genetic technology contributes to the flourishing of moral character in sport, for by leveling the genetic playing field such modifications decrease the importance of physiological prowess and increase the importance of moral character in determining athletic excellence. This is because victory under these modified genetic conditions would go to those most committed to their sport, and to the training and other sacrifices their sport requires, rather than to those most physically gifted.

The literature on performance-enhancing drugs in sport is abundant. Some of the better pieces on this controversial topic include Brown's "Practices and Prudence," Dixon's " Rorty, Performance-Enhancing Drugs, and Change in Sport," Gardner's "On Performance-Enhancing Substances and the Unfair Advantage Argument," Perry's "Blood Doping and Athletic Competition," and Schneider's and Tamburrini's contributions to *Values in Sport*.[1]

The literature on genetic technology and sport is understandably sparse. But two recent publications are well worth a close read: Miah's monograph *Genetically Modified Athletes*, which does an especially good and comprehensive job of introducing the bioethics and medical ethics literature to sport ethics; and Tamburrini's and Tännsjö's edited anthology, *Genetic Technology and Sport*, which contains several incisively argued essays on the subject of genetic modification.[2]

Notes

1. W. Miller Brown, "Practices and Prudence," *Journal of the Philosophy of Sport* XVII (1990): 71-84; Nicholas Dixon, "Rorty, Performance-Enhancing Drugs, and Change in Sport," *Journal of the Philosophy of Sport* XXVII, no. 1 (2001): 78-88; Roger Gardner, "On Performance-Enhancing Substances and the Unfair Advantage Argument," *Journal of the Philosophy of Sport* XVI (1989): 59-73; Clifton Perry, "Blood Doping and Athletic Competition," *The International Journal of Applied Philosophy* 1, no. 3

(1983): 39-45; Angela Schneider and Robert B. Butcher, "A Philosophical Overview of the Arguments on Banning Doping in Sport," and Claudio Tamburrini, "What's Wrong With Doping?" in *Values in Sport*, eds. T. Tännsjö and C. Tamburrini (London and New York: E&FN Spon, 2000) 185-199; 200-216.

2. Andy Miah, *Genetically Modified Athletes* (New York and London: Routledge, 2004); Claudio Tamburrini and Torbjörn Tännsjö, eds., *Genetic Technology and Sport* (London and New York: Routledge, 2005).

17

Listening to Steroids

◆

John Hoberman

For a decade after his reign as the premier American marathoner of the early 1980s, Alberto Salazar failed to win a major race, and no one could figure out why. His years-long quest for medical advice that might salvage a distinguished career became well known among those who follow the running scene. Finally, the long-awaited breakthrough came with a victory in the 56-mile Comrades Marathon in South Africa in June 1994. But this personal triumph was accompanied by an odd and, for some observers, unsettling piece of news. After consulting with a sports physician and an endocrinologist, Salazar had concluded that years of intensive training had "suppressed [his] body's endocrine system." The treatment that he and his advisers chose was a drug that had no previous association with athletic performance and did not violate international rules: the now-legendary antidepressant Prozac.

No one familiar with the history of drug use in sports will be surprised by an athlete's innovative use of a medication, especially one that is prescribed to create courage and self-confidence in timid, lethargic, or demoralized people. Over the past century there have always been athletes willing to ingest substances, including potential poisons such as heroin and strychnine, to boost their performance. That many of them have been assisted by physicians and pharmaceutical companies reminds us that sports medicine has always been part of what one German sports scientist has called "a gigantic experiment on the human organism." At the same time, we must not overlook the quasi-scientific or pseudoscientific character of most experimentation. Consider, for example, the fuzzy medical logic employed by Alberto Salazar and his counselors. While Dr. Peter D. Kramer's phenomenal best seller *Listening to Prozac* (1993) makes many claims for the drug, the treatment of endocrinological disorders is not one of them. Equally revealing is the vagueness of the self-diagnosis that pointed Salazar toward the world's most popular antidepressant: "It wasn't that I was depressed or sad," he told an interviewer. "I just never had any energy or zest. I knew there was something wrong with my whole system."

Reprinted, by permission, from J. Hoberman, 1995, "Listening to steroids," *Wilson Quarterly Winter '95*: 35-44.

Alberto Salazar's encounter with Prozac forged a high-profile link between doping in sport and the wider world of pharmacology that affects us all. The existence of powerful drugs forces us to think about human nature itself and how it can or should be transformed. As modern science increases our power to transform minds and bodies, we will have to make momentous decisions about how the human beings of the future will look and function, how fast they will run, and (perhaps) how fast they will think. To what extent do we want to preserve—and to what extent do we want to alter—human traits? It is already clear that in an age of genetic engineering advocates of the medical transformation of human beings sound reasonable, while the proponents of preserving human traits (and, therefore, human limitations) are likely to sound naive and opposed to progress in principle. The unequal contest between those who favor experimentation upon human beings and those who oppose it will be the most profound drama of 21st-century postindustrial society. Yet few people are aware that its essential acts have already been rehearsed during the past century of scientific sport.

Drugs have been used to enhance sexual, military, intellectual, and work performances as well as sportive ones. Yet sport is somehow different. Its exceptional status as a realm of inviolable performances becomes clear if we compare it with some other vocations. Consider, for example, another group of performers for whom mental and physical stress is a way of life. Their life expectancy is 22 percent below the national average. They suffer from tendinitis, muscle cramps, pinched nerves, a high incidence of mental health problems and heart attacks, and anxiety levels that threaten to cripple their performance as professionals. These people are not fire fighters or police officers or athletes; they are orchestral musicians, and many use "beta-blocker" drugs to control their stage fright and thereby improve their performances. The use of these same anti-anxiety drugs has been banned by the Medical Commission of the International Olympic Committee as a form of doping.

What accounts for this discrepancy? What makes sport the one type of performance that can be "corrupted" by pharmacological intervention? One might argue that an orchestral performance, unlike a sporting event, is not a contest. Since the performers are not competing against one another, deceit is not an issue. Yet even if we leave aside the prominent international music competitions, this argument overlooks the fact that an entire field of equally doped runners who knew exactly which drugs their competitors had taken would still violate the ethics of sport, which require both fair competition and the integrity of the performance itself—an untainted, and therefore accurate, measure of human potential. But why is the same requirement not imposed on the orchestral musician? Indeed, one would expect "high" cultural performances to carry greater ethical and anthropological significance than sportive ones. Sport's role as a special index of human capacity makes drug use by athletes uniquely problematic.

The "doping" issue within pharmacology thus originates in a tension between the licit and the illicit, a conflict that is inevitable in a society that both legitimizes and distrusts pharmacological solutions to human problems. The enormous market for substances that are supposed to boost the human organism in various ways benefits from the universal presumption that almost any attempt to expand human capacities is worth trying. Technological civilization always tends to turn productive activities into measurable performances, catalyzing an endless search for performance-enhancing technologies, from psychotherapy to caffeine tablets.

The modern obsession with performance enhancement is reflected in the wide range of substances and techniques enlisted on behalf of improving the human organism and its capacities. Commercial "brain gyms" employ stress-reduction devices such as flotation tanks, biofeedback machines, and somatrons (which bombard the body with musical vibrations) in an attempt to affect the brain waves and thereby increase intelligence, boost memory, strengthen the immune system, and combat phobias. So-called "smart drugs," none of which have been proven effective in scientifically valid trials, are sold to promote "cognitive enhancement."

The never-ending contest between the performance principle and the cultural restraints that work against it blurs the line separating the licit and the illicit. Consider, for example, the response in 1993 to charges of steroid doping among Chinese swimmers. A Chinese newspaper responded that the swimmers' world-class performances had been made possible by a "multi-functional muscle-building machine" that sends electronically controlled bursts of electricity through the muscles. That is to say, an accusation of illicit performance boosting of one kind was met with earnest assurances that Chinese athletes had succeeded by employing an equally artificial (but still legal) procedure. Few anecdotes could better illustrate the prevailing opportunism in the field.

Doping in sport has been banned for the past 25 years, yet less than a century ago European scientists were discussing pharmacological aids to athletic performance without any qualms. The physiologists of that time understood that the pharmacologically active substances they worked with displayed a range of effects: they could be medicines, stimulants, depressants, intoxicants, antiseptics, narcotics, poisons, or antagonists of other drugs. But during this phase, physicians and others had little interest in using drugs to improve athletic performance. Sports simply did not have the social and political importance they have today. At the same time, the athletic world did not yet recognize drugs as a threat to the integrity of sport. The distinction between performance-enhancing and therapeutic medications—a prerequisite of the doping concept—was not yet established.

The absence of such a norm explains why the French scientists who gave experimental doses of drugs such as alcohol and kola nuts to cyclists in the 1890s were untroubled by ethical doubts. The pioneering sports physician Philippe Tissié, for example, could both carry out experiments on human subjects and warn against the medical dangers of stimulants. Tissié saw athletic physiology as one approach to the study of the human organism. His attempt to prolong a cyclist's endurance by feeding him rum and champagne during a 24-hour distance trial may have been the first scientifically controlled experiment of its kind. Yet he was consistently cautious on medical grounds about the use of stimulants.

Tissié's attitude toward athletic stimulants appears strangely conflicted to those of us accustomed to the antidrug propaganda of the sports world today. How could the same physician who had urged his cyclist around the track for the purpose of identifying effective stimulants also condemn them as dangerous? To dissolve this apparent contradiction, we must abandon our conditioned reactions to the idea of doping and project ourselves back into Tissié's world. If he had no qualms about energizing his cyclist, it was because his experiment occurred before stimulants had come to be regarded as a threat to equitable competition. In any event, Tissié was not interested in producing record-breaking cyclists. It was medical prudence, not morality, that prompted his frequent cautionary remarks about stimulants. Indeed, his condemnation of alcohol is immediately followed by a recommendation that "the better beverage" for boosting performance is sugar water.

A similar ethical nonchalance is evident in a 1913 article, "Sport and Stimulants," by the early German sports physician Ferdinand Hueppe. Modern life is impossible without stimulants, he wrote, and the task of the physician is to replace harmful substances with more benign alternatives. Hueppe's disapproving references to "doping"—an internationally understood term even at this early date—concerned the uselessness or potential dangers of drugs, not their possible use as illicit performance-enhancers.

Condemnation of doping on ethical grounds appeared during the 1920s as sport became a genuine mass-cultural phenomenon. The growth of international sporting events after the first modern Olympics, held in Athens in 1896, created a new arena for nationalistic competition that served the interests of various governments. Larger financial investments and the prominence of sport in the emerging mass media gave elite athletes a new social and political significance, which helped foster new suspicions about the competitive practices of others. Having left its age of innocence behind, sports medicine was now embarked upon a new experimental phase involving the collaboration of athletes, trainers, physicians, and the pharmaceutical industry. At the same time, a new international sports establishment arose championing an ideal of sportsmanship that was threatened by the use of drugs.

The debate over doping in Germany during the 1920s and '30s anticipated today's doping controversy in almost every respect. Drug use among German athletes was widespread and openly discussed. The German sports literature of this period offered antidoping sermons, justifications for the use of various substances, and rationales for drawing lines between what should and should not be forbidden. Some German physicians dearly believed that certain substances did improve athletic performance, and they were not reluctant to prescribe them. The prominent sports physician Herbert Herxheimer, for example, claimed in 1922 that the commercial product "Recresal" (primary sodium phosphate) produced a detectable increase in physical fitness. More interesting than his endorsement, however, were the verbal gymnastics that followed. With the approach of the spring sports season, he said, the aspiring athlete would need his full dose of phosphates. Without mentioning the word "doping," he went on to assure his readers that this ergogenic "aid" was not comparable to the many "stimulants" in use, since it merely "supported" basic physiological processes. Echoes of Herxheimer's argument have been heard in recent years from former East German sports scientists who still seek to portray steroid use as a form of beneficial "hormonal regulation" for athletes under stress.

By 1930 a less restrained attitude toward the use of Recresal was evident. W. Poppelreuter, a professor of medicine in Bonn, claimed that wartime tests on German troops and later experiments on mountain climbers had confirmed positive laboratory results. Feeding this substance to horses, cows, and pigs had caused them to grow larger, look better, sweat less, work harder, give more milk, and produce better litters. Poppelreuter's own experiments indicated that Recresal also improved arithmetic performance: the speed of mental calculations rose while the number of errors went down—an important finding, he said, because the mental dimension of athletic performance had become increasingly clear. He was adamant about the propriety of Recresal therapy, which he called "a normal hygienic procedure" that merely supported basic physiological processes.

The most controversial technique in Germany at this time was the use of ultraviolet radiation (UV) to invigorate all or part of the athlete's body. From one standpoint, UV was about as invasive and "artificial" a procedure as standing in sunlight. But from another perspective, UV light was the product of "technical and machine-like devices" that threatened to destroy the "honorable competition" sport was meant to be. The debate over UV became a textbook confrontation between the antidoping purists and their more up-to-date opponents for whom performance was the first priority.

Such problematic distinctions between "nutrients" and "stimulants," between supplemental nutrition and more ambitious regimens, constitute the core of the "doping" issue. The sports medical literature of the interwar period is filled with arguments over variations on this fundamental dichotomy: the "natural" versus the "artificial," rehabilitation versus performance enhancement, restoring the organism versus boosting it, and so on. Then as now, debates over specific drugs or techniques were less important than the larger question of whether society should impose limits on athletic ambition and certain methods that serve it, whether athletes should attempt to improve performances by resorting to what one German physician of this period called "deviations from a natural way of life."

Medical objections to doping in Germany did not command universal support among physicians for two reasons. Some of these medical men, like their modern counterparts, were simply spellbound by the prospect of boosting athletic performance in ingenious new ways. But the more fundamental problem, then as now, was that there were simply too many ways to rationalize the use of what were believed to be performance-enhancing drugs within the standard guidelines for medical practice. The line between healing the organism and "improving" it could not be drawn in a clear and definitive way.

Lacking a systematic definition of doping, biomedical conservatives adopted a position based on a kind of moral intuition. Dr. Otto Riesser, director of the Pharmacological Institute at the University of Breslau, was one of the few who understood the biochemical complexities of doping and its uncertain effects. In an address to the German Swimming Federation in 1933, he deplored widespread doping in German sport and blamed physicians for their collusion in these unethical practices. Riesser's response to the problem of defining doping was to say that in difficult cases "common sense and conscience must be the final judges." Such homespun wisdom, though it could not always prevail over the temptation to cheat, was an important statement of principle. Similarly, when Riesser wrote about digitalis in 1930, he speculated that it might help the long-distance skier. "I don't know whether that sort of thing has been tried," he commented. "But all of us feel a healthy inner resistance to such experiments in artificially boosting athletic performance, and, perhaps, a not unjustified fear that any pharmacological intervention, no matter how small, may cause a disturbance in the healthy organism."

The history of doping tells us that our "healthy inner resistance" to such temptations is constantly being subverted by the problem of distinguishing between licit and illicit techniques. The idea of doping—and its notoriety—are, after all, cultural constructs. The rise of an antidoping ethos during the 1920s shows that the culturally conservative response to drug use in sport required about a generation to formulate itself. The culturally conservative response to performance-enhancing drugs, in society at large as well as in sport, is today under siege as it has never been before. In *Listening to Prozac,* Peter Kramer makes a point of undermining what he calls "pharmacological Calvinism," defined as "a general distrust of drugs used for nontherapeutic purposes." Pharmacological Calvinism, he suggests, "may be flimsy protection against the allure of medication. Do we feel secure in counting on our irrationality—our antiscientific prejudice—to save us from the ubiquitous cultural pressures for enhancement?" As Kramer (and his critics) well know, we do not. Indeed, the transformation of Otto Riesser's "healthy inner resistance" into "antiscientific prejudice" is one more sign that Kramer's enormously popular brief on behalf of "cosmetic psychopharmacology" has benefited from (and strengthened) an increasingly activist view of therapeutic intervention.

The rise of the therapeutic ideal has made the stigma attached to performance-enhancing drugs seem increasingly implausible. In the therapeutic model, the distinction between enhancement and the treatment of specific disorders is blurred. Therapy aims at human improvement, not necessarily the curing of a specific malady. Precisely because we now treat the legitimacy of "therapy" as self-evident, we overlook its expanded role in modern life. Drugs in particular have a vast range of applications that extend far beyond the treatment of organic diseases. Drugs now in wide use help people cope with such "normal" challenges of daily life as work performance and mood control. The elastic concept of therapy easily accommodates the physiological conditions and psychological stresses experienced by high-performance athletes, and the fusion of everyday stress and extreme athletic exertion makes it difficult to condemn doping in sport on a priori grounds. We simply do not employ a typology of stressful experiences that distinguishes on a deep enough level between the pressures of everyday life and sportive stress. The modern English (and now internationalized) word "stress" homogenizes an entire spectrum of experiences and simultaneously implies the need for "therapies" to restore the organism to its original healthy state.

The power of this therapeutic ideal is already transforming the status of the male hormone testosterone and its anabolic-androgenic steroid derivatives. These hormonal substances have been leading a double life as (legitimate) medications and (illegitimate) doping agents for almost half a century. Over the past three decades, steroid use by male and, more recently, female elite athletes has become epidemic, covertly supported by a prosteroid lobby among sports physicians that has received almost no media coverage outside Germany.

The legitimate medical career of synthetic testosterone compounds began within a few years of the first laboratory synthesis in 1935. By the early 1940s, methyl testosterone and testosterone propionate were being promoted by pharmaceutical companies and administered to patients as an experimental therapy for a variety of disorders both real and imagined: to treat the "male climacteric" (fatigue, melancholia, and impotence) in older men, to deal with impotence in younger men, to treat hypogonadism (testicular deficiency), to restore libido in women, and to reverse homosexuality—a particularly problematic use of testosterone, as was recognized at the time. Early practitioners groped toward safe and effective treatments, sometimes administering megadoses (for breast cancer) that dwarfed the lifetime consumption of the most heavily doped East German athletes of the 1970s and '80s. These clinicians divided into more and less cautious factions, but no one questioned the legitimacy of hormonal therapy as a medical technique.

Even at this early date, ambitions for testosterone transcended strictly clinical uses. The idea that synthetic testosterone might become a restorative therapy for millions of people dates from the early period of its commercial development. In 1938 a Yale scientist told a meeting of the American Chemical Society that testosterone propionate "rejuvenated" old men by relieving depression. While the idea of using testosterone to boost athletic performance does not appear in the medical literature, it was becoming apparent to this generation of scientists that testosterone played a role in physical fitness. In 1942, for example, three American researchers correctly guessed that the combination of megadoses and exercise would alter "responses to fatiguing exercise"—an early harbinger of steroid use in elite sport.

Paul de Kruif's popular book *The Male Hormone* (1945) promoted the idea that testosterone would soon become a mass therapy for the fatigue and waning sexual potency of aging males, and pharmaceutical companies advertised testosterone preparations in professional journals during the decade. Yet testosterone never caught on as a mass-market drug.

A half-century later, new developments are again encouraging the widespread use of testosterone. For one thing, hormone therapy is now a conventional procedure, even if certain applications remain controversial. Pediatric endocrinologists, for example, treat thousands of children of subnormal stature with synthetic human growth hormone (HGH). At the same time, they face increasing demands from parents to prescribe the same therapy for children who are only somewhat short. Such pressures are likely to legitimate the wider use of HGH. Inevitably, some parents will want HGH to boost the athletic potential of their children. Others have already requested steroids for the same purpose. A National Institutes of Health (NIH) plan to recruit healthy children to test the efficacy of biosynthetic HGH is yet another sign that social barriers to hormonal treatments are falling. According to the NIH panel that approved this clinical trial several years ago, "There is substantial evidence that extreme short stature carries distinct disadvantages, including functional impairment and psychological stigmatization." The commercial interests of drug companies also play a role in promoting hormone therapies. In October 1994, less than a week before the federal government was to outline complaints at a congressional hearing against the two major manufacturers of synthetic HGH, Genentech and Caremark, Inc., both companies agreed to curtail aggressive marketing campaigns.

Testosterone therapy is now a standard treatment for hypogonadal males. The resulting demand has stimulated a growing market for testosterone patches that athletes (among others) can use for nonclinical purposes. But again the significance of hormonal therapy extends far beyond the clinic and into the public sphere, where medical "disorders" and "crises" are defined in accordance with social and commercial demands. Thus in 1992 the National Institutes of Health requested research proposals to test whether testosterone therapy can prevent physical ailments and depression in older males. We may now ask whether the aging process itself is about to be officially recognized as a treatable deficiency disease. "I don't believe in the male midlife crisis," commented Dr. John B. McKinlay, an epidemiologist at the New England Research Institute who is a specialist on aging. "But even though in my perspective there is no epidemiological, physiological or clinical evidence for such a syndrome, I think by the year 2000 the syndrome will exist. There's a very strong interest in treating aging men for a profit, just as there is for menopausal women." The emergence of such a syndrome would bring with it new definitions of physiological normality and male identity, and it would help to legitimize other grand ambitions to "boost" the human organism.

The advent of mass testosterone therapy would represent a dramatic cultural change. The use of sex hormones as a "popular nutritional supplement" (as one German expert has put it) to strengthen aging muscles would be a major step toward equating therapy with performance enhancement. And if testosterone products proved to have a restorative effect on sexual functioning in the elderly, this would surely foster a new ideal of "normal" sexual capacity that many people would regard as a "health" entitlement. The certification of low doses as medically safe would transform the image of these drugs, "gentrifying" testosterone products and paving the way for wider use by athletes and body builders.

The meteoric career of Prozac is culturally significant because Prozac is regarded not strictly as a treatment for a specific disorder but as a performance-enhancing drug for a competitive society. The history of Prozac is a case study in how the legitimization of a performance-enhancing drug proceeds. *Listening to Prozac* is a fascinating book because it presents in autobiographical form the entire cycle of initial discovery, ethical doubt, therapeutic concern, and transformative ambition that constitutes the history of doping in the 20th century. (Whether Prozac has actually transformed the lives of a large number of patients remains a matter of dispute.) The author's periodic references to his own doubts about the ethics of prescribing Prozac function as evidence of his bona fides: "I became aware of my own irrational discomfort, my sense that for a drug to have such a pronounced effect is inherently unnatural, unsafe, uncanny." The resolution of this ethical discomfort is an important aspect of Kramer's narrative, and it is achieved by witnessing the relief afforded his patients by Prozac therapy. The transformative phase is where real ethical peril lies, and once again Kramer sees himself swimming with the historical tide. "If I am right, we are entering an era in which medication can be used to enhance the functioning of the normal mind." It will take bravery for human beings to decide to change themselves, he suggests, but history is on the side of Prozac and psychobiological transformation.

By now the voice of a famous cultural diagnostician from the last century has become faintly audible. We return to the text for further clues and read that Prozac "seemed to provide access to a vital capacity that had heretofore been stunted or absent." The trail grows warmer. We read on and find that Prozac "lends people courage and allows them to choose life's ordinarily risky undertakings." Now the voice is more distinct. Finally, on the last page of the book, the missing theme falls into place. The most profound moral consequence of Prozac, we learn, will be "in changing our sense of constraints on human behavior, in changing the observing self." The idea of human self-transcendence has been the key all along. Now we understand that Kramer is the prophet of a Nietzschean pharmacology that exalts a more dynamic, biochemically enhanced human type.

Doping is Nietzschean pharmacology because it defies biomedical conservatism in the name of a biochemically engineered superperson. But the legitimization of doping takes place not under the charismatic banner of the Nietzschean superman but under the humane rubric of therapy. The use of doping substances is driven by the ambiguous status of drugs that have (or may have) legitimate medical applications as well as performance-boosting value for elite athletes. The "dual-uses" of such drugs make it difficult to argue that they should be banned from sport as medically hazardous. Medical researchers have already confirmed the benefits of human growth hormone for AIDS patients. The amino acid L-carnitine, which appears on a list of legal "steroid alternatives" compiled by the U.S. Food and Drug Administration, is another "dual-use" drug that is targeted at both the physically powerful and the physically enfeebled. Sold to athletes in Europe as "supplementary nutrition," it has also been promoted by researchers who claim that it may play a role in preserving mental and physical capacities in the elderly. Making L-carnitine a standard part of geriatric medicine would certainly promote its legitimacy as a performance-enhancing drug for both athletes and the general public.

The gradual "gentrification" of such drugs will have diverse effects. Testosterone products will be more available to the elderly and thus more acceptable to everyone, creating a market much larger than the estimated one million American males who now buy these drugs on the black market. Gentrification will also undermine the campaign against doping in sport. At the same time, destigmatizing these drugs will enable physicians to treat large groups of patients in new ways. Ironically, the criminalization of steroids has been an obstacle to their use for legitimate purposes. At the Ninth International Conference on AIDS, held in Berlin in 1993, physicians urged that anabolic steroids become a standard treatment for AIDS patients and people who are HIV-positive. The potential market represented by these patients already numbers in the tens of millions around the world.

The official pharmacological Calvinism of organized sport is thus under siege from within and without. While drug use has been epidemic among elite athletes since the late 1960s, the new respectability of testosterone products will put international sports officials in an unprecedented bind. How will the Medical Commission of the International Olympic Committee maintain the official notoriety of steroids once these drugs have become a standard medical therapy for millions of ordinary people? In a word, the hard line against doping is not likely to survive the gentrification process. This outcome of the contest between our "healthy inner resistance" to doping and ambitions to "improve" the human organism will have fateful consequences. New roles for drugs will promote the medicalization of everyday life at the expense of our sense of human independence from scientific domination. It will certainly affect our thinking about licit and illicit applications of genetic engineering.

While it is easy to endorse the medical wisdom of warnings against the widespread use of steroids and other potentially dangerous drugs, the history of athletic doping in this century shows that it has been very difficult to enforce such pharmacological Calvinism in the face of growing demands for the "therapeutic" benefits of enhanced performance. The elastic concept of therapy will help to legitimize hormonal manipulation as a mass therapy of the future. It is interesting to speculate about how the advertising experts will promote these products. It is hard to imagine that they will not turn to elite athletes, portraying them as pharmacologically improved examples of supercharged health. One can see the athletes now, lined up at the start of an Olympic final early in the next century, their drug-company logos gleaming in the sun.

Good Competition and Drug-Enhanced Performance

Robert L. Simon

Competition in sport frequently has been defended in terms of the search for excellence in performance.[1] Top athletes, whether their motivation arises from adherence to the internal values of competition or desire for external reward, are willing to pay a heavy price in time and effort in order to achieve competitive success. When this price consists of time spent in hard practice, we are prepared to praise the athlete as a worker and true competitor. But when athletes attempt to achieve excellence through the use of performance-enhancing drugs, there is widespread condemnation. Is such condemnation justified? What is wrong with the use of drugs to achieve excellence in sport? Is prohibiting the use of performance-enhancing drugs in athletic competition justified?

The relatively widespread use of such drugs as anabolic steroids to enhance performance dates back at least to the Olympics of the 1960s, although broad public awareness of such drug use seems relatively recent. Anabolic steroids are drugs, synthetic derivatives of the male hormone testosterone, which are claimed to stimulate muscle growth and tissue repair. While claims about possible bad consequences of steroid use are controversial, the American College of Sports Medicine warns against serious side effects. These are believed to include liver damage, atherosclerosis, hypertension, personality changes, a lowered sperm count in males, and masculinization in females. Particularly frightening is that world-class athletes are reportedly taking steroids at many times the recommended medical dosage—at levels so high that, as Thomas Murray (4: p. 26) has pointed out, under "current

Reprinted, by permission, from R.L. Simon, 1984, "Good competition and drug-enhanced performance," *Journal of the Philosophy of Sport 11*: 6-13.

federal regulations governing human subjects. . . no institutional review board would approve a research design that entailed giving subjects anywhere near the levels . . . used by the athletes."

The use of such high levels of a drug raises complex empirical as well as ethical issues. For example, even if steroid use at a low level does not actually enhance athletic performance, as some authorities claim, it is far from clear whether heavy use produces any positive effects on performance. At the very least, athletes who believe in the positive effects of heavy doses of steroids are not likely to be convinced by data based on more moderate intake.

As interesting as these issues are, it will be assumed in what follows that the use of certain drugs does enhance athletic performance and does carry with it some significant risk to the athlete. Although each of these assumptions may be controversial, by granting them, the discussion can concentrate on the ethical issues raised by use of performance-enhancing drugs.

I. What Is a Performance-Enhancing Drug?

If we are to discuss the ethics of using drugs to enhance athletic performance, we should begin with a clear account of what counts as such a drug. Unfortunately, a formal definition is exceedingly hard to come by, precisely because it is unclear to what substances such a definition ought to apply.

If it is held to be impermissible to take steroids or amphetamines to enhance performance, what about special diets, the use of coffee to promote alertness, or the bizarre practice of "blood doping," by which runners store their own blood in a frozen state and then return it to their body before a major meet in order to increase the oxygen sent to the muscles?

It is clear that the concept of an "unnatural" or "artificial" substance will not take us very far here, since testosterone hardly is unnatural. Similarly, it is difficult to see how one's own blood can be considered artificial. In addition, we should not include on any list of forbidden substances the use of medication for legitimate reasons of health.

Moreover, what counts as a performance-enhancing drug will vary from sport to sport. For example, drinking alcohol normally will hurt performance. However, in some sports, such as riflery, it can help. This is because as a depressant, alcohol will slow down one's heart rate and allow for a steadier stance and aim.

Rather than spend considerable time and effort in what is likely to be a fruitless search for necessary conditions, we would do better to ignore borderline cases and focus on such clear drugs of concern as amphetamines and steroids. If we can understand the ethical issues that apply to use of such drugs, we might then be in a better position to handle borderline cases as well. However, it does seem that paradigm cases of the drugs that are of concern satisfy at least some of the following criteria.

1. If the user did not believe that use of the substance in the amount ingested would increase the chances of enhanced athletic performance, that substance would not be taken.

2. The substance, in the amount ingested, is believed to carry significant risk to the user.

3. The substance, in the amount ingested, is not prescribed medication taken to relieve an illness or injury.

These criteria raise no concern about the normal ingestion of such drugs as caffeine in coffee or tea, or about medication since drugs used for medicinal purposes would not fall under them (1). The use of amphetamines and steroids, on the other hand, do fall under the criteria. Blood doping seems to be a borderline case and perhaps this is as it should be. It is employed only to enhance performance, is not medication, is not part of any normal training routine, yet seems to pose no significant risk to the user.[2]

However, the important issue for our purposes is not the adequacy of the three criteria as a definition for, as I have suggested, any search for a definition in the absence of the correct normative perspective will likely turn out to be a fruitless hunt for the nonexistent snark. Rather, the major concern is not with defining performance-enhancing drugs but with evaluating their use. In particular, it is one thing to claim that the three criteria (or any other proposed set) are satisfied to a particular degree. It is quite another to make the normative claim that use of the substance in question is morally questionable or impermissible.

Why should the use of possibly harmful drugs solely for the purpose of enhancing athletic performance be regarded as impermissible? In particular, why shouldn't individual athletes be left at liberty to pursue excellence by any means they freely choose?

II. Performance-Enhancing Drugs, Coercion, and the Harm Principle

One argument frequently advanced against the use of such performance-enhancing drugs as steroids is based on our second criterion of harm to the user. Since use of such drugs is harmful to the user, it ought to be prohibited.

However, if we accept the "harm principle," which is defended by such writers as J.S. Mill, paternalistic interference with the freedom of others is ruled out. According to the harm principle, we are entitled to interfere with the behavior of competent, consenting adults only to prevent harm to others. After all, if athletes prefer the gains that the use of drugs provide along with possible side effects to the alternative of less risk but worse performance, external interference with their freedom of choice seems unwarranted.

However, at least two possible justifications of paternalistic interference are compatible with the harm principle. First, we can argue that athletes do not give informed consent to the use of performance-enhancing drugs. Second, we can argue that the use of drugs by some athletes does harm other competitors. Let us consider each response in turn.

Informed Consent

Do athletes freely choose to use such performance-enhancing drugs as anabolic steroids? Consider, for example, professional athletes whose livelihood may depend on the quality of their performance. Athletes whose performance does not remain at peak levels may not be employed for very long. As Carolyn Thomas (6: p. 198) maintains, "the onus is on the athlete to . . . consent to things that he or she would not otherwise consent to. . . . Coercion, however, makes the athlete vulnerable. It also takes away the athlete's ability to act and choose freely with regard to informed consent." Since pressures on top amateur athletes in national and world-class competition may be at least as great as pressures on professionals, a comparable argument can be extended to cover them as well.

However, while this point is not without some force, we need to be careful about applying the notion of coercion too loosely. After all, no one is forced to try to become a top athlete. The reason for saying top athletes are "coerced" is that if they don't use performance-enhancing drugs, they may not get what they want. But they still have the choice of settling for less. Indeed, to take another position is to virtually deny the competence of top athletes to give consent in a variety of sports related areas including adoption of training regimens and scheduling. Are we to say, for example, that coaches coerce athletes into training and professors coerce students into doing work for their courses? Just as students can choose not to take a college degree, so too can athletes revise their goals. It is also to suggest that *any* individual who strives for great reward is not competent to give consent, since the fear of losing such a reward amounts to a coercive pressure.

While the issue of coercion and the distinction between threats and offers is highly complex, I would suggest that talk of coercion is problematic as long as the athlete has an acceptable alternative to continued participation in highly competitive sport. While coercion may indeed be a real problem in special cases, the burden of proof would seem to be on those who deny that top athletes *generally* are in a position to consent to practices affecting performance.

Harm to Others

This rejoinder might be satisfactory, critics will object, if athletes made their choices in total isolation. The competitive realities are different, however. If some athletes use drugs, others—who on their own might refrain from becoming users—are "forced" to indulge just to remain competitive. As Manhattan track coach Fred Dwyer (3: p. 25) points out, "The result is that athletes—none of whom understandingly, are willing to settle for second place—feel that 'if my opponent is going to get for himself that little extra, then I'm a fool not to.'" Athletes may feel trapped into using drugs in order to stay competitive. According to this argument, then, the user of performance-enhancing drugs is harming others by coercing them into becoming users as well.

While the competitive pressures to use performance-enhancing drugs undoubtedly are real, it is far from clear that they are unfair or improperly imposed. Suppose, for example, that some athletes embark on an especially heavy program of weight training. Are they coercing other athletes into training just as hard in order to compete? If not, why are those athletes who use steroids "coercing" others into going along?[3] Thus, if performance-enhancing drugs were available to all, no one would cheat by using them; for all would have the same opportunity and, so it would be argued, no one would be forced into drug use any more than top athletes are forced to embark on rigorous training programs.

Perhaps what bothers us about the use of drugs is that the user may be endangering his or her health. But why isn't the choice about whether the risk is worth the gain left to the individual athlete to make? After all, we don't always prohibit new training techniques just because they carry along with them some risk to health. Perhaps the stress generated by a particularly arduous training routine is more dangerous to some athletes than the possible side effects of drugs are to others?

Arguably, the charge that drug users create unfair pressures on other competitors begs the very question at issue. That is, it presupposes that such pressures are morally suspect in ways that other competitive pressures are not, when the very point at issue is whether that is the case. What is needed is some principled basis for asserting that certain competitive pressures—those generated by the use of performance enhancing drugs—are illegitimately imposed while other competitive pressures—such as those generated by hard training—are legitimate and proper. It will not do to point out that the former pressures are generated by drug use. What is needed is an explanation of why the use of performance-enhancing drugs should be prohibited in the first place.

While such arguments, which describe a position we might call a libertarianism of sports, raise important issues, they may seem to be open to clear counter-example when applied in nonathletic contexts. Suppose for example that your co-workers choose to put in many extra hours on the job. That may put pressure on you to work overtime as well, if only to show your employer that you are just as dedicated as your colleagues. But now, suppose your fellow workers start taking dangerous stimulants to enable them to put even more hours into their jobs. Your employer then asks why you are working less than they are. You reply that you can keep up the pace only by taking dangerous drugs. Is the employer's reply, "Well, no one is forcing you to stay on the job, but if you do you had better put in as many hours as the others" really acceptable?

However, even here, intuitions are not a particularly reliable guide to principle. Suppose you have other less stressful alternatives for employment and that the extra hours the others originally work without aid of drugs generate far more harmful stress than the risk generated by the use of the stimulant? Perhaps in that case your employer is not speaking impermissibly in telling you to work harder. If not, just why does the situation change when the harmful effects are generated by drugs rather than stress? Alternatively, if we think there should be limits both on the stress generated by pressures from overtime *and* the risks created by drug use, why not treat similar risks alike, regardless of source? Similarly, in the context of sport, if our goal is to lower risk, it is far from clear that the risks imposed by performance-enhancing drugs are so great as to warrant total prohibition, while the sometimes equal risks imposed by severe training regimens are left untouched.

Harm and the Protection of the Young

Even if athletes at top levels of competition can give informed consent to the use of performance-enhancing drugs, and even if users do not place unfair or coercive competitive pressures on others, the harm principle may still support prohibition.

Consider, for example, the influence of the behavior of star athletes on youngsters. Might not impressionable boys and girls below the age of consent be driven to use performance-enhancing drugs in an effort to emulate top stars? Might not high school athletes turn to performance-enhancing drugs to please coaches, parents, and fans?

Unfortunately, consideration of such remote effects of drug use is far from conclusive. After all, other training techniques such as strict weight programs also may be dangerous if adopted by young athletes who are too physically immature to take the stress such programs generate. Again, what is needed is not simply a statement that a practice imposes some risk on others. Also needed is a justification for saying the risk is improperly imposed. Why restrict the freedom of top athletes rather than increase the responsibility for supervision of youngsters assigned to coaches, teachers, and parents? After all, we don't restrict the freedom of adults in numerous other areas where they may set bad examples for the young.

III. Drugs and the Ideal of Competitive Sport

Our discussion so far suggests that although the charges that use of performance-enhancing drugs by some athletes harms others do warrant further examination, they amount to less than a determinative case against such drug use. However, they may have additional force when supported by an account of competitive sport which implies a distinction between appropriate and inappropriate competitive pressures. What we need, then, is an account of when risk is improperly imposed on others in sport. While I am unable to provide a full theory here, I do want to suggest a principled basis, grounded on an ethic of athletic competition, for prohibition of paradigm performance-enhancing drugs.

My suggestion, which I can only outline here, is that competition in athletics is best thought of as a mutual quest for excellence through challenge (2: pp. 133-139). Competitors are obliged to do their best so as to bring out the best in their opponents. Competitors are to present challenges to one another within the constitutive rules of the sport being played. Such an account may avoid the charges, often directed against competitive sports, that they are zero-sum games which encourage the selfish and egotistical desire to promote oneself by imposing losses on others.

In addition, the ideal of sport as a *mutual* quest for excellence brings out the crucial point that a sports contest is a competition between *persons*. Within the competitive framework, each participant must respond to the choices, acts, and abilities of others—which in turn manifest past decisions about what one's priorities should be and how one's skills are to be developed. The good competitor, then, does not see opponents as things to be overcome and beaten down but rather sees them as persons whose acts call for appropriate, mutually acceptable responses. On this view, athletic competition, rather than being incompatible with respect for our opponents as persons, actually presupposes it.

However, when use of drugs leads to improved play, it is natural to say that it is not athletic ability that determines outcome but rather the efficiency with which the athlete's body reacts to the performance enhancer. But the whole point of athletic competition is to test the athletic ability of persons, not the way bodies react to drugs. In the latter case, it is not the athlete who is responsible for the gain. Enhanced performance does not result from the qualities of the athlete *qua* person, such as dedication, motivation, or courage. It does not result from innate or developed ability, of which it is the point of competition to test. Rather, it results from an external factor, the ability of one's body to efficiently utilize a drug, a factor which has only a contingent and fortuitous relationship to athletic ability.[4]

Critics may react to this approach in at least two different ways. First, they may deny that drug use radically changes the point of athletic competition, which presumably is to test the physical and mental qualities of athletes in their sport. Second, they may assert that by allowing the use of performance-enhancing drugs, we expand the point of athletic competition in desirable ways. That is, they may question whether the paradigm of athletic competition to which I have appealed has any privileged moral standing. It may well be an accepted paradigm, but what makes it acceptable?

Drugs and Tests of Ability

Clearly, drugs such as steroids are not magic pills that guarantee success regardless of the qualities of the users. Athletes using steroids must practice just as hard as others to attain what may be only marginal benefits from use. If performance enhancers were available to all competitors, it would still be the qualities of athletes that determined the results.

While this point is not without force, neither is it decisive. Even if all athletes used drugs, they might not react to them equally. The difference in reaction might determine the difference between competitive success and failure. Hence, outcomes would be determined not by the relevant qualities of the athletes themselves but rather by the natural capacity of their bodies to react to the drug of choice.

Is this any different, the critic may reply, from other innate differences in athletes which might enable them to benefit more than others from weight training or to run faster or swing harder than others? Isn't it inconsistent to allow some kinds of innate differences to affect outcomes but not the others?

Such an objection, however, seems to ignore the point of athletic competition. The point of such competition is to select those who do run the fastest, swing the hardest, or jump the farthest. The idea is not for all to come out equally, but for differences in outcome to correlate with differences in ability and motivation. Likewise, while some athletes may be predisposed to benefit more from a given amount of weight training than others, this trait seems relevant to selection of the best athlete. Capacity to benefit from training techniques seems part of what makes one a superior athlete in a way that capacity to benefit from a drug does not.

Competition and Respect for Persons

At this point, a proponent of the use of performance-enhancing drugs might acknowledge that use of such drugs falls outside the prevailing paradigm of athletic competition. However, such a proponent might ask, "What is the *moral* force of such a conclusion?" Unless we assume that the accepted paradigm not only is acceptable, but in addition that deviance from it should be prohibited, nothing follows about the ethics of the use of performance-enhancing drugs.

Indeed, some writers seem to suggest that we consider new paradigms compatible with greater freedom for athletes, including freedom to experiment with performance-enhancing drugs. W.M. Brown seems to advocate such a view when he writes,

> Won't it [drug use] change the nature of our sports and ourselves? Yes. . . . But then people can choose, as they always have, to compete with those similar to themselves or those different. . . . I can still make my actions an "adventure in freedom" and "explore the limits of my strength" however I choose to develop it. (1: p. 22)

I believe Brown has raised a point of fundamental significance here. I wish I had a fully satisfactory response to it. Since I don't, perhaps the best I can do is indicate the lines of a reply I think are worth considering, in the hope that it will stimulate further discussion and evaluation.

Where athletic competition is concerned, if all we are interested in is better and better performance, we could design robots to "run" the hundred yards in 3 seconds or hit a golf ball 500 yards when necessary. But it isn't just enhanced performance that we are after. In addition, we want athletic competition to be a test of *persons*. It is not only raw ability we are testing for; it is what people do with their ability that counts at least as much. In competition itself, each competitor is reacting to the choices, strategies, and valued abilities of the other, which in turn are affected by past decisions and commitments. Arguably, athletic competition is a paradigm example of an area in which each individual competitor respects the other competitors as persons. That is, each reacts to the intelligent choices and valued characteristics of the other. These characteristics include motivation, courage, intelligence, and what might be called the metachoice of which talents and capacities are to assume priority over others for a given stage of the individual's life.

However, if outcomes are significantly affected not by such features but instead by the capacity of the body to benefit physiologically from drugs, athletes are no longer reacting to each other as persons but rather become more like competing bodies. It becomes more and more appropriate to see the opposition as things to be overcome—as mere means to be overcome in the name of victory—rather than as persons posing valuable challenges. So, insofar as the requirement that we respect each other as persons is ethically fundamental, the prevailing paradigm does enjoy a privileged perspective from the moral point of view.

It is of course true that the choice to develop one's capacity through drugs is a choice a person might make. Doesn't respect for persons require that we respect the choice to use performance enhancers as much as any other? The difficulty, I suggest, is the effect that such a choice has on the process of athletic competition itself. The use of performance-enhancing drugs in sports restricts the area in which we can be respected as persons. Although individual athletes certainly can make such a choice, there is a justification inherent in the nature of good competition for prohibiting participation by those who make such a decision. Accordingly, the use of performance-enhancing drugs should be prohibited in the name of the value of respect for persons itself.

Notes

1. This paper was presented at the Olympic Scientific Congress in Eugene, Oregon (July, 1984) as part of a symposium, sponsored by the Philosophic Society for the Study of Sport, on the use of performance-enhancing drugs in sport. Some of the material in this paper is included in Robert L. Simon, *Sports and Social Values* (Englewood Cliffs, NJ: Prentice-Hall, 1985), and published by permission of Prentice-Hall.

2. The ethical issues raised by blood doping are discussed by Perry (5).

3. The charge of coercion does seem more plausible if the athlete has no acceptable alternative but to participate. Thus, professional athletes with no other career prospects may fit the model of coercion better than, say, a young amateur weight lifter who has been accepted at law school.

4. Does this approach have the unintuitive consequence that the dietary practice of carbohydrate loading, utilized by runners, also is ethically dubious? Perhaps so, but perhaps a distinction can be made between steroid use, which changes an athlete's capabilities for athletically irrelevant reasons, and dietary practices, which enable athletes to get the most out of the ability they have.

Bibliography

1. Brown, W.M. (1980). "Ethics, Drugs and Sport." *Journal of the Philosophy of Sport,* VII, 15-23.

2. Delattre, Edward. (1975). "Some Reflections on Success and Failure in Competitive Athletics." *Journal of the Philosophy of Sport,* I, 133-139.

3. Dwyer, Fred. (1982). "The Real Problem: Using Drugs to Win." *The New York Times,* July 4, 2S.

4. Murray, Thomas H. (1983). "The Coercive Power of Drugs in Sports." *The Hastings Center Report,* 13, 24-30.

5. Perry, Clifton. (1983). "Blood Doping and Athletic Competition." *International Journal of Applied Philosophy,* 1, 39-45.

6. Thomas, Carolyn E. (1983). *Sport in a Philosophic Context.* Philadelphia: Lea & Febiger.

Paternalism, Drugs, and the Nature of Sports

◆

W.M. Brown

During the marathon run at the 1972 Munich Olympics, Frank Shorter is said to have sipped decarbonated Coca-Cola provided along the route by his assistants as he headed for a gold medal. Clearly, for Shorter, caffeine was the drug of choice for that most demanding of running events. Since that time, caffeine has become one of an increasingly long list of banned drugs no longer permitted by the International Olympic Committee for competing athletes.[1] The list includes both a variety of chemically synthesized drugs as well as naturally occurring substances that are artificially prepared for human use.[2] The central issue of the use of such substances is not their so-called recreational use, the most prominent example of which is probably the widely publicized use of cocaine by some professional athletes. (Alcohol is apparently not currently a prohibited drug for Olympic athletes.) Rather, the issue is the use of drugs to enhance the benefits of training and to improve peak performance in competition.

Controversy on this issue centers on several factors which have both an empirical aspect and a moral one. The empirical questions concern both the effectiveness of drug use for training and competition and the possible harm such use can have for users.[3] The moral questions concern the appropriateness of the use of drugs in sports, especially when their use is seen as a kind of cheating, a breach of principles of fair play. It is sometimes claimed, too, that the use of drugs in sports is somehow unnatural or incompatible with the very nature of sports. I intend to discuss these matters, but from the perspective of the moral principle of paternalism that I believe motivates many people who are concerned with this issue. First I want to look closely at the issue of drug use in sports by children and young people—cases

Reprinted, by permission, from W.M. Brown, 1984, "Paternalism, drugs, and the nature of sports," *Journal of the Philosophy of Sport, 11:* 14-22.

which may appear to justify paternalistic choices—and then turn to the harder case of the paternalistic control of drug use by adults in sports.

Even John Stuart Mill (7), in his sustained attack on paternalistic restrictions on individual liberty, limited the application of his principles to mature individuals, adults in the full possession of their cognitive and emotional capacities. In the case of children, and perhaps others whose mature development of these capacities and a wider experience of life's possibilities has yet to be achieved, restrictions on individual liberty may be justified as preventing significant harm that might not otherwise be recognized and avoided. In such cases it seems clear that paternalistic interference is not only permissible but may indeed be obligatory to prevent harm and allow for a full flourishing of the child's potential development. Of course, judgment must be balanced: An important part of growing up is making mistakes and learning from them. All parents know the anguish of allowing failure to help guide the maturation of their children. Following Joel Feinberg and Gerald Dworkin, we can distinguish between "soft" and "hard" paternalism (2;3;4).[4]

Soft paternalism is defined by Dworkin (3: p. 107) as "the view that (1) paternalism is sometimes justified, and (2) it is a necessary condition for such justification that the person for whom we are acting paternalistically is in some way not competent." The key element here is clearly the determination that the person for whom we are acting is in fact not acting voluntarily, perhaps due to various circumstances including immaturity, ignorance, incapacity, or coercion. It may be that the nonvoluntary character of the behavior is evident or justifiably assumed on other grounds. This is typically the case with young children; but it is sometimes also true of adults whose situation makes clear that their actions are not fully voluntary. The more problematic cases are those of adult behavior that is not obviously nonvoluntary, but whose consequences are potentially dangerous or serious enough to call for careful deliberation. In these cases, as Feinberg (4: p. 8) suggests, we may be justified in intervening at least temporarily to determine whether the conduct is voluntary or not.

If soft paternalism is most clearly relevant to intervention in the lives of children and incompetent persons, hard paternalism must deal with cases of fully voluntary action and show nevertheless that paternalism is justified. Here we may have every reason to suppose that the action in question is voluntarily undertaken by someone who has carefully appraised the consequences, weighed all available information, is emotionally responsive to the circumstances, but still opts to act in ways that involve the probability of serious harm, degradation, or impairment of opportunity or liberty. The most frequently cited cases are of those who seek to sell themselves into slavery, or persist in ignoring basic safety precautions such as wearing helmets while riding motorcycles. I shall return to the hard paternalistic thesis and its application to the case of adult sports after considering first the view of the soft paternalist and its application to the case of children and young people and their participation in sports. I shall not be directly concerned with the soft paternalist attitude toward adult sports except as an extension of its application to the case of children.

The soft paternalist argues that limitation of one's liberty is justified when one's behavior or actions are not fully voluntary because they are not fully informed, or because one is not fully competent or is in some relevant way coerced. All of these factors may plausibly be seen as present in the case of children's sports. By virtue of their youth, limited education, and inexperience, young people may frequently act in imprudent and potentially harmful ways, ways that may have unforeseen but long-term or irreversible consequences. Before considering the case of drugs, let me review several other cases in which the soft paternalist has what seems to be a strong argument for intervention or control of the young athlete's participation in sports.

The first kind of situation can best be called "safety cases."[5] These involve efforts by coaches, trainers, parents, and others to ensure that young players are provided with proper safety equipment and that they use it while engaged in playing the sport. Especially in contact sports such as football or hockey, such equipment as helmets and padded uniforms may be essential to protect the players against serious injury. Other sports may require other kinds of precautions. For example, swimmers may be prohibited from training alone in a pool, runners may be required to wear proper shoes, contact lenses may be forbidden, and so on. Some of these precautions may simply be prescribed by thoughtful parents or coaches, but others may be written into the rules of the sports by athletic associations, schools, or boards of education, thereby restricting participation to those who are properly equipped, or prohibiting certain kinds of play as too dangerous.

Indeed, most of the rules governing contact between players are formulated with the intention of ensuring the safety of enthusiastic and energetic players. The reasons for these requirements and rules are evident. Young athletes are frequently marvelously competent and talented in performing the intricate or arduous or swift feats called for in their sports. But they are typically equally unaware of their own limitations, their susceptibility to injury, and the long-term consequences of injuries to their development or effective participation. What justifies intervention in these cases, of restrictions on what young athletes may do, is precisely the belief that they are thus being prevented from harming themselves and that on mature reflection they themselves will come to see the reasonableness of the restrictions now placed on them. As their own experience broadens, and as their knowledge of themselves and their actions deepens and their values mature, they are, we anticipate, likely to join in accepting the restrictions they may have seen before as irksome and unnecessary.

A second set of cases I propose to refer to as "health cases." Insofar as injuries are closely connected with our views of health, there is clearly a considerable overlap between these two types of cases. Nevertheless, I believe there are some significant differences that warrant a separate category. Even in the absence of injuries and of circumstances likely to promote them, other matters of health rightly should concern the parent or coach of young athletes. I have in mind here matters that concern training, medical examinations and corresponding medical treatment or therapy, and nutrition and rest. They may involve the need for periodic medical examinations, the proper treatment of injuries, insistence on adequate nutrition and rest, and thoughtful organizing of training schedules that carefully consider the age, preparation, and health of the athlete.

In these cases, the young person typically lacks information to make adequate judgments—information that may be the purview of specially trained persons with long experience working with athletes and others. Furthermore, the young person is not generally expected even to be aware of his or her own ignorance or of the importance of acquiring medical or other information at an age when health may be taken for granted. Moreover, even when information is available, its significance may not be readily appreciated, habits of restraint and caution may be ill-formed, and self-discipline in maintaining therapeutic or training regimens may be minimal. The opposite may also occur. Youthful determination may manifest itself in excessive restraint, debilitating training, or stubborn persistence. Here ancient wisdom of balance, moderation, measure or variation may be the needed antidote, provided by more experienced people who insist on more wholesome approaches to sports preparation.

Of course, other factors than ignorance and inexperience may need to be overcome in paternalistic control of youthful sports. Peer and perhaps especially adult pressures are often a critical factor that adult advisors must deal with firmly and sensitively. One other important distinction should be mentioned here. So far, I have ignored the difference between health as the absence of disease or injury and health as a positive feature of growth and development. If it is clear that adults are justified in controlling the sports activities of young people in the interest of preventing injuries or speeding recuperation, and in maintaining the health of their children and students in the sense of keeping them injury-free and minimally healthy, it is also plausible that they are justified in seeking a greater degree of health or fitness for them. This seems to involve more centrally an educational function, though this feature is clearly present in the other two kinds of cases I have discussed, and I now turn to consider what might be called "educational cases."

Sports in our schools and universities, even when they involve intercollegiate competition, are almost invariably associated with departments of physical education. I mention this because it seems that a neglected but focal role for parents and coaches is educational, and the educational function goes far beyond the training of skills to include the inculcation of attitudes and values, the dissemination of information, and the formation of habits of mind as well as of body. It is difficult to illustrate cases in which paternalistic issues arise here, because the guidance of parents and coaches is often so subtle and pervasive as to be unnoticed by those it influences. Its character as interfering with or controlling the behavior of unwilling charges is more difficult to discern. Nevertheless, I think there are some fairly clear cases.

One type of case brings us back to efforts to prevent injury and to foster wholesome development by prescribing training schedules and nutritional standards designed to maximize training effectiveness. The effort here should never be merely to prescribe, but also to educate by explaining the rationale for the requirements, presenting the evidence available to substantiate the judgments, and requiring that the student understand as much as possible how the decisions were made. What can be expected here will vary with the age and educational level of the student; but resistance can often be expected, not only to following the requirements but to making efforts to understand them. I offer no formula for success in these efforts. As in all educational contexts many options are available to gifted teachers: cajolery, punishment, rewards, example, the inducements of affection, friendship, and respect, and lessons of failure and success. But I do wish to stress that these efforts are made because we believe the lessons should be learned, willingly or not, in the gym and playing field as well as the classroom. In doing so we counter the thoughtless or irrational or emotionally immature behavior of our students with paternalistic measures we believe are acceptable to fully rational and emotionally mature individuals.

A second type of educational case involves values. I have in mind instances of cheating or foul play in which adults may intervene to correct unfair, dishonest, or unsportsmanlike actions. Here again the goal is not merely to remedy or referee but is fundamentally educational. We should seek to instill values of fairness and honesty, countering whatever tendencies to the contrary we observe on the grounds that such action is not in the best interest of the players, whatever they may think about it. The development of values like the acquisition of knowledge in general is but one aspect of the central aim of education, which is the discovery of self-knowledge. Since, especially in young people, this is inextricably bound up with what they will become as well as with what they now are, the paternalistic guidance by adults must both inform and shape in light of what the adults believe to be the characteristics of persons in the fullness of their cognitive and emotional powers.

We are now ready to discuss control of the use of drugs by children and young people as an aspect of their participation in sports. Although I think a good general case can be made for proscribing drug use by young people, and even that a recreational use of drugs has some negative relevance to participation in sports, I plan to limit my remarks to a consideration of the use of drugs to influence athletic training and performance. I have not hesitated to offer here what I consider to be defensible moral judgments on the topics and issues I have raised. My point is not to insist that these judgments are unavoidable, but to suggest that they correspond with widely held intuitions relating to the acceptability of paternalism in regard to children and their sports activities.

Two aspects of drug use can be distinguished in advance, one being the use of drugs as medication. When medical treatment does not prevent sports participation entirely, it may significantly curtail that involvement. And when injury or illness requires medication which nevertheless will allow some sports activity, the decisive criterion will be improvement of the participant's health, not athletic achievement. There may also be times when use of medication is unrelated to sports and seems in no way to affect participation, except perhaps to allow it where otherwise it might not be possible. (An example might be drugs used to control mild epilepsy.) Here, too, the primary concern is the health and safety of the child. Such use may enhance participation in the limiting sense of making it possible, but where the purpose and effect of such usage is limited to medically justifiable ones, we may reasonably disregard this trivial enhancement. In the event that a medication did significantly improve performance over what would otherwise be expected, we could consider it in the next category.

This category involves cases in which drugs are used by otherwise healthy people for the express purpose of enhancing training or competition. There are a number of reasons why such usage should be prohibited. Foremost, of course, are the clear threats to the health and safety of the persons taking them. Among the many drugs available to athletes are some that have a powerful effect on the balance of the hormonal system, such as testosterone and other steroids, or human growth hormone, or L-dopa and b-blockers which can stimulate such hormones. Psychomotor or central nervous system stimulants can have a variety of powerful effects on the human body. Young people are especially vulnerable not only to the primary effects of such drugs but also to many deleterious side effects and to possible long-range effects that in many cases are only now beginning to be determined.[6] Damaging effects on growth patterns, and on psychosocial development, are probable high risks of such drugs for children and young people—risks far outweighing any possible benefits of temporary superior athletic prowess.

I should mention that in this respect, drugs are not different in kind, though perhaps in degree, from other features of sports which conflict with our values of health for young people. Arduous and extreme training methods, excessively rough contact between players, and insufficient recuperation or recovery from illness or injury, for example, may all violate our reasonable standards of wholesome athletics. Indeed a paramount concern for any tendency to overemphasize achievements in young people's sports is that it encourages a disregard for the health and balanced development of the young players.

I suspect that these judgments are relatively uncontroversial. But I now want to renew our discussion of the relation of such possible drug use and the development of attitudes and values by young players which I have already defended as among the legitimate paternalistic concerns of guardians and athletic supervisors. Drug use of the kind we are discussing (and of course many other features of training and competition) is clearly associated with winning, indeed with winning at virtually all costs. The chief consideration will always be how use of drugs will enable a young athlete to develop more quickly and effectively the strength, speed, or endurance needed to win, and how subsequent use will provide an improved competitive performance. This attitude is one that we can fairly consider to be nearly a defining characteristic of professionalism as it has come to be understood.

This use of drugs therefore carries with it, or encourages the development of, attitudes and values that conflict with those we hope to instill in children and young people through their very early participation in athletics. Among these latter values are sportsmanship, honesty, fairness, self-reliance as well as cooperation, grace under pressure, and health. Others could also be mentioned. But a central value is that of experiencing achievement through personal effort, of responding willfully to challenge, and thereby of coming to realize, that is, both to create and to understand, one's self, the complex bundle of skills, dispositions, beliefs, values, and capacities which constitute a personality.

Merit in a young athlete should reflect factors that are fully within his or her control. Ability and achievement should be a reflection of the amount of effort and self-motivation that are consonant with a normal life not characterized by fanaticism (an unreasonable purposiveness). We seek to stress a history of training and competitive effort that may to some extent cancel the uncontrollable differences among people so that superior skill is the result of a growing strength or personal resolve. In our paternalistic limiting of the freedom of young athletes, we are not emphasizing freedom to do anything or to have anything done to one, but rather the freedom of self-determination which accords with ideals of a reasoned, autonomous, well-balanced life, led in relation to a sensible ranking of values. It is because success due to some special technique or technology is only marginally reflective of athletic skill or training or motivation that we discount it or forbid it in the repertoire of young athletes.[7]

I want to emphasize that sports are not the only context in which these values are developed; indeed, they may not even be the best one. But they are a place, and for many people a very important one, where this learning process does occur. The conflict raised by drug usage of the kind we are discussing is that, by emphasizing one value over all others, it skews the context of learning and growth so as to deny sufficient credibility to other values. Moreover, it may conflict directly with efforts to encourage the young athlete to grasp the relation between personal effort and achievement so closely tied to both the experience of joy, excitement, and satisfaction of the athletes themselves, and to a similar appreciation by spectators.

It should be clear that we can extend the claims of soft paternalism, which I have so far discussed in regard to children, to various cases of adult behavior which presume incapacity of some sort, for example, ignorance, lack of opportunity or resources, or immaturity. But these are the easy cases for the soft paternalist and I shall not dispute them here. The difficult cases are surely those that give us every reason to believe that the actors are rational, informed, emotionally mature adults. The soft paternalist in turn must dispute such presumptions. We could of course hold that adult athletes who take drugs to enhance training or performance are in some way irrational, that they do not fully appreciate the dangers of such actions or the seriousness of side effects, or cannot adequately weigh the evidence that drug usage is not beneficial to performance. Moreover, we could claim that such athletes, in addition to ignoring relevant information, are unable to resist the pressures of others to succeed at all costs, that their weakness of will warrants paternalistic interference.

But such a reply is unconvincing, at least in many readily imaginable cases. It cannot be the very use of drugs which is the sole evidence for irrationality or self-destructiveness or weakness of will, on pain of begging the central question. And the evidence, once in, is very unlikely to support the claim that all cases of drug use are nonvoluntary in the requisite way. Rather, the truth seems to be that in these cases other values come into play. Adult values and motivations are not always the same as those we may encourage for young people. Adult life is more complicated, and though we intend the training in values and skills of childhood and youth to carry over to maturity, we are well aware that they will inevitably compete with other values that are often at odds with those we can reasonably insist on earlier. Often for adults winning *is* more important, and the circumstances of life may encourage a new range of motives: fame, wealth, power, social mobility, patriotism, pride of class, or race or ideology.

We may not accept such values or wish to encourage such motivations, but in a free society they are permissible; we may not deny them, to those who choose them, on grounds of paternalism. Where such values predominate, the risks of drugs may be outweighed by the benefits they may bring. Perhaps we come here to one of the sources of the distinction between "amateur" and "professional." If so, the distinction does not match the one I am suggesting between the values of youth and adulthood. Some professional skills and the knowledge of professional experience are clearly applicable to youth sports, and, conversely, professional values need not conflict with other values. It is always a matter of emphasis, role, age, commitments, and goals that determine which values dominate.

Indeed, even in our approach to sports for children, and especially of youths, we will at some point begin to anticipate some of the competing values that will increasingly vie for their attention and commitment as they grow older. As always, there are important questions of timing, emphasis, role, and age. But teachers and parents must at some point help facilitate the transition to full autonomy at which earlier limits to freedom can no longer be tolerated.

The soft paternalist could of course insist that where drug use or sports activities carry with them high risk, even risk of death or permanent injury, we are justified in intervening to prevent serious costs to the rest of us even when the athletes are willing to take the risks.[8] But society does not typically support the costs of such injury, and we could in any case require proper insurance for the athletes. Moreover, the psychic cost to others is surely minimal and, even in cases such as boxing, it is normally outweighed by the psychic gains of the spectator: the vicarious thrill and excitement, the shared pride, the satisfactions of knowledgeable viewing. In any case the balance of risks and benefits concerning drug usage is not likely to be clear. Efforts are no doubt being made to control for undesirable side effects, and the benefits may often need to be measured only in fractions of seconds. And why should we single out one class of risks when others, perhaps equally great, are already tolerated for the sake of excellence? Finally though it involves interference in the lives of others, such a response does not seem paternalistically motivated.

At this point, we may resort to something like a principle of "hard" paternalism if we are to persist in our efforts to control the choices and options of athletes. We are in effect seeking to impose on those who resist it an alternative set of values. But what would justify such an imposition? There seems no reason to suppose that taking risk in sports, even great risk, is inevitably irrational, self-destructive, or immature, as we have seen. Nor is it plausible to suggest that we forbid all of the sports which involve such risk, such as mountain climbing, sky-diving, or even boxing. As Mill argued, such intervention in people's lives would itself be a greater wrong than the possible injury of activities voluntarily chosen.

It may nevertheless be argued that the use of drugs is somehow inconsistent with the nature of sports, and that sports in turn are linked with a broader set of values—a conception of the good life—which is betrayed by the use of drugs, so that interference in the choices of athletes in this respect is done to preserve a greater good, one they may have lost sight of in their preoccupation with the more narrow concerns of training and competition. Such an argument a priori, as I have argued elsewhere, is not cogent (1). There is, I believe, no single conception of sports on which we need agree. In competitive sports we stress fairness and balanced competition; but in more solitary pursuits these values seem irrelevant. In the case of drugs, fairness may dictate equal access and widely available information. But even this is not clear: athletes and coaches seem justified in keeping secret their training regimens, and even, when permitted by the rules, equipment modifications.

Often, too, we stress human factors such as determination, fortitude, and cooperativeness over risk taking and technology. But in other cases—luge, skiing, mountain climbing, hang-gliding—risk and technology dominate. We believe in the capacity of sports to promote health and fitness, but many originated in the practice of war and routinely involve stress and injury, sometimes death. We fashion rules and continually modify them to reduce hazards and minimize serious injury, but few would seek to do so entirely. Perhaps we are tempted to require in athletes only what is natural. But our sports have evolved with our technology and our best athletes are often unnaturally, statistically, endowed with abilities and other characteristics far beyond the norm. It seems artificial indeed to draw the line at drugs when so much of today's training techniques, equipment, food, medical care, even the origin of the sports themselves, are the product of our technological culture.

Nevertheless, something more may be said for the claim that sports reflect a broader set of values. In discussing the justification of paternalism in coaching the young, I have stressed the formation of the values of honesty, fairness, and autonomy, values central to my conception of personhood. But they are not the only ones that might be stressed. Obedience, regimentation, service to others, or sacrifice might have been proposed. These, too, in the proper context, might also be developed together with the skills of athletics. The values, perhaps even a conception of what is good for human life, are associated with sports, not because of their nature, but due to the way we choose to play them. We can indeed forbid the use of drugs in athletics in general, just as we do in the case of children. But ironically, in adopting such a paternalistic stance of insisting that we know better than the athletes themselves how to achieve some more general good which they myopically ignore, we must deny in them the very attributes we claim to value: self-reliance, personal achievement, and autonomy.

Notes

1. The current ban on caffeine is defined in terms of a maximum level in urine of 15 mg/mL. For athletes this certainly means no direct ingestion of caffeine tablets, but also a need to avoid combinations of coffee, soft drinks, and over-the-counter medications like Anacin or Empirin which could lead to excessive accumulations of the drug.

2. A good example of such substances is the hormone testosterone. Since it occurs naturally in the body, it has been difficult to detect exogenous testosterone. A new test, however, now measures the ratio of testosterone to a metabolite, epitestosterone, which normally occur in a one-to-one ratio. Since exogenous testosterone isn't converted as readily to epitestosterone, it changes the ratio. The IOC requires the ratio of testosterone to its epimer in urine to be less than six to one. See Zurer (10).

3. Much of the evidence available to athletes in this regard is anecdotal, based on the personal experience of coaches, trainers, a few sports physicians, and the athletes themselves. The research literature is skimpy and the results conflicting. See Zurer (10) for a brief discussion of the conflicting views on the evidence. See also Williams (9).

4. These articles are conveniently reprinted in (8). Dworkin makes the distinction between "soft" and "hard" paternalism in (3). A slightly broader definition of paternalism is defended by Gert and Culver (5). (A version of this article appears in [6: Ch. 7].)

5. Dworkin (3: p. 108) uses this rubric, but for a different type of case.

6. Among the side effects of anabolic steroids are acne and liver tumors. For children and adolescents who are still growing, premature bone fusing and precocious puberty are likely results. See Zurer (10: pp. 73-75).

7. I'm grateful to Bill Puka for discussing this point with me, though in a somewhat different context.

8. Dworkin (3: p. 109) briefly discusses this argument for a different kind of case.

Bibliography

1. Brown, W.M. (1980). "Drugs, Ethics, and Sport." *The Journal of the Philosophy of Sport,* VII, 15-23.

2. Dworkin, Gerald. (1972). "Paternalism." *The Monist,* 56, 64-84.

3. Dworkin, Gerald. (1983). "Paternalism: Some Second Thoughts." *Paternalism.* Edited by Rolf Sartorius. Minneapolis: University of Minnesota Press.

4. Feinberg, Joel. (1971). "Legal Paternalism." *Canadian Journal of Philosophy,* 1, 106-124.

5. Gert, Bernard, and Culver, Charles. (1976). "Paternalistic Behavior." *Philosophy and Public Affairs,* 6, 45-57.

6. Gert, Bernard, and Culver, Charles. (1982). *Philosophy in Medicine: Conceptual and Ethical Issues in Medicine and Psychiatry.* New York: Oxford University Press.

7. Mill, J.S. (1978). *On Liberty.* Indianapolis: Hackett Publ.

8. Sartorius, Rolf. (1983). *Paternalism.* Minneapolis: University of Minnesota Press.

9. Williams, Melvin H. (1974). *Drugs and Athletic Performance.* Springfield, IL: Charles C. Thomas.

10. Zurer, Pamela S. (1984). "Drugs in Sports." *Chemical and Engineering News,* April 30, pp. 69-79.

Sports and Drugs

Are the Current Bans Justified?

◆

Michael Lavin

This paper explores some rationales for regulating drug use by athletes in order to determine what lessons the current drug crisis may have for philosophers of sport. I will proceed as follows. First, I distinguish between three classes of drugs in order to argue that only drugs in two of these classes raise special issues for sports. Second, I argue against some widely accepted distinctions regarding drugs, but argue that even if those distinctions are rejected it is still reasonable to be concerned about substances that give a player an edge or those which Robert Simon has called "paradigm" drugs.[1] Third, I discuss how edge-giving substances do raise issues of concern for philosophers of sport. I relate these issues to some arguments in favor of regulating, and even prohibiting, the use of certain substances by athletes. Finally, I reject those arguments, but conclude by offering a different kind of argument for regulation. My positive position strives to show that the failure of standard arguments for substance regulation does not force one to adopt the substance libertarianism of W.M. Brown (1, 2), even if one also rejects Robert Simon's contention (6) that regulation of substances may be justified in terms of *the* ideal of competitive sport.

To think clearly about drugs in sports, it is wise to distinguish three classes of drugs: (a) recreational drugs, (b) restorative drugs, and (c) additive drugs. Examples are perhaps the easiest way to grasp the differences between these three classes. Recreational drugs are drugs such as alcohol, cocaine, heroin, marijuana, and a host of other street drugs. Typically, recreational drugs are taken without medical supervision, and many are illegal. Restorative drugs, by contrast, are drugs such as aspirin and antihypertensive medications. These typically permit people suffering

I wish to thank K.V. Meier and three anonymous referees for many helpful suggestions.

Reprinted, by permission, from M. Lavin, 1987, "Sports and drugs: Are the current bans justified?," *Journal of the Philosophy of Sport, 14:* 34-43.

from a medical disorder to approximate their normal functioning. Additive drugs, such as anabolic steroids, are the third class of drugs. These drugs let users reach performance levels exceeding what they might otherwise reach when healthy.

Once one keeps these intuitive distinctions in mind, it should be relatively easy to see that recreational drugs pose no special problems for philosophers of sport, who presumably care about issues relating to sport itself or men and women qua athletes. But athletes abusing recreational drugs do not use these drugs to further their careers qua athletes any more than drug-abusing certified public accountants do. Recreational drug abuse may be a national tragedy; it is not peculiar to sports. So, it is of no special concern for the philosopher of sport.

If drugs raise special issues for the sports philosopher, then the issues relate to the use of restorative and additive drugs. It at least seems that real issues are lurking here. Athletes, far more than other people, have incentives to keep their bodies functioning at peak levels. For professional athletes, their very livelihood depends on being at their best. So, let me further investigate restorative and additive drugs.

Despite what conventional wisdom might think, in practice distinguishing restoratives from additives and drugs from nondrugs proves difficult. Consider these four items:

Item 1—The International Olympic Committee (IOC) stripped Rick Demont of his 1972 Gold Medal in the 1500-meter Freestyle for swimming while under the influence of Marax, an antiasthma medication containing ephedrine. Ephedrine is a stimulant proscribed on the IOC's "dope list."

Item 2—Bill Walton, formerly a star for the Portland Trailblazers, sued the team on the grounds that its doctor concealed the hazards of playing on a fractured foot. The doctor, evidently complying with management's preference, prescribed analgesics. Walton's foot was further damaged.

Item 3—A scandal occurred at Vanderbilt University when informed sources alleged that some players on the football team were using anabolic steroids in conjunction with their strength training.

Item 4—Italian distance runners participated in the 1986 New York City Marathon though suspected of blood doping. This technique involves reinfusing athletes with their own red blood cells, previously removed and saved for this purpose. Although outlawed by the governing bodies of track, blood doping is presently undetectable.

These items should serve to induce at least a modest skepticism about the basis for distinguishing between (a) restorative and additive drugs and (b) drugs and nondrugs.

To begin with, consider what might be thought of as an obvious difference between restorative and additive drugs: Restorative drugs, unlike additives, do not take athletes beyond their natural potential. Hence, although Marax may seem to be a restorative, it is not, since the stimulant, ephedrine, would permit nonasthmatic athletes to exceed natural peaks. However, if a natural peak is to be the litmus test for distinguishing between restoratives and additives, it should be possible to determine what a natural peak is. The necessity of doing this is most obvious if one is trying to determine whether an unfamiliar drug is a restorative or an additive. For athletes that will be no easy task. Athletes already engage in a multitude of practices specifically designed to take them beyond natural peaks. Nautilus training, high distance mileage, interval training, special diets, vitamin supplements, special equipment, and so on all converge to bring athletes far beyond anything remotely resembling a natural peak. If anything, the purpose of training is to improve what nature has provided.

Worse still, what is an athlete's peak, natural or otherwise? Athletic prowess is susceptible to myriad influences. Weather, time of day, training stage, age, emotional state, and so on vary constantly, but indisputably alter performance. Would one conclude that whenever an addition to an athlete's training program is followed by a peak performance, the addition counts as an additive? In that case far too many devices and drugs would count as additives. Moreover, distinguishing between restorative and additive drugs on the basis of their potential to alter performance for the good seems to lead to other undesirable results. It is indisputable that many restoratives could be used by healthy athletes with advantage. In the final analysis, who knows who might benefit from using a particular drug? In item 2, Walton made use of an analgesic in order to play in a championship match. Without the drug he could not have played at all. Healthy athletes could also use some analgesics to better their performance. After all, a common limiting condition on peak performance is pain.

Of course other proposals might successfully distinguish between restoratives and additives. For example, many people might not object to additives per se but to additives whose collateral effects are dangerous—without there being compensatory health benefits for the user. Hence restoratives do improve the health of an unhealthy athlete but do not improve the health of a healthy athlete. Additives of special interest to sports regulators would be those that place users at uncompensated health risk. Unfortunately, the notion of a health risk, as opposed to a nonhealth risk, is far from clear. Walton's use of analgesics made him more susceptible to injury, not less. In fact, it is safer for a noninjured player to play on painkillers than for an injured player to do so. The healthy player has no injury to aggravate. So the present proposal would yield the result that analgesics are additives when they are clearly restoratives. In the end, as Norman Fost (5) has noted, it is probably difficult to sustain a sharp distinction between restoratives and additives for superathletes.

Item 4 raises issues of a slightly different sort. Can drugs be distinguished from nondrugs? If blood counts as a drug, what does not? Attempts to make out a principled distinction do not inspire confidence. The federal Food and Drug Administration (FDA), which presumably has a passionate interest in the subject, opines that drugs are "articles (other than food) intended to affect the structure or any function of the body." Foods, one learns, are "articles used for food."[2] I presume articles other than drugs.

The FDA proposal has one feature easily overlooked. Drugs are identified not in terms of chemistry but in terms of intended effects. Specifying the chemistry of a substance will not enable one to distinguish drugs from foods. In practice, the FDA often has to list drugs. The current boom in designer drugs illustrates the difficulty. Drug peddlers produce a substance not on the FDA's list of controlled substances. The FDA then has to rush to get the new substance placed on the list. All of this suggests, but does not establish, that "drug" is a normative term used to identify what people buy from their pushers rather than their pharmacists, a term most likely to be used colloquially when one disapproves of a substance's effect. Simon (6), who defends regulating some drugs, is alert to this difficulty. He proposes to minimize it by limiting his attention to what he calls paradigm case drugs.[3] Although I believe it would be beneficial to stop talking about the regulation of drugs in sport and to start talking about what ought and ought not be regulated substances in sport, I doubt whether it ultimately matters whether one sides with me or with Simon on the seriousness of the definitional difficulty. Regulators in either case would have to keep in mind that there is no universally agreed upon objective criteria for identifying drugs and only drugs.

For Simon or me, the right question to ask is whether the traditional prohibitions against the use of substances such as anabolic steroids, amphetamines, and so on, Simon's paradigm drugs, are defensible. I contend that the traditional prohibitions are defensible, but not for either the traditional reasons or quite for Simon's reason.

Conventional wisdom recognizes a set of fairly common rationales as underwriting regulation of certain edge-giving substances in sport. Although other rationales certainly exist, the following are archetypical.

1. The argument from fairness: the substance gives the user an unfair advantage.

2. The argument from danger: the substance endangers the user to an undue degree.

3. The argument from coercion: the substance, if its use were permitted, would force athletes to use a dangerous substance that they would otherwise not genuinely wish to use.

These rationales are the common ones and are often jointly employed. They capture, I think, first-try justificatory defenses of traditional substance regulations in sport. Once the distinctions between drug and nondrug and restorative and additive substances are blurred, however, these rationales are far from compelling.[4]

The argument from fairness objects to the use of certain substances on the grounds that users secure an unfair advantage, and fails because it explains nothing. When athletes avail themselves of means that rules prohibit, they do act unfairly. Nobody doubts that. But the present demand is for a compelling rationale for making the use of certain substances against the rules in the first place. It is beside the point to say that use is against this or that nonconstitutive rule, for it is just such rules for which justifications are being requested. When people claim that using a particular drug is unfair, if they do not mean that its use is against the rules, they probably mean that it is either unnatural or secures players an advantage at grave risk to themselves or, ultimately, coerces others into taking those same risks.

I have already indicated above the appropriate reply to the claim that advantages secured by use of traditionally banned substances is unnatural. Many "unnatural" practices mark the athlete's regimen. It boggles the mind to believe that the routines or diet of a runner for Athletics West or a tackle for the Los Angeles Raiders is natural. In any case, the response leaves it a mystery as to why only some unnatural substances are banned. But the remaining two objections, which focus on dangers to the players, amount to the arguments from danger and coercion. I will now argue that they do not provide compelling rationales for current bans either.

Athletes striving for excellence incur health risks. High mileage jeopardizes the distance runner's knees. Sumo wrestlers become obese. Modern training regimens often keep players on the edge of injury. The phenomenon is an accepted part of athletic life. Traditional bans on drugs are, to be sure, often offered out of paternalistic concern. Sports regulators wish to protect athletes from undue risks. But serious reflection on the risks that regulators permit a player to run strongly suggests that risk alone does not select the present prohibitions and only the present prohibitions. Consider football. Players vary considerably in size and weight. These disparities, as many quarterbacks discover, can cause serious injuries. In principle, risks could be considerably reduced by placing size and weight limitations on players. That is not done. Now it might reasonably be claimed that most sports do not specify any limitations on who may or may not play in their constitutive rules. Competition is open to all. Suppose one accepts that. The principles for regulating what substances a player may ingest or inject are still difficult to justify if the justification is player safety.

As previously mentioned, players routinely resort to analgesics and anti-inflammatories, even though using them to play puts players at far higher risk than nonuse would. After all, without medicine's helping hand, in many cases the player could not play at all, which would indeed be the safest policy. To this the response may be made that it is up to the player to decide whether to play injured. But if that is the response, it does not explain why players are allowed to determine what risks they wish to run in that case, but not, say, in the training case. A straightforward response would be that permitting players to make the latter judgment would force others, out of a desire to remain competitive, to resort to using whatever means, however dangerous, as are necessary to remain competitive. Although similar considerations might appear to apply to the use of painkillers during a match, the fact that matches are the goal of training justifies permitting players to run extraordinary risks. If that is so, then the present objection amounts to the third rationale for prohibition.

Ordinarily, philosophers who offer the arguments from danger and coercion do so on paternalistic grounds. W.M. Brown (2), for example, seems to think that substance control involves weak paternalism in Dworkin's sense (4), and hence requires that a judgment be defended that adult players are unfit to judge their own good. However, Brown overlooks that Dworkin himself recognizes that not all apparently paternalistic practices are paternalistic. Players themselves may have a collective interest in securing freedom from certain risks. To do this, players might have to relinquish the use of something they would gladly forego if they were confident that most everybody else would also relinquish its use. Hence football linemen might prefer to stop using anabolic steroids if they had assurance that their competitors would likewise abstain. But even if that is so, the resulting prohibitions would presumably not coincide with the traditional list of banned substances. When one remembers the amount of money involved in professional sports, it should be clear that the amount of risk that is rational for athletes to endure will depend, in large measure, on their pay.

Consequently, there would be considerable disagreement about which substances to ban as one moves from one sport to another. But that is not the case. Prohibited substances tend to be the same for all sports. I should add that many athletes might prefer not to stop using even highly dangerous substances for a simple reason: namely, their ability to participate in the sport at all depends on their use, say, of hormones and what not. And if some athletes win their advantage by running the risks of extra training, why may not others win them by ingesting or injecting what they want? It will not do to claim, yet again, that extra training is unnatural. An American athlete undoubtedly owes many of his advantages over thirdworld athletes to diet and even nutritional advice that may put him at risk. Body builders have long known this. Is there then no rationale for the current prohibitions? I believe there is. My solution builds on a suggestion of Robert Simon (6) but does not depend, as Simon's solution does, on spelling out the details of a particular ideal of competitive sport.

In one way or another, the previous rationales for banning certain substances in drugs focus on morally objectionable properties that those substances, unlike other substances, are alleged to have. The root idea seems to be that certain prohibitions on substance use are morally required. Not surprisingly, it has turned out to be very difficult indeed to justify prohibitions along these lines. Entirely too many substances, not to mention activities, have the relevantly objectionable properties. Simon (6) tries to avert this difficulty by proposing to segregate appropriately regulated substances in terms of the ideal of competitive sport. As Simon has it, sports involve a mutual quest for excellence on the part of the competitors. He sees this as an attempt to bring out the best in a *person*. Drugs circumvent this ideal by showing only whose body responded best to performance enhancers.[5]

W.M. Brown (3: pp. 33-34) has offered the obvious, and to my mind correct, objection to Simon's account. No account of the ideal of sport has good enough credentials to do the work Simon wants it to do. There is, though, an alternative route to prohibitions. It is mindful of Simon's suggestion to segregate objectionable substances in terms of the ideal of sports, but accepts Brown's charge that no current ideal has good enough credentials. The alternative begins by recognizing the permissibility of imposing certain prohibitions. Consider, to take one instance, the length of baseball bats. Nobody could credibly claim that it is impermissible to limit the kinds of bats players use. Granted, that is an example involving a nonconstitutive rule of a particular game.

All the same, there is no reason to suppose that governing bodies of sport might not concur in what substances athletes may use. It is even relatively easy to discern a principle at work as soon as one forgets the traditional rationales. Prohibitions on what substances players may use typically do concern substances whose use endangers players or puts them at what most perceive, rightly or wrongly, to be an unfair advantage. But one further feature is involved. Prohibited substances share the property of being commonly, or at least publicly, disapproved. Other substances may very well be just as dangerous as forbidden substances but fail to meet the test of pervasive disapproval. Nobody seriously maintains that playing on painkillers is a boon for players. It does endanger them. Still, there is very little agreement on the permissibility of regulating the use of analgesics. If there were agreement, then regulations could, I claim, be justified.

As I would want to put it, something approximating democracy operates to justify prohibitions. However, what might *explain* why certain substances become subject to democratic regulation and prohibition while others do not? It is implausible, for example, to suppose that prohibitions on the use of caffeine by track athletes reflect a puritan abhorrence for coffee, tea, or Coke.

I propose that some core set of ideals of sport covertly operates to favor the adoption of certain prohibitions rather than others. Current prohibitions, then, do not capture a timeless ideal of sport. Nevertheless, they are explained, at least in part, if viewed as the product of covert, but quite commonly held, ideals of sport. Since those ideals may change, so may what is regulated. One might say that regulation is a democratic attempt to enforce and perpetuate widely accepted ideals. Insofar as the fostering of widely accepted and morally permissible ideals is defensible, the regulation and even prohibition of certain substances is also defensible. Hence, there being no one ideal of sport does not lead to Brown's pharmacological libertarianism. I believe Simon was on the right track, but his approach is needlessly ambitious if the goal is justifying the current prohibitions.

Some philosophers will undoubtedly have a patrician disdain for my proposal. After all, democracy poisoned Socrates, segregated schools, and prefers Rock to Bach. And so it is that no sane person equates what ought to be with what most people want. Accordingly, I might be asked to make assurances that my reliance on consensus does not pander to irrational aversions against the use of drugs. For consensus to justify an interference in the means athletes use to achieve their ends, the objection continues, it must be supplemented with good argument. However, since the arguments typically advanced to support drug regulation in sport are embarrassingly inadequate, my opponents might wonder what moral force the existence of a consensus without good arguments as a bodyguard can have.[6]

There is a sense in which I cannot give a fully satisfying response to this plea for good reasons. Let me suppose, though, for the sake of argument, that there would be a consensus on the desirability of regulating some subset of currently regulated substances. If there is no consensus, then my suggestion cannot serve to justify regulation. But given a consensus, I claim that its best explanation would refer to an unconsciously grasped ideal of competitive sport. It would of course require empirical investigation to determine the core content of the currently prevailing ideal or ideals. An example or two may help to get across what I have in mind.

In their own native tongue, people seldom have difficulty distinguishing grammatically correct from incorrect sentences. But few can articulate the rules employed to distinguish the one from the other. All the same, linguists such as Chomsky have demonstrated the fruitfulness of explaining linguistic competence with internalized rules. Similar strategies may help to explain moral competence. Americans, for example, tend to exhibit considerable agreement on what is right and wrong. It may be useful to try to explain such agreement on the basis of their having internalized many of the same moral rules. Of course, as in the case of grammar, it will often be difficult for those who have internalized such rules to articulate them. Take an example: My students invariably think it wrong to sell huge whole-life policies to the retarded, but have trouble offering good arguments against the practice. Nevertheless they remain (to my mind, rightly) attached to their judgment even after I point out how bad their arguments for it are.

Now to return to the ideals of competitive sport, I conjecture that (a) there is a core of current ideals of competitive sport, (b) it will help explain the consensus on what substances to regulate, and (c) discovering it will reveal the ends in terms of which it is possible to develop good arguments justifying the regulatory consensus. That is my hypothesis.

To assess its plausibility, it is essential to keep one previously made claim in mind. Earlier I argued that the imposition of regulation on substance use may be no more than morally permissible rather than morally required. That that is so does complicate my argument. How? Suppose that research reveals a consensus on what substances are appropriate for regulation. Suppose further that investigation has identified a set of ideals of sport in terms of which substance regulations are justifiable. It is important to notice that my proposal does not require regulation of all similarly damaging substances. Rather, regulation *furthers* achieving the end of realizing the current ideals of competitive sport. And since it is unreasonable to expect that every morally permissible and effective means to an end must be adopted, the beginning of an explanation as to why similar substances do not have to receive the same regulatory treatment is at hand, namely, these regulations secure the end well enough. Only controversial principles that mandate adopting all the most efficacious, morally permissible means to an end would require regulation of all relevantly similar substances.

The situation might be compared to setting a college's curriculum. Although I am sure it would be mad to maintain that my university's general education requirements are the very best means for achieving the ideal of an educated citizen (students will not, alas, fail the republic if they no longer have to take Philosophy 1511 or college algebra), I maintain that universities may impose requirements that reasonably work to secure that ideal. If a current ideal of competitive sports exists, it could serve to justify regulation in much the same way that the ideal of an educated citizen serves to justify a university's general education requirements. The ideal rationalizes, without mandating, specific regulations or requirements.

At this point the importance of having a consensus on what substances to regulate in sports may be clearer. For without a consensus, individuals and groups subject to regulation will tend to view it as a capricious imposition of values alien to them. Unfortunately, I do not know how to specify what is required to establish that a consensus exists, but three features seem important.

First, consensus should involve widespread and shared opinions of diverse interest groups. It will not do to let owners, players, the IOC, fans, the NCAA, and so on singularly proclaim a consensus. A consensus should, then, invoke a pervasive opinion. Widespread disregard of a regulation, when combined with frequent criticism of it, is surely an excellent sign that a consensus is lacking. Second, as it becomes clearer what the current ideals of competitive sports are, the use of substances targeted for regulation should evoke a visceral dislike. An almost instinctive and pervasive dislike of a substance may be taken as a fallible indicator that its use does run contrary to the current ideal. Third, regulation should respect history. Generally there will be scant support for the regulation of longstanding practices. Democratic regulation requires that regulation be mindful of a sport's history. Regulations indifferent to history threaten to undermine regulatory authority. Regulators will be perceived as unmindful of what competition in that sport requires. Longstanding practices become, as it were, natural. These practices tend to become the context in which athletes pursue excellence in their chosen sports. But of course opinion can change with time on the desirability of continuing a practice. In the absence of these three features of consensus, disillusionment with regulations will probably arise. Such disillusionment, in turn, will tend to express itself in abuse.

My discussion of ideals of competitive sport has assumed that these ideals do not involve morally impermissible ends. It seems reasonably safe to say that the ends are at least morally innocuous, being ends that some agents might wish to adopt. Consequently the only obvious objection to these ends must, I think, consist in saying that it is objectionable to impose them on all athletes. The insistence on a deep consensus is meant to meet this objection. What is more, it should be remembered that participation in professional and amateur sports is *voluntary* participation in a group activity. Those who do not share the core ideals of the group need not participate.

Still, one might grant that athletes should respect the prevailing ideals, but that they should be free to select the means for attaining those ideals. That claim, though, requires justification. Groups routinely set limitations on what means participants may employ for attaining a group end. So long as this is done democratically, it needs to be shown that such limitations are morally impermissible. This is especially so when no regulation would make the end less well achieved. If a group's end is to limit pollution, it may be necessary to specify what forms of polluting are permissible; otherwise, a failure to coordinate may result in a failure to achieve the end at all. Regulating substance choice by athletes, when in the pursuit of the current ideal of competitive sport, may make coordination possible. If it does, then the objection against restricting means has misfired.

This paper set out to identify drug issues of special interest to sports philosophers. To a large extent, the results have been negative. Recreational drug use poses no special issues. The common distinction between restorative and additive drugs, and for that matter between drugs and nondrugs, does not aid sports philosophers if they wish to justify regulating substances. And so it goes. But despite these negative results, justification is possible. Consensus often can do the work of reason. Sports philosophers do have a special interest in understanding the regulatory practices of sports bodies. Consensus, I believe, permits understanding in areas where that possibility seemed bleak. And although some philosophers may suspect that my proposal will be stillborn, I hope I have given reasons for rejecting that diagnosis. So, perhaps, regulating substances can be justified.

Notes

1. Simon (6: p. 7) believes that these drugs (a) increase the probability of superior performance, (b) put users at significant risk, and/or (c) are not prescribed for an illness or injury.

2. Cited in Fost (5: p. 6).

3. See Note 1 for what Simon takes the characteristic features of these drugs to be.

4. In fact writers less skeptical of those distinctions than I have rejected these rationales. See, for example, W.M. Brown (1) and Robert Simon (6). They differ over the appropriate response to the failure of the common rationales. Brown draws the skeptical conclusion. Simon seems to want to use an ideal of competitive sport to select out a class of unfair, coercive, or dangerous substances as appropriately subject to regulation or prohibition.

5. It should, in view of the arguments offered in this paper, be clear that Simon will have to put heavy stress on the possibility of distinguishing restoratives from additive substances. But even if he intends, as he does, to limit his concern to relatively uncontroversial instances of "restoratives," his regulatory justification is still open to the objections discussed above.

6. I am indebted to an anonymous referee for pressing me to respond to some variant of this argument.

Bibliography

1. Brown, W.M. "Drugs, Ethics, and Sport." *Journal of the Philosophy of Sport*, VII (1980), 15-23.

2. Brown, W.M. "Paternalism, Drugs, and the Nature of Sports." *Journal of the Philosophy of Sport*, XI (1984), 14-22.

3. Brown, W.M. "Comments on Simon and Fraleigh." *Journal of the Philosophy of Sport*, XI (1984), 33-35.

4. Dworkin, G. "Paternalism." *The Monist*, 56 (1972), 64-84.

5. Fost, N. "Banning Drugs in Sports: A Skeptical View." *The Hastings Center Report*, 16 (1986), n.4, 5-10.

6. Simon, R.L. "Good Competition and Drug-Enhanced Performance." *Journal of the Philosophy of Sport*, XI (1984), 6-13.

Selected Champions

Making Winners in the Age of Genetic Technology

◆

Christian Munthe

Introduction

One of the most lively current controversies within sports concerns those interventions with the human body (and mind) that are acceptable in a 'fair competition' and those that are not so acceptable. On the philosophical level, this issue actualises the more basic query regarding the underlying criteria for demarcation between acceptable and unacceptable interventions. Traditionally, the controversies in this field have regarded intake of achievement-enhancing substances (some, like water, are allowed; others, like steroids, are prohibited; and yet others, like transfusion of one's own blood from a period of 'top shape', are controversial), but also peculiar forms of 'designed environment' in training (such as the 'low oxygen, low air pressure' house made so, famous by the Norwegian cross-country skier Bjorn Dählie). In this essay I will take the discussion at least one step beyond these issues and consider the prospect of using various forms of gene technology in the making of winners in elite sports.

The second section of the paper describes various opportunities to use gene technology in sports. As will be evident, genetic interventions may proceed in very different ways, and it is not obvious that they can all be treated alike in the context of sports. In the third section, I discuss to what extent ideals and values within sports used to back up reasons for prohibiting doping may also be a basis for rejecting genetic interventions. My conclusion, summed up in the last section, is that this may be plausible regarding some interventions, but not by a long way is it plausible regarding them all.

In fact, genetic interventions in order to enhance athletic achievement in many ways seem to *promote* important values within sports! Moreover, even for those interventions which in theory may be classified as analogous to doping, in practice it will often be impossible to check whether or not an athlete has made use of them or not.

Gene Technology: Present Realities and Future Prospects

Every living organism is a product of environmental impact and genetic inheritance. For a long time, our way of coping with obstacles for the attainment of various ends (such as winning an athletic competition) has been manipulation of the environment (intake of substances, bodily exercise, change of climate, technical tools, etc.). However, up till now, it has seldom been possible to 'fine-tune' environmental interventions on the basis of *precise* knowledge about how they interplay with genetic factors. Either it has been impossible to detect the genetic factors, or the impact of these factors in different environmental settings has been not well enough known. Even less has it been possible to change by 'design' the genetic basis for an individual's potential for achievement in sports. However, as will be described, this is a situation that will most probably be radically changed during the course of just a couple of decades.

For many years, a huge international research project, popularly called the HUGO-project, has been working on mapping the entire human genome.[1] Already, it has given considerable input to the management of various genetic diseases. However, a good deal of the information obtained does not relate to health as we normally perceive it. The genes uncovered govern the function of the cells in our body (more precisely, the production of various proteins in these cell). When a gene is abnormal this may cause dysfunction, disease or death. However, another abnormality may instead cause the *enhancement* of bodily traits and /or functions, many of which are particularly relevant in sports. For example, a gene governing the propensity for muscular growth may in some variants (or *mutations*, as the geneticist say) have normal effects, but in other variants cause serious muscular diseases, and in yet other variants cause a higher than normal propensity for muscular growth. Of course, muscular growth may also be influenced by other factors (other genes or environmental influence). However, recent molecular biological research has indeed revealed a gene having tremendous impact on the volume of muscle mass (indeed, even the *number* of muscles!) in mammals (this gene explains the enormous muscle mass of the famous Belgian Blue Bull). Higher than normal propensity for muscular growth is, of course, of relevance for any sport where muscle mass to some extent influences achievement. An example of another trait with high relevance for many sports which is already known to be strongly genetically determined is capacity of oxygen uptake. In fact, there are even well-known *natural* mutations present in the human population that predispose for lower- or higher-than-average capacity for oxygen uptake significant enough to influence athletic achievement.

There are at least four ways in which this kind of knowledge may be used in order to increase the likelihood of superior achievement in athletic competitions.[2]

Background for Environmental Interventions ｜∧丿

In the medical field of genomics, genetic information is used to fine-tune normal types of medical interventions (such as the use of drugs). In the ideal case, the chemical composition of a drug is fine-tuned in relation to a particular patient's genetic makeup (which in turn influences metabolism, sensitivity to various substances, etc.). Similarly, it is quite possible to perceive a peculiar 'genomics of sports', aimed at optimising the effect of training, nutrition, etc. in relation to the individual athlete's genetic makeup. The increased knowledge in such a field might also lead to discoveries of completely new nutritional and metabolic aspects of relevance for athletic achievement.

Genetic info can optimize effect of training & nutrition

Somatic Genetic Modification

In the field of gene therapy, procedures are developed in order to modify the genome in very specific ways. Although already implemented within the industrial cultivation of crops (e.g., the well-known soya bean) and animal breeding, the use of such procedures in health care is still limited. However, there is aggressive development regarding the treatment of somatic cells—that is, the 'normal' cells making up our tissue, blood, various organs, etc. (but not our gametes). Interventions on such cells will always be 'local' and will not be inherited by the modified individual's offspring. However, with access to appropriate genetic knowledge such procedures may still be useful for athletes interested in improving their physical fitness in very specific ways; for example, 'blood-doping' with genetically modified red blood cells (which can be infinitely multiplied and stored in freezers, thus completely eliminating the need for excessive training in order to get enhanced red blood cells) or increased 'in-body' production of various hormones.

Germ-Line Genetic Modification

Many basic structures of the human body (in turn determining the limits of various physical capabilities) are founded very early in life. In particular, this concerns the metabolic capabilities of cells and their basic chemical structures in other respects. For this reason, in order to achieve more drastic improvements built into the organism from the start, genetic modification has to be performed before the genome of the cells starts to become specialised (or *differentiates*) for various purposes. Simply put, interventions must be made on sperm, unfertilised eggs or, at the very latest, the newly fertilised egg (so-called germ-line cells). As a side effect, the modification has to be performed before the affected individual actually exists and will also be inheritable. Up till recently, this possibility has remained theoretical, since germ-line cells very soon begin to differentiate. However, the successful somatic cloning resulting in the famous sheep Dolly (and the recent repetition of this experiment in USA on mice) has radically changed the situation. The idea of genetically modifying 'ordinary' somatic cells (which are already fully developed and therefore do not differentiate further), the nucleus of which is inserted into an 'emptied' (or *enucleated*) unfertilised egg and then 'reprogrammed' to the germ-line stage with the 'Dolly-procedure', is now considered technically feasible among most experts in the field and may soon be applicable to human beings.

Genetic Selection of Individuals

While reliable and specific gene therapy is still a vision for the future, selection of individuals on genetic grounds (without modifying their genome) is already quite feasible. Indeed, it has been a part of the routine management of genetic diseases for many years: techniques for testing (a very small cell sample is usually sufficient) are already in place and the only limit is set by the available genetic knowledge. Thus, forthcoming knowledge regarding genes influencing traits relevant for athletic achievement can be implemented in order to select among different people on such grounds. For example, when a national Olympic committee or commercial sponsor initiates support programmes for promising young athletes, those whose genome makes it unlikely that they will ever reach the elite (no matter what the amount and quality of training) can be sorted out from the very beginning, thereby ensuring that scarce resources are not 'wasted' on such 'hopeless cases'. In fact, the selection may actually be undertaken before the individuals to be selected among even exist. Genetic testing of potential parents, sperm or ova donors in assisted reproduction, early embryos in in vitro fertilisation (so-called pre-implantation genetic diagnosis, or PGD), or foetuses in already initiated pregnancies (regular prenatal diagnosis), are all examples of techniques already in use which (assuming the availability of the appropriate knowledge) may be applied for the purpose of pre-selecting future children whose genetic makeup is particularly fitting for a successful career in (certain) sports.

Genetic Interventions and Arguments Against Doping

The extent to which arguments in favour of prohibiting the use of certain substances' (such as steroids) within sports may be extended to various genetic interventions depends, of course, on what these arguments are. Generally, there seem to be four kinds of reasons advanced in order to motivate regulations within sports (such as bans on the use of certain substances)—reasons of safety, reasons of 'moral purity', pragmatic reasons and reasons of athletic tradition. I will consider these in turn, and apply them to the various forms of genetic intervention described above.

Reasons of Safety

One argument for banning the use of substances such as steroids is simply that such use is dangerous—for the athlete, for others, or both. It may, of course, be debated whether or not this is a good reason for such bans. But the fact remains that this reason is actually in use and, furthermore, that it connects to a widely recognised value, namely the avoidance of harm and the promotion of well-being. This is reason enough to investigate its range of applicability to the issue at hand.

Genetic interventions in sports may, of course, be objected to on this ground inasmuch as they are dangerous for athletes. This is easiest to imagine in the cases of genomics, somatic genetic modification and selection of existing individuals. Genetic modification may bring side effects that the athlete would have been significantly better off without. The 'fine-tuning' of nutrition in a genomics of sports may go wrong and endanger the health and well-being of the athlete. The genetic testing underlying the selection of individuals for athletic support programmes may be misleading, thereby causing individuals to be 'tricked' into believing that they are more/less promising candidates for success than they in fact are. And, since 'no athlete is an island', such effects will in turn mean that other parties are also harmed: family, trainers, supporters, sponsors, etc.

At the same time, however, it should be observed that all these interventions may equally well *increase* safety compared with presently used methods. Genetically uninformed nutritional directions and selections of athletes, as well as excessive training in order to compensate for genetic 'shortcomings', may all be *more* dangerous than any genetic intervention. One reason for believing so is that present practices are based on a more crude and less nuanced collection of knowledge than any working genetic intervention would be. One real-life example of this is the detection of athletes with the genetic trait for the hereditary blood disease Sickle Cell Anemia, which may be life-threatening in combination with certain kinds of physical exercise. But, of course, *new* methods are always *especially* sensitive to failure and that fact cannot be ignored when pondering whether or not to welcome their introduction.

When moving on to germ-line genetic modifications and genetic *pre-selection* of *future* individuals, the analogy to safety arguments against doping becomes more tricky to uphold. The reason for this is that these interventions influence not only the genome of future individuals, but also *which* individuals actually exist in the future.

This fact is most easily demonstrated in the case of pre-selection. Suppose that a couple is very interested in having children well suited for athletic achievement in sports requiring a high degree of physical strength (perhaps because they have themselves failed in this sport and want their children to secure the success they themselves failed to achieve). Evidently, if sports organisations, teams, sponsors, etc. use genetic tests for selecting which athletes to support, this will constitute a further reason for such a couple to use genetic pre-selection. Suppose further that genetic tests have established that both the man and the woman are carriers for a gene which leads to increased propensity for muscular growth in their offspring if inherited from both of the parents (who themselves only carry the gene in one copy each). According to the laws of heredity, there is a 75 per cent probability that normal procreation (through sexual intercourse) will not lead to this result. Therefore, the couple uses PGD in order to select one specific 'test-tube' embryo among many (available after a round of in vitro fertilisation) meeting their desires. As a result, a child is born with a good genetic basis for becoming physically very strong later on in life. Now, had this couple instead procreated in the normal way, it is extremely probable that *that* child would have resulted from the joining of a *different sperm and a different unfertilised egg* than the child they in fact have (through PGD). In consequence, the use of PGD secures not only that the child born has a certain genetic makeup, but also that this child is a *different individual* from the one who would have been born had the couple instead elected not to use PGD.

The implication of this phenomenon for the applicability of reasons of safety is the following. Suppose further that the child resulting from the PGD suffers some physical damage due to the impact of the PGD procedure.[3] At first glance, it is tempting to conclude that the child has therefore been harmed by the use of PGD. However, since *this* child would never have existed had PGD not been used (though *another* child might have existed in its place), this conclusion seems very hard to sustain unless the harm is of extreme severity, guaranteeing a short life dominated by the most dreadful agony, so that it is plausible to suggest that such a life is actually worse for the child than no life at all.[4] It does not seem unreasonable to suggest that such *grave* risks of PGD are in fact very small. The explanation is that such grave damage has to occur very early in physical development and that no child born after PGD (presently around 200) has been reported to be so damaged. In short, therefore, since existing with some physical damage or handicap may very well be preferable to not existing at all, it is hard to see how PGD could be harmful to resulting children even if it actually causes some damage to them. This does not exclude the claim that the damage may still be claimed to be *undesirable,* although unharmful. However, it is extremely controversial whether and how such a claim can be supported.

The same reasoning partly repeats itself regarding germ-line genetic modifications, again powered by the fact that the peculiar technical procedures involved will most probably mean that a different individual results than if procreation had been achieved by sexual intercourse. This is not to suggest that one isolated modification of an individual's genome *in itself* makes it into another individual. Since two different persons can have the same genetic makeup (namely, genetically identical twins), our individuality cannot be that closely connected to our genome. All I am claiming is that, since germ-line genetic interventions will mean that procreation proceeds so differently (and at a different time) compared to procreation by sexual intercourse, chances are they will not result in the same sperm and egg joining to give rise to an embryo.

In connection with germ-line genetic modifications, the fear of actual harm to resulting children is more warranted, since *nothing* is known about the severity of possible damages to the offspring due to genetic modifications (since such modification of human beings has never been accomplished). However, should risks for extremely severe damage prove to be very low, this reason will disappear.

Not even athletes are islands, as I said above, and this, of course, is relevant also regarding the presently considered interventions. Here, it seems obvious that all risks of damage to the resulting child will mean that its parents are harmed by being disappointed, feeling cheated, and having to cope with the child's special needs arising out of the damage done to it. Moreover, the reproductive technologies used may physically harm the woman. However, none of this will, of course, apply when the intervention is a success. And, therefore, when these procedures in the future are safe and reliable (which they undoubtedly will become, sooner or later) reasons of safety will no longer be applicable.

In conclusion, therefore, reasons of safety may at best support a strong requirement of precaution in the *introduction* of new procedures for genetic intervention in the context of sports. This requirement should, it seems reasonable to suggest, in general be stronger than in the context of health care, since enhancement in order to secure greater chance of superior athletic achievement is not an important human need in the same way as greater chance of preventing or curing diseases. However, when the risks are clarified and the methods are reliable and safe, the introductory phase is over and the reasons for precaution disappear.

Reasons of 'Moral Purity'

In some cases, bans within sports on the intake of certain substances mainly seem to be motivated from demands for a kind of 'moral purity' on the part of athletes. This, for example, seems to be the case with bans against marijuana or when soccer and ice-hockey players are expelled from a team or tournament because of excessive drinking. Can this kind of reason be extended to genetic interventions? In order to answer that question, we must first look closer into what is involved in these kinds of reasons.

Obviously, a ban within sports against marijuana-smoking or excessive drinking cannot be supported on the ground that these practices enhance athletic performance in an illegitimate way. On the contrary—the moral dislike within sports against such activities seems, rather, to arise from the fact that they *decrease* the chance of winning, thereby indicating that athletes engaging in such activities are not strongly committed to an aim of superior athletic achievement (victory, in other words). The underlying premise here, of course, is that it is a moral virtue of athletes to have such a strong commitment to 'a sound mind in a sound body'. One peculiar thing with this kind of argument is that it seems to point in the opposite direction compared with arguments against doping (steroids, hormones), which typically stress the desirability of athletes *tempering* their commitment to victory (such reasons will be discussed below).

From this it seems evident that reasons of 'moral purity' cannot be used against genetic interventions in sports, since their use will obviously be governed by strong desires for superior athletic achievement. The only possible exception I can see is in the case of genetic pre-selection, when the technical procedures used mean that embryos or foetuses are killed. It *might* be argued that, *if* such actions are generally immoral (as some indeed claim them to be), someone engaging in them does not have a 'sound mind' in the way that athletes should have (in virtue of their being athletes). I gladly confess that such a line of reasoning is questionable at best (not least because the pre-selection, for obvious reasons, is never decided on by the athlete). However, it does seem to be a *possible* extension of reasons of 'moral purity' covering at least *some* genetic interventions.

Pragmatic Reasons

Some years ago, the track and field discipline of javelin got into problems because of the increased length of the throws—the standard field was simply not long enough any more. The simple solution to this problem was new regulations regarding the characteristics of the javelin, which made it much harder to make such long throws. This is one example of pragmatic reasons for regulations in sports. Another example is when the rules of soccer changed so that the goalkeeper was no longer allowed to catch the ball with his or her hands as much as before. The reasoning behind this was that the old rules tended to make the games boring to watch (since they made too much room for extremely defensive tactics). In this case the pragmatic reason clearly connected to the role of elite sports as a section of the contemporary entertainment industry.

Could there be similar objections to genetic interventions? For example, would an increased use of such interventions within sports constitute a threat to their entertainment value?

In my view this is mistaken. Genetic interventions could in many ways *contribute* to the entertainment value of sports! The simple reason is that they will (if they work as intended) increase the level of excellence of athletes. This might have the side effect of making some sports very impractical in the same way as the increased strength and skill of javelin throwers did. However, as we have seen, this may be handled by changes of rules regarding competitive procedures, materials, etc. If necessary, particular disciplines may be taken away altogether and replaced by other ones where the impractical effects do not occur.

I can see only one possible scenario where genetic interventions would seriously threaten the pragmatic value of sports. If all athletes were to be genetically identical clones and equally well skilled, trained, nurtured and prepared in other respects, then many sports would become extremely boring. However, it is hard to believe that any such 'perfection' would ever be actualised. Rather, small differences in relevant factors would determine who would win—so small that it is practically impossible to guarantee that all athletes are equal in all respects that influence results. One simple reason for this is that even genetically identical clones (twins, for instance) do not remain so identical for a very long time (as we all do, they already begin to mutate in the womb). Another reason is, of course, that it is practically impossible *perfectly* to control *all* environmental factors that may influence athletic results (such as the wind, the angle of the sunlight, the temperature, etc.).

This, I conjecture, is enough for most fans of sports to maintain their interest. Add to this the increased level of excellence and excitement (the latter due to the closeness in strength and skill of the competing athletes), and we may certainly look forward to even more engaging sports in the future.

Reasons of Athletic Tradition

Sports, it is often said, should be a fair competition between athletes (or teams of athletes). Such fairness in turn seems to be seen as a function of the athletes' competing under similar conditions. Now obviously this cannot be taken to imply a requirement of similarity in all respects (relevant to the outcome of the competition). Rather, it must be understood as a similarity in certain selected respects (traditionally these have not included the genetic makeup of athletes). Some of these conditions are included, everyone agrees, in the very definition of different sports (100m necessarily includes running no less than 100m, ice hockey cannot be executed without ice skates, etc.). However, many of the conditions are such that it seems perfectly possible to deviate from them but still be executing the sport in question, although not in a *proper* way. Such conditions are thus less semantic or ontological in nature than they are normative. This difference is, of course, one of degree, but nevertheless it seems clear to me that, for example, the game of soccer could very well continue to exist even if soccer players were to be allowed to use steroids, although they *should not* be so allowed.

What, then, determines whether or not some procedure or substance *is* improper as a means to winning in sports? One simple suggestion could be that nothing more can be said about this than 'look at the list of presently prohibited procedures'. Regarding forthcoming procedures we have to wait and see what the high-and-mighty ones in the world of sports will eventually decide, and then we will have the only answer we can get. Evidently, this suggestion is potentially compatible with *any* view regarding the appropriateness/inappropriateness of genetic interventions.

However, the majority of people would almost certainly feel rather discontent with such a bleak approach to normative issues. Surely, even the high and mighty of the world of sports may have *better or worse reasons* for deciding one way rather than the other. Normative issues are not only a question of 'Who's in charge?', but a question of whether or not those in charge make *well-founded* decisions. What, then, would characterise a well-founded decision regarding the issue at hand? What would constitute good reasons for deciding one way rather than another regarding genetic interventions in sports?

One possible way of approaching this question is to invoke traditional basic ideas from normative ethics, such as utilitarianism, ethics of rights, theories of justice, etc. However, it seems extremely clear to me that such basic ideas are miles away from the norms usually applied in order to resolve normative issues within sports. Take, for example the celebrated idea of justice as fairness put forward by John Rawls.[5] Rawls suggests that we would rationally prefer a just social arrangement under conditions of ignorance regarding our own situation in this arrangement. We are then forced to reason from the assumption that we might as well be losers as winners and will, Rawls claims, therefore prefer arrangements that give large opportunities for the worse off to compensate for the shortcomings which make them worse off. Clearly, this is no basis whatsoever for arguing against the use of steroids or other achievement-enhancing substances in sports, since such substances are means of compensation for, say, economic shortcomings. Regarding other normative ethical theories, it is even harder to see how they could ever motivate bans on doping in any simple manner. Even less, I claim, can they so motivate bans on genetic interventions in sports, unless they are used for arguments against the whole phenomenon of elite sports.

My suggestion, therefore, is the following. Decisions regarding which things are to be included in the 'competition on similar conditions' clause indeed *are* guided by a set of basic normative considerations. However, these considerations are hard to spell out in the form of some traditional basic ethical view—indeed, they are hard to spell out *at all*, since they have never been explicitly formulated. Rather, they are implicit in the actual practice of decision-making in sports management. And, I suggest, what we see in this practice is the expression of a peculiar and partly vague *conservative* ideal, aimed at preserving the athletic tradition shaped by practices of the past. Not in such a way that radical changes of 'sports policy' are never made—on the contrary. Rather, the conservative attitude is directed at *patterns of reasoning* that have been employed in the past when making decisions. Moreover, this conservatism is not absolute in any way, but rather of the *precautionary* kind, requiring small steps and a slow pace when changing such patterns. In this way decisions will never involve a complete break with athletic tradition: even if a change of some rule is radical in comparison with how it was before the change, it is still motivated from a pattern of reasoning that connects it to past decisions.

What, then, is the pattern of reasoning underlying bans against the intake of various substances (besides reasons of safety, moral purity and pragmatics, that is)? This, of course, is hard to say for sure, but it seems to me that one important *part* of the answer is that intake of such substances directly influences the biochemistry of the body in a way *very different* from the influence of this kind one would have been exposed to *had one lived an average life rather than ventured into the athletic elite.* This pattern of reasoning is vague, of course, but nevertheless seems to capture an important part of what the sports community finds objectionable in the use of steroids, hormones, etc. The vagueness also explains why some procedures are controversial. It is not easy to answer either yes or no to questions regarding whether or not 'high-altitude houses' and blood-doping can be fitted into the pattern of reasoning just spelled out. However, this pattern is still *suffiiciently* clear and intelligible in order to function as a basis for the further treatment of the specific case of genetic interventions—to which I now return.

May we object to genetic interventions using the above pattern of reasoning? I will claim, yes in some cases, but mostly not. *Somatic* genetic modifications may be described as just another way of messing with the biochemistry of the body. In this case we have an individual with certain initial bodily functions which are then changed by the use of gene technology. Say, for example, that the result of this is that the in-body production of some hormone is increased. From the point of view of the pattern of reasoning underlying bans against the *intake* of such hormones, it seems quite sensible to suggest that attaining a similar result (increasing the amount of such hormones in the body) by modifying the molecular structure of some cells is insignificantly different. The important thing is the upshot (the biochemistry of the body is much too different compared with the individual who had not been involved in elite sports), not the means of production.

However, when turning to the other brands of genetic intervention such analogies seem much harder to sustain. A genomics of sports seems no different in essence to the use of nutritional and other kinds of scientific knowledge already employed today in training and preparatory procedures. What has been added is only further background knowledge which enables even more fine-tuned procedures of preparation. Thus, as long as these procedures do not lead to biochemical changes in the athlete which are comparable to 'regular' doping, to undertake them against a background of precise genetic knowledge seems unobjectionable.[6]

Something similar is true regarding genetic *selection.* There is no ban on selecting individual athletes for training camps or support programmes on the basis of hypotheses about their potential for future success, in turn based on knowledge about their physiology, bodily biochemistry, etc. In fact, it is perfectly permitted to use the more crude genetic information one can get from knowledge about an athlete's family for this purpose. Thus, it is hard to see how the adding of more precise knowledge by the use of genetic testing could involve any break with athletic tradition. Moreover, procedures for selection can in no way be described as involving *changes* of the initial biochemistry of the body. All it means is that information about individuals (whose biochemistry has not been improperly changed) is used to decide which of these shall be the subject of support. The same reasoning applies with even greater force regarding pre-selection on the basis of genetic information, since, in this case, the selective decision can be taken even before the individual exists. Thus, here, there are no initial bodily functions to interfere with when the selection is undertaken. Rather, the selection determines *which* initial bodily functions *will* exist in the future (by determining which individual will exist).

How about germ-line genetic modifications, then? On the one hand, such interventions surely involve interference with the bodily biochemistry of some individual (through the modification of genes). But, on the other hand, it is not likely that the individual interfered with is the same individual as the one who may reap athletic profit from this interference. This is most easily seen in the case when the athlete is the child of parents who have undergone germ-line genetic modification. To be true, the *parent's* biochemistry has been interfered with, maybe even to an improper extent. However, this does not imply that the bodily biochemistry of their *child* has been changed, at least not in a way analogous to presently prohibited forms of doping. The child's bodily biochemistry is the same, no matter if he or she ventures on a career in elite sports or not.

This line of reasoning can be extended also to the case in which the intervention is performed on the embryo from which the athlete has sprung. First, it may be debated whether or not this embryo and the grown-up athlete really are the *same* individual. One basis for doubt regarding this is that it seems hard to sustain the claim that a grown-up is the same *person* as the embryo from which he or she once evolved. Another basis is that it is debatable whether embryos in their early stages can be ascribed any *individuality* at all, since they may split into twins, triplets, etc. Second, even if they *are* the same individual, it is hard to sustain the claim that this individual's biochemistry has been changed in a way that makes it different compared with if he or she had not ventured on an athletic career. Since the intervention is undertaken at such an early stage of the individual's existence, it will affect his or her biochemistry in the same way, no matter what paths he or she will follow in life. Third, it is even impossible to say that, because of the germ-line genetic modification, the resulting individual's biochemical bodily characteristics have been changed compared to if the modification had never been undertaken. This is due to the fact mentioned above that, due to the procedures used to attain the modification, *another* individual will exist compared with if no such procedures had been used. Therefore, the situation is very much similar to the case of genetic preselection.

The End of Elite Sports?

There are good reasons in terms of safety for being extra cautious when introducing procedures for genetic interventions in sports. However, when a sufficient degree of reliability and unharmfulness has been proven, it is hard to see any convincing way of arguing *generally* against the use of such interventions, no matter if the basis be reasons of safety, 'moral purity' or pragmatic concerns. Somatic genetic modifications *may* be analogous to more regular forms of doping (and objected to on the same ground as these are commonly objected to). However, other types of genetic interventions seem completely immune to such criticism. In all, therefore, I conclude that, with the possible exception of certain ways of performing genetic interventions and certain types of somatic genetic modifications, there are within sports no good reasons for objecting against the use of genetic technologies for increasing athletic excellence. Indeed, athletic virtues and pragmatic reasons even seem to support the *desirability* of such a development!

However, in practice, these differences between various types of genetic interventions do not matter very much. For, even if some athlete should use somatic genetic modification, for example, in order to increase the in-body production of some hormone, how are we to distinguish this person from one who has a *natural genetic mutation* with the same biochemical effect? The answer is that, as long as the modification has been skilfully done, we cannot make this distinction in practice. Moreover, we cannot plausibly exclude people from athletic competitions merely because they have exceptionally favourable genetic makeups, since that would most probably mean that we would have to expel the large majority of *today's* champions! In practice, therefore, it seems unavoidable that the sports community will eventually have to accept *all* genetic interventions for the purpose of selecting champions and making winners.

What, then, will this mean for the future of elite sports? Does the arrival of genetic technology signal the beginning of the end for this, the most successful entertainment project of the twentieth century? Much of what has been said above suggests that the answer to this question is negative, if safe, genetic interventions fit traditional athletic virtues like a glove and may even promote some important pragmatic values within sports.

Acknowledgments

For factual guidance, many thanks to Mikael Andäng and Lars Ährlund-Richter at the section for Mammalian Embryology and Genetics, Department of Bioscience, Karolinska Institutet/NOVUM in Stockholm and Jan Wahlström, Section of Clinical Genetics, Department of Selected Specialities, Sahlgrenska University Hospital/East Göteborg.

Notes

1. See, for example Cooper Grant, *The Human Genome Project: Deciphering the Blue Print of Heredity.* Mill Valley, University Science Books, 1994.

2. One possibility which will not be mentioned further is genetic modification of food (such as crops and meat) in such a way that it 'naturally' contains achievement-enhancing substances today only available as drugs.

3. At the present state of knowledge, risks for such damage due to PGD cannot be ruled out (mainly because children born after PGD are still very young).

4. This presupposes a certain idea regarding what makes a life better and worse for the individual living this life. I assume that this is determined mainly by the subjective well-being/suffering enjoyed/suffered by this individual. It should be noted, though, that other views are possible, so pre-selection in sports connects to deep philosophical issues.

5. John Rawls, *A Theory of Justice,* Cambridge, MA: Harvard University Press, 1971.

6. It should be observed though, that it is not unreasonable to expect that a genomics of sort will also give rise to a number of *new* ways for nutritional athletic preparation some of which may resemble doping.

After Doping, What?

The Morality of the Genetic Engineering of Athletes[1]

Claudio Tamburrini

Introduction

I intend to discuss a new "threat" to the ideal of sports that has entered into the scene lately: the transformation of the genetic makeup of athletes. Because of this possibility, current doping techniques will not certainly become obsolete in the near future. Similar effects, and even better can be achieved by means of genetic engineering.

To say that gene technology evokes instant rejection from people would indeed be an understatement. Rather, the terms in which this new technique is rejected borders on moral panic. Comparisons are made with a Nazi, elitist society, or with an Orwellian world projected into the next century. Gene modification is seen as a practice belonging in an inhuman and technological society with no place for human freedom.

In this article, I will defend gene technology against this attack. First, I intend to scrutinize the practice of genetically manufacturing winners in the light of an argument traditionally advanced by the sporting community against doping, namely that the ban is necessary to prevent harm, for the athletes themselves as well as for others.[2] In this regard, I will argue that, while antipaternalism recommends lifting the ban on doping, the same argument does not apply automatically to all cases of genetic

Adapted from *Sport technology: History, philosophy and policy,* Volume 21, Claudio Tamburrini, pages 253-268, Copyright 2002 with permission from Elsevier.

engineering. This notwithstanding, my conclusion will be that the harm-prevention argument is no objection to the adoption of genetic engineering in sports.

Nor are there any other reasons, general or sport-related, that might support banning the new genetic techniques. This discussion will be conducted in the final sections of this article.

Thus, the final conclusion will be that the new performance-enhancing techniques should not be proscribed by sport officials and leading sport organizations. As a matter of fact, gene technology probably leads to the flourishing of human character in the realm of sports. Or so I will argue.

What Is Genetic Engineering?

Let us begin by distinguishing the different kinds of applications gene technology may have in order to improve athletic performance.[3] They are:

(a) *Genomics:* information on the patient's/athlete's genetic makeup is used to fine-tune medical interventions (for instance, the use of drugs) to obtain a better treatment result.

(b) *Selection of individuals:* here it is appropriate to distinguish between selecting: (i) actual, and (ii) future individuals, on grounds of genetic information. In the first case, genetic information is used by sport institutions and/or sponsors in order to sort out those individuals whose genetic makeup makes it unlikely that they will ever reach elite level in their particular discipline. Thus, resources can be concentrated on those 'good prognoses' who are in possession of the right physiological conditions to become top athletes. In the second kind of genetic selection, individuals are chosen at an embryo level on grounds of their (eventual) predisposition for athletic performance. Embryos with genetic characteristics inappropriate for a sport career are simply aborted.

(c) *Somatic genetic modification* (hereafter SGM): with the help of gene therapy, we can modify the genome (genetic structure) of *existing* individuals in order to make them more resistant to some diseases or, in the realm of sports, to help them achieve better sporting performances. This sort of intervention is local (it is performed on somatic cells) and is therefore not inherited by the modified individual's offspring.

(d) *Germ-line genetic modification* (hereafter GL-GM): modifications are made on the so-called germ-line cells (sperm, unfertilized eggs or the newly fertilized embryo) in order to improve their metabolic capabilities with the aim of, again, either improving health or enhancing athletic achievements for the individuals whose germ-line cells are so modified. This modification has to be performed before the affected individual is born, as most physical capabilities are determined very early in the cell development. Thus, the results of this sort of genetic intervention will be inheritable and can therefore be passed on from one generation to the next.

Two different techniques of GL-GM can be distinguished. The first one proceeds by in vitro-fertilization of embryonic stem cells from the foetus. These cells are genetically modified, as it is done with somatic cells, and then introduced into a blastocyst, thereby changing the germ-line of the future individual. The other procedure involves cloning. An adult somatic cell is genetically modified and, then, the DNA of this cell is introduced into an embryo by way of cloning, from which the new individual originates, free from the genetic disorder prevented by such procedure. GL-GM, in both forms, has not been applied to human beings yet.[4]

In the future, we will be able to perform (rather safe) genetic interventions, either on an already existing person or at an embryo level, in order to ameliorate certain physiological characteristics that enhance athletic performance (for instance, the capacity for oxygen uptake and the propensity for muscular growth). In the case of GL-GM, as the transformed genetic structure will not be discernible from a naturally originated one, there will be no test or technique capable of tracking this kind of intervention at a gene level.

Genomics and the selection of individuals on genetic grounds, though they are applications of gene technology, do not imply transforming the genetic structure of either existing or future individuals. I will therefore concentrate my discussion on somatic and germ-line genetic transformations, that is (c) and (d) above. Both these techniques involve risks for the health of the individuals submitted to them. Should they therefore be rejected on grounds of safety?

What's Wrong With Genetic Engineering?

Genetic modification may be dangerous for the individual. Is this particularly disturbing for *somatic gene modifications?* I do not think so. The desirability of strengthening personal autonomy—itself a warrant against intrusive State intervention on individuals' private sphere—speaks for allowing every individual to decide for herself which risks she is willing to take in order to achieve professional success and recognition. Restrictions imposed on the exercise of professional activities can only be justified by the need of protecting others from harm. This should not be different in the realm of professional sports. Nor can more prudent sport practitioners complain on grounds of unfairness in competition either. They are of course entitled to decide not to sacrifice themselves for an Olympic gold medal. But then they should not get it either! Those who sacrifice most should get the most rewards. There is nothing odd about this. On the contrary: this is the way in which most of us reason when assigning benefits, praise and recognition to our fellow-persons. Of course, this does not automatically mean that this stance is a sound one. But, in my opinion, the fact that we seem to accept it in other professional areas puts the burden of prooof on those who deny its validity in the world of professional elite sports.[5]

It is instead *germ-line genetic modification* that, at first sight, presents almost insurmountable difficulties from a harm-prevention point of view. Here, antipaternalism does not seem to apply, as the individual who might be harmed by the technical procedures apparently is not the same individual who makes the decision. Does this mean that it is wrong to resort to germ-line genetic modification in order to, say, have a child who will excel in certain physiological characteristics that are highly relevant for sporting performance?

Let us first dispose of the argument that it won't do to support GL-GM, at least not all the way. It might be stated as follows:

> Germ-line genetic modifications are burdened with certain risks for the person who is submitted to it. Things can go wrong and health damages may occur. However, even then, at least provided the individual still lives a life that is worth living, no wrong has been committed. Had GL-GM not been used, the genetic structure of the embryo would

have remained as it was before the technique was applied. By implementing GL-GM, however, the embryo may undergo major genetic transformations. The person originated from this transformed embryo will then be a different individual from the one who would have existed had we not applied GL-GM. That means that *this* particular person (the one who actually is born): suffered no damage, as the alternative for her would have been not to be born. And, although that damage may be undesirable, a life with a bearable health problem is preferable to no life at all.

At first sight, this argument suggests that the traditional preventing-harm-to-others objection directed against, for instance, performance-enhancing substances does not automatically apply to GL-GM. Here, the individual suffering from a (minor) disability due to the application of GL-GM cannot reasonably be said to be *harmed*, as the alternative would have been not coming into existence.

Opponents of genetic engineering in general, and of GL-GM in particular, might resort here to two different strategies. First, they might point out that, when the transformations undergone by the embryo are not of such a magnitude as to change the identity of the person developed from it, the person suffering from a disability caused by the implementation of GL-GM is *the same individual* than the one who would have come into existence, had we abstained from resorting to GL-GM. In those cases, they will therefore underline, the preventing-harm-to-others-principle still applies in all its strength. Had the parents not resorted to GL-GM, the same child would have been born, but without the disability.

Second, opponents of genetic engineering could rely on utilitarianism to support their cause. Even when the genetic transformations are so comprehensive as to give rise to a different individual, they might argue, GL-GM fails to maximise total utility, from an impersonal point of view. Confronted with the above defence of GL-GM, a partisan of total utilitarianism would argue that two different issues are being conflated here: welfare maximization and non-complainability. Maybe the disabled person cannot *complain:* how could she, if the alternative would have been not to give birth to her! But, this total utilitarian would say, that is not the issue at stake here. Rather, what matters is whether there were some alternative course of action that the parents could have chosen to act upon, and that—*from an impersonal point of view*—would have produced more happiness (or avoided more pain) than the action they actually chose. Seen from this perspective, it becomes evident that the defence of GL-GM outlined above assumes the so-called person-affecting view. This view states that what is *bad,* must be bad for *someone.* As existing with a minor disability resulting from genetic transformation is better than not exising at all, genetically modified people are not harmed. (As a matter of fact, if we assume that, provided they live lives that are worth living, coming into existence is better than not being born, these genetically modified individuals might even be said to benefit from GL-GM). Furthermore, the people who might have been born instead without the disability (if we had refrained from genetic engineering) are not harmed either, as they simply do not exist. When we choose to genetically transform some individuals, we thereby make it happen that some future individuals will come to exist instead of others. But *future* (existing) individuals is not all that matters morally. *Possible* individuals (that is, those who might have existed, had we acted otherwise, though they will never exist, because we do not act otherwise) are equally relevant from a welfare maximizing point of view. This means that, in the case of germ-line genetic modification, when we cause harm to future individuals by genetic procedures, we act wrongly from an impersonal, universalistic point of view, *not because we harm these particular individuals (we certainly do not!), but rather because we fail to give birth to other individuals who would have been free from the disability caused by genetic modification techniques.* Or so would the total utilitarian argue.

In my view, these two arguments are not successful in showing genetic engineering should be banned. To begin with, the total utilitarian position is far from being unproblematic. Derek Parfit (1984) made us aware of the fact that maximizing welfare (or happiness, or pleasurable experiences) demands that we give birth to a steadily increasing number of persons, at least as long as they have lives that are worth living. The result of this would be a world populated by an enormous number of individuals, all of them living lives just barely above the limit below which life becomes not worth living. This repugnant conclusion (as Parfit called it) is now a standard argument against the total utilitarian point of view.[6] It is true that some authors do not see this particular situation as repugnant (as a matter of fact, some among them do not even see it as morally problematic).[7] I do not intend to take a stand on that dispute in this article. But the fact that the total utilitarian view is rejected, not only by non-utilitarians, but even by people prone to adopt a consequentialist approach to moral matters, is sufficient to weaken this line of attack against the genetic engineering of athletes.

Besides, it is also doubtful whether total utilitarianism actually implies rejecting GL-GM. As this technique will help to cure and prevent serious diseases, it seems justified to adopt a liberal stance regarding its use and implementation in health care system in general. But then the adoption of this new technology in the world of sports will be just a matter of time. Before they are introduced in sports medicine, new techniques are first developed and tested in the health care system. Even if germ-line genetic modification (unlike somatic genetic modification) in some cases may involve risks for others than the agent herself, in the future this technique will probably become as harmless as a medical technique can be, as a consequence of its medical applications. At that stage of development, opponents of genetic modification will no longer be able to resort to 'avoid-harm' considerations to reject the genetic engineering of winners in sports.

Finally, it is easy to see that this same argument also neutralises the first objection raised by opponents of genetic engineering. Even when embryo trans- formations are not so comprehensive as to alter the identity of the person stemming from it, the genetically transformed individual will probably not be exposed to any morally relevant risks, provided (acceptably) safe techniques are developed. At any rate, no more than what is involved in standard medical treatments at present.

What (Else) Is Wrong With Genetic Engineering?

But, even if the genetic design of athletic winners might prove to be innocuous in the future, is that all there is to say against this technique? Maybe the gains of adopting this new technology would surpass the costs. But are there not other, more compelling moral reasons against genetically manufacturing sport winners? And do those reasons not neutralise the summary utilitarian calculus outlined above? What will happen with human freedom, for instance? And what will happen with sports? In the remaining sections of this article, I intend to discuss: (a) general, and (b) sport-related objections against the genetic engineering of athletes.

General Objections

In the future, it will be possible to ameliorate certain physiological characteristics in human beings by means of genetic interventions. The new technology will also have applications within sport medicine. Modifications in human genetic structure might be performed that enhance athletic performance (for instance, the capacity for oxygen uptake and the propensity for muscular growth). In the case of GL-GM, the transformed genetic structure will not be discernible from a naturally originated one. Therefore, no test will be capable of tracking this kind of intervention. GL-GM designed athletes will not differ from naturally endowed ones. Will that be the end of sport, as we know it? And—more generally—would not such a world, in which people are pre-programmed to become excellent in a certain professional field (for instance, the one preferred by parents) be an awful place to live indeed? Probably not. Indeed, such a world might even be expected to be a place in which human character could flourish. We can of course choose to describe that world as a place which (no longer?) allows room for human freedom. But we could also depict it as a universe in which humans, and not the whims of nature, have the power at last to decide over their destinies. The very idea of changing the genetic structure of our species fills us with fear. But what would be so bad in eliminating our genetic defects, and turning humans into healthier beings? Who would wish to object to genetic technology, if it were performed on an embryo to prevent future suffering for the individual in gestation?

Of course, even if most of us probably share these intuitions, this does not mean that we are disposed to condone the use of genetic engineering to produce better people. In that respect, there seems to be an asymmetry in our preferences: we find it justified to interfere with nature to alleviate pain, but not to enhance our skills or capacities.

This asymmetry seems to me unreasonable. Enhancing human capacities might directly reduce the pain experienced by human beings. This would be the case, for instance, if we proceed to modify humans genetically, in order to produce more peaceful and empathetic individuals. Most probably, the utilization of new genetic techniques to enhance individuals' athletic capacities will lead to further developments in physiology and medicine. This might, albeit indirectly, help many sick people to experience pain reduction and even recover their health. Thus, the distinction between reducing suffering and enhancing human capacities is not only difficult to draw, but even of doubtful moral relevance.

But, is not enhancing *sport performances* through genetic engineering after all an obvious case of improper intervention in the natural order? Would not pre-programming an individual to excel in the exercise of a sporting activity be a powerful denial of *personal autonomy?* Should we not, therefore, abstain from using that technique, and leave the decision on whether or not to take up a particular sport discipline to the individual herself?

The problem with this objection is that it is too comprehensive. As it is stated, it equally affects the sort of specialization in a certain activity— and the predisposition for it so generated—that characterizes education of children. As we educate them, at school or in daily life at home, we also inculcate certain skills and attitudes in children that, in most cases, will influence their professional choices in the future. Why is this kind of 'pre-programming' generally seen as less objectionable than genetic engineering?

For many people, the answer is obvious. The good pedagogue offers guidance and support to the child, but does not compel her to go in a certain professional direction. A good education helps the child to develop a variety of skills, and instills in her the self-confidence required to make a free decision. The good pedagogue does not pre-programme, she does not even predispose the child for a particular career. Rather, she is attentive to the preferences and skills of the child, and supportive of her development. At least ideally conceived, education—unlike manipulation of all sorts—leaves the final decision to the student. Or so it could be argued.

In my view, genetic technology does not run counter to this ideal. In fact, the only difference from traditional education is that a genetically modified child would know *from the very beginning* that, if she so chooses, she can be really good in, say, field and track disciplines. But genetic modification does not compel her to become a sportswoman, any more than the good pedagogue 'compels' a child to become a lawyer when she tries to make the child interested in legal issues. In fact, many adolescents might even feel relieved to know that, if they so wish, there is a professional area in which they can excel.

But, is it not disturbing to know in advance what one is good at? Will not such a piece of information cause anxiety in the child? And is there not a risk that knowing that one could become excellent at a particular sport discipline could influence one's decision too much?[8] A similar discussion is carried out in the context of genetic counselling and whether individuals ought to be given the information relating to their susceptibility to specific kinds of disease. It is affirmed that the psychological trauma invoked by such knowledge can be more detrimental than the disease itself and even, provoke the onset of the disease in question. However, genetic counselling should be distinguished from the issue discussed in this section. Unlike being informed of what diseases one might develop in the future, knowing in advance what one is good at cannot reasonably be expected to have the same triggering effect. I tend to give a negative answer to all these questions. In that regard, genetic technology is not a problem, at least no more than vocational testing is. Vocational tests also tell the child in advance what she could do well at. Should we then forbid these tests too?[9]

There is a further objection to elite sports that seems particularly suited to be included in the weapon arsenal against genetic technology. It has been formulated by Torbjörn Tännsjö in his widely discussed article "Is it fascistoid to admire sports heroes? He says:

> . . . our admiration for the achievements of the great sports heroes, such as the athletes who triumph at the Olympics, reflects a fascistoid ideology. While nationalism may be dangerous, and has often been associated with fascism, what is going on in our enthusiasm for individual athletic heroes is even worse. Our enthusiasm springs from the very core of fascist ideology: admiration for strength and contempt for weakness (Tännsjö 2000b, p. 10).

Thus, the argument runs, the widespread implementation of genetic technology might give rise to an elitist society in which only the best human specimens will be respected and admired. The weak, the less intelligent, even the ugly, will be despised, as they will fall short (indeed, much more than they do at present) from the ideal of strength, intelligence and beauty that most people today see as norm-giving and try to live up to. Is that really so?

Probably not. Genetic technology makes it possible to reduce current gaps in skills and inherited traits between individuals. Thus, it might reasonably be expected that its application will have an equalizing effect among individuals. However, the present objection might be restated as exclusively referring to those who—for different reasons—will choose to abstain from genetic technology, either for themselves (as in somatic gene transformations) or for their off-spring (as in GL-GM). Regarding them, it will still be true that there will exist a substantial gap between their abilities and qualities, and those of the rest of the population. Will not they be seen with contempt by the stronger, the more intelligent, the more beautiful?

I am not sure. Indeed, it could turn out to be the other way around, that is, that these (in that future, gene-technological society) highly divergent people might become admired precisely for their (freely chosen) divergence.

The possibility of choosing one's own genetic structure will bring about a situation in which one will be able to decide for oneself whether to be a weak, less intelligent or an ugly person. Thus, what is today seen as a negative trait might come to be considered as an utmost personal and idiosyncratic preference in the future. The fact that someone would choose to be (or to remain, if the genetic choice was made before the individual was born) weaker, less intelligent or uglier than average, when the possibility of choosing otherwise is open for all, might yield respect for the individual who so chooses. The characteristics that most people at present regard with disdain could then become tokens of a particularly strong personality and, therefore, a source of admiration from others. Genetic technology could therefore contribute to eliminating much of the prejudices against not-up-to-the-mark people that seems to permeate societies at present.

This line of reasoning leads us into a, in my view, powerful argument in favour of genetic technology. When fully developed, these new techniques might give us the possibility of (perhaps once and for all) overcoming the injustices of the genetic lottery. Is it not remarkable that, while many of us support social and political reforms to promote equality between people, we are strongly reluctant to eliminate the inequalities brought about by genetic inheritance? Seen from this perspective, genetic technology might be seen as a complement to political action. Through political changes, we try to equalize social and economic conditions for people. Through genetic technology, perhaps we could get rid of the most profound inequality of them all, namely the one that originates in that some people are (probably *by birth*) smarter, healthier, more intelligent and more beautiful than others. Admittedly, genetic technology might go wrong. But so can political action. Should we refrain from political reform work because of the fact that, say, there was a Hitler? If the answer is no, then we should not refrain from genetic technology either.

Opponents of genetic technology will argue that this optimistic scenario is indeed a naïve representation of how things might evolve in the future. The new technology will cost large sums of money. Thus, it will not be available for the majority of individuals: only a selected, economically powerful group of people will have access to it. No equalizing effects can possibly follow from that.

Maybe these opponents are right. Who will have access to new medical technologies is, no doubt, one of the most decisive political battles to be fought in the future. But even if that battle were won by the economic elite, it still remains to be seen what effects this might have on society. The upper class will be smarter, healthier, more beautiful and intelligent than economically deprived people. But everyone will know these qualities are bought, rather than stemming from dedication and hard work. It is not obvious to me that this will increase social prestige for members of the economic elite.

Sport-Related Objections

Opponents of genetic technology might also resort to different sport-related arguments in their attempt to stop current technical developments in sport medicine. The first argument says that, with genetic pre-programming of athletes, they do not need to make any efforts, or endure any sacrifices, to achieve good sporting results. The second argument, instead, rests on reasons of fairness. It states that genetic technology in sports creates a situation in which competitions are not won by the best athletes, but instead by those who were genetically designed to win at an embryo stage. Do these arguments hit the mark?

Not at all. The objection from endured sacrifices and efforts is, indeed, a caricature. In fact, the physiological equalization yielded by genetic technology leads to a situation in which effort, dedication and sacrifice become even more decisive for sporting performance than they are at present. As athletes will not differ so much from each other genetically, the tiny difference on which victory depends will be totally dependent on excellence of character, and not on the fortuitous circumstance that one happens to be the lucky winner in the genetic lottery.

The objection from unfair competitive conditions is not tenable either. What could be more unfair than the present situation, in which—no matter how many sacrifices she undergoes—a sport practitioner is unable to beat a genetically superior competitor? Is it not more fair that, starting from similar genetic characteristics, the more dedicated athlete wins? What's so fair about genetic superiority? Until opponents of genetic technology answer that question, the argument of fairness will not have any bite.

There is another aspect of the objection based on unfairness that deserves to be discussed. It says that, even if athletes might, in theory, become rather equal physiologically, this will not be the case in practice. Some athletes have more resources at their disposal than others; some countries can spend more money on developing the new genetic techniques than others. Thus, if they paved the way for gene technology, sport officials will be introducing yet another economic inequality in sports that threatens to further disrupt the ideal of fair conditions of competition between athletes.

I believe this argument to be tenable. However, I have doubts regarding its relevance. Which are the scenarios sport officials have to choose between, depending on whether genetic technology is allowed or not? On the one hand, they might keep the present situation, with profound *inequalities* between athletes (we should not forget that not all of .them have access to the newest doping techniques) and *harmful* performance-enhancing substances and techniques. On the other hand, if sport officials do not reject genetic technology, we will have a similar inequality, but without much of the harmful effects that follow from outdated doping techniques. It is evident to me that, if the election stands between two (similarly) unfair policies, we should choose the one that is less harmful. The alternative of choosing a sporting scenario that is *both* fair and harmless is, in my opinion, unrealistic. Sport officials waived that possibility at the very moment they let sponsorship and business interests enter into the world of sports.

Another sport-related objection to genetic engineering says that implementing these techniques will spoil the game. In order to establish whether this is so, we need first to say something on how a good sporting game is characterised. A tentative characterization of the good game will have to include the following elements (Tamburrini, 2000c, pp. 23-24):

(1) Flow: a good game needs to have a certain fluidity to allow different game combinations to arise, and to let the development of game skills flourish.

(2) Skill: in a good game, participants have to display a relatively high level in the display of the relevant skills.

(3) Challenge: a good game has to be a (roughly) even competition between rivals. An uneven match is not a good match, as it will lack intensity and the outcome will almost be given in advance.

(4) Excitement: if the outcome is uncertain, and if the skill level is high, then the game will probably turn out to be exciting.

(5) Drama: in very disputed and even games, the outcome could be decided only in the final moments of the competition, thus adding drama to the game.

(6) Joy: when the game has flow, skill level is high and the contest even and exciting, both competitors and the public will experience joy, a sensation of having fun as a consequence of being engaged in a practice of great hedonistic quality.

Now, there is no reason to assume a priori that genetic engineering of athletes will decrease the quality of the game, as characterized in (1)–(6) above. Regarding flow and skill, the situation will be the same, regardless of whether athletes have been genetically designed to be excellent in their sport disciplines or not. As a matter of fact, it might even be argued that the level of skill will be enhanced by genetic design.[10]

In reference to challenge, excitement, drama and joy, I think there are good reasons to suppose the balance will turn over in favour of gene technology. Even if some physiological differences will probably continue to exist between genetically transformed athletes, it is not far-fetched to expect that these differences will be much less marked than they are at present, in a sports world ruled by biological lottery. Thus, competitions might be expected to be more even, more exciting and dramatic, thereby contributing to the pleasure of the game. Environmental factors will probably have more influence on the sporting results than they have at present, where genetics probably play an almost decisive role in the outcome. Of course, it is not possible to produce unequivocal evidence that it will be the case. But there is at least a presumption of truth in favour of the judgment that more equal physiological conditions will yield more challenging games.

Perhaps there is another sense in which it might be said that the quality of the game will decrease if genetic technology were introduced in the world of sports. Even if not affecting the characteristics of the game directly, the new techniques might nonetheless lower the popularity of sports. Admittedly, it cannot be doubted that genetic engineering of winners will weaken the general illusion that sportspersons are exceptional. In the future, the excellent sport star might simply be seen as a person endowed with the appropriate genetic makeup by the choice of her parents. Could not that fact alone lead to a loss of popularity for sports?

I do not think so. Again, I cannot give any conclusive reasons in favour of this empirical speculation. However, two factual arguments can be put forward to support my intuition. First, the on-going commercialization and professionalization of sports do not seem to have affected their popularity. Second, even in such sports where overwhelming technical improvements have been introduced in recent decades (for instance, motor sports such as Formula 1), the public still follows competitions with the same, if not more, enthusiasm than before. Thus, it looks like sports can stand a greater amount of disillusion than the present objections seem to assume.

Yet, even if it were true that the public's interest for sports would decline as a consequence of genetic engineering, it is not obvious to me that such a development would be for the worse. As a matter of fact, knowing that athletic winners are genetically designed from the embryonic stage might make us adopt a more sound stance towards elite sports. We will no longer admire sport starts for their outstanding physical traits (they will be genetically designed). Rather, we will continue to admire then for all the sacrifices endured to actualize their genetic predisposition. In the same way that today's natural talents cannot do without hard training, the genetically transformed athlete will have to devote herself to her discipline in a goal-directed and professional manner. As everyone will be genetically designed, physiological excellence will probably cease to be the basis of our fascination with elite athletes.[11] Character excellence will take its place instead. Our admiration for sport heroes will, to a much higher degree than today, concentrate on their dedication and efforts, rather than on a fortuitous physiological predisposition. I cannot see anything unsound in such a development.

Conclusions

My conclusions are therefore as follows:

(1) Regarding somatic genetic modification, the eventual harmful effects of the practice are not decisive arguments to support its prohibition by sport officials. The athlete who decides to change her genetic makeup brings the damage, if any, upon herself.

(2) Also regarding germ-line genetic interventions, I have argued that the arguments usually advanced for proscribing it are insufficient. Developments in medicine technology will turn this technique into a (rather) safe and reliable therapeutic alternative. That means that there will no longer be any safety reasons for rejecting gene technology in sports, even when implemented on unborn individuals. Detractors of performance-enhancing substances and techniques are thus deprived of their strongest argument. Unlike doping, gene technology will probably offer to athletes the possibility of improving their performance without taking considerable health risks. At any rate, no more risks than incurred by today's standard training techniques.

(3) There are no conclusive reasons, either social or sport-related, on which sports officials might reject genetic technology either. The new techniques do not run counter to the ideal of personal autonomy, and they probably will not contribute to an elitist society. On the contrary, genetic technology might even lead to a more enlightened and positive evaluation of personal traits (such as lack of intelligence, physical weakness and ugliness) that are considered as overwhelmingly negative today. Genetic engineering of athletes does not yield unfairness in competition either. Quite the contrary, by neutralizing the effects of the genetic lottery to a high degree, the new techniques might even enhance equality in competition between athletes.

If these conclusions are correct, it follows that sport officials should adopt an open stance towards new developments in sport medicine. Members of the IOC and other world sport federations have now a golden opportunity to put an end to the health problems related to traditional doping techniques. There is, however, a certain risk that they will repeat the errors of the past, when current doping bans were adopted. In order to indulge a public opinion affected by moral panic, they chose then to forbid a considerable number of substances and techniques on weak grounds. Such a policy is, no doubt, good for business, as it gives customers what they demand. But it resulted in an ever-increasing doping list that now appears to be impossible to handle.

Therefore, the only right thing to do is to welcome the introduction of genetic engineering in the realm of sports.

Notes

1. A first version of this article was presented at the Annual Meeting of the International Association for the Philosophy of Sports, held in September 2000 at Melbourne, Australia. A revised version was discussed at the doctoral seminar at the Dept. of Philosophy, Univ. of Gothenburg, Sweden. I am particularly indebted to Christian Munthe for a thorough critique and revision of the viewpoints advanced in this article.

2. Throughout this article, by the sporting community I will understand a (rather vague) conglomerate including athletes, officials, trainers, sport journalists and the public.

3. In doing this, I will be following Munthe (2000), as he presents the different uses of genetic technology in sports.

4. For more on these two different methods of GL-GM, see Munthe (1999).

5. I will not comment on this further, as I already discussed this subject in my previously mentioned article. For a more thorough discussion of the arguments on fairness and desert in sports, see "What's wrong with doping?"

6. See Parfit (1984), particularly Ch. 17, pp. 381-390.

7. See, for instance, Tännsjö (1998).

8. A similar discussion is carried out in the context of genetic counselling and whether individuals ought to be given the information relating to their susceptibility to generate specific kinds of disease. It is affirmed that the psychological trauma invoked by such knowledge can be more detrimental than the disease itself and even provoke the onset of the disease in question. However, genetic counselling should be distinguished from the issue discussed in this section. Unlike being informed on what diseases one might develop in the future, knowing in advance what one is good at cannot reasonably be expected to have the same triggering effect.

9. Besides, even if they were tenable, the above objections would only apply to pre-natal genetic modification (that is, transforming the genetic structure of an embryo). But they do not affect the genetic transformation of adults.

10. See, for instance, Munthe (2000), particularly pp. 224-225.

11. On the morally disturbing connotations of this sort of admiration for sport heroes, see Torbjörn Tännsjö's already quoted article, in: Tännsjö, Torbjön and Tamburrini, C. M. (Eds), op. cit.

References

Munthe, C. (1999). Genetic Treatment and Preselection: Ethical Differences and Similarities. In: A. Nordgren (Ed.), *Gene Therapy and Ethics, Vol. 4: Studies in Bioethics and Research Ethics* (pp. 159-172). Acta Universitatis Upsaliensis.

Munthe, C. (2000). Selected Champions—Making Winners in the Age of Genetic Technology. In: T. Tännsjö & C. M. Tamburrini (Eds), op. cit. (pp. 217-231).

Parfit, D. (1984). *Reasons and Persons*. Oxford: Clarendon Press.

Tamburrini, C. M. (2000b). What's wrong with doping? In: T. Tännsjö & C. M. Tamburrini (Eds), *Values in Sport—Elitism, Nationalism, Gender Equality and the Scientific Manufacture of Winners* (pp. 200-216). London & New York: E. & F. N. Spon.

Tamburrini, C. M. (2000c). *The "Hand of God"?—Essays in the Philosophy of Sports.* Göteborg Sweden: Acta Universitatis Gothoburgensis.

Tännsjö, T. (1998). *Hedonistic Utilitarianism.* Edinburgh: Edinburgh University Press.

Tännsjö, T. (2000b). Is it Fascistooid to Admire Sports Heroes? In: T. Tännsjö & C. M. Tamburrini (Eds), op. cit. (pp. 9-23).

Tännsjö, T., & Tamburrini, C. M. (2000a). *Values in Sport—Elitism, Nationalism, Gender Equality and the Scientific Manufacture of Winners.* London & New York: E & F. N. Spon.

IV
PART

Gender and Sexual Equality in Sport

The group of essays in this section tackles the thorny issues of what constitutes sexual equality in sport and how best to achieve it. Also examined are gender roles perpetuated by sport that are harmful to women both in and outside the athletic arena.

Jane English's classic essay, "Sex Equality in Sports," begins by noting that what haunts efforts to achieve equity for women in sport are the obvious physiological advantages men enjoy over women in most sports. It is precisely because the traditional accounts of equal opportunity in the relevant philosophical and social science literature presume men and women have roughly the same capacity to succeed at any given endeavor, if given the fair chance to do so, that English finds these accounts wanting in the case of sport. She offers two remedies to ensure equal opportunity for women in sport that are intended to neutralize the physical advantages men hold over women in certain sports. The first remedy is to group participants in sport by ability alone and provide enough of such ability groupings to accommodate everyone who wants to participate. English argues this is a good way to distribute the basic benefits of sport (health, development of motor skills, cooperation, character, and fun), which can only be acquired if women actually participate in sport. The second measure is to group individuals by gender and thus set up separate and protected groups of women's sports. English contends that this is a good way to distribute the scarce benefits of sport (principally, fortune and fame) and thus to make sure there are a sufficient number of women athletic stars who can serve as role models for other women. Although this latter measure discriminates against male athletes whose ability is on par with more-able female athletes but below that of more-able male athletes, English justifies this practice by arguing that the integration into women's sports by these male athletes would have an adverse impact on the self-respect of all women. However, English concludes that because most sports privilege the male physique, a society that creates alternative sports that privilege the female physique is more just than one that simply offers protected classes of women's sports.

Raymond Belliotti's contribution, "Women, Sex, and Sports," takes aim at English's second proposal to establish gender-segregated sports for women in order to ensure an ample supply of athletic role models for women that might help to disabuse them of the crippling notion that they are inferior to men. Although sympathetic to most of what English has to say regarding women's rights to the basic benefits of sport and about how best to honor that right, Belliotti is both puzzled and troubled by English's self-respect argument to justify equal prize money and press coverage for elite women athletes. His objection to this idea is both moral and empirical. To begin with his moral misgiving, he argues that neither women nor men should respect themselves because of their own or their particular group's attainments in high-performance sports; as he sees it, this gives more weight to sports than they warrant. His empirical objection is the simple one that as a matter of fact women do not base their self-respect on the achievements of elite women athletes. If these moral and empirical objections hold water, then they pose obvious and serious problems for this feature of English's argument.

"Title IX: Equality for Women's Sports?" by Leslie P. Francis views the issue of providing more opportunities for women in sport, and in intercollegiate sport circles in particular, as a problem regarding the morality of affirmative action when the social practice in question is a flawed one. Sports at the college level are flawed practices in Francis' view, and she provides a two-pronged argument to back up her claim. The first prong seeks to support the case for affirmative action for women in sport, and so to defend Title IX legislation that led to a remarkable upturn in women's participation rates in high school and intercollegiate sports, on the grounds that so long as male athletes are allowed and even encouraged to participate in these practices women should be similarly allowed to pursue them. To deny women such opportunities would not only deprive women of the benefits of athletic participation but, perhaps more important, deny women the same autonomy men enjoy to live their lives as they see fit. This defense of Title IX, Francis argues, is a limited one, but it is also, to her mind, "powerful" because it steadfastly insists that women not be treated differently from men in the athletic arena. However, because there is no denying that sports as presently structured and conducted leave much to be desired morally and socially speaking, Francis thinks justice would be better served if these sports were radically restructured—a plea that goes well beyond the purview of Title IX. She ventures four such reformation schemes, all of which seek to redress the main abuses of elite sports and thereby transform these practices into worthwhile ones that would be attractive to both women and men.

Leslie Howe's "Being and Playing: Sport and the Valorization of Gender" interrogates the stereotypes of masculinity and femininity churned out with regularity by traditional sports, which leads her to concede Francis' point that such sports are indeed flawed practices we should be ever wary of, even as we seek to overturn the inequities that are surely one of their chief flaws. However, Howe's defense of women's continued participation in these sports is stronger and runs deeper that Francis' more temperate and limited defense. Howe's position rests on her interesting claim that despite their considerable drawbacks these same sports furnish women "an immensely valuable opportunity for redefinition of the female self." So it is that Howe takes as her point of departure the sport of ice hockey, a sport whose repressive stereotypes and yet, improbably, potential for gender transcendence she can personally attest to because this is the sport she plays and loves. Hockey is, as she aptly puts it, not just a masculine game but a "hypermasculine" game in which such quintessential male features as strength, courage, physical power and skill, and aggression are on constant display. Of these, perhaps aggression stands out above all and is exemplified by the desire to hit one's opponent with all the physical force one can muster, to fight at the slightest provocation, and to pursue victory at all costs. It is thus not surprising that hockey doesn't take kindly to anything that smacks of the effeminate; in fact, many see the sport as stubbornly and unrelentingly antifeminine in its outlook. Yet for all that, insists Howe, women who play hockey, who love it in spite of its unmistakable masculine bent, cannot be written off as hopeless masochists. Far from it, for by playing hockey such women not only manage to challenge the dominant male stereotype of the "passive" female body but as well are able to telegraph to their male counterparts that they don't need them to affirm who they are, what they want, or what they find of value. Moreover, by playing this traditional sport in an untraditional way—by emphasizing skill and finesse over brute force—women, Howe argues, are able to challenge headlong both dominant male and female stereotypes that not only subordinate women and pigeonhole men but impoverish sports such as hockey by preventing them from becoming all that they might be.

Torbjörn Tännsjö begins his provocative essay "Against Sexual Discrimination in Sports" with the innocent enough claim that the sexual discrimination that evidently is still directed at women in sport should be abolished. But we soon realize that his plea is far from innocent once we understand how he is using the notion of sexual discrimination—which is, to use Tännsjö's words, in "a neutral, purely descriptive sense"—to mean whenever men and women are treated different from one another, no matter if that different treatment is justified. So in calling for the end of sexual discrimination in sport Tännsjö is not only calling for the end to the familiar inequalities women suffer in sport but also to the remedies that writers like Jane English insist are crucial to end such unequal treatment by, for example, setting up protected classes of sport for women. The latter part of this claim is, to say the least, controversial, but it is one that Tännsjö backs up with arguments that aim to show the weaknesses of arguments and arrangements such as those ventured by English. His main argument in this regard is to take moral and nonmoral qualities that are admittedly more often found in women's sporting practices than in men's (such as greater fairness and regard for one's opponents as well as more emphasis on skill rather than physical power) and instead of enforcing sexual or other restrictions on who may play these ennobling sports change all sports to incorporate such qualities. So if we, for instance, institute such practices as more weight and height classes in all sports, and modify existing sports such as tennis by eliminating the scorching first serve that often decides men's contests, we will end up with better sports in both a moral and nonmoral sense. Tännsjö thus concludes that the best way to purge sports of abuses such as sexual inequality is not to treat men and women differently in this regard but to treat the sports themselves differently by introducing moderations like those suggested above.

Despite the pressing moral importance of gender equality in sport ethics, the subject has still not received the attention it deserves. There is, however, a small but impressive body of literature devoted to these issues. Iris Young's relatively early and classic contribution, "The Exclusion of Women from Sport: Conceptual and Existential Dimensions," is a noteworthy example, as is Betsy Postow's "Women and Masculine Sports."[1] Postow also edited a useful collection of essays, entitled *Women, Philosophy, and Sport*, which critically examines the role of women's sports.[2] Robert

Simon's "Gender Equity and Inequity in Athletics" provides an acute analysis of some ethical problems in the ways in which athletic departments have sought to comply with the requirements of Title IX,[3] and provides a more general and searching overview of the issue of sexual equality in sport in a revised chapter in the second edition of his book, *Fair Play: The Ethics of Sport*. Berit Skirstad's "Gender Verification in Competitive Sport" examines the often degrading manner in which gender tests in sport are carried out, and Angela Schneider's "On the Definition of 'Woman' in the Sport Context," both of which appear in *Values in Sport*,[4] argues against the idea that sex equality can be achieved in sport by modifying sports rather than sexually segregating men's and women's sports. A more recent and insightful series of essays that explores the themes of gender, sexuality, and sport is Dennis Hemphill's and Caroline Symons's edited collection, *Gender, Sexuality, and Sport: A Dangerous Mix*.[5] Finally, Tamburrini's and Tännsjö's recent publication, *Genetic Technology and Sport*, contains a collection of four provocative essays that analyze the issue of gender equality in sport from the perspective of gene doping.[6]

Notes

1. Iris Young, "The Exclusion of Women from Sport: Conceptual and Existential Dimensions" *Philosophy in Context* 9 (1979): 44-53; Betsy Postow, "Women and Masculine Sports," *Journal of the Philosophy of Sport* VII (1980): 51-58.

2. Betsy Postow (Ed.), *Women, Philosophy, and Sport* (Metuchen, NJ: The Scarecrow Press, 1983).

3. Robert Simon, "Gender Equity and Inequity in Athletics," *Journal of the Philosophy of Sport* XX-XXI (1993-1994): 6-22; Robert Simon, *Fair Play: Ethics in Sport*, 2nd ed. (Boulder, CO: Westview Press, 2004).

4. Berit Skirstad, "Gender Verification in Competitive Sport: Turning from Research to Action" in *Values in Sport*, eds. C. Tamburrini and T. Tännsjö (London and New York: E&F Spon, 2000), 116-122; Angela Schneider, "On the Definition of 'Woman' in the Context of Sport," in *Values in Sport*, eds. C. Tamburrini and T. Tännsjö (London and New York: E&F Spon, 2000), 123-138.

5. Dennis Hemphill and Caroline Symons, *Gender, Sexuality and Sport: A Dangerous Mix* (New South Wales: Walla Walla Press, 2002).

6. Claudio Tamburrini and Torbjörn Tännsjö, *Genetic Technology and Sport* (London and New York: Routledge, 2005).

Sex Equality in Sports

✦

Jane English

What constitutes equal opportunity for women in sports? Philosophers have developed three major positions concerning equal opportunity, but they have focused on fields in which the sexes are either known or assumed to have equal potentialities. In sports, some relevant differences between the sexes, though statistical, do appear to be permanent. All three of the most widely held views on equal opportunity are deficient when applied to this area. Since there may be other permanent differences between the sexes, in such areas as spatial perception or verbal ability, it is useful to examine the problems of equal opportunity in sports.

I

One account of equal opportunity identifies it with nondiscrimination. On this view, if we do not pay any attention to the race of applicants to law school, for example, then our admissions are "color blind" and give blacks equal opportunity. Admission should be based on characteristics relevant to law school, such as intelligence and grades, while irrelevant characteristics such as sex and race should be ignored entirely. Most philosophers have rejected this account as too weak. If women lack motivation because they never see female lawyers on television, "sex blindness" alone will not provide equal opportunity. Although "formal" equality is necessary for justice, it is not sufficient. These philosophers would permit temporary violations of this ideal, but only in the transition to a just society.

When applied to sports, however, their view proves inadequate. If our sports were made sex-blind, women would have even less opportunity to participate than at present. Given equal incentives and more role models, women would have more interest in athletics, but few would qualify for high school, college, professional and

Reprinted from J. English, 1978; "Sex equality in sports," *Philosophy & Public Affairs* 7(3): 269-277, with permission of Blackwell Publishing.

Olympic teams. Statistically speaking, there are physiological differences between the sexes that are relevant to sports performance. Remedial programs and just institutions cannot obliterate all differences in size and strength. So far from being necessary for equal opportunity, sex-blindness can actually decrease it.

A second account of equal opportunity identifies it with equal chances. Oscar and Elmer are said to have equal opportunity to become brain surgeons if it is equally probable that they will become brain surgeons. Most philosophers have rejected this conception of equal opportunity as too strong. If Oscar is a genius with great manual dexterity and Elmer is uncoordinated and slightly retarded, then they should not have an equal chance to become brain surgeons. Our society is not unjust if it encourages Oscar and discourages Elmer from this profession, because these skills are relevant to the job.

When we turn to women in sports, however, the model of equal probabilities seems to have some merit. Sports offer what I will call *basic benefits* to which it seems everyone has an equal right: health, the self-respect to be gained by doing one's best, the cooperation to be learned from working with teammates and the incentive gained from having opponents, the "character" of learning to be a good loser and a good winner, the chance to improve one's skills and learn to accept criticism—and just plain fun. If Matilda is less adept at, say, wrestling than Walter is, this is no reason to deny Matilda an equal chance to wrestle for health, self-respect, and fun. Thus, contrary to the conclusion on the example of the brain surgeon, a society that discourages Matilda from wrestling is unjust because it lacks equal opportunity to attain these basic benefits.

The third account of equal opportunity calls for equal chances in the sense of equal achievements for the "major social groups." Blacks have an equal opportunity to be lawyers, on this view, when the percentage of lawyers who are black roughly equals the percentage of blacks in the population. Like the "equal probabilities" view, this one calls for equal chances, but it interprets this by averaging attainments across the major social groups.

When this third account is applied to sports, it seems to have the undesirable consequence that a society is unjust if less than half its professional football players are women. If we had to provide sufficient incentives or reverse discrimination to achieve this result, it would create a situation unfair to 170-pound males. (They may even clamor to be recognized as a "major social group.") More important, it seems wrong to argue that a low level of health and recreation for, say, short women, is compensated for by additional health and recreation for tall women; one might as well argue that women are compensated by the greater benefits enjoyed by men. Rawls and Nozick have argued against utilitarianism by pointing out that society is not a "macro-individual" such that the benefits of some persons cancel out the sufferings of others. But the major social groups are not macro-individuals either. Proponents of the third account have not, to my knowledge, replied to this objection.

Beyond the basic benefits of sport, some athletes reap the further benefits of fame and fortune. I shall call these the *scarce benefits* of sport. The term is not meant to imply that they are kept artificially scarce, but that it is simply not possible for prizes and publicity to be attained equally by everyone at once. Although everyone has an equal right to the basic benefits, not everyone can claim an equal right to receive fan mail or appear on television. For this, having the skill involved in the sport is one relevant factor. In short, I shall maintain that the second account, equal probabilities, should be applied to the basic benefits; whereas the third model, proportional attainments for the major social groups, should be applied to the scarce benefits. And I shall construct an argument from self-respect for taking the "average" across the major social groups in the case of scarce benefits.

II

The traditional accounts of equal opportunity are inadequate because men and women are physiologically different in ways relevant to performance in sports. What is a fair way to treat physiologically disadvantaged groups? Two methods are in common use, and I shall suggest a third option.

One common method is to form competition classes based on a clear-cut physiological characteristic, such as weight or age, well known to be a hindrance in the sport in question. For example, middleweight boxers receive preferential treatment in the sense that they are permitted to move up and compete against the heavyweights if they desire, while the heavyweights are not permitted to move down into the middleweight class.

Sex is frequently used to form separate competition groups. If we apply the boxing model, several conclusions about this practice follow. Women should be allowed to "move up" and compete against the men if they wish. Since sex is not relevant to performance in all sports, the sport should be integrated when it is not. For example, it is probably irrelevant in dressage, riflery and car racing. In other sports, the differences between the sexes may be too small to justify separate classes—as in diving and freestyle skiing. In still others, the sexes have compensating differences. In channel swimming, for instance, men are advantaged in strength, but women profit from an insulating layer of fat. Additional sports could be integrated if the abilities characteristic of the two sexes were valued equally. In many areas, such as swimming, it is simply unknown whether the existing differences are due to permanent physiological characteristics or to cultural and social inequalities. Additional empirical research is needed before it will be known where integration is appropriate.

An objection to the use of groupings by sex is that it discriminates against those males whose level of performance is equal to that of the abler females. For example, if we have a girls' football team in our high school, is it unfair to prohibit a 120-pound boy who cannot make the boys' team from trying out for the girls' team? If we provide an additional team for boys under 140 pounds, does that discriminate against girls under 100 pounds? Against short boys over 140 pounds? It is impossible to provide a team for every characteristic that might be relevant to football performance. The objection has force because the differences between the sexes are only statistical. Our 120-pound boy is being penalized for the average characteristics of a major social group to which he belongs, rather than being treated on the basis of his individual characteristics.

The justification for maintaining separate teams for the sexes is the impact on women that integration would have. When there are virtually no female athletic stars, or when women receive much less prize money than men do, this is damaging to the self-respect of all women. Members of disadvantaged groups identify strongly with each other's successes and failures. If women do not attain roughly equal fame and fortune in sports, it leads both men and women to think of women as naturally inferior. Thus, it is not a right of women tennis stars to the scarce benefits, but rather a right of all women to self-respect that justifies their demand for equal press coverage and prize money.

This provides a justification for applying the third account of equal opportunity to the distribution of scarce benefits. It also explains why the "major social groups" have this feature, while arbitrary sets of individuals do not. A group singled out for distinctive treatment and recognized as a class tends to develop feelings of mutual identification which have an impact on the members' self-respect. It also affects the respect and treatment they get from others. In an androgynous society, we might be as unaware of a person's sex as we now are of left-handedness. Then roughly equal attainments would no longer be required, on my reasoning, for unequal attainments would not injure self-respect. Conversely, although there is some evidence of late that blacks have physiological traits such as a longer calf that give them an advantage in jumping and sprinting, I do not conclude that we should form separate track or basketball leagues for whites, since the self-respect of whites is not endangered by this modest advantage possessed by blacks.

III

A different method often used to give the disadvantaged equal access to the basic benefits of sport is to group individuals by ability alone. This occurs when we find second- and third-string games, B-leagues, intramural meets or special matches for novices or amateurs. Groupings by age, sex, or weight are often just attempts to approximate ability groupings in a convenient and quick way. When convenience is the intent, then, it must not be rigidly imposed to keep talented girls off the first string.

Groupings by ability are much easier to justify than groupings by the specific characteristics just discussed. There is no discrimination against less able members of the dominant group. Ability groupings take into account all the traits that may affect performance. Competition with those close to one's own ability usually provides the most incentive and satisfaction, except where style of play is very different. It is imperative to make recreational leagues on all levels of skill available to people of all ages, sexes, income levels, and abilities, because everyone has an equal right to sport's basic benefits.

Groupings by ability must not lead to disrespect for those playing in the lower ability groups, however. Sports is an area in which we have tended to confuse respect with what has been called "esteem." I may have a low (and accurate) estimate of myself as a tennis player without losing respect for myself as a person. Although competition does entail winners and losers, it does not entail disrespect for the losers. Much has been said recently about this among other evils of competition. But competition per se is not bad. It offers fun, excitement, entertainment, and the incentive to perform at one's best. The problems arise when losers are scorned or discouraged from playing, and when winning becomes the end rather than the means to basic benefits. It is ironic that sports, long recommended for building character and teaching how to be a good loser and winner, have often taught aggression and elitism. Experts have become idols and millionaires, while the rest of us watch rather than participate. With effort, the entry of women into sports could foster a reawakening to these values, which are widely shared but have been lost lately in the shuffle of big business sports. Some such reawakening is necessary if ability groupings are to be effective.

IV

So far I have assumed that women are a physiologically disadvantaged group in need of protection or special handicaps. In recent years, women have been making impressive progress in narrowing the gap between male and female performance. But there are apparently some permanent biological differences that affirmative action and consciousness raising will never change: women are smaller than men, they have a higher percentage of fat, they lack the hormones necessary for massive muscle development, they have a different hip structure and a slower oxygenation rate.

Before we conclude that women are permanently relegated to inferiority, however, let us note that what is a physiological disadvantage in one activity may be an advantage in others: weight is an asset to a Sumo wrestler and a drawback for marathon running; height is an aid in basketball but not on the balance beam. In some sports, women have natural advantages over men. The hip structure that slows running gives a lower center of gravity. Fat provides insulation and an energy source for running fifty-mile races. The hormones that hinder development of heavy muscles promote flexibility. Even small size can be an asset, as jockeys and spelunkers know.

An example of an athletic activity which emphasizes the female advantages is ballet. Some ballerinas can stand on one toe while extending the other leg up into a vertical position where it touches the ear! While admittedly few women can do this, even fewer men can. Men are simply physiologically disadvantaged in the body flexibility that ballet emphasizes. Perhaps the most extreme example of a sport favoring women's natural skills is the balance beam. Here, small size, flexibility and low center of gravity combine to give women the kind of natural hegemony that men enjoy in football.

This suggests a third approach to aiding physiologically different groups. We should develop a variety of sports, in which a variety of physical types can expect to excel. We tend to think of the possible sports as a somewhat fixed group of those currently available. Yet even basketball and football are of very recent invention. Since women have been virtually excluded from all sports until the last century, it is appropriate that some sports using women's specific traits are now developing, such as synchronized swimming.

This method is different from forming handicapped groups or second-string leagues, and it is superior in its impact on the self-respect of the affected groups. It contributes to a woman's self-respect to see or read about the best women golfers. But this pride is tempered by the knowledge that they are "only" the best *women*. The very need for a protected competition class suggests inferiority. The pride and self-respect gained from witnessing a woman athlete who is not only the best woman but the very best athlete is much greater. Perhaps most white male readers have not experienced this sort of identification characteristic of "minority" groups. But it is clearly displayed in the extraordinary interest in gymnastics among adolescent girls inspired by Olga Korbut, and the pride blacks derived from Jackie Robinson.

V

In calling for the development of new sports, I am suggesting that our concept of "sports" contains a male bias. Historically, this is understandable, because sports were an exclusively male domain, probably based on war and hunting, and actually used to assert male dominance. The few athletic activities permitted to women—mostly forms of dance—were not thought to fall under the *concept* of sport, and are still classified as arts or entertainment instead. Speed, size, and strength seem to be the essence of sports. Women *are* naturally inferior at "sports" so conceived.

But if women had been the historically dominant sex, our concept of sport would no doubt have evolved differently. Competitions emphasizing flexibility, balance, strength, timing, and small size might dominate Sunday afternoon television and offer salaries in six figures. Men could be clamoring for equal press coverage of their champions.

Here it might be argued that our concept of sport cannot be altered to make women equal, because speed, strength, and size are inevitable elements of *spectator* appeal. But it is participating rather than watching that is central to sport. Although speed is exciting, so is precision. Nor do audiences always choose to watch the experts. More important, spectator interest is a cultural product, tending to follow rather than lead media attention.

VI

The just society, in my view, would contain a greater variety of sports than we now have, providing advantages for a wider range of physical types. The primary emphasis would be on participation, with a wealth of local teams and activities available to all, based on groupings by ability. Only where style of play is very different would groupings by weight, age, or sex be recommended. The goal would be to make the basic benefits of health, teamwork, and fun equally available to everyone. Just distribution of the scarce benefits is somewhat more complex. Level of skill, audience appeal, and the self-respect of major social groups all have to be considered.

Current problems of the real world are far removed from such a utopia. Rights to the basic benefits dictate immediate changes in the distribution of our sports resources. Most obvious is the need for equal facilities—everything from socks to stadiums. If this means we must disturb a "Pareto optimal" situation—selling the football team's videotape machine if we are to provide a jogging path for the middle-aged—so be it. More subtle is the need for equal incentives. As well as equal scholarships and prizes, women need peer approval and changed sex-role stereotypes.

In short, I have suggested a division of the benefits of sport into the "basic" and the "scarce" ones. From the assumption that everyone has an equal right to the basic benefits of health and recreation, I have argued that the access to participator sports should not be based upon having the ability to play the sport well. And this ability is only one factor in the attainment of the scarce benefits. Since I believe that the right of women to roughly half of the scarce benefits, overall, stems from the right to self-respect, I have argued that a society which invents alternative sports using women's distinctive abilities and which rewards these equally is preferable to a society which only maintains protected classes for women in sports at which men are advantaged.

Women, Sex, and Sports

Raymond A. Belliotti

Jane English (2) has presented several arguments related to sexual equality in athletics. Crucial to these arguments is the distinction between basic and scarce athletic benefits. Basic benefits are those to which everyone has an equal right; scarce benefits are those to which everyone does not have an equal right. Examples of basic benefits are health, the self-respect to be gained by doing one's best, learning cooperation and competition by working with teammates and battling against opponents, and the opportunity to improve one's skills. Examples of scarce benefits are fame and fortune. It is clear that basic benefits, at least in theory, can be available to all and are achievable by all; scarce benefits by their very nature cannot be attained by all (2: pp. 270-71).

I

English (2: p. 273) advances the following argument in defense of the claim that women have a justifiable demand for equal coverage and prize money:

The Argument From Self-Respect

1. Members of disadvantaged groups identify strongly with each other's successes and failures.

2. If women do not attain roughly equal fame and fortune in sports, it leads both men and women to think of women as naturally inferior.

3. When there is a wide disparity in these attainments between men and women, this is damaging to the self-respect of all women.

4. All women have a right to self-respect. This right to self-respect justifies the demand for equal press coverage and prize money for women.

Reprinted, by permission, from R.A. Belliotti, 1979, "Women, sex, and sports," *Journal of the Philosophy of Sport 6*: 67-72.

Premises (1) and (4) can be quickly accepted. Self-respect is an indispensable factor for both enjoying our lives and living fruitfully with others. And, surely, it is true that individuals are often classified into groups, and that this group affiliation often leads them to be treated in particular ways and also leads them toward certain expectations and goals—hence the call for "role models" by many advocates for affirmative action.

Premises (2) and (3) are much less convincing. Even if the performances of the most capable women in sports in which objective performance measurement is possible (e.g., golf and bowling) are below the performances of the most capable men, we should not conclude that women are naturally inferior. Past cultural and social inequalities may well account for at least some of the disparity. And if women do not attain equal fame and fortune because of this performance disparity and because of market conditions, this need and should not lead anyone to conclude that women are *naturally* inferior as athletes; and it should certainly not lead anyone to conclude that women are inferior *people.*

Why should *all* women lose self-respect because of a dearth of female athletic stars or because professional women athletes receive less prize money than men receive? It is only when society teaches us that our self-respect is connected integrally with athletic attainments that this might occur. It is one thing to say that members of disadvantaged groups identify strongly with each other's successes and failures, and quite another to say that unequal financial attainments in athletics will result in a loss of self-respect for all members of the group.

The fact is that we should not respect ourselves because of our own or our group's attainments of fame and fortune in professional sports; we should respect ourselves and those we identify with on the basis of the kind of people we are, the kind of moral lives we lead, and the characters we possess. And the strange part of all this is that English (2: p. 274) seems to recognize this later in her article, for she states, "I may have a low (and accurate) estimate of myself as a tennis player without losing respect for myself as a person." Here she is certainly correct.

All women may have low estimates of themselves as athletes and athletic attainers without losing respect for themselves or their sisters as people. There simply is no necessary connection between a person's athletic attainments and that person's degree of self-respect; and there should not be any empirical connection. Again, there is an empirical connection only if society as a whole or the major social group itself teaches and values athletic performance measured by fame/fortune as an important aspect of the group's or individual's self-respect. But society and the major social groups need not and should not teach this and, hence, there need be and should be no empirical connection between athletic attainments and self-respect.

However, it should be rejoined that even if there is no *necessary* connection between athletic attainments and group self-respect, and even if there *should* be no empirical connection, there still *is* an empirical connection, at least in our society.

But I think that this is false, at least in the case of women. Do all women, or even a majority of women, really lose self-respect because Chris Evert Lloyd does not make as much money as Bjorn Borg; or because Nancy Lopez is in a lower tax bracket than Jack Nicklaus; or, if we look to the past, because Mickey Wright received far less press coverage and prize money than did Arnold Palmer? I would conjecture that the vast majority of women could care less about Chris Evert Lloyd and Nancy Lopez, and that very few even know who Mickey Wright was. I believe that the majority of women do not even take an active interest in female professional sports, much less lose self-respect because of disparities in female and male sports attainments. So, I do not think there is any empirical connection between female athletic attainments and female self-respect.

II

English (2: p. 270) identifies properly the role of self-respect in athletics when she states that "self-respect (is) to be gained by doing one's best." The notion of individual self-respect being connected with effort expended in fulfilling athletic potential is much sounder than the attainment principle (3). Much athletic ability is natural, personally undeserved, and such that we cannot take credit generally for our possession of it. It seems inappropriate and mistaken to allow our self-respect to hinge upon so arbitrary a factor. However, much of what we personally deserve is directly determined by the effort and energy we expend in certain pursuits. That is why we often praise a less gifted competitor who is making the most of her ability and denigrate a more talented performer who seems to be an underachiever.

Athletics, if it is to be a factor in determining our self-respect, should be valued for its basic, and not for its scarce, benefits.

The argument from the right to self-respect does not concentrate on equality of performance between men and women professional sports stars, but rather upon equality in press coverage and financial rewards. To those who believe that fame/ fortune in professional sports should be proportionate to performance, it would not seem unjustified to compensate women less, or to allow them less media coverage, if the reason for doing so is not simply that they are women, but rather that they do not perform as well. At least in some sports objective performance is clearly measurable and comparable (e.g., golf, bowling, and skeet shooting); in other sports (e.g., basketball, tennis, and baseball) the top men professionals are held uncontroversially to be significantly superior to the top women. One could argue that the whole point of awarding prize money and lavishing fame is to single out the most proficient athletic performers. To reward equally the best men and women in a sport, when the former are objectively better performers than the latter, is to stray from the correlation of reward and performance.

I am assuming that in any occupation, professional athletics or otherwise, if females demonstrated that they could perform comparably to the top males, then unequal recognition and pay would clearly be justified, unless some special market conditions could be cited. Suppose that women could demonstrate this parity of performance, but were still denied equal recognition and pay. How would they respond? Rather than losing self-respect, I suspect, they would be outraged, angered, and indignant. Women under these circumstances would have no reason to lose self-respect, since they would have proven they were just as capable as comparable males. No one would conclude that women were naturally inferior in any respect. So I think that (2) is false. The connection between thinking women naturally inferior is connected, if it is connected at all, with inferior athletic *performance* and not inferior athletic *fame* and *fortune*. Further, as I have previously tried to indicate, even inferior performance in athletics need not lead everyone to conclude that women are *naturally* inferior athletes; and it should lead no one to conclude that they are inferior human beings.

Let us suppose that women could be shown to be inferior performers to comparable males in *all* occupations in which both groups labored. What would be the response of women in this case if they were recognized and rewarded less? The response might well be a loss of self-respect, since they might be led to conclude (rightly or wrongly) that women were naturally inferior to men in certain important skills. But note two things: (1) This loss of respect would be connected with inferior performance much more than with inferior fame/reward; (2) This loss of self-respect would not occur if women were judged inferior in only one, or a few, occupation(s), since they could point to other occupations in which they equalled or surpassed comparable male performers. So, again, I conclude that premises (2) and (3) are, at best, overstatements, and, at worst, simply false.

III

Recognition and monetary reward for athletics and all occupations are determined to a large extent by market conditions. Public demand for, and attendance at, sports contests determine in large part the money available to be awarded as prizes and the amount of media coverage for the event. But, of course, public interest can be altered by the media; increased media coverage of an event can have an important effect on increasing public demand for these types of events.

Do females have a justified demand for increased media coverage as a means of thwarting their loss of self-respect? Let us consider the case of high fashion models. There are several women who have recently become famous as models: Jean Shrimpton, Twiggy, Margeaux Hemingway, and Farrah Fawcett-Majors, among others. There are no relatively famous male fashion models. Female models at this level receive substantially more pay than male models. Yet this situation has not led all men to lose self-respect for several reasons: (1) Men are not taught that the rewards and recognition of this occupation are an integral part of their group's self-respect; (2) Even if it could be shown that male models perform less capably than their female counterparts—although I do not know how, if at all, the performances of models are measured—men can still point to other, more important, occupations in which they excel. Hence, they need not think themselves naturally inferior people; and (3) Men have been conditioned to regard all aspects of fashion less important to them than to women.

But suppose it were possible via an intensive program of public relations gimmickry to make fashion very important among men. Suppose by focusing a great deal of media coverage upon male fashion that the market could be manipulated and male demand for fashion increased greatly. Men would suddenly demand equal fame and recognition for male fashion models, since the self-respect of all men will be diminished if parity is not attained. However, the performance of male fashion models still lags behind the performance of comparable female models. So additional media and market manipulation is required in order to protect the self-respect of all men, and parity is achieved.

Would we really want all this to occur? I judge that if market and media manipulation in fashion is justified at all it should be concerned with deemphasizing the importance of fashion consciousness among both men and women. An individual's make-up, clothes, and sartorial style should play a very small role in determining one's self-respect. And so too with professional athletics. Instead of manipulating media and market influences to achieve a parity of fame and fortune for female stars whose objectively measured performances are inferior to comparable male stars, we might consider manipulating these influences (if at all) to achieve a deemphasis on professional sports themselves. Again, an individual's and a group's self-respect need not and should not be connected with the monetary attainments of professional athletic stars.

IV

Much of what English says is very perspicacious. The emphasis on athletics should be participation and not spectating; expenditures for big time male high school and college sports ought to be cut in deference to increasing the opportunities for participation for females, non-varsity males, and the community as a whole; equal opportunity for the *basic* benefits of athletics must be available to all; and sports other than those of traditional male domain should be considered valuable (2: p. 275).

However, she is wrong in arguing that the scarce benefits of athletics must be equalized for women in order to maintain the self-respect of all women. She is wrong because: (1) The attainments of top professional athletes need not and should not be a significant factor in determining the self-respect of all women; (2) As an empirical matter of fact, these attainments *are not* an important factor in the way the vast majority of women determine their respect for themselves; (3) Unequal objective performances, *ceteris paribus,* should not be rewarded and recognized equally; (4) Society should be more concerned with teaching us to identify our self-respect with our moral traits and characters, rather than vicarious identification with professional sports stars; and (5) Even if I am incorrect about the truth of (1)-(4), to say that X (women) have a right to Y (self-respect) and that Z (parity in attainments for female sports stars) is necessary for Y, it does not follow that X have a right to Z or a justified claim to Z.

To say that someone has a right to life and right to privacy, and to establish that certain things are necessary for that someone to continue living or continue to have privacy, does not establish that the person has a right or justified claim to these certain things.[1] Among other considerations, some of these necessary things may require that others perform supererogatory acts, and no one has a *right* that others perform supererogatory acts for her. Parity for female sports stars in terms of financial attainments may well require supererogatory acts on the part of society, especially in view of the fact that these stars have not demonstrated parity in terms of objectively measured performance.

There may be other arguments that can be advanced in support of equalizing the scarce benefits of professional sports (e.g., as *compensation* for past cultural and social deprivations); I suspect that these would not be successful. Finally, it seems clear that English's argument from the right to self-respect fails, or so I am claiming.

Note

1. For clarification of this point and related notions see my "Negative Duties, Positive Duties, and Rights" (1).

Bibliography

1. Belliotti, Raymond A. "Negative Duties, Positive Duties, and Rights." *The Southern Journal of Philosophy,* XVI (1978), 581-588.
2. English, Jane. "Sex Equality in Sports." *Philosophy and Public Affairs,* VII (1978), 269-277.

Title IX

Equality for Women's Sports?

◆

Leslie P. Francis

Since their beginnings in 1859 with a crew race between Harvard and Yale, intercollegiate athletics have been central to the mythology of American universities. Varsity football dominates the fall social calendar of student life; "homecoming," timed to coincide with an important football game, evokes alumni nostalgia. Winter is the season for varsity basketball, culminating in the National Collegiate Athletic Association (NCAA) national championship tournaments in early spring. Until quite recently, the participants in intercollegiate varsity sports were nearly all men.

The entry of women competitors into the apparently glorious haze of intercollegiate athletics has been belated and awkward. With the passage of Title IX in 1972, universities were required to provide equal opportunity in all of their federally funded programs. Most moved quickly to establish varsity sports teams for women in numbers roughly equal to their offerings for men. The near similarity in numbers, however, belies important continuing differences. Football remains a major source of attention, revenue, and expenditure. Men's basketball is also a high-profile activity; women's basketball, particularly with the NCAA tournament and television exposure, recently has taken some steps towards success on the male model. In nonrevenue sports, from skiing and ice hockey to swimming and water polo, although teams are fielded in roughly equal numbers, participation and expenditure rates remain higher for men, in ratios that far exceed the proportions of men in overall enrollments.

The rosy glow of college athletics, perhaps always exaggerated, has been fading of late. Even football is a losing proposition on most campuses. Sperber (27), Thelin (29), and others report mismanagement, overexpenditure, and corruption. The National

Reprinted, by permission, from L.P. Francis, 1995, "Title IX: Equality for women's sports?," *Journal of the Philosophy of Sport, 20-21:* 32-47.

Collegiate Athletic Association, the private body that regulates intercollegiate athletics, has been criticized for behaving as an economic cartel by Fleisher, Goff, and Tollison (8), Hart-Nibbrig and Cottingham (11), and Lawrence (13), among others. Colleges are rebuked for exploiting, not educating athletes; premier athletes themselves exit early, in increasingly greater numbers, to professional opportunities. Faculties and even university presidents seek, with uneven success, to establish greater control over intercollegiate athletics. As universities confront shrinking academic budgets, athletics expenditures, often more than 5% of the institution's total, are viewed with mounting concern (30). Universities are urged to sell off their money-making sports teams as separate businesses and to abolish the remainder, leaving only intramural activities that all can enjoy. Older and working students may view intercollegiate athletics as part of a romanticized past that never really was and may resent the dedication of large proportions of student fees to their continued support.

Given this critical picture of the current state of intercollegiate competitive sports, there is something of a paradox to women's claims for equal participation. These claims might be viewed as efforts to participate in a practice that is morally problematic on many counts—that is perhaps bad for, and most likely not beneficial for, participants; bad for their fellow students and the universities; and bad for society in general. If intercollegiate athletics in their current state are indeed an activity that universities should discourage, radically alter, or even eliminate, how should claims to equality on behalf of women be evaluated? In this paper, I take women's athletics as a problem about the morality of affirmative action within a social practice that is significantly morally flawed. I argue that within such a context, the case for affirmative action is limited but powerful, at least until there are serious social efforts to improve or eliminate the flawed social practice. I begin with an assessment of the case to be made for the current practice of intercollegiate athletic competition.

I. Why Intercollegiate Athletic Competition?

Since Greek times at least, sports have been thought to be an important part of the process of education. Athletic endeavors, it has been argued, promote discipline and health. They clear the mind for other learning, it is said. For women, athletic participation may also be important in counteracting historical images of weakness and passivity. If this or a similar paean to the educational glory of sports is to be believed, then there are arguments for physical education, health, and intramural sports activities on university campuses. Arguments for the general educational importance of athletics, however, do not necessarily provide support for intercollegiate competition. Indeed, if the development of intercollegiate competition draws money and enthusiasm away from more widespread participation in sports, education and intercollegiate sports may come into conflict. The critical analysis that follows is aimed at intercollegiate sports competition of the kind found in schools offering athletic scholarships, not at the general educational value of sport or at the intramural or club programs open to the entire student body.[1]

Universities typically offer both intrinsic and instrumental arguments for the promotion of intercollegiate varsity competition. Some arguments are based on the value of the activity itself to those involved. Athletics on the competitive level, it is said, develop skills and self-discipline to the highest degree possible for those participating. Team sports encourage cooperation and develop friendships. For many, competitive sports are an enjoyable, even a thrilling, activity. Without further support, however, these arguments do not explain why universities ought to provide such intrinsically valuable activities. Skill development and teamwork surely can be learned outside the university; and there are many valued activities, from good parties to good horse racing, that universities are not generally expected to offer. More complete defenses of intercollegiate competition rely either on the benefits it provides to athletes—benefits which are thought in some way to be relevant to the educational function of the university—or on overall benefits to the university as an institution.

One quite traditional, and perhaps rather quaint, argument for intercollegiate competition is that it develops character traits in athletes—and, by example, in other students—in a way appropriate to the function of the university. The "Battle of Waterloo was won on the playing fields of Eton," the Duke of Wellington once opined.[2] Some recent empirical work by sociologists, however, questions whether the kinds of character traits that are developed in intercollegiate competitive athletes today are appropriate sequelae of a liberal education. Chu (4) and Stevenson (28) report data suggesting that as athletes become more successful, they increasingly value winning rather than fair play, and that coaches tend to model authoritarian rather than autonomous behavior patterns. Both the focus on winning for its own sake, and the authoritarian coaching behavior might seem to be at odds with the values of a liberal education.

An argument that relies heavily on the social role of the modern university is that intercollegiate athletics are a source of upward mobility for otherwise disadvantaged participants. Varsity athletes receive scholarships and academic support that often are not generally available to other students. Premier athletes may parlay their college success into lucrative professional athletic careers. The experience of intercollegiate competition may also prove a useful basis for job opportunities more generally. Unfortunately, the data indicate that these claims are unjustifiably optimistic. Although varsity athletes do receive scholarships and other support, Purdy, Eitzen, and Hufnagel (23) report that graduation rates are low, particularly for minority students in the sports of football and basketball. Women athletes graduate in rates comparable to rates of students overall, but the picture is worsening for women playing basketball as their sport becomes increasingly successful and emulates the model of a male, revenue-earning sport. Dubois's (6) study of post competition occupations of male varsity athletes in comparison to occupations of male students who did not participate in varsity sports shows no advantage for the athletes, whether white or minority. Intercollegiate sports have also been argued to be an important source of opportunities in professional sports. College football and basketball serve to some extent as a farm system for the professional leagues, although professional opportunities are limited. For women, there are few professional sports opportunities, and even fewer lucrative possibilities. If increasing numbers of women are well trained in college competition, however, perhaps they will become a source of pressures for changes in professional sports. Thus the desirability of pressures for increased professional athletic opportunities for women might be an argument for increased opportunities on the university level.

Another argument for varsity competition is the positive contribution it makes to attitudes towards athletes. Successful competition may be a source of self-esteem for the athletes themselves. Competition may also help change attitudes towards historically underappreciated groups. Both university and professional sports have been important forums for the admiration of minority male athletes. Female sports heroes such as Jackie Joyner-Kersee have also emerged from the college ranks into professional and Olympic competition. They are exemplars of achievement and strength, rather than weakness and passivity. If intercollegiate competition contributes to changes in attitudes towards women and minorities, it is arguably linked to the social role of the university in opening opportunities for underrepresented groups in society and should be supported on that ground.

Intercollegiate athletics are also thought to be of significant instrumental benefit for universities. The "big game" is part of the mythology of campus life. Defenders of intercollegiate competition argue that winning sports teams garner respect for the institution, encourage better potential students to apply, and augment alumni donations. One recent survey of the data (30) suggests that this optimism is not borne out. Evidence for the contention that successful teams increase alumni gifts is very mixed. Contributions to booster clubs go to underwrite athletics rather than to bolster academic budgets. In a few cases, the investment in revenue-producing sports is profitable; in most schools, however, even high-profile sports are a losing proposition. In the end, claims that intercollegiate athletics contribute to an overall aura of institutional success are very difficult to pin down.

Finally, defenders of intercollegiate sports competition argue that it fosters university identification and community. Students, who may lead very fragmented and separate lives, come together to cheer on their teams. They are joined by alumni reliving their loyalties to alma mater. Members of the local community may also identify with university sports teams and town-gown conflicts may thus be mitigated (4). Sports are a "safe" vehicle for affiliation, cutting across at least some religious, cultural, racial, and generational lines, and even linking students with alumni and members of the local community. Chu (4: p. 162) has argued that students who attend university athletic events are more likely to be involved with the institution in other ways, although the study does not indicate whether these are dependent or independent variables. Even so, however, overall student community might be fostered more successfully by an intense intramural system such as the one in place at the University of California at Davis. When they attract visitors from afar, university athletic events surely bring money into local businesses; but there may be other, more successful ways for universities to contribute to local economies.

The case for intercollegiate competition on its current scale is thus tenuous. The best case that can be made for the current practice of intercollegiate sports is that they are sought after by their participants and may open opportunities for them, although the empirical evidence in support of this is slim. Varsity competition may also contribute to changed social perceptions of women and minorities, and to an enhanced sense of university community. Many continue to believe that, despite their flaws, university intercollegiate sports make important contributions to institutional glory and community, besides being just plain fun. At the same time, others charge that varsity competition exploits athletes, drains revenue, and detracts from the educational programs of the university. Efforts to remedy discrimination against women and minorities in university athletics thus take place against a background of at best mixed support for the enterprise generally.

II. Title IX and University Athletics

Enacted in 1972, Title IX[3] prohibits discrimination in any educational program or activity receiving federal financial assistance. In part because of debates about Title IX's impact on athletics, universities were given six years from its adoption to develop compliance programs. Despite the phase-in, Title IX was met with resistance from coaches of men's teams, from university athletics directors, and from the National Collegiate Athletic Association. For example, the athletic director of the University of Maryland told a congressional subcommittee in 1975 that his department stood in staunch opposition to women's varsity sports because they did not want to market an inferior product (30). The NCAA lobbied Congress to exempt athletics from Title IX, and, when this effort failed, brought suit challenging the regulations issued by the Department of Health, Education, and Welfare (HEW) to implement Title IX.[4]

At the time Title IX was enacted, university athletic programs were heavily dominated by men's varsity sports. With the impetus of Title IX, many universities moved quickly to add a number of women's varsity teams. By the late 1970s, the typical pattern was for a university to offer roughly equal numbers of men's and women's teams in nonrevenue sports, men's and women's basketball teams, and a football team. Football of course consumed—and, in at least a few cases, produced—immense amounts of revenue. But differences persisted in the patterns of participation in, and support for, other men's and women's varsity teams. In 1985, the percentage of athletic budgets devoted to women's sports in Division I schools offering football was 12%; in nonfootball Division I schools, it was 23% (4: p. 103). Although expenses for women's sports rose after implementation of Title IX, Chu (4) reports that expenses for men's sports also rose by multiples of two to five times as much at different institutions during the same period. As late as 1993, NCAA (19) statistics indicate that only 34.8% of varsity university athletes were women, up from 31.3% in the 1984-85 academic year. In 1992, the NCAA (19) reported that only 30% of athletic scholarship money, 23% of operating dollars, and 17% of recruitment funds went to women. Nationally, the NCAA (19) calculated that the most frequently offered women's sport was basketball (289 schools; 3,873 athletes) and the sport with the most female participants was outdoor track (249 schools; 6,250 athletes). At individual institutions, participation rates over the entire period since the enactment of Title IX have departed noticeably from enrollment rates. At the University of Illinois in the Big Ten Conference, for example, although 56% of the student body was male, over 75% of the varsity athletes (including football players) were male.[5] Pieronek (20) reports that these rates were typical in the Big Ten Conference, which in 1992 proposed to require a proportion of at least 40% female athletes by 1997. At Colorado State University in the Western Athletic Conference, there was a better than 10% disparity in participation rates, a quite low difference by national and Big Ten standards, but insufficient for Title IX.[6] Moreover, with the merger of men's and women's programs at many institutions, Acosta and Carpenter (1) and Lapchick and Slaughter (12) have reported that the number of women coaches and women athletics administrators has dwindled.

By the early 1980s, over 100 Title IX challenges to gender differences in university athletics had been filed with the Office of Civil Rights of the Department of Education (32). In 1984, however, the United States Supreme Court held that Title IX applied only to specific program(s) receiving federal funding, rather than to entire institutions.[7] Because university athletics programs rarely received federal funding on their own, this holding largely deflated the Title IX challenges to them. In 1988, however, the program-specific interpretation of Title IX was superseded by Congress in the Civil Rights Restoration Act.[8]

Since 1988, a new set of Title IX complaints has been brought against university athletics programs, by both male and female athletes. These complaints have forced courts to rule directly on what is meant by nondiscrimination in athletics programs under Title IX and, ultimately, to confront difficult ethical questions about the meaning of equal opportunity in university athletics.

The renewed ability to challenge athletics programs under Title IX coincided with a period of significant retrenchment in university athletics budgets specifically and university budgets more generally. Much of the Title IX litigation was instigated by athletes seeking to block their schools from dropping their chosen sports. Female members of varsity teams objected to cutbacks that eliminated the teams in equal numbers for both sexes. Male members protested cutbacks that were imposed unilaterally on men's teams. In several other cases, women members of club teams sought to compel their university to upgrade their teams to varsity status, a step that the university was unwilling to take for financial reasons.

Judicial analyses of these Title IX claims have followed a pattern set out in the federal regulations and interpretive policy manuals.[9] Athletics programs must not discriminate in awarding financial aid—although they may structure awards differently for separate male and female teams provided that reasonable and proportional aid is available for each.[10] Second, programs must provide equal opportunity in a range of important supportive services: equipment, practice times, travel and per diem allowances, coaching and tutoring, locker rooms, medical and training facilities, housing and dining services, and publicity. Finally, programs must offer a "selection of sports and levels of competition [that] effectively accommodate[s] the interests and abilities of members of both sexes."[11] Relying on a policy interpretation issued by the Office of Civil Rights of the Department of Education,[12] courts have developed a three-prong test for effective accommodation of the interests of a sex that has been underserved historically in an athletic program: universities must offer varsity opportunities in proportion to representation in the student body; or, universities must demonstrate continuing progress in adding opportunities for the underserved sex; or, universities must demonstrate the interests and abilities of the underserved sex are in fact fully met.

This structure of analysis reflects an uneasy compromise between exactly equal levels of participation and the historical differences between men's and women's sports. First, it allows football to remain a sport apart, as long as there is equal opportunity in the program overall, by allowing separate teams in contact sports, along with separate scholarship and revenue functions for those teams. Second, this analysis also permits ongoing, quite large differences between percentages of participation by sex in varsity sports and percentages in the overall student body, that is, if the university can bear the burden of proving that existing interests and abilities are met for the underrepresented sex. This allowance, too, is important to the perpetuation of large football programs.

On the other hand, where there are ongoing disproportionalities between participation rates and the student body, the university will be virtually compelled to accede to demands by women for a sport to be upgraded, or for a sport to be protected from cuts. In the view of the Department of Education (32),

> Institutions where women are currently underrepresented in the athletics program will have a difficult time maintaining compliance with Title IX while eliminating women's teams unless they make comparable cuts, and, in some cases, deeper cuts in the men's program. . . . Institutions that plan to eliminate the same number of sports for men and women may also have compliance problems if women are already underrepresented in the athletics program.

Women ice hockey players, for example, obtained a court order in line with this analysis, compelling Colgate University to upgrade their club team to varsity status, against a background of differential participation in varsity sports by women and men.[13] Women gymnasts and field hockey players at Indiana University of Pennsylvania successfully fought elimination of their varsity teams (in tandem with the elimination of men's tennis and soccer), despite a university proposal to replace them with women's soccer.[14] At Colorado State University, women blocked the elimination of fast-pitch softball;[15] at Brown University, they fought off cuts in women's gymnastics and volleyball.[16] On the other side, male athletes have not found Title IX a particular ally in their efforts to stall cuts, even when the counterpart women's team was spared. Male swimmers at the University of Illinois, for example, failed in a challenge to their team's elimination despite the continuation of the women's team, because the Illinois athletics programs were predominately (75%) male.[17]

Thus as Title IX is currently implemented, unless a university provides varsity opportunities in proportion to enrollments (which schools fielding football teams are unlikely to do), women's varsity sports are virtually guaranteed protection when women express interest in varsity competition. This bottom line has been characterized by Thro and Snow (31) as a form of affirmative action and criticized as an unfair burden on straitened athletics budgets. A quick but facile reply to this criticism is that universities can do much to end participation rates that are disproportional to enrollments by cutting football rosters.[18] A deeper set of concerns is prompted by the observation that mandated varsity teams may be quite expensive yet benefit only the few athletes who participate in them. Pieronek (20) estimates that in order to achieve proportionality with enrollments but still leave men's varsity sports untouched, universities would need to add on average six sports (and 128 varsity spaces) for women. Is Title IX, as currently interpreted to barter football for women's varsity teams, a desirable model for equality in athletics? Is it an example of affirmative action at all, much less of justifiable affirmative action? Should universities cut football, cut other men's sports, or add women's sports? Should revenues from football, when football is profit-making, be dedicated to football or be used to underwrite the remainder of the academic program?[19] Would models of equality that require major changes in the organization of intercollegiate athletics be morally preferable within the current context?

III. Affirmative Action in University Athletics

The term *affirmative action* encompasses a wide range of positive steps that might be taken in response to discrimination.[20] In university athletics, in addition to the provision of varsity sports opportunities for women, affirmative action might include efforts to evoke women's interest and develop their skills, to encourage intramural participation by more women, to form coeducational teams, and even to reassess the entire way that intercollegiate competition is structured and understood. In comparison, affirmative action in employment has ranged from reassessment of frankly biased selection criteria, to job training and recruitment, to redefinition of entire job categories.

I have argued elsewhere (10) that the case for affirmative action in education can be made on at least three different moral grounds. Affirmative action may be used to compensate identified victims of past injustices; the creation of remedial programs for individuals who have been unjustly denied opportunities is an example. In athletics, Lapchick and Slaughter (12) suggest the example of providing enhanced scholarship opportunities for women who have been discriminatorily denied them. It may serve to correct ongoing discrimination; faculty recruitment or hiring goals may be required when patterns of selection indicate subjective, difficult-to-eradicate bias. An example here might be the recruitment of more women coaches and athletic administrators. A third moral justification for affirmative action is that it may be a method for improving overall distributive justice in society. The United States Supreme Court had held, however, that a concern for social justice is not a legally compelling interest that can justify the state's use of reverse racial preferences in such areas as government contracts.[21] Nonetheless, educational diversity may remain a legally compelling state interest that justifies university consideration of multiple factors, including race, in making admissions decisions.[22] An example from athletics might be increasing participation by women to further the likely development of women's opportunities in professional sports.

These arguments for affirmative action typically are made within contexts in which the activity at issue is thought to be worthwhile both to the individuals seeking increased access and to society more generally. Compensatory affirmative action gives victims something of value, such as a training opportunity. Moral objections to compensatory affirmative action generally rest on the claims of others to the means of compensation, such as admission to a training program, or on whether the source from which compensation is sought is any way responsible for the past victimization, not on whether the means of compensation is itself a good. Corrective affirmative action roots out continuing bias in order, it is hoped, that everyone is treated fairly. Here, the chief moral objection lies not with what is being distributed, but with the risk that affirmative action will introduce new forms of bias. Redistributive affirmative action aims to move society towards more just distribution of the benefits and burdens of social living. Here, too, objections that affirmative action is unjust rest on who wins and loses under the change and why and how they lose, rather than on whether it is a good thing for anyone at all to experience the benefits being redistributed.[23]

What happens to these justifications for affirmative action if an historically disadvantaged group seeks fuller participation in an activity that is socially problematic or that should be reduced or eliminated for good social reasons? If criticisms of the current practice of university athletics are to be believed, this is the problem posed by affirmative action for women in intercollegiate varsity competition. I will argue here that the case for affirmative action is limited, but not entirely vitiated, under such circumstances. Moreover, how the case is changed depends on the nature of the reasons for discouraging the activity; several importantly different reasons are that it is risky to participating individuals, that it is costly but unlikely to yield any benefits to participants, or that it has undesirable consequences for others in society.

First, take activities that are risky to participants. Such risks have been offered as objections to including women in high-injury or high-stress sports.[24] They may be at least part of the explanation for the continued accommodation of separate teams for men and women in contact sports.[25] Risks to participants are, however, unjust reasons for exclusion, so long as the activity is left open to men. Medical experiments with human subjects are an illuminating analogy.[26] Some experiments simply are not permitted by federal regulations because their risks outweigh their potential benefits.

Researchers may not enter any subjects in such experiments, even with the subjects' informed consent. In medical research, however, there has been a long-standing practice of routinely excluding women from experiments, allegedly because of the risks of pregnancy or the need for a uniform subject population. This exclusion has been criticized as unwarranted paternalism, because it substitutes the experimenter's risk judgments for the judgments of the excluded group of women subjects, but not for the included men subjects. It thus continues stereotypes of women as less capable of responsible decision-making. Moreover, as Merton (15) and others have argued, the insistence on exclusion to ensure a uniform patient population is misguided because it significantly limits the information that is available about the responses of women to new medical therapies and limits women's access to the therapies themselves in their developmental stages. The National Institutes of Health (NIH) have recently issued policy guidelines requiring equal participation of women in studies it sponsors and analysis of relevant differences in results by gender, unless there is a compelling justification to the contrary.[27] Thus, in medical research, affirmative action has not been required when experiments are prohibited across the board, but is demanded when a study is open to men but not to women. Applying this analogy to sports, the conclusion would be that universities may decide that some sports are too risky to offer at all, but not that their risks warrant limiting them to men.

A second concern about the assumption that it is desirable to increase opportunities for varsity competition is that there is little evidence that such competition benefits participants with increased educational or job opportunities. This lack of evidence at least undercuts the argument that affirmative action in women's varsity athletics will give more women these benefits and thus increase overall social justice. The fact remains, however, that Title IX only requires a university to protect women's varsity sports when its athletic program is disproportionate, when it has not made continued progress towards improvement, or when there is unmet need among able women competitors. A university can avoid a Title IX order if it can show that there is insufficient interest or ability to field a given women's team. Nonetheless, a university with a problematic history will need to respond to expressions of women's interest despite a lack of evidence that the women will ultimately benefit. Such universities will be ordered to make quite substantial expenditures because a few women want the opportunities. In times of tight budgets, there is something unfortunate about costly expenditures that respond to the desires of a few. This argument could be the basis for the elimination of all varsity sports that respond principally to the interests of their participants—all of what might be called "vanity" sports. The trouble with applying this argument to the present situation, however, is that universities continue to offer at least some low-interest varsity sports for both men and women. As long as universities continue the pattern of funding for "vanity" sports, it is wrong for them to offer this desired benefit disproportionately to men. Title IX's requirements are therefore justified. At the same time, it might be preferable from the point of view of justice to eliminate all "vanity" programs and spend the money saved on more important opportunities for a larger group of students such as intramural sports, an issue to which I shall return in the final section.

Universities opting to eliminate all intercollegiate competition in "vanity" sports, however, would also confront the problem of whether they could choose, legally or ethically, to retain football as a revenue-producing sport.[28] Under current legal standards, they probably could not make this choice; although Title IX permits differently structured and financed programs, it also requires that there be equal accommodation of the interests of women athletes, including provision of teams at competitive levels and efforts to develop women's teams as revenue-producers on the model of men's teams. It would also be ethically troublesome to retain football while abolishing the remainder of the intercollegiate program for both men and women. This choice would leave the university with a high-profile, highly sought after (albeit most likely not beneficial) showcase for male athletes, with no comparable opportunities for women. An alternative might be to take up the suggestion of critics of university athletics that some allegedly profitable sports enterprises be privatized.

Finally, what are the consequences for affirmative action if the activity to which increased entry is sought is one that there are good social reasons for discouraging entirely? As the initial section of this paper argued, intercollegiate athletic competition might well fall into this category because it is expensive, provides little or no educational benefit, and may foster problematic images of excellence and fair play. If society is genuinely discouraging the activity, then the argument for affirmative action would be undercut. But if society is not working to discourage the activity, the case for affirmative action remains. It is worse from the point of view of justice to continue sponsoring the activity, but leave women out, than to sponsor it without women. It is worse still if one of the concerns about the activity is that it contributes to problematic images of women or other disadvantaged groups. Thus even if it would be best overall to phase out intercollegiate athletic competition, it is better to make serious efforts to include women, even if they increase the resources committed to the enterprise, than to continue it with disproportionate participation by men. In short, universities that stick with football are stuck with Title IX.

There are, to be sure, moral difficulties with phasing out intercollegiate competition, just as there are with phasing out any cherished benefit. Athletes, both male and female, have been recruited with promises of scholarships and competition. They have what I have argued elsewhere (9) might be viewed as legitimate expectations that these opportunities will continue during their time as students; at least, they have been encouraged to form these expectations by those providing the benefits—they have had no reason to believe the assurances were dubious or that they themselves were benefiting as perpetrators of injustice. These expectations might be the basis for constructing a phase-out so as to cushion the impact on present athletes, while not creating a new set of expectations for incoming students. Recruited athletes might, for example, be able to keep their scholarships for four years; or, universities might continue to field competitive teams at least through the junior years of recruited athletes in sports slated for discontinuation.

Phase-outs such as the abolition of all or most "vanity" sports face tremendously difficult issues of coordination, however. Unless all of the schools within a conference—or, perhaps, within a region—adopt similar phase-out strategies, athletes recruited by one school will find themselves left out, while athletes at other schools will continue to compete. They may well believe that they have been treated unfairly by their own schools. While they have no entitlement to continue to compete, and of course are free to transfer, it is true that they are losing a cherished benefit that others just like them continue to enjoy. The situation is perhaps worst when a men's sport is cancelled and women at the same school continue to enjoy the opportunity to compete in that sport.[29] The alternative that avoids the apparent unfairness of differential treatment of athletes with similar expectations is to continue to provide the competitive opportunity until a coordinated system of cuts is in place. Athletes already recruited could continue to enjoy their sport until it was gradually phased down in a coordinated way, and new recruitment efforts would cease. Such coordination strategies are difficult to implement, however, because as Fleisher, Goff, and Tollison (8) argue, individual athletic departments have incentives to keep their budgets as large as possible. Thus the fairest of the likely outcomes is to continue to support men's "vanity" sports, while increasing support for women's sports—an outcome that is expensive and that may lead universities in the long run to reconsider the wisdom of their support for intercollegiate competition.

IV. Beyond the Title IX Model of Equality

The strong protection given women's varsity sports by Title IX is thus justified despite—and perhaps even because of—the flaws of the current system of competition. A better alternative, however, might be to consider ways of radically restructuring intercollegiate athletic competition. In this concluding section, I explore four possibilities for reconstruction and argue that all are preferable, from the point of view of justice, to affirmative action within the current context.[30] None, however, are explicitly supported by the current interpretation of Title IX.

First, universities might increase efforts to encourage women to participate in skills training and sports activities. If women's historical underrepresentation in competitive athletics is in part a result of earlier educational programs and attitudes that discourage them from participating in athletics at all, such efforts are an important form of affirmative action. Because the aim would be to increase exposure to a real benefit, the focus of such encouragement would be fitness and skills activities that are of lifelong importance and simply not short-term competitive opportunities. An analogy might be the programs at many universities to increase interest and training in science and mathematics among women and minority students. The focus of the Title IX regulations, however, is the provision of levels of competition that "effectively accommodate the interests and abilities of members of both sexes."[31]

A second initiative for universities might be the development of intramural sports programs that expand participation and competition widely throughout the student body. A typical pattern at universities today is the contrast between lavish support for varsity athletics and little support for intramural activities. An alternative would be to improve intramural facilities, to make educational opportunities (such as skills training) available in conjunction with them, and to increase the amenities associated with them. The University of California at Davis is an example of how widespread intramural programs can help to develop a sense of community among students. While Title IX requires the provision of appropriate levels of competition at all levels, including the intramural level, its emphasis, as it has been interpreted in litigation, has been varsity teams, not the overall expansion of athletic participation across the student body.

A more radical option might be the reconsideration of what are considered sports. Sports today emphasize physical characteristics such as bulk (football) and height (basketball)—characteristics that are predominately male—rather than characteristics such as finesse, agility, or endurance. Women athletes confront what Martha Minow (16) has called the "difference dilemma": either they play by historical rules, which fail to acknowledge differences between women and men, or they are stigmatized for calling attention to differences. Women basketball players, for example, have moved into a sport constructed for tall bodies. Although they have in many respects been successful in constructing a different kind of sport—one that emphasizes ball movement, for example—they might have constructed an even more exciting sport had basket height or angle been adjusted. Nonetheless, there have been some encouraging signs in the direction of changed sports emphases. For example, women's soccer has become far more popular, as have endurance track events such as the marathon for women. Gymnastics tests different skills for men and women; women's gymnastics has become a popular sport on some campuses, although sometimes one that advertises based on the sexuality of the women athletes involved. Title IX, as it has been interpreted, however, does not require implementation of new sports for women, except in response to demand; it may even be an obstacle to new sports to the extent that it protects established ones.[32] Moreover, there is no mandate in Title IX for the identification or development of entirely new sports.

Finally, university sports programs might consider the introduction of coeducational teams. Such teams are of course a mainstay of recreational and intramural programs. They emphasize teamwork and complementary skills—both characteristics that are arguably beneficial and useful educationally. Such teamwork opportunities might also be highly useful in acculturating women and men to work together in other contexts, especially if the opportunities are spread widely throughout the student body. Yet no intercollegiate competition today features coeducational teams, although parallel teams are fielded in such sports as tennis, swimming, diving, track, golf, and skiing. Even mixed doubles, a staple of both professional and recreational tennis, is ignored on the college level. Title IX accepts the separation of men's and women's teams outright, with one exception: in noncontact sports in which no team is fielded for the underrepresented sex, members of the excluded sex must be permitted to try out on a skills basis for the team of the other sex.[33]

V. Conclusion

In this article, I have argued that university athletics for women should be treated as a case of affirmative action within a morally flawed practice. So long as the practice continues in its present form, the case for affirmative action remains. But there is a stronger case to be made for radical changes in the current practice. Title IX, the statute requiring equality in federally funded educational programs, does not propose such radical changes and may even in some contexts be a roadblock to them.[34]

Notes

1. As such, my criticism is directed principally at NCAA Division I and Division II schools, which mount large-scale competitive programs. It may not apply to Division III schools, which do not offer athletic scholarships per se, and which adhere to much more stringent limits on funding and other participation in intercollegiate athletics. However, to the extent that Division I practices operate covertly in Division III schools (for example, by using school tours to recruit athletes and suggest the possibility of athletic scholarships), the analysis applies to them also.

2. Quoted in Chu, Segrave, and Becker (5: p. 215); Martin (14) also examines the argument that sports build character.

3. 20 U.S.C. § 1681(a) (1993).

4. *NCAA v. Califano,* 622 F.2d 1382 (10th Cir., 1980).

5. *Kelley v. Board of Trustees of Univ. of Ill.,* 832 F. Supp. 237 (C.D. Ill. 1993).

6. *Kelley v. Board of Trustees of Univ. of Ill.,* 832 F. Supp. 237 (C.D. Ill. 1993); *Roberts v. Colorado State University,* 814 F. Supp. 1507 (D. Colo.), *aff'd* sub nom. *Roberts v. Colorado State Bd. of Agric.,* 993 F.2d 824 (10th Cir.), cert. denied, 114 S.Ct. 580 (1993).

7. *Grove City College v. Bell,* 465 U.S. 555 (1984).

8. 20 U.S.C. § 1687 (1993); P.L. No. 100-259, 102 Stat. 28 (1988).

9. Policy Interpretation, 44 Fed. Reg. 71413 (December 11, 1979; United States Department of Education, 33).

10. 34 C.F.R. § 106.37(c) (1993).

11. 34 C.F.R. § 106.41(c) (1993).

12. 44 Fed. Reg. 71413 (December 11, 1979).

13. *Cook v. Colgate University,* 802 F. Supp. 737 (N.D.N.Y. 1992), vacated and remanded on other grounds, 992 F.2d 17 (2d Cir. 1993). (The other grounds were graduation of the athletes involved in the suit.)

14. *Favia v. Indiana University of Pennsylvania,* 812 F. Supp. 578 (W.D. Pa. 1993), *aff'd* 7 F.3d 332 (3d Cir. 1993). Although the undergraduate population at IUP was 55.6% women, only 38% of the varsity athletic slots and 21% of the athletic scholarships went to women. The court suggested in dicta that Title IX probably not only forbade the cancellation of women's varsity sports when interested athletes were available but also mandated the addition of further women's varsity sports.

15. *Roberts v. Colorado State University,* 814 F. Supp. 1507 (D. Colo.), *aff'd* sub nom. *Roberts v. Colorado State Bd. of Agric.,* 993 F.2d 824 (10th Cir.), cert. denied, 114 S.Ct. 580 (1993).

16. *Cohen v. Brown University,* 809 F. Supp. 978 (D.R.I. 1992), *aff'd,* 991 F.2d 888 (1st Cir. 1993).

17. *Kelley v. Board of Trustees of Univ. of Ill.,* 832 F. Supp. 237 (C.D. Ill. 1993).

18. The NCAA allowed 88 football scholarships in 1993; at many universities, this is equivalent to the total number of scholarships awarded members of women's teams. When nonscholarship players are allowed to join football teams, squad size may balloon to 145. In comparison, National Football League teams are allowed only 45 players. See Pieronek (20).

19. *Blair v. Washington State University,* 740 P.2d 1379 (Wash. 1987) held that the state's equal protection clause and nondiscrimination statute did not require football revenues to be shared within the athletic program; this approach is endorsed by Pieronek (20).

20. The term comes from the remedy section of Title VII of the Civil Rights Act, 42 U.S.C. § 2000e-5 (1993).

21. *City of Richmond v. J.A. Croson Co.,* 488 U.S. 469 (1989).

22. *Regents of the University of California v. Bakke,* 438 U.S. 265 (1978).

23. Where there are no common paradigms of social benefits and burdens, it may be impossible to find agreement on basic principles of justice, much less on when redistribution is justified under conditions of injustice. The theoretical shifts from Rawls (1971) to Rawls (1993) are instructive on this point.

24. An example is the rejection, until quite recently, of the women's marathon in Olympic competition.

25. Or are concerns about sexual contact the real explanation?

26. Another analogy might be inclusion of women in combat positions in the military.

27. "NIH Guidelines on the Inclusion of Women and Minorities as Subjects in Clinical Research," 59 Fed. Reg. 14508 (March 28, 1994).

28. Basketball isn't really an issue here, since women's basketball is so well established and a university could achieve equality by retaining both women's and men's basketball.

29. Cases that are examples are *Kelley v. Board of Trustees of Univ. of Ill.,* 832 F. Supp. 237 (C.D. Ill. 1993), and *Gonyo v. Drake University,* 837 F. Supp. 989 (S.D. Iowa 1993).

30. These possibilities are suggested in English (7), Moulton (18), and Postow (21, 22). They have been criticized by Belliotti (3) and Simon (26).

31. 34 C.F.R. § 106.41(c) (1) (1993).

32. In *Roberts v. Colorado State University,* 814 F. Supp. 1507 (D. Colo.), *aff'd* sub nom. *Roberts v. Colorado State Bd. of Agric.,* 993 F.2d 824 (10th Cir.), cert. denied, 114 S.Ct. 580 (1993), for example, the university sought to substitute women's soccer—a sport that included more athletes and afforded more competitive opportunities—for women's fast-pitch softball. The court refused to allow the substitution and suggested in dicta that CSU might be required to provide both sports for women. If budgets are tight, however, the result might be continued protection of the fast-pitch team, with little development of soccer. For criticism of this outcome, see Chu (4).

33. 34 C.F.R. § 106.41(b) (1993).

34. I am grateful to the University of Utah College of Law for a faculty summer stipend that supported the research on this project. I am also grateful to Peggy Battin, Frances Garrett, and Bob Simon for helpful comments on earlier drafts of this article.

Bibliography

1. Acosta, R.V., and Carpenter, L.J. "Women in Sport." In *Rethinking College Athletics.* Edited by J. Andre and D. James. Philadelphia: Temple University Press, 1991, pp. 313-325.

2. Andre, J., and James, D. (Eds.). *Rethinking College Athletics.* Philadelphia: Temple University Press, 1991.

3. Belliotti, R.A. "Women, Sex, and Sports." *Journal of the Philosophy of Sport,* VI (1979), 67-72.

4. Chu, D. *The Character of American Higher Education and Intercollegiate Sport.* Albany: State University of New York Press, 1989.

5. Chu, D., Segrave, J.O., and Becker, B.J. (Eds.). *Sport and Higher Education.* Champaign, IL: Human Kinetics Publishers, 1985.

6. Dubois, P.E. "The Occupational Attainment of Former College Athletes: A Comparative Study." In *Sport and Higher Education.* Edited by D. Chu, J.O. Segrave, and B.J. Becker. Champaign, IL: Human Kinetics Publishers, 1985, pp. 235-248.

7. English, J. "Sex Equality in Sports." *Philosophy and Public Affairs,* 7 (1978), 269-277.

8. Fleisher, A.A., Goff, B.L., and Tollison, R.D. *The National Collegiate Athletic Association: A Study in Cartel Behavior.* Chicago: University of Chicago Press, 1992.

9. Francis, L. "Consumer Expectations and Access to Health Care." *University of Pennsylvania Law Review,* 140 (1992), 1881.

10. Francis, L. "In Defense of Affirmative Action." In *Affirmative Action in the University.* Edited by S. Cahn. Philadelphia: Temple University Press, 1993.

11. Hart-Nibbrig, N., and Cottingham, C. *The Political Economy of College Sports.* Lexington, MA: Lexington Books, 1986.

12. Lapchick, R.E., and Slaughter, J.B. *The Rules of the Game: Ethics in College Sport.* New York: American Council on Education, 1989.

13. Lawrence, P.R. *Unsportsmanlike Conduct: The National Collegiate Athletic Association and the Business of College Football.* New York: Praeger, 1987.

14. Martin, W.B. *A College of Character.* San Francisco: Jossey-Bass, 1982.

15. Merton, V. "The Exclusion of Pregnant, Pregnable, and Once-Pregnable People (a.k.a. Women) from Biomedical Research." *American Journal of Law & Medicine,* XIX (1993), 369.

16. Minow, Martha. *Making All the Difference.* Ithaca, NY: Cornell University Press, 1990.

17. Miracle, A.W., Jr., and Rees, C.R. *Lessons of the Locker Room.* Buffalo, NY: Prometheus Books, 1994.

18. Moulton, J. "Why Everyone Deserves a Sporting Chance: Education, Justice, and College Sport." In *Rethinking College Athletics.* Edited by J. Andre and D. James. Philadelphia: Temple University Press, 1991, pp. 210-220.

19. National Collegiate Athletic Association. *Gender Equity Task Force Report.* 1993.

20. Pieronek, C. "A Clash of Titans: College Football v. Title IX." *Journal of College and University Law,* 20 (1994), 351.

21. Postow, B. "Women and Masculine Sports." *Journal of the Philosophy of Sport,* VII (1980), 51-58.

22. Postow, B. (Ed.). *Women, Philosophy, and Sport: A Collection of New Essays.* Metuchen, NJ: Scarecrow Press, 1983.

23. Purdy, D.A., Eitzen, D.S., and Hufnagel, R. "Are Athletes Also Students: The Educational Attainment of College Athletes." In *Sport and Higher Education.* Edited by D. Chu, J.O. Segrave, and B.J. Becker. Champaign, IL: Human Kinetics Publishers, 1985, pp. 221-234.

24. Rawls, J. *A Theory of Justice.* Cambridge, MA: Harvard University Press, 1971.

25. Rawls, J. *Political Liberalism.* New York: Columbia University Press, 1993.

26. Simon, R. *Fair Play: Sports, Values, and Society.* Boulder, CO: Westview Press, 1991.

27. Sperber, M. *College Sports Inc.: The Athletic Department vs. The University.* New York: Henry Holt, 1990.

28. Stevenson, C.L. "College Athletics and 'Character': The Decline and Fall of Socialization Research." In *Sport and Higher Education.* Edited by D. Chu, J.O. Segrave, and B.J. Becker. Champaign, IL: Human Kinetics Publishers, 1985, pp. 249-266.

29. Thelin, J.R. *Games Colleges Play.* Baltimore, MD: Johns Hopkins University Press, 1994.

30. Thelin, J.R., and Wiseman, L.L. *The Old College Try: Balancing Academics and Athletics in Higher Education.* Washington, DC: Clearinghouse on Higher Education, 1989.

31. Thro, W.E., and Snow, B.A. "*Cohen v. Brown University* and the Future of Intercollegiate and Inter-scholastic Athletics." *Education Law Reporter,* 84 (1993), 611.

32. United States Department of Education. *Technical Assistance Documents for Title IX Intercollegiate Athletics, National Enforcement Strategy.* 1993.

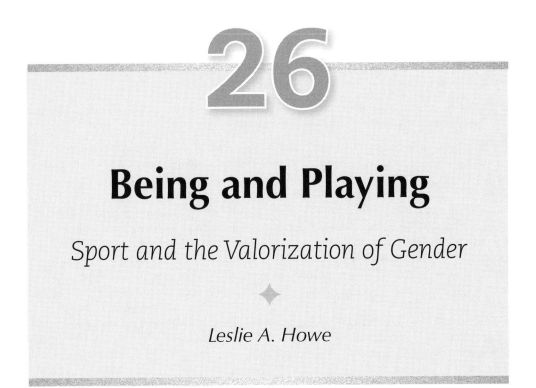

Being and Playing

Sport and the Valorization of Gender

◆

Leslie A. Howe

We tend to think of sports as mere trivial addenda to our lives, but sport reflects who we are at a particularly deep level and serves as a vitally important medium in shaping our personal and cultural identities. It so happens that for Canadians the sport that does this above all is hockey; in most of the world it is soccer. For Americans, matters are more complicated: baseball, football, and basketball carve up the collective psyche in variously complementary and perhaps contradictory ways. I will be talking about hockey because that is the *sport* I know and love, but most of what I say will, I think, be applicable in one way or another to other sports and other societies. No matter what *sport* we are talking about, however we participate in it, whether as spectators or players, its influence is at once subtle and profound. For women, the definitions of self that sport provides are frequently negative and even destructive (as indeed they are also for men, in some respects). But the direct involvement of women in sports, especially the traditional competitive ones, also presents an immensely valuable opportunity for the redefinition of the female self.

Hockey and Gender

Most of us can recognize quite readily how sport fashions our national, civic, and economic identities. What we usually manage to avoid reflecting on, however, is the way sport shapes us as individuals, that is, as individuals of a particular gender. Sports, as we humans play them, are never simply a series of purely physical motions of the body. Rather, they are complex normative structures of social interaction that effectively define, embody, and enforce the socially appropriate limits of human

Reprinted, by permission, from L.A. Howe, 2001, Being and playing: Sport and the valorization of gender. In *Philosophy and everyday life: The quest for meaning,* edited by L.D. Kaplan (New York, NY: Seven Bridges Press), 108-126.

being and behaviour. And the most notable way in which traditional sports, at least, do this is by telling us what it means to be male or female.

> "Only real men play hockey." These are the words from a popular song that appropriately became the anthem of ice arenas. (Tretiak, 28)

Hockey, as it is commonly conceived, as it is sold to the public, and as it is taught to young boys, is a hypermasculine game. Playing hockey, where it is a culturally significant sport, carries ultimate social validation for males. To play hockey is to be a man. In fact, the virtues extolled for hockey players are those most central to the traditional conception of masculinity ("manliness"): strength, courage, physical skill, solidarity, and, especially, aggression. These have become exaggerated, and heavily romanticized, to the point where "heart" (the most valued characteristic for North American players) is equated with a willingness to hit every opposing player in sight with as much punishing force as possible (preferably, to take him right out of the game), to play despite injury, and to fight whenever challenged, even when the game is well lost. It is a game where the smart player is one who knows how to do all these things "at the right time," that is, when it will most advantage his own team. Size and power are valued above all; skill, finesse, and careful playmaking are secondary and frequently suspect qualities. A player who is a superior skater and puckhandler, but hesitant to drop the gloves if pushed around, is assumed to be not tough enough (not man enough) to play the game and a target for the other team, as well as a liability to his own. "Character" in this context means a willingness to "mix it up," whether on one's own or one's teammates' behalf. One must not show any weakness, physical or otherwise, as this will be construed as a failure of masculinity, which failure demonstrates one to be unfit for the game. Hockey defines itself not only in terms of exaggerated masculine traits, but it interprets those traits as being in absolute opposition to any that might, in the remotest way, be thought of as being feminine or, more to the point, effeminate. Thus, at the most fundamental level, hockey excludes as antithetical to itself any trace of the feminine, and exalts itself as the pinnacle of purely masculine attainment.

Except . . . not all hockey players are men. Women have played hockey almost since the game was invented, though in considerably smaller numbers and without any significant encouragement. In fact, the gender disparities in funding, recognition, and opportunities continue to be grotesque even as women's involvement in the sport mushrooms at local, national, and international levels. The root cause of this continuing pattern of neglect is our socially constructed definitions of gender. These definitions of gender are maintained and deepened by the exclusionary self-definitions of our traditional sports. For example, women's hockey is not funded properly or supported because "obviously" hockey is a man's game. Such a circular definition works against women who seek to participate in the sport.

Every Tuesday and Thursday morning for two seasons I get up at 6:30, eat a bowl of cereal and a handful of aspirins, and head for a freezing arena in the west end of Montreal to play recreational "oldtimers" hockey. It's supposed to be the faculty and staff of the university, but few of the players are. Some are students, some are just guys who know guys: overweight and middle-aged accountants, realtors, dog food salesmen. It's mostly men, but usually, one of the women from the varsity team plays with us. We play on opposite sides most of the time; she plays left; I take right wing or defense. I'm supposed to check her. Sometimes I manage it; most of the time I don't. She doesn't do anything really extraordinary; she just does everything really, really well. That's a very significant accomplishment in a game as complex as hockey. Most of the guys I've played with have only one, maybe two, good moves, usually flashy ones, and if you play with them enough, you can always see it coming. She's on the national team, and later this particular year she will win a gold medal at the world championships in Lake Placid. Now, she's here, pulling a deke on me that I will remember for the rest of my life, and I have to decide whether to be humiliated or inspired. Ultimately, I choose to be inspired. But I suspect that she's really only playing at quarter speed—just getting in a light workout before class. So, there's a women's tournament here, and some of us go to watch her play for real. The teams are good ones, from Canadian and American universities. The Americans have expensive equipment and drill like the Red Army. But our team goes out and whips them all. Our player double-shifts, plays the point, and looks at the end of each game like she's ready to start another. We cheer excessively when she scores—as if we somehow had something to do with it. At one point, one of the guys turns to the rest of us and, his voice full of genuine admiration, offers the highest praise he can think of for her: "You know, when she skates you can't tell she's not a man."

———————

How do women deal with the problems associated with trying to participate in a sport that is not only masculine, but antifeminine?

> My plan for a deck of hockey tarot cards failed for want of the truly feminine. I could make some figure a woman in the game; Canada's women's team is the best in the world, and maybe I could push the notion until it does not matter, woman or man—just The Player. But I'd be lying. This is not why I love the game, or why its symbols work like runes in my language. This is a game the women watch, its gender moments taken in their image: The Trainer, running to the Fallen Man Beside the Boards, cradling the face now loose and looking skyward in his hands, smoothing his hair with a towel; the Equipment itself, stockings, girdles, garters. At the time I did not understand what the woman next to me at a hockey game was trying to teach when she wondered aloud whether she would find a better lover in another woman as the players below us skated the warm-up, around and around their own side of Centre, lofting long, lazy Pucks at their Goalie. There is a Mask on my face, the game divides us. Again I've come to a profession of love in words I cannot use for you, with all the women left in the stands where I demand that you sit and love it all. (Harrison, 19)

I first heard these words spoken by their author in a nationally broadcast presentation of his poetic interpretation of the game and its embedded emotional culture. What came across most clearly to me, as a hockey player and a woman, was at once the poetry's heightened sentimentality and its unquestioning celebration of the masculine mythos of hockey. I noticed that women featured only as a superfluous and confusing complication of the rapturously male experience. Indeed, even "The Feminine" in the above poem is represented preferentially by a male. It seemed to me that I had just been told that I did not exist, and that what I had thought I had loved all these years and worked so hard at was really something to which I could have no intuitive access. To add to the insult, not only had I been dismissed from something that is as central to my being as oxygen, but my own identity had been ludicrously misappropriated in order to valorize that from which I had been so summarily excluded. In short, I was infuriated.

When I was a little girl, the skating proprieties were communicated very clearly: boys got hockey skates and girls got figure skates. At the local park, there were two ice surfaces: one reserved for hockey and the other open to everyone—unless it was needed for hockey. I wasn't very interested in either figure-8's or frilly little dresses, so I hardly skated past the age of 9 or 10. It would never have occurred to me to be interested in hockey. That was for boys, much more obviously than the other "boy" things I was interested in: science, construction sets, and so on. It was almost 20 years later that I started to skate again, on hockey skates this time, playing shinny and, sometime later, hockey proper, at first recreationally and then competitively. Usually I would be the sole woman, or one of only a very small number of women, playing with men until I gradually shifted into women's hockey, joining a local women's league and eventually playing on a university women's team.

The Epistemology of Respect

What I found through all my various hockey experiences was that there was almost always a profound dissonance between male perceptions of the game (which are inevitably assumed to be normative) and those of women. We would look at the same action and offer radically different descriptions of what had happened; we would look at the same player and make quite incompatible assessments of his or her abilities. It seemed as though we were seeing different things.

When I later met other women hockey players, I found that they would tell similar stories. It seemed to be a recurrent experience for many women playing the game with men. What they would frequently find is that the men would not respect them—no matter what their relative skill level. It seems as though the male players come to the game with a pre-formed readiness to see the women as unqualified, compared to men, even when they do in fact play as well or better. What all this suggests is the influence of an epistemology underlying the attitude of respect.[1]

I'm sitting in the referees' room where I change after the game, listening to the guys in the next room yelling about the game, each other, about whether Patrick Roy can carry the Habs again this year, whatever. The walls don't go all the way to the ceiling, but they've never noticed and don't realize that I can hear everything they say. Their enthusiasm for their own athletic accomplishments leaves me more breathless than the game does. I resolve never to make assumptions about my own standard of play. They have decided that I'm useless because I can't pick up a pass (what pass?) and that the varsity player is so good she's almost as good as them. I cringe with embarrassment when I realize how pleased I am when they say I skate like her. At the end of the season they decide to go to a strip-joint on St. Jacques to celebrate.

Our respect for other persons is normally based on certain judgments we make about them, based on our experience of them. But those judgments about what we experience are themselves contingent on a network of presuppositions we carry with us about what it is that we are likely to experience. For the most part, we do not see what we do not expect to see. Very often, we anticipate what our senses actually present to us, leaping to conclusions about what we are seeing before we see it. Thus, if we expect a person to act in a certain way, or to do well at a specific activity, we are inclined to "see" them do *so;* that is, we interpret what we do see as satisfying that expectation. Our world works so much more smoothly if it follows regular and predictable patterns, and so we look for confirmation of pattern in our experience. What doesn't fit is discarded or discounted, usually without our being fully conscious of what we are doing. To a great extent this is unavoidable—if we didn't do this, we simply wouldn't be able to function: Information has to be ordered in some way or other to be information, that is, informative, and this means fitting what we get into some pattern that we can recognize and use without a great deal of epistemic fuss.

Most of the patterns we use are underdetermined by experience. In other words, either they are preconceived or they elaborate on whatever it is that is really presented to us. We have to remind ourselves now and again that this is what we are doing and be ready to revise the patterns we use since there is no a priori reason to suppose the patterns we are presently using to be optimal. Where the accepted patterns have not been consistently challenged or circumstances change sufficiently that they no longer adequately reflect reality (i.e., allow us to function and communicate optimally), they can become oppressive and regressive, as well as just plain false.

On the ice women encounter the expectation that they won't be any good at the game because they are women, whereas a man is always assumed to be competent. For a woman to show that she is as good or better is a nearly hopeless cause, because it is not the "facts" that are at issue. Rather, she is up against an embedded epistemological framework that makes it virtually impossible for the others to see those facts as facts—except in the rare cases where she is so overwhelmingly superior that she must be granted that strange sometime status of honorary male. That many women look different from men on the ice doesn't help, either. Given a set of confusing clues about the gender identity of a particular player, as well as a predisposition to discount the evidence as evidence, the easiest epistemic solution is to discount the player altogether.[2] When we see something that doesn't make any sense to us, doesn't fit any ontological category available to us, what we do is to conclude that we didn't really see it.[3]

> "Everybody has to have a little respect in order to get the room they want" [says Mark Messier]. To win space and respect the player must show both opponents and teammates that he will not be pushed around. The new player, especially, has to demonstrate at the very least that he can't be put off his own game, and preferably that he can and will retaliate. . . . The player, like Messier or the legendary Gordie Howe, who can make opponents hurt for such transgressions will be accorded a certain space, while those unable or unwilling to do this will be attacked with enthusiasm. (Gruneau and Whitson, 183-84)

It's my first year playing intramural hockey and the only other woman in the league is a goaltender. Next year I will be alone. Well, I wanted a challenge. There are people who don't want me to be here, but mostly I'm getting knocked around the rink because I'm a little smaller, a step slower, and I don't put up enough resistance. I'm discovering one of those dirty little secrets of the macho mystique—tough men beat up on the smallest guys first. Tripping, elbows, hooks and spears, innumerable crosschecks and bodychecks, especially from behind. For a noncontact league, I'm picking myself up off the ice a lot. In one game, I get flattened nine times, finally getting crosschecked into a goal post—and that's just the first period. No one ever gets a penalty for any of this. I play shinny two or three times a week, too. The play in shinny is extremely clean because no one wears protective equipment. Except, one of my teams defencemen always plays on the opposite side from me, and every game he keeps chopping at my feet with the stick, or putting his elbow in my ear, giving me a shove in the back. I'm trying to figure out if he's just confused about my age, and trying to get to know me in some awkward 19 year olds way. Eventually, it becomes clear that he's decided to do something about my being a target. "You've got to be tougher." He's trying to teach me to protect myself, to clear space for myself, by being more aggressive and hitting back. One time I've managed to get him pinned up against the boards and he's yelling "yeah, yeah, that's it! That's it!" He's 8 inches taller and 90 pounds heavier than me, so after a couple of months of this it's lost most of its charm. But it works. Next season I take my first penalty—in a women's game.

"Respect" is also a weasel word for fear. The behaviour referred to by Gruneau and Whitson is perhaps one of the most notable differences between men's and women's hockey. I do not mean to suggest that it is absent from the women's game, as if intimidation and violence were foreign to women. This is quite simply false: Some of the most disagreeable people I have ever met on the ice were women, and what I learned in men's hockey has been invaluable to me in competing against women. But testing behaviour, that is, pushing the rules as well as the opposing players to see how much you can get away with, and physical intimidation have an integral and institutionalized role in the men's game that is comparatively absent in women's hockey. Fighting is part of the game in men's hockey, but not in women's. In part the stricter rules, which forbid open-ice bodychecking, inhibit such behaviour in the women's game; in part outright in-your-face physical aggression is something that a great many women have to learn to do deliberately, in opposition to their normal socialization. Thus, I found that to compete effectively in the environment of the men's game, I had to learn to adopt, at least for the duration of the competition, what was to me a comparatively foreign frame of mind. I had to find a way to act and react "like a man," while being aware that I would also be expected to abandon that attitude once I left the rink. I resisted this for a long time, at first because I was reluctant to admit to my own inherent competitiveness, but also because I regarded the hyperaggressive, "get out of my way, this game is mine" attitude as an indefensible one to take toward other people. I thought it was wrong. But, in time, I found my own accommodation to the fact of competition. No way would I be a goon, but I would stand my own ground. No one was going to get a free shot at me and no one was going to run me off the ice. I wanted to play the game, and to play it I had to be in it, and that meant claiming my patch of ice, no matter who wanted to take it away from me.

In the women's game as well, one of the most important and sometimes the most difficult thing to learn is the controlled use of aggression: the determination to beat the opposing player to the puck, to win the struggle along the boards, and so on. Aggression, in the sense of the determination to "get there first," to take control of the movement of the game, to be the active force, is crucial to success in a competitive sport, but it is something that many women besides myself have to struggle to recognize as existing within themselves and learn to use. Without it, they will be spectators rather than competitors. But with it, they will find that the rewards for success in this struggle are often ambiguous.

Gender and Sex

We're changing after the game, and this student is telling me about a guy she plays broomball with. He's always making sure she knows that he thinks women are useless as athletes and that they shouldn't be allowed to play on any of the men's teams, 'cause they just drag everything down, and all chicks in sports are lesbos anyway, and on and on. But he keeps trying to get her to sleep with him.

Woman's participation in athletic endeavour of any sort presents a problem for traditional conceptions of gender and for traditional conceptions of appropriate sexual identity. Female athleticism challenges male sexual priority by supplanting the active role that is central to the traditional conception of male sexual identity. Traditional conceptions of woman emphasize her existence as body, with man as mind or spirit. This gets turned on its head by woman's participation in sport. For although woman is (supposedly) body, she is also defined as passive body. This is clearest in her definition as fundamentally sexual, where this sexuality is conceived as primarily receptive, and hence again, passive. Yet an athletic woman is clearly active and, as we have seen above, aggressive in her activity.

It is the traditional province of the male to be active in sexual matters as well as social ones. Traditional notions of male sexuality, and about virility and manliness, are located around the assumption of the active part. Thus, athletic women are an utter confusion to male identity. If maleness is defined by its exclusion of feminine qualities, and these are understood to be characterized by passivity, in contradistinction to the masculine qualities of activity, aggression, initiative, and so forth, the presence of women with masculine qualities threatens the male's understanding of what he is and what his role should be. Athletic prowess in women not only suggests that they might be able to supplant men in fields previously thought to be masculine (such as sport), but perhaps that they might also be able to usurp the male role in determining sexual activity. The abandonment of overall physical passivity hints at an abandonment of sexual passivity, which in turn whispers the terrible thought that women might no longer depend on men for their own sexual affirmation.

This is why one sees such a marked hostility toward particularly strong or successful female athletes and a determination in the media to present them less as powerful and self-realized athletes than as potential sexual objects for the gaze of men. Consider the case of goaltender Manon Rheaume, the first woman to be signed by an NHL team. Shortly after signing, she was approached by *Playboy* magazine to do a photo session, which she politely refused. What would have been accomplished by Rheaume's participation in such an exercise (profit aside)? Here was the first woman to break through a previously thought unbreakable boundary in one of the most conservative sports in North America, and now it was proposed that she should be displayed naked on glossy pages for anyone who cared to see. In other words, in recognition of her hard-won fight for an active role, she would now be reduced to a completely passive one. From spirit she would be reduced to mere flesh, and the threat to male identity and hegemony (apparently) removed. Indeed, although strong women present a challenge, their strength also occasionally lends them a certain kind of eroticism for the male spectator. The prospect of sexual conquest, actual or metaphorical, over such a woman becomes all the more compelling.[4]

Validation, Heterosexism, and Bonding

A woman playing the men's game is likely to face a significant amount of hostility from many of those men who feel their sacred territory to be invaded, and this hostility can be manifested in many ways: as physical abuse, the blindness of officials, intimidation, and the ordinary campaign of groundless gossip. Her every action in such a situation takes on a significance that it would not otherwise have. In my own case, when I was the only woman playing in an eighteen-team university intramural league, I had the deepest moral conviction that I could not possibly quit or even fail to show up for a game no matter how fed up I got with what was going on. Indeed, I could not even complain because of the way in which I knew that this would be interpreted, and because of my awareness that this interpretation would only make things more difficult for any woman coming after me.

There are other ways in which the desire of many men (and women) to preserve traditional divisions between the sexes makes the participation of women in traditionally male sports difficult, even when participation is segregated. Of major significance is the difference in validational import of participation in such sports for men and women. Masculinity is clearly at issue in the men's game; success gives superior validation, but merely participating also grants an instant warrant of masculine achievement. Femininity, however, is never part of the picture at any point in the women's game in the sense that there is no gender-value advantage to be gained by playing well, or even by playing at all. One never gains status as feminine for playing hockey. Rather, one runs a very high risk of losing feminine validation altogether, particularly if one is good at the game; women who play badly are not on that account perceived as being more feminine, just as more ridiculous.

This difference in validational import is reflected in the quickness with which charges of homosexuality are made against female athletes in general, but especially against female hockey players.[5] The same charge is almost never made (except as all-purpose verbal abuse) against male hockey players. It is a commonplace that there are no gays in men's hockey. This is because it is "obvious" that you can't play hockey unless you are a "real" man. The reasoning goes like this. To be a man is to be untainted by effeminate qualities, and all gays are effeminate. Thus, a gay man simply couldn't play hockey. Therefore, there are no gay hockey players. This, of course, is absurd, as is the converse assumption that the vast majority of female hockey players are lesbians. Nevertheless, both popular assumptions work to enforce very strict and often destructive codes of behaviour.[6]

For women hockey players, especially younger ones, who are unsure of their own identity in any case, the fear of being labelled a "dyke" sometimes encourages a great deal of overcompensation and aggressive heterosexuality. They become more concerned to prove themselves off the ice than on it and occasionally manifest a profound degree of hostility toward homosexuals, real or suspected. Someone once told me of a friend of hers, a hockey player who played for a team at a prominent Canadian university and who had been unapologetically public about her lesbianism since high school. She was beaten up by her teammates who were, one supposes, concerned to emphasize (to whom, exactly?) their own unreproachable heterosexuality. Obviously, the "team" atmosphere of conformity can exaggerate these sorts of tendencies even further. A particularly destructive manifestation of these tendencies to overexaggerate heterosexual conformity is the institution of team initiation practices that involve women making other women, their own teammates, into objects for the use of men. In this way, they re-enforce the rigid gender lines that their own participation in a traditionally male sport challenges, as if to demonstrate that whatever they may accomplish, they are still no threat to male hegemony and perhaps most important, to demonstrate to themselves that they really are still "normal girls."

It should be said, though, that not all team situations are the same. Social milieus vary widely and so do the kinds of social attitudes encountered. Many women—gay and straight—find a tolerance of their difference among other women hockey players that they do not often find elsewhere, and I myself have played on teams that were highly tolerant as well as those that were narrowly sexist and homophobic. Obviously, the level of personal maturity on the part of the players makes a considerable difference; but, this maturity itself is usually a reflection of a deeper set of conditions, in particular, the extent to which the team members have taken possession of and responsibility for their own identities.

The year I agreed to play on the women's team of a small university taught me more than I had anticipated learning about the relationship between personal maturity and athletic success, not to mention the relative insignificance of chronological age. Being nearly twice the age of the rest of the players, I expected there to be difficulties but not the ones that actually came up. In the local city league I would frequently play with teammates who were even younger, but we had no great problem adjusting to each other because we were all there for the same reason: to play hockey. With the university team, it was sometimes hard to tell.

I can't believe what's happening here. We're on our way to being thumped 7-0 by a local club team and we have totally disintegrated. Everyone's bitching about everyone else and I'm having a fight with one of my own players on the bench about who's yelling at whom. No one's taking any responsibility; everything that goes wrong is someone else's fault. The egos are all size XXL and eggshell thin. The other team can't believe their good fortune: we don't pass! Commiserating with me the next night the club teams coach says of my teammates, "mais, elles sont träs jeunes . . ."

It seemed at this time that I would go through this strange cultural shift every week. First it was between men's and women's hockey. Now, the discontinuity was more subtle, but I still seemed to be trying to negotiate myself between two worlds that were a great deal more different than I had anticipated. During the week I practiced and played with the varsity team; on the weekends I played in the local women's league. The two frequently played against each other, and in different years I have played on either side of these games. There were linguistic, age, and socioeconomic differences, but the most significant one had to do with the level of mutual respect for teammates and opponents. The league teams played together and were successful because the players respected one another enough, trusted one another enough, to combine for the complex sequences of interaction that form the core of the game. They became a team even when technically they were not, but were simply playing in pick-up situations with players they didn't know. This allowed them not only to win but to experience the most joyful aspects of a game that is fundamentally dialectical in nature.

Where this engagement between the players is lacking, where they do not value each other as partners in the play, all this is denied to them. When a player thinks that she (or he) is so much better than anyone else on the team that it is invariably her best play to hang on to the puck rather than pass it to an "inferior" player, she has negated the possibility of team play, and that team is not only likely to lose but to become miserable and internally divisive. If everyone plays like this, it's a disaster. Because this kind of individualistic attitude is so destructive, athletic teams of all sorts very often try to eliminate it by, in effect, eliminating individuals. This is the explicit purpose of initiation rituals: the artificial inducement of team spirit, the submergence of individual into collective identity. But these are necessarily counterproductive. Of course, as one goaltender put it to me, "they always go too far." Whatever the explicit intent of such practices, it is inevitably subverted by the more hidden and twisted motivations of power and dominance. (Imagine! Just this once, you can use another person however you like, make then do whatever you want—without any consequences!) What is needed for team play is mutual respect between the players, and you can't manufacture this by having them degrade and humiliate each other. What you get instead is mutual contempt and fear, a collection of individuals who cannot respect themselves, much less each other, and a mean-spirited satisfaction at seeing a teammate screw up. This team defeats itself.

One of the varsity team players is trying to explain to me why the team's initiation is not degrading. She describes how the soccer-teams' initiation involved the men and the women dancing and stripping for money. "And it was really great, because some girls made as much as $300!!" A couple of years ago, the women's rugby initiation involved rookies walking around campus in their underwear, wrapped in bits of toilet paper, with holes marked on their foreheads and the words "insert dick here," and signs on their butts saying "fuck me here." I'm trying to explain to my team captain why the involvement of the stickboy in a systematic process of degrading women is perverse. She doesn't get it. I tell her that this is the only team, men's or women's, I've ever been on that does this and that this is probably why it is also the most uncohesive. I explain that I cannot be part of a team that thinks that any of this is the right way to treat other people. I'm trying really, really hard to stay calm and reasonable and not to lose my temper. None of it is getting across. I can get out of participating by just refusing, but then how do I say "that's immoral if you do it to me, but go ahead and do it to her?" Finally, I walk off the team. The coach is furious; he thinks I'm overreacting. Then someone fills him in and he moves to ban initiation. I rejoin the team in time for the next game. Then someone else higher up overrules him. The university thinks they've already solved the problem (which is apparently worst with the women's teams) by requiring that the veterans get the rookies' consent. When you tell a 17 year old that the team she really wants to be a part of has an initiation, but that she can refuse to be involved and then she says "I don't mind" do you think she consents?

Before I started playing women's hockey, teammates were just the jerks you had to put up with in order to play the game. That doesn't mean I never liked any of them, but you always knew that you just weren't part of their team, and you couldn't be, because "team" is a guy-thing. It depends on a kind of supernatural communication or intuition, a sympathetic vibration between y-chromosomes that you could never partake in. When I started playing with women, everything changed. All of a sudden, I was aware of the assumption of respect, that I was being taken seriously. I had nothing to prove, only myself to live up to. The game itself was the only thing at issue. In a way, this made things tougher—if it is assumed from the start that you are incapable of reaching the same level as everyone else, you always have a ready excuse for not working harder. However, if you are expected to succeed, your failure to carry your own weight is all down to you. A poor showing becomes a matter of character, not biology. Although this puts a tremendous amount of responsibility on a person for herself; for me it was a relief. But for many of the younger players I know, letting go of the spurious comfort that the excuses offer is not only difficult in the ordinary way, but there are some fairly heavy influences pushing them down the easier path.

> There is nothing more corrupting for a young girl than associating a great deal with other young girls. . . . The woman's fundamental qualification is to be company for the man, but through association with her own sex she is led to reflection upon it, which makes her a society lady instead of company. (Kierkegaard, "Johannes the Seducer," p. 340)

It is a popular truism that women can't get along with each other, and thus a women's team cannot possibly bond the way a men's team can. There are indeed obstacles in the way of female bonding, but these are due more to an ideologically programmed gender divisiveness and the pressures of heterosexist expectations than anything else. As Kierkegaard's fictional protagonist noticed, if women spend too much time together, they may well find that they can exist separately from men, that they can have an existence that is not defined in relativity to their men-folk. And this must be prevented if men are to get first call on their attentions.

One male coach of my acquaintance once remarked that the women he coached tended to find it more difficult to bond in the team situation, but that when they did, they did so more strongly than men. One explanation for this, if true, might be that team bonding is a reflex taught to boys at an early age, through games and other activities, so many of which are team-oriented. Little girls, on the other hand, are taught to find their primary associations with males rather than females. Playing "house" and "dress-up" are activities that, though engaged in with other little girls, in many ways revolve around the assumption of a central relationship with a definitively male other. This centrality of the other gender to play and consequently the construction of identity is much less evident in the play of little boys (at least where play is to some degree segregated). It is assumed that a girl will forego female–female relationships in favour of those she has with certain significant males. Indeed, the former are more likely to be seen as immature or even selfish. Male–male relationships, by contrast, retain normative import. For the adult worlds of business and politics, being able to be a team player is a requisite for success. These values filter back again into the culture of sport. The football player who keeps his girlfriend waiting is acting appropriately, and he probably won't lose the girl over it; the hockey player who keeps her boyfriend on hold is significantly less likely either to keep him or to be well spoken of. The secondary aspect of female–female relationships as compared to male–male relationships thus militates against the likelihood of the sort of all-or-nothing, one-for-all-and-all-for-one bonding that takes place on male teams and that is vital to successful team competition. Contingency is injected into the heart of the female team experience: A woman must never put team above other obligations, particularly those she has to males.[7]

Women are still very often expected to find their self-worth in the subordination of their interests to those of others whose interests are valued more highly. To the extent that this is so, it becomes proportionately more difficult for them to develop the means to form a solidly cooperative relationship between themselves. The key to male bonding is denial of self in association. For women it seems to be just the opposite: learning to value oneself as distinct from others and not as merely contingent. Self-respect is the first step in the respect for others, and trust in others, that is the real basis of female bonding. This is the crucial step in forming an effective team, but it is also crucial to becoming a person who can be herself, taking the responsibility for that self and for her relations to others. Without self-respect one does not make decisions for oneself. Without self-respect one does not say no. Self-respect is the beginning of moral autonomy, it is the beginning of active self-determination, and it is the beginning of effective cooperation. It is a deeply empowering discovery.[8]

Self-respect, then, is the first thing needed for mutual respect between players and athletes as for anyone else. If the players on a team each respect themselves, then they also know that they can respect each other because this means that they can trust one another. If I know that my teammates respect themselves, I know that they will work hard in practice, will show up fit and ready for a game, that my winger will remember to cover the defenceman on the point, and that our goalie won't give up just because the rest of us can't find the other team's net. I can trust my teammates to do what they can to be where they're supposed to be and to at least try to make the play they're supposed to make. If it doesn't work, it's no big deal—there are far more things that you have no control over than things that you do. As it happens, a team has the ability to control more than does any number of individuals, but only if it cooperates and effective cooperation begins with the self-respect of individuals. In short, then, once these players can shake off their need to seek personal validation from an ideology of gender that incorporates a not merely differential but hierarchical structure of valuation, they can begin to develop themselves fully as responsible human beings and as athletes capable of trust and cooperation between themselves.

Praxis and Selfhood

We send children off to play sports under the pretext that it builds character. And so it does. But the character that sport builds is not always positive. Thus, it is worth rethinking not only how sport transmits messages about how we ought to be and how we ought to behave, but how sport itself ought to be. There is an important sense in which sport is not separate from us, and questions about structure, purpose, organization, etc. are not trivial ones. The issues are not simply technical or bureaucratic, but ontological, moral, and political.[9]

In the case of hockey, then, how do women appropriate or reconstitute this game for themselves? It seems that the first answer is that they cannot do it by simply trying to play the men's game as it stands now, but must find a way of playing their own game. But I think it would be misleading to suggest that the women's game either is or ought to be feminine. In the main, this is because our understanding of the feminine is shaped by what we think constitutes the masculine, and the masculine that the traditional male game presents to us is a deeply distorted and, indeed false, ideal of human organization. That being so, it is unlikely that any uncontested conception of the feminine would be any less distorted and false. And certainly, hockey (for one) simply cannot be a feminine game as that term is commonly understood: It does require at least some so-called masculine attitudes and characteristics, such as aggression and competitiveness. Since playing the game at all means learning traits not normally attributed to women, this means that the women's game will be not so much feminine as balanced, that is, more human in the sense that those women who play it have to develop a wider range of their inherent human capacities than they have traditionally been encouraged to do. These are already feminine qualities in the sense that women have them and are capable of developing them; we simply have to be more ready to acknowledge them as such. The women's game, with its structural emphasis on skill over force, already incorporates a rejection of both stereotypically masculine and feminine characteristics; it embraces active self-assertion in a competitive environment while also emphasizing highly cooperative play—as well as the use of careful playmaking and precise control of the puck—over violence and goon tactics.

Maintenance of a distinct women's game may prove more difficult in the future. The growth of women's hockey, as of other sports, along with an increased gender integration of sports programmes, has meant, amongst other things, an increase in the number of men coaching and controlling women's hockey. These men very often expect women's hockey to conform to the prototype of men's hockey. The demands of mainstream media and a public raised on rock 'em-sock 'em hockey also places pressure on a sport that needs greater public support and commercial recognition in order to finance itself. The commodification of sport that is going on everywhere is in danger of forcing the women's game to accommodate itself to the dominant hockey paradigm of force, power, and brutality. Such an accommodation would guarantee the women's game permanent second-class status. Women have to find a way to take control of their own game and determine their own future in it. If they do, there is at least the chance that we might affect the future of the men's game as well. Professional hockey is already seen by many who love the game to be spiritually bankrupt. By contrast, women's hockey still beats with its own heart. Since there are so many costs involved and so little external reward, those involved can only play for the pure love of the game.[10]

Finally, then, it is not just that women must claim the game for themselves, they must also lay claim to a collection of *human* traits that have been denied to them because of a spurious association with masculinity. Appropriating areas of human activity previously denied is inseparable from the redefinition of the *humans* performing that activity. Questions about what we do are always questions about what we are. But adequate answers to such questions require a loosening or even outright rejection of familiar categories. Women who play "men's" sports are rarely, if ever, doing it because they secretly wish that they were men. What they want is to be able to develop their own abilities and potential just as men have; while they may admire men's accomplishments and envy their opportunities, what they want is the chance to become themselves, not someone else. Even when they compete with men, as many prefer to do, the aim is not to be a man, but to take advantage of the opportunities that situation presents in order to become better as women athletes, or as athletes simpliciter. Thus the question of whose game women are to play has both a straightforwardly political dimension, reflected in the issue of who controls the continued development of the game, and a moral–metaphysical one, raising the questions, "Who are we to be?" "What am I to create of myself?" Such questions clearly extend beyond the comparatively narrow category of sport; they confront all of us, at every point in our lives. I contend that women playing or competing in male-defined/definitive sports are already engaged in a deeply practical way in the task of redefining what it means to be themselves and what it means for any of us to be women. And in doing so, they are actively reconstructing for all of us the definitions of woman, man, and human.

Afterword

After all I have described, some may be wondering, "Much of this sounds so miserable—just one struggle after another; if the cost is so high, why do you keep playing?" This is difficult to explain in any straightforward way. I know now that I enjoy the competition. Yes, I like to win. But what is absolutely central to my love of hockey is not competition, even though the competitive situation is the condition of its occurring. I play because you can do things on skates you can't do anywhere else: It is the closest anyone can get to flight while remaining on the ground. It's the incredible speed, and the extraordinary defiance of gravity that comes with it, that lets you turn your body at impossible angles to the surface of the ice, that you can move sideways without taking a step. It's because it seems as though I can will myself into a place and be there, instantly. It's the inevitability of time and the cessation of time in the same moment. There's a pure joy of movement, the dialectical interaction of action and reaction, with my teammates, the opposing players, the rhythm and grace of completely integrated movement, balletic in its complexity of communication, forward and back. It's the wonder of those few, rare and exhilarating moments when you feel as if you have complete mastery of your own body, all of your faculties open at once. There is in the game, at times, an experience of the sheer ontological immediacy of being which excludes the possibility of the noise of reflection but which is also a transcendence of pure physicality—you know your body as completely yours. It's a perfection of unity with your body, with being, which does not reduce you to it alone, but which gives it over to you utterly. I exist in this game and I will play it until I die.[11]

Notes

1. This issue has obvious parallels elsewhere. One of the most compelling reasons for the institution of affirmative action policies for hiring is the fact that candidates who are fully qualified for employment in a particular position are often not *seen* as qualified simply because of their difference from the norm anticipated by the employer.

2. I recall a pick-up game of shinny played in grad school where one male student offered the following solution for dividing the players fairly; "just put a woman on each team and then they'll be even."

3. Compare Ken Dryden and Roy MacGregor's description of the Canadian attitude to the Soviets in the 1950s: *"We were better.* It was through this optic that we saw everything. We shot harder and more often; we rushed the puck solo in great end-to-end dashes; we bodychecked. If they passed more, shot and bodychecked less, it could only mean that they passed *too* much, shot and bodychecked *too* little. Because *we were better"* (p. 199).

4. For a related sort of example, consider the closing scenes of the Ridley Scott movie *Alien*. After fighting off a dangerous creature that has destroyed all her shipmates, Second Officer Ripley prepares herself and the ship's cat for the voyage home to earth, only to be forced—*in her underwear*—into a final battle to the death with the alien. Why exactly? To show that, although she may be strong, courageous, and a dab hand with a flame-thrower, she's still (really) a babe, boys.

5. I say "especially" because hockey is a sport that is notably masculinized, but this is true of any sport explicitly defined as male. Rugby, basketball, track, tennis, and even golf display the same problematic to one degree or another.

6. In view of recent scandals in junior hockey regarding the sexual abuse of players by coaches, it is worth pointing out that the hypermasculine ethos of the game goes some way to strengthening the hold that the abuser has over the player. The primary means of enforcing both compliance and silence is the player's fear of losing his chance at a pro career, but the same of any association with activities regarded as homosexual is also overwhelming. And it is notable that while much entirely appropriate rage has, been expressed on the issue of the sexual exploitation of these young men, little concern is ever voiced over the incidence of heterosexual rape by those same players.

7. Except, sometimes, where that team obligation is to a male coach.

8. It is not my intention to defend some high libertarian notion of moral selfhood here, as if we were utterly distinct, atomistic individuals, ideally autonomous centres of rational self-interest maximization, who either can or should act wholly separately from the needs of interests of others. I think such a view is both manifestly false and morally wicked. But I do wish to emphasize that our relationships with others do have to be entered into, accepted as *our* relationships, by self-aware, self-choosing persons, i.e., those who do not acquiesce in a definition exhausted by contingency.

9. However, it should not be forgotten that not all sports are the same, and that the socializing structure inherent in traditional competitive team sports like hockey, football, basketball, etc, is not universal. The participants in certain individual sports, such as kayaking or rock-climbing to name just two, would argue that much of the ideological gender baggage of traditional team sports is either undercut or substantially transformed in these activities by the relationship the athlete has to the medium of competition. That is to say, even when racing (as in whitewater kayaking) the athlete is required to "compete," not so much against another human being but a natural object: the river, or

the rock-face for the climber. However, this is inevitably less an act of competition than of opportunistic cooperation: One does not defeat such an object, but must adapt to and cooperate with what is given to one by the river or the cliff in order to maximize one's own performance in relation to it. In this case, success (and the spiritual core experience that ultimately motivates athletic endeavor of all kinds) is the outcome of an openness on the part of the athlete to perceive what is offered by the other (the river, the rock) and to, in effect, cooperate with it; overpowering the other is simply not an option.

10. Dryden and MacGregor: "In the late 1940s, Tarasov, in fact, had had no choice but to go his own way. To copy meant not only to be second best, but to adopt a system that was philosophically unacceptable" (p. 200). In the end, of course, the Soviets significantly transformed the style of play of North American hockey.

11. This essay owes much to the many people, especially teammates past and present, whose play and experiences have contributed to my thinking about the game—most of them unknowingly and no doubt in a few cases, unwillingly. But thanks are also particularly due to Claire Grogan and to Jeanette Ettel who read and provided invaluable commentary on various earlier versions.

References

Dryden, Ken, and Roy MacGregor. *Home Game: Hockey and Lift in Canada.* Toronto: McClelland & Stewart, 1989.

Gruneau, Richard, and David Whitson. *Hockey Night in Canada: Sport, Identities, and Cultural Politics.* Toronto: Garamond, 1993.

Harrison, Richard. *Hero of the Play.* Toronto: Wolsak and Wynn, 1994.

Kierkegaard, Soren. *Either/Or Vol I.* Trans. Howard V. Hong and Edna H. Hong. Princeton, NJ: Princeton University Press, 1987.

Tretiak, Vladislav. *Tretiak: The Legend.* Edmonton: Plains Publishing, 1987.

Against Sexual Discrimination in Sports

◆

Torbjörn Tännsjö

Introduction

Sexual discrimination is a widespread and recalcitrant phenomenon. However, in Western societies, explicit sexual discrimination, when exposed, is seldom defended straightforwardly. There is one remarkable exception to this, however. Within sports sexual discrimination is taken for granted. It is assumed that, in many sports contexts, it is appropriate to discriminate (distinguish) between women and men and to have men competing exclusively with men, and women competing exclusively with women.[1] Even by radical feminists this kind of sexual discrimination has rarely been questioned. This is strange. If sexual discrimination is objectionable in most other areas of our lives, why should it be acceptable within sports?

The thesis of this chapter is that it is not. Even within sports, sexual discrimination is morally objectionable. No sexual discrimination should take place within sports. At least, the International Olympic Committee (IOC) and the leading national sports organisations should give it up.

The reasons for giving up sexual discrimination within sports, and for allowing individuals of both sexes to compete with each other, is simple. In sports it is crucial that the best person wins. Then sexual differences are simply irrelevant. If a female athlete can perform better than a male athlete, this female athlete should be allowed to compete with, and beat, the male athlete. If she cannot beat a certain male athlete, so be it. If the competition was fair, she should be able to face the fact that he was more talented. It is really as simple as that. Sexual discrimination within sports does not have any better rationale than sexual discrimination in any other fields of our lives.

From: Values in sport: Elitism, nationalism, gender equality and the scientific manufacture of winners, Torbjörn Tännsjö and Claudio Tamburrini, Copyright 2000 Taylor & Francis. Adapted by permission of Taylor & Francis Books UK.

However, arguments against giving up sexual discrimination within sports are not hard to come by, and in this chapter I will focus on such arguments. My thrust here is that, in various different ways, these arguments against abolition of sexual discrimination within sports are flawed. However, I will not restrict my argumentation to a discussion of arguments for sexual discrimination.

One important argument against sexual discrimination, apart from the general observation that, from the point of view of sports itself it is irrelevant, will also be developed.

These are the main arguments *for* sexual discrimination within sports—some of them, no doubt, striking an indistinguishable (yet false) chord of special concern for women:

- Sexual discrimination within sports is no different from the use of, say, different weight classes in certain sports, intended to make the result *less* predictable. We use sexual discrimination because we seek, to use Warren Fraleigh's term, 'the sweet tension of uncertainty of outcome'.

- If women and men compete, and women defeat men, then this will cause violent responses from men. So we had better retain the discrimination.

- If we give up sexual discrimination in sports, then probably all women will find (because on average they perform poorly in comparison with men) that they are always defeated by some men. This will be discouraging for women in general and for female athletes in particular.

- Female sports are different from male sports. They represent a unique value, and if we gave up discrimination this unique value would be foregone. A similar argument can be devised with reference to male sports, of course.

I will discuss these arguments in order. After having done so I will give my positive argument in defence of giving up sexual discrimination, which is that the rationale behind sexual discrimination is simply too good. If we consistently hold on to it, we are led to all sorts of discrimination which, upon closer examination, we do not want to accept. So a kind of reductio ad absurdum leads us to the conclusion that sexual discrimination within sports should be given up.

I conclude the chapter by summing up the main tenets of my argument and by proposing, constructively, that sport as a phenomenon should not be conceived of as static. A development of various different sports takes place, and has to take place. We should consciously mould the phenomenon of sports in a certain desirable direction. We should mould sports in a direction of more moderation (in ways indicated by Sigmund Loland). If we do, then we will be able to abolish sexual discrimination altogether within sports, thereby gaining a great deal from the point of view of gender equality and fairness, without having to pay any price at all for this timely reform.

If sexual discrimination within sports is abolished, this will not only be an advance from the point of view of feminism and the women's rights movement, I conclude, but from the point of view of sport itself. For the abolishment of sexual discrimination may render natural a development of sport in a direction which is, even if we put the matter of sexual discrimination to one side, of the utmost importance for sport itself, conceived of broadly as a cultural phenomenon. It may well be the case that, unless some sports develop in a direction where women and men *can* compete safely on equal terms, then there will be no future for these sports at all—or so I will argue, at any rate.

Sexual Discrimination As no Different to the Use of Weight Classes?

When I have proposed that sexual discrimination within sports should be abolished, I have sometimes met the objection that sexual discrimination in some sports is no different to the use of weight classes in, say, boxing. We have such weight classes in order to ascertain that the outcome of a competition is not too easily predictable. This (evasive) argumentative strategy is completely misplaced, however. I have no objection to weight classes in boxing and some other sports. As a matter of fact, I think we should develop this kind of system even within other sports. There should be weight classes even in running, and height classes in basketball, and so forth. Such classes are constructed with reference to crucial characteristics of the individual athlete, characteristics with relevance for the capacity to perform well in the sport in question, and they are created in the interest of making the outcome of the competitions less predictable. It is crucial that the classes are constructed on the grounds of characteristics actually exhibited by the people who get sorted with reference to the characteristics in question, and that these characteristics are of *immediate* relevance to the capacity to perform well within the sport in question.

Sexual discrimination is different: it takes place on the ground that, *on average,* women perform less well than men in certain sports. This is objectionable. First of all, this putative fact, that women perform less well than men, is hard to ascertain beyond reasonable doubt. Perhaps this is a mere statistical accident. Perhaps it is due to socially constructed gender differences rather than biological sexual differences and, hence, could be abolished. And even if the statistical correlation is due to biological sexual differences (more below about sexual differences, and how to define them), and even if it has a law-like character, it is still only a *statistical* difference. It is only indirectly, then, that sex is relevant to the outcome of a fair competition. It is relevant in the sense that it predisposes, statistically, for more or less of a certain characteristic, crucial to performing well in a certain sport. But then, if we should discriminate at all, we should discriminate in terms of this characteristic itself and not in terms of sex.

This means that some women, who are not (statistically speaking) 'typical', perform better than many (most) men do. They do so because to a considerable degree they possess the characteristics that are crucial to winning, and possess more of these characteristics than do most men. Consequently, there are some rare women who perform better than most men in the sport in question.

It is 'discrimination', then, not only in a factual sense (in the way the term is used in this chapter), when a competent woman, who can and wants to defeat a certain man, is prohibited from doing so, on the ground that women in general do not perform as well as men in general. But it is also 'discrimination' in a *moral* sense, and such discrimination is morally reprehensible.

So while there is nothing objectionable in having weight classes in boxing (a sport in which weight is of direct relevance to winning), it *is* objectionable to have sexual classes (sex is only indirectly and statistically relevant to winning in boxing).

If boxing should be allowed at all, it should be allowed in a form where individuals of both sexes can compete safely with each other. To render this possible we would have to retain weight classes, of course. We may also have to make some other improvements of this noble art of self-defence, but I will not elaborate on this point in the present context. However, I conjecture that, unless boxing can be performed in a manner where men and women can compete safely against each other, there will (and should) not be any such thing as boxing in the future.

Sexual Discrimination Because of Male Aggressiveness?

What I have just said connects with a second argument against abolishing sexual discrimination within sports. Not only boxing, but also many other sports, are aggressive and involve a considerable amount of physical contact and encounter between competing athletes. Now, if women and men are allowed to compete against each other, and if some women defeat some men, then this would trigger violent responses from these men, or so the argument goes. In order to protect women against such outbursts of male aggressiveness, we had better let women and men compete apart from each other.

Is this a good argument? I admit that there is something to it, and it points at a real danger. However, it would be wrong to surrender to the argument, for there is another way of responding to the phenomenon of male aggressiveness against women. I am thinking here of the possibility of rendering impossible the aggressive response. This could be done if the rules of the game in question were changed. Aggressive assault on competitors could be punished much more severely than it is in many sports currently. One physical assault could mean a red card—and the aggressive male competitor would be out.

The rules of the game could be modified in other ways as well, so that the assault would be made more difficult to perform in the first place. Then there would be little need for punishment. And the sports could be modified to render aggressiveness within the sports, even within the limits that are permitted, less rewarding and also never decisive.

Take tennis as an example. In modern tennis, the service is of enormous importance: an efficient service presupposes a lot of physical strength from the server. At the same time, an effective service tends to render the sport rather boring: it kills the game by taking the elegance out of it. An obvious solution to this problem would be to introduce a rule saying that a service is not successful unless the receiver has successfully returned it. Until it has been successfully returned, the server is granted a new opportunity. This would certainly reintroduce certain desirable qualities in tennis, and at the same time such a change in the rules of the game would mean better possibilities for women to compete successfully with men. Men would not defeat women merely by virtue of their superior strength and aggressiveness.

Were all this to be accomplished, I think we could make great strides in the general aim for sexual equality in society. *Some* women can defeat *most* men who perform any sport. Because of sexual prejudices, this is a hard lesson for a man to learn. It is hard even for me, a middle-aged man who regularly goes jogging, to be defeated now and then by a female jogger. As a matter of fact, I hate the defeat, and I go to considerable lengths to avoid it—but I sometimes fail. When I do, I get angry. I am enlightened enough to realise, however, when I do get defeated by a female jogger, that this teaches me a lesson. It is good for my mental development to be defeated by female runners: it teaches me to control my anger and it shows me something about the relation between the sexes. Some sexual stereotypes and (my) prejudices get exposed in the most efficient manner.

If this is correct, then we have good reasons not to surrender to this male aggressiveness argument regarding sexual discrimination within sports. We should allow women to defeat men in sports, and we should render it impossible for men physically to punish the women who do defeat them.

If we do so, in the long run certain sexual prejudices will hopefully wither.

Women Will Be Discouraged?

The response to the argument relating to male aggressiveness may be considered overly optimistic. It is true that in most sports there are some women who can beat most men, but it is also true that in many sports some men can beat all women. So, even if it is a good thing from the point of view of sexual equality when a woman beats a man, is it not a bad thing, from the same point of view, when the best women in certain sports find that they cannot compete with the best men? Wouldn't this fact be disappointing for these women?

Well, I suppose this depends on whether (due to sexual differences) it is *impossible* for these women to defeat the best man, or whether there is something that can be done about this fact (the problem lies not in the sexual differences themselves but in socially constructed gender differences, which could be abolished). If there is something that can be done about it, if the problem is socially constructed gender differences rather than sexual differences, then these women may view the fact that they get defeated as a challenge. And they may take it as their mission to abolish the gender bias within sports.

This is basically the case in many other fields of society. There are men within certain sciences and arts, such as mathematics and musical composition, who perform better than all women (there is no female Gödel or Bach, for example). Should this be disappointing for women? I think not. I think rather it should be considered a real challenge, for we do not believe that it is because of their biological sex that no women solved logical problems like Gödel or composed like Bach. Typically, the lack of outstanding female logicians and composers is due to socially constructed gender differences, not to biological sexual differences as such.

There are reasons why women do not perform as well as some men do in these fields, of course, and these reasons, which are to do with gender rather than sexual differences, should come under close scrutiny; Angela Schneider describes many of the obstacles that meet female athletes. Such obstacles, when identified and publicly recognised, should come under severe attack. Schneider has correctly observed that these obstacles are the outcome of a deeply entrenched ideal, according to which, from inception, 'the ancient and modern Olympic Games, and the ideal Olympic athlete, applied specifically and exclusively to men'. This is how she describes this ideal:

> From Pausanias' references to dropping women from the side of a cliff if they even observed the ancient Olympic Games, to de Coubertin's ideal that the goals that were to be achieved by the athletes through participation in the Olympic Games were not appropriate for women (de Coubertin 1912), one can easily see that the place of women in sport has been, for the most part, foreign at best. It is this basic idea, the idea that sport (or sometimes even physical activity), particularly high-level competitive sport, is somehow incompatible with what women are, or what they should be, that must dominate any discussion of the unique issues for women in sport. Philosophies of ideal sport, and ideal women, lie behind discussions of permitting women to compete, of choosing the types of sport in which women can compete, in developing judging standards for adjudicated (as opposed to refereed) sports—contrast gymnastics and basketball—in attitudes to aggression, and competition, and indeed to the very existence of women's sport as a separate entity at all.

I believe that, if such obstacles are eliminated, if new weight and length classes are introduced in many sports, if the rules are changed so as to render it impossible for aggressive athletes to punish their competitors, and if severe punishments are introduced for violations of the rules, then women can actually compete successfully and safely with men in many sports. In fact, they do so today in some sports, such as some shooting events, all the equestrian sports, parachuting, and so forth, and the list of these sports is growing all the time—and is likely to continue to get longer in the future.

But what if this belief is not borne out by realities? What if there are some sports where the elite is made up of men exclusively—would this be disappointing to women?

Yes, of course it would. But, for all that, this seems to me to be a kind of disappointment that should be acceptable as a natural part of life. Sexual distinctions are genetic in origin, and so are racial distinctions. After all, there may be all kinds of genetic distinctions of importance for how on average people of various different kinds perform in sports, and one of these is race. Perhaps black Africans perform better on average than Caucasians in some sports. This is disappointing to white people, of course, but is no reason to introduce racial discrimination within sports. But if this is not a reason to introduce racial discrimination in sports, then we should not retain sexual discrimination either.

To elaborate this point, allow me to return to the comparison with the sciences and the arts and take my own subject, philosophy, as an example. Women are poorly represented, not only among logicians and composers, but also within the philosophical world in general. Most people believe that the reason for this is to do with gender rather than with sex, and this is what I happen to believe. It is because women have been met with the wrong expectations, when they have taken up philosophy, it is because they have not been given proper credit for their achievements, and so forth, that they have had difficulties in performing well within philosophy. However, what if it turned out that, even after this kind of gender bias had been successfully abolished, women were still poorly represented within (a certain field of, say) philosophy, would this be disappointing for women?

Perhaps it would be (to some women), but then I think it should be possible for them to live with this kind of disappointment. It would be absurd, for this reason, to have sexual discrimination within philosophy and to have female positions and special journals for women in these fields of philosophy specially designed for them because they do not perform well enough to hold standard positions or to publish in ordinary journals within (these fields of) philosophy.

Maybe it would not be at all disappointing to (other) women however, if it turned out that a kind of philosophy exists that is just poorly suited to the female brain or heart. Another reaction from women (and many men) upon finding this out could be the following. If this philosophy is essentially without appeal to one of the sexes, if it does not fit women, then this indicates not that there is anything wrong with women but that there is something wrong with this kind of philosophy.

We could adopt the same stance towards the more plausible putative fact that there are some sports that simply suit (on average) men better than women; that is, we could say of these sports, 'So much worse for them!'

One of my colleagues, who likes to go to further extremes than I do,[2] has objected to my argument in the following way. If we should abolish sexual discrimination within sports, he asks, why not abolish species discrimination as well? Why not have men competing with animals? Why not have Carl Lewis running over 100m against a hunting leopard?

Well, the reason not to arrange such competitions is not only (or mainly) that it would be a difficult task to arrange them, or that such competitions are hardly likely to be rewarding to animals. Perhaps the difficulties could be overcome and perhaps some animals would take some pleasure in competing with men. The main reason for not arranging such competitions is that *no* man can beat *any* (healthy) hunting leopard. This is not merely a matter of a statistical generalisation. If there were a system similar to weight classes for running, then people and hunting leopards would have to compete in different classes.

However, if the differences between men and hunting leopards were merely statistical, so that some men could beat some hunting leopards, then I am not sure that competitions between men and beasts would seem so outlandish; after all, they used to have such competitions during antiquity. It is a delicate question for the animal liberation movement, of course, whether they should promote (because of an interest in abolishing species discrimination) such competitions or oppose them (because they may fear that the animals would not take pleasure in them).

To return to the human case. It is hard to assess finally how important the statistical genetic differences are between human beings within sports. And the assessment should not be made in any simplistic manner, where gender gets conflated with sex, nor should it be taken for granted that sport is a static phenomenon. The sports evolve, to some extent in a natural way, and to some extent as the result of our active and intentional intervention. If we do not like the fact that statistical genetic differences, such as sexual or racial differences, are decisive within sports, there is a lot we can do about it.

This leads to the next argument.

Female Sports Represent a Unique Value

It may seem that female sports are different from male sports, and so they represent a unique value. To give up sexual discrimination would therefore be like giving up valuable existing sports. It would be like giving up soccer or baseball, or basketball or hurdles in running.

How should we assess this argument? The answer to it is that, largely speaking, it is false and, to the extent that there is a grain of truth in it, this grain of truth does not warrant the conclusion that we should retain sexual discrimination in sports. Rather, it does warrant the conclusion that many aspects of sports need to be reformed, so that 'female' qualities are exchanged for 'male' ones.

Let me first comment on the major aspect of this objection—the mere falsity of it. In many ways, female sports are no different from male sports.

To a considerable and frightening extent, in many sports the male is simply the ideal. The good athlete is the hunter, the warrior, the man. And the conception of the masculine warrior is a narrow and simplistic one. In most athletic sports, Achilles could easily beat Ulysses. The cunning of the latter counts for nothing, whereas the superior strength of the former is decisive. This is also true when women take up these sports, and this is why women have to compete against each other and not against men. To put it drastically, therefore, I think it is fair to say that, in many sports, women compete against each other in masculinity, narrowly conceived. It is hard to find any special feminine qualities in *such* competitions.

What is the appropriate reaction to this obvious but little-publicised fact? Of course, this is hard to say. Some may find it unobjectionable. For my own part, I have to admit that I don't: I find the fact simply degrading, to both women and men. I also find that, if some women do want to compete in masculinity, why should they restrict themselves to a competition against each other? Why not compete also with men? After all, the best among them are capable of defeating most men even in masculinity. So why not do so?

It is not far-fetched to believe that, even if we *were* to do away with all kinds of gender bias within sports, in many sports a genuine sexual bias would remain. Statistically, men *are* better than women in many existing sports. I will return to this fact below and to the question of what to do about it.

However, there may still be a grain of truth in saying that women's sports in some aspects have unique qualities, I think, then of qualities that have less to do with mere physical strength and more to do with inventiveness, sensibility, cooperation, strategy, playfulness, wit, and so forth. There may be more room for these qualities in women's competitions And, to the extent that this is true, I think we are dealing with genuine and unique (female) qualities. However, there exists an obvious and better way of retaining these qualities than to retain sexual discrimination within sports. These qualities should be introduced in *all* sorts of sport, and they should not only be added to existing qualities, but, in many cases, be exchanged for existing qualities.

It may be fruitful to speak of these unique qualities, which I suspect are more frequent in women's sport than in men's sport, as qualities of—to use Sigmund Loland's term—'moderation.' Moderation in terms of what, though? Here I would like to be a bit more specific, in terms of gender, than Loland is himself. The object of the moderation, that which ought to be moderated, is arrogant outbursts of (male) aggressiveness and (mere) strength. These phenomena need not go away altogether, to be sure, moderated in the direction of values such as inventiveness, sensitivity, cooperation, playfulness and wit.

I think we are facing a happy coincidence here. Moderation is of great and growing importance within sports, not only as a means of rendering possible the abolition of sexual discrimination, but also as a means of saving sports as such, as a cultural phenomenon, from the most obvious threat to its continued existence.

The observation that moderation and sexual equality should go together is in accordance with a suggestion put forward in Jane English's much-discussed article, 'Sex Equality in Sports', even though (eventually) English reaches the conclusion that sexual discrimination within sports is necessary. She suggests that we develop a variety of sports in which an array of physical types can expect to excel:

> We tend to think of the possible sports as a somewhat fixed group of those currently available. Yet even basketball and football are of very recent invention. Since women have been virtually excluded from all sports until the last century, it is appropriate that some sports using women's specific traits are now developing, such as synchronized swimming.

A similar view has been put forward by Iris Marion Young, with reference to Mary E. Duquin. Young describes Duquin's position eloquently as follows:

> Androgyny in sport means for her the incorporation of virtues typically associated with women into the symbols and practices of sport—such as expressiveness and grace—along with a corresponding decline in the present overly aggressive and instrumentalist aspects of sport which are typically associated with masculinity.

Sports without moderation means competition in aspects such as mere strength. The problem with this is not that there is no public interest in competitions in strength; I think there is too *much* interest in such competitions. The problem with our fascination with strength is that it has a 'fascistoid' value basis. A further problem, of importance in the present context, is that mere strength, or the disposition for it, is a very simple and congenital quality, so mere strength is what we could call a *non*-moral virtue: either you have it or you don't. Moreover, there is every reason to believe that, not only is the disposition for strength congenital, but it has a rather simple *genetic explanation.* If this conjecture is borne out by realities, this means trouble for sports. For, certainly, once we can identify the genes for strength, which are really genes for winning in many existing sports, then it becomes possible genetically, not only to pre-select the winners, something that may seem frightening as such, but to *design* them. And, considering the enormous amounts *of* money and prestige that are invested in winning in sport, once the genetic design *of* winners becomes possible, it will take place. However, *if* we do design the winners genetically, then the public interest in sports competitions is likely to wither, or so I believe.

Genetic engineering, once it becomes possible, will be just as inevitable in sports as doping—unless we can render its application to sports impossible, And a way of rendering the genetic design *of* winners impossible is to change sports and to allow *moral* virtues to become crucial, for there are hardly any genes for inventiveness, sensitivity, cooperation, playfulness and wit in sports. All these virtues are true moral virtues: they can be learned (through training, to follow Aristotle) and, since there is a use for them outside the sports arenas as well, there is a point in learning them. To a considerable extent it is fair to say that these moral virtues, in contradistinction to the non-moral ones in sports, are typically 'female' (in the sense that there exist more *of* them in female sports than in male sports). So, at the same time, when we introduce more moderation into sports, in order to save sports from going extinct, we abolish the rationale behind sexual discrimination in sports, and we deepen the inherent value *of* sports as a cultural phenomenon.

All this means that, when we admire the winners of reformed (moderated) sports, our fascination for the winners will no longer bear a similarity to fascism, which is certainly an additional gain to be made.

Once we have reformed sports, by introducing more moderation into existing branches, and by adding new games to (and subtracting old ones from) the IOC list, we may safely give up sexual discrimination within sports and allow men and women to compete against each other on equal terms.

A Reductio Ad Absurdum of Sexual Discrimination

We have seen that the standard arguments in defence of sexual discrimination within sports are weak. Let me just add one more positive argument in defence of abolishing sexual discrimination; an argument that is a reductio ad absurdum of the rationale behind sexual discrimination.

What are we to test for, when we test whether a certain athlete qualifies as female or male? Three options are open to us. We could test for genitalia, for gender, or for chromosomal constitution.

There are obvious difficulties with all three options. However, we need to stick to some of them, otherwise we will not be able to guard ourselves against athletes who want to cheat—against athletes who are really men, but prefer to compete with women under the false pretext that they *are* women. Moreover, if we have a system of sexual discrimination, and do not perform tests, there is a positive risk that women who excel in sports are being mistakenly suspected of really being men rather than women. These excellent women need the chance to reject, once and for all, these kinds of rumours and false allegations, and only efficient tests can accomplish this task.

There are many problems connected with testing for genitalia. First of all, the criterion is vague. We are operating here with a continuum. After all, even if rare, there are examples of hermaphroditism. Second, it is not clear that the test for genitalia is a valid one. In what sense are genitalia relevant? In what sports *could* genitalia be relevant? I blush when I seek an answer to that question. Finally, genitalia can easily be manipulated: such tests are bound to be inefficient when it comes to people who (in an attempt to cheat) are prepared to undergo surgery.

The problems associated with testing for gender are even more obvious. First of all, this criterion is extremely vague. Perhaps the test should be the subjective sexual identification of the person in question, but this identification may be indeterminate. Furthermore, it may change over time. And then, once again, it is difficult to see any validity of such a test. In what sense does gender matter within sports? Finally, like a test for the appropriate genitalia, a test for appropriate gender would be only too easily fiddled with.

What, then, about chromosomal tests? These tests are what we rely on today, and I suppose that if we want to retain a system of sexual discrimination within sports, then chromosomal tests are what we have to rely on even in the future. The problem with chromosomal tests is not that they are vague or that they are easily manipulated. They rate high on measurements of specificity and sensitivity, if conducted in a meticulous way. They are also fairly easily conducted, they are not very invasive and, from the point of personal integrity, they are certainly less intrusive than tests for the appropriate genitalia.

Are chromosomal tests valid? Well, if we want to find variables that statistically speaking, correlate with sports performances, chromosomal tests may well be valid in some sports. I have argued that we should not discriminate on these grounds but, for the sake of the argument (for the sake of our reductio ad absurdum) let us assume that we should. Then a problem with our sex chromosomes is that, even if most people conform to a typical male constitution (they have the genotype XY) or a typical female constitution (they have the genotype XX), not everyone does. There are individuals with only one X chromosome (they have the genotype XO; that is, they suffer from what has been called Turner's syndrome), and there are individuals with two X chromosomes and one Y chromosome (they have the genotype XXY; that is, they suffer *from* what has been called Klinefelter's syndrome). Even these aberrations are of interest here. For it is natural to believe that, statistically speaking, people (women?) suffering from Turner's syndrome perform, in many sports, less efficiently than do 'ordinary' women, and it is also likely that, statistically speaking, people (men?) suffering from Klinefelter's syndrome perform less efficiently than do 'ordinary' men in many sports. There may also be sports where some of these groups have, statistically speaking, a slight advantage. This may have been true of a well-known Polish sprinter, Ewa Klobukowska, who turned out to have the chromosomal pattern XXY. This person may well have had an advantage in certain sports over most people with the XX chromosomal pattern because of her extra Y chromosome (she held the world record for the women's 100m).

All this means that, if we want to be consistent, and if we want to be true to the rationale behind sexual discrimination, we should go a step further and even introduce new discrimination categories (people suffering from Turner's syndrome and Klinefelter's syndrome, and people exhibiting other aberrations such as XYY, to mention just three examples). And, as was alluded to above, we may even have to introduce other kinds of genetic discrimination, such as racial discrimination, within sports, for different human races may on average perform more or less efficiently in certain sports.

However, this may strike most of us as downright absurd. But if it does, it means that we must give up the premise that led us to this conclusion. We must give up the very rationale behind the idea of sexual discrimination within sports. We must drop the assumption we adopted, for the sake of the argument—that it is appropriate to discriminate on grounds of genetic characteristics that, statistically speaking, favour or disfavour certain kinds of individuals in a certain sport.

We could add an even simpler argument to this. If we have sexual discrimination in sports, then (in order to avoid cheating and fraud) we need to have tests for sex. We have seen that these tests need to be chromosomal tests. However, it runs counter to a highly plausible idea of genetic integrity that information about a person's genetic constitution should ever be forced upon him or her (Schneider and Skirstad both seem to agree about this). We have a right *not* to know our genetic makeup, if we do not *want* to know it. Compulsory chromosomal tests for athletes violate this right.[3]

Conclusion

I have argued that, if we reform sports in the direction indicated by Sigmund Loland, and introduce more moderation into all kinds of sports, then we may safely give up sexual discrimination within sports. This is something that the IOC and the national sports organisations should do. And even if moderation in sports will prove to be utopian, I think we should give up sexual discrimination. But then the appropriate reaction from women may be to turn their backs on those kinds of elitist sports where males (on average and for simple genetic reasons) have the upper hand.

Certainly, this abolition of sexual discrimination is consistent with there remaining a possibility for those who like to arrange sports competitions for one sex exclusively, just as there exists a possibility for arranging special sports competitions for certain races, political beliefs or sexual orientations. However, in more official settings there should exist a strict ban on *all* such sorts of (from the point of view of sports itself) irrelevant discriminations. It should be incumbent upon the sports organisations themselves to make sure that such a ban becomes a reality. And it should also be a condition of obtaining public funding that a sport organisation does not discriminate between women and men.

The reform of sports indicated here does not guarantee that there are no branches where, statistically speaking, men will perform better than women (just as there may exist sports where, say, black people perform better than Caucasians), but this does not warrant that we retain a system of sexual discrimination, nor that we introduce racial discrimination within sports. We should all be perfectly capable of living with the truth that such differences exist—and freely allow them to surface in sports competitions. Yes, there are also likely to exist examples of sports where the order is reversed. This is certainly true of some equestrian sports, such as dressage. There has been only one male Olympic winner in dressage since 1968 but surely this is no reason to reintroduce sexual discrimination in dressage.

What should the reform of sports look like in more detail? I will leave this as an open question. The examples I have given (additional weight and height classes, the abolition of the winning service in tennis, and so forth), are mere speculations on my part. To develop this line of thought takes a kind of expertise that I do not possess. And the method of reform must of course be piecemeal rather than utopian. The various different sports events should be put under scrutiny, one at a time. However, the direction of change should be the same all over the field of sports events. Three desiderata of moderation should be met, when interventions in the development of sports take place:

• Non-moral virtues (such as strength) should be given a less important role, and moral virtues, (such as playfulness, inventiveness, sensitivity, cooperation and wit) a more important role, within sports.

• Sports should be developed in a direction that renders our admiration for the winners of sports competitions more decent.

• Sports should develop in a direction that makes it possible to abolish without any cost all kinds of sexual discrimination within sport.

If, and only if, these desiderata of moderation are met, will sports be able to thrive and flourish in the future and continue to add to the quality of our lives.

If these desiderata are (arrogantly) rejected, then, in a world where genetic engineering is quickly becoming a reality, the future prospects for athletics are bleak.

Arrogance and continued sexual discrimination will mean the marginalization of athletics, or so I suggest here. In particular, unless women are given an equal chance to compete with, and defeat, males within elitist sports, they have a good reason to turn their backs on elitist sports. And unless sports are made immune to the threat posed by genetic engineering, they will be looked upon with little interest by the general public, and will lose their role as important cultural phenomena.

Notes

1. I use the word 'discrimination' in a neutral, purely descriptive sense. Sexual discrimination takes place whenever men and women are treated differently, no matter whether or not this difference in treatment is warranted.

2. Hans Mathlein, Stockholm University

3. I defend the right in this strong form—which forbids insurance companies and employers to ask for information about the genotype of people or to use such information for any purposes whatever—in my book *Coercive Care,* London and New York; Routledge, 1999.

PART

V

Select Issues in the Social Ethics of Sport

Violence, Exploitation, Race, Spectatorship, and Disability

The essays in this section cover a wide range of controversial ethical issues associated with contemporary sport that touch on and thus implicate the larger social context in which they are conducted and organized. Alan Wertheimer's "The Exploitation of Student Athletes" begins this section by taking on one of the most contentious of such questions: whether the claim that student athletes are exploited by the colleges and universities that sponsor them can be made good. Wertheimer argues that it can, and he spins out his own detailed and complex account of exploitation to prove his point. But first he recounts two versions of the exploitation story commonly told about intercollegiate sports. In the first story, the exploitation of student athletes concerns the notion that colleges and universities receive significant economic and other social benefits from the performance of these athletes in return for which they often receive a shoddy education and seldom graduate. In this example, only bad institutions of higher education can be rightfully said to exploit their student athletes. In the second story, colleges and universities exploit student athletes because the benefits these institutions receive are significantly out of proportion to those the athletes receive, even if they manage to get a decent education and earn a degree. According to this example, practically all institutions of higher education can justifiably be said to exploit student athletes. Wertheimer's own account requires we critically revise what counts as exploitation of student athletes. Roughly put, exploitation for Wertheimer assumes the following form: "A exploits B only if A gains an advantage." In the particular terms of intercollegiate sports, that means only those colleges and universities that reap a surplus financial and social return off the performance of their student athletes can be justifiably charged with exploiting them.

At a minimum, this would most certainly include colleges and universities that run big-time athletic programs.

The next two selections, Robert L. Simon's "Violence in Sports" and Nicholas Dixon's "Boxing, Paternalism, and Legal Moralism," tackle headlong the question whether boxing, a sport that differs from all other sports, including contact sports such as football, in so far as its competitors intentionally aim to inflict physical harm on one another, should be morally sanctioned by a civilized society. Although clearly troubled by the violent bent of boxing, Simon is not persuaded that the two main arguments for banning boxing—that boxing harms the participants and also harms larger society—go through because of the very real threats they pose to our individual liberties. Nevertheless, although there might not be any good arguments to eliminate boxing, Simon thinks there are good reasons for morally reforming it so as to blunt its violent edges and sharpen the skills it brings into play. As a model here he ingeniously points to the case of fencing, which not so long ago was known as "dueling" and was a bloody encounter that usually ended in one of the combatant's death and in the maiming of all concerned. Today, however, fencing not only carries a new name but a new cachet, as a sport which puts a premium on skill and hardly ever results in physical harm to any of its participants. Perhaps, Simon surmises, a similar path could be charted for boxing in which the skills it employs are played up and the violence toned down by requiring, among other things, mandatory headgear, outlawing blows to the head, and an emphasis on skill rather than the infliction of physical damage.

Dixon's paper follows a similar line of argument as Simon's as he, too, doesn't think there are any compelling arguments to justify a ban on boxing—specifically, a ban on professional boxing, which is his primary focus here—and because he thinks there are, contrarily, good arguments to be made on behalf of morally reforming boxing, especially outlawing blows to the head. So it comes as no surprise that Dixon is not swayed by arguments from harm, nor from arguments that insist boxers are coerced or unduly pressured to pursue careers in boxing because most of them come from disadvantaged backgrounds. His analysis of coercion in this regard is the most sophisticated of any published account of boxing that I am familiar with. But if we cannot ban boxing because the harm it causes participants and fans alike is morally neutralized by the consent of those who participate in and watch it, we can seek to place moral constraints on how it is executed—that is, we can ban blows to the head, because of the morally offensive attitudes it fosters (the view that we can prohibit certain actions if they are immoral is precisely the view known as "legal moralism," which explains why this notion appears in Dixon's title). After all, the aim of boxing is to incapacitate one's opponent, preferably by knocking him or her unconscious. Here we can speak of moral wrong rather than simple harm because to treat others as mere objects to be physically pummeled is genuinely morally offensive. And this goes as much for the boxers themselves as it does for spectators, since to take pleasure in the physical misfortune of others (schadenfreude) from the safety and comfort of one's ringside seats or living room couch is morally wrong and borders on sadism.

John Valentine's "Darwin's Athletes: A Review Essay," is a review of a controversial book of the same name by John Hoberman that critically examines the role race plays in modern sports. But in an important respect Valentine's essay is more than a review of a provocative book, though one of its main strengths is its concise rendering and articulation of Hoberman's arguments. It is also an important critique of arguments such as those found in *Darwin's Athletes* that paint, according to Valentine, too bleak a picture of race in sport. Valentine begins by setting out the main two-part argument Hoberman advances in his book:

1. African-Americans have had imposed on them by Western racism a damaging primitive "physicalized" identity from which they still have not been able to extricate themselves.

2. In the contemporary era, this crippling identity has been "athleticized" through black Americans' own engagement in and patronage of sports.

As Hoberman sees it, then, it is black Americans' own fixation on sports that makes them at least in part complicit in their own subordination, a sport-induced complicity that has managed to co-opt, Hoberman further argues, not just black intellectuals but even black critics of sports, such as Harry Edwards. There are many problematic features of this African American obsession with sport, but perhaps the two most worrisome features for Hoberman have to do with its stifling of the intellectual expression of black Americans that plays directly into the stereotype of "black intellectual inferiority," as well as its fostering of the dangerous illusion that more racial progress has occurred in America than actually has been achieved. Although Valentine is largely supportive of much of what Hoberman argues for, he does think that Hoberman's analysis overreaches in at least two senses. First, it overstates both sport's complicity in the racial suppression of African Americans and the lack of progress in racial affairs in this country. Although Valentine thinks we have a long way to go before there is genuine racial equality in America, he also thinks that some important progress has been made in this regard that would be foolhardy to deny. Second, he argues that Hoberman's critique moves from the plausible view that the life of the mind should not be underestimated in a knowledge-based society such as our own to the far less plausible, and most likely implausible, view of the superiority of intellectual expression over physical expression. And it is this latter supposition, Valentine concludes, that explains much of the resistance Hoberman's book has encountered in the African American community, a claim which he neatly gets across with the following rhetorical question: "How would Jewish Americans, for example, countenance the assumption that the value they place upon intellectual expression is to be viewed first and foremost as a compensation for the limitations placed upon Jews by the diaspora?"

Gerald Early's "Sports, Political Philosophy, and the African American" chimes with Valentine's more balanced treatment of this complex topic. In an interesting twist, however, Early begins by noting that in the nineteenth century whites mostly regarded blacks as the "lady of the races," as mainly feminine in character and disposition. That is to say, black Americans were seen by their white counterparts as more religious, as more inclined to the arts and oratory, as more emotional than whites, and as less athletic even though physically powerful—which explains why blacks were barred from participating in sports dominated by whites on the grounds of their supposed athletic inferiority. This image of the effeminate black was popularized by the best-selling novel of 1852, Harriet Beecher Stowe's *Uncle Tom's Cabin*, in the persona of Uncle Tom himself—which today, of course, survives mainly as a racial epithet. Although an imposing physical specimen, Uncle Tom was not an aggressive man and certainly not an athlete. Early shows how it didn't take long for this image of the effeminate black to be transposed, through the magic of what he calls "romantic racialism," into its opposite: the hyper-masculinized black athlete and "showy" black mass cultural entertainer of the contemporary period. The point of romantic racialism, Early tells us, is primarily to allay the anxieties of whites by presenting blacks in nonthreatening terms. For Uncle Tom, that meant rendering his massive physique safe by passing him off as a passive nonathletic being. For the modern day black athlete, that meant, and here he directly connects up with Hoberman's argument, ensuring that their ample physicality and attitude was controlled by the presence of white authority figures (coaches, league officials, and, of course, owners). Safely cordoned off from the rest of white America, whites were now more than willing to grant black Americans athletic superiority, especially because that black advantage was considered conclusive evidence of white intellectual superiority. In this respect at any rate, Early concurs in Hoberman's negative assessment of sports as contributing to the romantic racialist assumption of the "natural black athlete." But like Valentine and contra theorists of Hoberman's persuasion, Early thinks this is a much too one-sided view of American sports that overlooks the important role sports played in "widening the concept of democracy in America."

The next set of essays, Torbjörn Tännsjö's sensibility-jarring "Is Our Admiration for Sports Heroes Fascistoid?" and Nicholas Dixon's more sobering "The Ethics of Supporting Sports Teams," present radically different views of the morality of sports spectatorship. Tännsjö's piece wastes no time going for the jugular, essentially arguing that anyone who shows more than a passing interest in the exploits of elite individual athletes is probably a fascist, or to use his neologism, a "fascistoid" (which means "tends to or resembles fascism," just as the analogous word "schizoid" means "tends to or resembles schizophrenia"). To see this seemingly strained connection, it is first necessary to recognize that fascism has much more to do with contempt for weakness than it does with chauvinism. Once we get our arms around this point, Tännsjö thinks we are two short steps away from confirming his striking thesis. The first step is the simple one, or so he claims, of recognizing that athletic excellence is all about demonstrating one's physical superiority over others, which (it should not go unremarked because it makes the admiration of such athletic accomplishments all that much worse) is a largely undeserved superiority because only those who come out on top in the genetic lottery are capable of the Herculean physical feats regularly performed by high-performance athletes. The second and perhaps more difficult step is to see that in admiring winning elite athletes we spectators cannot but help hold those they defeat, the losers, in contempt. This is evidenced, according to Tännsjö, by the fact that in contemporary sports the winner is accorded all the spoils of wealth and fame while the loser gets literally nothing save the wrath of irate fans. This point is also supported by the markedly pernicious way we spectators brand losers (even those who are highly successful athletes but fail, for whatever reason, to win the "big" one), as is apparent in such familiar but hardly innocuous scolds as that coming in second is like being first among losers.

As noted, Dixon's article comes down on the other side of this moral estimate of sport spectatorship, arguing that such attachment to teams is not only morally permissible but, under certain conditions, "positively virtuous." However, Dixon's moral defense of sport spectatorship is a qualified one and thus restricted to what he calls the "moderate partisan," a particular type of fan who embodies certain qualities of both the so-called "purist" fan and the "partisan" fan. Purist fans are those who reserve their allegiance to the team playing best, and who are, therefore, moved only by displays of superior athletic performance. Purists are far less interested in the outcome than the typical partisan fan and far more concerned that the games they watch are "good" ones in which the winners prevail because they are the most talented and excellent players. By contrast, partisan fans are not only moved by displays of athletic excellence but factor into their allegiance as well whether the team they support and root for has some relevant connection to them—for instance, whether they personally know or follow the players or whether the players represent the community in which they live. Whereas, then, partisan fans stick by their teams come hell or high water, no matter how badly they might fare in a given game, purist fans maintain a more neutral posture to ensure that whatever team they support is the best one, which is why they switch their allegiance whenever the teams they follow fall short of demonstrating athletic superiority. Given the impartial stance of the purist fan, it is tempting to say they deserve greater moral acclaim than their partisan counterparts who are anything but impartial in judging what teams they will support. But in an illuminating analogy to romantic love, Dixon persuasively shows why we should resist this temptation. For in certain relevant ways the partisan fans' devotion to their team is akin to the devotion lovers have for one another, in which our initial attraction to our partners on some set of qualities important to us grows into a much more profound connection that no longer pivots around those qualities per se but around our partner's "unique instantiation of those qualities." That is why if we truly are in love with our partners, we do not "trade up" for someone else who happens to come along and scores higher on such qualities. Rather, we maintain our love for and commitment to our partners owing to the special place they hold in our lives. This same stick-to-it-ness characterizes partisan fans who refuse to relinquish their support for their teams for another team that scores higher on the athletic excellence scale. However, just as love can be blind, so can partisan spectatorship, which is why Dixon thinks we need a blend of the kind of team loyalty we associate with the partisan fan and the devotion to athletic excellence we associate with the purist fan. That blend yields, argues Dixon, the "moderate" fan who will withdraw support from a team when they no longer morally deserve it, such as when their players violate the moral virtues and qualities on which "good" sport depends.

The last essay of this section, Anita Silver's and David Wasserman's "Convention and Competence: Disability Rights in Sports and Education," turns our attention to the oft-ignored legal and moral problems posed by the accommodation of disabled athletes. The passage of Title III, the Americans With Disabilities Act (ADA), was a landmark event in American jurisprudence, prohibiting discrimination against disabled persons in public accommodations, which covered not just institutions but various cultural practices and events as well. The key question this act raised is whether "reasonable" accommodations can be made to such institutions and practices to include disabled people. By "reasonable" was meant can such accommodations be enacted without "fundamentally altering" the "essential nature" of the activity or good in question. The authors single out here the much-publicized case of the professional golfer Casey Martin who petitioned the Professional Golf Association (PGA) to allow him to use a golf cart on the tour because of a disability he had that not only made walking difficult for him but also exposed him to serious physical harm. The obvious question raised by this case is what fundamental role, if any, walking plays in determining excellence in golf, which, in turn, requires consideration of just what is the main point and purpose of golf. The court found in favor of Martin, and the authors concur in that legal judgment. For like the court they were persuaded that walking plays little role in assessing excellence in golf and certainly in no way compares to shot-making in determining such excellence. They argued further that using a cart did not give Martin an unfair advantage over his competitors; after all, Martin suffered excruciating pain on practically every shot he attempted. And finally they argued that there is no credible doubt regarding Martin's obvious competence in golf. In cases like these then, Silvers and Wasserman are convinced and convincing that there are good reasons to argue that certain sports be modified in certain ways to accommodate highly skilled disabled athletes.

Despite the importance of social ethical analyses of sport that take seriously how ethical controversies in this carefully demarcated sphere of life touch on larger ethical controversies in society, the philosophical writing devoted to these salient issues is, to say the least, rather sparse. It is with this fact in mind that Peter French's recent monograph, *Ethics and College Sports*, represents a welcome addition to ethical inquiries that focus on intercollegiate sports. Judith Andre's and David James' important collection of essays, *Rethinking College Athletics*, should be mentioned in the same breath with French's here, not to mention Robert Simon's second edition of *Fair Play: Ethics in Sport*, whose penetrating analyses of the ethical role and place of intercollegiate athletics warrant a close read.[1] The controversial sport of boxing has attracted a number of critical pieces, but again the philosophical literature here is rather spotty. Herrera's "The Moral Controversy Over Boxing" and Davis' "Ethical Issues in Boxing" are notable exceptions.[2] Race in sport is yet another example of a contentious social issue that has drawn wide notice especially in the social science and social theory of sport literature but very little notice in the philosophical or ethical literature. Hoberman's controversial rendering of this controversial issue in *Darwin's Athletes* is something of an exception to this trend, notwithstanding its critical historicist aims, as is Mosley's "Racial Differences in Sports: What's Ethics Got to Do With It?"[3] The ethical literature dealing with sports spectatorship is also underdetermined, consisting mostly of critical responses to Tännsjö's essay featured in this section. In particular, Tamburrini's "Sports, Fascism, and the Market" and Holowchak's "'Fascistoid' Heroism Revisited: A Deontological Twist to a Recent Debate" follow this critical line, while Jones' "The Traditional Football Fan: An Ethical Critique of Selective Construction" goes chasing after different quarry.[4] Finally, ethical explorations of sport from the standpoint of disabled athletes are as far as I can tell practically nonexistent aside from Silver's and Wasserman's essay included in this section. This is a curious omission because this issue is garnering more and more attention in philosophical and ethical circles, as evidenced in part by the most recent issue of the critically acclaimed journal *Ethics*, which features a "Symposium on Disability."[5]

Notes

1. Peter A. French, *Ethics and College Sports* (New York: Rowman & Littlefield Publishers, 2004); Judith Andre and David James, eds., *Rethinking College Athletics* (Philadelphia: Temple University Press, 1990); Robert Simon, *Fair Play: Ethics in Sport*, 2nd ed. (Boulder, CO: Westview Press).

2. C. D. Herrara, "The Moral Controversy Over Boxing," *Journal of the Philosophy of Sport*, XXIX, no. 2 (2002): 163-173; Paul Davis, "Ethical Issues in Boxing," *Journal of the Philosophy of Sport*, XXI, (1984): 48-63.

3. John Hoberman, *Darwin's Athletes: How Sport Has Damaged Black America and Preserved the Myth of Race* (New York: Houghton Mifflin, 1997); Albert Mosley, "Racial Differences in Sport: What's Ethics Got to Do With It?" in *Philosophy of Sport: Critical Readings, Critical Issues.* ed. M. A. Holowchak (Upper Saddle River, NJ: Prentice Hall, 2002), 437-445.

4. Claudio Tamburrini, "Sports, Fascism, and the Market," *Journal of the Philosophy of Sport*, XXV, (1998): 23-34; M. Andrew Holowchak, "'Fascistoid' Heroism Revisited: A Deontological Twist to a Recent Debate," *Journal of the Philosophy of Sport*, XXXII, Issue 1 (2005): 96-104; Carwyn Jones, "The Traditional Football Fan: An Ethical Critique of a Selective Construction," *Journal of the Philosophy of Sport*, XXX, no. 1 (2003): 37-50.

5. "Symposium on Disability," *Ethics*. 116, no. 1 (October 2005): 1-213.

The Exploitation of Student Athletes

◆

Alan Wertheimer

The claim that American universities exploit student athletes is frequently made and sometimes denied. In capsule form, the exploitation story goes something like this. "Big-time" college athletic programs—a description that is typically limited to football and men's basketball at a limited number of institutions—provide significant financial benefits to the institution. The athletic programs generate direct revenue from ticket sales, television contracts, trading cards, and a growing business in royalties for licensing the university's seal, logo, and colors.[1] Athletic programs may also generate indirect revenue in the form of contributions from alumni/ae, whose commitment to the institution is said to be tied to the success of the athletic programs. In addition, a state's willingness to appropriate funds for public institutions may reflect the importance of the institution's athletic program.

In exchange for these benefits to the institution, the universities give several benefits to the student athletes. The athletes receive the opportunity to obtain a college education and a college degree, and this at institutions to which they may not have been admitted on the basis of their academic record. They are provided with full scholarships, covering tuition, room, and board. And because professional football and basketball recruit virtually all their players from the college ranks, some student athletes receive the opportunity to play in professional sports.[2] In exchange for those benefits, student athletes must practice for as much as thirty hours per week during the athletic season, keep in condition during the off season, maintain their academic eligibility, and, of course, perform.

Why is this arrangement thought to be exploitative? There are two versions of the exploitation story. One version maintains that the institution receives substantial

Reprinted, by permission, from A. Wertheimer, 1996, *Exploitation,* (Princeton, NJ: Princeton University Press), 77-95.

benefits from the performance of these student athletes, while the student athletes fail to receive a genuine college education and a college degree. True, some universities (e.g., Penn State, Michigan, Notre Dame, Duke) have reputations as the "good guys," as schools that have reasonably high admissions standards for student athletes and from which most student athletes graduate.[3] These institutions seem to make reasonably high academic demands on their athletes and provide the support necessary to enable most student athletes to meet them. By contrast, other institutions (e.g., North Carolina State, Nevada–Las Vegas, Oklahoma) have reputations for low admission standards, little concern for the academic progress of their athletes, and low graduation rates for the athletes.[4] This version of the exploitation story claims that only the "bad" institutions are exploitative because the university profits while the student athletes do not receive "anything lasting in return."[5]

The second version of the exploitation story claims that universities exploit student athletes because the gains to the institution and its student athletes are grossly asymmetrical: even if the student athletes receive a high-quality education and a college degree, they do not receive an appropriate return on the financial surplus that they generate. This version of the exploitation story applies to both "good" and "bad" institutions. Are student athletes exploited? If so, which version of the exploitation story is correct?

The University's Gain

I have suggested that A exploits B only if A gains from the transaction. Let us first consider the gains to the university. We can categorize university athletic programs on two dimensions: scope and surplus. With respect to scope, I distinguish between big-time and small-time athletic programs. A big-time athletic program is one that competes at the highest level, seeks national prominence, and provides almost all student athletes (in the major sports) with full scholarships. I consider virtually all the institutions in the major conferences (e.g., Big Ten, Big Eight, Southeast, Atlantic Coast, Pacific Ten, etc.) and some independent institutions (e.g., Notre Dame) to be big-time programs. By contrast, small-time programs do not aspire to national rankings, and few student athletes receive financial aid unrelated to financial need, although many would not have been admitted to the institution on the basis of their academic record alone. These institutions include almost all small private colleges, most small public universities, and some major private universities (e.g., Harvard, Yale, Chicago) that do not emphasize their athletic programs (although there may be intense athletic rivalries among them). With respect to surplus, I distinguish between those athletic programs that actually produce surplus revenue (direct and indirect) for the institution and those that do not. As we shall see, whether athletic programs produce surplus revenue will depend upon the breadth of our conception of surplus revenue. On a broad conception, more athletic programs produce surplus revenue than a financial analysis would suggest. But let us start with surplus financial revenue, as it is ordinarily understood. Given the two distinctions, four types of institutions are theoretically possible: (a) big-time, with surplus revenue; (b) small-time, with surplus revenue; (c) big-time, without surplus revenue; and (d) small-time, without surplus revenue (see figure 28.1).

I place a question mark in cell (b) because it may be empty. I do not know that any small-time programs produce significant surplus financial revenue. More important for present purposes, there may be many type (c) programs, big-time programs that do not produce a significant financial surplus. Big-time athletic programs are very expensive. An unsuccessful team is not likely to generate significant revenues from television and postseason (or tournament) play. In addition, the ability of athletic programs to generate alumni/ae donations (particularly donations from which academic programs benefit) appears to be vastly overstated.[6]

If we concentrate on big-time programs, it should be noted that there is no necessary correlation between the

	Big-time	Small-time
Surplus	(a)	(b) ?
No surplus	(c)	(d)

FIGURE 28.1

Reprinted, by permission, from A. Wertheimer, 1996, *Exploitation* (Princeton, NJ: Princeton University Press), 81.

capacity of the program to generate a surplus and the institution's commitment to the academic progress of its student athletes. There are "good" and "bad" institutions in both the surplus and nonsurplus categories. But the distinction between surplus and nonsurplus institutions raises a central issue with respect to exploitation. I have argued that one person can exploit another only if the alleged exploiter gains from the relationship. If this is so, then nonsurplus institutions do not exploit student athletes because their student athletes do not produce a net surplus for the institution.

To say that nonsurplus institutions do not exploit their student athletes is not to let them off the moral hook. They may be callously indifferent to the interests of their student athletes. We might say that these institutions are attempting to exploit student athletes or are acting exploitatively because they are trying to generate a surplus from the efforts of the athletes. And we may say that attempted (or unsuccessful) exploitation is seriously wrong, just as we regard attempted (unsuccessful) crimes as both wrong and punishable.[7] Note, however, that while the victim of a battery may have a civil claim for compensation against the offender, the intended victim of an attempted battery (where A throws a punch at B but misses) has no such civil claim. Similarly, even though nonsurplus institutions may be acting wrongly, their student athletes could not complain that they are being denied a fair share of the profits they generated for their institution, for no profits were generated.

It might be objected that I have adopted an excessively narrow view of exploitation. It may be thought that A exploits B when A "uses" B merely as a means for A's own ends and without proper regard for B's interests, even if A does not gain or does not gain unfairly from A's use of B. I believe that this objection fails. First, it is not clear that A violates the Kantian maxim if A respects B's capacity to consent to a transaction, even if A uses B's situation as a means to A's own ends. Second, so long as we can say that it is wrong for A to act exploitatively toward B, I see no reason for the Kantian to resist the view that successful exploitation requires an actual advantage to A. Third, acting "exploitatively" in that sense does not always seem wrong. We typically treat others primarily as a means to our own ends in ordinary market transactions. Even if we would prefer a world in which buyers and sellers treated each other as ends in themselves rather than merely as means to their own ends (although, and depending upon what this all means, I'm not sure that we would prefer such a world), the supermarket does not take unfair advantage of the customer (or vice versa) if A does not gain an advantage from B, whatever the spirit in which the parties undertake the transaction.

It is worth noting that the argument I am advancing here is consistent with a Marxian account of exploitation. On a Marxist view, "exploitation is the appropriation by a class of nonworkers of the surplus product of a class of workers."[8] On this view, if workers generate no surplus product beyond what is necessary for their subsistence, there can be no exploitation. And this, says Richard Arneson, is a disturbing implication of that account:

> This implies there is no exploitation in a slave society *in extremis* in which conditions of production have declined so that slaves do not produce more than is needed for their subsistence but are continually starved so that their master may live sumptuously. In the ordinary sense of the term there could hardly be exploitation more brutal that this.[9]

It is not clear that Arneson has reason to be concerned about the implications of his example. First, although there is no surplus product, when surplus is defined technically in terms of what is required for the slaves' subsistence, the masters are extracting a surplus from the slaves because the slaves are receiving less than subsistence requires. It is true that such a practice might be self-defeating from the master's perspective but that is a different matter.

But suppose that the masters continue to provide for the slaves' subsistence during the decline in productivity, say, so that they can have a group of productive slaves when better times return. During this period, the masters continue to live well off the surplus accrued previous periods, but they extract no surplus from the current slaves. I see no reason to resist the view that the slaves are not exploited during this unusual period. We have other terms available to describe the wrongful treatment of the slaves.

Although I am comfortable with the view that exploitation requires a surplus, the previous discussion raises the question as to how to define, measure, and locate that surplus. Suppose that a big-time but nonsurplus institution correctly claims that its football program generates no financial surplus, given the high salaries that are paid to a coaching staff, but that there would be a substantial surplus if the revenues were not used to pay exorbitantly high salaries to an excessive number of persons.[10] If the surplus is effectively "hidden" in the cost structure of the enterprise, there still exists precisely the sort of financial surplus that makes exploitation possible, although it might be more accurate to say that it is the recipients of the salaries who are exploiting the student athletes and not the "institution" as such.[11]

This gives rise to a more general point. To say that the "university" is reaping the surplus is to speak metaphorically. Does the surplus go to the library? To faculty salaries? The Classics Department? To scholarships for needy students? Does the surplus pay for gender equity by subsidizing women's athletic programs that run a financial deficit?[12] It is, of course, extremely difficult to identify the recipients of a surplus in an organization with a complex budget, although we do not need to know who receives the benefits in order to know that the student athletes do not. This also suggests that we need to distinguish between those who make the decisions that generate and allocate a surplus and the recipients of the surplus themselves. The recipients maybe entirely unaware that they are benefiting from a surplus derived from the efforts of others.

In addition to issues connected to *financial* surpluses, it might be claimed that the student athletes are generating nonfinancial benefits for which they are not compensated. They provide entertainment for students, faculty, alumni/ae, and the general public, some of whom receive the benefit on television or radio. They may assist in recruitment of students (and dare I say faculty?). A state's major public institutions may be an important source of "state pride." In these cases, it is not that the universities are hiding financial revenues. Rather, the student athletes create important benefits that are not converted into financial revenues. If nonfinancial benefits to the universities should be regarded as the sort of surplus gain that makes exploitation possible, then many institutions that appear to be of type (c) are actually type (a), and perhaps some type (d) institutions are actually type (b) institutions. In addition, if the non-revenue-generating benefits to others (entertainment, state pride) should be regarded as the sort of surplus gain that makes exploitation possible, then it is possible that other persons are receiving benefits through the institution's activities apart from any benefits to the university itself. In any case, this suggests that moral criteria are required not only to evaluate the distribution of a social surplus but to establish the presence and magnitude of a social surplus.

The Student Athlete

Suppose that the student athlete, B, is a football player enrolled at University A, a type (a) institution that generates a significant surplus from its football program. Let us also assume that B contributes to the competitive and (therefore) financial success of the athletic program.[13] Is B exploited? And, if so, is it a case of harmful exploitation or mutually advantageous exploitation?

Before we can consider these questions, I think that we need to confront directly the character of the educational and athletic benefits that B receives from A. Let us consider the educational opportunities first. We should understand such benefits in terms of their *ex ante* value rather than their *ex post* value. In one sense, educational opportunities are like a lottery ticket. There is no guarantee that anyone admitted to an institution will succeed, athlete or nonathlete. If A were to give B a lottery ticket that has a .50 chance of winning a $100 prize, it would be wrong for B to claim, *ex post,* that he or she had received nothing of value just because the ticket didn't win. Similarly, it would be a mistake to claim that University A gives nothing of value to Student B merely because Student B does not graduate or receive an education. And that, of course, brings out the sense in which a college education is unlike a lottery ticket: For whether B actually receives an education or a degree depends in large part although not altogether upon whether B makes the appropriate effort. The *ex post* value of the educational opportunity is at least somewhat subject to B's control.[14] Thus the question is not whether B actually receives an education or graduates, but specifying that *ex ante* value of the educational resources or opportunities that are provided to B.

The value of educational opportunities to B is, of course, not only a function of B's efforts; it is also a function of B's capacity to use those opportunities. Some students, whom I shall call "low-ability" students, are not capable of succeeding in an academic environment. Some such students have considerable natural ability, but are woefully underprepared to succeed in an academic environment. Others may lack the natural ability to succeed. In any case, and whatever the source of the deficiency in capacity to succeed, it is distinctly possible that some students lack the capacity to profit from college courses and do not have a reasonable chance of obtaining a college degree, even with good support.

Are low-ability students vulnerable to exploitation?[15] On the assumption that low-ability students can somehow maintain their academic eligibility and thus continue to engage in intercollegiate athletics, it is arguably unfair for A to receive a benefit from B's services when B cannot receive a compensating benefit from A. It might be replied that A does not exploit B if B voluntarily assumes the risk of not benefiting from the educational opportunities provided by A. But this is wrong. First, I believe that A can exploit B even if B consents to the exploitation. Second, it is not clear that this exploitation is genuinely consensual. If it is not B's intention to make a gift of his or her services to A, if we assume that B expects to gain from the educational opportunities offered by A, then we may also have reason to think that B does not have the information or judgment necessary to voluntarily assume such risks.

There is, of course, another package of benefits that the university provides to student athletes, and those are related to athletic participation itself. First, student athletes may value playing college sports in its own right. Second, big-time athletic programs also provide the opportunity for student athletes to become professional athletes. They provide training facilities, coaching, publicity, and exposure. It is true that only a small proportion of student athletes ever become professional athletes, so the value of the athletic opportunity may be relatively low. But it is not nothing. Indeed, for some students, the value of the athletic opportunity, low as it may be, will be greater than the value of the educational opportunities.

Suppose that the value of the athletic opportunities to student athletes is reasonably high. It might nonetheless be argued that an adequate moral accounting of a relationship requires a principle for allocating credit for the values that are received in the context of that relationship. Thus it might be argued that we must distinguish between the athletic opportunities that are *provided by* A and opportunities that B receives from *having been* at A, and that when we make this distinction, we will find that the benefits provided by A are less than they may seem. Alumni/ae may believe that they should acknowledge and reciprocate the value of the education they received from their universities, but do not think that they need to acknowledge and reciprocate the university because it provided the context in which they made lifelong friends or their spouses. Similarly, it is arguable that the university not receive (all) the credit for the exposure that student athletes receive, even if it provides the context in which they receive exposure.

Let us put the previous worries aside. Let us assume that we are able to evaluate the *ex ante* value of the educational and athletic opportunities received by B at surplus generating institutions (however that surplus is measured). Let us assume that the value of those opportunities at what I shall call a "good" institution, A_G, is equivalent to X and that the value of the opportunities provided at a "bad" institution, A_B, is much less, say, .2 X. Are student athletes exploited at A_B and A_G? If so, is it a case of harmful exploitation or mutually advantageous exploitation? Table 28.1 lists the plausible possibilities (where HE = harmful exploitation, MAE = mutually advantageous exploitation, and NE = no exploitation).

For case 1 or 2 or 3 to be the case, it must be true that student athletes are typically harmed by their relationship with their institutions at both A_G and A_B (case 1) or at A_G (cases 2 and 3). What would that mean? On the most natural reading, to say that student athletes are harmed by their experience is to say that they are typically less well off as student athletes than they otherwise would have been. To verify that claim, we would require some counterfactual information. We need to know what would B's life would have been like if B had

TABLE 28.1

	A_G	A_B
1	HE	HE
2	NE	HE
3	MAE	HE
4	MAE	MAE
5	NE	MAE
6	NE	NE

Reprinted, by permission, from A. Wertheimer, 1996, *Exploitation* (Princeton, NJ: Princeton Univesity Press), 87.

not gone to college.[16] This is important. For despite all of the commentaries on the myriad ways in which student athletes are mistreated, I know of no studies that attempt to compare the overall life prospects of student athletes with others who are similar to them in terms of relevant variables (e.g., race, class, academic ability, and athletic ability) but who do not attend college or attend as nonathletes. Suppose that things go badly for Student B at A_B or A_G. B rarely attends classes and learns very little, does not graduate, and does not receive an offer to play professional sports. It is still possible that B's life goes better if B becomes a student athlete than if B does not.[17] If, for example, B would otherwise be unemployed or employed in a low-skill job, it is arguable that four or five years of free room and board and some degree of local fame is not a bad deal. And even if the student does not graduate, having some additional educational experience may prove to be a long-term benefit.

And this suggests still another consideration. In attempting to determine whether the typical student athlete is harmed by the college experience, we must take a view that aggregates the college years and the postcollege years. It is possible that the effects on B are similar in both periods, that B's life goes better (or worse) during both the college and postcollege years than it otherwise would. But it is also possible that these two periods have different effects on B's life. It is possible that B's life in college goes better than it would have gone had B not attended college, but that B's subsequent life prospects are worse, say, because B gives up the opportunity to learn a trade or join the military. On the other hand, it is possible that B's life in college goes worse than it otherwise would have gone, but that B's postcollege life goes better because of the knowledge and contacts that B acquires. Bracketing such aggregation problems, we can say that if B's life goes worse if he or she attends A_G or A_B than if he or she had not attended college at all, then we may have a case of harmful exploitation. Otherwise, not.

Suppose that the typical student athlete is not harmed by the college experience. Does it follow that B is not exploited? One writer has maintained that a student athlete is exploited only if "he would have otherwise done something else more constructive with his time."[18] On this view, only cases 1, 2, and 6 are conceptually possible—no harm, no exploitation. But this view assumes what has to be shown and what I have denied, namely, that mutually advantageous exploitation is not possible. Moreover, most critics do not claim that student athletes are worse off as a result of their college experience than they otherwise would have been. They do not claim that the students are harmed. Rather, they say that the student athletes are not as well off as they should be, given that they attend college, particularly given the benefits that these students provide to their universities. The problem is to determine just what that might mean. After all, even if we were to say that student athletes are not exploited because they are not harmed, we must still determine whether their package of benefits is adequate.

Figure 28.2 represents the value that B receives from A_G or A_B along a continuum. X represents the value that B receives from College A_G.

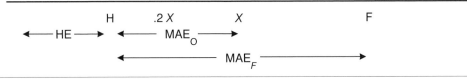

FIGURE 28.2
Reprinted, by permission, from A. Wertheimer, 1996, *Exploitation* (Princeton, NJ: Princeton Univesity Press), 89.

A_G provides its student athletes with appropriate educational opportunities. Its graduation record is high. Its students take rigorous academic programs. Its coaches demand that students attend classes, and so on. By contrast, A_B provides .2 X to its student athletes. Its record is low. Its students take nonrigorous courses. Its coaches take a laissez-faire attitude with respect to students' academic progress and so on. H represents the point below which B is harmed by the college experience. F represents what B would receive if B were to receive a "fair share" of A's surplus on whatever theory of fairness should turn out to be most acceptable. On one view (what I label MAE_O), B is exploited only when B receives less than X, an "objective" or "independent" standard as to what a student should receive from an institution. On another view (what I label MAE_F), B is exploited if B receives less than F, if B does not receive a fair share of the surplus that his or her performance has generated. If we accept MAE_O, then case 5 is true: A_B exploits its student athletes, but A_G does not. If we accept MAE_F, then case 4 is true: A_G and A_B both exploit student athletes.

Which is the better account of exploitation? There are several reasons for thinking that MAE_O is to be preferred. First—although this is technically not a reason for preferring MAE_O—it should be noted that when critics claim that colleges exploit student athletes, they typically imply that when colleges provide genuine educational opportunities, they are not engaged in exploitation.[19] And MAE_O distinguishes between A_G and A_B with respect to exploitation whereas MAE_F does not.

Second, MAE_F implies that type (a) (surplus and big-time) institutions exploit their students whereas type (c) and (d) (nonsurplus) institutions do not, even though students at type (c) and (d) institutions may be worse off than students at A_G (and even A_B). It requires us to say that whether B is exploited turns not on the value of the educational resources that B is receiving, but on how well the *institution* is doing. And on the assumption that B is receiving a solid package of educational resources, it might seem mean-spirited to claim that B is exploited if the institution also happens to receive a benefit from his or her performance, but that B is not exploited just because the institution does not.

A third argument for preferring MAE_O to MAE_F is that our very conception of college athletics seems to bar a university from sharing its surplus with student athletes. We may think that student athletes should receive no less than X if they are to be treated fairly, but that they should receive no more than X if we are going to remain true to the ideal of the amateur student athlete. Perhaps the "amateur" ideal cannot be defended. Many think that it would be less hypocritical if universities were to treat their student athletes as (quasi-)professionals and simply pay them for their services.[20] But if the amateur student athlete represents a better ideal, then it would seem that A_G should not share its surplus with student athletes. And, it may be argued, we can hardly claim that A_G is exploiting its student athletes when it does not do what it should not do. So MAE_O must be the better account of exploitation.

Is that correct? I am not sure. First, that MAE_F does not allow us to distinguish between A_G and A_B with respect to exploitation is not a persuasive reason for preferring MAE_O. We may simply have to confront the possibility that A_G and A_B are both exploitative, although it would not follow that there are no other important moral distinctions between A_G and A_B.

Is MAE_F mean-spirited because it makes exploitation turn on the gain to the institution rather than the value of the educational resources that are provided to B? I do not think so, at least not unless a concern with justice is mean-spirited. Perhaps, as Hume remarked, justice is the "cautious, jealous virtue."[21] Perhaps it would be a better world in which B does not worry about A's gain and simply asks whether his or her own situation is satisfactory. But if we think that there are reasons to worry about the distribution of a social surplus, then we can hardly reject MAE_o because it reflects such a concern. Moreover, and to emphasize that exploitation is only one moral concern, even if A_G exploits student athletes (under MAE_F), and thus is worse with respect to exploitation than type (c) and (d) institutions (which, by definition, cannot exploit their student athletes), it does not follow that exploitative "good" institutions are worse than nonexploitative "bad" institutions, all things considered.

The third argument for MAE_o appeals to the ideal of amateur intercollegiate athletics. The view that A_G should not share its surplus with B can be understood in two ways. It might mean that B has no moral claim whatever to share in A_G's surplus, that X represents both the minimum and the maximum of what a student has any legitimate claim to receive. On a second interpretation, the argument concedes that B may have some moral claim to share in A_G's surplus, but maintains that there are overriding moral reasons for not allowing such sharing to occur. On the latter view, we could maintain that MAE_F represents the better understanding of exploitation and still maintain the amateur ideal.

Which is the better account? I do not think that we are in a position to make a compelling case for either MAE_F or MAE_o at this point. But the analysis does underscore the need to distinguish between the truth conditions of the claim that someone is exploited and the moral weight and moral force of that claim. To the extent that one is exploited when one does not receive a fair share of the surplus one helps to generate, there may be less moral weight to exploitation than meets the eye. First, the athletic talent that enables student athletes to contribute to a surplus is arguably arbitrary from a moral point of view, at least to the extent that it is a function of natural abilities as contrasted with the sorts of efforts that have a greater claim to be morally relevant. Second, the extent to which any individual athlete's performance serves to generate a surplus depends on background factors for which an individual athlete cannot plausibly claim credit, for example, the performance of the other athletes, the coaches, the reputation of the institution (which may have allowed it to successfully recruit other, excellent players), and so on. Third, and more generally, whether B's performance generates a surplus is a function of the society's demand for such performance, and that, too, is at least somewhat arbitrary from a moral point of view. Consider men's basketball and women's basketball. Because the public's demand for women's basketball is significantly less than its demand for men's basketball, even successful big-time women's basketball programs may not generate a surplus. Is it morally troublesome that some male basketball players are exploited whereas virtually no female basketball players athletes are exploited? Perhaps, but probably not very much. Indeed, it might be argued that it is undesirable, nay, unjust, that student athletes in surplus programs should fare better than student athletes in nonsurplus programs. We may think it more important to ensure equality between male and female student athletes than to eliminate this form of exploitation.[22]

The Bargaining Process

We have seen that even if student athletes are not harmed by their college experience, they may be exploited nonetheless. Under MAE_o, B is exploited if he receives less than X. Under MAE_F, B is exploited if he or she receives less than F. How do student athletes find themselves in such a position? If universities do exploit student athletes, why are they able to do so? Does it occur voluntarily?

One commentator has suggested that colleges are in a "superior bargaining position" with respect to student athletes.[23] Is that so? Suppose that MAE_o is the better view. Suppose as well that B is a high school senior and is being recruited by several major institutions, including A_B and A_G.[24] It would seem that B should have some room for choice. And if B wants to attend an institution (A_G) that promises genuine educational opportunities, it would seem that B could do so.

Even though B may be in a position to choose A_G over A_B, there is a problem of knowledge and foresight. B may not know that A_G is superior to A_B with respect to educational opportunities or that he or she will be better off attending A_G. Second, there is a problem of desire. Even if B could choose A_G, B may not want to do so, preferring an institution that will make fewer academic demands. That B chooses A_B over A_G may do something to mitigate the force of the claim that B has been exploited by A, but it is arguably unreasonable to expect that an impressionable seventeen-year-old will make the choice that will best promotes his or her overall life prospects, particularly when the better long-term choice may be the less pleasant short-run choice. If we do not want students to be exploited in this way, then the best strategy is to (paternalistically) require all institutions to provide appropriate educational opportunities, even if students are willing to settle for less.

But suppose that we believe that MAE_F represents the better account of exploitation, that student athletes are exploited if they receive less than F. Here there are two questions: (1) What is the best account of F? and (2) Why do they receive less than F? It is possible that the answers to both questions may be located in the bargaining structure, in the fact that prospective students cannot bargain for more than X because NCAA rules do not permit institutions to offer more than X.

It would, I think, be a mistake to describe this situation as an "inequality of bargaining power," at least as between any particular institution and any particular athlete, for there is no bargaining at all. Just as students cannot bargain for financial incentives (including a share of the institution's surplus) when they might otherwise want to do so, institutions cannot (legitimately) offer special incentives to lure prospective students when they might want to do so.[25]

To say that there is no inequality in bargaining power as between institutions and student athletes is not to say that the bargaining structure is morally acceptable. No bargaining at all may be worse than an inequality in bargaining power. In effect, NCAA rules require that the contract between institutions and student athletes be made at a fixed maximum price. By creating a cartel among the universities, NCAA rules solve a collective action problem among institutions and make possible a surplus that might otherwise not exist. Although each institution might prefer to be able to offer a financial incentive in a given case, all institutions prefer a regime in which none are allowed to offer financial incentives to one in which all are allowed to offer financial incentives.

Just as the cartelization of the relationship between universities and students may explain why students receive less than F, it also presents us with a way to understand the value of F itself. We can define F as the (hypothetical) value that B would receive if institutions were free to bargain with prospective students without regard to limitations on financial incentives or rewards. In other words, we can define F as the value that students would receive in a competitive market. The students would not be exploited because they would be setting an appropriate return on their contributions (as defined in this manner), and—what amounts to the same thing—the institution would no longer be receiving an exorbitant surplus on student athletes services. Now, a competitive market in student athletes might not be desirable, all things considered. But if, among other things, a competitive market in student athletes provides the criterion for defining a fair wage or fair price (at least under certain conditions), then we have learned something important about the relation between competitive markets and exploitation.

The parenthetical clause in the previous sentence is critical. The moral quality of the wages and prices generated by a competitive market depends, at least in part, upon the moral quality of the background conditions that are in place. In evaluating the claim that student athletes are exploited, we have assumed a background in which student athletes exchange their athletic services for educational opportunities (admission and/or scholarships) that would otherwise not be available to them. Given those background conditions, a competitive market may give student athletes a certain value for their athletic services—a value that is likely to be greater than what some students now receive (those whose contribution is particularly high) and lower than the value that other students now receive (those whose contribution is relatively low). But the background conditions might be different. Suppose that we assume hypothetical background conditions in which all qualified students were able to attend a university without charge.[26] Under these background conditions, a competitive market would generate a different "wage" (or value for F) for student athletes than they would receive under the present background conditions, just as the wages that workers receive in competitive equilibrium will turn on whether society provides a safety net for the unemployed and, if so, at what level.

The background conditions are important even if we reject the view that students should receive the value that would be generated by a competitive market. Suppose that we assume that student athletes should not be paid for their services, but that we also assume hypothetical background conditions in which all qualified students are able to attend a university without charge or are guaranteed sufficient financial resources to pay for a university education. I think it fair to say that at least some students who enroll as student athletes under existing background conditions would not enroll as athletes under these hypothetical background conditions. If this is so, then intercollegiate athletic programs are importantly parasitic on the existing background conditions that make it attractive to enroll as student athletes. If the society is morally required to provide the hypothetical background conditions described above, then intercollegiate athletic programs are taking advantage of an unfair situation.

Would that constitute (wrongful) exploitation? I am inclined to think that the answer may be no with respect to the universities but yes with respect to society. I think that the answer is no with respect to the universities, because it is not always wrong or unfair for A to enter into a mutually advantageous transaction with B even though B would not enter into such a transaction under fair background conditions, particularly if A has not caused B's unfair background conditions and has no special responsibility to remove them. We must distinguish between *taking advantage of unfairness* and *taking unfair advantage* (of unfairness). And it does not follow that just because the universities are taking advantage of a background injustice to those who become student athletes that the university is taking unfair advantage of those student athletes. Of course, even if the individual institutions are themselves not acting unfairly given the extant background conditions, it would remain the case that the *system* of inter-collegiate athletics is built upon these unfair background conditions. It would be society's responsibility (and here we could expect universities to play a major role) to change the background conditions so as to eliminate this systemic form of exploitation. On this view, student athletes may be exploited, but it may not be the universities that are or even primarily to blame.

Notes

1. Some college football stadiums hold approximately 100,000 persons and are filled for every game. During the 1993–1994 academic year, the University of Michigan received nearly $5.8 million from such licenses. *New York Times,* September 11, 1994, sec. 3, p. 5.

2. Major league baseball continues to recruit many of its players from its minor league system.

3. On the "good guys," see "Jocks with Books," *Newsweek,* January 9, 1989, p. 60. Frederick Schauer pointed out to me that there are several different criteria for being a "good guy": (1) scrupulous adherence to NCAA rules; (2) high admission standards; (3) high graduation rates, which may be a function of safe-harbor programs, demanding coaches, and compliant faculty; (4) genuine opportunity for the typical athlete to get a real education; and (5) no academic breaks for athletes. These criteria do not always correlate with one another.

4. Nand Hart-Nibbrig and Clement Cottingham, *The Political Economy of College Sports* (Lexington, Mass.: Lexington Books, 1986), p. 88. Indeed, many student athletes fail to gain the most basic educational skills. It has been estimated that 20 to 25 percent of African American athletes at four-year colleges are functionally illiterate. See Derek Quinn Johnson, "Educating Misguided Student Athletes: An Application of Contract Theory," 85 *Columbia Law Review* 96 (1985).

5. Kennedy, "So What If College Players," sec. 4, p. 21.

6. See Roger G. Noll, "The Economics of Intercollegiate Sports," in Judith Andre and David N. James, eds., *Rethinking College Athletics* (Philadelphia: Temple University Press, 1990). At most institutions, only football and basketball generate surplus income, and that surplus is used to fund other athletic programs. For a survey of research on the relationship between successful athletic programs and alumni/ae giving, see James H. Frey, "The Winning-Team Myth," *Currents,* January 1985, pp. 32–35.

7. See Lawrence Becker, "Criminal Attempt and the Theory of the Law of Crimes," 3 *Philosophy & Public Affairs* 262 (1974). Becher argues that attempted crimes may be as wrong—qua crimes—as successful crimes and that there are good reasons for punishing attempted crimes as severely as successful crimes.

8. Richard Arneson, "What's Wrong with Exploitation?" 91 *Ethics* 202 (1981), at 203.

9. Ibid., pp. 203–4.

10. Less than one-third of Division I-A football programs break even. John Underwood, "Reading, Writing and Remuneration," *New York Times,* September 11, 1994, sec. 5 p. 13.

11. Although there is no competitive market among players, there may be a highly competitive market among coaches. Bobby Bowden, coach of Florida State University's 1994 national championship football team, received a salary of $700,000.

12. Because Title IX of the Education Amendments of 1973 requires that "all aspects of a university education, including athletics, should be free of gender discrimination," federal law might be characterized as requiring that universities use financial surpluses generated by male athletic programs to subsidize women's athletic programs rather than for other purposes. Jill K. Johnson, "Title IX and Intercollegiate Athletics: Current Interpretation of the Standards of Compliance," 74 *Boston University Law Review* 553 (1994), at 553. I thank Fred Schauer for raising this issue with me.

13. It is an interesting question whether B might validly claim to be exploited even if B did not contribute to A's surplus (say, because B is injured) if, given the *ex ante* value of B's contribution to A, B receives less than he should.

14. As Mike Garrett put it, "For a kid to get a scholarship . . . is a great, great opportunity. To some degree, it has to be up to the kid to take advantage of it." Quoted in Phil Taylor and Shelley Smith, "The Black Athlete Revisited," *Sports Illustrated,* August 12, 1991, p. 46

15. We might want to say that colleges should not admit low-ability students because it violates what should be the standards of an academic institution, but that is a different issue.

16. Perhaps more accurately, we would need to compare an *ex ante* probability distribution of B's life prospects in the world in which B attends the college A_G or A_B and the *ex ante* probability distribution of B's life prospects in the world in which B does not go to college.

17. Fred Brown, who played basketball at Georgetown University, put it this way: "If you come into a school, you may not be on an academic par with the general population of the school, but if you as an individual can sit there and learn something and better yourself, that's an education. . . . I always ask my mother, 'If I hadn't played basketball, what would have happened?' Ninety percent of the people I grew up with are dead or in jail, and I would have been the same way." Quoted in Ted Gulp, "Foul," *Time*, April 3, 1989, p. 60. It should be noted that Georgetown University has a reputation as one of the "good" athletic programs.

18. Elbert B. Smith, a professor of history at the University of Maryland, in a letter to the editor, *Washington Post*, November 17, 1986, p. A12.

19. Consider Representative Collins's statement: "Colleges [must] not exploit our youngsters for victories and profits. Instead, colleges must provide an opportunity for a real education." Quoted in *USA Today*, August 17, 1992, p. 10A.

20. The scandal . . . is not that someone paid [Ramsey] $100 here and there. He earned more and deserved more." David Kindred, *The Sporting News*, December 7, 1972, p. 5. It should be noted that this change would not leave everything else as it is. Intercollegiate athletics is immensely popular "because it can still be sold with the idea that these athletes really do represent and care about their universities. Otherwise, they're the French foreign legion." Underwood, "Reading, Writing, and Remuneration," New York Times, September 11, 1994, sec. 8, p. 13.

21. David Hume, *An Inquiry Concerning the Principles of Morals* (1777; reprint, New York: Hafner Publishing Co., 1948), sec. III, pt. I.

22. See Chapter 1, text accompanying note 93.

23. Johnson, "Educating Misguided Student Athletes," p. 111.

24. After all, if B has not been heavily recruited, he or she is not likely to be a major contributor to the institution's financial success, and so will not be exploited even it he or she does not receive (at A_B) the appropriate educational opportunities.

25. Because institutions cannot compete with one another by bargaining, they attempt to differentiate themselves in other ways, by emphasizing their high (or low) commitment to academics, the likelihood of national exposure, the size of the stadium or arena, proximity to family, the quality of coaching, the likelihood of becoming a starting player early in one's career, and so on.

26. For example, the society (or government) might pay for their college education up front on condition that they pay back a share of their future income as a fair return on society's investment in their education.

Violence in Sports

◆

Robert L. Simon

The Case Against Boxing

What is the case against boxing? Actually, there are several arguments for the conclusion that boxing ought to be prohibited. A not atypical point of departure for our discussion is the following passage from an editorial in *The New York Times:*

> Some people watch boxing to see skill, others just for the blood. Far worse than the blood is the unseen damage. Retinas are dislodged, kidneys bruised and . . . the cerebral cortex accumulates damage to the higher functions of the brain, leading to loss of memory, shambling walk: the traits of the punch drunk boxer. Can a civilized society plausibly justify the pleasure it may gain from such a sport?[1]

This passage suggests two kinds of reasons for prohibiting boxing. The first is the protection of the boxers themselves. The violence inherent in boxing may make it too dangerous for the participants. In this view, society ought to protect boxers from harm by banning the sport. The passage also suggests a second line of argument. Might we somehow become less civilized, or morally more insensitive, if boxing is permitted to continue? The question concerning what civilized societies ought to permit implies that the practice of boxing may have social consequences that are harmful, not just to boxers, but to others as well. Do either of these lines of argument justify the prohibition of boxing?

Paternalism and Mill's Harm Principle

There is little question that boxing can be harmful to the participants. Every boxer who enters the ring faces the real possibility of serious injury. Doesn't society have the right as well as the duty to legally prohibit boxing in order to protect boxers themselves from harm and even death?

Before we agree too quickly, however, we should consider the following examples. Should your friends prevent you from ordering ice cream and fatty meats when you go out because such foods contain too much cholesterol? Should your friends prevent you from trying out for the basketball or football team because other sports you might play, such as golf, are much safer? On a broader level, suppose the state passes legislation requiring that reasonably healthy adults who do not exercise for at least thirty minutes a day must pay substantial extra taxes. This legislation is justified as an attempt to save the sedentary from themselves by requiring participation in a healthy life style.

The issue at stake here is one of *paternalism*. Roughly stated, paternalism refers to interference with the liberty of agents for what is believed to be their own good. A major objection to paternalism, however, is that it wrongly disregards the liberty and autonomy of those very agents who are interfered with for their own good.

Perhaps the most influential case against paternalistic interference with the liberty of competent agents was presented by the British philosopher John Stuart Mill (1806-1873) in his eloquent defense of personal freedom, *On Liberty*. Mill himself claimed to be a utilitarian in ethics, committed to the view that the sole criterion of right and wrong is the social utility of acts or practices. At first glance, utilitarianism does not seem to be particularly hostile to paternalism or especially protective of the freedom of the individual. It seems that paternalistic interference with liberty would be justified on utilitarian grounds whenever it produced better consequences for all affected than the available alternatives. Utilitarians might turn out to be interfering busybodies on the individual level and benevolent versions of Big Brother on the state level, interfering with freedom whenever necessary to bring about the best results.

However, in *On Liberty*, Mill advanced important arguments against applying utilitarianism so crudely. Even if, as many suspect, Mill was unable to consistently remain within the utilitarian framework, he did advance important arguments against paternalistic interference with the individual based on respect for the liberty and autonomy of the individual.

In one of the most widely discussed passages of *On Liberty*, Mill declared that

> the sole end for which mankind are warranted individually or collectively in interfering with the liberty of action of any of their number is self protection. . . . The only purpose for which power can be rightfully exercised over any member of a civilized community, against his will, is to prevent harm to others. His own good, either physical or mental, is not a sufficient warrant.[2]

According to Mill, as long as another person's acts are self-regarding, so long as they do not harm or constitute a threat to the welfare of others, interference with them is unjustified.

Why did Mill reject what would seem to be the position most in harmony with utilitarianism, namely, that paternalistic interference with freedom is justified whenever it produces better consequences than alternatives? Perhaps the line of argument Mill advances that is most compatible with his official utilitarianism is one of efficiency. Paternalistic interference is likely to be inefficient. After all, agents generally know their own interests better than others do. Moreover, paternalists may often be influenced by their own values and prejudices or by fear for the safety of others, and so are unlikely to properly calculate the consequences of interfering. As a result, allowing paternalism will create a society of busybodies who, in their efforts to do good, will interfere in the wrong place at the wrong time for the wrong reasons. In a sense, Mill can be read here as advancing a *rule utilitarian* argument. A society following a rule prohibiting paternalistic interference will actually promote utility more efficiently than one adopting a rule allowing it, for in the second society, the good produced by the few cases of justifiable paternalism will be swamped by the harm promoted by unjustifiable paternalistic interferences constantly carried out by utilitarian busybodies.

Although this argument is not implausible, it may not accomplish as much as Mill thinks. After all, wouldn't paternalism still be justified in those few cases where we are convinced it would do more good than harm?

In fact, Mill advanced a second line of argument, not easily reconciled with utilitarianism, which has perhaps been more influential than the approach sketched above. Even if paternalistic interference would produce more good than harm, constant interference with our liberty will stunt our moral and intellectual growth and eventually make us incapable of thinking for ourselves. As Mill maintained,

> the human faculties of perception, judgment, discrimination, feeling, mental activity, and even moral preference are exercised only in making a choice. . . . The mental and the moral, like the muscular powers, are improved only by being used. . . . He who lets the world . . . choose his plan of life for him, has no need of any other faculty than the ape-like one of imitation.[3]

Here, Mill seems to be appealing more to the value of the idea of autonomy than to social utility understood in the sense of a balance of pleasure or satisfaction over pain or frustration of desires. Arguably, the appeal to autonomy is more fundamental than the appeal to utility, since one must first be autonomous in order to evaluate any moral argument at all, including utilitarian arguments. Autonomy is a fundamental value, it can be argued, precisely because it is presupposed by the practice of moral argument itself.[4]

Finally, one can reinforce Mill's case by arguing that paternalism interferes with the fundamental moral right of individuals to control their own lives. Although moral rights may themselves be sometimes justified by the degree to which they promote utility, or as protections for autonomy, they also can be justified as basic moral commodities which protect individuals from being regarded as mere resources to be used for the good of the greater number. In a sense, rights function as political and social "trumps" which individuals can play to protect themselves from being swallowed up in the pursuit of the social good.[5] Individual rights to liberty protect the ability of persons to live their lives as they choose rather than as someone else, however benevolent, thinks such lives should be led.

Accordingly, supporters of boxing can appeal to the arguments suggested by *On Liberty* to reject the claim that boxing ought to be prohibited. In particular, they can maintain (a) it is unclear whether prohibition really will promote the most utility, (b) even if it does, it prevents both boxers and spectators alike from making the moral choice of whether to engage in and support the sport, and finally (c) it ignores the rights of the boxers and spectators to live their own lives as they themselves see fit. Are such arguments decisive?

Exceptions to the Harm Principle

Is it possible to accept the Harm Principle and still maintain that paternalistic interference with boxing *sometimes* is justified? For one thing, Mill himself acknowledges that the Harm Principle "is meant to apply only to human beings in the maturity of their faculties."[6] Thus, interference with the behavior of children and the mentally incompetent for their own good would be allowed by the Harm Principle. This surely is a plausible restriction because such persons are not in a good position to rationally evaluate their desires so as to determine their real interests, and they are not (yet) capable of making rational and autonomous choices.

However, such a restriction would not allow interference with the behavior of competent adults, some of whom can and do choose to box. Of course, one could argue that the mere fact that some persons choose to box demonstrates their irrationality and lack of competency and thus disqualifies them from protection by the Harm Principle. However, if the only reason for thinking such people are irrational is that they make a choice others of us don't like, such an argument must be rejected. The very point of the Harm Principle is to protect individuals from having the values of others imposed upon them, so we must have independent reason to think that agents are incompetent or immature before we are justified in interfering with their behavior; the mere fact that we don't like their choices is not enough.

A second kind of exception to the Harm Principle might allow interference with the choice of competent adults to participate in boxing. That is, perhaps paternalism is acceptable when its goal is not simply to benefit the people being interfered with but rather is to protect their status as rational and autonomous agents.[7] For example, suppose a person of sound mind and body is about to take a drug which, while causing pleasurable experiences, is highly addictive and will eventually destroy her capacity to reason. Aren't you justified in interfering to remove her supply of the drug, even against her will? After all, your goal is not to impose your conception of happiness upon her but to preserve her capacity to choose her own conception of the good life for herself.

How does this argument apply to the prohibition of boxing? In particular, repeated blows to the head produce brain damage, leading to the symptoms associated with the behavior of the "punch drunk" fighter. Long before those symptoms become evident, however, irreversible brain damage, and gradual diminishment of rational capacities, might have taken place.[8]

Although this sort of argument does provide grounds for interference, whether these grounds are sufficiently strong or weighty to justify interference with liberty is controversial. In particular, unlike the case of a mind-destroying addictive drug, the effects of boxing on mental capacity are long term and uncertain. Moreover, the rewards that some professional fighters can obtain are potentially great. Why is it less justifiable to risk one's capacity for rational choice to secure a great gain than it is, say, to risk shortening one's life span by following an unhealthy but pleasurable diet, or putting oneself under unhealthy stress in order to succeed in business?

Perhaps a third ground for making exceptions to the Harm Principle provides a stronger justification for interference with boxing. We have been assuming that athletes freely and autonomously choose to engage in boxing. But there are grounds for doubting the truth of that assumption.

For one thing, many boxers may be ignorant of the risks of engaging in their sport. Hence, they no more freely consent to run those risks than the person who drives over an unsafe bridge in the mistaken belief that it is safe consents to being thrown into the raging river below.

Of equal importance, many of the participants in professional boxing come from severely disadvantaged backgrounds. These men see boxing as their main chance of escape from the economic and social disadvantages of the ghetto, many of which are due to the injustice of racial discrimination. In this view, the athlete who chooses to box is not responding to an offer or opportunity, i.e., "you can better yourself by becoming a boxer," but rather is reacting to a threat, i.e., "if you don't become a boxer, you will continue to be a victim of social injustice and neglect." Accordingly, since boxers are not autonomous freely choosing agents, but rather are victims of societal coercion, they are not covered by the Harm Principle in the first place.

However, proponents of individual liberty will regard such a view as too extreme. Carried to its logical limits, they will point out, it implies that the poor and deprived should have less liberty to direct their own lives than the rest of us because they are not "truly free" to begin with. In other words, in the name of protecting them from themselves, we would be depriving the disadvantaged of one of the most basic elements of human dignity, the ability to have some control of their own lives. By viewing them only as victims, we would no longer see them as persons in their own right. Would we go so far as to paternalistically deprive them of taking any risks to better themselves since they are, we are told, not able to freely choose to begin with?

This point does have force, but it also must be remembered that poverty and deprivation can lead people to take risks that no one would take unless desperate. The *justice* of a system that presents people with such cruel choices can be called into question. Thus, a proponent of prohibition might agree that the poor and deprived are not mere victims and can make choices but might regard the choice between becoming a boxer and living a life of deprivation as itself unjust. Perhaps a prohibition on boxing could be justified to prevent the imposition of such unjust choices upon the disadvantaged.

The evaluation of this point will depend upon whether one regards the athlete from a disadvantaged and perhaps minority background as having a reasonable set of available choices in our society. If one believes that the alternative to boxing is not starvation, or even welfare, but that educational opportunities are available for those who want to take advantage of them, then one will view the chance to become a boxer as an opportunity. If one regards alternate opportunities as shams, one will be inclined to see boxers as the victim of societal coercion. In any case, to the extent that alternate opportunities are available, it is the responsibility of coaches and parents to inform young athletes of them and of the relatively infinitesimal chances of being successful in professional sports.

Be that as it may, it is doubtful if the current argument supports an across-the-board ban on participation in boxing, even if one makes highly pessimistic assumptions about the range of opportunities available to disadvantaged youth in our society. This is because not everyone who chooses to participate in boxing need be from a disadvantaged background. At most, the argument justifies closing boxing only to certain classes of people, namely, (a) those for whom it is a last resort and who may be "forced" into it because of social or economic pressure, and (b) those who lack the education or have not had the opportunity to fully understand the risks of participation.

We can conclude, then, that although paternalistic arguments in favor of prohibition of boxing are not without force, they are not conclusive either. On the contrary, concern for individual liberty and autonomy justifies us in placing the burden of proof on the paternalist. Although further discussion might warrant us in revising our opinion, it appears from what we have seen that the burden has not yet been met where participation in boxing (and other risky activities) is at issue.

Boxing and the Protection of Society

So far, we have been assuming that the only grounds for prohibition of boxing are paternalistic. But what if the participation in boxing is not simply self-regarding but has harmful effects on others? The Harm Principle permits interference with the individual liberty of some to prevent them from harming others.

But how can boxing harm others? At first glance, it may appear that the only ones boxers can harm are themselves.

However, first glances can be deceiving. To see how boxing can harm society, consider the imaginary sport of Mayhem. The rules of Mayhem are simple. Adult volunteers, who have given their informed consent to participate, are placed in an arena with swords and spears and are divided into two teams. They then fight until only members of one team are left alive. The players on the winning, i.e., surviving, team then get to divide $10,000,000.

Does it follow that if there are no paternalistic reasons strong enough to justify prohibiting Mayhem, there are no reasons at all to justify prohibition?[9] Isn't it plausible to think that even though there is no direct harm to spectators—the gladiators refrain even from attacking those fans who boo—the indirect harm is substantial. Children might come to idolize (and imitate) trained killers. (Would youngsters collect gladiator bubble gum cards with kill ratio statistics on the back side?) Violence would be glorified and the value of human life inevitably would be cheapened. Such effects may not be inevitable, but the likelihood of eventual harm to others seems sufficient to justify a civilized society in banning Mayhem.

Can't a similar argument be applied to boxing, for as one newspaper editorial exclaimed, "the public celebration of violence cannot be a private matter."[10] After all, although many sports involve the use of force and risk of injury, only boxing has violence in the sense of intentional attempts to injure opponents at its core. Do we want our society to glorify such an activity in the name of sports?

How powerful are these sorts of considerations? In fact, they can be understood as supporting two distinct kinds of arguments. According to the first, public exposure to boxing causes nonparticipants to be influenced adversely and as a result to be more violent or tolerant of violence themselves, thereby increasing the risk for others. In this way, exposure to boxing contributes to the rise of violence throughout society. According to the second kind of argument, adulation of the violence inherent in boxing undermines the standards constituting our community. The public glorification of violence debases our society and changes it into one that is more vulgar and less civilized.

The difference between these two arguments is that the first is more *individualistic,* the second more *communitarian.* That is, the first stresses harm to individuals. The second emphasizes that the social context in which individuals are formed is adversely affected, and so a new and less worthy kind of individual will emerge from the debased social context that results.

The first argument needs to be supported by empirical evidence, which is likely to be inconclusive. In fact, many psychologists have maintained for some time that we can be and often are influenced by models, and, accordingly, if society presents persons engaging in violence as its heroes, toleration of violence and the tendency to commit it will increase.[11] On the other hand, it is unlikely that the normal boxing fan is going to act violently after watching a match. Thus, it is unlikely that any *direct and immediate* tie between boxing and broader social violence exists.

However, conceptual and moral issues are at least as important as empirical ones. Thus, even if participation in or observation of boxing does have subtle long-term effects on the amount of violence committed elsewhere in society, does it *follow* that boxing ought to be prohibited? In answering this question, we must consider its implications for regulation generally if our overall moral view is to be systematically consistent. Suppose, for example, that a book advocates a kind of undisciplined secondary-school education, which, contrary to the author, would actually be educationally harmful to most youngsters. The book's author is highly respected, and it is likely that the book will be widely read and will influence many educators. Are we justified in banning the book because its publication is believed to have harmful effects? On the contrary, it seems that if we prohibit activities like boxing or reading a controversial book because they might have harmful long-term effects, our right to liberty is drastically restricted. We would have ceded to others the ability to make up our own minds for us and to interfere with our lives in a broad range of areas where direct and immediate harm to others is not at issue.

However, to communitarians, advocates of the second argument sketched above, the role of individual liberty has been misrepresented in our whole discussion. We have proceeded, according to this criticism, as if the individual is an autonomous atom who can step back from social institutions and make choices in isolation. It is this individualistic choosing self who is seen as the locus of value, yet, according to the communitarian, such a self is in many ways a fiction. Rather, selves are formed within communities and are constituted or defined by their relationships with others in their social settings. Thus, one is a parent, teacher, coach, member of a religious group, and citizen rather than an isolated individualistic pure agent, allegedly capable of stepping aside from all roles and autonomously evaluating them. What would such an abstract individual be but a mysterious "0" stripped of all distinguishing human characteristics?[12]

What has this roughly sketched communitarian picture of the self have to do with the critique of boxing and with violence in sports? Although the specific implications for policy of theoretical communitarianism are not always clear, the communitarian approach at least emphasizes the need to preserve the common values that bind society together. Boxing and the public celebration of violence undermine the standards of the community and hence transform the kind of individuals it produces. There is no asocial individual who can stand outside his or her community to evaluate boxing. If we tolerate boxing, as well as violence in other areas, we will end up with individuals who no longer share the standards and traditions that lead to the condemnation of violence. Our community will gradually be replaced by one that tolerates and may even welcome behavior that the previous community would have regarded as degrading, threatening, and blatantly immoral.

Although all aspects of the debate between communitarians and what they regard as their liberal individualistic opponents cannot be touched on here, two important points should be kept in mind.[13] First, if the communitarian's major point is that we are so tightly situated within specific communities and traditions that free, rational, and autonomous choice is impossible, we cannot freely, rationally, and autonomously choose to believe communitarianism. That some of us accept a communitarian approach would be just another social fact, to be explained by reference to our social situation, rather than by the truth of communitarianism or the strength of the rational justification for it.

Presumably, the communitarian would not want to accept such a conclusion. But, then, some weight must be given to free, rational, and autonomous choice within communitarianism, even if the account of such choice differs in substantial ways from that of more individualistic approaches to political theory.

However, and this is the second critical point that should be kept in mind, what weight should be given to liberty by communitarians? If their reply is "It's up to the standards of one's community," then they must be reminded that many communities are oppressive, racist, intolerant, and fanatical. On the other hand, if they are to avoid giving weight to the standards implicit in the practices of immoral communities, they seem to be committed to some standard, such as Mill's Harm Principle, or liberal rights to free choice, which is relatively independent of the standards of particular societies. Thus, they cannot settle the issue of whether boxing ought to be prohibited by appealing to the standards of the community, for even assuming there is just one community in our society, the moral question of why its standards *ought* to be obeyed still remains to be answered. (In fact, it can be argued plausibly that many communities in the United States do find the violence in boxing acceptable. Does that settle the moral question of whether it is acceptable?)

Boxing, Morality, and Legality

Our discussion has not provided any conclusive reason for thinking boxing ought to be *legally* prohibited. Paternalistic arguments do not seem strong enough to justify a general prohibition, the link between boxing and individual violence is too tenuous and indirect to support such a general prohibition, and the standards of the community are an insufficient guide to action. On the other hand, while most of us regard individual liberty as of the greatest value, we probably would agree that society does have the right to prohibit such practices as professional gladiatorial contests (such as Mayhem), perhaps on communitarian grounds or perhaps because we doubt that the choice to participate can be truly free or informed. The trouble is that boxing seems to be a borderline case. It is not quite as dangerous as Mayhem, the harm is not as certain or direct, and we can at least begin to understand how a participant can voluntarily accept the risks involved. Thus, the arguments both for and against prohibition seem to be at something of a standoff. Given the dangers of interfering with liberty, perhaps the best policy would be one not of legal interference but of moral sanction and reform.

Thus, whether or not the case for legal prohibition is determinative, many reasons have been given for moral concern about boxing. It is perfectly appropriate for those who share such moral concerns to refuse to support boxing, to urge others to refrain from supporting it, and to advocate strong reforms in the practice of boxing. For example, reformers may want to direct boxing in the direction of becoming an example of the constrained use of force rather than of violence. On this view, boxing as a sport should be distinguished from boxing as a form of violence, just as we now distinguish fencing from actual dueling. Reforms that work in this direction include mandatory use of helmets by fighters, prohibition of blows to the head, and emphasis on scoring points through skill rather than on inflicting damage to opponents. Although boxing probably never will be sedate, it can be modified so it bears a much closer resemblance to fencing than to Mayhem.

To conclude, even if boxing should be immune to legal prohibition on grounds of respect for individual liberty, radical reform of the sport seems to be morally justified. Boxing, as presently constituted, has the goal of infliction of harm by one opponent on another at its core, and so makes violence central. If society should not glorify violence, and if violence in sports might contribute however indirectly to greater tolerance and commission of violence throughout society, or to the erosion of *defensible* community standards, we can be led by such considerations to freely, rationally, and autonomously choose to reduce the level of violence in sports.

Notes

1. *New York Times,* December 14, 1982, p. 30. © *New York Times.* Reprinted by permission.

2. John Stuart Mill, *On Liberty* (1859), edited by Elizabeth Rappaport (Indianapolis: Hackett Publishing Company, 1978), p. 9. Many other editions of *On Liberty* are also in print.

3. *Ibid.,* p. 56.

4. A committed utilitarian might reply, however, that on the contrary, autonomy itself is valuable only because a society of autonomous individuals is likely to generate more utility than one in which the autonomy of individuals is suppressed, perhaps through tyrannical means.

5. The account of individual rights as political trumps has been advanced by Dworkin in *Taking Rights Seriously.*

6. Mill, *On Liberty,* p. 9.

7. For a defense of such a position, see Gerald Dworkin, "Paternalism," in Richard A. Wasserstrom, ed., *Morality and the Law* (Belmont, Calif.: Wadsworth, 1971), pp. 107-126.

8. An accessible discussion of the medical evidence on the effects of boxing, and of the implications of the evidence for policy, can be found in Robert H. Boyle and Wilmer Ames, "Too Many Punches, Too Little Concern," *Sports Illustrated,* April 11, 1983, pp. 42-67.

9. The example of Mayhem is based upon a similar illustration employed by Irving Kristol in his essay, "Pornography, Obscenity, and the Case for Censorship," *New York Times Magazine,* March 28, 1971, reprinted in Joel Feinberg and Hyman Gross, eds., *Philosophy of Law* (Encino, Calif.: Dickenson Publishing Company, Inc., 1975), pp. 165-171.

10. *New York Times,* December 14, 1982, p. 30.

11. An influential account of the role of models in learning is found in Albert Bandura's *Social Learning Theory* (Englewood Cliffs, N. J.: Prentice Hall, 1977).

12. The views presented here represent only a rough sketch of communitarian approaches, but recent communitarian criticisms of liberal individualist approaches to political theory include Alasdair MacIntyre, *After Virtue* (Notre Dame, Ind.: University of Notre Dame Press, 1984) and Michael Sandel, *Liberalism and the Limits of Justice* (New York: Cambridge University Press, 1982).

13. For extended critical discussions of communitarianism, see Amy Gutmann, "Communitarian Critics of Liberalism," *Philosophy and Public Affairs,* Vol. 14 (1983), pp. 308-322; George Sher, "Three Grades of Social Involvement," *Philosophy and Public Affairs,* Vol. 18 (1989), pp. 133-157; Alan E. Buchanan, "Assessing the Communitarian Critique of Liberalism," *Ethics,* Vol. 99 (1989), pp. 852-882; and Patrick Nil and David Paris, "Liberalism and the Communitarian Critique, A Guide for the Perplexed," *Canadian Journal of Political Science,* Vol. 23, No. 3 (1990), pp. 419-439.

Boxing, Paternalism, and Legal Moralism

Nicholas Dixon

Studies have shown that blows to the head cause boxers chronic brain damage, due to the rapid movement of the brain within the skull, tearing vessels and nerve fibers.(n1) Nor are those who suffer knockouts the only fighters at risk for brain damage: "the number of bouts rather than knockouts correlates best with the development of chronic brain damage."(n2) 64-87% of current and former boxers tested in studies done in the 1980s suffered from measurable brain damage, leading Robert Glenn Morrison to conclude that "the evidence is indisputable that modern boxers do suffer brain damage as a result of their profession, despite improved safety standards."(n3)

Interestingly, while any death from boxing is a tragedy, it appears that the risk of death is fairly remote. For instance, in absolute numbers, fewer boxers died in various time periods and places than participants in such other sports as American football and baseball. And the number of deaths per 1,000 participants is similar to or lower than the numbers for such other high-risk sports as mountaineering and motorcycle racing.(n4) The risk of such injuries as cuts, bone fractures, and damage to the cornea and retina is much greater. However, since these injuries are generally treatable and rarely if ever debilitating, debate over whether we should ban boxing has focused on the problem of brain damage. Largely due to its concern over the risk of brain damage, in 1984 the American Medical Association House of Delegates proposed that professional and amateur boxing be banned.(n5)

This paper is devoted to examining arguments supporting the ban on boxing proposed by the AMA. My major focus will be on professional boxing, because,

Reprinted, by permission, from N. Dixon, 2001, "Boxing, paternalism and legal moralism," *Social Theory and Practice* 27(2): 323-345.

with its longer fights and greater tolerance of punishment of fighters before bouts are stopped, it is more dangerous than amateur boxing, and also because only the professional sport raises questions about the autonomy of decisions to risk injury in order to gain untold wealth. Because his fierce defense of the liberal view—"[t]he harm and offense principles, duly clarified and qualified, between them exhaust the class of good reasons for criminal prohibitions"—provides such a stringent test of any proposal to restrict liberty, I will make extensive reference throughout this paper to Joel Feinberg's arguments against legal paternalism and legal moralism in his monumental work, *The Moral Limits of the Criminal Law.*(n6) I will conclude that we should impose a single legal restriction that would effectively eliminate boxing's main medical risk: a complete ban on blows to the head.

Paternalistic Arguments for Restricting Boxing

The most obvious rationale for restricting boxing is to protect boxers from harm. The initial paternalistic case for prohibition—that is, that the risks of brain damage are so severe that we have a duty to protect fighters from the harm that they are likely to suffer—falls foul of Mill's famous defense of individual freedom in *On Liberty.* According to Mill, we should respect the right of autonomous adults to exercise their ability to rationally guide their behavior by their own freely chosen values. To interfere with the career choices of adults who wish to take up boxing is wrong, on this view, because it treats them as children and not as autonomous beings.(n7) To justify restricting boxing, then, we need to turn to more sophisticated paternalistic arguments.

The entire paternalism v. respect for autonomy debate as it applies to boxing is cast in nonconsequentialist terms. Confining our attention to the results of boxing for the fighters, a cost-benefit analysis seems to indicate that the utilities are stacked overwhelmingly against allowing boxing. In return for the psychological benefits of being allowed to live according to their own lights, and the minuscule chance of becoming rich, boxers face the likelihood of irreversible brain damage. The proautonomy, anti-governmental interference view gains its strength not from the claim that it will produce the best results for boxers, but rather from the claim that boxers should be free to act on their own decisions, even if those decisions will probably end up hurting them.

Soft Paternalism

Even the liberal view, though, as defended by Mill and Feinberg, allows for paternalistic restrictions in the case of people whose decisions lack autonomy, for example, children, the mentally ill, and people acting under duress or in predicaments. In such cases, respect for autonomy may actually require paternalistic intervention. Following standard usage, let us call paternalism to protect people from the results of inautonomous requests or actions "soft paternalism," in contrast to "hard paternalism," which permits interference with fully voluntary, autonomous requests or actions. The question we have to consider, then, is whether we have any reason to suspect that boxers' decisions to enter the profession are lacking in autonomy.

Many boxers probably fail to clear the very first hurdle required for an autonomous decision: having adequate information. Boxers are unlikely to have subscriptions to the *Journal of the American Medical Association,* whose detailed accounts of the medical dangers of their profession are cited above, while promoters, managers, and trainers have a vested interest in not drawing their potential breadwinners' attention to information that might deter them from entering the ring. At best, the majority of boxers are aware that some fighters have died in the ring, and that some have suffered serious injuries, but they likely share—doubtless due to an understatement of risks on the part of the boxing business as well as their own self-deception—the popular misconception that brain damage is a rare occurrence that happens only to fighters who suffer repeated knockouts. However, boxers' ignorance of the full extent of the dangers of prizefighting will not persuade the liberal to support prohibition. A far better remedy, according to the liberal view, would be to institute mandatory education on these dangers—supervised by a neutral boxing commission that has no financial stake in minimizing the risks—as one of the requirements for receiving a boxing license. These educational programs should also include detailed information on the likely career earnings of boxers and the very low percentage of fighters who ever reach the level of lucrative title fights. Such an approach, which parallels government health warnings on cigarette packs and bottles of alcohol, would enable boxers to make autonomous decisions and would show maximal respect for their autonomy.[n8]

A far stronger paternalistic argument arises from the fact that an autonomous decision must flow from the agent's own values, without undue pressure from other people or external circumstances. When such pressure is too great, it becomes coercive and precludes autonomous action. In this light, we must consider the argument that since boxers often come from severely disadvantaged backgrounds and may see boxing as their only means of escaping from dangerous, poverty-stricken neighborhoods, their decision to become boxers may reflect their desperation, rather than an authentic desire that flows from their own considered values.[n9] Can the offer of a career in professional boxing ever be coercive?

The idea of a coercive offer seems paradoxical, since an offer that actually increases a person's options hardly seems capable of forcing him or her into an action. However, as Joel Feinberg has argued, increasing people's freedom is sometimes compatible with coercing them.[n10] He asks us to consider the example of a millionaire who offers to pay for the expensive surgery necessary to save the life of a woman's child, on the condition that the woman agree to have sexual relations with him for a period of time. By hypothesis, the woman has no other means to save her child's life. In these circumstances, Feinberg suggests, the woman is indeed forced to do something she would far rather not do—have sex with a lecherous, exploitative stranger—by her desperate desire to save her child's life. From her point of view, the situation is just as coercive as one in which a man kidnaps her healthy child and threatens to kill him unless she agrees to have sex with the kidnapper.[n11]

The "lecherous millionaire" example belongs to the clearest category of coercive offers: those in which the coerced person is pressured to choose an option she does not desire in order to avoid an alternative that she desires even less. The "differential coercive pressure" is greatest when the offered option is vastly less unattractive than the option avoided by taking up the offer. More difficult to categorize are situations in which the offered option is mildly attractive in its own right to its recipient. Suppose, Feinberg asks us, that the woman with the dying child would have regarded an affair with the millionaire as somewhat desirable independently of his offer. (Let us assume for the sake of argument that her mild attraction to the millionaire is not destroyed by the crass opportunism of his offer.) In this event, he suggests, while the differential coercive pressure is even greater than in the original example, making the offer even harder to refuse, the fact that the woman would have had a mild desire to have an affair with him regardless of the offer relegates this case to the status of "impure" coercion. The "coercive minimum"(n12)—the degree of unpleasantness of the action that the offer induces the woman to perform—is negligible or even negative. The situation is coercive, but her choice is made willingly, and not because of the coercion.(n13) One measure of the degree of coercion exerted by any given offer is a function of the amount of differential coercive pressure and the unpleasantness of the coercive minimum.(n14)

Into which category—relatively harmless impure coercion or morally problematic coercion—does the pull that boxing exerts on poor youths and adults fall? It all depends on the attitude that boxers take toward their profession. There are doubtless some boxers who thoroughly enjoy fighting and would do so anyway as members of amateur clubs even if the rich rewards of professional boxing were unavailable. They may be driven by a variety of motivations: the desire to hurt and physically dominate opponents or gain the status of macho cult heroes, or pride in the skill, courage, and discipline that successful boxers require.(n15) Such boxers are subject only to morally innocuous impure coercion. I suspect that the majority of fighters, while they may share some of all of these motives, are more ambivalent toward their occupation. They regard the pain and injuries that they suffer, the damage that they inflict on opponents, and the indignity of performing in public in their underwear before a crowd that wants to see at least one of the two fighters get hurt, as unpleasant necessities to be endured in order to achieve financial and physical security and have a shot at the rich rewards that are available to highly successful boxers. This is the likely attitude of the large number of boxers known as "opponents," whose role is primarily to provide opposition for rising stars who are working their way up through the ranks, compiling impressive win-loss records as they go. These opponents, who are an integral part of the boxing world (after all, not everyone can be a champion or contender), occasionally score upset victories but are usually content to survive a fight and collect their paycheck with a minimal amount of injuries. That many fighters, even successful ones, harbor reservations about their profession is strikingly supported by Michael Burke in the context of his impassioned defense of the sport as viewed by boxers themselves:

> [T]he quasi-religious link of the boxer to his craft is not without tension, and sometimes resentment, which the fighters suggest is produced by the "barbaricness" (sic) of the sport, the grind and torture of the body resulting in its breakdown, the physical abuse of self and others, and the ruthless and despotic exploitation of the boxer by his manager and controllers for the enjoyment of others. The boxers understand it as a coerced affection, a poor man's love . . . There are no rich, white boxers in the semi-professional game . . . Boxers leave parts of themselves in the ring. The body which has been trained and disciplined to perform the "sweet craft" does not survive intact. The contradiction in this ruination of the cherished masculine body creates a further ambivalence toward boxing. As a result, the overwhelming majority of boxers [in the study by Lois Wacquant that Burke cites], who speak of the love of their craft, do not want their sons to follow in their footsteps . . . Therefore, the boxers' passion is a skewed and malicious one. It is tainted by the idea that boxing, for all of its benefits, exacts too high a price.(n16)

For such boxers, plying their trade requires that they endure a coercive minimum of varying degrees of unpleasantness and grave doubts therefore arise about the autonomy of their decision to enter the ring.

If boxers are primarily motivated by the intrinsic enjoyment that they gain from the activity, we would expect that they would be evenly distributed throughout all socioeconomic classes. The reality that the vast majority of fighters come from poor backgrounds lends credence to the claim that economic motivations are the primary ones for their choice of occupation. As Colin Radford, a defender of boxing, concedes,

> for most boxers . . . boxing was their only escape from hard labor—or, as it is more likely to be these days, unemployment. (Whether a country has a lot of good boxers, or few, is a pretty good indicator of the state of its economy, or of the economic opportunities available to some community within that country.)(n17)

The very small number of fighters who come from affluent backgrounds would not be subject to coercion at all, but, for the majority of the others, the offer of boxing contracts creates a strong differential coercive pressure with a more or less significant coercive minimum. A plausible soft paternalist argument for restricting boxing, then, is to protect boxers—those who regard fighting as an unpleasant necessity in order to escape poverty—from acting on inautonomous decisions.

However, does the argument just presented not have the unfortunate consequence that all offers of menial work, which often brings little intrinsic satisfaction and is performed largely out of economic necessity, are coercive? In response, while a Marxist would indeed regard the need to find a job in a capitalist society as coercive, no particular job offer is coercive. The reason I have singled out the offer of a career in boxing as coercive is that it provides a unique opportunity for a slim chance of vast wealth and, thus, exerts vastly greater differential coercive pressure than the prospect of poorly-paid menial jobs. Moreover, for many fighters boxing exacts a far more burdensome coercive minimum than unskilled jobs in order to enjoy the rewards: physical pain, the risk of serious injury, and moral qualms about injuring opponents, as opposed to the tedium of menial jobs. When, as in the case of most minimum-wage jobs, the coercive minimum that an offer induces a person to perform is only mildly unpleasant, little if any coercion occurs. Similarly, the view that people can be coerced by offers to become professional boxers does not entail that lucrative contracts for such other sports as basketball would also be coercive for youths from disadvantaged backgrounds. While such offers may indeed be hard to refuse, basketball contracts impose negative coercive minimums and are, therefore, only impurely coercive. For most people, accepting such contracts would impose no costs at all, since they regard playing basketball as a positively pleasant experience. Hence offers of professional boxing contracts can be coercive in a way that offers of minimum wage jobs and professional basketball contracts are not.

However, Feinberg argues that the coerciveness of an offer does not necessarily invalidate its recipient's consent. When the coercer deliberately creates the situation that makes the coercee unable to refuse the offer—for example, if the millionaire had actually caused the child's illness that now requires expensive medical care—the coercee's consent is indeed involuntary and invalid. But when the coercer merely takes advantage of the coercee's pre-existing predicament—and such is clearly the case for any coercion that promoters, managers, and trainers exert over those whom they persuade to become professional boxers—their exploitation does not preclude an autonomous decision by the coercee to accept the offer.(n18) Since boxing promoters, managers, or trainers, who are not the cause of a potential fighter's socioeconomic disadvantages, merely provide him with an opportunity to overcome those disadvantages, he can surely make a voluntary decision to accept their offer as the best (though unfortunate) solution to a sorry situation.

Nonetheless, even though exploitative coercers who take advantage of their coercees' pre-existing predicaments do not normally prevent coercees from voluntarily accepting their offers, Feinberg concedes that in the case of "unconscionable contracts," coed' voluntariness may be so impaired as to make their consent to the contract invalid.(n19) An offer is unconscionable when it is coercive and imposes harsh conditions on the coercee or confers unfair benefits on the coercer. Feinberg argues that the lecherous millionaire's offer is unconscionable if the woman is coerced into sexual relations, which constitutes a harsh cost for her. This unconscionability reduces her voluntariness in consenting to the agreement to a level that renders it null and void. If she broke the agreement once the millionaire had paid for her child's medical care, courts should dismiss his claim for compensation for her breach of contract.

Since offers to become professional boxers are sometimes coercive, and since the medical evidence cited at the outset of this paper gives ample reason to consider the costs imposed on boxers as harsh, these offers therefore do indeed sometimes qualify as unconscionable. Does the unconscionability of the contracts that boxers sign reduce boxers' voluntariness to a sufficiently low level to justify outlawing such agreements? By analogy with Feinberg's treatment of the lecherous millionaire example, if the contracts are unconscionable, courts would be justified in denying promoters et al. any legal recourse should a boxer break a contract. And the same reasoning—protecting boxers from the effects of agreements to which they have not given sufficiently voluntary consent—justifies pre-emptive protection of boxers, in the form of banning such contracts in the first place. In the case of the lecherous millionaire, we could allow the woman to benefit from the offer (since denying her the opportunity to save her child seems wrong) and then protect her from the millionaire's harsh demand by declaring the agreement void on the ground of its unconscionability when he sues her after she refuses to fulfill her end of the contract. In contrast, in the case of boxing the benefits are inseparable from the unduly harsh cost: the only way that boxers can enjoy the chance of earning a fortune in the ring is by simultaneously risking the probability of irreversible brain damage. Consequently, the only way we can protect boxers from the effects of unconscionable contracts is to prohibit such contracts.(n20)

Since some boxers—those who are not socioeconomically disadvantaged and those who find fighting intrinsically enjoyable and do not experience its hardships as costs—may make fully voluntary decisions to become boxers, restricting boxing would reduce their freedom in order to protect others from the effects of inautonomous decisions. While this interference is regrettable, it is justified by the need to protect the large number of fighters who currently enter the ring under varying degrees of de facto coercion. In defense of a cautious, paternalistic approach, since boxers run the risk of serious, irreversible harm, we are entitled to demand a high standard of autonomy before we allow them to do so.(n21) Given the socioeconomic realities in which most fighters enter the profession and given the brutality that most fighters regard as a necessary unpleasantness to be endured, many of them do not meet that standard, and we are entitled to restrict boxing in order to protect them.

Pre-Emptive Paternalism

If the previous soft paternalistic argument fails, on the ground that many or most boxers do indeed choose their profession autonomously, the case for restricting boxing in order to protect boxers from harm will have to resort to the far more controversial principle of hard paternalism: the permissibility of interfering with people's fully autonomous choices in order to protect them from harm.

The most defensible type of hard paternalism was originally proposed by John Stuart Mill, in the context of his famous anti-paternalistic argument in *On Liberty*. Mill argues that we are permitted to prevent people from acting on their desire to become slaves, even in the unlikely event that their decision is fully voluntary.(n22) Mill points out the irony of letting our desire to respect people's freedom to live their lives according to their own values lead us to permit people to perform a single act, however voluntarily, that would irrevocably relinquish this freedom. If autonomy really is important, we are surely justified in this minor restriction on people's current autonomy in order to prevent the complete loss of autonomy that occurs in slavery. We could compare this paternalistic restriction with the act of pruning a tree in order to facilitate its future growth. Let us call restrictions on autonomous actions in order to preserve greater future autonomy pre-emptive paternalism.

If pre-emptive paternalism is ever justified, restricting boxing seems to fall well within its rationale. According to the recent studies cited above, most boxers will suffer from irreversible brain damage, and brain damage is the most direct way to reduce a person's autonomy. And preemptive paternalism itself seems to be well established in our legal system, since it is the most obvious rationale for our prohibition on dangerous, addictive drugs and our laws requiring the use of car seat belts and motorcycle safety helmets.(n23) A landmark judicial opinion on informed consent recognized, on the same ground of pre-emptive paternalism, that exceptions to physicians' normal duty of disclosure exist in the case of currently autonomous patients

> when risk-disclosure poses such a threat of detriment to the patient as to become unfeasible or contraindicated from a medical point of view. It is recognized that patients occasionally become so ill or emotionally distraught on disclosure as to foreclose a rational decision.(n24)

Boxers face a considerably higher probability of autonomy-reducing injuries than do automobile drivers and motorcycle riders, whom we already protect with paternalistic laws. For instance, whereas motorcycle riders face a relatively small lifetime risk (2%) of serious injury or death,(n25) we have seen that boxers face the probability of brain damage.

However, we need to consider Feinberg's powerful and original critique of any pre-emptive paternalism.(n26) He insists that we should respect a fully autonomous decision to embark on a course of action that a person knows may result in a loss of autonomy. While liberty is obviously the central value that the liberal position is designed to protect, "liberty too is a means to a person's good which a sovereign chooser might voluntarily decide to trade off for some other value."(n27) Even though a fully voluntary decision to risk the probability of a loss of future autonomy may lead to a life with diminished autonomy, it would be an autonomously chosen life in any case, and to interfere with its choice would be to infringe the chooser's autonomy at the time he makes the choice, that is to treat him in a manner precluded by respect for him as an autonomous agent.(n28)

Feinberg argues that we must give priority to the autonomous wishes of my current self, even if I explicitly "disenfranchise" my future self by waiving my right to revoke my decision.

[T]he earlier choice, being the genuine choice of a sovereign being, free to dispose of his own lot in the future, must continue to govern. After all, the earlier self and the later are: the same self, not morally distinct persons, but rather one person at different times.(n29)

Feinberg presents a reductio ad absurdum argument against banning slavery on pre-emptive paternalistic grounds. He fears that the rationale of preserving future autonomy would also justify banning suicide and euthanasia, imposing "a 'Spartan regime' of enforced health and hygiene" including bans on fried food and smoking, and forbidding any agreements that would commit a person to narrowing his or her future options.(n30) However, Feinberg's attempt to show that all pre- emptive paternalism has absurd consequences is vulnerable to several objections.

First, it does not entail a ban on suicide and euthanasia. Calling death a curtailment of autonomy sounds odd, since the paradigm case of losing autonomy is a living person whose ability to determine her own future is diminished. The harm that is inflicted by death, when it is indeed harmful, is not so much loss of autonomy as the cancellation of any future experiences at all. However, one might object, being alive is a necessary condition for exercising autonomy and the autonomy-preserving rationale for pre-emptive paternalism might, after all, require that we prohibit suicide and euthanasia. In response, a crucial difference exists between suicide/euthanasia and the type of harm that I propose to prevent by preemptive paternalism. Whereas we may safely assume that boxers do not desire the loss of future autonomy that they risk suffering, terminally ill people seek to end their own lives precisely because they no longer value their burdensome existence, and regard the permanent loss of their autonomy as a release from suffering. Allowing suicide or euthanasia is, therefore, quite consistent with protecting people like boxers from losses of autonomy that they do not desire. But what about people who want to become slaves, who presumably desire to irrevocably give up their freedom? Does not the view that I am defending have the embarrassing consequence that we should allow such people to become slaves? We can, fortunately, avoid this unwanted entailment. A good number of those who voluntarily enter servitude are likely to come to regard their irreversible relinquishment of freedom as a terrible mistake, perhaps made in a moment of recklessness or depression. Terminally ill people are, by contrast, far less likely to undergo changes of heart: most patients suffering from painful terminal or degenerative diseases will desire even more strongly to die as their suffering increases, rather than being grateful to society for forbidding euthanasia, thus giving them the opportunity to change their minds about dying. Moreover, to anticipate a similar argument from Feinberg that I endorse later in this section, the request to become a slave is so self-destructive as to create a presumption of irrationality in the requester. Protecting such incompetent people from inautonomous decisions outweighs the occasional injustice done to those who make genuinely autonomous requests to become slaves.

Second, it isn't clear why we can't distinguish between dramatic differences in degree between different losses of future autonomy. A boxer's chronic brain damage over several decades is a far more serious loss of autonomy than that suffered by a junk food eater whose capacity to think rationally is not at all diminished during a life that is less healthy and slightly abbreviated as a result of unwise eating habits. Allowing pre-emptive paternalism to prevent such catastrophic losses of future autonomy as irrevocable slavery agreements and irreversible brain damage caused by boxing does not commit us to allowing paternalism to prevent trivial reductions in future options, any more than the harm principle commits us to draconian laws punishing such trivial harms to others as rudeness. A more appropriate comparison would be between boxing and a food that was known to cause irreversible brain damage in the majority of people who eat it. Agreeing that we should indeed ban such a food would be a relatively easy bullet to bite for the proponent of restricting boxing on the ground of pre-emptive paternalism. The FDA already prohibits foods and drugs that are known to have far less dramatic harmful effects.

Third, even if using pre-emptive paternalism to ban slavery does have the absurd consequences that Feinberg alleges, this does not taint the parallel argument for restricting boxing, because of a crucial difference between the cases. Slavery is certainly a catastrophic renunciation of liberty that prevents slaves who live to regret their enslavement from acting on their newly formed values. But, unlike brain damage caused by boxing, it does not impair slaves' ability to reflect on and form values and life plans in the first place, which is the most fundamental element of autonomy. Boxing is especially pernicious in that it impairs intellectual and moral autonomy, whereas slavery, repugnant though the permanent relinquishment of freedom of action is, does not impair slaves' ability to think for themselves. As pointed out above, precisely this desire to protect people from irreversible loss of intellectual and moral autonomy may well underlie our current prohibition on dangerous, addictive drugs and our laws requiring seat belts and safety helmets.

So pre-emptive paternalism provides a plausible rationale for several of our current legal requirements and restrictions and, if justified, it makes a strong case for restricting boxing. Restricting boxing on the ground of pre-emptive paternalism entails neither a controversial ban on suicide and euthanasia nor unduly invasive laws designed to prevent trivial losses of autonomy. And Feinberg's claim that all pre-emptive paternalism is a violation of competent adults' right to choose their own life plans depends on the controversial assertion that, even in the case of such dangerous activities as taking addictive drugs, driving without seat belts or safety helmets, and boxing, the autonomous decisions of my current self always take precedence over my future self's intellectual and moral autonomy.

Feinberg argues that we may justify banning slavery contracts and requiring motorcyclists to wear helmets on grounds other than preemptive paternalism. Even if we accept Feinberg's rejection of preemptive paternalism, we can construct parallel rationales for restricting boxing that do not involve hard paternalism. The first argument is based on the premise that we should demand that people demonstrate an especially high level of autonomy before we allow them to engage in activities that create a substantial risk of serious, irreversible harm. Feinberg reasons that we may refuse to recognize slavery contracts, which involve the ultimate act of permanently renouncing one's autonomy, on the ground that inevitably fallible tests for autonomy would wrongly allow some inautonomous people to become slaves.(n31) On the same soft paternalist ground that is acceptable to liberals, we could argue that, especially in light of the concerns about de facto coercion of fighters from disadvantaged backgrounds discussed above in section 1a [see p. 390], any legal tests that we devise may be too inexact for us to be sure that boxers have displayed the requisite level of autonomy for us to allow them to risk irreversible brain damage. Second, in an argument that anticipates our harm principle-based discussion in section 3, Feinberg warns against recognizing slavery contracts on the further ground that society's abandonment of those people who are reckless enough to become slaves would send a dangerous message of indifference to the plight of others that could lead to a general decrease in care and compassion in our society.(n32) Similarly, we could justify restricting boxing by appealing to the moral insensitivity that is caused by our government's willingness to let fighters suffer the probability of brain damage in their most likely unsuccessful pursuit of fame and fortune. Third, Feinberg justifies both the prohibition of slavery and laws requiring safety helmets for motorcyclists by appealing to the "psychic costs" to other people who are distressed when they see or learn of those who are harmed by the absence of such protective laws.(n33) A parallel argument would justify restricting boxing due to the distress and indignation it causes to third parties. I do not endorse the second and third arguments for restricting boxing and I present them only to show that they are entailed by Feinberg's nonpaternalistic arguments for banning slavery and requiring the use of safety helmets.

If, on the other hand, we reject Feinberg's absolute opposition to hard paternalism, we can combine the arguments for restricting boxing on the ground of pre-emptive paternalism presented in the current section with the soft paternalistic arguments of the previous section to provide a compelling case. If boxing creates the probability of a severe and irreversible loss of autonomy and if serious doubts exist about the autonomy of many fighters' decisions to enter the profession in the first place, we should restrict the sport in order to protect them.

Arguments Based on Legal Moralism

Even if we reject all paternalistic arguments for restricting boxing, another ground for prohibition deserves consideration: the objection that professional boxing is morally repugnant. If so, fighters, managers, trainers, promoters, and fans alike are complicit in perpetrating or supporting an immorality. Why exactly is boxing morally wrong? It cannot be the mere fact that brain damage and other injuries are the probable result, because the consent of the participants arguably prevents these harms from constituting wrongs (though, as we have seen, whether many boxers' consent is fully voluntary is doubtful). To locate any immorality in boxing we should look beyond the consequences of the actions involved and focus instead on the attitudes that these actions express. I will focus on the attitudes displayed by boxers and by fans.

Boxing, along with such offshoots as full-contact karate and ultimate combat, is unique among sports in that competitors' primary goal is to incapacitate their opponents. American football players sometimes use the morally dubious tactic of legal but bone-shattering hits designed to intimidate and shake up star opponents and, better still, force them out of the game. However, while this tactic may facilitate victory, the goal of the game remains to score more points than the opponent. In boxing, in contrast, incapacitating the opponent—by knockout or technical knockout—is sufficient for victory. By far the most effective way to incapacitate opponents is by inflicting blows to the head, thus causing (at least) temporary damage to the brain. Even winning by points is best achieved by punching opponents' heads, making knockdowns—which judges often consider decisive in awarding a round to a fighter—more likely to occur, while also reducing opponents' ability to fight back.

In attempting to injure their opponents, boxers treat them as mere objects to be disposed of in order to achieve victory. No amount of post-fight embraces and mutual congratulations can erase the savage, brutal attitude that, for the duration of the fight, each displayed toward the other.(n34) Whereas the usual wrongness of injuring another is arguably avoided by each fighter's consent to participate in an activity known to be dangerous, this consent in no way diminishes the inherent wrongness of regarding another person as a subhuman object to be damaged. Consider, by analogy, a TV show (not too far removed from reality) in which participants hurl a torrent of racist, sexist, or homophobic abuse at other people. The voluntary participation of these victims of abuse would not lessen our moral repugnance at the attitude of contempt that the abusers display.

The attitude of many spectators of boxing is just as problematic as that of the boxers themselves. Spectators pay for the privilege of watching two half-naked humans in a ring attempt to incapacitate one another by means of punches. "Purist" fans who appreciate the high level of skills that a talented boxer displays no doubt exist, and even less knowledgeable fans can admire the genuine courage that fighters sometimes exhibit. But many fans are especially eager to see cuts, knockdowns, and knockouts—that is, pain and injury—often standing and baying with bloodlust when one fighter gets in trouble. Promoter Mike Jacobs said in 1935 that he looked for fighters who injure opponents, because fans do not "come out to see a tea party. They come to see a man hurt."(n35) We have little reason to believe that the majority of boxing fans today are any different. TV promotions for upcoming fights, which we may presume are based on market research and designed to attract as many viewers as possible, highlight brutal knockdowns rather than deft footwork and adroit evasions of blows. Mike Tyson, for all his misdeeds outside the ring and his failing powers within it, still commands more attention than nearly all other fighters because of his ability to inflict gruesome punishment on opponents. Sitting in comfortable ringside or living-room seats and reveling in the sight of one man hurting another is a paradigm case of the wonderful German word *schadenfreude*—pleasure derived from another person's misfortune. That this attitude is reprehensible needs no argument. Indeed, it is not far removed from sadism.

Legal moralism is the principle that would allow us to prohibit such "free-floating" evils,(n36) even if (because of the consent of those who are adversely affected by them) no one is wronged by them. Legal moralism permits us to restrict actions solely on the ground of their immorality, even though they might be harmless.

Legal moralism is normally associated with a conservative agenda, as in the case of its most famous proponent, Patrick Devlin, who argued for the continued legal prohibition of prostitution and homosexuality on the ground that these practices tend to cause social disintegration by violating values held by the majority.(n37) The problem with this type of legal moralism is that it gives blanket approval to the majority for imposing groundless prejudices on minority groups.(n38) Strictly speaking, this rationale for restricting liberty is not legal moralism at all, since it is based not on moral arguments as such, but on the desire to preserve prevailing morality. For this reason, Feinberg refers to it instead as moral conservatism.(n39) However, rejecting moral conservatism does not entail rejecting the argument for restricting boxing presented above based on strict legal moralism (i.e., arguments that boxing is immoral, regardless of whether prevailing morality approves or disapproves of it). First, let us examine whether strict legal moralism is ever defensible.

Feinberg considers a graphic hypothetical example of a free-floating evil—Kristol's imaginary gladiatorial contests held in Yankee Stadium, ending in the death of the losing combatants(n40)—which makes a good prima facie case for strict legal moralism.(n41) If anything is so inherently immoral, regardless of the voluntary participation of both fighters and spectators, as to justify prohibition, such gladiatorial contests are. A society that allowed such barbaric contests to occur would be so morally base that the knowledge that it at least held fast to the liberal ideal of respect for individual autonomy would be small comfort. If this example allows a foot inside the door for strict legal moralism, may we not use the same principle to justify restricting the brutal business of professional boxing, which differs from gladiatorial combat only in the severity of the injuries inflicted? Granted, the difference in degree is huge—the certainty of death for the losing gladiator v. the probability of brain damage for both boxers if they fight many contests—but the morally troubling feature is the same in both cases: the infliction of pain and injury for the pleasure of onlookers.

Feinberg's strategy in responding to this attempted counter-example to his liberal position is to argue that our intuition that we should indeed ban gladiatorial contests can be explained on grounds that are perfectly acceptable to the liberal, without resorting to strict legal moralism. The kind of people whom we allow to delight in watching brutal displays of maiming and homicide, he argues, are likely to show a similar, callous disregard for other people's welfare in their own private lives.

We cannot hold an image of these wretches in our minds without recoiling, for each of them alone will seem threatening or dangerous, and thousands or millions of them together will be downright terrifying. It is highly difficult, if not plain impossible, to think of widespread indifference to suffering as a mere private moral failing unproductive of further individual and social harm... [M]oral corruption as such is not a relevant ground for preventive criminalization, but when the moral dispositions that are corrupted include concern about the sufferings of others, then the interests of others become vulnerable, and the corrupting activity can no longer be thought to be exclusively self-regarding.(n42)

This corrupting effect is amplified by the fact that legal toleration of these contests, even and perhaps especially if accompanied by government regulations, would seem to send a tacit message of official approval of violence and cruelty. Moreover, the probable effects on impressionable children, who (even if they are barred from witnessing the contests "live") are likely to idolize successful gladiators, are even more alarming. Consequently, the harm principle itself, which any liberal can embrace without fear of unjust intrusions on individual autonomy, is sufficient to justify banning Kristol's hypothetical practice of modern gladiatorial contests.

Although Feinberg's arguments do not refute legal moralism—they show only that a liberal can give a plausible analysis of hard cases without using this principle—I will not use it as an independent reason for restricting boxing. While strict legal moralism is intuitively attractive in the case of boxing, we might have difficulty avoiding sliding down a slippery slope to interferences with harmless self-regarding behavior for trivial reasons, and to the same danger of the legal enforcement of groundless prejudices that is created by moral conservatism. If strict legal moralism is not necessary to explain why we should ban gladiatorial contests, we are even less justified in using this controversial principle in arguing for restricting the far less dangerous business of boxing. In the next section, I will consider instead whether we can formulate arguments for restricting boxing based on the harm principle similar to the ones that Feinberg uses to argue for prohibiting gladiatorial contests.

Arguments Based on Harm to Society at Large

Boxing is considerably less violent than gladiatorial contests, primarily in that the death of the loser is only an occasional tragedy, rather than the inevitable result of each bout. Any brutalizing effect of boxing, then, will be considerably less severe than that of gladiatorial contests. Nonetheless, as pointed out above in our discussion of legal moralism, the morally troubling feature is the same in both cases: the infliction of pain and injury for the pleasure of onlookers. And it is precisely the message that it is acceptable to take pleasure in watching the suffering of others that creates a very real danger that it will increase anti-social behavior. And, unlike Kristol's hypothetical gladiators, boxers are real people who are idolized by real children, who learn that hurting and injuring opponents is an admirable thing to do. The number of people present at fights may be relatively small, but the television audience, including pay-per-view, closed circuit, and sports bars, is huge. Moreover, the mere knowledge that public displays of the attempts of fighters to incapacitate one another are legally tolerated may lower the inhibition to anti-social behavior of even those with no interest in boxing. Unlike boxers, the public at large does not consent to the practice and any harm that it may cause, so an uncontroversial application of the harm principle may justify restricting boxing in order to protect society as a whole.

However, this argument invites the objection that concern for freedom of expression has quite properly prevented us from banning violent films despite comparable fears that viewing them causes an increase in violent behavior. The same concern should also prevent us from restricting boxing. In response, a huge distinction exists between the depiction of violence, which is all that happens in films, and violence itself, which is what happens in the boxing ring. Restricting actions is less problematic than restricting the portrayal of actions in movies. A more apt analogy would be between boxing and either "snuff films" in which actors are allegedly injured or killed, or pornographic films in which unwilling actors are allegedly coerced to appear, both of which we would have less hesitation in restricting than mainstream films.

Robert Simon raises a related objection, asking whether the same reasoning that led to restricting boxing wouldn't also commit us to banning books that we have determined will have a pernicious effect, for instance, one that proposes educational reforms that would be disastrous if implemented, which is likely, given the prestige of its author. Simon claims that such restrictions would seriously impede our ability to make up our own minds on educational and other issues.(n43) In response to Simon's reductio ad absurdum, while the alleged consequence that he describes is indeed unacceptable, it does not follow from the argument for restricting boxing that we are considering. The reason that his example of book banning is alarming is that it involves the outright censorship of ideas, which undeniably does interfere with our ability to exercise intellectual autonomy in reaching our own views. In contrast, restricting boxing in no way precludes the publication of books describing the alleged beauty of the activity, explaining its physical and emotional benefits, and demanding its legalization. Prohibiting boxing restricts people's actions, not their access to ideas.

The weakness of the argument for restricting boxing on the ground of its brutalizing effect on society is not that it entails indefensible instances of censorship. Nor is there any problem in principle with restricting behavior that fosters attitudes that lead to tangible harm to other people. The Achilles Heel of this argument is the lack of evidence that boxing actually leads to an increase in violence and other anti-social behavior. Whether boxing incites such behavior or reduces it by acting as a harmless cathartic outlet is an empirical question that is hard to answer. In particular, finding a pure control group so that we can isolate the influence of boxing on, for instance, violence is especially difficult. Comparisons between states and countries that do allow professional boxing and those that do not are of limited value, since television coverage is ubiquitous worldwide. The best evidence would come from a comparison of the level of violent and anti-social behavior in an experimental group that watches many boxing matches and a carefully matched control group that watches none. In the absence of such evidence, the argument for restricting boxing because of the danger that it harms society by lowering inhibitions to anti-social behavior is too slight to justify restricting people's freedom.

Conclusion

We have found two substantial paternalistic arguments for restricting professional boxing: first, the need to protect boxers from serious losses of future autonomy due to irreversible brain damage, which is all the more urgent because, second, many boxers' decisions to enter the profession in the first place are of questionable autonomy because of de facto coercion resulting from their socioeconomic disadvantages. While legal moralism does not by itself provide a defensible rationale for restricting boxing, the argument presented in section 2 that boxers and fans have inherently immoral attitudes bolsters the paternalistic argument. That is, if strong reasons exist for protecting boxers from harm, then if, furthermore, far from having redeeming value, boxing is inherently immoral, the case for restricting it is stronger still.

I propose a single legal restriction—a complete ban on blows to the head—which would allow boxing to continue, while eliminating its single most harmful aspect.(n44) Injuries could still occur, of course, as a result of body blows, but they would not have the devastating effect on boxers' well-being and future autonomy that brain damage has. Given this vast reduction in the risks of boxing, we could require potential boxers to demonstrate a considerably more relaxed standard of autonomy, one that even the most socioeconomically disadvantaged people would probably meet. Imposing this restriction would thus neutralize the two paternalistic arguments for prohibiting boxing.

Granted, boxing would remain a violent activity the goal of which is to incapacitate the opponent, so the argument for restricting boxing because of the inherently immoral attitude that boxers adopt toward one another would remain operative. However, as I argued at the end of section 2, legal moralism is not by itself a sufficient reason for restricting boxing. Moreover, the attitude of boxers and spectators is likely to be less troubling under the proposed reform. Knockouts and stoppages arise far more commonly as a result of blows to the head than from body blows. The likely result of restricting boxers to body blows is to reorient their strategy in favor of scoring points with frequent blows, rather than trying to injure opponents with heavy shots. Thus the role of skill and strategy will be increased, with a corresponding decrease in violence and intimidation.

Market forces may give rise to fighters who will meet fans' demand for violence by specializing in punches that crack ribs and cause other painful injuries. However, the many fans who are currently drawn to boxing by the prospect of seeing bloody fighters become groggy and drop to the canvas after repeated blows to the head would most likely lose interest if boxing became a relatively safe sport in which knockouts are rare and skill and strategy, rather than the infliction of injuries, are the major determinants of victory. And boxing purists who continue to like, and even prefer, this safer form of boxing would probably be too rare for professional boxing to continue to be a profitable business. The likely result of eliminating blows to the head, then, is the withering away of professional boxing, which depends on attracting large numbers of spectators to pay fighters and their handlers.

This would leave amateur boxing, which is already—with its short three-round bouts, mandatory protective headgear, and referees' greater willingness to stop fights to prevent injuries to outmatched fighters—considerably safer than professional fighting.(n45) It would become even safer with a prohibition on blows to the head, which would make protective headgear superfluous. Amateur boxing would continue as a recreation for boxers who enjoy the sport, but the number of participants would probably dramatically decline, since many boxers currently use the amateur arena as a prelude to the professional business that would, under my proposal, most likely soon cease to exist. The elimination of financial motives for entering the ring would completely disarm one of my major objections to today's professional boxing, namely the danger that socioeconomically disadvantaged boxers might be acting inautonomously due to de facto coercion. And pre-emptive paternalism would be out of the question, since no significant danger of irreversible brain damage would exist.

A salutary aspect of my proposal is that it achieves its carefully targeted goal of eliminating the morally objectionable components of boxing while imposing minimal legal restrictions on the actions of competent adults. The single regulation, a ban on blows to the head in any type of boxing, is justified by the uncontroversial goal of protecting boxers from acting on inautonomous decisions and suffering a permanent reduction in future autonomy. And the likely disappearance of professional boxing would be the result of market forces rather than governmental coercion, as would the likely reduction in the number of participants in amateur boxing.(n46)

Notes

(n1) Peter W. Lampert, MD, and John M. Hardman, MD, "Morphological Changes in Brains of Boxers," Journal of the American Medical Association, vol. 251. no. 20 (May 25, 1984), p. 2676.

(n2)   Ibid. See also Robert Glenn Morrison, "Medical and Public Health Aspects of Boxing," Journal of the American Medical Association, vol. 255, no. 18 (May 9, 1986), pp. 2476-77.

(n3) Morrison, "Medical and Public Health Aspects of Boxing," p. 2478. For more on the medical dangers of boxing, see also Ira R. Casson, MD, et al., "Brain Damage in Modern Boxers," Journal of the American Medical Association, vol. 251 no. 20 (May 25, 1984); and Jeffrey T. Sammons, "Why Physicians Should Oppose Boxing: An Interdisciplinary History Perspective," Journal of the American Medical Association, vol. 261, no. 10, (March 10, 1989).

(n4) Morrison, "Medical and Public Health Aspects of Boxing," p. 2475.

(n5) RESOLVED, That the American Medical Association: 1. Encourage the elimination of both amateur and professional boxing, a sport in which the primary objective is to inflict injury; 2. Communicate its opposition to boxing as a sport to appropriate regulatory bodies; 3. Assist state medical societies to work with their state legislatures to enact laws to eliminate boxing in their jurisdictions; and 4. Educate the American public, especially children and young adults, about the dangerous effects of boxing on the health of participants.

(n6) Joel Feinberg, The Moral Limits of the Criminal Law, vol. 3, Harm to Self (Oxford: Oxford University Press, 1986), and vol. 4, Harmless Wrongdoing (Oxford: Oxford University Press, 1990). The definition of the liberal view comes from Harm to Self, p. xvii.

(n7) For good objections to banning boxing based on Mill's argument against paternalism, see Russel H. Patterson, Jr., MD, "On Boxing and Liberty," Journal of the American Medical Association vol. 255, no. 18 (May 9, 1986); and Robert L. Simon, Fair Play: Sports, Values, and Society (Boulder: Westview Press, 1991), pp. 54-57.

(n8) Thus, while the AMA's proposal to ban boxing is obviously contrary to the liberal position, its call to educate the public, especially children and young adults, on the dangers of boxing (item #4) is entirely consistent with liberalism.

(n9) See Simon, Fair Play, pp. 59-60.

(n10) See Feinberg, Harm to Self, chap. 24, esp. pp. 229.49.

(n11) Ibid., pp. 229-33. As Feinberg says, "one person can effectively force another person to do what he wants by manipulating his options in such a way as to render alternative choices ineligible and, in so doing, quite incidentally enlarge his freedom in general" (p. 233).

(n12) Following Feinberg (ibid., p. 211), I base both the coercive minimum and the differential coercive pressure on boxers' subjective assessment of the harms of boxing and of the poverty that it enables them to escape. As I explain in the next paragraph, boxers' assessments of these harms may vary.

(n13) Ibid., pp. 233-40.

(n14) For more detail on the nature of differential coercive pressure and coercive minimums, see ibid., pp. 199-205.

(n15) For sympathetic accounts of the pride that some boxers take in their sport, see Michael Burke, "Is Boxing Violent? Let's Ask Some Boxers," and Baydon Beddoe, "'In the Fight': Phenomenology of a Pugilist," both in Dennis Hemphill (ed.), All Part of the Game: Violence and Australian Sport (Sydney: Walla Walla Press, 1998).

(n16) Burke, "Is Boxing Violent? Let's Ask Some Boxers," pp. 118-19.

(n17) Colin Radford, "Utilitarianism and the Noble Art," Philosophy 63 (1988): 63-81, p. 70. For more on the link between boxing and poverty, see Stephen Brunt, "Boxing is not to blame: A fighter died of his injuries this week, but the culprit isn't pugilism, it's poverty," The Globe and Mail (Toronto), December 10, 1999, p. A19.

(n18) Feinberg, Harm to Self, pp. 244-48.

(n19) Ibid., pp. 249-53.

(n20) I refer here to contracts in today's sport of boxing, in which boxers risk the probability of brain damage. I have no objection to professional contracts in the reformed sport of boxing that I propose in the conclusion, since the ban on blows to the head virtually eliminates that danger.

(n21) See Feinberg on variable standards for voluntariness, Harm to Self, pp. 117-21.

(n22) John Stuart Mill, On Liberty (Indianapolis: Hackett Publishing Co., 1978), p. 101.

(n23 See Gerald Dworkin, "Paternalism," in Richard Wasserstrom (ed.), Morality and the law (Belmont, Cal.: Wadsworth Publishing Co., 1971), section VI.

(n24) Canterbury v. Spence (U.S. Court of Appeals, District of Columbia Court, 1972). The quotation is from the reprint in Thomas A. Mappes and David DeGrazia (eds.), Biomedical Ethics, 4th ed. (New York: McGraw-Hill, 1996), p. 87.

(n25) Feinberg, Harm to Self, p. 392, n. 38.

(n26) Ibid., pp. 71-87.

(n27) Ibid., pp. 76-77.

(n28) Ibid., p. 78.

(n29) Ibid., p. 83.

(n30) Ibid., p. 77. See also Simon, Fair Play, p. 58, where he raises similar concerns about using pre-emptive paternalism to justify banning boxing.

(n31) Feinberg, Harm to Self, pp. 79-80.

(n32) Ibid., pp. 80-81

(n33) Ibid., pp. 81, 139-41

(n34) See Paul Davis, "Ethical Issues in Boxing," Journal of the Philosophy of Sport 20-21 (1993-94): 48-63, pp. 51-56, for an excellent account of the morally problematic attitude that boxers display toward each other.

(n35) Quoted by Jeffrey T. Sammons, "Why Physicians Should Oppose Boxing: An Interdisciplinary History Perspective," Journal of the American Medical Association vol. 261, no. 10 (March 10, 1989), p. 1486.

(n36) Free-floating evils" is Feinberg's expression. See Harmless Wrongdoing, p. 125.

(n37) Patrick Devlin, "The Enforcement of Morals," The Enforcement of Morals (London: Oxford University Press, 1965), chap. 1.

(n38) See H.L.A. Hart, "Immorality and Treason," The Listener, July 3D, 1959. For a critique of similar "communitarian" arguments for banning boxing (on the ground that it violates community standards), see Simon, Fair Play, p. 63.

(n39) For more detail on the difference between moral conservatism and strict legal moralism (see text below), see Feinberg, Harmless Wrongdoing, pp. 124-26.

(n40) See Irving Kristol, "Pornography, Obscenity, and the Case for Censorship," The New York Times Magazine, March 28, 1971. Simon presents a similar example in Fair Play, pp. 60-61.

(n41) Feinberg, Harmless Wrongdoing, pp. 129-33.

(n42) Ibid., pp. 131-32.

(n43) Simon, Fair Play, pp. 61-62.

(n44) My conclusion is thus similar to George D. Lundberg's disjunctive proposal to either ban boxing outright or ban blows to the head. See "Boxing Should Be Banned in Civilized Countries," Journal of the American Medical Association vol. 251, no. 20 (May 25, 1984), p. 2697. Robert L. Simon also proposes banning blows to the head as one of several ways of improving safety in boxing. See Fair Play, p. 64. I differ from Simon in that, whereas he suggests only that the ban be enacted voluntarily by boxing authorities, I claim that the arguments presented in this paper are strong enough to justify a government-enacted legal prohibition.

(n45) See Robert Ludwig, MO, "Making Boxing Safer: The Swedish Model," Journal of the American Medical Association vol. 255, no. 18 (May 9,1986), p. 2482, for an account of the extensive safety precautions already in place in amateur boxing in Sweden.

(n46) I presented earlier drafts of this paper at the International Association for the Philosophy of Sport 1997 meeting in Oslo, Norway and the Central States Philosophical Association 1998 meeting in Des Moines, Iowa. I am grateful to audience members at both conferences, CSPA commentator Jim Swindler and referees for Social Theory and Practice for helpful comments.

Darwin's Athletes

A Review Essay

◆

John Valentine

Darwin's Athletes, written by John Hoberman, is a learned, courageous, and original work that should be read by everyone who is a serious student of either race or sport. The thesis of *Darwin's Athletes* is provocative: sport has done more harm than good to African-Americans. Hoberman argues that sport has played an important role in leading African-Americans to embrace the damaging idea that physical self-expression is the essence of being black. He also argues that sport has helped to preserve deep seated racial myths among whites, while at the same time fostering an illusory view of racial integration in the U.S. For Hoberman, these factors outweigh the contributions that sport has made to racial integration, to promoting friendships among blacks and whites, to teaching values such as deferred gratification and fair play, and to paving the way to higher education. Although one might ultimately disagree with one or more of the positions that Hoberman takes in his book, it is unlikely that one can read *Darwin's Athletes* without a serious reassessment of one's own views on race and sport.

I will review and cite page numbers from the Mariner paperback edition, as it features a new Preface in which Hoberman formulates replies to African-American critics of the hardcover edition. Hoberman's efforts to reply to his critics are especially fitting, in that he characterizes the whole of his book as "an exercise in racial dialogue." As such, *Darwin's Athletes* is a call to the African-American middle class and its intelligentsia to mount a campaign against the "damage" caused to African-Americans by the "pathology" of white racism.

Darwin's Athletes is divided into three parts. Part I, entitled "Shooting Hoops Under the Bell Curve," is the most provocative and controversial section of the book, as it asserts that pride in black athletic achievement "is damaging black America in ways that African-Americans in particular find hard to acknowledge."

Adapted, by permission, from J. Valentine, 1999, "Review Essay," *Journal of the Philosophy of Sport,* 26: 105-112.

In Part I Hoberman argues that Western racism has inflicted upon African-Americans a "physicalized" and thus "primitive" identity from which they have yet to escape. In the 20th century this physicalized identity has become "athleticized" through African-American engagement in sport. Thus Hoberman characterizes Jesse Jackson as "breathing new life" into the industrial education movement of Booker T. Washington when Jackson asserts that young black athletes "create a tremendous industrial base for black America" (p. 9). Similarly, Hoberman quotes Charles S. Farrell, national director of Jackson's Rainbow Coalition for Fairness in Athletics, who states, "Athletics is to the black community what technology is to the Japanese and what oil is to the Arabs" (p. 9). Hoberman concludes:

> The black athletes today who refine their athletic skills and little else at American universities are thus the damaged inheritors of an educational philosophy that once promoted manual training as the highest cultural achievement to which black youngsters should aspire. (p. 17)

This physicalized identity of African-Americans became athleticized, Hoberman argues, as African-Americans became increasingly entrapped in a "sports fixation." He continues:

> The sports fixation is a direct result of the exclusion of blacks from every cognitive elite of the past century and the resulting starvation for "race heroes"; it has always been a defensive response to the assault on black intelligence, which continues to this day. That is why the sports syndrome has made athleticism the signature achievement of black America, the reigning symbol of black "genius." (p. 6)

As evidence of the power of this sports fixation, Hoberman not only puts forth the athleticized prose of writers such as Amiri Baraka and Ishmael Reed, he points out the intellectual vacillations of academics such as Harry Edwards.

> Even Harry Edwards, who has spoken out against the fixation for many years, has declared that the highest form of human genius is athleticism: "If I were charged with introducing an alien life form to the epitome of human potential, creativity, perseverance and spirit, I would introduce that alien life form to Michael Jordan." (p. 9)

This sports fixation, which disposes African-Americans to identify "blackness" with "physical prowess" and "physical expression," has had profound consequences for the African-American community. First, it has engendered a physicalized form of anti-intellectualism. This physicalized anti-intellectualism, asserts Hoberman, damages black children "by discouraging academic achievement in favor of physical self-expression, which is widely considered a racial trait." Studying academics in school, then, becomes a form of "acting white."

This physicalized anti-intellectualism, Hoberman argues, has prompted "compensatory efforts" by African-American writers and academics "to convert black physicality into intelligence." He quotes the black sportswriter Edwin Bancroft Henderson who wrote the following in a 1936 article on Joe Louis entitled "The Negro Athlete and Race Prejudice":

> The great boxer was a human replica of Rodin's "Thinker." In the ring he associates ideas and responds with lightning-like rapier thrusts about as rapidly through the medium of mind and muscle as an Einstein calculates cause and effect in cosmic theory. (p. 53)

Hoberman also discusses the compensatory efforts of Afrocentrists who respond to doubts about black intelligence by positing a theory of cognitive "styles." Among the work he cites is that of Alice M. Scales who, in a 1987 article in the *Negro Educational Review*, distinguishes between "reflective" cognition, which is a white style of cognition, and "impulsive" cognition, which is a black style of cognition. In the last analysis, Hoberman asserts, these compensatory efforts simply reenforce the white racist folklore that "has always made the body the essence of black humanity and a sign of its inferior status."

Finally, Hoberman argues, even African-American writers and thinkers who consciously reject the identification of blackness with physicality can be entrapped by a fixation on sport that undercuts their rejection. Kariamu Asante, an Afrocentric professor at Temple University is a case in point. It is Asante's position, stated in his own words, that "when you see Michael Jordan going to the hoop . . . you're seeing the African-American approach to things" (p. 46). Now Asante explicitly states that Jordan's going to the hoop is not a "natural" phenomenon but a "cultural" phenomenon rooted in the role that rhythm plays in traditional African culture. Yet what all too often gets communicated by Asante's use of Michael Jordan as a cultural paradigm is the message that to be black is to be physical. It is as if African-Americans had heeded the advise of Charles Murray and Richard Hernstein, authors of *The Bell Curve*, who argue that the "wise" cultural response to residence at the bottom of the mental ability scale would be to develop a "clannish self-esteem" based on the demonstrated aptitudes of one's group (p. 3). Hoberman concludes:

> A black middle class (and its intelligentsia) that remains infatuated with sports cannot campaign effectively against racial stereotyping that preserves the black man's physicality as a sign of his inherent limitations. (p. 46)

Whether consciously or unconsciously, the African-American fixation on sport has fostered a physicalized form of anti-intellectualism that, for most of this century, has diverted interest away from "the life of the mind." As we have come to live in a modern, "knowledge based society," this fixation has held a large number of African-Americans in a "premodern condition" by limiting their own sense of "developmental possibilities" to the world of "physical expression." For example, given the racist "defamation and devirilization" of the black fighting man in American history, the black athlete has become the "primary male action figure" for black Americans and, as such, has served to obscure the achievements of black aviators and astronauts, whom whites reluctantly allowed to demonstrate "technological competence" and "intellectual mastery."

This physicalized anti-intellectualism, Hoberman continues, has subverted "more productive developmental strategies founded on academic and professional development," and it has discouraged "more productive cultural and intellectual interests" that are driven by "theory," "argument," and "concept-creating." It is for these reasons that Hoberman dedicates *Darwin's Athletes* to Ralph Ellison:

> Ellison saw the physicality of black self-expression as an unsatisfactory substitute for unhampered intellectual development. Here, as elsewhere, he opposed a notion of racial essence that is conducive to both black and white separatism. (p. 20)

Physicalized anti-intellectualism, however, is not the only consequence of the African-American sports fixation. For Hoberman it is a small step from the idea that physical expression and physical prowess are the essence of being a black man, to the black practice of physical exhibitionism and the black exercise of physical violence. This step has been made all the easier to take by white commercial interests. Hoberman writes:

> Convinced that black athleticism alone cannot sustain market appeal, these commercial interests dramatize and embellish the physical and psychological traits of athletes whose public personalities come to embody the full spectrum of male pathology. (p. xxvii)

Thus, according to Hoberman, the African-American fixation on sport has facilitated:

> the merger of the athlete, the gangster rapper and the criminal into a single black persona that the sports industry, the music industry, and the advertising industry have made into the predominate image of black masculinity in the U.S. and around the world. (p. xxvii)

A third consequence of the African-American sports fixation is that it has fostered an illusion of racial progress or, as Hoberman puts it, "a virtual integration" that serves as a racial coping strategy for blacks as well as whites. "The presence of large numbers of black athletes in the major sports," Hoberman writes, "appears to have persuaded almost everyone that the process of integration has been a success." But this "sense of closure," he goes on to argue, is "wishful thinking" that is rooted in "black apathy" and "white auto-intoxication." Thus he writes of the Reverend Jesse Jackson:

> "We believe," Jackson wrote in 1993, "that sports can help change the despair in our communities into hope, replace low self-esteem with confidence and rebuild a true sense of community that transcends neighborhood and racial boundries." For all its noble intentions, this declaration revealed a stunning lack of historical perspective. Could Jesse Jackson not have known that he was invoking the millennial hopes for sport that the NAACP had proclaimed back in the 1920s and 1930s? Had the passage of most of a century taught him nothing about what the African-American engagement in sports could and could not do for his people? The recycling of noble rhetoric is, in fact, a constant byproduct of the black sports fixation precisely because it has produced so little of permanent value for most black Americans. (pp. 9-10)

Hoberman, then, comes down squarely on the side of the "justly famous" 1968 *Sports Illustrated* series on the black athlete, which concluded that the social utility of integrated sport has proven to be largely fraudulent and illusory. Although he acknowledges that the importance of pursuing integration within the sports world "varies by historical period," he concludes that the integration of sport "has long served as a distraction" that has obscured the racial struggles directly affecting the rights and dignity of the far larger numbers of black Americans who do not dwell within the sports world.

Hoberman, however, is not done. He argues that there is a "dirty little secret" associated with the integration of sport. Within the integrated sports world itself, the subordinate racial status of the black athlete has been "preserved." It has been preserved in two ways.

First, integration of the world of sport has not fundamentally changed the attitudes of whites toward black athletic performers once these performers leave their stage. To this effect, he quotes the critic Martha Bayles who wrote of "the simple fact that whites can genuinely appreciate black cultural styles without necessarily acquiring new sympathy or liking for their black fellow citizens." (p. 31)

Second, there is a racial imbalance of power within college and professional sport that is the product of a "genuine colonial arrangement" that has preserved a traditional white hierarchy of owners, general managers, coaches, trainers, writers, and broadcasters. Thus Hoberman goes on to characterizes the NBA in language similar to that recently employed by some critics of the owner imposed lockout:

White supremacism, which denigrates the black man's capacity to lead, is part of a long racist tradition that survives within the officially biracial world of the NBA as a determination to reserve almost all leadership positions for whites. This monopoly on managerial and technological competence is the essence of any colonial arrangement, and it is instructive to see how effectively the managers of the most "integrated" sports industry have been able to preserve it a full generation after the breakthrough of the civil rights movement. (pp. 36-37)

The one positive role that Hoberman can see for virtually integrated sport today is to "keep alive" the idea that racial integration can actually work. "If integrated sport boosts the morale of a multiracial society in this way," he writes, then it may "buy time" for more significant bridge building measures to take effect.

Hoberman's argument about "virtually integrated sport" roughly parallels the argument made by Marx in 1843 regarding the "integration" of German Jews into the world of German state officials. Marx supported this integration as being historically progressive. At the same time, however, he argued that this integration would foster a regressive "false consciousness" among Jews and Christians alike as to the true extent of their liberation unless it was accompanied by a deep and comprehensive "critique."

In Part I of *Darwin's Athletes*, Hoberman calls for a deep and comprehensive critique of the entire relationship between African-Americans and sport, and in Parts II and III he attempts to lay the historical and anthropological foundations for such a critique. Part II of *Darwin's Athletes* is entitled "Prospero and Caliban" after the characters in Shakespeare's *The Tempest*, and it presents the past century of sport as an "arena of racial competition." Hoberman writes:

> The ascendancy of the black athlete and the growing belief in his biological superiority represents a historic reversal of roles in the encounter between Africans and the West. White European preeminence during the 19th century included the presumption of physical as well as intellectual and characterlogical superiority over other races, and athletic ability played a significant role in establishing white male authority in colonial societies. (p. 99)

This historic "reversal of roles" in the arena of sport, however, did not undermine the myth of white superiority. Instead it "preserved" it. How can this be? Hoberman's answer is prefigured in Part I when he writes about the "physicalization" of black identity through the "athleticizing" of the black essence. As long as African-Americans think of themselves first and foremost in terms of their bodies, the myth of white racial superiority will be preserved. The brutish Caliban, who is so closely identified with the physical as to be subhuman, will always be inferior to the scholarly Prospero who used his mind to discover the secrets of white magic that makes him all-powerful.

Part III of *Darwin's Athletes* is entitled "Dissecting John Henry," and is subtitled "The Search for Racial Athletic Aptitude." In this final section of his book, Hoberman shows how ideas about black athletic superiority belong to a "more comprehensive racial folklore that has long imagined black people to be a hardier, physically stronger, and biologically more robust human subspecies than other races." Today, this racial folklore is often put forth in the form of "tabloid science." Unlike "genuine science," tabloid science "streamlines its presentations" and "feigns omniscience" in order to excite its readers.

As an example of tabloid science, Hoberman cites Amby Burfoot's cover story in the August 1992 issue of *Runner's World* magazine entitled, "White Men Can't Run." This article claimed to scientifically demonstrate the physiological superiority of East

Africans in distance events and West Africans in the sprints. The most significant evidence presented in the article was unpublished muscle fiber research done by the Swedish physiologist Bengt Saltin. The research results, as published by Burfoot in his article, were "purged of uncertainty," asserts Hoberman, whereas the research results eventually published by Saltin "raised more questions than they answered."

Hoberman goes on to argue that Saltin subsequently cast a shadow on the whole muscle fiber theory by calling into question the representative character of any given muscle biopsy sample. This did not, however, dampen the splash made by Burfoot's article, which has subsequently been featured by right wing proponents of differential evolution and innate racial differences such as the Canadian psychologist J. Phillip Rushton.

Here we get to the nub of the matter. "One of the cleanest tests" of differential evolution, writes Rushton, "comes in the realm of athletic competition." If we can demonstrate that the races have evolved differently in this realm, then it is more likely that they have evolved differently in other realms as well. As it stands, of course, this is a relatively weak inductive argument.

Hoberman points out, however, that racial folklorists also fashion a deductive argument using the premise of differential athletic aptitude in conjunction with the Darwinian "law of compensation," which postulates an inverse evolutionary relationship between brain and brawn. This deductive argument would take the following form:

Premise 1: If Africans have evolved with superior physical aptitude, then they have evolved with inferior intellectual aptitude.

Premise 2: Africans have evolved with superior physical aptitude.

Conclusion: Africans have evolved with inferior intellectual aptitude.

Hoberman then examines the scientific literature on nerve fibers, muscle fibers, bone density, human growth hormone, testosterone, hip width, leg length, calf size, and so on, and their possible links to athletic performance and intelligence. On the basis of his examination of the literature, he concludes that we should reject the folklorists' argument.

In short, it is Hoberman's position in Part III of *Darwin's Athletes* that genuine science has not yet demonstrated that biological differences in racial athletic aptitude exist and that it has provided no evidence to support a Darwinian law of compensation. He writes:

> This is not to say that bioracial differences of athletic significance do not exist. It is possible that there is a population of West African origin that is endowed with an unusual proportion of fast-twitch muscle fibers, and it is somewhat more likely that there are East Africans whose resistance to fatigue, for both genetic and cultural reasons, exceeds that of other racial groups. But these hypotheses are not even close to scientific confirmation, and there is no scientifically justified reason to tie such plausible athletic traits to mental aptitudes, despite the promptings of the racist heritage that says we should. (p. 240)

Although I am sympathetic to much of what Hoberman writes, I do have the following quibbles and concerns. Hoberman, I believe, overstates his case for the growing dominance of athletes of black African ancestry, and on one occasion he misleads his readers in the process. He cites as evidence for "Caucasian athletic inferiority" the recent achievements of "North Africans such as Nourddine Morcelli, the invincible Algerian middle distance specialist, and Kahlid Skah the Moroccan distance star" (p. 134). Morcelli and Skah, however, are Arabs, and as such, are Caucasian. Similarly, Hoberman overstates his case when he asserts that white racism survives in the biracial world of the NBA as a "determination to reserve almost all leadership positions for whites" (p. 36). Hoberman supplies no evidence in support of this assertion; and, although white racism may still play a pivotal role in the world of professional sports, does it still take the form of a "determination" to keep leadership white?

Moreover, when discussing the Darwinian Law of Compensation, Hoberman refers to the "classic muscle/mind tradeoff Darwin presented in the *Descent of Man*" (p. 230). The only mention of a law of compensation on the part of Darwin that this reviewer has been able to find occurs in *The Origin of Species*, where Darwin takes pains to argue that "there is hardly any way of distinguishing" between the effects of a purported law of compensation and the effects of natural selection, whereby one part of an organism develops over time through use and another reduces over time through disuse (1: p. 71).

In Part III, Hoberman argues correctly, I believe, that we must overcome our fear of racial biology if we are to combat racism, and he states in a footnote that he is "inclined to agree" with the view that biological race can be studied independently of ethnicity. Now it is true that we might be able to study biological races independently of ethnicity in isolated geographic areas in East Africa, West Africa, or Scandinavia. Things are more problematic, however, when we study race in North America, where biraciality and multiraciality are widespread and spreading, and where race is defined in terms that characterize persons of predominately Caucasian ancestry as Negro. This would be true whether the study of race as a biological category independent of ethnicity is conducted by students of sport, medical doctors, or psychologists. Indeed, this is one of the major issues regarding *The Bell Curve*. Do its findings on intelligence speak to biology or ethnicity?

Although Hoberman is careful to argue for the superiority of the life of intellectual expression ("theory," "argument," and "concept-creating") over the life of physical expression ("sport") in terms of its utility in a knowledge based society, *Darwin's Athletes* in fact represents intellectual expression as *intrinsically* superior to physical expression. This is manifest in Hoberman's assumption that the value placed upon physical expression in African-American life is to be viewed first and foremost as a compensation for the limitations placed upon blacks by slavery, Jim Crow, and racism. It is further manifest in Hoberman's assumption that African-American assertions of a non-intellectual life of the mind or "genius" in sport are simply compensatory efforts to "convert black physicality into intelligence" (p. 60). Finally, it is manifest in Hoberman's willingness to accept the traditional identification of the physical with the primitive (p. xxvi). Hoberman at no point argues for the intrinsic superiority of intellectual expression as a way of being in the world; he simply assumes it in much the same way that Freud assumes that sublimating the instinctual demands of the id through art and science is higher and finer than sublimating them through business and commerce.

This assumption of the intrinsic superiority of intellectual expression on the part of Hoberman is a source of major resistance to his work on the part of those for whom physical expression, as a way of being in the world, is as intrinsically valuable as intellectual expression. How would Jewish Americans, for example, countenance the assumption that the value they place upon intellectual expression is to be viewed first and foremost as a compensation for the limitations placed upon Jews by the diaspora? Until we confront the issue of the relationship between intellectual and the physical expression in human life, we cannot fully address the issues of race and sport that John Hoberman so courageously and insightfully raises for us in *Darwin's Athletes*.

Bibliography

1. Darwin, C. *The origin of species*. Chicago: William Benton, 1952.

Sports, Political Philosophy, and the African American

Gerald Early

There was a time in the United States, particularly in the nineteenth century, but not exclusively so, for the idea persisted in some sociological and anthropological circles well into the twentieth century, when blacks were referred to by whites as the "lady of the races." That is to say, blacks or African Americans, were seen as exhibiting qualities as a, group that were considered-feminine or associated with the female side of nature. Blacks, like women, were seen as being deeply religious, much more naturally religious than whites; tending more towards the arts and oratory; more musical than whites; more emotional than whites; more attracted to colors; to physical sensations rather than to abstract ideas. In short, blacks, like women, couldn't think but they could feel deeply. While this idea of blacks as the lady of the races was pervasive in some nineteenth century white intellectual circles, no one popularized it more than Harriet Beecher Stowe in her 1852 novel, *Uncle Tom's Cabin,* one of the best-selling novels of the nineteenth century, although now neglected, if not a book that has fallen into disfavor except among a group of feminist scholars who argue about whether the feminist vision of the novel is truly radical. And the novel that has given us the epithet, "Uncle Tom." The impact of this novel, despite the fact that few people read it now, cannot be overstated.

In this novel, we are given the picture of the African as the epitome of non-aggression, the African as the sacrificial saint, in the person of Uncle Tom himself. Tom is described as "a large, broad-chested, powerfully-made man, of a full glossy black,

Reprinted, by permission, from G. Early, 2003, Sports, political philosophy, and the African American. In *A companion to African-American philosophy,* edited by T.L. Lott and J.P. Pittman (Oxford: Blackwell Publishers), 436-449.

and a face whose truly African features were characterized by an expression of grave and steady good sense, united with much kindliness and benevolence." In short, Tom is described as having the physique of, well, an athlete. He is, of course, no athlete, although his appearance might bring to mind the legendary African-American boxer, former slave, Tom Molineaux, who fought British open-weight champion Tom Cribb for the world championship in 1810 and 1811, losing both times and who died a lonely and dissipated death a short time after his defeats. Professional athletics for a black person, with the exception of prizefighting and horseracing, scarcely existed in the United States before the Civil War. (Indeed, professional and amateur sports as we understand them today are largely the result of industrialization and urbanization that occurred after the Civil War, in the later third of the nineteenth century.) Uncle Tom is not only a top field supervisor and clerk; he is a minister, a deeply religious man who believes whole-heartedly in his Bible. He is, moreover, looked up to on the various plantations where he works during the course of the novel by both the whites and the blacks. He is a leader, although he does not seem to comprehend clearly how much of a leader he is. And while his religious beliefs give him authority; it is his physical presence that gives him stature and brings him to the notice of others. Simon Legree, for instance, wishes to make Tom a slave driver on the basis of Tom's appearance. He is a big man whom other slaves will obey without questions, is how Legree thinks.

Yet, Tom is suitably humble to his station. He wants to be free but not in an assertive or daring way. He is far different from George Harris, the other black man who is described at length and featured prominently in the novel. Harris is described in a fugitive slave poster as "six feet in height, a very light mulatto, brown curly hair; is very intelligent, speaks handsomely, can read and write; will probably try to pass for a white man." Harris is naturally aggressive and outgoing as Tom is "naturally patient, timid, and unenterprising." Harris flees from slavery to escape a cruel master and to rescue his family; Tom does not. Harris stands up to white slave hunters and even shoots one of his pursuers. Tom is beaten to death by Simon Legree's slaves and forgives them before he dies. The difference between the two men is that George Harris has hot, hasty Saxon blood. After all, as James Baldwin remarked about the character in his famous essay on the novel, "Everybody's Protest Novel," we have only the author's word that Harris is black. In no way does he seem different from the standard white fictional male hero of the mass-market literature of this period. Tom, on the other hand, is a full-blooded African. Alas, that difference is the only difference that matters. In an odd paradox in the novel, Tom is referred to as "Father Tom" and seems a father figure to everyone, white and black. Yet, in this novel that is a celebration of motherhood, Tom is the grandest mother of them all. He is maternal with everyone, including, most famously, Little Eva, the doomed daughter of the paternal, effeminate planter, Augustine St. Clair. This is why Baldwin called Tom "de-sexed," despite the fact that Tom has a wife and children. Everything about him glows with the aura of the feminine: his gentleness, his patience, his willingness to sacrifice. It seemed that Harriet Beecher Stowe was saying that the only way a black man could be a father was by being, in effect, a mother. It might be said, of course, that Tom is meant to be a Christ figure which is simply saying the obvious. What we have in Tom is the feminization of Christ himself as a savior figure, much in keeping with the nineteenth-century view, the Victorian view of Christ. It is also much in keeping with the rampant feminization of Christianity that is taking place in the nineteenth century that Ann Douglas wrote about so incisively in her book,

The Feminization of American Culture. Religion is no longer complex theology but simply speaking from the heart; in the womanly sphere of domesticity is where true religious virtue lives because it was in the sphere of domesticity and the hearth and home that one found refuge from the money values of the marketplace and from the corruption of outside the world of politics. Remember the novel is called *Uncle Tom's Cabin,* the scene in which we are given this domicile in the novel is not a picture of masculine asceticism but womanly domesticity, a peaceable kingdom of family relations. In the stage shows and films that have been made based on *Uncle Tom's Cabin,* Tom is so "de-sexed" that he is usually portrayed as an old man, well beyond the age of an active sex life, not as the strong-limbed black man in the prime of life that he actually is.

This un-manning of the black man in what became not merely a popular novel but a virtually unstoppable force in American popular culture may have led to blacks using "Uncle Tom" as a vituperative epithet. Baldwin was right that the book seemed to give the black man his humanity by denying his human nature, by making him the personification of moral good while being completely non-threatening. Tom never said he hated the conditions he had to endure, the unfairness of his life. For some like Baldwin, this seemed to be asking a bit too much of the victims of oppression, particularly oppressed men who always had to bear the burden of being non-threatening and non-aggressive in order to gain the sympathy of their oppressors. The feminization of Uncle Tom was not the only factor that led to "Uncle Tom," the term, being used in the way that it currently is but I believe it is one of them.

What we realize right away with *Uncle Tom's Cabin* is that the muscular black man was an icon in American popular culture before the Civil War, who, even in the guise of being meek and mild, evolved as popular culture representations into an old man without virility. In this regard, he was a man whose presence generated a specific need to confine him, indeed, the presence seemed to have been evoked in order to confine it. The philosophical and political issues surrounding the muscular black man, and, in turn, the assertive black man, for the muscularity became an outward symbol of an assertiveness that had to be placed under white social control, were to achieve their highest resonance in the realm of sports.

In his controversial study of the intersection of race and sports, John Hoberman, in *Darwin's Athletes: How Sport has Damaged Black America and Preserved the Myth of Race,* writes: "The muscular black male for whom certain white men felt a kind of nostalgia long after Emancipation can thus be seen as a kind of domesticated noble savage, and it is likely that our own culture's taste for *Mandingo* style images of the black man is to some degree a legacy of this: an idealized black muscularity that was once safely confined by whips and chains is now financially controlled by the white businessmen who own and operate the professional sports leagues" (italics Hoberman). Here Hoberman is openly suggesting that sports exist as a form of white hegemonic ideology, a representation within the sphere of entertainment and popular culture of the same political arrangement that exists elsewhere and everywhere in American society. If this muscularity is no longer confined by religion, as we now live in more secular age, then it is dominated by, what some scholars have argued is, one of the major mass cultural activities that have replaced religion by taking on the characteristics of a religion: namely high-performance athletics.

What Stowe did in her novel, this transformation of the muscular black man to Jesus Christ, is called romantic racialism or romantic racism, dressing up blacks in sentimental clothing to make them more palatable, more acceptable to whites.

Historian George M. Fredrickson provides a detailed historical overview of romantic racialism in his book on nineteenth-century American racial attitudes called *The Black Image in the White Mind*. The impact of this concept of romantic racialism has been wide and deep in this society and for the most part very pernicious. Although there have been subtle changes in the idea of romantic racialism, it has largely remained the same over the years and the major racial trait it emphasizes is the physicality of blacks. While perhaps not apparent at first blush, it would seem inevitable that blacks as slaves in the United States who were largely manual agrarian laborers, "primitives," if you will, in a country that was rapidly transforming itself from something agrarian to a highly complex industrial society would be seen through the haze of romantic racialism, a view reflecting its own anti-intellectualism and fear of modernity while emphasizing the lack of black intellectual capacity.

Blacks themselves have found it difficult to overcome this view of themselves. Its persistence has been intense. First, many blacks have adopted a version of romantic racialism where they themselves believe that blacks or Africans are more caring, more spiritual, more musical, more family-oriented, more emotional, less interested in abstract concepts than whites. At one time this was called Negritude. At another, it was called the Black Aesthetic. Now, it is called Afrocentrism. All of these racial orthodoxies suggests, in some of their aspects, that blacks are "the lady of the races," that they are somehow more "humane" than aggressive, competitive whites. Second, the enormous presence and success that blacks have achieved in two fields that are perceived in our culture as being both "charismatic" and "anti-intellectual"—popular music and sports—has further intensified the idea of blacks as primitives, as somehow more in tune with their bodies and more in tune with their feelings and their intuitions, their instincts, than whites. Many blacks, seizing these areas of achievement as sources of pride, have stressed their physical superiority. Many whites have granted blacks this physical superiority as a sign of their mental inferiority. Perhaps one of the most famous exchanges in the matter of black physical superiority was black sociologist Harry Edwards's "The Sources of the Black Athlete's Superiority," written in 1971 in response to another *Sports Illustrated* article by Martin Kane called "An Assessment of 'Black is Best'" (January 18, 1971). But this has been an ongoing discussion since the nineteenth century (Frederick Douglass's 1854 "The Negro Ethnologically Considered" as a response to the racist assessment of the black body and black mind by such racist intellectuals of the day as Josiah Nott, Louis Agassiz, Samuel Morton, and others). The most recent subtle but elaborate assertion of a black physical superiority as an explanation for a lower black IQ is Murray and Herrnstein's *The Bell Curve*, which has received numerous critical responses from blacks. There can be no real understanding of African Americans and sports or how African Americans see sports without a fundamental understanding of how the body of the African American has become the subject of racist philosophical and political beliefs, of romantic racialism.

Whites of course adopted these beliefs in romantic racialism for other reasons as well, in large measure, because they saw blacks as a kind of alter ego to themselves. Black faced-minstrelsy, the most popular and powerful theater in nineteenth century American, is proof of that. It gave whites a great deal of pleasure and psychic relief to pretend to be blacks and from this form of grotesque impersonation, rooted in European mummery, emerged a form of mass entertainment. If whites saw blacks, on the one hand, as beasts, rapists, murderers, and potential rebels against the slave order who must be put down at all costs, this could be disguised by seeing them as child-like, emotional beings, full of Christian grace. Moreover, if whites, especially white males, felt that they lived in a super competitive society that demanded aggression and shrewdness to survive, that was so fluid as to produce acute anxiety and a deep sense of insecurity, blacks, especially slaves, became for them a kind of psychological escape. Here whites could fantasize about a group of people who did not need aggression to survive, who did not suffer anxiety and a sense of insecurity, who were timid, peaceful, and unenterprising in a land that was obsessed with enterprise, a land where aggression was highly valued because the United States, until the twentieth century, was largely a frontier society, rapidly expanding its space in hostile encounters against the indigenous peoples who lived here. In eighteenth- and nineteenth-century America, and the same remains true today, the main obsession was "making it." In some ways, the creation of high-level professional and amateur athletics in the latter-part of the nineteenth century was a dramatization and representation of the very values of aggression, enterprise, ingenuity, and improvisation that American society prized. Of course, as blacks began more and more to excel in athletics, they became associated with these values but in a somewhat perverse way; certainly not in a way that freed them from romantic racialist assumptions.

Eldridge Cleaver, in *Soul on Ice,* was to make much of this idea of romantic racialism as a primary force in American social thinking when it comes to sex and the physicality of blacks and whites. The twist was that, by the twentieth century, the black man was no longer quite "the lady" but a kind of romantic version of an exaggerated masculinity, a version of American machismo. This idea of the black man as exaggerated masculinity intensified as black men achieved fame in popular music and athletics that both, in their unique ways, sold, among other things, sex and sexual taboos to the American public. The black male as a superior form of masculinity to the white man was certainly an idea that Norman Mailer was trying to sell in his famous 1957 essay, "The White Negro," which was just a new expression of romantic racialism. But this was all still rooted in the old nineteenth-century idea of romantic racialism: for Norman Mailer and others like him, the African-American male was less repressed, more intuitive, more natural, more rhythmic, more in touch with his sexuality than the white man. And of course he was still less intellectual than the white man. Blacks don't deal with abstractions and highly complex ideas: the burden of the over-civilized white man. One can easily see the connection to Stowe's romantic racialism: in each instance, the black man is seen as a primitive, a kind of noble savage, as Hoberman suggested. The biggest difference is that with the rise of hipsterism and the cool, it was no longer necessary to see the black man as virtuous in Victorian terms, that is to say, in bourgeois Christian terms. Indeed, now the black man as an iconic symbol of masculinity, through his superlative performances in sports, was reified in even starker terms than before as something decidedly pagan and anti-bourgeois.

The shift in romantic racialism that changed a popular view of black men from naturally humble Christians to, using Eldridge Cleaver's phrase, super-masculine menials was largely the result of the creation of the huge entertainment machinery that was erected in the United States starting in the late nineteenth century. Today, we call this conglomerate, popular culture or mass culture. This machinery was created as America became a more urban society in the late nineteenth and early twentieth centuries, as it became a society with more leisure time that needed to be filled, and more consumer-oriented. The creation of popular culture as we understand it today occurred at the same time that black men were encouraged to exercise authority as heads of their own households in order to bring stability to the black family, that is, during Reconstruction. It must be remembered that black men, even though they may not have been able to exercise it as much as they would have liked, were able to vote and hold elective office, a good fifty years before black women could. In other words, black men had a kind of civic authority in their communities that black women lacked. Moreover, the Freedmen's Bureau and the white philanthropic foundations that financed black education in the south were very much interested in having black men hold authority in their communities. Finally, because the black church was, by far, the most powerful, most autocratic institution in the black community, the ascendancy of black men was assured as the black church is a deeply patriarchal institution. All of this effort to raise the black man as an authority figure in his own community helped produce, by way of cultural and political paradox, the many terrible lynchings and acts of terrorism that occurred during Reconstruction and after, most of these being crimes committed against black men. These lynchings were, of course, acts of political intimidation and social control.

So, what was this popular culture that came into existence? By the early twentieth century, the film industry was firmly established. Recordings made their appearance by the very early twentieth century (Enrico Caruso made records at the turn of the century, for instance) and this changed forever how popular music was packaged and sold in the United States and eventually the world. Another major component of popular culture was the rise of professional and collegiate sports. Black men were by and large shut out of most team sports. Organized baseball, the most popular sport in America, banned interracial play in the early 1880s and hardly encouraged it before. Scarcely any blacks played collegiate football because hardly any blacks were admitted to white colleges at this time. Blacks had a huge presence as jockeys in horse-racing but were driven from the profession in the early twentieth century by angry whites who wanted the jobs. As a result of this discrimination, the one sport where blacks were disproportionately represented was professional boxing. Blacks generally were able to fight for championships in boxing. George Dixon, Joe Gans, and Joe Walcott were all famous black champions at the turn of the century in the lighter weight divisions. The heavy-weight title was considered the supreme title in sports by those who followed sports even casually. Blacks were largely banned from fighting for the heavyweight title for the same reason they were banned from other sports. Athletics were considered a sign of white male superiority. Sports existed symbolically, politically, to show the world that whites were the better race, the more aggressive race, the conquering, imperial, more masculine race. In other words, it was whites, not blacks, who first attached political significance to sports by banning blacks from competition. (Blacks were to interpret sports politically and symbolically in the years to come, especially as more blacks began to write on the subject.) In these days, African Americans were thought to lack the nerve and skill to beat whites in head-to-head competition.

The color line was drawn in heavyweight boxing until 1908 when Jack Johnson defeated Tommy Burns and became the first black heavyweight champion. Johnson's winning the title and the controversy that ensued is very important in understanding the shift that eventually occurred where black men became more associated with being superior athletes. Johnson not only beat the best white fighters of his day but he had white girlfriends. This did not make him unique among black public figures of the day. George Walker, for instance, of the successful black comedy team, Williams and Walker, had many white girlfriends. George Dixon, the famous black boxer, had a white wife. What made Johnson unique was that he flaunted his attraction to white women and their attraction to him. This tied together in our popular culture the idea of the black man as superior athlete and superior sexual competitor to the white man. It was the actualization of a secret fear that had played at the edges of white entertainment and American popular culture for years, the white hegemonic implications of this secret fear were to reach a new level of intensity with the emergence of the modern black athlete.

These ideas of black athletic superiority and black ultra-masculinity have remained with us ever since with an ever-growing luridness. As blacks like Joe Louis, Jesse Owens, Fritz Pollard, Jackie Robinson, and others continued to demonstrate great black athletic ability, whites began more and more to promote the idea of a natural black athletic superiority, that blacks were physically superior to whites. Most whites were willing to accept this because they always thought blacks were their intellectual inferiors. Black supremacy in sports proved black intellectual inferiority in the eyes of many whites. Besides, since big-time, high level sports are nothing more than a form of entertainment in our society, to be a sports performer is certainly not an expression of power; it was nothing more than a part of the mass culture machine, many whites thought that black sports prowess simply confirmed the idea that blacks were natural, showy entertainers. Thus, blacks as sports performers did not threaten white hegemonic assumptions embedded in the symbolism of sports themselves. Sport was the African American niche in American life, to show themselves off as flamboyant physical presences.

This was the new twist on the old romantic radicalism of the nineteenth century. As blacks became a more and more dominant presence in American's most popular sports, the idea that they were natural athletes gained more currency, as did the idea that the sports black dominated, and the positions they dominated in those sports (a practice known as stacking), required no particular intellect to play. This idea even now has a powerfully and complex hold in our society. Here is a recent example. The stories in the *New York Times* (July 7, 1997, page C9) and the *St. Louis Post-Dispatch* July 7, 1997, page C5) that covered young black golfer Tiger Woods' recent win at the Motorola Western Open had these headlines, respectively: "Woods Wins in Triumph of Mind Over Matter" and "Brain, not Brawn, Captures Western Open for Woods." There are two important points being made here: first, golf, as a game dominated by white men who do not have to demonstrate spectacular physical gifts is implicitly more intellectual than most sports. Certainly, most people probably believe that although there is not a shred of objective evidence that says playing eighteen holes of golf in a professional tournament is more mentally taxing than being a major league catcher or a major league centerfielder or a wide receiver in pro football. Second, the newspapers as well as Woods himself seem to be stressing the fact that he has great mental abilities that explain why he is able to play this game well. Both the newspapers and Woods seem very aware of the dumb black jock stereotype and seem to be think that Woods, as the brainy champion in the white man's game, can counter-act it. This is all implicit in the headlines. Once again, there is not a shred of evidence that the considerable mental toughness and competitive spirit that Woods exhibits differ in either kind or degree from the mental toughness and competitive spirit necessary for a high-performance athlete to succeed in any sport where the pressure is intense and the risk of failure high. In other words, it might be said that a certain mentality, if not intelligence, wins any athletic contest (if not, luck). One must strategize to win any sports competition. It might also be said that brawn, physical ability, wins golfing matches as it does any sporting endeavor. After all, the pro golfer, like the centerfielder or the wide receiver, or the concert pianist, for that matter, is relying on muscle memory, on rote training, on automatic responses, as much as anything else. Naturally, there are many Hispanics and some Asians who are famous in American sports but the issue of race and sports in America is not: a "minority" issue but a black and white one, which is why Woods's half-Asian ancestry is a political irrelevancy.

Broadly speaking, the main attitudes of blacks themselves towards sports might be seen, predictably enough, as, on the one hand, a fierce opposition to sports and play as both a waste of time, unenterprising and unproductive, and a form of racial degradation, as, in most instances, sports competition between blacks was being performed for a white audience or at the behest of whites. Such an attitude was expressed by Frederick Douglass in his 1845 *Narrative,* and generally so in most anti-slavery literature written by blacks. If one were to interpret the Battle Royal scene in Ralph Ellison's *Invisible Man* (1952) as, in part, a representation, both politically and aesthetically, of blacks in athletic competition in this country, one finds, in a much more sophisticated and intellectually complex way, the same concerns about sports as a form of race degradation that the slave narrators like Douglass expressed in the nineteenth century. This anti-sports attitude is not uncommon among many blacks today largely fueled by a strict sense of Protestant or religious sobriety and propriety (many black religious denominations—including Baptists, on the one hand, and the Holiness Church, Black Muslims, Moorish Americans, on the other, discourage or prohibit their members from attending or watching sporting events) as well as a strong sense of race mission and race dignity.

On the other hand, blacks have seen sports as a means of access, a way to or route for social and economic mobility or they have seen it as a way of widening democracy, of spreading democratic values and ideals. The first view, studied as a sociological phenomenon in Othello Harris's "Race, Sport, and Future Orientation?" in the *Journal of African American Men,* largely supports sports as a way of giving black men, who have limited occupational opportunities in this country a chance not only to succeed in a high-paying, high visibility career but also to get a college education. Indeed, according to this view, many black men finish high school only because of the sports option and would exhibit very little interest in school if it were not there. The second view, championed most famously by long-time black sportswriter A. S. "Doc" Young in *Negro Firsts in Sports* (1963), sees sports as an arena where blacks compete with whites as equals, thus providing the country, through daily coverage of sporting events in the local papers, an opportunity to see, in action, the ideal of blacks and whites working together. Moreover, not only does the opening of sports to the black athlete, particularly after World War II, show the triumph of democratic ideals of fair play and the like but sports themselves are a representation of democratic ideals, the individual's interest balanced against that of the team, the same application of rules for both sides, the ultimate rewarding of superior merit, and so forth. This set of arguments was used by black and white sportswriters in support of the integration of major league baseball, a major cause for both the left and black sportswriters of the 1930s and they were to be used to interpret the significance of Jackie Robinson and baseball as symbols of American democratic values once baseball was integrated on the minor league level in 1946 and the major league level in 1947. This was an argument that saw no real hegemonic expression of white power in sports as a representation but rather located all hegemonic expression in its corporate structure of ownership which could be, by public pressure forcing the corporation to redefine its self-interest, made to change.

A new note was sounded in the African-American view of sports with the emergence of the civil disobedience phase of the civil rights movement. Famed black sportswriter Wendell Smith, who had campaigned hard for the integration of professional baseball and served as Jackie Robinson's companion during the first year of Robinson's career as Brooklyn Dodger, wrote in the *Pittsburgh Courier* on March 14, 1964 that "the Negro athlete in this country has, with a few exceptions, been conspicuously silent in the fight for civil rights. . . . most of them seem to hold themselves above the Negro masses with respect to civil rights and do nothing to help correct existing evils." If, at one time, the black athlete was a political and folk hero simply by virtue of his professional accomplishments or because he competed head-to-head against whites, by the 1960s, this was no longer a sufficient sign that he was committed to his people or a representation of the virtue of their struggle. In his article, Smith particularly criticizes baseball players: "on the whole, the Negro baseball player has been remiss in his responsibilities in the area of civil rights, even to the extent that he was voluntarily acquiesced to racial segregation and discrimination in certain instances." Smith is the black boxer as the political vanguard: "When Floyd Patterson was the champion, he went to Alabama with Jackie Robinson to march and demonstrate against racial bigotry. Joe Louis, Ray Robinson, and other Negro boxers contributed similarly toward the cause when they were in their prime. Cassius Clay has, unfortunately chosen the 'Muslim Way' to fight bigotry. But that does not obliterate the fact that he has had the fortitude to take a position. While you may not agree with his form of protest, you have to agree that Cassius is at last (sic) protesting."

It was, without question, the emergence of heavyweight boxer Muhammad Ali, known before 1964 as Cassius Clay, that generated the entire issue of how publicly political any black athlete should be. One month earlier, in February 1964, Clay, a huge underdog, defeated Sonny Liston and won the heavyweight boxing title. Immediately after the fight, Clay announced that he was a member of the Nation of Islam, a militant, separatist black group whose leading spokesman was Malcolm X. By 1967, Ali had taken a stance against the Vietnam War and refused to be inducted in the US Army. He was convicted of violation of the Selective Service Act and sentenced to five years in prison. Arguably, the famous athlete and probably the most famous black person in the world by this time, Ali had become also the world's most famous political dissident. As the civil rights movement grew increasingly more militant and disruptive as the decade of the 1960s progressed, with the rise of Black Power and an increasing number of urban race riots and political assassinations, there was, as a result of the example of Ali, more and more pressure on the black athlete to take public political stances that identified him clearly with the mood of black people at this time. Most of these athletes were young and more inclined to identify with this more pronounced expression of militancy as largely the black freedom struggle in the United States at this time was dominated or at least very much energized by young people. Indeed, many began to look at earlier black athletes such as Jackie Robinson, Jesse Owens, and Joe Louis as Uncle Toms or decidedly compromised heroes. One culmination of this was at the 1968 Olympic Games when sprinters Tommie Smith and John Carlos gave clenched fist salutes during the playing of the Star Spangled Banner when they were awarded their medals.

A full account of this overt politicization of the black athlete in the 1960s is given in Harry Edwards's *The Revolt of the Black Athlete* (1969). Since this period of the

1960s, black athletes have never been openly political again. There remains some who think that the black athlete should be more blatantly political (which generally among those who: espouse this position means more blatantly left-wing or anti-establishment) because he is a role-model, a highly influential and publicized person, who can do much to bring together what some see as a fractured black community or who could publicly advocate for the black community. Basketball stars are most commonly criticized by those who take this position for not being more publicly political. For instance, some bitterly complained when Michael Jordan, from North Carolina, refused to publicly support Harvey Gant, a black who ran for the Senate twice in the 1990s, feeling that someone of the stature of Jordan not only had a responsibility to do so but could have made a difference as Gant lost both times. Black sports historian Jeffrey Sammons is one of the most ardent supporters of this view of the political engagement of the black athlete. The representation of the black athlete as a political figure or, more accurately, because he comes from an oppressed group, a political rebel or dissident, leads to questions about whether sports themselves are the expression or representation of a political ideology or white corporate hegemony which the black athlete must both conform to as a public performer while he criticizes it as a public citizen. The inherent contradictions and difficulties of such a position rarely dawn on those who espouse the political engagement of the black athlete. There would seem to be nothing inherent in the performance of any sport that would be considered the expression of an explicit political ideology. As a performance, sports seem to transcend any given political system or political ideas. Free market democracies, Communist regimes, right-wing dictatorships have all supported professional sports and have all lionized star athletes. This, of course, does not mean in the act of attaching immediate or transcendent meaning or values to sports or in the structure created to support sports or the athlete, there is not a great deal of political ideology or at least some number of political issues.

Currently, the issue of race and sports revolves around the political and social meaning attached to the issue of black athletic superiority or the general perception of such supposed superiority. The cover story of the March 24, 1997 issue of *U.S. News and World Report* was "Are Pro Sports Bad for Black America?" which dealt with the preoccupation with sports in the black community. According to the story, "66 percent of all African-American males between the ages of 13 and 18 believe they can earn a living playing professional sports," while only 33 percent of white boys in the same age bracket think this. Doubtless, the over-representation of blacks in the major team sports (80 percent of all NBA players, 6 percent of all NFL players, and 20 percent of all baseball players) contributes to this. Moreover, as our society continues to debate heatedly the need for Affirmative Action, sports offers a curious dimension to the subject for it is the only competitive field where merit unquestioningly determines one's fate. And it is one of the few fields of endeavor in American life, in its performance aspect, where no one, especially no one white, questions the ability of blacks. Blacks themselves may feel less pressure pursuing athletics because of this: no one questions their ability; indeed, many are willing to grant their superiority.

To understand why our society is having this problem with young black males' over-determined aspiration to be athletes, one must, of course link this to the equally difficult battle to fight their intense anti-intellectualism. These boys generally think intellectualism and mental accomplishment are white, such thinking being largely the result of the romantic racialism that has shaped our culture. Oddly, the young black boys who think that being intellectual, that being literate and learned is "white," actually are right, for our society has promoted that every image, that very idea, that very concept, since, at least, the early days of colonial America.

An examination of two recent articles should put this issue of blacks over-pursuit of sports in perspective. "Great Black Hopes," written by Steve Sailor, a Chicago businessman was published in the August 12, 1996 issue of the famous conservative magazine, *National Review.* Sailor had, in the April 8, 1996 issue of the same magazine, written a piece called "How Jackie Robinson Integrated America" that argued that Robinson's integration of baseball was a victory for free market principles. In the piece entitled "Great Black Hopes," Sailor argues that "equality of opportunity in America's top team sports has led not to equality of results but to black superiority. For example, a random American black is currently 10 times more likely to reach the National Football League and 25 times more likely to reach the National Basketball Association that a random non-black." Sailor argues that sports is, in essence, black people's market niche in American society and that they should exploit their "natural edges" and "sizable cultural advantages." He further argues that in a multiracial society such as the United States, it is no surprise that certain professions will become the specialties of certain ethnic or racial groups. He cites the fact that Asian Indians manage about half of America's hotels. He is cognizant of the fact that many believe that a black superiority in sports indicates or implies a general intellectual inferiority for the group. He counters this by asserting that "much of black sports success seems to originate above the neck, in certain common mental advantages blacks tend to have over whites." This superior intelligence that blacks have is for "creative improvisation and on-the-fly interpersonal decision-making." Blacks seem to be able to respond to situations quicker than whites. "These black cerebral superiorities in 'real time' responsiveness also contribute to black dominance in jazz, running with the football, rap, dance, trash talking, preaching, and oratory." These are, of course, the very "intelligences" that whites have granted to blacks since the days of Harriet Beecher Stowe's *Uncle Tom's Cabin.* In short, blacks are good at entertaining. Sailor is doing nothing more but giving us the old romantic racialist line but calling these so-called black or African qualities by the euphemism, intelligence. He ultimately suggests that black men, charismatic by nature, ought to go into sales. Black men are generally ill-suited for paper-pushing bureaucratic jobs. "Natural leadership," writes Sailor, "is practically synonymous with something black guys have in abundance: masculine charisma." This sounds a great deal like the view of black men in Mailer's "The White Negro," the modern hipster's version of romantic racialism.

Sailor argues that because black men are so over-represented in certain sports, they should exploit this advantage by steering themselves toward these sports. This is tantamount to saying that because there are several prominent Hollywood filmmakers who happen to be Jewish, Jewish boys should be pushed toward filmmaking in school. Because an ethnic or racial group dominates a particularly small industry really says nothing about what the majority of people in the group should do, especially' as the majority clearly will have insufficient talent to go into that industry for a living. Asian Indians may manage half the hotels in the United States but what that means is that the vast majority of Asian Indians have nothing to do with hotel management and are not especially helped by the fact that Asian Indians dominate that field, any more so than the average African American is in any way much affected by the fact that the

NBA teams are 80 percent black. The reasoning may be less than persuasive here. Sailor's essay, nevertheless, is a common white conservative view. It was espoused, for instance, by Murray and Herrnstein in *The Bell Curve.*

Neither Sailor, Herrnstein, or Murray understand the implications of what they are suggesting. Blacks do not wish to be seen merely as America's entertainers or merely as people who are good at athletics. They want to explore the whole range of career possibilities. This is especially important because they have been denied access to so many careers for so long. In other words, it will not solve the race problem or ease it simply to tell blacks to exploit their natural "charisma" and go into sports and sales because such a solution does not address fundamentally the frustration and unhappiness many black people feel about their lives and the nature of the opportunities open to them in America. Black people have already proven to themselves and to the world that they can play sports. They feel a need to prove to themselves and to the world that they can do other things just as well. This is why the fact that so many black boys wish to play sports constitutes a serious problem in the black community.

The Winter 1995/96 issue of *Journal of African American Men,* a new academic publication, featured an article by Billy Hawkins entitled "The Black Student Athlete: The Colonized Black Body." In this piece, which, whether consciously intended or not, is a real counterpoint to the Sailor essay, Hawkins argues that black men historically have existed as a colonized presence, to be exploited like a physical resource. "The Black Body is the source of revenue for many Division I NCAA athletic departments," writes the author. They themselves cannot exploit being athletes for their own benefit in this society because they have virtually no power. To be a high-level college athlete, Hawkins asserts, by its very nature, is to be exploited. "Though the exploitation is disguised at the professional level by designer clothes and multi-million-dollar contracts the exploitation is even greater at the collegiate level where black athletes are only granted year-to-year scholarships that cover tuition, books, room and board while these institutions are benefiting to a far greater extent than the athletes." He says this is particularly true of black athletes at predominantly white, Division I NCAA schools where they rarely get a decent education, nor are they adequately compensated for the labor they provide as athletes. He goes into some lengthy discussion of the black man as the Body in the American mind, a truncated and somewhat distorted historical account. This discussion of the issue it seems to me is very flawed, equally as flawed as the white conservative view of Sailor's.

First, while black people are seen largely as physical presences in the United States, they are not really the Body in the American mind. Women, particularly white women, serve that purpose. It is their physical beauty that is central to American advertising and to the entertainment world. This is why women's dieting and women's beauty culture are such multi-billion dollar industries in this country. It is because of this emphasis on women as the body that women are generally so insecure about their looks and suffer a great deal from low self-esteem and depression. There is a need for greater precision in the matter of what type of physical presences blacks actually are in the white mind and in their own. Moreover, was the NCAA a colonizing/regulation body when white colleges exclusively recruited white student–athletes? Is it a form of exploitation when white student–athletes are recruited today? If not, why so? "Black student athletes are, in most cases, heavily recruited because of their athletic abilities; token interest, if any, is given to their academic abilities." But is not the same true for white student–athletes who are recruited by these schools? If this is not so, the author should explain as the difference is crucial to his argument.

Hawkins's discussion is further flawed by his attempt to make an analogy between being a college athlete and colonialism. Colleges exploit the labor of many other students including, most notably, their Ph.D. and their post-doctoral students. One might argue that the Ph.D. students' exploitation is, after all, related to education, whereas the athlete is brought to the college to do something which is not really part of the primary mission or purpose of any college or university. But this is to suggest that intercollegiate competition cannot be a legitimate part of a college education and this would be incorrect. Only certain college athletics, such as football and basketball, are much the cause of the problem. Colleges almost never go on probation for recruitment violations in fencing, volleyball, women's gymnastics, or tennis. Athletics might, on the whole, be helpful to a university's mission. Certainly, sports are not a priori harmful or inimical to such a mission. Thomas Sowell makes this clear in his argument about sports and education in his book on American education. The existence of athletics at the university is not a self-evident case of exploitation: And exploitation of labor, as in the case of Ph.D. student, in and of itself, is not prima facie evidence of colonialism; for "colonialism," as understood as a policy of one nation dominating the indigenous people of another in the latter's own nation, is a philosophical and cultural system of social control and degradation. "Exploitation," a leftist cant word, does not even mean that those who are being exploited are suffering because of it. Hawkins's argument works only if we accept the premise that black participation in high-level sports is, in and of itself, an act of degradation which he seems to suggest because of the fixation by the white public on the physicality of the black body: To believe this is not the affirmation of a fact about sports but the acceptance of an attitude or stance toward the value of sports.

The explosive expansion of professional and high-level amateur sports may have intensified racism in this country through its romantic racialist assumptions about blacks being natural athletes and it may have made it very difficult for blacks to be seen as equals, having equal merit with whites, in other arenas of human endeavor. On the other hand, sports may have widened the concept of democracy in America and given blacks greater visibility and more access than they might otherwise have had. How the issue of race and sports will be resolved is nearly impossible to say. John Hoberman's controversial *Darwin's Athletes* has sparked considerable debate among black scholars, even outrage in some quarters. Whether such response is justified is not as important a concern as that a full engagement of this issue by black thinkers may not lead to a solution but it may lead to a fuller understanding of why things are the way they are and how the black community might intelligently be able to make changes.

References

Baldwin, James. 1955. "Everybody's Protest Novel." In James Baldwin, *Notes of A Native Son.* Boston: Beacon Press.

Cleaver, Eldridge. 1968. *Soul on Ice.* New York: Dell Publishing Co.

Douglas, Ann. 1997. *The Feminization of American Culture.* New York: Knopf.

Douglass, Frederick. 1848. *Narrative of the Life of Frederick Douglass, an American Slave.* New York: Penguin, 1982 rpt.

_____.1854. "The Claims of the Negro Ethnologiclly Considered." Rochester: n. p.

Edwards, Harry. 1969. *The Revolt of the Black Athlete.* New York: The Free Press.

_____.1971. "The Sources of the Black Athlete's Superiority." *Black Scholar.* November.

Ellison, Ralph. 1952. *Invisible Man.* 1948/75. New York: Vintage Books.

Fredrickson, George M. 1971. *The Black Image in the White Mind.* New York: Harper & Row.

Harris, Othello. 1996/97. "Race, Sport, and Future Orientation." *Journal of African American Men* 2.2/3. Fall-Winter.

Hawkins, Billy: 1995/96. "The Black Student Athlete: The Colonized Black Body." *Journal of African American Men* 1.3. Winter.

Hoberman, John M. 1997. *Darwin's Athletes: How Sport Has Damaged Black America and Preserved the Myth of Race.* Boston: Houghton Mifflin Co.

_____.1984. *Sports and Political Ideology.* Austin: University of Texas Press.

Kane, Morton. 1971. "An Assessment of 'Black is Best'." *Sports Illustrated,* January 13.

Mailer, Norman. 1956. "The White Negro: Superficial Reflections on the Hipster." In Norman Mailer, *Advertisements for Myself.* New York: Putnam, 1959.

Murray, Charles and Richard Herrnstein. 1994. *The Bell Curve: Intelligence and Class Structure in American Life.* New York: The Free Press.

Sailor, Steve. 1996. "Great Black Hopes." *National Review.* August 12.

Smith, Wendell. 1964. *Pittsburg Courier:* March 14.

Sowell, Thomas. 1993. *Inside American Education: The Decline, The Deception, The Dogmas.* New York: Free Press.

Stowe, Harriet Beecher. 1852. *Uncle Tom's Cabin; or Life Among the Lowly.* New York: Collier Books, 1962 rpt.

_____.1856. *Dred: A Tale of the Great Dismal Swamp.* Boston: Phillips, Sampson.

Young, A. S. 1963. *Negro Firsts in Sports.* Chicago: Johnson Publishing Co.

Is Our Admiration for Sports Heroes Fascistoid?

◆

Torbjörn Tännsjö

Introduction

Already looking forward to the Olympic Games in Sydney at the turn of the millennium, I try to recollect what happened last time in Atlanta. How did I react? I realize that once again I was swept away with enthusiasm and admiration for those heroic athletes who had stretched the limits of what is physically possible for humans to achieve. Some have run faster than anyone has done before. This is true of Michael Johnson. Others have excelled and shown that, contrary to what should have been expected, they are—still—invincible. This is true of the greatest of them all, Carl Lewis. My query is: Is my enthusiasm for Johnson, Lewis, and all the other athletic heroes, respectable? Upon closer examination, my answer is *no*. My enthusiasm is not respectable. On the contrary, it is of a fascistoid[1] nature. So the problem is really what to do about it. The problem is pressing, for my attitude toward the Games is not exceptional. I share it with a great many other people who walk this planet. This is why the games were so widely broadcast.

Many people have pointed out that there is something unhealthy in much of the public interest in team sports on an elitist level. There was a time in many European countries when the Workers' Movement fought actively against the growing interest in sports. This concern has withered, but the rationale behind it remains relevant. As a matter of fact, team sports have often been used by nationalist governments to create a chauvinist zeal in their own populations. This zeal has rendered easier the

Reprinted, by permission, from T. Tännsjö, 1998, "Is our admiration for sports heroes fascistoid?," *Journal of the Philosophy of Sport, 25:* 23-34.

formation of totalitarian government, oppression of minorities at home, and imperialist adventures abroad. National sports teams have become emblems of their respective nations. These facts are rather obvious. It is also obvious that some of the interest that most people take in elitist sports events is nourished by these kinds of nationalistic sentiments. The interest as such reinforces the nationalism. This is indeed a vicious circle. But what about the public interest in the individual athletes in the Olympics? Should it be condemned because it reinforces an unhealthy nationalism?

To some extent it certainly does. Even individual athletes may become the target of these kinds of sentiments. Johnson and Lewis have reinforced U.S. nationalist sentiments. I am, on my part, more interested when a Swede succeeds in the Olympics, than when someone else does. But this cannot be the only source of my interest in the Olympic games. For my main interest is in the achievements of people like Johnson and Lewis. So perhaps much (the main part) of my admiration for their achievements is, after all, respectable? Perhaps much of the general interest taken in the games is respectable?

If this were the case, there would be room for optimism. For it seems to be part of the received wisdom that nationalism within sports withers. When big business in the form of international enterprises enter the arena, in the manner of sponsoring, advertising, and selling and buying television rights, national governments have to go. Often, the foreign NHL professionals do not bother to take part with their respective national teams. Instead of nationalism and interest on the part of the public in one's "own" team, admiration comes for the achievement of the outstanding individual. Local teams turn into corporations. And these corporations are seen as places where the outstanding individual can excel. However, this interest in the achievement of the outstanding individual is really no better than our (perhaps outmoded) nationalistic interest in the fate of "our" own team. Or so I will argue in this paper.

My thesis is that our admiration for the achievements of the great sports heroes, such as the athletes that triumph at the Olympics, reflects a fascistoid ideology. While nationalism may be dangerous and has often been associated with fascism, what is going on in our enthusiasm for individual athletic heroes is even worse. Our enthusiasm springs from the very core of fascist ideology.

Note that my thesis is not that there is anything fishy about the motives of the athletes themselves. I say nothing about this. Nor do I condemn those who organize sports events, those who train young people to become members of the athletic elite, or those who profit from the games, and so forth. In the present context, the *exclusive* target of my criticism is what goes on within the enormous, world-wide public, watching sports, usually through television. My interest is in the values entertained by you and me, we who tend, over and over again, to get carried away by such events as the Olympic Games.

Traditional Team Sports on an Elitist Level

Before developing my main argument, let me briefly comment on why it is a bad thing to have nationalistic values expressed and reinforced by publicly broadcast sports events. If this is a kind of danger in relation to elite sports that is becoming outmoded, and so it seems to be, it might be interesting to reflect on what it is we are getting rid of. When we see this more clearly, we are on firmer ground in our investigation of the new kind of danger we exchanged for the old one.

The main problem with nationalism is its orientation towards abstract symbols: the flag, the team (seen as an emblem), and yes, even the nation conceived of abstractly. When such entities are celebrated, the individual tends to become replaceable. The nation can get strong, it can be successful, even if each and every one of its citizens suffers. This individual suffering need not matter in the very least to the nationalistic ideology. In a similar vein, when the team becomes a representative of the nation, *its* individual members tend to become replaceable. When our football or soccer heroes are successful, we cheer for them. When they fail "us," we despise them.

This way of regarding our sports stars as representatives of our country, conceived of abstractly, fits with a common view of the military force. It may easily spread and permeate all the relations between people in a country. Young women are treated as potential instruments that shall safeguard the strength and survival of the nation; young men are viewed merely as potential soldiers, and so forth.

One might object that this is only a description. What is actually *wrong* with celebrating abstract symbols? Why not stress the interests of the nation rather than the interests of individual beings? Why not stress the survival of a race or species rather than of individuals making it up?

The answer is, as far as I can see, that abstract entities as such are of no value. What matters, ultimately, from a moral point of view, is what happens to individuals capable (at least) of feeling pleasure and pain. Only *individual* values are genuine. In order to be good absolutely, something must be good *for* an individual, capable of feeling (at least) pleasure and pain.

This is not to say that there exist no positive examples of nationalism. The U.S. struggle, say, for national independence was a worthy aim. But in those times, nationalism had a content. It was possible to see over and above the flags and the marches a point to the struggle, a point relating, in the final analysis, to respectable individual interests (in avoiding oppression, of various kinds). Even so, the flags and the marches are dangerous things. When the struggle is over, they tend to stay with us and live their own lives in the form of fetishes.

I will not try to argue the point in the present context that all respectable values are individual. I have discussed it in detail in *Hedonistic Utilitarianism* (2). It is here simply taken for granted. This means that if someone claims that the strength of his or her nation is of value in itself, he or she makes a value mistake. This mistake is dangerous if it leads to actions where individual interests actually get sacrificed for the sake of abstract, symbolic values. And this kind of sacrifice is the rule rather than the exception when a nationalistic ideology gets a firm hold of the members of a nation—in particular, if the nation in question does not face the least *threat* from any other nation.

Even if this be conceded, it might perhaps be argued that the kind of nationalism fostered by the public interest in team sports events is innocent. It might even be argued that nationalism in relation to sports is a good replacement for political nationalism (i.e., the kind of nationalism that is truly dangerous). It is better if people live out their nationalism in front of their television sets or on the seats around the sports arenas, than if they channel their nationalism through political parties and movements. Only in the latter case does their nationalism pose a real threat to important values.

I do not believe that this argument is tenable. The nationalism fostered by our interest for our "own" national team, and the nationalism we exhibit on the political arena, tend to reinforce each other. In particular, in periods where political nationalism is strong, what happens on the sports arenas tend to become politically important. There is only a small step from being a soccer hooligan to joining a fascist organization modeled on the Hitler Jugend. I will not develop this line of thought, however. The reason for not developing it has already been adumbrated. I think the common observation, that nationalism is becoming less and less important in relation to sports, is correct.

Why is nationalism within sports becoming less important? This has to do with commercialization and internationalization. The best sportsmen and the best teams earn enormous amounts of money. They can afford to allow themselves a considerable independence from political authorities and interests. They can take liberties with their own sports organizations. They rely rather on their own impresarios than on elected authorities of the Olympic Committee. However, when the old nationalism gives way, it gives way to something no less problematic. Let me now develop this main theme of my paper.

Contempt for Weakness

Nationalism, or chauvinism, has sometimes been thought to be a defining trait of nazism. However, in his seminal book, *Our Contempt for Weakness*, Harald Ofstad has argued, convincingly it seems to me, that the nationalism of the Nazis was only a contingent fact. To be sure, Hitler put the German nation before all other nations. And he put the so-called Aryan race before all other races. However, the hard core of nazism was different. The hard core of nazism was a contempt for weakness. This is shown by Hitler's reaction when the Third Reich broke down. In Hitler's own opinion, the defeat showed, not that there was something basically wrong with the Nazi ideology, but that there was something basically wrong with the German Nation. The German Nation had proved to be weak rather than strong. So eventually Hitler came to feel contempt for it (1: p. 24).

My thesis is: When we give up nationalism as a source of our interest in elite sports activities, when we give up our view of individual sportsmen and teams as representatives of "our" nation, when we base our interest in sports on a more direct fascination for the individual winners of these events—we move from something that is only contingently associated with nazism (nationalism) to something that is really at the core of nazism (a contempt for weakness).

Obviously, in my argument, a premise is missing. It is one thing to admire the person who wins the victory, who shows off as the strongest, but another thing to feel contempt for those who do not win (and turn out to be weak). I believe, however, that in doing the one thing, we cannot help but do the other. When we celebrate the winner, we cannot help but feel contempt for those who do not win. Admiration for the winner and contempt for the loser are only two sides of the same Olympic medal.

This is not to say that those who win the contest feel contempt for those who don't. It is one thing to compete and to want to win and quite a different thing to admire, as a third party, the winner. My argument relates to those who view sports, not to those who perform. Those who perform may well look upon each other as colleagues. They may feel that they are doing their job, and that is all. The winner may well feel respect for the loser. Or the winner may entertain any other feelings. It is not part of my project to speculate about this at all. My argument does not relate to the responses of the athletes; it relates to *our* responses to what they are doing. We, who comprise the public *viewing* the sports events, are the ones who admire the winner and feel contempt for the loser. If we are sincere in our admiration, and we often are, we cannot *help* but feel contempt for the losers. We would be *inconsistent* if we did not feel any kind of contempt for the losers, once we sincerely admire the winner.

To see why this is so we ought to think critically about *why* we admire those who excel in the Olympics. Our feeling is based on a value judgment. Those who win the game, if the competition is fair, are *excellent*, and their excellence makes them *valuable*; that is why we admire them. Their excellence is, in an obvious manner, based on the strength they exhibited in the competition. And the strength they exhibit is "strength" in a very literal sense of the word.

But our value terms are comparative. So if we see a person as especially valuable, because of his excellence, and if the excellence is a manifestation of strength (in a very literal sense), then this must mean that other people, who do not win the fair competition, those who are comparatively weak, are *less* valuable. The most natural feeling associated with *this* value judgement is—contempt. It is expressed in the popular saying: Being second is being the first one among the losers.

Contempt can take very different forms, of course. It may be of some interest in the present context to distinguish between three forms of contempt. First, contempt can take an aggressive form, as was the case with the Nazis. They wanted to exterminate weakness (by exterminating those who were weak). Second, contempt can take a negligent form. We try not to think at all about those for whom we feel contempt. We "think them away." We treat them as nonexistent. We do not care about them at all. Third, contempt can assume a paternalistic form. We want to "take care" of those "poor creatures" for whom we feel contempt. Common to all these reactions (all based on the idea that some individuals are of less value than others) is a tendency not to treat those who are considered less valuable with respect. They are not treated as full persons.

The surer we are that "we" are among the strong ones, among those who are valuable, the more prepared we are, I conjecture, to adopt the paternalistic reaction to those whom we consider weak. The more we fear that we might really belong to the weak ones, I also conjecture, the stronger our inclination to treat the weak ones negligently, as nonexistent—or even aggressively, with hatred: We want to exterminate them (i.e., *make* them nonexistent).

This is what is going on when enthusiastically we stay up half the night watching the athletes compete. To be sure, to some extent what takes place does so only in a symbolic way. We admire Carl Lewis for his excellence, and we feel some contempt for those who fall behind. However, we know that we would never stand a chance of beating Carl Lewis. Does this mean that we realize we are among those who are weak? It means, probably, that we fear this. But many of us believe we have other skills that compensate for those Carl Lewis possesses. Even if we are not physically as strong as he is, we may possess other kinds of strength. We may excel in respects that are (in our own opinions) more valuable than "strength" in the literal sense of the word.

But what if we do not? I believe that some of us may fear that we might fail on *all* relevant accounts. Those of us who do, I conjecture, are those who cheer most loudly for people like Carl Lewis.

What respects are relevant? This question is not possible to answer in a general manner. The Nazis had one (rather vague) notion about what kind of strength was important. We may have a differing view. As a matter of fact, each person may have his or her own opinion about this. But there is really no *need* to give a general answer to the question: What kind of strength is important to exhibit? As soon as we hold one opinion or another about it, we are vulnerable to the kind of argument I want to level in the present paper. Any person who is eager to be strong, who is prepared to feel contempt for those who are weak, and who fears that he or she may belong to those who are weak—any person who feels that those who are in any sense "strong" are better than those who are "weak"—are open to the criticism that he or she has fallen prey to the core of Nazi ideology.

There is a kind of betterness that is moral. A person, S, is (morally) better than another person, P, if and only if S is more praiseworthy, admirable, or deserving of the good things in life than is P. This notion is given a fascistoid twist when moral betterness is conceived of in terms of *strength*.

But must we feel contempt for those who are less successful (valuable)? Can we not just admire them less? I think not. For there are normative aspects of the notion as well. Those who are less valuable have to stand back when some goods (and evils) are to be distributed. And when resources are scarce, treating one person well is tantamount to treating another person badly. In a sports situation, this is clearly the fact. The setting is competitive. Olympic medals (and the money and reputation that go with them) are a scarce resource.

If we want to be sure that we do not get carried away by our admiration for winners, we ought to resist the very idea of moral excellence and betterness. In particular, we ought to resist the idea that moral excellence consists of *strength*.

To be sure, the idea of moral excellence in general and of moral excellence as (at least partly) a matter of strength of some kind, is an idea with deep roots in the history of philosophy, playing a crucial role for example in the ethical thinking of Aristotle. Yet an ethical theory can be constructed without having recourse to it. The utilitarian tradition, for example, bears witness to this.

Of course, even a utilitarian must concede that a life can be better or worse, for the person who lives it, depending on the content of the life, as experienced "from inside"; but this does not mean that a *person* can, as such, be (morally) better or worse. A certain kind of character can be more conducive to happiness than another kind of character, and should for this reason be encouraged; however, this has nothing to do with moral worth. In particular, it has nothing to do with strength of any kind. And the idea that strength is a proper grounds for admiration, the idea that underlies our fascination for the winners of sports events, is one that we ought to resist.

Objection: Similarities in the Arts and Science

Those who are prepared to concede that there is something to the argument stated above may still want to protest. They may want to argue like this. Even if there is something fishy about the reaction of the sports public to athletic achievements, it is unfair to single out sports for exclusive concern. After all, even within science and the arts we meet with the same phenomenon. Some people exhibit an unusual scientific or creative skill (strength). They make important contributions to science or create valuable pieces of art. They are then met with admiration. Does that not mean we value these persons in a manner similar to the way we value successful athletes? And if we do, does this not mean we think of those who are less successful in these areas as less valuable? Do we not exhibit contempt for weakness, then, when, for example, we give Nobel Prizes and the like to some "outstanding" persons?

At least to some extent I think this argument sound. And to the extent that it is sound, we ought to be ashamed of ourselves. But I think it sound only to some extent. For, to be sure, when we become enthusiastic about scientific and cultural achievements, we *need* not have scientists or artists as the focus of our attention. We can admire Frege's theories and Mozart's operas without feeling that Frege and Mozart are valuable persons. We can value the *products* of their ingenuity, not their genius itself. We can say truthfully that what they produced is of the utmost value but still retain the view that *they* are not more valuable than anyone else. They are merely *instrumental* to things of importance in themselves.

To be sure, even within science and the arts there are ugly manifestations of the phenomenon I have criticized within sports. Some people tend to get carried away with their admiration for lonely, heroic "geniuses" in the development of human science and art. Philosophy is not free of this phenomenon. There are people who speak with admiration of philosophers such as Nietzsche, Heidegger, and Wittgenstein, not because of any clear thoughts they have absorbed from the writings of these philosophers, but because they feel confident that these philosophers are especially "deep" and "inspired" thinkers. All this, like the actual Nazi ideology, is part of the legacy of the romanticism of the 19th century. However, while this phenomenon within science and the arts may be seen as a kind of corruption, it belongs in a more essential way to sports.

We can and we ought to admire the *products* of skillful scientists and artists, not these persons themselves, at least not because of their skill. (Perhaps some of them deserve our admiration because of their moral qualities, but Frege is not among those.) However, we cannot but admire the winning athletes themselves or else give up our interest in watching sport. Or can we? Why not consider the sports as simply a (very popular) part of human culture, where the results (products) of the individual achievements are what count?

Objection: We Admire Results, Not Athletes

I believe that there may be something to the objection that sport is not very different from art. In both cases there is excitement over the results of people's strivings. However, while the results are often, and should always be, the main focus of our attention within the arts, sports are different. There is an aesthetic aspect even to sport, to be sure. Some people are met with admiration not only because of their strength, but also because of the beauty with which they perform. Juantorena ran more beautifully than anyone before him. Why not say that it is the beauty of his running we admire, not himself? We admire the beauty in his running in the same way that we admire the beauty in a piano concerto by Mozart.

This line of argument is tenable to some extent. The Juantorena example is not a very good one, however. Had Juantorena not also been, for the time being, the fastest, we would not have remembered him for the beauty in his way of running. In the final analysis, what counts is who breaks the tape. But in some team sports, such as soccer, the aesthetic dimension may be considered more important. I believe that it might be of considerable importance, particularly among skilled audience members. After a match, they can discuss for hours the beauty in a single rush, irrespective of the outcome of the match where it took place. However, even *their* interest in the aesthetics of the play tend to be secondary, in the final analysis, to the outcome of the match. Remember that during the Chinese Cultural Revolution, there was a period when soccer competitions were reviewed with no mention of the outcome. At least among the majority of the sports public, this policy met with little approval and soon had to be changed.

As a rough approximation, then, we may say that, though there is room in science and the arts for admiration both of scientists and artists for their skill (their metaphorical "strength") and for their results, within sports there is room only for admiration of performers. The "results" they produce are not genuine; they are mainly results of measurements, measurements intended, first of all, to establish who won. But winning (a fair competition) is only a means. It is a means to prove excellence. So what we admire in sports is really the excellence shown by the winner.

Take away our admiration for the winner of the genetic lottery, who has proved his superiority in a big sports manifestation, and you take away most of our interest in the manifestation. This is true in particular for those of us who are not experts in the field and who tend to get carried away only now and then when we are informed by media that something remarkable is going on in a sports arena (like the Olympics).

But could it not be argued that what we admire is not really the *excellence* of the winner but what the winner has achieved *given* his natural endowments? And would not this kind of reaction on our part be morally more acceptable?

There is a grain of truth in this objection. And this grain of truth explains that there is a public interest in such things as female competition, competition between seniors, competition between handicapped persons, and so forth. When someone wins the Olympics for handicapped persons and we admire him or her for winning, we admire the achievement (given the constraints). In spite of the obstacles, this person made quite an achievement, we concede. However, the relatively weak public interest in such competitions, as compared to the interest in competitions of the absolute elite, shows that this kind of public interest in sports is of minor importance.

As a matter of fact, I suspect that there is even an element of contempt for weakness underlying many people's interest in this kind of handicap sport—but that it takes a paternalistic form. We do not take those who perform in handicap competitions seriously. We encourage them to go on but only in order that they develop into something less worthy of our contempt. In any case, if we are forced to choose, what we, the vast majority of us, want most to watch are competitions involving the *absolute* elite, not the Olympics for handicapped people.

Moreover, even if we are prepared to admire people who have worked hard, at least if they succeed in the competition (and the ability to work hard need not be anything that must be explained with reference to genes), I believe we will admire even more a person who excels *without* having worked hard for it. If a middle-aged member of the audience who never exercised unexpectedly walked down from the stadium and joined the Olympic 10,000-meter race and, because of superior natural talent, defeated all the finalists, the success would be formidable. Our admiration for this person would be unlimited. It is talent (which can be genetically explained), not achievement, we admire most. The point of the contest is to show who has the most superior talent.

This elitism of ours is also revealed by our way of reacting to doping. We want the competition to be fair. We are not prepared to admire Ben Johnson only because he has run 100 meters faster than anyone before or after him. Why? We suspect that Carl Lewis is genetically more fit than Ben Johnson. This is why we condemn Ben Johnson. He cheated.

But how do we know that Carl Lewis did not cheat too? Perhaps he was only more clever and got away with it. If doping were allowed, we would avoid *this* problem. We would not need to fear that the winner was not the strongest individual. If everybody were free to use whatever drugs they find helpful, then the crucial test, the competition, would show who is most fit. The competition is then fair.

For this reason, it is not at all implausible that doping, the deliberate use of drugs intended to enhance our strength, will rather soon be permitted. At least it is plausible to assume that drugs that do not pose any threat to the health of those who use them will be allowed. This seems only an extrapolation of a development that has already taken place. After all, there was a time when training was looked upon with suspicion. No one questions training today, and all athletes engage in it. Then came a time when *massive* training, on a professional basis, was condemned; I can vividly recollect the disdain with which swimmers from Eastern Germany were regarded by Western media during the 1960s. These days are also gone. Today, all successful athletes train on a professional and scientific basis. To the extent that all have the same resources at their disposal (an ideal we are far from having realized, of course, because of social differences and differences between nations), the competitions remain fair. But if training, even on a professional and scientific basis is all right, then why not accept doping as well, at least so long as the drugs used are not especially dangerous to the user?

If we were to permit such performance-enhancing drugs, we would no longer need to entertain the uneasy suspicion that the winner used prohibited drugs and managed to get away with it. We could then watch the games in a more relaxed manner.

A special problem, of course, is posed by the possibility of genetic engineering. What if those who win the Olympic Games in some not too distant future are not winners in a natural genetic lottery but genetically *designed* to do what they do? Would we still be prepared to stay up half the night to watch them perform? Would we still be prepared to admire those who make the greatest achievements? Would we still be prepared to cheer for the winners?

My conjecture is that we would not. Interestingly enough, then, genetic engineering may come to pose a threat not only to elitist sport but to the fascist ideology I claim underlies our interest in such sports.

Objection: Contempt for Weakness Is Human Nature

A fourth objection to my thesis that our admiration for sports heroes is at its core fascist needs to be addressed. Is not our admiration for strength, and a corresponding contempt for weakness, only natural? Are these feelings, moreover, not natural as well? Hence, is not a criticism of them misplaced? Since our nature is given to us by evolution, and since that nature dictates that we admire strength and feel a contempt for weakness, it hardly seems fair to criticize the possession and expression of these kinds of feelings.

This objection is flawed, but it renders necessary some important distinctions. It may be true that most of us are, by nature, competitive. We compete with each other, and we enjoy doing so. But there is nothing wrong in this, or at least, this competitiveness is not the target of my criticism. The competitiveness might go to an unsound extreme in certain circumstances, of course, but I do not intend to say that our competitiveness, as such, is immoral. Our competitiveness engenders important achievements, and it is a source of excitement and joy. It is also, of course, a source of disappointment and dissatisfaction. However, this is only as it should be; without *some* disappointment and dissatisfaction our lives would feel rather empty. I can readily concede this, for my criticism, in the present context, is not directed against competitiveness as such, nor to competitiveness in sports. I accept that scientists compete in a struggle to be the first to solve a certain problem, and I accept that athletes compete to win an important race. What I protest against is the admiration we show for the winner, be they scientists or sports heroes—and the corresponding contempt we feel for the losers. This reaction of *ours,* not the natural pride felt by *the winner himself,* is immoral. And the stronger our enthusiasm for the winner (and the stronger our corresponding contempt for the losers), the more immoral our reaction.

However, is not also this admiration for the winner, and the corresponding contempt for the loser, only natural? Well, this may depend on what we mean by calling a disposition "natural." Here we need another distinction.

One way of talking about "natural" dispositions is as follows. A certain disposition is "natural" if nature (evolution) has provided a species with it in the form of a blind *instinct.* If this is how the disposition is given to the species, then there is no room for blame when individual members of the species act on it. There is no point in blaming the lion for preying on the antelope. Under the circumstances, the lion can't help doing what it does. And it cannot help finding itself under the circumstances, either.

Another way of taking the idea that a certain disposition is "natural" is as follows. Evolution has provided the species with the disposition, but not as a blind instinct. Individual members of the species tend to act on it to be sure. And there exists a good evolutionary explanation *why* they do. However, sometimes they do not. When they don't, we need an explanation for this fact, an explanation cast, not in terms of evolutionary biology, but rather in cultural or psychological terms.

It seems highly implausible that our admiration for strength and contempt for weakness is natural in the former sense. Human beings are not driven by instinct when they cheer for the winners of the Olympics. If people choose not to do so, then they often succeed. Some people do choose, for one reason or another, not to join in, when the public hysteria is raised by main sports events. And they succeed in not joining in. So this is a possible course of action.

However, it might well be that we need an explanation why they do not join in, and the explanation may have to be cast in psychological or cultural terms. For snobbish reasons, say, they do not want to go with the crowd. Be that as it may, they *can* stay out of the events and they *do.*

So it might well be that our admiration for strength and our contempt for weakness, exhibited most prominently in our reaction to sports, is natural in the sense that is has been given to us by evolution: It takes education of some kind to avoid developing it. From an evolutionary perspective, it might have been advantageous to show contempt for weak individuals. It might have been advantageous to cheer for those who are skilled in aspects that relate to human survival. To borrow a phrase, if you can't beat them, join them. In particular, it might have been advantageous, alas, to despise handicapped children, not to feed them—and even to kill them, rather than to raise and nurture them.

This does not show, however, that such admiration for strength and contempt for weakness is morally acceptable. On the contrary, such kinds of contempt are *not* acceptable. They are morally evil. And to the extent we can through education counteract the influence of them, we ought to do so.

This raises an important and strongly contested question. If contempt for weakness is immoral, in particular when it is directed against individuals who are "weak" in a very literal sense of the word (people who are physically or mentally handicapped), does this mean that selective abortion (of fetuses with defective genes) is not acceptable?

It does not. It does mean, however, that some grounds for selective abortion are not respectable. It is not respectable to abort a fetus because one feels a "natural" contempt for the kind of handicap one knows it will be born with. Instead, one ought to convince oneself to accept and treat with respect individuals with this handicap. However, in rare circumstances, it can be obligatory to abort a fetus selectively, because one knows that the child it will develop into, if carried to term, will lead a miserable life, one filled with pain and devoid of pleasure. But then the abortion should not be carried out because of contempt for this (possible) child but, rather, out of compassion.

There may also exist selective abortions that are morally legitimate on the account that they save the family from unnecessary burdens, or, simply, because it allows a healthy child to be born rather than a handicapped one.

However, in all these kinds of selective abortions, as has been repeatedly and correctly noted by representatives of the handicapped people's movement, there is a risk that we might well be acting on an immoral contempt for weakness, rather than on a morally admirable compassion. Selective abortions provide much room for rationalization and wishful thinking. This is something we should always keep in mind.

Conclusion

I conclude, then, that our enthusiasm for our sports heroes is fascistoid in nature. It is not respectable. Our admiration for strength carries with it a fascistoid contempt for weakness. There are relatively innocent (paternalistic) forms of this contempt, but there is always a risk that they might develop into more morally problematic kinds, where we choose not to acknowledge those who are weak, or to reject them as unworthy of our respect, or worse yet, to seek their extermination (as did the Nazis).

It is true that sports are not the only place where this admiration for strength and a corresponding contempt for weakness is exhibited. We see the same phenomenon in the sciences and the arts as well. And when we do, what we see is no less morally depraved than what is exhibited in our enthusiasm for the winners of the Olympics. However, there is a rough but crucial difference between sports, on the one hand, and science and the arts, on the other. In sports, admiration of the winner is essential. If we do not admire the winners, and admire them *qua* winners of a genetic lottery, there is no reason to watch the games at all. For the aesthetic dimension of sports, however important it might be as an additional value, commands very little interest of its own. If our admiration for strength and contempt for weakness were somehow purged from sports, there would, I contend, be little reason to watch them. There will be little reason to watch sports competitions.

This is not to say, of course, that there will be little reason to take part in sports. We can all take joy in the exercise and excitement they provide. There is always someone to compete with. (If with no one else, one can always compete against oneself.) But if we get rid of our unhealthy enthusiasm for strength and corresponding contempt for weakness, no one will be able to arrange the kind of Summer Olympic Games that we witnessed in Atlanta in 1996.

Recommendation for the Future

Suppose we are now convinced that there is something wrong with our enthusiasm for sports heroes like Carl Lewis and Michael Johnson—what should we do about it?

Well, our enthusiasm for sports is much like an addiction. How do we defeat addictions? There is little help in imposing sanctions and using force. We cannot compel a person not to smoke, at least not if there remains a physical possibility for him or her to continue the habit. The only way to make someone give up a bad habit is to *convince* the person in question that the habit *is* bad. Then a possibility opens up that this person might, himself or herself, overcome the habit. This may take a lot of strength, skill, time, control, and cunning. However, eventually many people succeed in giving up even deeply entrenched bad habits. I suppose that something of the kind is what we ought to do with regards to our enthusiasm for sports heroes.

In sum, we ought to realize that our enthusiasm for sports heroes is fascistoid in nature. That is why it is no exaggeration to say, in closing, that if we are to grow as moral agents, we need to cultivate a distaste for our present interest in and admiration for sports.

Note

1. My neologism *fascistoid* should be understood in analogy with the word *schizoid*. Just as something schizoid tends to or resembles schizophrenia, something fascistoid tends to or resembles fascism.

Bibliography

1. Ofstad, H. *Our Contempt for Weakness. Nazi Norms and Values—And Our Own.* Stockholm, Sweden: Almqvist and Wiksell, 1998.
2. Tännsjö, T. *Hedonistic Utilitarianism.* Edinburgh, Scotland: Edinburgh University Press, 1998.

The Ethics of Supporting Sports Teams

Nicholas Dixon

Many people devote considerable amounts of time and emotional energy to following their favourite sports teams. However, the role of the fan or supporter of a team has received surprisingly little attention in the literature on the ethics of competitive sport. In a recent paper I defended an attitude of "moderate patriotism" on the part of supporters of their countries' national teams [1]. This paper addresses more fundamental questions about the ethics of supporting a team, whether it be local or national. Why do fans support a particular team, and are any reasons for doing so more worthy than others? Indeed, is any sporting team a worthy object of allegiance? I will defend the view that, provided certain conditions are met, loyal support of a team is not only permissible but also positively virtuous.

1. Different Motivations of Fans

I distinguish two main categories of fan: the "partisan" and the "purist." The "partisan" is a loyal supporter of a team to which she may have a personal connection or which she may have grown to support by dint of mere familiarity. The "purist," in contrast, supports the team that he thinks exemplifies the highest virtues of the game, but his allegiance is flexible.

The most grassroots level of partisan support occurs among fans of a local amateur team, whose players may include friends and relatives of the fans. The reason for support is a pre-existing relationship with the team's players. Fans of school or college teams may either fall into the previous category or else have a direct connection with the institution, as is the case with current or past students. Both these

Adapted from N. Dixon, 2001, "The ethics of supporting sports teams," *Journal of Applied Philosophy* 18(2): 149-158, by permission of Blackwell Publishing.

two types of fandom are straightforwardly explicable by reference to a concern for the wellbeing of people for whom one cares or institutions with which one identifies. Support for regional and national teams seems similar to support for school and college teams, in that fans may feel enlarged, albeit slightly, by the successes of teams representing the region or country to which they belong.

The motivation for supporting modern professional sports teams such as football clubs is more complex. While many fans support their local team, the link between fan and team is more tenuous than in the case of local amateur teams, school, college, regional or national teams. The professional team may be located in a fan's hometown, but players are typically not homegrown. In the English Premier League, for instance, the majority of players are not English, and many of those who are did not grow up in the club's area. North American professional sports teams—baseball, basketball, American football and hockey—also draw the majority of their players from other states and countries. Their fans cannot, then, feel enlarged by their team's success in the same way as fans of school, college [2], regional or national teams, since there is no obvious group to which fans and the majority of players both belong, allowing the players' credit to reflect on the fans.

Yet the absence of this kind of connection clearly does not prevent millions of fans from supporting professional teams in Europe, North America, and throughout the world. The basis for their support seems to be simple proximity and familiarity. The local team gets more coverage than others in local media and is the easiest one—for purely geographical reasons—for the local sport enthusiast to see live. The local sport enthusiast gets to know the local team's players and their strengths and weaknesses. She grows fond of her team's ground/stadium, which she starts to associate with the pleasure of the exciting moments she has spent there watching the sport that she enjoys. Even when players retire or are traded and new players arrive, a sense of continuity remains by virtue of the core of remaining players and also the club's style of play and its tradition. These factors combine to lead her to identify with the team by "adoption," as it were, as opposed to the first type of partisan fan who has more of a "family" connection with her team. This process of adopting a team is no more mysterious than the increasing concern for the wellbeing of another that is central to the beginning and deepening of friendship. It also parallels the very process of becoming proud of one's town, region or country, which usually develops gradually over a person's life, that underlies support of local amateur, or regional or national teams. Whereas support of such local amateur, regional or national, or school and college teams is based on a pre-existing loyalty to a region or institution, support for modern professional sports teams is more likely to be based on an organic allegiance that *originates in* and grows with familiarity with the team.

An interesting feature of modern professional sport is that a team's fans are no longer confined to inhabitants of its region. Famous clubs like Manchester United, the New York Yankees and the Chicago Bulls have avid supporters throughout the world. Now some of these long-distance partisan fans have doubtless become supporters by means of the same process of gradual familiarity as home town fans, thanks to satellite television and other worldwide media coverage. The fact that the world's most famous, successful teams—i.e., those that are more likely to be featured in the world's media—have far more long-distance fans than their more modest rivals supports this hypothesis. And other long-distance fans, just like some local ones, are doubtless motivated by apparently trite, superficial reasons for becoming supporters: the desire to support a winning team, infatuation with a matinee idol who plays for the team, etc.

However, national and worldwide television coverage of team sport has increased the probability of another motivation for becoming a fan: namely, admiration for a team's skill and style of play. Free from local, regional or patriotic biases, this second type of fan chooses his allegiance on purist grounds [3]. While the purist may well have a favourite team, he effectively watches each game as a neutral: his main desire is to see an exciting, skilful contest in which the better team prevails.

2. Evaluation of Partisan v. Purist Fans

I turn next to a moral evaluation of the two main motivations for supporting teams that are outlined in the previous section. I will focus on support for professional clubs and high-profile American college teams, since this level of sport attracts far more fans' attention than any other. How does the purist fan, who chooses his team based solely on admiration for the quality of its play, compare to the partisan fan, whose allegiance to her team arises from a person or geographical connection or by virtue of gradual familiarity with the club?

The purist appears to have staked out the moral high ground, since his choice of team is based only on sporting excellence. His allegiance is flexible and will switch if his team falls short of the high standards that he expects. His is the attitude of the neutral fan who genuinely wants the best team to win in an exciting, skilful contest. In contrast, the partisan will stick by her team even when it is performing badly. She would rather see her team win, even when playing poorly against a far more talented, attractive side. We are tempted to call the purist, but not the partisan, the true "fan of the game," since he is untainted by hometown bias and desires only to see an excellent contest in which the team that is superior in the central skills of the game prevails. Alongside him, the partisan appears superficial and parochial. When we teach children that playing the game fairly and to the best of our ability is more important than winning, the attitude we are nurturing is parallel to that of the purist, whereas the win-at-all-costs mentality that we discourage is more akin to that of the partisan.

However, in another respect the attitude of the partisan seems preferable and that of the purist curiously lacking. To elucidate this desirable feature of the partisan's attitude, let us consider a surprising analogy with romantic love. Our love for our partners begins with an appreciation of their good qualities. However, with time, our love becomes less dependent on our partners' qualities and fixes instead on their unique instantiation of those qualities: in other words, on their special identity. As Robert Nozick says, "[A] romantic mate eventually comes to be loved, not for any general dimensions or 'score' on such dimensions . . .— but for his or her own particular and nonduplicable way of embodying such general traits." [4] Our love becomes, as it were, *imprinted* on the particular person, just as a duckling regards as its mother the first living being that it sees, even if (as has happened on occasion) that being is a human. Two considerations give strong support to this characterization of romantic love.

First, a person in love does not seek to "trade up" to a different partner who scores higher than her current partner on the most significant evaluative scales. In other words, even if we meet someone who has even more of the good qualities that we admire in our partner, we will not reject her in favour of this new person. Even if objective appraisal of our potential new partner's qualities reveals that she really does score higher on the scales that we consider most important, a willingness to trade up to her would indicate that we were not, after all, in love with our original partner.

Second, love can endure a considerable amount of change. Some changes in our partner would doubtless make the continuation of our love impossible: attempted murder, chronic abusive behaviour, significant betrayals, etc. However, people change significantly in the course of long-term love relationships and this clearly does not prevent all such relationships from continuing. The very qualities that led us to fall in love may diminish or even disappear; they may be replaced by new qualities that we come to love; and even those qualities that we originally considered as minor faults in our partner may gradually seem endearing. The constant nucleus that remains the object of our love throughout all these changing attributes is our partner's identity.

The surprising conclusion of the analogy between this analysis of love and the attitude of fans is that the purist barely qualifies as a fan at all. His support for a team is purely conditional. He trades up at the drop of a hat: namely, whenever a rival starts to play better than his current team. The partisan, in contrast, is willing to stick with her team despite significant changes in personnel and fortune. Nor is she tempted to "trade up" to a more successful, skilful team, except in unusual circumstances discussed below. Indeed, we regard the willingness to continue supporting a team despite hard times as a sign of admirable loyalty. Granted, the purist is no fair-weather supporter who jumps ship in the superficial pursuit of a winning team. His changes of loyalty are based on love of the game and admiration for attractive, skilful play. Nonetheless, and unlike the partisan fan, he lacks an allegiance that is imprinted on a given team and remains in spite of changing qualities. A loyalty that is so contingent is a fleeting, tenuous type of support.

Lacking the commitment to support flesh-and-blood players, despite their losses of form, the purist's support for his team is too ethereal. Just as retaining affection for one's partner despite changes and disappointments is essential to love, a certain amount of unconditional loyalty—the kind that the partisan has—is essential to genuine support of a team. Rather than being a genuine fan, the purist approaches each game as a neutral, hoping that his team will continue its excellent play, so that he will be able to continue supporting it.

Perhaps, analogous to a rule-utilitarian, a purist could recognize that even the best team will occasionally falter and fail to live up to its usual high standards. He would then choose to support the team that *on the whole* plays the most skillfully and entertainingly. However, as has been famously pointed out in criticism of rule utilitarianism, a consistent utilitarian must favour breaking the optimizing rule on those occasions when obeying it would have negative results [5]. Similarly, the fan who is truest to his purist principles would confine his support for his team to those occasions when it really does live up to his high standards. And even a rule-utilitarian purist would be prone to change allegiance from season to season, as the talent and form of different teams wax and wane.

Such tenuous, contingent support is unlikely to sustain a team that requires, for purely financial reasons, a solid base of loyal fans. And it may well be psychologically impossible for actual fans to maintain such a detached attitude toward games. The allegiance that arises from familiarity in the case of the partisan fan is a perfectly natural human response that may be hard to suppress even in the case of the purist fan. The purist fan may find that, in spite of himself, his concern for his team's wellbeing will continue even when it falls below his expectations of athletic excellence.

Having criticized the attitude of the 100% purist fan, we need to realize that the attitude of the purely partisan fan is also problematic. Admirable loyalty and a willingness to stick by her team during hard times can spill over into stubbornness and overzealous partisanship. If allegiance to her team is the only motivating factor, she may continue to support her team when the team's actions are not worthy of support. By analogy, while continuing to cherish a partner even after he or she has undergone considerable changes can be a worthy sign of true love, such love need not be unconditional. A person who was genuinely in love can lose that love in the face of betrayal or abuse on the part of the partner, and indeed self-respect may *require* that we withdraw our love from such mistreaters. Similarly, a genuine fan may nonetheless withdraw her support if her team starts to engage in such indefensible practices as violent play or other forms of cheating, or even if it starts to use cynical, negative tactics, which may be within the letter of the law of the game, while violating its spirit. A modicum of the purist's attitude will provide a healthy safeguard against any tendency the partisan may have toward blind allegiance to a team that is unworthy of such support. Such withdrawal of support is far removed from the fair-weather fan's abandonment of his or her team when it hits hard times. It is based instead on love of the game and a belief that how it is played is more important than achieving a good result at any cost.

In sum, a completely purist fan has an admirable concern for sporting excellence and a commendable disdain for blind, parochial support for one's own favourite team. However, his support for the team that he judges to be most excellent is so contingent and tenuous that he barely qualifies as a fan at all. The completely partisan fan, in contrast, exhibits the great virtue of steadfast allegiance to her team even if its fortunes decline. The downside of her approach is that it can easily degenerate into blind support of a team whose conduct is unworthy of it. The ideal attitude for fans, then, appears to be the tenacious loyalty of the partisan, tempered by the purist's realization that teams that violate the rules or spirit of the game do not deserve our support. Let us call such a fan the "moderate partisan." In reality, many fans already contain elements of both the partisan and the purist. The purpose of this section has been to show *which* elements of each motivation are worth preserving.

3. Should We Be Fans of Particular Teams at All?

The previous section made clear that, if conventional fandom is desirable, then the loyalty of the partisan fan is an essential component. If, however, we have good reasons to believe that persistent allegiance to a particular team is undesirable, then the purist paradigm of fandom—i.e., that we should support athletic excellence wherever it occurs, rather than a favourite team—may be, for all its limitations, the only one that is morally permissible. In this section I consider, then, several arguments against loyal support of a particular team and respond on behalf of the type of fan defended in the previous section—the moderate partisan.

The first objection concerns immoral actions and attitudes that partisan fans sometimes perform and hold. Little doubt exists that partisan fandom can sometimes lead to atrocities, for instance the acts of violence that have sometimes been committed by supporters of club and national teams. And some partisan supporters have a hostile attitude toward rival teams and their supporters, which is indefensible, even if it never leads to any tangible harm. However, there is nothing inherent in supporting a team that requires its fans to act violently and it would be unfair to tar all supporters, the vast majority of whom never act violently, with the same brush that we justly apply to hooligans. Similarly, merely being a partisan fan—identifying with and having a special concern for the success of our team—in itself implies no negative attitudes toward rival teams and players, just as people's special concern for their loved ones does not preclude having moral respect for strangers. Even though some fans fail to live up to this ideal, being a fervent, committed supporter of a team is perfectly compatible with showing respect for opponents and even admiring the excellence of their play. The moderate partisan fans defended in this paper expect their teams to maintain high ethical standards and are especially unlikely to be so hypocritical as to act violently or disrespectfully toward rival teams or fans.

Torbjörn Tännsjö has criticized the attitude of sports fans, but not because of their hostility toward rival teams and fans. He argues, rather, that the admiration we have for Olympic champions and other "sports heroes" necessarily goes hand in hand with contempt for athletes who do not achieve such dizzying levels of success [6]. While Tännsjö focuses on champions in individual sports, we can nonetheless extend his argument to team sports and ask whether our admiration for elite clubs like Real Madrid or the Michael Jordan era Chicago Cubs is accompanied by morally indefensible contempt toward their less illustrious rivals. However, to the extent that Tännsjö's argument succeeds—and his central claim that admiration for outstanding athletes entails contempt for others is highly controversial [7]—it is a problem for the purist, not the moderate partisan defended in this paper. When Tännsjö describes our attraction to and fascination with Olympic champions he is describing the attitude of the purist, who admires athletic excellence wherever it occurs, regardless of the athletes' nationality. The corresponding fan in team sports is the one who watches a team competition like the European Champions' League as a neutral and is won over by the excellence of the winners. The moderate partisan, in contrast, observes competitions as anything but a neutral. While she is able to appreciate good play by other teams, her defining feature as a partisan is support for her own team, whether or not it performs better than other teams and whether or not it wins. Since her support is contingent on her team's performing fairly and within the spirit of the game, her loyalty is unobjectionable and even commendable. Moreover, in contrast to the fans whose attitude Tännsjö criticizes, the moderate partisan's primary motivation for following sport is loyalty to her team rather than a fascination with winners.

A more fundamental concern is that even moderate partisan support of a team appears to do precisely what impartiality rules out: it involves giving special treatment to a favoured group of people. And impartiality—giving equal respect to the interests of all people—is central to all non-egoistic moral theories. In this light, the purist fan's approach seems preferable, since he only favours teams whose quality of play merits their being singled out and treated differently from other teams. In response: impartiality is primarily a restraint on our behaviour that prevents us from harming those who are not part of our "in-group." It dictates that in the pursuit of our own interests and those of the people whom we specially favour—including a fan's favourite team—we may not trample on the rights of outsiders. However, giving special preference to certain people is in itself unobjectionable. If I choose to bestow benefits on a particular person or people, I am morally free to follow my whim, as long as the cause that I support is not itself immoral. Thus the undoubted preference that partisan fans give to their team in no way violates any moral duty of impartiality, since fans do not *owe* their support to any team at all. The moderate partisan fan's moral concern for her team, like any other exercise of moral regard for others, is a *prima facie* good. Its goodness is not diminished by the fact that she does not extend it to other teams, provided, of course, that it is unaccompanied by negative attitudes toward or violations of the rights of rival teams and fans [8].

So not only is the moderate partisan fan's support for her team unobjectionable, but it is also a positive good. Moreover, while no one is obligated to become a supporter of any team at all, we have reason to be wary of the completely purist fan who has no lasting attachment to a single team. A fan who regularly watches a local team but never identifies with its fortunes fails to exhibit the perfectly natural, healthy tendency to form a bond with those with whom we are familiar. While this is innocuous enough in the case of a sporting team to which no one owes any allegiance, it may betoken an inability to develop empathy for other people. A person who lacks this ability may have difficulty forming friendships and lasting romantic attachments. Granted, no one has a moral obligation to form such close personal relationships in the first place, but being unable to do so seems to be a character flaw that would be condemned from a standpoint of virtue ethics.

The completely purist fan who has no ongoing allegiance to any team resembles the moral fanatic parodied by Richard Taylor [9]. This fanatic is perfectly obedient to moral rules, to the point of obsession, but his tangible lack of empathy for others makes him a moral monster. The purist shows a commendable appreciation for the fine points of the game but seems to lack the passion and commitment that is the lifeblood of competitive sport. As does the moral fanatic, he seems to appreciate the cognitive elements of the enterprise but not its emotive force.

However, even if we grant that the capacity for empathetic identification with individuals and groups of people is morally permissible and even desirable, the purist or other critics might still object that being a moderate partisan fan is an inappropriate exercise of a generally desirable capacity. Isn't sport too trivial an entertainment to justify making teams of highly-paid professionals the object of fans' devotion? In the absence of a morally worthy object of allegiance, doesn't the support of even moderately partisan fans amount to a form of tribalism: the division of sports fans into arbitrary opposing factions? At a time when tribalism is manifesting itself in ugly ways in conflicts between ethnic groups such as those in the former Yugoslavia, we hardly want to encourage the formation of cliques that further divide populations.

I have three responses to this criticism of moderate partisan fans. First, the objection gives no support for its assertion that the pursuits of sporting teams are too trivial to make them a suitable object of fans' allegiance. Teams provide entertainment and excitement for spectators, which is already enough to take their enterprise out of the category of the mindless. More important, their displays of physical excellence—skill, conditioning, etc.—can be comparable to those of performers, such as ballet dancers, whom we are far less tempted to dismiss as unworthy of devotion. Athletes can also display mental qualities, such as astute strategy and coolness under pressure, that are fit objects for fans' admiration. Some philosophers have argued that sport has an aesthetic element [10] and this suggests an analogy with other practitioners of the performing arts, such as musicians and actors. Supremely fit and skilful athletes who perform efficiently and gracefully seem to be ennobling of human nature and hence worthy of admiration and support for similar reasons as artistic performers.

Furthermore, just as the partisan fan has her favourite team, so the patron of the arts may well be a regular supporter of a local orchestra or theatre or dance company. The arts lover may well have his favourite performers and follow their careers with interest, looking forward to each new role or piece that they perform. Thus the arts lover's allegiance to the local performing arts company may well develop by the very same process of increasing familiarity as the partisan's support for her team. Consistency requires that we extend to the moderate partisan sports fan the same admiration, or at least respect, that we accord to the loyal supporter of a local arts group.

Second, this criticism unfairly singles out support of sporting teams when many other allegiances would be vulnerable to the same objection, if we were willing to describe them in similarly unfavourable terms. Romantic love, for instance, is to some extent an arbitrary, irrational attachment to a person. While our love may originate in our appreciation of our beloved's good qualities, it gradually takes on a life of its own that transcends these qualities. As we saw earlier, our love becomes fixed on our beloved as a person and may remain even if her qualities change quite significantly. The key point is that we do not normally regard such love as groundless or undesirable. On the contrary, we regard the commitment and devotion to another person in romantic love as a *prima facie* good. To be fair, we should similarly regard a fan's dedication to her team as in itself virtuous, rather than condemning it as an empty-headed, blind affiliation. Such dedication is no more inherently divisive or tribalistic than is people's devotion to their romantic partners.

The previous two responses do not depend on any controversial assertions that sport has the same aesthetic and moral value as the performing arts and love, respectively. They assume only that sport has at least *some* aesthetic and moral value and this is sufficient to answer the objections that (1) sport is such a trivial pursuit that teams are not worthy objects of fans' support and that (2) fans' allegiance to their teams lacks moral worth and is an undesirable form of tribalism.

A third and final consideration that helps to further allay the concern that sport has too little value to justify the fierce allegiance of fans to their teams arises from the purist approach to sport that tempers the zeal of moderate partisan fans. While the loyalty of the partisan fan is admirable, it should not be unconditional. Teams that engage in morally reprehensible behaviour—e.g., violent play, cheating, verbal abuse of opponents and referees—do not deserve support and moderate partisan fans will boycott them until the teams end these wrongful actions. Other teams may stay within the game's laws but play in a manner that violates the spirit of the game and interferes with the emergence of the game's most skilful, exhilarating features, by using professional fouls or other cynical tactics. These violations of the ethos of games also justify, and in extreme cases require, the withdrawal of support by fans of the perpetrating teams. Moderate partisan fans' use of such moral and aesthetic criteria in determining whether to support a team helps to ensure that, even though their choice of allegiance may originally have been made on the arbitrary ground of familiarity, their continued loyalty depends on whether the team's actions are worthy of it. Furthermore, fans who restrict their support to teams that perform according to certain moral standards are likely to be equally exemplary in their own conduct while supporting their teams. Such fans are unlikely to regard rival fans and teams with hostility and exhibit the tribalism that is currently displayed by some narrow-minded supporters.

4. Conclusion

The ideal attitude for sports fans is that of the moderate partisan, who restrains the commendable loyalty of the partisan by the purist's insistence that the game be played skillfully, fairly and with style. While partisan support is sometimes accompanied by negative attitudes toward rival teams and their fans, the connection is contingent and being a loyal supporter is quite compatible with treating rivals with respect. Moderate partisans who use ethical criteria in their choice of team are especially unlikely to act immorally in their role as fans. Like any expression of concern for other people, moderate partisan support of sports teams is a *prima facie* good. Indeed, the inability to give such support may signify a moral flaw. Finally, while sport is indeed a recreation, teams that moderate partisans support are worthy objects of their fans' allegiance. Such teams strive for physical, intellectual and aesthetic excellence, while restraining their actions by the demands of morality. To support such teams is a positive virtue.

Notes

[1] NICHOLAS DIXON (2000) A justification of moderate patriotism in sport, in Claudio Tamburrini and Torbjörn Tännsjö (eds.), *Value in Sport* (London, E & FN Spon), pp. 74-86.

[2] Granted, many American colleges recruit athletes from distant states thousands of miles away, and so U.S. college teams in this regard resemble European professional football teams. However, current and past students of these colleges do at least share a significant identity—that of being/having been a student at the college—with the college's athletes, who are also, at least nominally, students at the same institution.

[3] Of course, basing support for a professional team on familiarity can coincide with purist motivations. In other words, my local team, or the one to which I have become most accustomed by media coverage, may also be the one that I most admire because of its excellent play.

[4] ROBERT NOZICK (1989) The *Examined Life: Philosophical Meditations* (New York, Simon and Schuster), p. 237.

[5] See, for example, J. J. C. SMART (1973) An outline of a system of utilitarian ethics, in J. J. C. Smart and Bernard Williams, *Utilitarianism: For and against* (Cambridge, Cambridge University Press), pp. 10-12; and BERNARD WILLIAMS (1972) *Morality: An introduction to ethics* (New York, Harper and Row), p. 102.

[6] TORBJÖRN TÄNNSJÖ (1998) Is our admiration for sports heroes fascistoid? *Journal of the Philosophy of Sport* xxv, pp. 23-34.

[7] For a cogent critique of Tännsjö's main thesis, see CLAUDIO M. TAMBURRINI, Sports, fascism, and the market, *ibid.*, pp. 35-47, esp. pp. 39-44.

[8] For more detail on my reconciliation of particular allegiances with the demands of impaniality, see my A justification of moderate patriotism in sport, pp. 76-77.

[9] DIODORUS CRONUS (Taylor's pseudonym) (1971) The governance of the Kingdom of Darkness, *Southern Journal of Philosophy* 9, pp. 113-18.

[10] See, for example, JOSEPH KUPFER (1975) Purpose and beauty in sport, *Journal of the Philosophy of Sport* II, pp. 83-90; and DREW A. HYLAND (1990) *Philosophy of Sport* (New York, Paragon House), ch. 5.

Convention and Competence

Disability Rights in Sports and Education

◆

Anita Silvers and David Wasserman

In the last six months, federal district courts have issued decisions in two highly publicized cases alleging discrimination on the basis of disability. In one, the Professional Golfers Association (PGA) was ordered to allow Casey Martin, a talented contender with a serious leg impairment, to use a golf cart in its championship tournaments, in contravention of its existing rules. In the other, Boston University (BU) was permitted to maintain its foreign language requirement without exceptions for learning-disabled students after a court-mandated faculty committee determined that the requirement was "fundamental to the nature of a liberal arts degree" at that university.

Both cases were brought under Title III of the Americans with Disabilities Act (ADA), which prohibits discrimination in "public accommodations," a term which covers a wide range of facilities, institutions, and organized activities. Both addressed the same issue under Title III: Was the proposed exception a "reasonable modification," or would it "fundamentally alter the nature" of the good, service, or activity in question?

The drafters of the ADA expected the meaning of "reasonable modification" to be fleshed out in the courts, and the two rulings were made in the context of the distinct bodies of case law governing organized sports and higher education. Still, the cases *look* similar, at least from the distance of a newspaper report, and so it may seem puzzling that they were resolved differently. Why should the PGA not be allowed to

Reprinted, by permission, from A. Silvers and D. Wasserman, 1998, "Convention and competence: Disability rights in sports and education." *Report from the Institute for Philosophy and Public Policy* 18(4): 1-7.

decide that walking is fundamental to tournament play, if BU is allowed to decide that a foreign language requirement is fundamental to its liberal arts program?

Several explanations suggest themselves. The courts may be more deferential to the judgment of faculty committees, given the greater prestige of academics and the long tradition of university self-government, than to professional athletic associations. The nature of Casey Martin's disability was clear and undisputed while the diagnosis of "learning disability" on which the BU students' ADA claim rested remains deeply controversial. Finally, the opportunities available to the plaintiffs in the two cases were strikingly different. While there is only one PGA Tour (the most prestigious of the four tours offered by the PGA, and arguably the most prestigious in golf), there are lots of places to obtain a liberal arts degree—some more prestigious than BU, and many not requiring two years of a foreign language. For these reasons, the courts may have been more inclined to require inclusiveness and accommodation on the part of the PGA, while holding BU to a less demanding standard.

Ultimately, however, we cannot explain the appearance of inconsistency, or assess the merits of these decisions, without some understanding of how the ADA defines discrimination and what it requires for its redress.

What the ADA Demands

In enacting the ADA, Congress found that people with disabilities had been systematically denied "the opportunity to compete on an equal basis" by pervasive discrimination, involving not only "outright intentional exclusion" but also "architectural, transportation, and communication barriers," "exclusionary qualification standards and criteria," and the "failure to make modifications to existing facilities and practices." The ADA thus treats discrimination against people with disabilities as, in part, a sin of commission—the imposition of exclusionary practices and standards—and, in part, a sin of omission—the failure to remove barriers and to make reasonable modifications. This understanding of discrimination reflects a recognition that our society has deliberately or negligently excluded its disabled members from a wide range of activities by structuring those activities in a way that makes them needlessly inaccessible.

Eliminating such structural discrimination often requires significant changes in the physical and social environment. The most visible accommodations required by the ADA are the design features that ensure access for people in wheelchairs or people who are blind: curb-cuts, ramps, accessible entrances and bathrooms, braille signs, and computers that read their own screens aloud. But the ADA also requires less tangible accommodation, in the "design" of jobs, tasks, and activities. As one recent law review article observes, "By contrast to earlier prohibitions against discrimination, the ADA incorporates a more explicit understanding of the contingency of existing job configurations: that they need not be structured the way that they are. Rather than taking job descriptions as a given, reasonable accommodation doctrine asks how the job might be modified to enable more individuals to perform it."

The demand for restructuring may make the ADA look more "affirmative" than other civil rights laws; the measures required to accommodate people with disabilities appear more extensive, and less directly linked to the redress of prior intentional discrimination, than those required to protect the rights of women and minorities. But in fact, the changes mandated by the ADA are more circumscribed than those mandated by other civil rights legislation. For example, the ADA requires job restructuring only for those disabled individuals "otherwise qualified" to perform the job's "essential functions." Moreover, it requires modifications only if they are "reasonable," if they do not impose an "undue burden," and, to bring us back to the present cases, if they do not "fundamentally alter the nature" of the activity, good, or service being offered.

These exceptions make the antidiscrimination mandate of the ADA a good deal more conservative than it initially appears, but they still demand a bracing exercise in institutional self-examination. They require employers, public and private service providers, and, ultimately, the courts to decide what constitutes the essential functions of a job or the fundamental nature of an activity, good, or service. Because the functions of a job, the requirements for a degree, the rules of a game or social practice depend to a large extent on convention, habit, and the practical imperatives of bygone eras, it will often be difficult to say whether they are essential, or why. And because the ADA places the burden of proof on those who seek to maintain exclusionary practices, the difficulty of establishing that such practices are essential will often work to the benefit of those demanding accommodation.

Demonstrating Competence

If the implementation of the ADA has been complicated by uncertainty about the essential nature of various activities, goods, or services, it has also been complicated by uncertainty over what constitutes competence or qualification in those persons who are excluded from them. Formally, the second concern might not appear independent of the first: the competence or qualification of a person with a disability would seem to depend on the essential requirements of the job or the fundamental nature of the activity. But competence is not always assessed with reference to the requirements of a particular task or job. We will sometimes be more certain about a person's talent for achieving the outcomes associated with an activity than about the activity's fundamental nature; even those who claimed that walking was fundamental to the PGA Tour conceded that Casey Martin had already shown himself to be a formidable golfer. It may also be that our understanding of an activity's fundamental nature will be decisively *shaped* by our convictions about an individual's achievement. If we are more certain of the consummate skill that Casey Martin displays in playing golf than we are about the specific skills which golf requires, we may deny that the highest-level professional golf could possibly require any skill that Martin lacks. Along with his defenders, we may conclude that the PGA Tour is essentially a shotmaking competition.

There is a second reason why the assessment of competence is so uncertain: competence is more likely to have been attained and exhibited in some domains than in others. This may be the most striking contrast between the PGA and BU cases. Golfers who seek to compete in the PGA Tour will have had abundant opportunity to demonstrate their talent in other tournaments, while students at a liberal arts college most likely have promise rather than actual accomplishments to show. Admittedly, some college students can boast a Westinghouse Science Prize or a poem published in the *New Yorker*. But they are the exception. A liberal arts education offers few venues for precocious achievement, and talent in its specific domains may simply take longer to cultivate and display. The PGA case thus appears closer than the BU case to the ADA's paradigm injustice of a talented person with a disability denied an opportunity to "participate in, and contribute to, society."

In saying this, we do not mean to suggest that the ADA requires plaintiffs to display competence as clearly as Casey Martin did. Indeed, most people who claim discrimination based on disability will probably fall somewhere between Martin and the BU students, with achievements more concrete than the students' but less compelling than Martin's. Our suggestion is simply that in close or disputed cases—particularly cases where the fundamental nature of the activity is at all uncertain—plaintiffs are more likely to prevail if they can clearly display competence or qualification in the activities from which they have been excluded.

The "Fundamental Nature" Test

However unfair Casey Martin's exclusion from the PGA Tour might have appeared, it might not have been illegal if walking were indeed fundamental to the highest-level professional play. On this point, there was conflicting and ambiguous evidence. The PGA rules clearly stated that contestants were to walk the course, and some players regarded that as a formidable challenge in hot, humid weather and difficult terrain. But walking was not (otherwise) part of the competition: players did not get lower scores for faster walking, and no minimum pace or time was specified. Moreover, many players felt that walking was actually advantageous, giving them a feel for the course they would lack if they rode in a cart. Finally, the fact that other tournaments permit carts did not settle the issue of how to regard the walking requirement in the PGA Tour. That requirement may be seen as gratuitous, since walking is deemed essential in no other tournament, or, no less plausibly, as a defining requirement of the PGA Tour, distinguishing it from other tournaments.

Behind this specific clash of interpretations lies the more general question of how the courts could ascertain the fundamental nature of a conventional activity like PGA Tour golfing. This question invites comparison with the inquiry mandated under Title I of the ADA as to whether a given requirement is an "essential function" of a job. Title I prohibits employers from refusing to hire or retain "otherwise qualified" individuals on the basis of their disabilities; an individual is otherwise qualified if she can perform the "essential functions" of the job with reasonable accommodation. If the person with a disability cannot perform an essential function even with accommodation (such as the provision of assistive technology), the individual is not qualified.

Though many of the functions that people with disabilities cannot perform are clearly incidental to the jobs they seek to do, such as walking up a flight of stairs to work as a computer programmer, there is often disagreement about whether a particular function is incidental or essential (e.g., is the ability to quickly analyze a fact pattern and apply complex rules essential to lawyering, or is speed incidental, and extra time on bar examinations therefore a reasonable accommodation for applicants with learning disabilities?). Such questions—which were rarely asked before civil rights laws forced employers to address them—will sometimes be difficult to answer. But generally they can be resolved by examining a company's past practice, its productive and financial goals and constraints, and the practice of similar organizations: Does the employer really need this employee to perform this function in order to maintain its productivity or market share, comply with OSHA or EPA standards, or increase its dividends?

The inquiry may be less straightforward when a person with a disability seeks access to an activity, good, or service rather than a job. Formally, the language of Title I (regarding employment) and Title III (regarding public accommodations) is quite similar. Where the former requires "reasonable accommodation," the latter requires "reasonable modification"; both make an exception for undue burdens. And much as an employer is not required to accommodate a person with a disability who cannot perform the essential functions of the job, an organization is not required to modify the activity, good, or service it offers if that change would "fundamentally alter [its] nature." If walking indisputably had as incidental a role in golfing as it has in computer programming, the Casey Martin case would be an easy one under either section of the ADA.

The demand for reasonable modification suggests that the ADA recognize the same contingency in the "existing configurations" of activities like sports and education as it does in employment. But the contingency in such activities is different from that found in jobs. Sports are conventional in a way that jobs are not (or are not generally thought to be). Their features are not dictated by the external objective of making a product or a profit, but are shaped by tacit consensus and informal practice of the participants themselves. Education falls somewhere in the middle: closer to employment if we see it in more instrumental terms as job training; closer to sports if we see it as a constituent of a good, cultured, or civilized life, e.g., "Part of being an informed and cultured member of our society is having learned (or at least having been exposed to) a foreign language or the Classics of Western Civilization."

The more conventional character of sports, and arguably of education, may appear to make them more flexible, more amenable to modification, than the production- or profit-driven operations of a business. But their conventional nature is double-edged. The rules and practices that define a sport or a liberal arts education may be in some sense arbitrary, but they may also acquire a non-instrumental value that few job descriptions possess. The ADA's exemption for modifications that fundamentally alter the nature of an activity, good, or service can be seen as protecting, perhaps too categorically, the attachments and expectations that develop around conventional activities.

In the BU case, the court deferred to the considered judgment of a faculty committee that the foreign language requirement was essential to a liberal arts education at Boston University. There was ample precedent for this deference in other cases addressing the fundamental nature of an academic or professional program, based in part on the tradition of academic autonomy. (Indeed, that deference might have been greater if the BU president had not provoked the controversy with a wholesale attack on his school's program for students with learning disabilities and on the very idea of accommodating such disabilities.) Such deference may look elitist if we see the nature of a liberal arts degree as no less conventional than a golf tournament—why should academics be allowed to judge which of their conventions are fundamental while sports organizers must yield to the court's judgment? It will look a little less elitist if we see the requirements for a liberal arts degree as instrumental—developing the skills needed to succeed in civic or commercial life outside the academy (or within it, as professors). But the university might be reluctant to justify its foreign language requirement in instrumental terms. If the question is whether students perform better at various life pursuits with the minimal proficiency that two years of a foreign language confer, the BU faculty has no more expertise than other educators in providing an answer. Rather, the university may see the foreign language requirement as an essential constituent of a liberal education *as BU defines it.* In that case, its authority to impose the requirement is a matter of prerogative, not expertise.

Protected Values

We would like to conclude with some reflections on the values that may be protected by the "fundamental nature" exception of Title III. If the law were simply concerned with equitably distributing the costs of reasonable accommodation and modification among people with disabilities, employers, public accommodations, and the larger society, it is not clear why it would need such an exception in addition to that for "undue burden," as well as the overall requirement of reasonableness. If a public accommodation can modify its activity, service, or good without undue burden, what does it matter that the modification alters its fundamental nature?

This impatience with convention is found in some feminist writing on sports, which challenges the need for rules that limit the participation and success of women. Thus, Janice Moulton maintains:

> As it is now, athletes are used to adjusting their play to rule changes, and systems of scoring now exist to allow players at different levels to compete together. Informal games of many kinds are played with whoever shows up, and every school athlete has played in such games. The rules are freely revised to take into account the number of players, the playing field . . . , the level of skill, and anything else considered important. People who object to making changes in the standard rules may not realize how very often such rules are altered in practice.

As anyone who has followed the protracted controversies about rule changes in many sports will appreciate, however, players and spectators are often fiercely attached to the status quo, and regard even minor changes as threats to the integrity of the sport. Changes far subtler than those needed for the inclusion of people with various disabilities might well alter the style of play and the character of the game. The point is not that such changes would make the sport intrinsically better or worse, or would impose any tangible burden on the players, spectators, or organizers, but that they would alter familiar and cherished conventions. Moulton recognizes how sports talk pervades our social lives and civilization, but fails to recognize how much of that talk concerns the very details she would so readily alter in the interest of greater inclusiveness. It is not the improvised pick-up games that are debated in the barbershops and the tabloids; it is organized sports with highly specific rules and other conventions, a knowledge and acceptance of which is presupposed in the spirited discourse Moulton observes. This hardly renders those conventions sacrosanct, but it does suggest that changes can be wrenching and disruptive.

Moreover, one does not have to be a fetishist about existing conventions to worry about the broad postwar trend, in work, school, and sports, toward specialization. American sports used to place a premium on endurance and versatility, just as American universities once imposed a comprehensive liberal arts curriculum. A football career required a full 60 minutes on the gridiron, on defense and offense; a B.A. once required not only proficiency in Latin and Greek, and a familiarity with the classics of Western Civilization, but also an ability to swim several laps in an Olympic-size pool. The specialization that has overtaken many domains may be a welcome trend for those with finely honed but narrow talents and capabilities. But in these domains, many well-intentioned people fight to preserve an emphasis on versatility or well-roundedness, lest the participants become technicians instead of scholars or athletes. And even those not disposed to rearguard actions may feel some sense of loss when excellence in golf is confined to shotmaking or when pitchers no longer have to come to the plate to face their opposite numbers on the mound, leaving that task to designated hitters. Whether or not we believe that the law should attempt to take cognizance of such costs, it must recognize the danger of deforming a practice so extensively that it is no longer one in which previously excluded or included people wish to participate. At that point, the attempt to reshape the practice becomes self-defeating. If the ADA does give weight to convention in exempting public accommodations from changes that would fundamentally alter the nature of their activities, goods, and services, this is consistent with the generally conservative and incremental character of that statute. The ADA is committed to opening up existing employment, facilities, activities, goods, and services to people with disabilities, but it was not designed to equalize opportunities in more radical ways. While the interests of people with specific disabilities might be well served by the creation of new sports emphasizing skills in which they were likely to have developed compensatory superiority—the rough analogue of a proposal made by Jane English for reducing sex inequality in sports—or of more universities like Gallaudet, the ADA requires nothing of the sort. Rather, it calls for the maximum feasible integration, and leaves it to the courts to decide whether what is of distinctive value in an enterprise can be preserved by changes that permit people with a given disability to participate, and even to compete and win. Will the singular virtues of the highest-level professional golf be compromised if players use carts to go from hole to hole? Would a BU liberal arts degree lose its special character if it were conferred without two years of a foreign language? Such questions will often be difficult ones, both for disabled individuals who seek inclusion and for institutions which are pressed to change. Nevertheless, they provoke a valuable exercise in institutional appraisal.

Making Exceptions

One issue close to the surface but rarely discussed in cases like these is why we should have to choose between excluding people with disabilities from an activity, or altering its rules and conventions for everyone so that people with disabilities can be included. Why not simply make an exception to those rules or conventions for participants with disabilities? What does it matter if a few people are allowed to depart from the conventions that govern a sport or an academic program?

The most obvious concern is that exceptions would give some participants an unfair advantage, thereby imposing an undue burden on the others. Suppose that Casey Martin won a game on the PGA Tour by one stroke, pulling ahead on the final hole to beat a player exhausted by walking a long course on a hot, humid day. Or suppose that the two top seniors at BU had equal GPAs, but that one was a learning-disabled student who had gotten A's in foreign culture but would probably have gotten C's or D's in a foreign language, the other a non-LD student who had gotten B's in a foreign language, but would probably have gotten A's in foreign culture. Would it be fair to award Casey Martin the trophy, and to make the learning-disabled student valedictorian?

A second concern is that exceptions would alter the fundamental nature of an activity. Clearly, this could happen if an "exception" were available to all—and if there were some advantage to non-disabled participants in the alternative way of engaging in the activity. But it could also happen even if the exception were limited to disabled participants, since our notion of what constitutes achievement in that activity would be affected by their success. BU, for instance, would be hard-pressed to claim that two years of a foreign language were integral to its conception of liberal arts education if several of its recent valedictorians were learning-disabled students who lacked that coursework.

Operating in a legal framework somewhat different from the ADA, the Ontario court faced both of these concerns when it was asked to decide whether the province's Youth Bowling Council could exclude Tammy McLeod, a girl with cerebral palsy, from tournament play. Tammy aimed and released the ball down a ramp rather than holding it in her hand. The judge concluded that the girl was "not able, because of handicap, to perform the essential act of bowling—manual control and release of the ball." Under the ADA, such a finding would have settled the matter. By analogy with Title I, the employment section, the bowling council would not be required to include Tammy if she was unable, even with accommodation, to perform the essential functions of the sport. But under the Ontario Human Rights Code, as the judge interpreted it, the bowling council *was* required to include her. A person with a disability is entitled to accommodation whether or not she can perform the essential functions of an activity, so long as the accommodation does not impose a hardship on the organizers or on other participants. In this case, the judge ruled that there was no hardship: Tammy's device gave her "no competitive advantage over others" (since it did not allow her to impart speed or spin to the ball), and her use of it did not require other bowlers to alter their manner of play in the slightest.

The judge went on to say, however, that if use of the ramp *had* given Tammy a competitive advantage, or if she were to adopt a more sophisticated device, the bowling council might well be allowed to exclude her. In effect, he ruled that Tammy could participate as long as she was not competitive. He gave her permission only to engage in a loosely parallel activity alongside real bowlers, in which she was unlikely to obtain a higher score than the real bowlers, and unlikely to be regarded as having won a bowling game even if she did. Though she could be a participant in some attenuated sense, she could never be a contender. This resolution is ironic in a case where the judge emphasized the inherently competitive nature of sports: "All sport at all levels involves competition; all participants strive to win." It may have been a fair resolution for a youth tournament, where winning is not the only thing, but if so, the decision was fair for reasons that belied its stated rationale.

It will, of course, be as difficult to say when an alternative way of performing an activity confers an unfair advantage as it is to say whether it departs from the fundamental nature of that activity. From the moment he began to dance around Sonny Liston in Las Vegas, to the moment he had the ropes loosened in the Kinshasa ring to defeat George Foreman with his rope-a-dope, Muhammed Ali was accused of gaining unfair advantage or threatening the fundamental nature of heavyweight boxing; he is now almost universally regarded as having improved it. A cart on a PGA Tour golf course is surely closer to looser ropes in a boxing ring than to ramps in a bowling alley. But closer cases and difficult judgment calls will inevitably attend the integration of people with disabilities.

Bibliography

1. Pamela S. Karlan and George Rutherglen, "Disabilities, Discrimination, and Reasonable Accomodation," *Duke Law Journal*, vol. 46. no. 1 (October 1996).

2. Ruth Shalit, "Defining Disability Down," *New Republic* (August 25, 1997).

3. Michael Grunwald, "U.S. Launches Drive for Disabled Golfer: Justice Dept. Invokes ADA in Martin Case," *Washington Post* (August 24, 1998).

4. Janice Moulton, "Why Everyone Deserves a Sporting Chance: Education, Justice, and College Sport," in *Rethinking College Athletics,* edited by Judith Andre and David N. James (Temple University Press, 1991).

5. Jane English, "Sex Equality in Sports," *Philosophy and Public Affairs,* vol. 7 (Sprint 1978).

6. *Youth Bowling Council of Ontario v. McLeod, 75 Ontario Reports* (2d).

INDEX

Note: The letters *f* and *t* after page numbers indicate figures and tables, respectively.

ABOUT THE EDITOR

 **William J. Morgan, PhD,** is a professor of sport humanities and interim director of the Center for Sport and Citizenship at Ohio State University in Columbus. He has served as editor and has published extensively in the *Journal of the Philosophy of Sport*. Currently he serves on its editorial review board. He has presented numerous papers on the topic of ethics in sport throughout the world and has written and edited several books on the topic: *Why Sports Morally Matter; Philosophic Inquiry in Sport; Leftist Theories of Sport: A Critique and Reconstruction; Sport and the Humanities: A Collection of Original Essays;* and *Sport and the Body: A Philosophical Symposium.*

Dr. Morgan is former president of the International Association for the Philosophy of Sport. In 1995, he received the association's Distinguished Scholar Award. In the same year, he was elected an active fellow of the American Academy of Kinesiology and Physical Education.